COURT-SUPERVISED RESTRUCTURING OF LARGE DISTRESSED COMPANIES IN ASIA

This book provides an in-depth analysis of four economically significant Asian jurisdictions: Mainland China, India, Hong Kong and Singapore. These jurisdictions have recently either reformed – or are considering reforming – their corporate restructuring laws to promote regimes conducive to restructuring financially distressed, but otherwise economically viable, companies.

Mainland China, India, Hong Kong and Singapore continue to adhere to a framework that requires the court's final approval but draw references from Chapter 11 of the Bankruptcy Code 1978 in the United States and/or the schemes of arrangement in the United Kingdom. However, the institutional and market structures are very different in Asia; in particular, Asia has a far higher concentration in shareholdings among listed firms, including holdings by families and the state, and a different composition of creditors.

The book explains how, notwithstanding the legal transplantation, corporate restructuring laws in these Asian jurisdictions have adapted and evolved due to the frictions in shareholder-creditor and creditor-creditor relationships, and the role of the state in resolving non-performing loans and financial distress of state-owned enterprises which are listed, or which issue public debt.

The study argues that any reforms must go beyond professionalising the insolvency professionals and the judiciary but must be designed to address fundamental issues of corporate governance, bank regulation and enforcing non-bankruptcy rules. It offers invaluable insights for academics and policy makers alike.

CONTEMPORARY STUDIES IN CORPORATE LAW

Series editors: Marc Moore, Christopher Bruner

Corporate law scholarship has a relatively recent history despite the fact that corporations have existed and been subject to legal regulation for three centuries. The modern flourishing of corporate law scholarship has been matched by some broadening of the field of study to embrace insolvency, corporate finance, corporate governance and regulation of the financial markets. At the same time the intersection between other branches of law such as, for example, labour, contract, criminal law, competition, and intellectual property law and the introduction of new inter-disciplinary methodologies affords new possibilities for studying the corporation. This series seeks to foster intellectually diverse approaches to thinking about the law and its role, scope and effectiveness in the context of corporate activity. In so doing the series aims to publish works of high intellectual content and theoretical rigour.

Titles in this series

Working Within Two Kinds of Capitalism: Corporate Governance and Employee Stakeholding: US and EC Perspectives
Irene Lynch Fannon

Contracting with Companies
Andrew Griffiths

The Law and Economics of Takeovers: An Acquirer's Perspective
Athanasios Kouloridas

The Foundations and Anatomy of Shareholder Activism
Iris H-Y Chiu

Corporate Governance in the Shadow of the State
Marc T Moore

Reconceptualising Corporate Compliance
Anna Donovan

Corporate Opportunities: A Law and Economics Analysis
Marco Claudio Corradi

The Making of the Modern Company
Susan Watson

Court-Supervised Restructuring of Large Distressed Companies in Asia

Law and Policy

Wai Yee Wan

•HART•
OXFORD • LONDON • NEW YORK • NEW DELHI • SYDNEY

HART PUBLISHING

Bloomsbury Publishing Plc

Kemp House, Chawley Park, Cumnor Hill, Oxford, OX2 9PH, UK

1385 Broadway, New York, NY 10018, USA

29 Earlsfort Terrace, Dublin 2, Ireland

HART PUBLISHING, the Hart/Stag logo, BLOOMSBURY and the Diana logo are trademarks of Bloomsbury Publishing Plc

First published in Great Britain 2022

A catalogue record for this book is available from the British Library.

A catalogue record for this book is available from the Library of Congress.

Library of Congress Control Number: 2022010748

ISBN: HB: 978-1-50995-233-5
ePDF: 978-1-50995-235-9
ePub: 978-1-50995-234-2

Typeset by Compuscript Ltd, Shannon

For Kian Tiong and Kai Jin

Preface

THE PRIMARY MOTIVATION for the book is to investigate the corporate restructuring law and practice of four Asian jurisdictions – Mainland China, India, Hong Kong and Singapore – and the optimal regulatory design of a restructuring framework. Many jurisdictions, when considering whether to reform their pre-insolvency or insolvency restructuring framework, continue to fundamentally adhere to a restructuring framework that requires the supervision of the court or a judicial body, but draw references from the Chapter 11 of the Bankruptcy Code 1978 of the United States (US) or to the schemes of arrangement in the United Kingdom (UK). Chapter 11 is a debtor in possession bankruptcy regime in which the managers remain in control of the debtor company. It is widely seen as the hallmark of a modern and progressive restructuring regime. The UK scheme of arrangement, which is described as a debtor in possession model for early-stage restructuring, but which continues to afford secured creditors significant rights, has proven to be very successful in the UK.

However, Asian companies operate in economies with very different institutions and market participants. Yet there is a dearth of academic literature on the optimal design of a corporate restructuring framework. With certain exceptions, there is little in the literature on the theoretical and empirical framework of an appropriate bankruptcy regimes in Asian jurisdictions with concentrated shareholdings and having to restructure diverse holdings of debt. In contrast, there is an influential and burgeoning work on corporate governance regimes in Asia. In prior works, together with others, I have argued that the legal transplantation of the Anglo-American corporate and securities laws (in particular, the use of independent directors and strengthening private securities action) in Hong Kong and Singapore does not take into account significant risk factors which are absent in the US and the UK. Hong Kong and Singapore are dominated by the presence of controlling shareholders, and a significant proportion of the companies use these two financial centres as places to raise capital, whilst locating their operations in other jurisdictions. Yet, the considerations for a legal framework when a company is solvent could be very different from a financially distressed company since the stakeholders are subject to different motivations. When a company is insolvent, shareholders may prefer a restructuring proposal that may be seen by creditors as gambling for resurrection since they (shareholders) have nothing further to lose while creditors wish to be repaid.

The key contribution of this book is the analysis of the solutions adopted by corporate restructuring laws in the US and the UK, to address the agency and coordination costs posed by frictions in shareholder–creditor, manager–creditor and the creditor–creditor relationships, have limitations in the context of Asian companies. These solutions also do not adequately consider the variations to the agency costs posed by the banking regulator's interests in resolving non-performing loans in emerging jurisdictions, the benefits and limitations of the independent gatekeepers operating in the insolvency and restructuring ecosystem, or the complex relationships between corporate restructuring law and other areas of the law.

The central thesis of this book is that an optimal design of corporate restructuring law must take into account the following factors and risks that are absent or not present to the same extent as in the US/UK: (1) the interaction between *concentrated shareholdings* and *widely-held debt* leading to significant risks of prejudice to outside creditors; (2) the incentives of the state in resolving non-performing loans for the purposes of bank regulation; (3) the benefits and limitations of the independent gatekeepers, being the insolvency practitioners and the courts; and (4) the interaction between restructuring law and non-restructuring law.

As economies around the world, including the four Asian jurisdictions under study, continue to grapple with COVID-19, these issues are even more relevant today as the number and variety of restructurings increase.

Acknowledgements

MY WORK ON this book was partially supported by the Collaborative Research Fund award from the Research Grants Council of the Hong Kong Special Administrative Region, China (Project No CityU C1115-20GF) for the project 'Hong Kong Insolvency Law and Policy in Times of COVID-19 and Beyond', and partially supported by a grant from City University of Hong Kong (CityU) (Project No 9380136) for the project 'Legal Transplantation of Chapter 11 of the US Bankruptcy Code'. I thank the Research Grants Council as well as CityU for providing funding to enable me to carry out the research.

Although my research for the project started intensively in early 2020, I have considered many of the ideas in the book for several years. I thank the many participants at the various academic forums, seminars and conferences I have attended who provided me with comments on my earlier insolvency and restructuring law papers, which have laid the foundations of this project linking corporate restructuring law, corporate governance and bank regulation. In particular, I thank colleagues at University of Cambridge, University of Leeds, Indian Institute of Corporate Affairs, Jinan University, Tsinghua University, Southwest University of Political Science and the Law and Wuhan University, where I presented and tested some of these very early ideas. I benefited from the discussions with insolvency practitioners, academic members and market professionals when I served on the Singapore Insolvency Law Review Committee in the early 2010s, and which published 'Report of the Insolvency Law Review Committee: Final Report' (Singapore Ministry of Law, 2013). That report, which together with a later report, formed the foundation of several changes to the insolvency and restructuring framework in Singapore in 2017. Together with Gerard McCormack and Casey Watters, I had the benefit of receiving the Singapore Judicial College Empirical Judicial Research Grant, which enabled the team to conduct in-depth empirical study on Singapore schemes of arrangement and the impact of the 2017 reforms in Singapore, and which was published in WY Wan, C Watters and G McCormack, 'Schemes of Arrangement in Singapore: Empirical and Comparative Analysis' (2020) 94 *American Bankruptcy Law Journal* 463. The empirical research has inspired me to later conduct a more wide-ranging study on the adoption of restructuring law changes in Asia. The views in this book are entirely my own.

Many friends and colleagues generously discussed aspects of my ideas or read draft chapters, including (but not limited to) Divyansh Dev, Simin Gao, Andrew Godwin, Aurelio Gurrea-Martinez, Gerard McCormack, Wei Shen, Neeti Shikha, Stacey Steele, Felix Steffek, Umakanth Varottil, Fang Wang, Jiangyu Wang, Bhargavi Zaveri, Jingchen Zhao, and Zinian Zhang (in alphabetical order by last names). In addition, I thank my co-principal investigators and collaborators involved in the Collaborative

Research Fund award, current colleagues at CityU and former colleagues at my previous academic institution, Singapore Management University (SMU), who have spent countless hours discussing with me the role of insolvency law in capital markets. I am also indebted to the various insolvency lawyers, insolvency practitioners, judges and market professionals in banks and distressed funds in Mainland China, India, Hong Kong and Singapore who have guided me to some of the information contained in this book and have spent a lot of time explaining to me the various aspects of the practice of restructuring, enforcing debt, corporate governance and the behaviour of stakeholders of firms facing financial distress in the respective jurisdictions. Despite the onset of COVID-19, which imposed severe travel restrictions in 2020 and 2021, I was able to conduct many of these discussions over emails, Zoom and conference calls with these stakeholders. As this book focuses not only on the rights under formal insolvency and restructuring law but also the effectiveness of these rights in practice, it would not be complete without insight from these market practitioners and judges. I have not mentioned them by name as many requested anonymity, and I believe that nearly all will prefer it.

In addition, I am deeply indebted to Professor Anthony J Casey of University of Chicago Law School, Professor Sarah Paterson of London School of Economics Law School, Professor Richard Squire of Fordham Law School and Professor Sally Wheeler of Australian National University for generously taking the time to review the book and provide comments and endorsements.

Several student research assistants at CityU have worked with me during the period of research, including Chloe Chan, Shuyi Cheng, Boris Chiu, Wenxuan Fan, Bella Lai and Ivan Sin. I thank them for their help. The students in my Cross-border Restructuring and Insolvency course in CityU and a related course, Law of Mergers and Acquisitions (given that one of the restructuring outcomes is a merger or an acquisition) in SMU, have constantly challenged me with perceptive and insightful questions and provided me with several ideas upon which I built the structure of the book.

I am grateful to Marc Moore and Christopher Bruner, the general editors of the Hart monograph series, Contemporary Studies in Corporate Law, for agreeing to include the book in the series, as well as the team at Hart Publishing, and in particular, Sinead Moloney, Roberta Bassi and Rosemarie Mearns, for bringing the project to fruition. I also thank the anonymous reviewers for my book proposal who have made extremely valuable comments and several suggestions which I have gladly incorporated.

Finally, my family provided the much-needed support during the period of this project.

I have attempted to state the law as of 31 August 2021.

Wai Yee WAN
Associate Dean and Professor of Law
City University of Hong Kong
December 2021

Table of Contents

Preface ... *vii*
Acknowledgements ... *ix*
List of Abbreviations ... *xv*
References to Judicial and Policy Guiding Documents in Mainland China (Bilingual) ... *xvii*
List of Tables ... *xxi*
List of Figures ... *xxiii*
Table of Cases ... *xxv*
Table of Legislation and Other Materials ... *xxxi*

1. Introduction and Theoretical Framework ... **1**
1.1. Overview ... 1
1.2. Restructuring Models in Anglo-America and Asia ... 8
1.2.1. The US Pure Debtor in Possession Regime ... 8
1.2.2. The Three UK Models ... 9
1.2.3. Transplanting US/UK Restructuring Concepts in Asia ... 10
1.3. Understanding the Interaction between Corporate Governance and Restructuring Law ... 12
1.4. Building an Analytical Framework ... 17
1.4.1. Management–Creditor and Shareholder–Creditor Conflicts ... 18
1.4.2. Creditor–Creditor Conflicts ... 18
1.4.3. Non-Performing Loans Management ... 19
1.4.4. The Gatekeepers ... 21
1.4.5. Non-Bankruptcy Rules on Enforcing Contracts and Directors' Duties ... 21
1.5. Methodology ... 22
1.5.1. Distinction between Deployment and Distribution ... 22
1.5.2. Court Restructurings of Large Companies ... 23
1.5.3. Choice of Asian Jurisdictions ... 24
1.5.4. Framework of the Book ... 26
1.6. Organisation of the Book ... 31

2. Development of Corporate Restructuring Law in Four Asian Jurisdictions ... **33**
2.1. Introduction ... 33
2.2. Emerging Jurisdictions ... 35
2.2.1. Mainland China ... 36
2.2.2. India ... 39

2.3. Advanced Jurisdictions 44
2.3.1. Hong Kong 44
2.3.2. Singapore 51
2.4. Conclusion 55

3. The Agency Costs of Manager–Creditor and Shareholder–Creditor Relationships in Restructuring 57
3.1. Introduction 57
3.2. Institutional and Organisational Background 60
3.2.1. The US and the UK 60
3.2.2. Asia 61
3.3. Strategies to Deal with Agency Costs of Manager–Creditor and Shareholder–Creditor Conflicts in Anglo-American Restructurings 66
3.3.1. The Hold-Out Problem 66
3.3.2. Heightened Friction between Creditors and Shareholders 70
3.4. Addressing Information Asymmetry and Hold-Out Problems in Asian Restructurings 73
3.4.1. Process of Bargaining: Mandatory Disclosure Regime 73
3.4.2. Distribution of Proceeds of Restructuring and the APR in Asia 75
3.4.3. Heightened Conflicts in Asian Restructurings 85
3.5. Enhancing the Restructuring Regime: Lessons and Implications 93
3.5.1. No One-Size-Fits-All Rule for APR and Cram-Down 94
3.5.2. The Example of Corporate Governance 94
3.6. Conclusion 99

4. The Agency and Coordination Costs of Creditor–Creditor Relationships in Restructuring 101
4.1. Introduction 101
4.2. Institutional and Organisational Background 103
4.2.1. The US and the UK 103
4.2.2. Asia 105
4.2.3. Distressed Debt and Loan Markets 113
4.3. Strategies to Deal with Agency and Coordination Costs of Creditor–Creditor Conflicts in Anglo-American Restructurings 114
4.3.1. The Deployment Question 115
4.3.2. The Distribution Question 118
4.3.3. Creditor Protection in Cram-Downs 121
4.3.4. Existing Bank Creditor Providing New Finance 123
4.4. The Features of Asian Restructurings 124
4.4.1. The Deployment Question 124
4.4.2. Distribution of Assets 131
4.5. Enhancing the Restructuring Regime in Asia: Lessons and Implications 143
4.5.1. The Advantages and Limits of the APR and Equal Treatment 143
4.5.2. Reducing the Costs of Negotiation Among Creditors 146
4.5.3. Recent Developments in Onshore and Offshore Restructuring 148
4.6. Conclusion 150

5. **Managing Non-Performing Loans and their Impact on Agency and Coordination Costs in Two Emerging Jurisdictions** 152
5.1. Introduction 152
5.2. Institutional and Organisational Background in the International Context for Resolving NPLs 154
5.2.1. AMCs as Debt Aggregation Vehicles 154
5.2.2. Developing the Market for Distressed Assets 155
5.3. Institutional Background to NPLs in India and Mainland China 156
5.3.1. India 156
5.3.2. Mainland China 160
5.4. AMCs and Variations to Agency and Coordination Costs in Restructuring 161
5.4.1. AMCs in India 162
5.4.2. CAMCs in China 171
5.4.3. Variations to the Agency Costs of CAMCs in China 177
5.5. Developing Active Distressed Loan Markets in India and Mainland China 181
5.5.1. India 181
5.5.2. Mainland China 183
5.6. Conclusion, Lessons and Implications for Managing NPLs 185
5.6.1. Incentivising CAMCs/ARCs 186
5.6.2. Future of the CAMC/ARC Model and Distressed Loan Markets 187
5.7. Postscript 187

6. **Insolvency Practitioners as Gatekeeper Intermediaries** 188
6.1. Introduction 188
6.2. Role of Insolvency Practitioners: A Comparative Perspective 191
6.2.1. The PIP Model 191
6.2.2. Schemes of Arrangement with Insolvency Practitioner Having a Statutory or an Intermediary Role 199
6.3. The Governance of Intermediaries: Accountability, Conflicts of Interest and Effectiveness 201
6.3.1. Appointment and Accountability 202
6.3.2. Fee Arrangements 204
6.3.3. Conflicts of Interest 206
6.3.4. Effectiveness of the Insolvency Practitioner 207
6.4. Lessons, Implications and Options for Reform in Asian Jurisdictions 210
6.4.1. Reconceptualising the Role of the Insolvency Practitioner 210
6.4.2. Reforms Addressing the Insolvency Practitioner's Conflicts of Interest 213
6.5. Conclusion 215

7. **Role of the Courts in Court-Supervised Restructurings** 217
7.1. Introduction 217
7.2. Legislative Framework and Judicial Discretion in the US and the UK: Strengths and Limitations 220

7.2.1. The Moratorium 220
7.2.2. Plan Confirmation or Sanction of the Scheme of Arrangement 223
7.2.3. Analysis 226
7.3. Legislative Framework and Judicial Discretion in Asia 227
7.3.1. Moratorium and Conditions 228
7.3.2. Sanction of the Scheme 234
7.3.3. Rescue Financing 236
7.4. Lessons and Implications 238
7.4.1. Leeway to Debtor's Management 239
7.4.2. Cram-Down of Dissenting Creditors and Valuation 240
7.4.3. Rescue Financing 241
7.4.4. The Choice and Objectives of Regulation 242
7.5. The Experience of Mainland China 245
7.5.1. Improving Certainty and Predictability of Plan Approval through Judicial Pronouncements 247
7.5.2. Addressing the Length of Time in Restructuring and Moratorium 248
7.5.3. Analysis and the Future of Pre-Packs 250
7.6. Conclusion 251

8. Relationship between Restructuring Law, Enforcing Contracts and Directors' Duties 253
8.1. Introduction 253
8.2. Impact of Enforcing Creditor Rights on Restructuring Law 255
8.2.1. Enforcement of Debts and Resolving Insolvency 255
8.2.2. Usage of Formal Insolvency and Restructuring Law 257
8.3. Analysis 268
8.4. Directors' Duties and Incentives to Invoke or Use Restructuring Law 269
8.4.1. Why should Incentives to Commence Insolvency Proceedings Matter? 269
8.4.2. Incentives in Asia 271
8.5. Conclusion 274

9. Restructuring Law, Implications for Reform and Conclusion 275
9.1. Introduction 275
9.2. Seven Propositions in this Book 276
9.3. Future Prospects for Reform in the Asian Jurisdictions 285
9.3.1. Mainland China 285
9.3.2. India 287
9.3.3. Hong Kong 289
9.3.4. Singapore 291
9.4. Conclusion 292

Appendices *294*
Bibliography *302*
Index *319*

List of Abbreviations

ABC	Agricultural Bank of China
AMC	Asset management companies
APR	Absolute priority rule
ARC	Asset reconstruction companies (in India)
BOC	Bank of China
BOCOM	Bank of Communications
BVI	British Virgin Islands
CAMC	Chinese asset management companies
CBIRC	China Banking and Insurance Regulatory Commission
CCB	China Construction Bank
Chapter 11	Chapter 11 of the US Bankruptcy Code 1978 (US)
CIGA	Corporate Insolvency and Governance Act 2020 (UK)
CIRP	Corporate Insolvency Resolution Process (India)
Companies Ordinance	Companies Ordinance, Cap 622 (HK)
CSRC	China Securities Regulatory Commission
DIP	Debtor in possession
EBL	Enterprise Bankruptcy Law 2006 (PRC)
GDP	Gross domestic product
Hong Kong	Hong Kong Special Administrative Region, China
HKMA	Hong Kong Monetary Authority
IBBI	Insolvency and Bankruptcy Board of India (India)
IBC	Insolvency and Bankruptcy Code 2016 (India)
ICBC	Industrial and Commercial Bank of China
IMF	International Monetary Fund
IP	Insolvency practitioner

IRDA	Insolvency, Restructuring and Dissolution Act 2018 (Singapore)
MAS	Monetary Authority of Singapore
MOF	Ministry of Finance (PRC)
MSMEs	Micro, small and medium-size enterprises
NBFC	Non-banking financial companies
NCLAT	National Company Law Appellate Tribunal (India)
NCLT	National Company Law Tribunal (India)
NPA or NPL	Non-performing assets or non-performing loans
PBOC	People's Bank of China
PIP	Practitioner in possession
PRC	People's Republic of China (for the purposes of this book, excludes Hong Kong Special Administrative Region, Macau Special Administrative Region and the territory of Taiwan)
RBI	Reserve Bank of India (India)
SAFE	State Administration of Foreign Exchange (PRC)
SARFAESI	Securitisation and Reconstruction of Financial Assets and Enforcement of Security Interest Act 2002 (India)
SEBI	Securities and Exchange Board of India
SEHK	Stock Exchange of Hong Kong
SGX	Stock Exchange of Singapore
SME	Small and medium-sized enterprises
SSE	Shanghai Stock Exchange
SZSE	Shenzhen Stock Exchange
UK	United Kingdom
UNCITRAL	United Nations Commission on International Trade Law
US	United States

References to Judicial and Policy Guiding Documents in Mainland China (Bilingual)

(In chronological order)

Organic Law of People's Courts of the People's Republic of China (Adopted at the 2nd session of the Fifth National People's Congress on July 1, 1979, amended for the first time according to the Decision of the 2nd Session of the Standing Committee of the Sixth National People's Congress on Amending the Organic Law of the People's Courts of the People's Republic of China on September 2, 1983; amended for the second time according to the Decision of the 18th Session of the Standing Committee of the Sixth National People's Congress on Amending the Organic Law of the Local People's Congresses at All Levels and Local People's Governments at All Levels of the People's Republic of China on December 2, 1986; amended for the third time according to the Decision of the 24th Session of the Standing Committee of the Tenth National People's Congress on Amending the Organic Law of the People's Courts of the People's Republic of China on October 31, 2006; and revised at the 6th session of the Standing Committee of the Thirteenth National People's Congress on October 26, 2018)

中国人民共和国人民法院组织法 (1979年7月1日第五届全国人民代表大会第二次会议通过 根据1983年9月2日第六届全国人民代表大会常务委员会第二次会议《关于修改〈中华人民共和国人民法院组织法〉的决定》第一次修正 根据1986年12月2日第六届全国人民代表大会常务委员会第十八次会议《关于修改〈中华人民共和国地方各级人民代表大会和地方各级人民政府组织法〉的决定》第二次修正 根据2006年10月31日第十届全国人民代表大会常务委员会第二十四次会议《关于修改〈中华人民共和国人民法院组织法〉的决定》第三次修正 2018年10月26日第十三届全国人民代表大会常务委员会第六次会议修订)

Notice of the People's Bank of China on the Guidance on Provisioning for Loan Losses No 82 [2002] of the People's Bank of China

中国人民银行关于印发《银行贷款损失准备计提指引》的通知 (银发[2002] 98号)

Notice of the Ministry of Finance about Issuing the Measures for the Administration of the Asset Disposal of Financial Asset Management Companies (Revision) [Expired] (No 41 [2004] issued by the Ministry of Finance on April 30th, 2004)

财政部关于印发《金融资产管理公司资产处置管理办法(修订)》的通知 （财金[2004] 41号 2004年4月30日）

Supreme People's Court, Provisions of the Supreme People's Court on the Judicial Interpretation Work [Revised], No 12 [2007] (Notice by Supreme People's Court on Issuing the Provisions of the Supreme People's Court on the Judicial Interpretation Work (No 12 [2007] of the Supreme People's Court))

最高人民法院印发《最高人民法院关于司法解释工作的规定》的通知 (法发〔2007〕12号)

Supreme People's Court, Provisions of the Supreme People's Court on Designating the Administrator during the Trial of Enterprise Bankruptcy Cases, Judicial Interpretation No 8 [2007]

最高人民法院关于审理企业破产案件指定管理人的规定 (法释 [2007] 8号)

Provisions of the Supreme People's Court on Determination of the Administrator's Remunerations: Announcement of the Supreme People's Court of the People's Republic of China No 129 [2007]

最高人民法院关于执行《最高人民法院审理企业破产案件指定管理人的规定》、《最高人民法院审理企业破产案件确定管理人报酬的规定》几个问题的通知（2007年4月12日　法明传[2007] 129号）

China Banking Regulatory Commission (CBRC), Relevant Questions Regarding CBRC Measures on Commercial Banks Transferring Loans to Social Investors, 2009, No 24.

银监会《中国银监会办公厅关于商业银行向社会投资者转让贷款债权法律效力有关问题的批复》（银监办发 [2009] 24号）

Opinions of the Supreme People's Court on Several Issues Concerning Correctly Trying Enterprise Bankruptcy Cases to Provide Judicial Protection for Maintaining the Order of Market Economy (No 36 [2009] of the Supreme People's Court)

最高人民法院关于正确审理企业破产案件为维护市场经济秩序提供司法保障若干问题的意见 [现行有效](法发〔2009〕36号)

Notice of the Supreme People's Court on the Summary of Minutes of the Symposium on the Trial of Cases concerning Bankruptcy Reorganisation of Listed Companies [Effective] (29 October 2012), promulgation (No 261 [2012] of the Supreme People's Court)

最高人民法院印发《关于审理上市公司破产重整案件工作座谈会纪要》的通知 [现行有效] (法 [2012] 261号)

The Management Measures on the Bulk Transfer of Non-performance Assets of Financial Enterprises (No 6 [2012] of the China Bank Regulatory Commission)

财政部银监会关于印发〈金融企业不良资产批量转让管理办法〉的通知 (财金〔2012〕6号)

Circular of the SAFE on Releasing the Provisions on Foreign Exchange Administration for Cross-border Guarantees (*Huifa* No 29 [2014])

国家外汇管理局关于发布《跨境担保外汇管理规定》的通知 (汇发 [2014] 29号)

Shenzhen Intermediate People's Court, Rules Governing Bankruptcy Administrators

深圳市中级人民法院破产案件管理人工作规范（2015年2月5日深圳市中级人民法院审判委员会民事行政执行 专业委员会第1次会议通过）(2018年10月19日)

Opinions of the State Council on Vigorously, Steadily and Properly Reducing Corporate Leverage Ratios [Effective] (No 54 [2016] of the State Council)

国务院关于积极稳妥降低企业杠杆率的意见 [现行有效] (国发[2016] 54号)

Notice of the Supreme People's Court on Issuing the Minutes of the National Court Work Conference on Bankruptcy Trials [Effective] (No 53 [2018] of the Supreme People's Court)

最高人民法院印发《全国法院破产审判工作会议纪要》的通知 [现行有效]（法〔2018〕53号）

Notice of the National Development and Reform Commission on Steps to Deal with Zombie Companies and Eliminate Over-Capacity (No 1756) [2018])

关于进一步做好"僵尸企业"及去产能企业债务处置工作的通知 (发改财金 [2018] 1756号)

Notice of the National Development and Reform Commission, the People's Bank of China, the Ministry of Finance and Other Ministries and Commissions on the Specific Policy Issues concerning the Implementation of the Market-Oriented Debt-Equity Swaps of Banks (No 152 [2018] of the National Development and Reform Commission)

国家发展改革委、人民银行、财政部、银监会、国务院国资委、证监会、保监会关于市场化银行债权转股权实施中有关具体政策问题的通知 (发改财金〔2018〕152号）

Provisions (III) of the Supreme People's Court on Several Issues concerning the Application of the Enterprise Bankruptcy Law of the People's Republic of China [Revised] Interpretation No 3 [2019] of the Supreme People's Court

最高人民法院关于适用《中华人民共和国企业破产法》若干问题的规定(三) [已被修订]（法释 [2019] 3号）

Notice by the National Development and Reform Commission, the Supreme People's Court, the Ministry of Industry and Information Technology and Other Departments of Issuing the Reform Plan for Accelerating Improvement of the Exit System for Market Participants [Effective] (No 1104 [2019] of the National Development and Reform Commission)

国家发展改革委、最高人民法院、工业和信息化部、民政部、司法部、财政部、人力资源社会保障部、人民银行、国资委、税务总局、市场监管总局、银保监会、证监会关于印发《加快完善市场主体退出制度改革方案》的通知 (发改财金 [2019] 1104号)

Notice of the Supreme People's Court on Issuing the Minutes of the National Courts' Civil and Commercial Trial Work Conference, [2019] No 254, effective 8 November 2019

最高人民法院关于印发《全国法院民商事审判工作会议纪要》的通知 [现行有效]（法〔2019〕254号）

Shenzhen Intermediate People's Court, Practice Directions on Reorganisations, 14 March 2019

【审理企业重整案件的共作指引】.

The Measures Relating to the Asset Management Business of Financial Assets Investment Companies (No 12 [2020] CBIRC)

中国银保监会关于金融资产投资公司开展资产管理业务有关事项的通知 (银保监发〔2020〕12号)

Notice by the Supreme People's Court on Issuing the Minutes of the National Courts Symposium on the Trial of Bond Disputes [Effective] (No 185 [2020] of the Supreme People's Court)

最高人民法院关于印发《全国法院审理债券纠纷案件座谈会纪要》的通知 [现行有效]（法 [2020] 185号）

Notice by the China Banking and Insurance Regulatory Commission, the National Development and Reform Commission, the People's Bank of China, and the China Securities Regulatory Commission of Issuing the Work Procedures of Financial Institutional Creditors' Committees [Effective] No 57 [2020] of the China Banking and Insurance Regulatory Commission

中国银保监会、发展改革委、中国人民银行、中国证监会关于印发金融机构债权人委员会工作规程的通知（银保监发[2020]57号）

Rules Governing the Listing of Shares on the ChiNext Market of Shenzhen Stock Exchange (2020 Revision)

深圳证券交易所创业板股票上市规则 (2020年修订)

Notice by the General Office of the China Banking and Insurance Regulatory Commission of Implementing the Pilot Work of Non-Performing Loans (No 26 [2021] of the China Banking and Insurance Regulatory Commission)

中国银保监会办公厅关于开展不良贷款转让试点工作的通知 （银保监办便函〔2021〕26号）

List of Tables

Table 1.1 Models of debt restructuring systems 4
Table 3.1 Schemes of arrangement for listed companies in Singapore (2015–20) 78
Table 3.2 Schemes of arrangement for listed companies in Hong Kong (2015–20) 85
Table 4.1 Bank and total credit to GDP for non-financial private sector 106
Table 4.2 Differential treatment of financial versus non-financial creditors 134
Table 4.3 Differential treatment of small debt-holders 135
Table 5.1 Shareholdings of asset reconstruction companies 168
Table 5.2 Shareholding of national Chinese asset management companies 179
Table 6.1 Role of the IP in PIP regimes 210

List of Figures

Figure 1.1 Interaction between shareholders and creditors in Anglo-American and Asian frameworks ... 14
Figure 2.1 Winding-up petitions presented and ordered from 1997 to 2020... 48
Figure 3.1 Number and amount of defaults in China's onshore bond market by SOEs and private enterprises ... 65
Figure 4.1 Onshore bond market for Mainland China ... 107
Figure 4.2 Status of issuers of bonds in default as at 31 December 2020... 108
Figure 4.3 Onshore bond market for India ... 109
Figure 4.4 Corporate local and foreign currency bonds outstanding in Hong Kong and Singapore... 110
Figure 4.5 Number of CIRPs filed ... 132
Figure 5.1 NPL ratios in India ... 158
Figure 5.2 Size of non-performing loans in India... 159
Figure 5.3 Recovery of NPAs through various channels ... 159
Figure 5.4 NPA ratios in China (%) ... 160
Figure 5.5 Size of NPLs in Mainland China ... 161
Figure 5.6 Special mention loans for commercial banks in China... 161
Figure 5.7 NPAs acquired and security receipts subscribed ... 163
Figure 5.8 Security receipts subscribed by parties ... 164
Figure 5.9 Time period in which single loan trades to ARCs take place before or after commencement of CIRP... 166
Figure 5.10 Time for sale of NPLs by classification of seller... 167
Figure 5.11 Sector distribution of CIRPS admitted 2016–20 ... 170
Figure 5.12 Number of single NPL sales to ARCs by sector... 170
Figure 5.13 NPLs of commercial banks by top five industries ... 180
Figure 5.14 Risk concentration of distressed assets of Cinda and Huarong... 180
Figure 7.1 Distribution of the number of days in Chapter 11 ... 222
Figure 7.2 Average time spent in CIRP ... 233
Figure 7.3 Distribution of the number of days spent in CIRP 2016–21 where resolution plans are approved ... 234
Figure 7.4 Length of time Chinese listed companies spent in restructuring in court... 249
Figure 8.1 Enforcement of contracts and resolving insolvency ... 256
Figure 8.2 Usage of formal insolvency and restructuring law ... 257
Figure 8.3 Bankruptcy petitions (leading to liquidation) over company exits... 258
Figure 8.4 Number of bankruptcy cases accepted by the Chinese courts... 267

Table of Cases

BERMUDA

Agritrade Resources Ltd, Re [2020] SC (Bda) 28 Com (17 June 2020) 231
Fidelity Advisor Series VIII v APP China Group Ltd [2007] Bda LR 35 72

CANADA

Toronto-Dominion Bank v Ty (Canada) Inc (2003), 42 CBR (4th) 142, 2003 Carswell Ont 371 (Ont SCJ) 126

CHINA

Dandong Intermediate People's Court, 'Dandong Port Group Debt Restructuring' [辽宁省丹东市中级人民法院民事裁定书：关于批准丹东港集团重整草案的裁定 (2019) 辽06破2-5号], dated 31 December 2019 .... 81, 91, 139
Shanghai Financial Court, 'Decision of the Court on Keepwell Deed', 上海金融法院涉"维好协议"香港特别行政区法院判决在内地申请认可和执行的认定标准—时和全球投资基金SPC-时和价值投资基金申请认可和执行香港特别行政区法院民事判决 (16 November 2020) 149, 150
Shenzhen Intermediate People's Court, Restructuring of Shenzhen Fuchang Electronic Technology [深圳市福昌电子技术有限公司破产重整案】 (14 April 2017) 93, 250

HONG KONG

Agritrade Resources Ltd, Re [2020] HKCFI 1967, [2020] 4 HKLRD 616 47
Albatronics (Far East) Ltd (in liq), Re [2001] 3 HKC 223 .... 47, 85
APP (Hong Kong) Ltd, Re [2005] 1 HKLRD 272 87
Century Sun International Ltd, Re [2021] HKCFI 2928 87
China Bozza Development Holdings, Re [2021] HKCFI 1235 .... 113, 137, 230, 232, 239, 243, 267, 271, 290
China Huiyuan Juice Group Ltd [2020] HKCFI 2940 .... 48, 49, 148, 243

China Oil Gangran Energy Group Holdings Ltd, Re [2021] HKCFI 1592, [2021] 3 HKLRD 69 243
China Singyes Solar Technologies Holdings, Re [2020] HKCU 548 234
China Solar Energy Holdings Ltd, Re [2018] HKCFI 555, [2018] 2 HKLRD 338 .... 46, 126
China Solar Energy Holdings Ltd, Re HCCW 108/2015, [2016] HKCU 465, CFI 27, 47, 200, 231, 290
China Solar Energy Holdings Ltd, Re HCCW108A/2015, [2017] 2 HKLRD 1074 .... 27, 290
Cyberworks Audio Video Technology Ltd, Re [2010] 2 HKLRD 1137, HKCFI 271
Da Yu Financial Holdings Ltd, Re [2019] HKCFI 2531 201
FDG Electric Vehicles Ltd, Re [2020] HKCFI 2931, [2020] 5 HKLRD 701 .... 47, 127, 231
Hsin Chong Group Holdings Ltd, Re [2019] HKCFI 805 .... 28, 47
Kaisa Group Holdings Ltd, Re [2016] HKCU 2765 234
KB (Asia) Ltd, Re [2014] HKEC 1192 87
Lamtex Holdings Ltd, Re. See Li Yiqing v Lamtex Holdings Ltd ....
Legend International Resorts Ltd, Re [2005] 3 HKLRD 16, HKCFI 113
Legend International Resorts Ltd, Re [2006] 2 HKLRD 192, HKCA 27, 47, 126, 200, 230, 290
Lehman Brothers Securities Asia Ltd (in liquidation), Re [2017] HKCFI 204, [2017] 2 HKLRD 871, HCMP 2266/2016 .... 130, 138
Lerthai Group Ltd, Re [2021] HKCFI 207 50
Li Yiqing v Lamtex Holdings Ltd [2021] HKCFI 622 .... 49, 50, 113, 137, 231, 242
Mongolian Mining Corporation, Re [2018] HKCU 3109 234
Moody Technology Holdings, Re [2020] HKCFI 416, [2020] 2 HKLRD 187 .... 28, 47
Rhine Holdings Ltd (in Liquidation), Re (2000) HCCW 510/1998 201
Rhine Holdings Ltd (in liq), Re [2000] 3 HKC 543 .... 47, 85
3D-Gold Jewellery Holdings Ltd, Re [2009] HKEC 1104 .... 130, 138
Trinity (Management Services Ltd), In the Matter of [2021] HKCFI 2207 .... 45, 50
UDL Argos Engineering & Heavy Industries Co Ltd v Li Oi Lin [2000] HKCFI 1568, [2001] 3 HKLRD 634 .... 122, 141, 234
Victory City International Holdings Ltd, Re [2021] HKCFI 1370 232
Winsway Enterprises Holdings Ltd, Re [2016] HKCFI 1915 234
Yaohan Hong Kong Corp (in liq), Re [2000] 4 HKC 488 .... 47, 85
Z-Obee Holdings Ltd, Re [2017] HKCFI 2204, [2018] 1 HKLRD 165, [2017] HKCU 3186 .... 28, 47, 231

INDIA

ArcelorMittal India Private Ltd v Satish Kumar Gupta, Civil Appeal No 9582 of 2018 (2019) 2 SCC 1 (4 October 2018), Supreme Court of India 83, 208
Bank of Maharashtra v Videocon Industries, Company Appeal (AT) (Ins) No 503 of 2021 236

Bhushan Power and Steel NCLT 26 July 2017, approved by the NCLT 5 September 2019 and by the NCLAT 17 February 2020 75
Committee of Creditors of Essar Steel India through SBI v Satish Kumar Gupta, Company Appeal (AT) (Ins) No 242 of 2019 96
DBS Bank Ltd v Shailendra Ajmera (Resolution Professional of Ruchi Soya Industries Ltd) Company Appeal (AT) (Insolvency) No 788 of 2019 ..... 140, 144, 244
Dharani Sugars and Chemicals Ltd v Union of India – Transferred Case (Civil) No 66 of 2018 in Transfer Petition (Civil) No 1399 of 2018 (2 April 2019), Supreme Ct of India 44
Edelweiss Asset Reconstruction Company Ltd v Synergies Dooray Automotive Ltd, Company Appeal (AT) (Insolvency) No 169 of 2017 89
Essar Steel India Ltd, Committee of Creditors v Satish Kumar Gupta & Ors, Civil Appeal 8766-67 of 2019 (SC), [2020] 8 SCC 531 ..... 43, 75, 82, 83, 84, 129, 130, 131, 140, 142, 144, 147, 196, 208, 211, 233, 235, 244, 245
Gujarat Urja Vikas Nigam Ltd v Amit Gupta & Ors Civil Appeal No 9241 of 2019 (21 March 2021), Supreme Ct 125
India Resurgence ARC Private Litd v Amit Metaliks Ltd Civil Appeal No 1700 of 2021 132
Jindal Steel & Power Limited v Arun Kumar Jagatramka & Gujarat NRE Coke, Company Appeal (AT) No 221 of 2018, NCLAT 84
Jaypee Kensington Boulevard Apartments Welfare Association & Ors v NBCC (India) Ltd & Ors Civil Appeal No 3395 of 2020 .....144, 206
JSW Steel Ltd v Mahender Kumar Khandelwal, Company Appeal (AT) (Insolvency) No 957 of 2019 96
Lalit Mishra & Ors v Sharon Bio Medicine Ltd, Company Appeal Insolvency No 164 of 2018 83
Maharashtra Seamless Steel Ltd v Padmanabhan Venkatesh & Ors, Civil Appeal No 4242 of 2019, Supreme Court 140
Pankaj Yadav v State Bank of India, Company Appeal (AT) (Insolvency) No 28 of 2018 89
Peter Beck & Partners v Sharon Bio Medicine Ltd [2018] 1 IBJ 254 (NCLT) 129
Phoenix Arc Private Limited v Spade Financial Services Ltd, Civil Appeal 2842 of 2020 (1 February 2020) 89, 95
Pratap Technocrats (P) Ltd & Ors v Monitoring Committee of Reliance Infratel Ltd (Civil Appeal 676 of 2021) 43, 130, 236
Saket Tex Dye Private Ltd v Kailash T Shah MA 705/2020 in CP 1981(IB)/MB/2019 ..... 129, 164, 196
Sashidhar v Indian Overseas Bank & Ors Civil Appeal 10673 of 2018 (Supreme Court, 5 February 2019) 130, 197, 235
SC Sekaran v Amit Gupta and Ors, Company Appeal (AT) Nos 495 and 496 of 2019 84
State Bank of India v Ram Dev International Ltd, Company Appeal (AT) (Insolvency) No 302 of 2018 207

State Bank of India vs M/s Metenere Ltd, Company Appeal (AT) (Insolvency) No 76 of 2020 207
Swiss Ribbons Private Ltd v Union of India (2019) 4 SCC 17 ....82, 84, 131
Union of India v Vijaykumar V Iyer Company Appeal (AT) (Insolvency) No 733 of 2020 133
Videocon Industries Ltd, Re IA 196 of 2021 (NCLT) 235, 244

SINGAPORE

Design Studio Group Ltd, Re [2020] SGHC 148 238
DSG Asia Holdings Pte Ltd, Re [2021] SGHC 209 ....88, 95
Empire Capital Resources Pte Ltd, Re [2018] SGHC 36 73
Hitachi Plant Engineering & Construction v Eltraco International [2003] SGCA 38 77
HTL International Holdings Pte Ltd, Re [2021] SGHC 86 198
IM Skaugen SE, Re [2018] SGHC 259 ....228, 229
Kobian Pte Ltd, Re HC/OS 1269/2020, unreported 228, 239
KS Energy Ltd and another matter, Re [2020] SGHC 198 197
nTan Corporate Advisory Pte Ltd v TT International Ltd [2018] SGCA 69 205
Ocean Tankers (Pte Ltd) v Rajah & Tann Originating Summons No 666 of 2020 (Summons No 4317 of 2020) 209
Pacific Andes Resources Development, Re [2016] SGHC 210 ....53, 54
Pathfinder Strategic Credit LP v Empire Capital Resources (Pathfinder) [2019] SGCA 29 ....73, 74, 228, 230, 240
Royal Bank of Scotland NV (formerly known as ABN Amro Bank NV) and others v TT ....
International Ltd and another appeal [2012] SGCA 9, [2012] 2 SLR 213 ....88, 130, 138, 141, 142, 200, 205, 206, 234, 235
SK Engineering v Conchubar [2017] SGCA 51 ....88, 235
TT International Ltd, Re [2012] SGCA 53, [2012] 4 SLR 1182 241
Yihua Lifestyle Technology Co, Ltd and another v HTL International Holdings Pte Ltd and others [2021] SGCA 87 198

UNITED KINGDOM

All Scheme Ltd, Re [2021] EWHC 1401 (Ch) 102, 122, 123, 225
Bluebrook, Re [2009] EWHC 2114 (Ch), [2010] 1 BCLC 338, [2010] BCC 209 ....9, 70, 120
BTI 2014 LLC v Sequana SA & others [2019] EWCA Civ 112, [2019] 1 BCLC 347 270
Charnley Davies Ltd (No 2), Re [1990] BCLC 760, [1990] BCC 605, ChD 193
Codere Finance II (UK) Ltd, Re [2020] EWHC 2441 (Ch), [2021] 2 BCLC 396 ....117, 118

Codere Finance II (UK) Ltd, Re [2020] EWHC 2683 (Ch), [2021] 2 BCLC 428 .... 118, 224
Debenhams Retail Ltd (in Administration) [2020] EWHC 921 (Ch), [2020] 3 All ER 319, [2020] 2 All ER (Comm) 409, [2010] 1 BCLC 747 .... 10, 193
Debenhams Retail Ltd (in administration), Re [2020] EWCA Civ 600, [2020] Bus LR 788, [2020] BCC 548, [2020] IRLR 524 .... 10, 193
DeepOcean I UK Ltd, Re [2021] EWHC 138 (Ch), [2021] All ER D) 08 (Feb) 121
DKLL Solicitors v HMRC [2007] EWHC 2067 (Ch), [2008] 1 BCLC 112, [2007] BCC 908 192
Four Private Investment Funds v Lomas and others [2008] EWHC 2869 (Ch), [2009] 1 BCLC 161, [2009] BCC 632 193
Gategroup Guarantee Ltd, Re [2021] EWHC 304 (Ch), [2022] 1 BCLC 98 191
Hawk Insurance Co Ltd, Re [2001] EWCA Civ 241, [2001] 2 BCLC 480, [2002] BCC 300 .... 122, 224, 225
House of Fraser (funding) PLC, Re [2018] EWHC 1906 (Ch), [2019] 2 BCLC 278 67
Hurricane Energy Plc, Re [2021] EWHC 1759 (Ch), [2022] 1 BCLC 36 .... 76, 121, 225
Indah Kiat International Finance Co, Re [2016] EWHC 246 (Ch), [2016] BCC 418, [2016] All ER (D) 144 (Feb) 67, 72, 95, 235
Lehman Bros Australia Ltd v MacNamara and others [2020] EWCA Civ 321, [2020] 3 WLR 147 193
Lehman Brothers Europe Ltd, Re [2017] EWHC 2031 (Ch), [2018] Bus LR 439, [2018] 2 All ER 367 192
Lehman Brothers International (Europe) (in administration), Re [2018] EWHC 1980 (Ch), [2019] Bus LR 1012, [2019] BCC 115 72
MAB Leasing Ltd, Re [2021] EWHC 379 (Ch) 102
Meem SL Ltd, Re [2017] EWHC 2688 (Ch), [2018] Bus LR 393, [2017] WLR(D) 718 193
Mytravel Group Plc, Re [2004] EWHC 2741 (Ch), [2005] 1 WLR 2365, [2005] 2 BCLC 123 120
New Look Secured Issuer plc, Re [2019] EWHC 960 (Ch), [2019] All ER (D) 91 Apr 122
Noble Group Ltd, Re [2018] EWHC 2911 (Ch), [2019] Bus LR 947, [2019] 2 BCLC 505 .... 117, 118, 123, 141, 225
Noble Group Ltd, Re [2018] EWHC 3092 (Ch), [2019] 2 BCLC 548 .... 224, 225
Practice Statement (Companies: Schemes of Arrangement under Part 26 and Part 26A of the Companies Act 2006) 122
Practice Statement (Companies: Schemes of Arrangement) [2002] 1 WLR 1345 122
Primacom Holding GmbH v Credit Agricole [2012] EWHC 164 (Ch) 122
SABMiller plc, Re [2016] EWHC 2153 (Ch), [2017] Ch 173, [2017] 2 WLR 837 123
Savoy Hotel Ltd, Re [1981] Ch 351, [1981] 3 All ER 646, ChD 224
Sea Assets Ltd v PT Garuda Indonesia [2001] EWCA Civ 1696 .... 121, 123
Sovereign Life Assurance Co v Dodd [1892] 2 QB 573, 62 LJQB 19 122
Sunbird Business Services, Re [2020] EWHC 2493 (Ch), [2020] Bus LR 2371 .... 67, 72, 118, 225, 235

Swissport Fuelling Ltd, Re [2020] EWHC 1499 (Ch), [2021] 1 BCLC 527 224
T&N Ltd, Re [2006] EWHC 1447 (Ch), [2007] Bus LR 1411, [2007] 1 All ER 851 67
Tea Corporation, Re [1904] 1 Ch 12, 73 LJ Ch 57, CA 121
Telewest Communications Plc, Re [2004] EWHC 924 (Ch), [2005] 1 BCLC 752 117
Virgin Atlantic Airways Ltd, Re [2020] EWHC 2376 (Ch), [2021] 1 BCLC 105 .... 121, 123, 131, 225
Virgin Active Holdings Ltd, Re [2021] EWHC 1246 (Ch), [2021] All ER (D) 100 (May) 76, 102
West Mercia Safetywear v Dodd [1988] BCLC 250, 4 BCC 30, CA 270

USA

Ad Hoc Committee of Non-consenting Creditors v Peabody Energy Corp 933 F 3d 918 (8th Cir 2019) 118
Aleris International, Inc, et al, Ch 11 Case No 09-10478 (BLS), In re (Bankr D Del 12 February 2009) 124
Breitburn Energy Partners LP, In Re 582 BR 321 (Bankr SDNY 2018) 118, 119
Czyzewski v Jevic Holding Corp 137 S Ct 973, 197 L Ed 2d 398 (2017) 69
Foamex International Inc, et al, Ch 11 Case No 09-10560 (KJC), In re (Bankr D Del 18 February 2009) 124
Kmart Corp, In re 359 F 3d 866 (7th Cir 2004) 120
Lyondell Chemical Company, et al, Ch 11 Case No 09-10023 (REG), In re (Bankr SDNY 6 January 2009) 124
Metromedia Fiber Network, Re 416 F 3d 136 (2d Cir 2005) 71
Midway Gold US, Re 575 BR 475 (Bkry Ct, D Colorado 2017) 71
North American Catholic Educational Programming Foundation, Inc v Gheewalla 930 A 2d 92, 101–02 (Del 2007) 270
Peabody Energy Corporation, Re 933 F 3d 918 (8th Cir 2019) 71
Revlon, Inc v MacAndrews & Forbes Holdings, Inc, 506 A 2d 173 (Del 1985) 227
SPM Mfg Corp, Re 984 F 2d 1305 (1st Cir 1993) 69
Tronox Incorporated, et al, Ch 11 Case No 09-10156 (ALG), In re (Bankr SDNY 12 January 2009) 124
United Airlines, Inc v HSBC Bank USA, NA 416 F 3d 609 (7th Cir 2005) 119
Uno Restaurant Holdings Corporation, et al, Ch 11 Case No 10-10209 (MG), In re (Bankr SDNY 20 January 2010) 124
Unocal Corp v Mesa Petroleum Co, 493 A 2d 946 (Del 1985) 227
US Bank National Association v Village at Lakeridge LLC 138 S Ct 960 (2018) 71
Worldcom, Inc, No 02-13533, In Re 2002 WL 1732646 (Bank SDNY 22 July, 2002) 104

Table of Legislation and Other Materials

CANADA

Bankruptcy and Insolvency Act, RSC 1985, c B-3
s 65.1(6) ... 126

CHINA

China Civil Procedure Law 1991 ... 36
Company Law 2013
Art 20 ... 273
Art 183 ... 273
Chinese Enterprise Bankruptcy Law 2006 (EBL) ... 7, 11, 12, 24, 27, 30, 34, 35, 36, 37, 38, 39, 49, 74, 81, 90, 91, 92, 96, 98, 99, 102, 108, 125, 127, 128, 139, 184, 188, 193, 194, 195, 199, 203, 209, 218, 220, 238, 246, 247, 248, 249, 250, 254, 256, 258, 263, 264, 265, 266, 268, 269, 273, 274, 285, 286
Art 1 ... 245
Art 2 ... 38, 193
Art 6 ... 245
Art 7 ... 193, 273
Art 10 ... 125, 265
Art 13 ... 38, 193
Art 18 ... 195, 199
Art 20 ... 125
Art 21 ... 125
Art 23 ... 194
Art 24 ... 194, 195
Art 27 ... 195
Art 31 ... 27, 269
Art 32 ... 27, 195
Art 33 ... 27, 195, 269
Art 34 ... 269
Art 42 ... 176, 238
Art 43 ... 176

Art 62 38
Art 67 128
Art 73 .... 12, 27, 38, 193, 195, 250
Art 75 .... 37, 125, 238, 264
Art 79 .... 12, 37, 248
Art 80 .... 12, 37, 59, 195
Art 82 245
Art 84 .... 38, 74, 79
Art 85 .... 74, 79
Art 86 .... 38, 74, 79
Art 87 .... 38, 50, 74, 79, 82, 128, 138, 245, 265
Art 87(1) 79, 138
Art 87(2)–(6) 79
Art 88 79
EBL (Trial Implementation) 1986 36
Property Law 2007 263

GERMANY

Insolvency Code 1999 .... 24, 38

HONG KONG

Application of English Law Ordinance 1966 45
Bankruptcy Ordinance, Cap 6 46
Basic Law 45
Art 8 45
Companies Ordinance 1865 45
Companies Ordinance 1932 45
Companies Ordinance, Cap 622
s 141 84
ss 297–298 267
s 673 45
s 674 45
Companies (Winding Up and Miscellaneous Provisions) Ordinance Cap 32 289
s 182 .... 47, 85
s 186 .... 46, 126, 200, 230, 231
s 192 126
s 193 231
s 232 .... 47, 85
s 275 272
s 276 271
Securities and Futures Ordinance, Cap 571
s 213 272
s 214 272

SEHK listing rules
listing rule 14.06A....48
listing rule 14.54....48

INDIA

Banking Regulation Act 1949 (India)....42, 64, 158
s 35AA....44
Civil Procedure Code....156, 157
Companies Act 1949
s 230....84
Companies Act 1956.... 40, 262
Companies Act 2013....11, 40, 63
s 188(1)....95
s 230....84
s 409....42
s 410....42
s 411....42
Debt Recovery Tribunals Act 1993....156
Indian Contracts Act 1872....83
Insolvency and Bankruptcy (Application to Adjudicating Authority for Bankruptcy Process for Personal Guarantors to Corporate Debtors) Regulations, 2019....83
Insolvency and Bankruptcy (Application to Adjudicating Authority for Insolvency Resolution Process for Personal Guarantors to Corporate Debtors) Rules, 2019....83
Insolvency and Bankruptcy Board of India (Insolvency Professionals) Regulations 2016....196
First Schedule, Code of Conduct
Para 25....196
Insolvency and Bankruptcy Board of India (Insolvency Resolution Process for Corporate Persons) Regulations, 2016 (CIRP Regulations)
reg 3....196
reg 27....196
reg 34....196, 197
Insolvency and Bankruptcy Board of India (Liquidation Process) (Amendment) Regulations, 2018....238
Insolvency and Bankruptcy Code 2016 (IBC)....3, 11, 16, 19, 20, 22, 24, 25, 27, 30, 34, 39, 41, 42, 43, 44, 59, 63, 64, 82, 92, 96, 102, 125, 128, 129, 131, 133, 140, 153, 158, 159, 162, 164, 166, 168, 181, 195, 207, 212, 219, 232, 233, 238, 251, 254, 258, 260, 261, 262, 268, 277, 287
s 3(19)....195
s 5(13)(a)....238
s 5(15)....238

s 12 ... 42, 125, 208, 260
s 12A ... 82, 92
s 13 ... 232
s 14 ... 125, 196, 212, 232
s 17 ... 195, 207
s 19 ... 207
s 20(2) ... 195
s 21 ... 89, 96, 131
s 22(2) ... 196
s 25 ... 196
s 28 ... 195
s 28(1) ... 238
s 29A ... 42, 43, 64, 82, 83, 84, 96, 208, 277, 288
s 30 ... 197
s 30(2) ... 131, 132, 140, 211, 235, 244
s 30(2)(a) ... 238
s 30(4) ... 42, 82, 132
s 31 ... 235
s 33 ... 125
s 53 ... 133, 140, 211
s 60 ... 84
s 61(3) ... 130
s 208(2) ... 197
s 238 ... 164
Insolvency and Bankruptcy Code (Amendment) Act 2019, No 26 of 2019 ... 158, 232
Insolvency and Bankruptcy Code (Amendment Ordinance) Act 2019 ... 260
Insolvency and Bankruptcy Code (Amendment) Ordinance, 2020 effective 5 June 2020 ... 132, 261
Insolvency and Bankruptcy Code (Amendment) Ordinance 2021 ... 24, 43, 92, 212, 268
Insolvency and Bankruptcy Code (Second Amendment Act) 2018 ... 144
Micro, Small and Medium Enterprises Development Act 2006 ... 83
Presidency Towns Insolvency Act 1902 ... 83
Prudential Framework for Resolution of Stressed Assets, RBI/2018-19/203; DBR.No.BP.BC.45/21.04.048/2018-19 ... 44, 64
Recovery of Debts due to Banks and Financial Institutions Act 1993 (RDDBFI) ... 25, 40, 156, 157
Recovery of Debts Due to Banks and Financial Institutions Act 1993 ... 262
Reserve Bank of India Act 1934
Sch 2 ... 156
Securitisation and Reconstruction of Financial Assets and Enforcement of Security Interest Act 2002 (SARFAESI) ... 22, 25, 39, 40, 41, 43, 156, 157, 162, 164, 165, 166, 168, 169, 259, 260, 262
s 2 ... 162
s 2(1) ... 165
s 13 ... 164

Sick Industrial Companies (Special Provisions) Act 1985 (SICA) 25, 40, 41, 63, 64, 156
s 3(o) 156
s 20..........41

MALAYA

Companies Act 1965 51

SINGAPORE

Application of English Law Act, Cap 7A, 1994 rev edn 51
Companies Act, Cap 50 1967..........51
Companies Act, 2006 Rev Ed, Cap 50 .... 93, 291
s 160..........77
s 161..........77
s 210..........51, 54
s 210(10)..........53, 86, 228
s 211B..........237
s 211E..........237
s 227C 52
s 227N..........52
s 227X..........52
s 339(3)..........272
s 340(2)..........272, 273
s 403..........267
Companies (Amendment) Act 1987 52
Companies (Amendment) Act 2017 54
Companies Ordinance 1948..........51
Insolvency, Restructuring and Dissolution Act 2018 (IRDA) 5, 24, 52, 54, 142, 200, 205, 228, 272, 291
Pt 5..........188
Pt 7..........197
Pt 9.......... 86, 198
s 47..........200, 208
s 64..........228, 229
s 64(6) 229
s 65..........228, 229
s 65(5) 228
s 67..........237
s 68..........206
s 68(9) 142
s 69..........241
s 70..........55, 77

s 70(3) 77
s 70(3)(c) 77
s 70(4) 77
s 70(5) 241
s 71.... 198, 199, 230
s 89....197
s 89(2) 198
s 91....197
s 91(3) 197, 209
s 94....23, 54, 197
s 96....52
s 96(4) 198
s 99.... 52, 198, 208
s 99(3) 86
s 99(6) 199
s 106....208
s 107.... 52, 198, 199
s 115....198
s 117.... 52, 198
s 230....198
s 232....198
s 239.... 54, 272, 273
s 440.... 54, 126
s 440(4)....126
First Sch 198
First Sch, para (f) 198
Insolvency, Restructuring and Dissolution (Amendment) Act 2020
(No 39 of 2020) 291
Insolvency, Restructuring and Dissolution (Amendment) Act 2021 24
Insolvency, Restructuring and Dissolution (Corporate Insolvency
and Restructuring) Rules 2020
r 44....142
r 46....142
Insolvency, Restructuring and Dissolution (Prescribed Contracts under
Section 440) Regulations 2020 126
Insolvency, Restructuring and Dissolution (Proofs of Debt in Schemes
of Arrangement) Regulation 2020
r 6 142
Second Charter of Justice 1826....51
Securities and Futures Act 2002 (Singapore)....87
Singapore Code on Takeovers and Mergers....77, 93
Singapore Exchange listing rules 93
Ch 10 77
Singapore Exchange Securities Trading Ltd Listing Manual Section B
r 704(22)....237

UNITED KINGDOM

Administration (Restrictions on Disposal etc to Connected Persons)
Regulations 2021 (SI 2021/427) 192
City Code on Takeovers and Mergers (UK) 227
Companies Act 1929 .... 45, 51
Companies Act 1862 45
Companies Act 2006 120
Pt 26....2, 4, 9, 58, 101, 188, 225
Pt 26A 4, 9, 18, 58, 75, 76, 101, 102, 115, 121, 188, 191, 225, 227
s 172(3)....270
s 901G(2)–(5) 225
Company Directors Disqualification Act 1986 271
Corporate Insolvency and Governance Act 2020 (CIGA) 2, 9, 10, 15, 70, 75, 115, 116, 124, 219, 223, 225, 237
ss 1–6 116
Schs 1–8 116
Enterprise Act 2002.... 9, 11, 13, 34, 52, 58, 59, 190, 191, 197
Insolvency Act 1986 ....9, 34, 46, 52, 116, 193, 197, 203, 214
Pt I.... 2
Pt II.... 2
Pt A1 ....9, 116, 223
Pt A1, ch 2, ss A3–A4.... 9, 116
Pt A1, ch 2, s A5 .... 9, 116
s 6 23
s 9(2) 223
s 12....223
s 38....223
s 174A 116
s 174A(4) 116
s 174A(11) 116
s 213....271
s 214....271
s 223A 10
s 233....10
ss 233–233A....116
s 233B.... 10, 116
s 233B(10).... 10, 116
ss 238, 239 191
s 435....192
Sch 4ZZA.... 10, 116
Sch ZA1, paras 13–14 116
Sch ZA2 223
Sch B1 191

Sch B1, para 3 .... 191, 214
Sch B1, para 3(1)(a)–(c) 191
Sch B1, para 5 191
Sch B1, para 11 191
Sch B1, para 14 191
Sch B1, para 49 192
Sch B1, para 52 192
Sch B1, para 59 191
Sch B1, para 60A 192
Sch B1, para 73 192
Sch B1, para 74 193
Sch B1, para 99 .... 116, 124
Insolvency Act 2000 190
Insolvency Practitioner Association, 'Statement of Insolvency Practice 16' (SIP 16) (2015) 192
Insolvency Rules 1986 (SI 1986/1925), as amended 192
rr 2.47–2.49 192
Joint Stock Companies Arrangement Act 1870
s 2 34

UNITED STATES

Bankruptcy Abuse Prevention and Consumer Protection Act 2005 (BAPCHA) 221, 222
Bankruptcy Code 1978 of the United States (US) 4, 18, 69, 119, 121, 226, 255
Chapter 7 259
Chapter 11 .... i, vii, ix, 1, 2, 3, 6, 8, 9, 10, 11, 12, 13, 15, 18, 21, 23, 24, 26, 27, 34, 36, 37, 38, 43, 54, 57, 58, 63, 66, 68, 69, 70, 71, 73, 74, 75, 76, 77, 78, 101, 102, 103, 104, 105, 114, 115, 116, 118, 119, 121, 122, 123, 128, 131, 135, 138, 150, 155, 189, 190, 197, 217, 218, 219, 221, 222, 223, 226, 227, 235, 237, 240, 242, 245, 251, 255, 258, 266, 269, 276, 278, 282, 286, 292
11 USC § 101(31)(B)(i)–(iii) 71
11 USC § 105 226
11 USC, § 1121(a)–(d) 8
11 USC § 361 .... 37, 221
11 USC § 362 221
11 USC § 362(a) 115
11 USC § 363 .... 222, 223
11 USC § 364 123
11 USC § 364(d) 9, 123, 236
11 USC § 365(e) and § 541(c) 8, 115
11 USC § 365(a) 8

11 USC § 1102 ... 117
11 USC § 1102(b)(1) ... 72
11 USC § 1121 ... 221
11 USC § 1121(a) ... 72
11 USC § 1121(b) ... 66
11 USC § 1121(d) ... 221
11 USC § 1122(a) ... 71, 121
11 USC § 1122(b) ... 71, 121, 135
11 USC § 1123(a)(4) ... 71
11 USC § 1124 ... 69
11 USC § 1125 ... 66
11 USC § 1126 ... 8
11 USC § 1126(b) ... 72
11 USC § 1129 ... 8, 79, 123, 223
11 USC § 1129(a)(7)(A)(ii) ... 8, 68
11 USC § 1129(a)(10) ... 71
11 USC § 1129(b) ... 68, 266
11 USC § 1129(b)(2) ... 101
11 USC § 1129(b)(2)(A)–(C) ... 69
11 USC § 1191 ... 69
Coronavirus Aid, Relief and Economic Security (CARES) Act 2020 ... 63, 69
Sarbanes-Oxley Act 2002 ... 213
Small Business Reorganizations Act 2019 ... 63, 69
US Uniform Commercial Code ... 14, 222
Fed R Bankr P 1007(b) ... 66

Delaware

Delaware General Corporations Law
s 173 ... 255

New York

New York Uniform Voidable Transactions Act ... 255

OTHER MATERIALS

Arrangement on Reciprocal Recognition and Enforcement of Judgments in Civil and Commercial Matters between the Courts of the Mainland and of the HKSAR pursuant to the Choice of Court Agreements between Parties Concerned ... 150
EU Restructuring Directive 2019/1023 of 20 June 2019 ... 75
Lugano Convention ... 191
Singapore Supreme Court, 'Guide for the Conduct of Applications for Moratoria under Sections 64 and 65 of the Insolvency, Restructuring and Dissolution Act 2018' (21 February 2021) ... 228
Sino-British Joint Declaration of 1984 ... 45

United Nations Commission on International Trade Law (UNCITRAL) Model Law on Cross-border Insolvency 231, 243, 291
UNCITRAL Legislative Guide on Insolvency Law (2005) 24, 33, 36, 276
Recommendation 112 37

BANKING REGULATORS

China Banking Regulatory Commission (CBRC)

CBIRC, 'Circular of the General Office of the CBIRC on the Pilot Work of NPL transfers' (2021) 176
China Banking Regulatory Commission (CBRC), Relevant Questions Regarding CBRC Measures on Commercial Banks Transferring Loans to Social Investors, 2009, No 24 银监会《中国银监会办公厅关于商业银行向社会投资者转让贷款债权法 律效力有关问题的批复》[2009] 24号 176

Reserve Bank of India (RBI)

Reserve Bank of India (Prudential Framework for Resolution of Stressed Assets) Directions 2019 11
RBI Circular of 12 February 2018 introducing a revised framework for resolution of stressed assets by scheduled commercial banks and all Indian financial institutions 44
RBI circular of 7 June 2019 11

OTHER MATERIALS – CHINA

Beijing No. One Intermediate People's Court, Beijing's Bankruptcy Courts Trial Cases [北京市 第一中级人民法院关于印发【北京破产法庭破产重整案件办理规范（试行）】 的通知]，北一中法 【2019】 437 号 250
China Banking Regulatory Commission (CBRC), Relevant Questions Regarding CBRC Measures on Commercial Banks Transferring Loans to Social Investors, 2009, No 24 银监会《中国银监会办公厅关于商业银行向社会投资者转让贷款债权法律效力 有关问题的批复》（银监办发 [2009] 24号） .... xvii, 176
Circular of the SAFE on Releasing the Provisions on Foreign Exchange Administration for Cross-border Guarantees (Huifa No 29 [2014]) 国家外汇管理局关于发布《跨境担保外汇管理规定》的通知 (汇发 [2014] 29号) .... xviii, 149
Management Measures on the Bulk Transfer of Non-performance Assets of Financial Enterprises (No 6 [2012] of the China Bank Regulatory Commission) 财政部银监会关于印发〈金融企业不良资产批量转让管理办法〉的通知 (财金〔2012〕6号) .... xviii, 174, 179

Measures Relating to the Asset Management Business of Financial Assets Investment Companies (No 12 [2020] CBIRC) 中国银保监会关于金融资产投资公司开展资产管理业务有关事项的通知 (银保监发〔2020〕12号) .... xx, 174
Notice by the China Banking and Insurance Regulatory Commission, the National Development and Reform Commission, the People's Bank of China, and the China Securities Regulatory Commission of Issuing the Work Procedures of Financial Institutional Creditors' Committees [Effective] No 57 [2020] of the China Banking and Insurance Regulatory Commission 中国银保监会、发展改革委、中国人民银行、中国证监会关于印发金融机构债 权人委员会工作规程的通知（银保监发[2020]57号） .... xx, 128, 146
Art 10 128
Art 12 128
Notice by the General Office of the China Banking and Insurance Regulatory Commission of Implementing the Pilot Work of Non-Performing Loans (No 26 [2021] of the China Banking and Insurance Regulatory Commission) 中国银保监会办公厅关于开展不良贷款转让试点工作的通知（银保监办便函 (2021) 26号） .... xx, 176
Notice by the National Development and Reform Commission, the Supreme People's Court, the Ministry of Industry and Information Technology and Other Departments of Issuing the Reform Plan for Accelerating Improvement of the Exit System for Market Participants [Effective] (No 1104 [2019] of the National Development and Reform Commission) 国家发展改革委、最高人民法院、工业和信息化部、民政部、司法部、财政 部、人力资源社会保障部、人民银行、国资委、税务总局、市场监管总局、银保监会、证监会关于印发《加快-完善市场主体退出制度改革方案》的通知 (发改财金 [2019] 1104号) ..... xix, 91
Notice by the Supreme People's Court on Issuing the Minutes of the National Courts Symposium on the Trial of Bond Disputes [Effective] (No 185 [2020] of the Supreme People's Court) 最高人民法院关于印发《全国法院审理债券纠纷案件座谈会纪要》的通知 [现行有效] （法 [2020] 185号） xx
Para 15 90
Notice of the Ministry of Finance about Issuing the Measures for the Administration of the Asset Disposal of Financial Asset Management Companies (Revision) [Expired] (No 41 [2004] issued by the Ministry of Finance on April 30th, 2004) 财政部关于印发《金融资产管理公司资产处置管理办法(修订)》的通知 （财金 [2004] 41号 2004年4月30日） .... xvii, 172
Notice of the National Development and Reform Commission on Steps to Deal with Zombie Companies and Eliminate Over-Capacity (No 1756) [2018]) 关于进一步做好“僵尸企业”及去产能企业债务处置工作的通知 (发改财金 [2018]1756号) .... xix, 25, 91, 92, 93

Notice of the National Development and Reform Commission, the People's Bank of China, the Ministry of Finance and Other Ministries and Commissions on the Specific Policy Issues concerning the Implementation of the Market-Oriented Debt-Equity Swaps of Banks (No 152 [2018] of the National Development and Reform Commission) 国家发展改革委、人民银行、财政部、银监会、国务院国资委、证监会、保监 会关于市场化银行债权转股权实施中有关具体政策问题的通知 (发改财金〔2018〕152号） .... xix, 174
Para VI 174
Notice of the People's Bank of China on Guidance on Provisioning for Loan Losses [中国人民银行关于印发《银行贷款损失准备计提指引》的通知 (银发[2002] 98号)], effective 1 January 2002 .... xvii, 160
Notice of the Supreme People's Court on Issuing the Minutes of the National Court Work Conference on Bankruptcy Trials [Effective] (No 53 [2018] of the Supreme People's Court) 最高人民法院印发《全国法院破产审判工作会议纪要》的通知 [现行有效]（法〔2018〕53号） .... xix, 74, 247
Para 18 80
Art 22 93
Paras 40–42 125
Notice of the Supreme People's Court on Issuing the Minutes of the National Courts' Civil and Commercial Trial Work Conference, [2019] No 254, effective 8 November 2019 最高人民法院关于印发《全国法院民商事审判工作会议纪要》的通知 [现行有效]（法〔2019〕254号） .... xx, 38, 93, 146, 247
Para 15 147
Arts 107, 108 246
Paras 109–110 125
Para 111 38
Art 112 37
Notice of the Supreme People's Court on the Summary of Minutes of the Symposium on the Trial of Cases concerning Bankruptcy Reorganisation of Listed Companies [Effective] (29 October 2012), promulgation (No 261 [2012] of the Supreme People's Court) 最高人民法院印发《关于审理上市公司破产重整案件工作座谈会纪要》的通知 [现行有效] (法 [2012] 261号) .... xviii, 80
Opinions of the State Council on Vigorously, Steadily and Properly Reducing Corporate Leverage Ratios [Effective] (No 54 [2016] of the State Council) 国务院关于积极稳妥降低企业杠杆率的意见 [现行有效] (国发[2016] 54号) .... xix, 174
Opinions of the Supreme People's Court on Several Issues Concerning Correctly Trying Enterprise Bankruptcy Cases to Provide Judicial Protection for Maintaining the Order of Market Economy (No 36 [2009] of the Supreme People's Court) 最高人民法院关于正确审理企业破产案件为维护市场经济秩序提供司法保障若 干问题的意见 [现行有效] (法发〔2009〕36号) .... xviii, 36, 80

Organic Law of People's Courts of the People's Republic of China (adopted at the 2nd session of the Fifth National People's Congress on 1 July 1979, last revised and adopted at the 6th session of the Standing Committee of the 13th National People's Congress on 26 October 2018 [中国人民共和国人民法院组织法 (1979年7月1日第五届全国人民代表大会第二次会议通过 根据1983 年9月 2日第六届全国人民代表大会常务委员会第二次会议《关于修改〈中华人民共和国人民法院组 织法〉的决定》第一次修正 根据1986年12月2日第六届全国人民代表大会常务委员会第十八次会议《关于修改〈中华人民共和国地方各级人民代表大会和地方各级人民政府组织法〉的决定》第二次修正根据2006年10月31日第十届全国人民代表大会常务委员会第二十四次会议《关于修改〈中华人民共和国人民法院组织法〉的决定》第三次修正 2018年10月26日第十三届全国人民代表大会常务委员会第六次会议修订)] .... xvii, 37

Provisions of the Supreme People's Court on Determination of the Administrator's Remunerations: Announcement of the Supreme People's Court of the People's Republic of China No 129 [2007] 最高人民法院关于执行《最高人民法院审理企业破产案件指定管理人的 规定》、《最高人民法院审理企业破产案件确定管理人报酬的规定》几个问题的通知（2007年4月12日 法明传 [2007] 129号） .... xviii, 195

Provisions (III) of the Supreme People's Court on Several Issues concerning the Application of the Enterprise Bankruptcy Law of the People's Republic of China [Revised] Interpretation No 3 [2019] of the Supreme People's Court 最高人民法院关于适用《中华人民共和国企业破产法》若干问题的规定(三) [已被修订]（法释 [2019] 3号） xix
- Art 2 238
- Art 10 74
- Art 11 79

Rules Governing the Listing of Shares on the ChiNext Market of Shenzhen Stock Exchange (2020 Revision) 深圳证券交易所创业板股票上市规则 (2020年修订) xx
- Ch X, section 2 95

SAFE, 'Notice regarding the Establishment of a Pilot Program by SAFE's Shenzhen Branch for the Cross-border Transfer of NPLs' (HuiFu (2017) No 24) (《国家外汇管理局关于深圳市分局开展辖区内银行不良资产跨境转让试点业务有关事项的批复》(汇复 [2017] 24 号)) 184

Shenzhen Intermediate People's Court, Practice Directions on Reorganisations, 14 March 2019 【审理企业重整案件的共作指引 .... xx, 27

Shenzhen Intermediate People's Court, Rules Governing Bankruptcy Administrators 深圳市中级人民法院破产案件管理人工作规范（2015年2月5日深圳市中级人民 法院审判委员会民事行政执行专业委员会第1次会议通过）(2018年10月19日) .... xix, 204

Shenzhen Intermediate People's Court, Shenzhen's Bankruptcy Courts Trial cases (Shenzhen Prepack Rules) [深圳市中级人民法院审理企业重整案件的工作指引（试行）] 2019 年3 月14 日本院审判委员会民事执行专业委员会2019 年第3 次会议讨论通过) 250
- R 28 251
- R 33 251

Supreme People's Court, Provisions of the Supreme People's Court on Designating the Administrator during the Trial of Enterprise Bankruptcy Cases, Judicial Interpretation No 8 [2007] 最高人民法院关于审理企业破产案件指定管理人的规定 (法释 [2007] 8号)
Arts 18, 19 194
Art 21 .... xviii, 193
Supreme People's Court, Typical EBL Cases [全 国 法 院 审 理 破 产 典 型 案 例] issued in 2018 and 2020 .... 12, 194, 247
Supreme People's Court of the PRC 'Judicial Transparency by People's Court' (14 March 2017) 30
Status Reports [在破产审判工作调研座谈会上的讲话：情况通报] (18 October 2016) 80

1

Introduction and Theoretical Framework

1.1. OVERVIEW

IN THE LAST two decades, several jurisdictions around the world have reformed or are considering reforming their corporate insolvency and restructuring laws[1] in order to promote legal regimes that are conducive to restructuring viable companies. Many jurisdictions, including significant economies in Asia, have court-supervised corporate restructuring frameworks that are drawn from Chapter 11 of the Bankruptcy Code 1978 (Chapter 11) in the United States (US) and/or schemes of arrangement or administration process in the United Kingdom (UK).

It is widely agreed that the key goal of corporate restructuring law is to preserve, as much as possible, the debtor company's viable (but financially distressed) business at the beginning of the restructuring process until it exits the process, and thus it is critical for the transaction costs to be minimised. Once the restructuring is resolved speedily and in a cost-efficient manner, capital and labour can be put to productive uses quickly. Companies that are no longer economically viable should proceed to liquidation. Further, even though restructuring is a relatively rare occurrence among businesses, the outcomes of restructuring have *ex ante* effects on the credit market since costly restructurings may lead to attempts by the creditors to avoid the process and instead charge high interest rates to compensate for their costs, or demand more collateral. Some of the early debates on agency costs of debt and inefficiencies in bankruptcy include Jensen and Meckling,[2] Baird,[3] Jackson,[4] Bebchuk,[5] Aghion, Hart and Moore,[6] and Bradley and Rosenzweig.[7] Bankruptcy scholars, particularly

[1] The terminology in the UK (and the former English law transplants) refers to 'insolvency law' whereas in the US it is known as 'bankruptcy law'. In this book, I use the terms 'restructuring law' or 'corporate restructuring law' broadly to refer to both instances. The expressions 'insolvency' and 'bankruptcy' are used interchangeably.

[2] MC Jensen, and WH Meckling, 'Theory of the firm: Managerial behavior, agency costs and ownership structure' (1976) 3 *Journal of Financial Economics* 305.

[3] DG Baird, 'The Uneasy Case for Corporate Reorganizations' (1986) 15 *Journal of Legal Studies* 127.

[4] TH Jackson, *The Logic and Limits of Bankruptcy Law* (Cambridge, MA, Harvard University Press, 1986).

[5] LA Bebchuk, 'A new approach to corporate reorganizations' (1988) 101 *Harvard Law Review* 775.

[6] P Aghion, O Hart and J Moore, 'The Economics of Bankruptcy Reform' (1992) 8 *Journal of Law, Economics and Organization* 523.

[7] M Bradley and M Rosenzweig, 'The Untenable Case for Chapter 11' (1992) 101 *Yale Law Journal* 1043 (arguing that the main beneficiaries of Chapter 11 are managers). Cf LM LoPucki, 'Strange Visions in a Strange World: A Reply to Professors Bradley and Rosenzweig' (1992) 91 *Michigan Law Review* 79.

the economically minded scholars, view the goal of restructuring law to be solving the coordination problem of the creditors. Under their normative Creditors' Bargain Theory, creditors may in their own self-interest prefer to race to grab the assets of the debtor in financial distress when they are better off bargaining over how the assets should be best used, and Chapter 11 is to solve their coordination or collective action problems.[8]

The model adopted by Chapter 11 in the US for restructuring is that of a single gateway, and is a debtor in possession model (DIP) where the management of the debtor continues to drive the restructuring post-filing of the petition, with the process ultimately being approved by the court. In the UK, the legislative approach allows for four gateways for restructuring: the scheme of arrangement, administration, the restructuring plan and company voluntary arrangement (CVA). The English scheme of arrangement[9] is a DIP model for early stage restructuring but the secured creditors retain significant rights to veto the restructuring and the administration process requires the insolvency practitioner to be in control of the restructuring, and thus the administration is a practitioner-in-possession (PIP) model.[10] The third is a recent addition that was introduced by UK Corporate Insolvency and Governance Act 2020; it is closer to Chapter 11 and shares many of its features. The CVA allows for a company to restructure its debts by compromising with certain creditors, and it is led by its directors unless the company is in liquidation or in administration.[11] In the UK, only the English scheme and restructuring plan (but not administration or CVA) require court approval. In this book, I will not focus on the CVA as the CVA is subject to minimal court involvement.[12]

The US Chapter 11 and the English schemes and administration have been influential in the exportation of their insolvency and restructuring laws globally. I refer to both the US and the UK systems as the 'Anglo-American' models, whilst recognising that there are differences between the two models in bankruptcy law. Four economically significant jurisdictions in Asia – Mainland China, India, Hong Kong and Singapore – are no exceptions. They have also recently reformed or are considering reforming their corporate restructuring laws to promote regimes conducive to restructuring financially distressed but otherwise economically viable companies, and draw concepts from the US and the UK. This book focuses on the restructurings of large distressed companies in the four Asian jurisdictions.

Both Hong Kong and Singapore are international financial centres in Asia. Mainland China and India rank second and sixth globally respectively in the terms of the nominal gross domestic product (GDP) in 2021.[13] These jurisdictions continue

[8] eg Jackson, *Logic and Limits* (1986); see also TH Jackson 'Bankruptcy, Non-Bankruptcy Entitlements, and the Creditors' Bargain' (1982) 91 *Yale Law Journal* 857.

[9] In this book, the UK or English schemes refer to the schemes of arrangement under Part 26 of the Companies Act 2006.

[10] Insolvency Act 1986, Part II.

[11] Insolvency Act 1986, Part I.

[12] See J Payne, *Schemes of Arrangement: Theory, Structure and Operation* (Cambridge, CUP, 2014) 195–200.

[13] International Monetary Fund, 'GDP, current prices', available at www.imf.org/external/datamapper/NGDPD@WEO/OEMDC/ADVEC/WEOWORLD (China's GDP is estimated at US$16.64 trillion and India's GDP is estimated at US$3.05 trillion).

to adhere to a framework that requires the court's final approval but draw references from US Chapter 11 and/or the English schemes or administration. Singapore's 2017 reforms to the insolvency and restructuring framework are the closest to Chapter 11. Mainland China, India and Hong Kong (in its proposed corporate rescue bill) have not adopted the full DIP regime, and insolvency practitioners continue to play an important intermediary role. These jurisdictions have very different governance structures and institutional frameworks from the origin jurisdictions. For instance, the shareholdings of large companies in Asia are far more concentrated and the debt that is sought to be restructured is often not identical to the US/UK restructurings.

The taxonomy of the comparisons of the various court-supervised models in the US, UK and each of the four Asian jurisdictions in Table 1.1.

Given the core aim of restructuring law is to preserve the business of financially distressed but otherwise viable business, the key motivation of the book here is the design of restructuring law and policy for large companies in Asia that minimises these transaction costs. These ex post transactional costs include the professional costs of the advisers and the administrative fees, costs to creditors in terms of time value of money, and the loss of opportunities that may arise if stakeholders are disincentivised from putting forward competing viable restructuring plans. *Ex ante* costs, which include loss of managerial time and increased overall cost of debt, are more difficult to quantify. Empirical studies have been carried out to isolate the effects of the impact on cost of lending involving a regime change (eg for Italy)[14] or using direct bank data on the interest rate chargeable on debt for the financially distressed firms.[15] However, this book will only be concerned with ex post costs.

In this book, I have concentrated only on large companies. The choice of restructurings of large companies is driven by the fact that the restructuring regimes are much more complex than those applicable for small and medium-size enterprises (where the owners and managers are the same persons). Inevitably, there is no standard definition of large companies across the Asian jurisdictions and the criteria is driven by both functions as to data availability and the amount of debt that is involved. For three of the four Asian jurisdictions studied in the book, I consider large companies to be those that are listed on a stock exchange and/or issue publicly traded debt. This is the criteria that is used for Mainland China, Singapore and Hong Kong. In these jurisdictions, often financial and other data is only available for listed companies and those that issue public debt because of the disclosure requirements imposed by the various stock exchanges or interest in the press due to their significance to the economies. For India, more information is available on the companies undergoing the resolution process pursuant to the Indian Insolvency and Bankruptcy Code 2016 (IBC) disclosed by the regulator, that is, the Insolvency and Bankruptcy Board of India (IBBI). In this book, large companies in the Indian context are those where the size of the financial claims is at least INR100 million (US$1.3 million). Throughout the book, to ensure comparability, I have attempted to convert the local currency in each of the four jurisdictions to US dollars.

[14] G Rodano, NAB Serrano-Velarde and E Tarantino, 'The Causal Effect of Bankruptcy Law on the Cost of Finance' (2016) 120 *Journal of Financial Economics* 363.

[15] See eg JR Franks and W Torous, 'An Empirical Investigation of U.S. Firms in Reorganization' (1989) 44 *Journal of Finance* 747.

Table 1.1 Models of debt restructuring systems

Classification	**Manager in control or DIP**	**Manager in control or DIP**	**Manager in control or DIP**	**Hybrid of DIP and Practitioner in possession (PIP)**	**Practitioner in control or PIP**	**Practitioner in control or PIP**	**PIP**	**Secured creditor-in- control**	**Secured creditor-in-control**
Jurisdiction and bankruptcy law	US Bankruptcy Code	UK Part 26A of the Companies Act 2006 restructuring plan	Singapore scheme of arrangement (post-2017 reforms)	Mainland China (EBL)	India (IBC)	Singapore judicial management*	UK administration	Hong Kong scheme of arrangement†	UK Part 26 of the Companies Act 2006 scheme of arrangement
Shareholder concentration‡	Low	To be determined as more cases invoke Part 26A	High	High	High	High	Low	High	Low
Diversity in debt§	High	To be determined as more cases invoke Part 26A plan	High (financial and operational debt; also retail debt)	Moderate (includes retail debt)	Moderate (only financial creditors are represented on committee of creditors)	High (includes financial, operational debt and retail debt)	Low (only financial debt)	High (financial and operational debt)	Low (only financial debt)
Size of the NPLs as a proportion to gross loans**	1.1%	1.2%	1.3%	1.8%	7.9%	1.3%	1.2%	0.9%	1.2%
Ease of enforcing contracts (ranking)††	17	34	1	5	163	1	34	31	34

* Judicial management can be within or out-of-court in Singapore. The out-of-court judicial management regime came into force via Insolvency, Restructuring and Dissolution Act 2018 on 30 July 2020.

† Excludes the soft-touch provisional liquidation that is used in Hong Kong.

‡ Assessment on shareholding concentration East Asian jurisdictions (Hong Kong and Singapore) is based on Chen and Wan (2018) (based on a sample of 25% of the companies that were listed on SGX during 2009–15; the mean of shareholding interests of the largest beneficial holder was 40.7%; based on a sample of 25% of the companies that were listed on Stock Exchange of Hong Kong (SEHK) during 2009–15; the mean shareholding interests of the largest beneficial holder was 45.98%). For India, I use U Varottil, 'The Nature of the Market for Corporate Control in India' in Varottil (2017) Table 11.5 (showing that, as of 31 March 2015, the average promoter shareholding of companies on CNX Nifty (50-stock index representing about 66.2% of the free float market capitalisation of stocks listed on NSE), CNX 100 (100-stock index representing 78.57% of the free float market capitalisation of stocks listed on NSE) and CNX 500 (representing about 95.77% of the free float market capitalisation of stocks listed on NSE) is 49.22%, 52.17% and 54.62%, respectively). For China, I use Jiang and Kim (2014) (data showing that, as of 2012, for the non-financial firms listed on Shanghai and Shenzhen stock exchanges, the largest shareholder held on average 36.8% of the shareholding and the five largest shareholders together held 53.2% of the shareholding).

§ Assessment on diversity in debt-holdings is based on the following: (1) for Singapore, assessment is based on the dataset of schemes of arrangement in Appendix D; (2) for Hong Kong, based on the dataset of judgments involving schemes of arrangement in Appendix C; (3) for India, based on the analysis of the dataset on the CIRPS in Appendix B; (3) US and UK data from Ivashina et al (2018).

** Figures from World Bank, as at 2020.

†† Figures from World Bank 'Doing Business 2020'. The World Bank announced that the 'Doing Business' reports would be discontinued on 16 September 2021 due to data irregularities. However, the figures are included here as the irregularities did not pertain to the indicators relating to enforcing contracts but to 'Starting A Business', 'Legal Rights – Getting Credit' and 'Paying Taxes'. See RC Machen, MT Jones, GP Varghese and EL Stark, 'Investigation of Data Irregularities in *Doing Business 2018 and Doing Business 2020* – Investigation Findings and Report to the Board of Executive Directors' (Wilmerhale, 15 September 2021) 1–16, available at thedocs.worldbank.org/en/doc/84a922cc9273b7b120d49ad3b9e9d3f9-0090012021/original/DB-Investigation-Findings-and-Report-to-the-Board-of-Executive-Directors-September-15-2021.pdf.

In US/UK scholarship, the restructuring process is traditionally characterised as either 'management-driven' (also known as debtor in possession)[16] or 'management-displacing' (also known as practitioner in possession).[17] As mentioned earlier, the DIP model is associated with the US Chapter 11 proceedings. In the latter, found primarily in the UK, it is also characterised as secured creditor-driven, particularly if secured creditors have a floating charge over all or substantially all of the assets of the company and may proceed appoint receivers to take over control of the collateral with a view of sale.[18] The DIP model is associated with a bias towards favouring reorganisation and the secured creditor-driven process has a pro-liquidation bias. The debates have centred on the trade-offs and optimal design of restructuring law and policy in addressing agency and coordination costs of various market participants in either model, and the literature has been updated to include modern bankruptcy practice by several scholars, including Skeel,[19] Baird and Rasmussen,[20] Skeel and Triantis,[21] and Paterson.[22] The PIP model was also discussed when the UK introduced administration as a gateway to restructuring in 2002 where the insolvency practitioner takes control of the restructuring.

However, the debates are largely located in the US/UK, focusing on the optimal structures in these two advance jurisdictions. With certain exceptions of emerging jurisdictions[23] and jurisdiction-specific studies,[24] there has been less focus on optimal designs of restructuring law in emerging jurisdictions, even though more emerging jurisdictions are favouring processes that promote reorganisation. Insolvency and restructuring law are also seen as a means to resolve a jurisdiction's non-performing loans so as to ensure the stability of its banking sector. In contrast, there is influential theoretical and empirical scholarship on addressing agency costs in corporate governance structures in Asia for solvent companies.[25] Insofar as the empirical evidence on

[16] See eg Franks and Torous (ibid); E Berkovitch and R Israel. 'Optimal Bankruptcy Laws across Different Economic Systems' (1999) 12 *Review of Financial Studies* 347.

[17] J Armour, BR Cheffins and DA Skeel, 'Corporate Ownership Structure and the Evolution of Bankruptcy Law: Lessons from the United Kingdom' (2002) 55 *Vanderbilt Law Review* 1699.

[18] Amour, Cheffins and Skeel (ibid). See eg I Welch, 'Why is bank debt senior? A theory of asymmetry and claim priority based on influence costs' (1997) 10 *Review of Financial Studies* 1203; DG Baird and RK Rasmussen, 'The End of Bankruptcy' (2002) 55 *Stanford Law Review* 751.

[19] DA Skeel, Jr, 'Creditors' Ball: The 'New' New Corporate Governance in Chapter 11' (2003) 152 *University of Pennsylvania Law Review* 917.

[20] DG Baird and RK Rasmussen, 'Anti-bankruptcy' (2009) 119 *Yale Law Journal* 648.

[21] DA Skeel, Jr. and G Triantis, 'Bankruptcy's Uneasy Shift to a Contract Paradigm' (2018) 166 *University of Pennsylvania Law* Review 1777.

[22] S Paterson, *Corporate Reorganization Law and Forces of Change* (Oxford, OUP, 2020).

[23] eg O Hart, R La Porta, F Lopez-de-Silanes and J Moore, 'Proposal for a New Bankruptcy Procedure in Emerging Markets' in RM Levich (ed), 'Emerging Capital Flows: Proceedings of a Conference held at the Stern School of Business,' New York University, 23–24 May (Springer US, New York, 1997) 401–19; S Claesens, S Djankov and A Mody (eds), *Resolution of Financial Distress: An International Perspective on the Design of Bankruptcy Laws* (World Bank Publications, 2001).

[24] The literature on restructuring law on the four Asian jurisdictions in this book, Mainland China, India, Hong Kong and Singapore, is listed in section 1.5.4.2 below.

[25] eg ML Lemmon and KV Lins, 'Ownership Structure, Corporate Governance, and Firm Value: Evidence from the East Asian Financial Crisis' (2003) 58 *Journal of Finance* 1445; see also references in C Chen, WY Wan and W Zhang, 'Board Independence as a Panacea to Tunneling? An Empirical Study of Related - Party Transactions in Hong Kong and Singapore' (2018) 15 *Journal of Empirical Legal Studies* 987.

insolvency and restructuring law, while there are English language monographs on jurisdiction-specific studies particularly on Mainland China, they have limitations in demonstrating *how* these frictions in the relationships *matter* in modern bankruptcy practice. For instance, Zhao focuses only on listed company reorganisations[26] and does not cover bond restructurings, which have drawn significant attention due the high-profile nature of these defaults on the wider economy and their implications on the future of bankruptcy reforms.[27] Since Zhang's work on reorganisations of Chinese firms up to 2015, the Chinese Government has taken a number of measures to use bankruptcy law to facilitate market reforms.[28] Mrockova discusses comprehensively the implementation of the Chinese Enterprise Bankruptcy Law 2006 based on extensive interviews with various stakeholders but does not address in-depth the diverse interests of creditors.[29] Additionally, none of the above authors deal with how reorganisations are impacted by the solutions of the jurisdictions in resolving non-performing loans.

In view of the differences in the share ownership and debt structures between Asian firms and the US/UK firms, as well as the differences in the legal institutions, the question arises as to whether the solutions adopted in the US/UK to respond to the agency and coordination costs posed by frictions of stakeholders in fact work as intended when transplanted to Asia. This book fills the gap by reference to experiences in Asia. The key contribution of this book is the analysis of the solutions adopted by corporate restructuring law and practice in the US and the UK that address the agency and/or coordination costs posed by frictions in shareholder–creditor, manager–creditor and creditor–creditor relationships, and how these costs have limitations in the context of Asian companies. These solutions also do not adequately consider the variations to the agency and coordination costs posed by the banking regulator's interests in resolving non-performing loans in emerging jurisdictions, the benefits and limitations of the independent gatekeepers operating in the insolvency ecosystem, and the complex relationships between corporate restructuring law and other areas of the law.

The central thesis of this book is that an optimal design must take into account the following that are absent or not present to the same extent as in the US/UK: (1) the interaction between *concentrated shareholdings* and *widely held debt* leading to significant risks of prejudice to outside creditors; (2) the incentives of the state in resolving non-performing loans for the purposes of bank regulation; (3) the benefits and limitations of the independent gatekeepers, being the insolvency practitioners and the courts; and (4) the interaction among restructuring law, enforcing contracts and duties of directors of financially distressed companies.

[26] H Zhao, *Government Intervention in the Reorganisation of Listed Companies in China* (Cambridge, CUP, 2019).

[27] E White, 'China's Courts Take Centre Stage as Defaults Shake $17tn Bond Market' *Financial Times* (24 August 2021), available at www.ftchinese.com/interactive/46668/en?exclusive.

[28] Z Zhang, *Corporate Reorganisations in China: An Empirical Analysis* (Cambridge, CUP, 2018).

[29] N Mrockova, *Corporate Bankruptcy Law in China: Principles, Limitations and Options for Reform* (Oxford, Hart Publishing, 2021).

1.2. RESTRUCTURING MODELS IN ANGLO-AMERICA AND ASIA

1.2.1. The US Pure Debtor in Possession Regime

The US Chapter 11, a DIP regime, is widely regarded as pro-debtor and pro-restructuring, and is highly flexible.[30] In particular, Chapter 11, the choice for large firm restructurings,[31] is designed to encourage efficient consensual bargaining by parties to maximise the debtor's assets and minimise the collection costs of creditors.[32] To this end, a set of comprehensive tools are in place. The debtor management remains in possession and the debtor has a strong automatic stay or moratorium[33] while the management has an exclusive right to propose a plan of reorganisation for the first 120 days of the case (which can be extended).[34] During this period, committees of creditors negotiate the plan, supported by a mandatory disclosure regime, as to how the assets are to be deployed. Other tools include prohibiting the exercise of termination rights of non-financial contracts as a result of filing for Chapter 11 or *ipso facto* clauses,[35] and allowing the creditors to cherry-pick certain executory contracts.[36]

Creditors' and/or shareholders' hold-outs on how assets are to be distributed are addressed by the court's ability to impose a cram-down, either within-class or by way of a cross-class cram-down.[37] Chapter 11 requires the impaired creditors to be classified according to their rights for voting purposes. When the majority of the creditors represent two-thirds in value in each class vote for the plan, the plan is binding on the minority of the class.[38] For the cross-class cram-down to be exercised, even if not all of the impaired classes vote for the plan, certain conditions must be satisfied. The plan must not discriminate unfairly and the plan must be fair and equitable.[39] The latter is satisfied if the absolute priority rule (APR) found in distributions in liquidation – that is, requiring that senior classes must be paid in full before junior classes can receive any payment in the absence of consent by the class in question – is respected. Other conditions include satisfying the 'best interests' test, that is, the creditor must receive at least what he/she would be otherwise be entitled to in the liquidation.[40] In theory, shareholders of a company that is insolvent should be wiped

[30] T Eisenberg and S Sundgren, 'Is Chapter 11 Too Favorable to Debtors? Evidence from Abroad' (1997) 82 *Cornell Law Review* 1532. For an analysis of the US Chapter 11, see generally, R Squire, *Corporate Bankruptcy and Financial Reorganizations* (New York, Wolters Kluwer, 2016).

[31] LM LoPucki and WC Whitford, 'Bargaining over Equity's Share in the Bankruptcy Reorganization of Large, Publicly Held Companies' (1990) 139 *University of Pennsylvania Law Review* 125.

[32] R Rasmussen, 'The Efficiency of Chapter 11' (1991) 8 *Bankruptcy Developments Journal* 319.

[33] This book uses the terms 'stay' and 'moratorium' interchangeably.

[34] 11 USC, §1121(a)–(d).

[35] 11 USC §365(e) and §541(c).

[36] 11 USC §365(a).

[37] 11 USC §1129; see Jackson (n 4) 216 (on the distinction between the deployment and distribution of assets):'The groups, moreover, are negotiating distributional issues in a bilateral monopoly context, and any time this is done there is some danger that the distributional conflicts will interfere with the optimal deployment result.'

[38] 11 USC §1126.

[39] 11 USC §1129.

[40] 11 USC § 1129(a)(7)(A)(ii).

out if the APR is strictly applied. DIP loans or rescue financing is well established in Chapter 11, where providers of the DIP financing may be existing lenders or new lenders, and may have their priority elevated to other creditors with the court's approval.[41]

1.2.2. The Three UK Models

In the UK, there are two possibilities for effecting a restructuring using a court-approved process. In addition, the debtor may also restructure under the administration framework pursuant to the Insolvency Act 1986 (amended by the Enterprise Act 2002), which allows for the appointment of administrators by the court. In the case of administration, it is also possible to appoint the administrator with an out-of-court process.

For restructuring that is to be ultimately approved by the court, Part 26 of the Companies Act 2006 (in existence at least since 1870)[42] provides only for a within-class cram-down for the English schemes of arrangement. In 2020, the new restructuring plan was introduced in Part 26A of the Companies Act 2006 via the Corporate Insolvency and Governance Act 2020 (CIGA), which has many of the Chapter 11 features described below.

In a traditional English scheme of arrangement, which model was transplanted to India, Hong Kong and Singapore, there are three stages to the approval process. First, the company applies to the court to convene a meeting of creditors. Second, the relevant class meetings are held and the scheme must be approved by a majority in number representing 75 per cent in value of the creditors within the class, in order to effect a within-class cram-down. Third, the scheme must be approved by the court for it to be effective.[43] In reviewing the fairness of the scheme, the court will normally give effect to the wishes of the creditors so long as the classes of creditors are properly formed, though the court does not serve as a rubber-stamp.

To effect a cross-class cram-down and to squeeze out the junior creditors and shareholders, the process is more complex and involves the English scheme being twinned with the English administration in a pre-packaged plan.[44] The English or English-modelled scheme is a DIP model but is classified as a secured creditor-in-control model, as there is no ability to stay enforcement by secured creditors against their consent while the debtor is attempting to seek a restructuring.

In 2020, with the enactment of the CIGA, many of the features found in Chapter 11 are incorporated in the UK's restructuring regime. These include a standalone moratorium in order to effect a restructuring[45] and a cross-class cram-down.[46]

[41] 11 USC §364(d).

[42] See J Payne 'Debt Restructuring in English Law: Lessons from the United States and the Need for Reform' (2014) 130 *LQR* 282, fn 36.

[43] See generally Payne, *Schemes of Arrangement* (2014).

[44] *Re Bluebrook* [2009] EWHC 2114 (Ch). See discussion in ch 3, section 3.3.1.2, ch 4, section 4.3.2.

[45] Insolvency Act 1986, Pt A1, Ch 2, ss A3–A4 (and for overseas companies) see s A5. Part A1 was introduced by CIGA.

[46] Companies Act 2006, Pt 26A.

In the former, it provides the company with an initial breathing space of 20 business days and the directors may file for an extension of a further 20 business days. Any extension beyond 40 business days requires the consent of the company's pre-moratorium creditors or the court. Under the restructuring plan introduced by CIGA, with the sanction of the court, it is possible to effect a cram-down across classes of creditors. The CIGA restricts the use of *ipso facto* clauses in contracts for not only the essential supply provisions that were previously found in the Insolvency Act 1986[47] but also the contracts for the supply of goods and services, though there are exemptions.[48] When a company becomes subject to a relevant insolvency procedure, including the statutory moratorium, administration and restructuring plan (but not the scheme of arrangement), the provisions apply to any clause in a contract for goods or services that automatically terminates the contract or entitles the supplier to terminate the contract upon the company being subject to an insolvency procedure. However, there is no wider ban on *ipso facto* clauses of the width that is found in Chapter 11.

Finally, there is administration. The objectives of administration stated in the legislation are: (1) to rescue the company as a going concern; (2) to achieve a better result for the company's creditors as a whole than would be likely if the company was wound up; or (3) to realise the company's property in order to distribute to its secured or preferential creditors.[49]

Once the company is put into administration, the administrator, who is a qualified insolvency practitioner, displaces the board of directors, has the powers to manage the business affairs of the company, and presents the plan (that will achieve at least one of the above-mentioned objectives) for the creditors to approve. While the English administration is a PIP regime (since the directors are displaced in favour of the insolvency practitioner), developments since the onset of COVID-19 pandemic show that the market practitioners are using a 'light touch' administration, where the administrator allows the management to exercise some of these powers while the administrator continues to have oversight.[50]

1.2.3. Transplanting US/UK Restructuring Concepts in Asia

The four Asian jurisdictions under study have all adopted restructuring regimes based on US and/or UK models. Hong Kong's scheme of arrangement draws on the UK case law on English schemes, being a secured creditor-in-control model, though

[47] Insolvency Act 1986, ss 233 and 223A.

[48] Insolvency Act 1986, s 233B. Financial services providers such as lenders are not subject to the *ipso facto* provisions; see the new s 233B(10) of the Insolvency Act 1986 inserting Sch 4ZZA.

[49] See ch 6.

[50] eg *Re Debenhams Retail Ltd (in Administration)* [2020] EWHC 921 (Ch) 20; *Re Debenhams Retail Ltd (in administration)* [2020] EWCA Civ 600 (where the company went into administration under a 'light touch' procedure that allowed the management of the company to stabilise the business during the period of uncertainty resulting from COVID-19).

Hong Kong may be moving ahead with a corporate rescue mechanism.[51] Under a secured creditor-in-control model, no restructuring is possible without the consent of the secured creditors. It is not possible to effect a cross-class cram-down in Hong Kong or (prior to 2017) Singapore due to the absence of an equivalent UK process which allows for administration that is twinned with schemes of arrangement.[52] In the case of Singapore, in fact, prior to the enactment of the amendments to the company legislation and insolvency law framework in 2017, its regime was a distinctly secured creditor-in-control model that was similar to Hong Kong. Since these reforms, Singapore's scheme of arrangement has shifted distinctly to a DIP model that is based on Chapter 11.[53]

There are currently three main gateways to restructuring in India: (1) via the Indian Insolvency and Bankruptcy Code 2016; (2) the scheme of arrangement under the Companies Act 2013,[54] and (3) Reserve Bank of India's 7 June 2019 circular on the Prudential Framework for Resolution of Stressed Assets, which is an out-of-court mechanism for banks' resolution of stressed assets involving large accounts.[55] Gateways (1) and (3) are used regularly in India. Gateway (2) is seldom used as a tool of debt restructuring in India due to the inefficiencies of the court system.[56] Gateway (3) is a mechanism for an out-of-court bank-led creditor restructuring, which is often used by RBI-regulated entities to resolve non-performing assets (NPAs) and take advantage of the prudential norms applicable for NPAs following restructurings where the borrowers have aggregate exposure of Rs 15 billion (USD$202 million).[57] The IBC, introduced in 2016, is by far the most significant piece of restructuring legislation. Its model is that the insolvency practitioner, known as the resolution professional, takes control of the assets, similar to the PIP model found in the UK's administration proceedings under the Enterprise Act 2002.[58] The IBC will be the focus of discussion in this book.

In Mainland China, the only method for corporate restructuring is prescribed under the Enterprise Bankruptcy Law 2006 (EBL), which became effective on 1 June 2007, as well as the judicial interpretations and notices issued by the Supreme People's

[51] E Yiu, 'Hong Kong resurrects Chapter 11-style corporate rescue bill after a 24-year hiatus as Singapore powers ahead with reforms' *South China Morning Post* (12 March 2020).

[52] See n 44 and accompanying text.

[53] See ch 2.

[54] U Varottil, 'The Scheme of Arrangement as a Debt Restructuring Tool in India: Problems and Prospects' (2018) 15 *European Company and Financial Law Review* 586.

[55] Reserve Bank of India (Prudential Framework for Resolution of Stressed Assets) Directions 2019.

[56] Varottil, 'The Scheme of Arrangement as a Debt Restructuring Tool in India' (2018).

[57] The RBI circular of 7 June 2019 creates a method for bank creditors to execute an out-of-court restructuring, including ownership changes, with the approval of creditors holding 75% in value of debt (and 60% by number); under this framework, banks are required to review the loan and come up with a resolution plan within a strict timeline of 30 days, and the resolution plan has to be implemented within 180 days. If the timelines are not met, additional provisioning is required to be made. To facilitate the restructuring, the bank creditors must enter into an inter-creditor agreement which blocks the creditors' enforcement, even if they are secured creditors. See also RBI, Reserve Bank of India (Prudential Framework for Resolution of Stressed Assets) Directions, 2019. The prudential treatment of the NPAs is set out in the framework.

[58] See ch 2.

Court (SPC) and the typical case lists that are issued by the SPC.[59] The EBL is the most significant piece of modern restructuring law in an emerging jurisdiction, and its inspiration was drawn from Chapter 11 of the US Bankruptcy Code 1978, the UK, Germany and Japan.[60]

The EBL is a hybrid of the DIP and PIP model where either the debtor or the administrator can propose the plan.[61] The debtor can continue to manage the business and operations whilst in reorganisation, with the approval of the court, whilst the administrator supervises the process.[62]

1.3. UNDERSTANDING THE INTERACTION BETWEEN CORPORATE GOVERNANCE AND RESTRUCTURING LAW

Given the goal of restructuring law is to minimise the costs of restructurings of financially distressed but otherwise viable companies, the key question is how to manage frictions among the stakeholders. There is a rich body of literature as to agency costs; in corporate governance literature, where the shareholdings have been dispersed, the key question is managing the agency costs relating to the conflicts between the shareholders and management. The most influential analysis was conducted by Jensen and Meckling,[63] who demonstrated that while the firm raises outside capital, it benefits from economies of scale. However, at the same time, agency costs arise because managers have an incentive to engage in conduct, such as shirking or taking, that benefits them personally, though such behaviour is value-destructive.[64] Debt is an important factor to mitigate these costs as debt limits the discretion of management in engaging in wasteful projects.[65] As long as the firm is solvent, the management will be kept in check; the creditor's standard contractual right against the firm to sue for repayment (with eventual liquidation if repayment is not made) is presumed to incentivise the debtor's manager to keep the company solvent.

In corporate governance literature on Asian firms where the shareholdings are concentrated in the hands of families or the state, the focus is on managing the agency costs between the controlling and minority shareholders.[66] The managers are

[59] Supreme People's Court, Typical EBL Cases [全国法院审理破产典型案例] issued in 2018 and 2020, available at pccz.court.gov.cn/pcajxxw/pcdxal/dxal.

[60] See ch 2.

[61] EBL, Arts 79–80.

[62] EBL, Art 73.

[63] Jensen and Meckling, 'Theory of the firm' (1976).

[64] See also J Armour, G Hertig and H Kanda, 'Transaction with Creditors' in R Kraakman et al (eds), *The Anatomy of Corporate Law: A Comparative and Functional Approach*, 3rd edn (Oxford, OUP, 2017) 109.

[65] See also BE Adler and V Capkun, 'Debt-Equity Conflict and the Incidence of Secured Credit' (2019) 62 *The Journal of Law & Economics* 551.

[66] eg, see generally the following articles and the references therein: F Jiang and KA Kim, 'Corporate Governance in China: A Modern Perspective' (2014) 32 *Journal of Corporate Finance* 190 (for China); A

appointed by the controlling shareholders and hence would be expected to be aligned to the interests of the controlling shareholders.

However, in either situation of controlled or dispersed ownership, once the company enters into financial distress (whether through fraud, managerial incompetence or unfortunate circumstances), the interests of shareholders and creditors diverge sharply. The shareholders are keen to gamble for resurrection and engage in risky projects, when creditors are interested only in getting repaid. Even if ownership is dispersed, it would be expected that management will side with shareholders since they may lose their jobs when the company goes into insolvent liquidation. Creditors may also engage in grabbing the assets of the debtor first, even if all of the creditors and other stakeholders would have been better off overall if the company remains economically viable and can benefit from restructuring. Insofar as creditor–creditor relationships are concerned, agency costs arise where the interests of the majority of the creditors (the agent) diverge from the minority of the creditors (the principal) or where the interests of one class of creditors diverge from the other classes. As the number of creditors increase, there will also be an increase in the costs of coordination.

While there is a rich body of literature discussing the trade-offs and optimal design of restructuring law and policy in addressing agency costs of creditor-shareholder, creditor-management and agency and coordination costs of creditor–creditor relationships, the literature is largely located in the US/UK. For example, in an influential paper, Skeel argues that the debtor in possession (DIP) or 'manager in control' model of Chapter 11 is complementary and is co-related to a dispersed ownership.[67] Nuance was added in a follow-up work by Armour, Skeel and Cheffins: the US model is both co-related to *dispersed ownership and widely held debt*, while the UK model of 'manager displacing' or creditor-driven bankruptcy regulation is co-related to its *dispersed shareholding* ownership but *concentrated debt structure*.[68] Since this work, the English scheme of arrangements have been widely used as early modes of restructurings. The English scheme may be twinned with administration under the Enterprise Act 2002, which displaces the managers in favour of the insolvency practitioner.

Figure 1.1 shows the interaction between shareholders and creditors in the Anglo-American and Asian frameworks.

Khosa, K Ahmed and D Henry, *Ownership Structure, Related-Party Transactions, and Firm Valuation: Evidence from Indian Business Groups* (Cambridge, CUP, 2019); C Chen, WY Wan and W Zhang, 'Board Independence as a Panacea to Tunneling? An Empirical Study of Related - Party Transactions in Hong Kong and Singapore' (2018) 15 *Journal of Empirical Legal Studies* 987 (for Singapore and Hong Kong).

[67] DA Skeel, 'An Evolutionary Theory of Corporate Law and Corporate Bankruptcy' (1998) 51 *Vanderbilt Law Review* 1325.

[68] Armour, Cheffins and Skeel, 'Corporate Ownership Structure' (2002).

Figure 1.1 Interaction between shareholders and creditors in Anglo-American and Asian frameworks

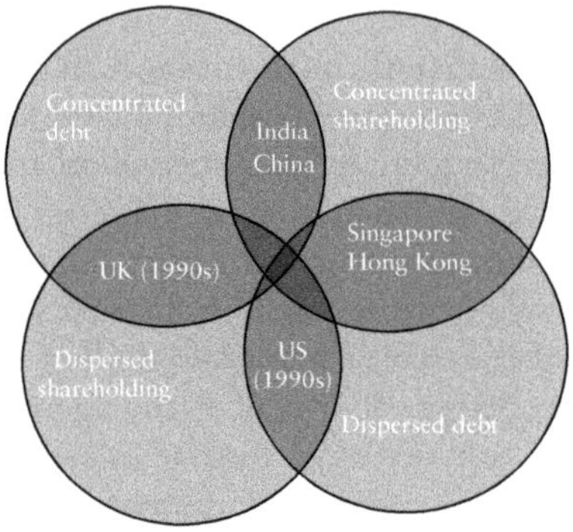

Since 1990s US/UK restructuring practice has undergone changes

Rise of private equity and portfolio companies – leading to greater concentration in shareholdings and debt in debt restructurings

1

After the publication of Skeel and his co-authors, the capital markets in the US and the UK underwent significant changes beginning from 2000. Private equity sponsors become very active in engaging in takeovers of publicly listed companies and subsequently taking them private or acquiring other privately held companies.[69] The shareholding structures of these firms, ie portfolio companies, become concentrated after the buy-outs, and the deals are highly leveraged, financed with a mix of equity and junior debt provided by the private equity sponsors and senior debt arranged by bank lenders.[70] Management is also often given incentive in the form of equity to align their interests with the private equity funds. The investment horizon is limited in time (three to seven years), and the aim of the investment is to re-list the company in a stock exchange or undertake a trade sale.[71] During the global financial crisis of 2008, these highly leveraged portfolio companies became susceptible to financial distress and had to be restructured.[72] At the same time, changes to the US Uniform Commercial Code in 2001 had improved the position of the secured creditor to take security over the whole of the assets of the company.

Paterson argues that there is some convergence between the US and UK models due to the presence of adaptive devices in both jurisdictions and certain other factors,

[69] See generally, BR Cheffins and J Armour, 'The Eclipse of Private Equity' (2008) 33 *Delaware Journal of Corporate Law* 1, and the references therein.

[70] The amount of equity financing tends to be small compared with the debt financing because equity ranks behind debt. Various estimates in the market have provided that the debt financing constitutes 70–80% of the total funding costs: see eg Corporate Finance Institute, 'Leveraged Buyout', available at corporatefinanceinstitute.com/resources/knowledge/finance/leveraged-buyout-lbo.

[71] See generally, S Beddow, D Carter and A Lewis, 'Private Equity Buyouts: An Overview' Practical Law for Companies, available at uk.practicallaw.thomsonreuters.com/6-518 0998?transitionType=Default&contextData=(sc.Default)&firstPage=true.

[72] See generally, S Paterson, 'The Paradox of Alignment: Agency Problems and Debt Restructuring' (2016) 17 *European Business Organization Law Review* 497 (for the UK financing market where the author identified 52 large or mid-size restructurings situations in the UK between 2008 and 2013, half of these situations involve portfolio companies); Paterson, *Corporate Reorganization Law* (2022) 55–56, 147–48 (for the US financing market).

including the increasing power of secured creditors in Chapter 11 proceedings and the rise of high-yield debt in the UK.[73] Further, finance scholars have pointed out that the debt in Chapter 11 restructurings may not be static; it could be widely held at the time of filing but becomes more concentrated as a result of distressed debt investors purchasing debt prior to the voting on the plan.[74] Most recently, the UK has introduced a new flexible restructuring process in CIGA, which is based on Chapter 11.

Influential as these theories are, it is doubtful if they can be applied to the restructuring of Asian companies. First, the theories by Skeel and his co-authors do not capture the interaction between corporate governance and bankruptcy/insolvency of financially distressed firms where the shareholders are *concentrated*, given that they dealt with Anglo-American firms in the 1990s. Since 2000, Anglo-American scholarship documents the changes in bankruptcy practice and, in particular, the increase in concentration in shareholdings in private equity portfolio as a result of the leveraged buy-outs occurring. However, much of the scholarship continues to be located in the US and UK, and in the case of the US, the emphasis is on sidelining the shareholders when the company is in financial distress. In this work, I explain how and why shareholders (being families or the state) have influenced the outcomes of restructurings of large companies and their associated transaction costs in the four Asian jurisdictions. For instance, even if assets are worth less than the debt, one may be in favour of by-passing the intermediate classes of junior creditors and award some of the distributions to old shareholders who may bring in new capital but will baulk if the old shareholders have been dishonest or are otherwise perceived to have contributed to the company's financial distress.

Second, as will be explained in this book, the debt that is sought to be compromised under restructuring in Asian companies is not identical to the debts that are sought to be compromised in the US and UK restructurings, and this debt has also been subject to changes in recent years. Even between the US and UK, there are differences. In the US, Chapter 11 restructures the whole balance sheet of the company, including the financial debt, operational debt and unpaid workers' wages. English schemes and pre-packaged administration plans are traditionally concerned with financial restructuring only and the company continues with its existing suppliers.

Mainland China is the closest to Chapter 11 in terms of restructuring both financial and operational debt. However, while, prior to 2015, the debt was still primarily bank debt for which restructuring was sought, the situation has since undergone significant changes as bond issuances have ramped up significantly. Post-2015, more companies have raised debt financing in the public markets and more companies have

[73] See S Paterson, 'The Adaptive Capacity of Markets and Convergence in Law: UK High Yield Issuers, US Investors and Insolvency Law' (2015) 78 *MLR* 431.

[74] V Ivashina, B Iverson and DC Smith, 'The Ownership and Trading of Debt Claims in Chapter 11 Restructurings' (2016) 119 *Journal of Financial Economics* 316.

defaulted on their bonds.[75] The creditors thus are much more diverse and include bondholders. Likewise, in India, onshore bond issuances have risen since 2010, and there is also an active market for distressed loans given that India is an emerging jurisdiction where it is possible for distressed investors to turn many of the distressed assets around for profits.[76]

In Singapore and Hong Kong, which have English-modelled schemes of arrangement, the debt that is sought to be compromised does not comprise only financial debt but also operational debt held by a number of trade creditors. Even among the financial creditors, there is no uniformity as they may include not only banks but also non-institutional creditors (such as retail bondholders). In India, the negotiation process under the Indian IBC only comprises the financial creditors; however, as can be seen from later chapters, financial creditors may also include the diverse group of home buyers in real estate development insolvencies.

Therefore, the rules governing the bargaining process by the stakeholders (creditors, shareholders and management) in Anglo-American restructurings may not be suitable for Asian restructurings where there are many (and different) conflicted parties. Yet, these rules are essential as they tell us *how* these negotiations are conducted (for example, through creditor committees or classes of creditors) and whose consent is required to negotiate to compromise the claims, in order for the bargaining process to be efficient and reduce transaction costs.

Third, with some rare exceptions, notably during the global financial crisis for the rescue of what are deemed systematically important companies, the literature on US[77] and UK restructuring in these strong market economies assumes that the creditors want to maximise the value of their assets in the bankruptcy outcomes, though there may be differences in views as to how maximisation should take place. Further, the assumption is that bankruptcy proceedings are not the sole debt collection devices for creditors; if restructuring fails, the creditors will enforce their rights elsewhere in the courts and ultimately put the companies into insolvent liquidation, though such enforcement may be less effective in achieving the desired recovery.[78] Both assumptions cannot always be relied on in emerging jurisdictions where the state is also a creditor and/or shareholder. In particular, in Mainland China and India where non-performing loans are a perennial problem in the banking sectors, mechanisms such as asset management companies (AMCs) are used to purchase these loans, which have an impact on agency and coordination costs as the AMCs serve as the new creditor in place of the lender. In the case of India, enforcement via the courts is often hampered by delays, making the Indian IBC the preferred (and often only) choice in recovery, and thereby creating pressures on the judicial systems administering the Indian IBC.

[75] ch 4. China accounts for the second largest onshore bond market in the world, after the US.

[76] ch 4.

[77] MJ Roe and DA Skeel, 'Assessing the Chrysler Bankruptcy' (2010) 108 *Michigan Law Review* 727.

[78] DG Baird, 'Loss Distribution, Forum Shopping, and Bankruptcy: A Reply to Warren' (1987) 54 *University of Chicago Law Review* 815, Section III.

While scholars have engaged with comparative insolvency law between the US and the UK,[79] save for certain exceptions,[80] there is a dearth of academic literature on optimal design of restructuring framework in Asia that takes into account the relationship between corporate governance and restructuring law and practice. This book aims to fill the gap in the literature on legal transplantation as applied to restructuring of financially distressed companies.

1.4. BUILDING AN ANALYTICAL FRAMEWORK

The luxury of the space afforded by this book allows an investigation on *how* agency conflicts arise and are resolved in Asian jurisdictions. The comparison is not made in a vacuum and takes place in a framework of established scholarship on agency and coordination costs in the US and UK, but with key institutional differences. The choice of jurisdictions is explained below.[81]

The central thesis of this book is that an optimal design must take into account the following that are absent or not present to the same extent as in the US/UK: (1) the interaction between *concentrated shareholdings* and *widely held debt* leading to significant risks of prejudice to outside creditors; (2) the incentives of the state in resolving non-performing loans for the purposes of bank regulation; (3) the benefits and limitations of the independent gatekeepers, being the insolvency practitioners and the courts; and (4) the interaction among restructuring law and enforcing contracts and duties of directors of financially distressed companies.

It is not the purpose of this book to weigh in on the debate on the wider question on whether the goals of restructuring law should be confined only to the economic outcomes (as encapsulated by the Creditors' Bargain theory) or should be progressive in using restructuring law as a tool to promote reorganisation.[82] This has been ably done by other scholars.[83] Rather, the book has taken the normative Creditors' Bargain theory as the starting point that the goal of restructuring law is to minimise transaction costs ex post the commencement of the restructuring process and up to the time of exit. The book assumes that even if a progressive approach is taken towards reorganisation, it must be the goal to minimise transaction costs.

These issues will be even more relevant today as each jurisdiction is expected to deal with the rise of restructuring filings due to the economic fallout from COVID-19.

[79] eg Paterson, 'The Paradox of Alignment' (2016); Paterson, *Corporate Reorganization Law* (2020); G McCormack, *Corporate Rescue Law – An Anglo-American Perspective (Corporations, Globalisation and the Law)* (Cheltenham, Edward Elgar Publishing, 2008) 1–42.

[80] See references in n 24 above. See also section 1.5.4.2 below.

[81] See section 1.5.3 below.

[82] The Creditors' Bargain theory argues that bankruptcy law should be limited to solving the problems caused by the lack of coordination among creditors faced by a firm in financial distress, and should not attempt to solve other wider problems. See for example, Jackson (n 4); TH Jackson, 'Bankruptcy, Non-Bankruptcy Entitlements, and the Creditors' Bargain' (1982) 91 *Yale Law Journal* 857. In contrast, other scholars, such as Warren, have argued that bankruptcy law has wider distributive goals. See E Warren, 'Bankruptcy Policy-Making in an Imperfect World' (1993) 92 *Michigan Law Review* 336.

[83] eg Paterson (n 22).

1.4.1. Management–Creditor and Shareholder–Creditor Conflicts

The aim of the DIP regime is to allow the management to drive the restructuring. In Anglo-American restructurings, shareholders of a distressed company are treated as having no economic interests of the company. In particular, where the company has dispersed shareholdings, and shareholders do not operate the firm but entrust the operations to professional managers, managers in any event are likely to pay more attention to creditors. The exception is where the management of the company is perceived as having brought about the distressed situation through fraud or incompetence. Even in the case of portfolio companies where the shareholdings are concentrated in the hands of private equity firms, the decisions will continue to be made based on market-oriented outcomes.

Controlling shareholders are dominant in Asian economies, in contrast to the dispersed shareholding structure found in the publicly listed companies in the US and the UK. Conventional US/UK scholarship has argued that concentrated shareholding is generally detrimental for corporate governance and the conversations have shifted to policing the private benefits of control between the companies and controlling shareholders. Many scholars have also argued that concentrated shareholdings are not appropriate for DIP models which may serve to entrench existing management, which led the company into financial difficulties in the first place.[84]

However, simply rejecting the DIP framework for jurisdictions with controlling shareholders is often not optimal since they are important in determining the outcomes of successful restructurings. Further, the absolute priority rule (APR), a cornerstone of the US Bankruptcy Code which allows the court to exercise cramdown of dissenting classes of creditors only if, among others, senior creditors must be paid in full before junior creditors or shareholders can receive anything, is not necessarily optimal if the interests of shareholders (including controlling shareholders) are to be wiped out after the restructuring.

Thus, the regime should incentivise controlling shareholders to participate if they are able to add value. However, the conflicts of interests posed by controlling shareholders need to be addressed, including controlling their participation in the outcomes, mandating disclosures of the debtor's financial information (and in early in the process), and addressing gaps in the enforcement of directors' duties.

1.4.2. Creditor–Creditor Conflicts

Until the 1990s, restructuring in the UK took place largely in the context of financial debt held by banks. Even with the rise of private equity portfolios after 2000, schemes of arrangement and pre-packaged administration plans were traditionally used to reorganise financial debt only. Only recently has there been a shift towards the reorganisation of operational debt, particularly under Part 26A. In contrast to the UK, Chapter 11 involves the restructuring of the whole of the balance sheet of the

[84] ch 3.

company and the debt has traditionally been more diverse than in the UK. In both the UK and the US, the developments in the markets, including the rise in leveraged debt financing and distressed debt trading, has weakened the dominating power of the banks.

The debt markets in the four Asian jurisdictions have also experienced increases in complexity in the last two decades. Until the late 1990s, Mainland China and India have concentrated debt markets dominated by bank lending. As chapter four demonstrates, bond issuances have increased dramatically since 2000, and it follows that onshore bond defaults become more prominent. In Mainland China, onshore bonds are often widely held across institutional and non-institutional holders. Partly to address concerns as to social unrest, the restructuring regime has resulted in departures from equal treatment of the same class of creditors, such as between smaller and larger bondholders.[85] Likewise, partly to address concerns of social unrest, different treatment also occurs between financial and non-financial creditors even among the same class. In India, while all of the creditors will be bound by the corporate resolution process under the IBC, the resolution process involves voting by financial creditors and not operational creditors as the latter could be extremely numerous and it is extremely time-consuming to coordinate the process.[86]

Even though Singapore and Hong Kong draw their schemes of arrangement framework from UK, the composition of the debt-holdings of large companies has some similarities but also key differences. In Singapore and Hong Kong, trade creditors routinely have their debts compromised. Further, bond debt in these two Asian markets is widely held by not only institutional creditors but also non-institutional investors (such as individual or retail investors) due to the several regulatory policies that encouraged non-institutional investment in corporate debt.

In addition, the creditors that are present in Asian restructurings often present risks of the scale that are not necessarily present in the US and the UK. Creditors in Asian restructurings are often related parties and face conflicts of interests because they or their affiliates are shareholders or are shareholders of affiliated companies. These creditors would also be privy to information that is not available to other outside creditors, and the debtor's management often have no incentives to disclose information (or to disclose information early) to the creditors in the absence of mandatory requirements.

1.4.3. Non-Performing Loans Management

If a creditor bank participates in a restructuring process, it would generally be expected that it would be motivated by market reasons to maximise its recovery. However, if a bank is not in good financial health due to its non-performing loans (NPLs), it may prefer to postpone the restructuring or may refuse to accept a haircut but take a longer tenure for the loan. How the banking regulator encourages speedy

[85] ch 4.
[86] ibid.

resolution of NPLs will affect the incentives of the bank creditors in participating in any restructuring.

However, where a jurisdiction's NPLs are unacceptably high, banking regulators have to intervene to ensure the stability of the country's banking market; high levels of NPLs depress credit growth, impede recovery and do not allow assets to be put to productive use.[87] In dealing with NPLs, it is well established that reforms to the insolvency and restructuring law framework for such NPL resolution is important.[88] However, it is also clear that insolvency law reforms are not, by themselves, the complete cure. Certainly, banking crises in the last three decades, including the savings and loans crisis in the US in the 1980s, the Asian financial crisis in 1997 and the global financial crisis in 2008, reveal that advanced and emerging jurisdictions will have to use other measures, including a series of bank regulatory measures (such as less favourable bank provisioning for NPLs and off-loading of the NPLs), bank bail-outs or bail-ins, tax measures and accounting rules.[89] In the bank regulatory measures to off-load the NPLs, two are prominent: using asset management companies (AMCs) or their equivalents to acquire the NPLs and thus taking the NPLs off the balance sheet of the banks; and increasing external investor participation in the secondary market for NPLs.

The analysis of the standard agency and transaction costs in restructuring proceedings must consider further the use of asset management companies and the consequences of opening up the market to distressed trading. AMCs and distressed debt market can reduce the agency and transaction costs in at least two ways. First, by mandating the banks to sell the NPLs only to the AMCs in the primary market, the AMCs can more easily aggregate debt and potentially reach faster resolutions for the NPLs. Second, the relationship between the lender and the debtor changes as the new lender has acquired the NPLs (usually at a discount). If the reason for the NPL problem is that the banks are not sufficiently disciplined to clean up the NPLs, AMCs (or the subsequent secondary purchasers of the NPLs) should instil the discipline in maximising recoveries, particularly if NPLs are acquired on market terms and these purchasers have to account to their own stakeholders.

In Mainland China, the national and provincial asset management companies, which are formed to take over the NPLs are largely state-owned. In the case of India, the equivalent counterpart are asset reconstruction companies though there is a higher degree of foreign or private ownership. The distressed loan market in India is particularly vibrant in view of the fact that it is an emerging economy (which means that there is great potential for certain assets to be turned around). The enactment of the IBC which allows the creditors a clearer path of recovery has certainly been very helpful.[90] Using asset management companies or their equivalents lead to an

[87] VV Acharya, T Eisert, C Eufinger and C Hirsch, 'Real Effects of the Sovereign Debt Crisis in Europe: Evidence from Syndicated Loans' (2018) 31 *Review of Financial Studies* 2855; S Aiyar et al, 'A Strategy for Resolving Europe's Problem Loan' IMF Staff Discussion Note 15/19 (International Monetary Fund, 2015).

[88] JC Bricongne, M Demertzis, P Pontuch and A Turrini, 'Macroeconomic Relevance of Insolvency Frameworks in a High-Debt Context: An EU Perspective' EU Publication (2016).

[89] ibid, 13.

[90] See ch 5 generally.

important change in the way the agency and coordination costs are played out in the restructuring as they purchase the NPLs and take the place of the original lender. However, state-owned asset management companies may face the same incentives as state-owned banks in their reluctance to resolve NPLs and adopt non-efficiency-based solutions. As jurisdictions seek to promote foreign investors to invest in asset management companies, purchase NPLs and/or create active distressed markets, it is even more critical to identify the agency and coordination costs that are posed by these companies.

1.4.4. The Gatekeepers

The successes of the US Chapter 11 and English scheme have been credited in significant part to the presence of the effective judiciary and the bankruptcy professionals. Law and economics scholars have argued that the jurisdictions with poor legal development and lacking in judicial expertise are better off with a more creditor-friendly regime.[91] The difficulties faced by Mainland China and India in their paths towards insolvency reforms have been attributed to, among others, the absence of the judicial expertise in handling commercial insolvencies (eg Li and Ponticelli[92] (China), and van Zwieten[93] (India)).[94] However, while an effective and competent judiciary and a highly developed profession of insolvency practitioners are important, they are not in themselves sufficient to ensure effective oversight and thus the success of the restructurings in Asia.

There are limitations to relying only on the courts and insolvency practitioners to enforce a transparent and consistent restructuring regime. The development of these mechanisms will take time and often even well-trained judges are often not in a position to decide who is acting opportunistically, nor can they assess proposals that are not even put on the table. Insolvency practitioners often face conflicts of interests and where enforcement of underlying contracts is unclear, administrators are not in the best position to determine the admission of claims for the purpose of voting.

1.4.5. Non-Bankruptcy Rules on Enforcing Contracts and Directors' Duties

It is well established in the literature that an assessment of a country's creditor protection depends on the efficacy of both the ability of the creditor to enforce their rights (and either liquidate the company or take possession of their security) as well as its

[91] eg K Ayotte and H Yun, 'Matching Bankruptcy Laws to Legal Environments' (2007) 25 *Journal of Law, Economics & Organization* 2.

[92] B Li and J Ponticelli, 'Going Bankrupt in China' (2020) PBCSF-NIFR Research Paper, available at ssrn.com/abstract=3251570.

[93] K van Zwieten, 'Corporate Rescue in India: The Influence of the Courts' (2015) 15 *Journal of Corporate Law Studies* 1.

[94] See ch 7 generally.

powers to influence the outcome of the reorganisation.[95] In the Anglo-American view of bankruptcy law, where restructuring fails, the creditors have alternative remedies in enforcing their debts in the courts, putting forth their claims in liquidation and repossessing the collateral. Thus, in analysing the shareholder–creditor, management–creditor or shareholder–creditor agency and coordination costs, the only concern will be in respect of the restructuring process.

However, in emerging jurisdictions, enforcement of unsecured debt may be weak, and liquidation takes a long time. Secured creditors may also not be able to repossess the collateral readily without obtaining court orders or jumping through other hoops (while continuing to have the power to vote to influence the outcome of the restructuring). In these cases when the alternative of recovery though enforcement or liquidation is not readily available, the agency costs of shareholder–creditor and agency and coordination costs of creditor–creditor relationships will be exacerbated. If creditors realistically only have the option of invoking the restructuring process in an attempt to receive their claims, the regime will be extremely protective of the debtor unless the restructuring process is efficient. For instance, in India, prior to the IBC, the non-bank unsecured creditors had little prospect of recovery of their claims through the courts and secured creditors faced many obstacles in repossessing the collateral. Thus, the regime was too friendly to the debtor (and its management and controlling shareholders). The Securitisation and Reconstruction of Financial Assets and Enforcement of Security Interest Act 2002 (SARFAESI) facilitated out of court enforcement by secured creditors but only for the financial institutions. If repossession of the collateral is difficult or challenging, the secured creditors in effect receive less protection (vis-a-vis the unsecured creditors and managers) and the effect is similar to that of an automatic stay on the assets against the secured creditors outside the restructuring process. These conceptual difficulties arise when analysing the appropriate reforms.

Further, how effectively the jurisdiction enforces directors' duties also impacts on when the directors invoke the insolvency or restructuring framework. If directors' duties are well enforced and there are adverse consequences for the directors if they continue to allow the insolvent company to continue trading, the likelihood is that such they will seek assistance early and the more likely it is that the company can be rescued, leading to savings in transaction costs.

1.5. METHODOLOGY

1.5.1. Distinction between Deployment and Distribution

In analysing the agency and coordination costs in this book, I deal with the questions as to deployment (how the assets should be used) and distribution (how much

[95] R La Porta et al, 'Law and Finance' (1998) 106 *Journal of Political Economy* 1113; R La Porta, F Lopez-de-Silanes and A Shleifer, 'The Economic Consequences of Legal Origins' (2008) 46 *Journal of Economic Literature* 285; S Djankov, O Hart, C McLiesh and A Shleifer, 'Debt Enforcement around the World' (2008) 116 *Journal of Political Economy* 1105.

creditors will receive) separately. This distinction is grounded from a long line of corporate finance literature, including a seminar paper by Modigliani and Miller[96] which established that the market value of a firm depends on its underlying assets and the present value of future cash flows and is thus independent of its capital structure. Using Modigliani and Miller's theory and extrapolating in the bankruptcy context, how the assets should be deployed and who has rights to those assets are separate questions.[97]

While Chapter 11 requires the creditors to bargain as to both deployment and distribution in the reorganisation process, this is not necessary the norm even in advanced economies. For example, in a PIP model in the UK administration proceedings (see Table 1.1), the process does not require the creditors to bargain over distribution and the question of deployment is carried out by the administrator.[98] The administrator has the power of sale of assets, and is able to leave behind the liabilities, and thus only negotiates the sale with the intended new purchaser in a pre-pack sale. The distribution of the proceeds of sale will follow the priority rules that apply in the case of liquidation.

1.5.2. Court Restructurings of Large Companies

In this book, I focus only on court restructurings and exclude, for example, UK company voluntary arrangements (which do not require the supervision of the courts).[99] Administration is included in the discussion, particularly in chapter six on the role of the insolvency proceedings since administration can be granted by the court,[100] corporate rescue is one of the possible outcomes of administration.

There are a number of reasons for focusing only on court proceedings. First, in the four Asian jurisdictions (see Table 1.1), excluding out-of-court workouts which are often difficult to study empirically due to the lack of data, the court-supervised restructuring remains the dominant mode of restructuring in comparison with the PIP models. Singapore is an exception as it is possible to effect an out-of-court judicial management.[101] Second, whilst many reorganisations take place consensually,

[96] F Modigliani, and MH Miller, 'The Cost of Capital, Corporation Finance and the Theory of Investment' (1958) 48 *American Economic Review* 261.

[97] DG Baird, 'Loss Distribution, Forum Shopping, and Bankruptcy: A Reply to Warren' (1987) 54 *University of Chicago Law Review* 815; DG Baird and TH Jackson, 'Corporate Reorganizations and the Treatment of Diverse Ownership Interests: A Comment on Adequate Protection of Secured Creditors in Bankruptcy' (1984) 51 *University of Chicago Law Review* 97.

[98] See G McCormack and WY Wan, 'Transplanting Chapter 11 of the US Bankruptcy Code into Singapore's Restructuring and Insolvency Laws: Opportunities and Challenges' (2019) 19 *Journal of Corporate Law Studies* 69.

[99] A company voluntary arrangement (CVA) can be challenged in court on the ground of unfair prejudice or procedural irregularity. See Insolvency Act 1986, s 6. However, as the CVA is not approved by the court and the court does not appoint the insolvency practitioner, the CVA is excluded from the discussions in the book. See text accompanying n 9 above.

[100] ch 6.

[101] IRDA, s 94.

bargaining ultimately takes place in the shadow of the law, which influences the outcomes of these bargains.[102]

Due to both space constraints and the availability of data (such as restructuring plans and related documents), I have only focused on large company restructurings in the four Asian jurisdictions. For the discussion on Indian restructuring, I have focused only on the IBC (as opposed to the schemes of arrangement because schemes are not widely used for debt restructurings).[103] I have excluded small and medium enterprise restructurings, which are increasingly subject to a different restructuring framework, as is the case in India[104] and Singapore.[105]

1.5.3. Choice of Asian Jurisdictions

I study Mainland China, India, Hong Kong and Singapore for the following reasons.

First, they are located in Asia and represent a mix of debt resolution in two economically advanced (Singapore and Hong Kong) and two emerging (Mainland China and India) jurisdictions. Mainland China and India are the second and fifth largest economies in the world, measured by GDP. Second, all four economies have listed companies that have concentrated shareholdings and vibrant capital markets whose companies regularly issue public debt.

Third, the four jurisdictions have explicitly drawn attention to the fact that they have transplanted restructuring models from UK/US, though there are differences. Mainland China enacted the Enterprise Bankruptcy Law (EBL) in 2006, which borrows from, among others, US Chapter 11, the UK administration and the German Insolvency Code of 1999, as well as the recommendations of the UNCITRAL Legislative Guide on Insolvency Law 2005.[106] Singapore amended its schemes of arrangement (originally based on the English schemes), drawing the features inspired from Chapter 11, and whose provisions are now found in the Insolvency, Restructuring and Dissolution Act 2018 (IRDA). India enacted the IBC in response to its NPL problems, and the solutions that India seeks are similar to the practitioner in possession (PIP) model found in the UK's administration proceedings. After almost two decades of consultation, Hong Kong (whose framework is based on English schemes) may be moving ahead with bankruptcy reforms which are likely to include a corporate rescue regime.[107] Currently, Hong Kong's regime is based on English schemes and with significant rights retained by secured creditors in vetoing the restructuring.

[102] See DG Baird and DS Bernstein, 'Absolute Priority, Valuation Uncertainty, and the Reorganization Bargain' (2006) 115 *Yale Law Journal* 1930.

[103] Varottil (n 54).

[104] IBC (Amendment) Ordinance 2021.

[105] Insolvency, Restructuring and Dissolution (Amendment) Act 2021, introducing the Simplified Insolvency Programme.

[106] L Qi, 'The Corporate Reorganization Regime under China's New Enterprise Bankruptcy Law' (2008) 19 *International Insolvency Review* 13, 16.

[107] Yiu, 'Hong Kong Resurrects Chapter 11-style Corporate Rescue Bill' (n 52).

Further, this book will explain how the experiences of the four jurisdictions are relevant to one another and how these lessons may be generalised in relation to other jurisdictions.

There is no question that Mainland China is firmly moving towards market-driven restructuring,[108] even though there are some accounts of Chinese bankruptcy practice focusing on governmental influence in bankruptcy process and the lack of institutional support in the restructuring process.[109] Ministries have issued notices for the clean-up of 'zombie companies' using market-based methods.[110] More recent scholarship also points out its remarkable progress towards market-based bankruptcy system and institutional capacity-building.[111] By early 2020, mounting levels of distressed debt, due to the slowdown in the economy and the trade war with the US, had led to NPLs in Mainland China exceeding US$1.5 trillion.[112] While China's asset management companies (AMCs) were set up to purchase the NPLs from the state-owned banks since 1999, the NPL market is opening up to foreign investors in order to clean up the bad debt problem. Phase one of the trade deal between the US and China (the Economic and Trade Agreement) allows for US financial services firms to apply for licences to set up AMCs. Foreign investors would expect predictability and transparency in the treatment of the distressed debts in the courts, whether through enforcement or bankruptcy,[113] and the recent experiences of China on resolving NPLs through insolvency law will be relevant for other emerging jurisdictions that are transitioning into market-based restructurings and facing high levels of NPLs.

In India, the Sick Industrial Companies (Special Provisions) Act 1985 was introduced, which by most accounts was a failure.[114] Later attempts, such as the Recovery of Debts due to Banks and Financial Institutions Act 1993 and SARFAESI, are only applicable to banks and financial institutions. In 2016, the Insolvency and Bankruptcy Code (IBC) was introduced, which laid down a time-bound insolvency procedure for companies to be resolved. The IBC has been transformational, both in moving the regime from a strong debtor-friendly regime to one that is creditor-friendly, and one that is led by insolvency practitioners as opposed to being controlled by debtors. The IBC is also an important tool to resolve some of the NPLs. How the distressed debts in the NPL market are dealt with in the courts (whether under the IBC or in enforcing contracts under general law) will be critical in the strategy towards moving to a more

[108] R Parry and Y Long, 'China's enterprise bankruptcy law, building an infrastructure towards a market-based approach' (2020) 20 *Journal of Corporate Law Studies* 157.

[109] eg Z Zhang, *Corporate Reorganisations in China: An Empirical Analysis* (Cambridge, CUP, 2018); H Zhao, *Government Intervention in the Reorganisation of Listed Companies in China* (Cambridge, CUP, 2019); Mrockova, *Corporate Bankruptcy Law in China* (2021).

[110] Notice of the National Development and Reform Commission on Steps to Deal with Zombie Companies and Eliminate Over-Capacity (No 1756) [2018]) [关于进一步做好'僵尸企业'及去产能企业债务处置工作的通知 (发改财金) [2018] 1756号).

[111] Parry and Long, 'China's enterprise bankruptcy law' (n 108).

[112] K Yeung, 'Coronavirus: China to open US$1.5 Trillion Distressed Debt Market as It Braces for Bad Loan Blowout' *South China Morning Post* (30 March 2020).

[113] World Bank (2016) 'Principles for Effective Insolvency and Creditor/Debtor Regimes', available at pubdocs.worldbank.org/en/919511468425523509/ICR-Principles-Insolvency-Creditor-Debtor-Regimes-2016.pdf.

[114] van Zwieten, 'Corporate Rescue in India' (2015).

market-based restructuring. The experience of India will be relevant to other emerging jurisdictions as to how insolvency law reform can dramatically impact the shift between a debtor-friendly to creditor-friendly regime.

Singapore's rationale for adopting Chapter 11 in its schemes framework was different from the other three jurisdictions: it was motivated by becoming a regional restructuring hub.[115] However, Singapore's debt market has significant retail investment, due to the institutional factors in encouraging the development of an active retail market for corporate bonds. The experiences of Singapore on Chapter 11-style restructurings in the context of concentrated shareholding structure and dispersed debt-holding demonstrates the lessons that can be learnt in jurisdictions with both concentrated shareholding and dispersed debt-holding. Its experiences on judicial management (which has some parallels with the administration process in the UK) will also be useful to jurisdictions considering the PIP model.

Hong Kong's restructuring law is largely based on the traditional English schemes of arrangement. The Hong Kong Government is proposing to enact legislative reforms to allow for provisional supervision and corporate rescue, which are out-of-court procedures, to facilitate restructuring if the major secured creditor consents.[116] As with Singapore, the lessons of Hong Kong in effecting schemes of arrangement of companies with concentrated shareholding structures and dispersed debt-holdings offers lessons for other jurisdictions. Hong Kong's experience with soft-touch liquidation (explained in the next section) also holds lessons of the future of a DIP regime.

In relation to the materials on Chinese bankruptcy law, I refer, where possible, to the English sources. Where the original sources are only available in the Chinese language, I include the Chinese language references as well to facilitate Chinese-speaking readers to locate the sources. I have included a bilingual list of judicial and policy guiding documents for readers so that Chinese language readers can refer to the original sources, since many of them do not have official English translations.

1.5.4. Framework of the Book

1.5.4.1. Theoretical and Comparative Framework

In the theoretical framework, the study engages with the theories of Skeel, Armour and Cheffins, as well as Skeel, Baird and Rasmussen, Skeel and Triantis, and Paterson, who consider the later developments in the debt markets,[117] and who seek to explain the UK and US bankruptcy models on the basis of shareholding dispersion and

[115] G McCormack and WY Wan, 'Transplanting Chapter 11' (2019).

[116] This proposal is not new; it first appeared in the recommendations of the Law Reform Commission (Law Reform Commission, 1996) and was attempted in 2000 and 2001, during the period immediately post-Asian financial crisis of 1997. Other previous consultations took place in 2009/10 to address the economic fallout post-2008 global financial crisis, but did not lead to legislative change. See generally Financial Services and Treasury Bureau, 'Consultation conclusions of improving corporate insolvency law and detailed proposals for introducing new statutory corporate rescue procedure' (2014); Financial Services and Treasury Bureau, 'Review of Corporate Rescue Procedure Legislative Proposals: Consultation Conclusions' (July 2010).

[117] See discussion in section 1.1 above.

different debt structures. The book tests whether these theories can be extended to Asia, by looking at the inefficiencies that arise due to shareholder–creditor, shareholder–manager, and creditor–creditor conflicts, the banking regulator's management of the NPLs, and the efficiency of the institutional structures.

In this book, the DIP model under study is Singapore's schemes of arrangement post-2017 reforms; a hybrid form of DIP and PIP models is Mainland China's EBL, and the PIP models in the Indian IBC and Singapore's judicial management.

Mainland China is classified as a hybrid form of DIP and PIP because while certain aspects of the EBL is modelled after DIP in Chapter 11, once the debtor enters into reorganisation proceedings, the court-appointed administrator directly manages the property and affairs of the debtor. However, the debtor can apply for its management to be in control but under the supervision of the administrator.[118] The latter will require court approval.[119] Either the debtor or the administrator is responsible for formulating the reorganisation plan, depending on which one manages the business.

Hong Kong utilises the English-origin schemes of arrangement to restructure both financial and operational debt, which I have classified as 'secured creditor-in-control', given that any scheme can only proceed with the consent of the secured creditors. As there is no free-standing automatic stay on enforcement proceedings, prior to *Re Legend International Resorts Ltd*,[120] a decision of the Hong Kong Court of Appeal, the market has used provisional liquidation (which allows for automatic stay of proceedings) to facilitate corporate rescues via schemes of arrangement. However, in *Re Legend*, by way of dicta, the Court of Appeal held that provisional liquidation cannot be used to effect a corporate rescue. This created uncertainty as to the use of schemes of arrangement for corporate rescue since the Hong Kong scheme does not carry with it a moratorium. Eleven years later, in a series of judgments arising from *Re China Solar Energy Holdings Ltd*,[121] the Court clarified that the limitation in provisional liquidation does not preclude its use when the assets are in jeopardy. However, it should be noted that provisional liquidation does not stay enforcement of secured debt but only the unsecured debt.

There is a further layer of complexity in Hong Kong, which is the use of the soft-touch provisional liquidation. Almost 80 per cent of the listed companies in Hong Kong are incorporated outside Hong Kong, notably in the Cayman Islands, the British Virgin Islands and Bermuda.[122] In recent years, debtors have gone to these

[118] EBL, Art 73. See also M Liu and C Wei, 'Towards a Better Future for Chinese Bankruptcy Law: Problems and Potential' Working Paper No 62 Lau Chor Tak Institute of Global Economics and Finance (2017).

[119] EBL, Art 73. The specific regulations issued by the specialist bankruptcy courts may provide the criteria to allow the debtor's management to continue managing the business. For example, the Shenzhen Intermediate People's Court provides that debtor management will not be able to manage if, among others, Arts 31–33 of the EBL are invoked (relating to the avoiding antecedent transactions). See Shenzhen Intermediate People's Court, 'Practice Directions on Reorganisation's【审理企业重整案件的共作指引】(14 March 2019), available at www.cbplaw.cn/show.aspx?info_lb=3&flag=3&info_id=4516.

[120] [2006] 2 HKLRD 192.

[121] [2016] HKCU 465; *Re China Solar Energy Holdings Ltd* [2017] 2 HKLRD 1074; *Re China Solar Energy Holdings Ltd* [2018] HKCFI 555. See CZ Qu, 'The court's power to appoint provisional liquidators to carry out rescue roles: Rethinking Legend' (2019) 28 *International Insolvency Review* 86.

[122] ch 4.

jurisdictions (being the place of their incorporation) to appoint provisional liquidators for the purpose of restructuring, though such appointment is not allowed in Hong Kong. Unlike provisional liquidation in Hong Kong, the appointment of soft-touch provisional liquidators does not displace the directors. Debtors have then proceeded to seek a recognition of such appointment in Hong Kong.[123] For reasons explained in chapters two and four, including the fact that the courts are cognisant that debtors may have abused the process in seeking soft-touch liquidation to delay proceedings as opposed to genuinely attempt restructuring, the impact of such recognition in staying winding-up proceedings to effect a restructuring is now becoming very unlikely.

Banking regulation has had a large impact on the development and impetus on the development of restructuring law in Mainland China and India. Mainland China and India have contributed to the largest NPL portfolio in Asia (collectively amounting to 75 per cent).[124] One key solution adopted by these jurisdictions is to set up AMCs to ringfence the non-performing assets and allow for these assets to be disposed or restructured. Existing literature has highlighted the potential advantages of the AMCs over other market-based solutions including the economies of scale in workouts, the granting of special powers to the AMCs to deal with loan resolution and having a disinterested third party to mediate between the bank creditor and the debtor.[125] However, as many of the AMCs in Mainland China are still state-owned, they have been criticised as lacking incentives to effectively restructure the NPLs that they have acquired from the state-owned banks.[126] But with China and India[127] opening up their economies by allowing greater participation in the AMCs by foreign investors, this book will address the changing incentives of AMCs.

Finally, the book will address the effectiveness of the institutional structures in place to support restructuring law, such as the judiciary and insolvency profession. The ease in which debts are enforced and how directors' duties are enforced are also addressed.

Due to limitations of space, I make certain omissions. First, I will not be covering the cultural factors behind the motivations of the Asian entrepreneurs in using credit and invoking insolvency and restructuring laws as compared with the US/UK, including whether there are differences in the perceptions of bankruptcy stigma. Readers will be advised to look at the literature discussing cross-cultural differences in their attitudes towards risk-taking.[128] Second, as the book focuses primarily on institutional structures and the framework, I exclude the broader discussion on the political

[123] eg *Z-Obee Holdings* [2017] HKCU 3186; *Re Hsin Chong Group Holdings* [2019] HKCFI 805; *Re Moody Technology Holdings* [2020] HKCFI 416.

[124] Deloitte LLP, 'Deleveraging Europe', Financial Advisory (2019).

[125] CW Calomiris, D Klingebiel and L Laeven 'Seven Ways to Deal with a Financial Crisis: Cross - Country Experience and Policy Implications' (2012) 24 *Journal of Applied Corporate Finance* 8.

[126] C Wei and Y Chen, 'The Predicament of Bank Creditors in Chinese Bankruptcy and the Way Out' (2019) 27 *International Insolvency Review* 110.

[127] S Shukla, 'Budget 2016: Foreign Investors Can Now Establish [Asset Reconstruction Companies] ARCs in India' *Economic Times* (26 February 2016).

[128] For the literature on risk-taking, see eg A Brumagim and X Wu, 'An Examination of Cross-Cultural Differences in Attitudes towards Risk: Testing Prospect Theory in the People's Republic of China' (2005) 13 *Multinational Business Review* 67; C Cheng, 'Are the Chinese Really More Risk Averse? A Cross-Cultural Comparison of the Risk-Return Relationship' (2009) 20 *Journal of Global Business Management* 37.

environment that may have influenced the choice of insolvency and restructuring law. Instead, the book will focus on the role of the state as a shareholder (particularly in the case of Mainland China), in the context of its highly visible roles in listed company and international bond restructurings. Third, as mentioned earlier in this chapter, the book is concerned with primarily ex post transaction costs when the company is in financial distress. Thus, the book will not go into detailed treatment as to how legal traditions and origins impact the choice of insolvency and restructuring law. Fourth, I have mainly concentrated on the domestic insolvency and restructuring framework in the jurisdictions and have not discussed cross-border elements of restructuring in the four jurisdictions, except in the context of Hong Kong and Mainland China, due to the fact that many large restructurings in recent years involve cross-border restructuring practice, and the practice has a substantial impact on the development of the jurisprudence in insolvency and restructuring law. Fifth, I have excluded discussions of restructuring of financially distressed financial institutions and banks as they are subject to specific bank resolution regulation. Sixth, the book is only concerned with corporate restructuring law, and not personal bankruptcy law.

1.5.4.2. *Empirical Studies*

In the empirical studies of the four jurisdictions, I examine the outcomes of the restructuring and analyse the outcomes using the framework set out above on resolving shareholder-creditor, shareholder-manager and creditor-creditor conflicts. With certain exceptions on Mainland China,[129] India[130] Hong Kong[131] and Singapore,[132] there are few empirical studies on the impact of the restructuring laws on creditor and shareholder outcomes as well as the impact of NPL regulation on restructuring law.

The main empirical sources of data for this book are set out below.

1.5.4.2.1. Mainland China

For Mainland China, my approach will build on prior studies which have focused that the outcomes of listed company restructurings are attributable to governmental intervention.[133] I have extended the dataset substantially to include companies that issued public debt. Thus, the dataset comprises the outcomes of the reorganisation of large companies (which will be the companies that issued public debt (in Panel A

[129] eg S Li and Z Zhang, *Law Review of Corporate Reorganization and Restructuring* [公司重整法律评论：上市公司重整专辑] vol 5 (Beijing, China Law Press [法律出版社], 2019), Z Zhang, *Corporate Reorganisations in China* (2018); Mrockova (n 29); Li and Ponticelli, 'Going Bankrupt in China' (2020); Zhao, *Government Intervention* (2019).

[130] eg S Chatterjee, G Shaikh and B Zaveri, 'An Empirical Analysis of the Early Days of the Insolvency and Bankruptcy Code, 2016' (2018) 30 *National Law School of India Review* 89.

[131] eg WY Wan and C Watters, 'Mandatory Disclosure in Corporate Debt Restructuring via Schemes of Arrangement: A Comparative Approach' [2021] 30 *International Insolvency Review* S111.

[132] eg WY Wan, C Watters and G McCormack 'Schemes of Arrangement in Singapore: Empirical and Comparative Analysis' (2020) 94 *American Bankruptcy Law Journal* 463; WY Wan and C Watters, 'Mandatory Disclosure' (ibid).

[133] Zhang (n 109); Zhao (n 109); S Li and Z Zheng, *Law Review of Corporate Reorganization and Restructuring* (n 129).

of Appendix A) and listed companies (in Panel B of Appendix A). The period under investigation will be 2015–19. 2015 is chosen as it is the year in which the Communist Party of People's Republic of China identified improving the implementation of EBL as one of its key priorities, given EBL's importance as a market-based mechanism to resolve insolvent companies.[134] Data will be the judgments and restructuring plans obtained through National Enterprise Bankruptcy Information Disclosure Platform ('Platform')[135] that was launched in August 2016 by the Chinese Supreme People's Court (SPC), which allows for the debtor companies and creditors to monitor the development of the cases,[136] as well as from *WIND* database, a subscription database and press articles. For the status of bond restructurings, I refer to *Fitch Blue Book*, which provides the status of bonds in default[137] and cross-checked with WIND database, which contains the announcements by the companies whose bonds are in default.

Data on the NPLs acquired by AMCs in China will be drawn from the public disclosures by the four national AMCs, comprising China Huarong Asset Management Co Ltd (Huarong), China Cinda Asset Management Co Ltd (Cinda), China Orient Asset Management Company Limited (China Orient) and China Great Wall Asset Management (Great Wall). Huarong and Cinda are listed on the Stock Exchange of Hong Kong and will have disclosures in respect of their NPLs. The companies within the Great Wall group and China Orient group have raised public debt and offering circulars in connection with the fundraising provide the information on the operations of the two AMCs respectively.

Chinese specialist bankruptcy courts also draw up the procedures in which the reorganisation takes place. As there were nine specialist courts as at June 2020 (excluding the bankruptcy tribunals),[138] I have been selective and focused on only certain of the practices of the specialist courts in Shenzhen and Zhejiang, which are economically advanced regions and which have been the subject of academic commentary.[139]

1.5.4.2.2. India

In the case of India, I will examine the outcomes of large-scale bankruptcy cases involving Indian companies that have been restructured under the Indian Insolvency and Bankruptcy Code 2016. The primary source of data on the corporate insolvency and resolution processes (CIRPs) will be *Debtwire India*, the Insolvency and Bankruptcy Board of India and the judgments from the National Company Law Tribunal and the National Company Law Appellate Tribunal. The period in question

[134] Mrockova (n 29) 253.

[135] pccz.court.gov.cn/pcajxxw/index/xxwsy.

[136] The Supreme People's Court of the PRC, 'Judicial Transparency by People's Court' (14 March 2017), available at english.court.gov.cn/2017-03/14/content_28552039_3.htm.

[137] Fitch Ratings, 'China Corporate Bond Market Bluebook' (2019), available at your.fitch.group/rs/732-CKH-767/images/china-corporate-bond-market-blue-book_fitch_10083315.pdf.

[138] Li and Ponticelli (n 92).

[139] S Steele et al, 'Trends and Developments in Chinese Insolvency Law: The First Decade of the PRC Enterprise Bankruptcy Law' (2018) 66 *American Journal of Comparative Law* 669.

is 2016 to March 2021. Appendix B, Panel A contains the 12 large accounts which RBI has ordered to utilise the IBC in 2017.[140] I collected the data on the large distressed companies that have been resolved under the IBC (as at 31 March 2021) and they are listed in Appendix B, Panel B. The large debtors are those whose claims from financial creditors exceed INR100 million (US$1.3 million) and where the claims cannot be determined, they are excluded from Appendix B, Panel B. Appendix B, Panel B has 154 cases.[141]

1.5.4.2.3. Hong Kong

For the schemes of arrangement sanctioned by the Hong Kong courts, I identify the publicly listed companies that have undergone debt restructurings via schemes of arrangement for the period 2015–20 from the court decisions, press information and stock exchange filings. The list of filings is found in Appendix C.

1.5.4.2.4. Singapore

The relevant dataset of schemes of arrangement sanctioned by the Singapore courts will be drawn from an earlier study by the author[142] (but in this study, I will focus only on the publicly listed companies and/or their subsidiaries), and I have substantially updated the dataset to include the schemes of arrangement up to 31 December 2020. The list of companies is found in Appendix D.

For both Hong Kong and Singapore, I identify the companies that have undergone debt restructuring through press articles, court judgments and stock exchange filings. I also use Perfect Information, a subscription database, and providers of management services for bond restructurings to obtain copies of the explanatory statements or descriptions of the schemes of arrangement. Copies of the shareholder circulars are reviewed in order to ascertain the dilution to the existing public shareholders. More generally, data relating to bond issuance, bank data and macroeconomic data for all four jurisdictions is obtained from Bank of International Settlements, CEIC Data, a subscription database, and Asian Bonds Online.

1.6. ORGANISATION OF THE BOOK

Chapter two sets the institutional background to, and the development of, restructuring law and practice in the four Asian jurisdictions since the 1980s. Due to constraints of space, the selection is highly selective but illustrates the main drivers and background for the development of the modern restructuring law.

[140] In 2017, RBI had directed the resolution of 12 large accounts, which constituted 25% of the total non-performing assets of the banking system in India. See 'RBI Lists 12 NPA Accounts For Insolvency Proceedings' *Hindu Business Line* (12 January 2018).

[141] The total number of all CIRPs (and not only the large cases) that have been resolved as at December 2020 is 347. Source: IBBI Newsletter (January to March 2021) 19.

[142] Wan, Watters and McCormack, 'Schemes of Arrangement in Singapore' (2020).

Chapter three analyses the agency costs of the shareholder–creditor and manager–creditor relationships. The chapter first sets the scene on the institutional background of share ownership in the US/UK as well as the four Asian jurisdictions, followed by a section explaining the strategies to deal with the shareholder–creditor and manager–creditor agency costs in the aforementioned jurisdictions. I then explain how the strategies developed in the US/UK will often not work as well in the four Asian jurisdictions in light of differences in their institutional structures. The chapter ends with lessons learned and implications for reform.

Chapter four analyses the agency and coordination costs of creditor–creditor relationships. Similar to chapter three, the chapter first sets the scene on the debt-holdings in the US/UK as well as the four Asian jurisdictions, followed by a section explaining the strategies to deal with the agency costs arising from the different creditors. I discuss the strategies involving the question of deployment of assets and distribution of assets separately. I then explain how the strategies to resolve the conflicts are used in Asia. The chapter ends with lessons and implications for reform.

Chapter five focuses on the NPL problem in Mainland China and India, and the ongoing efforts by the two jurisdictions to utilise the restructuring law to tackle these issues. I argue that the analysis of the standard agency and coordination costs in restructuring proceedings must further consider the use of asset management companies and the consequences of opening up the market to allow greater distressed fund participation.

Chapter six discusses the role of the insolvency practitioner or administrator and the limitations of such roles in the four Asian jurisdictions, including accountability, potential conflicts of interests and effectiveness. The chapter ends with a discussion of lessons learned and implications for reform to remove or mitigate the conflicts and interests and to enhance their effectiveness.

Chapter seven discusses the role of the courts (and other judicial bodies) in the supervision of the reorganisation process. It argues that the courts have several strengths in determining the outcome of the restructurings but also face several limitations: (1) determining which players are behaving opportunistically; (2) a preference to allow debtors to drive the restructuring in common law jurisdictions; and (3) the interest of the state in achieving certain objectives from the restructuring regime.

Chapter eight discusses the relationship among restructuring law and enforcing contracts and directors' duties. There are two dimensions. First, whether a regime is regarded as creditor-friendly or debtor-friendly will depend not only on the insolvency and restructuring framework but also the ease to which the debt is enforced in the jurisdiction. Where enforcement of the debt is weak or non-existent, the debtor protection features in restructuring law will only render the regime more inefficient by exacerbating the agency costs between managers and the creditors. Second, I discuss the incentives and disincentives that are put in place to nudge or mandate directors to address the problem of financial distress early and invoke the insolvency and restructuring framework before matters are too late.

Chapter nine concludes the book. It summarises the approach towards restructuring law and concluding observations. The current proposals for reforms that are being considered in each of the four Asian jurisdictions are also discussed.

This book aims to state the law as on 31 August 2021.

2

Development of Corporate Restructuring Law in Four Asian Jurisdictions

2.1. INTRODUCTION

IN THIS CHAPTER, I outline the key differences in the current restructuring regimes in Mainland China, India, Hong Kong and Singapore, and the practice that has been developed by the law-makers, market participants and the judiciary. I will also discuss the economic conditions, the institutions as well as the crises that exist immediately prior to modern corporate reorganisation law and practice in the four jurisdictions. Broader issues relating to the corporate governance and state of capital markets are addressed in later chapters. The influence of two well-known international organisations – the United Nations Commission on International Trade Law (UNCITRAL) and its 'Legislative Guide on Insolvency Law' (*UNCITRAL Guide*),[1] and World Bank and the now discontinued 'Doing Business Reports'[2] – is highlighted given their emphasis on resolving insolvency within a business-friendly environment.

It is the central thesis of this chapter that the economic and institutional conditions in the 1980s and 1990s significantly influence the making of modern restructuring law in three of the four jurisdictions, Mainland China, India and Singapore. In making the comparison of the development of corporate restructuring laws, I separately compare Mainland China and India, two of the emerging jurisdictions, and Hong Kong and Singapore, two advanced jurisdictions. For the two emerging jurisdictions, the choice of their current restructuring models, being the practitioner in possession (PIP) (India) and hybrid PIP/debtor in possession (DIP; China) models, are the outcomes of attempts to resolve the prevailing problems then relating to a debtor-friendly regime and external pressures to comply with international norms. However, in certain cases, past attitudes of market actors towards resolving problems continue to persist,

[1] UNCITRAL Legislative Guide on Insolvency Law (2005), available at uncitral.un.org/en/texts/insolvency/legislativeguides/insolvency_law (*UNCITRAL Guide*). See generally S Block-Lieb and TC Halliday, 'Harmonization And Modernization In UNCITRAL's Legislative Guide On Insolvency Law' (2007), available at papers.ssrn.com/sol3/papers.cfm?abstract_id=965710#.

[2] World Bank, 'Doing Business', available at www.doingbusiness.org/en/doingbusiness. The World Bank discontinued the 'Doing Business' series on 16 September 2021, when data irregularities were found: World Bank, 'World Bank to Discontinue Doing Business Report' (16 September 2021), available at www.worldbank.org/en/news/statement/2021/09/16/world-bank-group-to-discontinue-doing-business-report. For a critical view of Doing Business reports, see G McCormack 'Why "Doing Business" with the World Bank May Be Bad for You' (2018) 19 *European Business Organisation Law Review* 649.

making change difficult. For instance, in Mainland China, the choice of the hybrid PIP/DIP model in the Enterprise Bankruptcy Law 2006 (EBL) reflected the compromise to turn the administration of the debtor to an external administrator. However, as will be demonstrated in chapter three, in many of the state-owned enterprise (SOE) restructurings, the influence of local government persists.

India's general distrust of promoters (who are the controlling shareholders) stems from the fact that historically its regime was extremely debtor-friendly, and promoters had routinely used successive bankruptcy reforms to frustrate creditors' enforcement of the debt. In many situations, their arguments have found sympathy with the lower courts. In 2016, with the enactment of the Indian Insolvency and Bankruptcy Code (IBC) and the setting up of the Insolvency and Bankruptcy Board of India (IBBI), there was a clean break from past practice and a distinct shift into the PIP model. However, the rulings of the lower courts continue to indicate a pro-rescue culture. The Supreme Court of India and the legislature have corrected the rulings on appeal and by way of new amendments to the legislation respectively.

Hong Kong and Singapore are two financial hubs in Asia. Both are former British colonies, and their initial company legislation was derived from the United Kingdom (UK). Singapore gained its independence from Britain, first as part of Malaysia and then as an independent republic, whereas Hong Kong remained a British colony before reunifying with China on 1 July 1997. In the 1960s and 1970s, both jurisdictions had a very creditor-friendly regime, as in the UK, where prior to the enactment of the Insolvency Act 1986 that introduced the administration process, restructurings were carried out by either consensually or using the scheme of arrangement under the companies legislation, which was in existence for over a century and was present in the successive amendments and consolidations.[3]

However, the restructuring framework diverged during the 1980s. Singapore's reforms have been largely driven in response to crises and market needs. In 1986, Singapore introduced the judicial management, which is a PIP model, to deal with the aftermath of the Pan-Electric crisis.[4] Judicial management was based on the original UK administration order introduced in 1986 before it was revised by the Enterprise Act 2002. The next major reform introduced by Singapore came in 2017 to transform it to distinctly DIP procedure modelled after the features of Chapter 11 of the Bankruptcy Code of the United States (US). The 2017 reforms responded to the aftermath of the global financial crisis of 2008, when the Government of Singapore saw the opportunity to service companies in need of restructuring in the Asia-Pacific and to reform its laws to be an international restructuring hub. Further reforms were made in response to the COVID-19 crisis, including introducing a simplified restructuring framework.

In Hong Kong, there is no formal corporate rescue framework. There are proposals to introduce a new provisional supervision and corporate rescue bill, discussed as far back as 1996, which has been revitalised but not yet tabled before the Legislative Council at the time of writing. The differences in the two approaches lie in their

[3] Joint Stock Companies Arrangement Act 1870, s 2. See J Payne 'Debt Restructuring in English Law: Lessons from the United States and the Need for Reform' (2014) 130 *LQR* 282.

[4] See n 131 below (and accompanying text).

priorities – in Hong Kong, discussions on insolvency law reforms arose in connection with the Asian financial crisis of 1997, the global financial crisis of 2008 and most recently COVID-19, which is still ongoing. In the last two financial crises, when the consultations on the merits of the reforms concluded, the crises abated somewhat and the economy rebounded, lessening the urgency. In contrast, Singapore's reforms are driven to become an international restructuring hub.

Together with chapter one, the investigation of the different conditions and the institutional frameworks provide the foundation for the rest of the book. Later chapters explain why ownership and composition of debt-holdings matters and how they give rise to agency costs, how bank regulation influences the manner of development of the insolvency and restructuring law and policy, the role of insolvency practitioners and the courts, the relationship between insolvency and restructuring laws and other rules and implications for the corporate restructuring debate. Due to the limitations of space in this book, I refer the readers to the literature on economics and financial markets, as well as the historical roots of how insolvency is treated in the relevant Asian jurisdictions prior to the 1980s.[5]

2.2. EMERGING JURISDICTIONS

The modern insolvency reforms in Mainland China and India favour a PIP regime (though Mainland China offers a hybrid PIP regime), rather than a DIP regime. The reasons are largely historical due to the debtor-friendly regime that existed prior to the enactment of the modern restructuring framework, and the enactment of the unified insolvency and restructuring law is intended to represent a clean break from the past. The previous regime in both countries had failed to provide an efficient system for the exit of non-viable businesses or the revival of distressed but viable businesses, which proved to be extremely problematic when both countries had to transition to more free market-oriented economies and to promote regimes that put the assets to their most productive use. Both jurisdictions also had to deal with high levels of non-performing loans (NPLs) during the relevant time of the enactment, and these problems continue to persist even until today (see chapter five). While the primary method of dealing with NPLs will be prudential regulatory measures, insolvency and restructuring laws are also regarded as an important tool to ensure prudential stability by providing a venue of exit.

[5] For Mainland China, see TC Halliday and BG Carruthers, *Bankrupt: Global Lawmaking and Systemic Financial Crisis* (Stanford, Stanford University Press, 2009) ch 8; N Mrockova, *Corporate Bankruptcy Law in China: Principles, Limitations and Options for Reform* (Oxford, Hart Publishing, 2021) 15–45 on the discussion on China's political and economic history leading to the EBL. For an excellent account of the historical balance of powers between creditors and debtors in India, see RG Rajan, *I Do What I Do: On Reform, Rhetoric and Resolve* (Uttar Pradesh, Harper Business, 2018). RG Rajan was the former Governor of the Reserve Bank of India. See also J Armour and P Lele, 'Law, Finance, and Politics: The Case of India' (2009) 43 *Law & Society Review* 491–526. For Hong Kong, see A Tang, *Insolvency in China and Hong Kong: A Practitioner's Perspective* (Hong Kong, Sweet & Maxwell Asia, 2005). For Singapore, see V Yeo and P Gan, 'Insolvency Law in Singapore' in R Tomasic (ed), *Insolvency Law in East Asia* (Aldershot, England/Burlington, VT, Ashgate, 1986) ch 12.

2.2.1. Mainland China

In Mainland China, the bankruptcy code in effect is the EBL, which applies to all the enterprises, including SOEs and private enterprises. Prior to 2006, the then governing laws on bankruptcy were the EBL (Trial Implementation) 1986, which only dealt with SOE bankruptcies, and the China Civil Procedure Law 1991, which dealt with private company bankruptcies. Both the 1986 and 1991 laws were not regarded as effective due to their cumbersome processes, and were seldom used.[6] The 1986 law particularly was seen as not compelling financially distressed SOEs to enter restructuring or liquidation but a means of warning these SOEs, and the 1986 law was often not enforced.[7] There was considerable resistance to the enforcement of the 1986 law. SOEs employed as many as 70 per cent of workers in the cities, and it was estimated that half of the SOEs then were unprofitable.[8] The SOE managers did not want to make mass redundancies, local governments did not want to be saddled with social unrest arising from unemployed workers, and the state-owned banks were reluctant to write down the NPLs.[9] Further, as debt enforcement was particularly challenging due to the difficulties in verifying financial information and property rights in the 1980s and 1990s,[10] the regime then applicable was distinctly debtor-friendly.

When China acceded to the World Trade Organization in 2001, it became clear that a modern bankruptcy regime was required to ensure an orderly exit of companies that failed, as well as the rehabilitation of economically viable companies.[11] However, the drafting of the new comprehensive bankruptcy law, the EBL, proved to be protracted, and the main contentious issues related to whether the unified law should apply equally to SOEs and private enterprises and whether employee claims should have priority over secured debt.[12] Eventually, the EBL was passed; it recognised some of the compromises reached among the various stakeholders, and its chapter on reorganisation also had several features that were drawn from the US Chapter 11 of the Bankruptcy Code (Chapter 11), the UK, Germany and Japan.[13] The EBL provides three processes: (1) liquidation in which the company was sold either as a going concern or piecemeal; (2) conciliation where the parties could negotiate over the debt and the settlement be granted by the court; and (3) reorganisation. The EBL also explicitly drew on the *UNCITRAL Guide*, which borrows heavily from Chapter 11 on corporate reorganisation,[14] though it allows for different approaches towards reorganisation. For example, the *UNCITRAL Guide* recommends a menu of options,

[6] Mrockova, *Corporate Bankruptcy Law in China* (2021) 78. See also W Wang, 'Adopting Corporate Rescue Regimes in China: A Comparative Survey' (1998) 9 *Australian Journal of Corporate Law* 234 (noting that there were hardly any cases under the 1986 law).

[7] ibid.

[8] Halliday and Carruthers, *Bankrupt* (2009) 261.

[9] ibid, ch 7.

[10] Mrockova (n 5) 60–64.

[11] Z Zhang, *Corporate Reorganisations in China: An Empirical Analysis* (Cambridge, CUP, 2018) 6–7; see also DA Austin and C Lin, 'Bankruptcy with Chinese Characteristics: Insolvency Administration in the People's Republic of China' (2020) 94 *American Bankruptcy Law Journal* 85.

[12] Halliday and Carruthers (n 5).

[13] Mrockova (n 5) 72.

[14] Halliday and Carruthers (n 5) 394.

including a DIP model that is based on Chapter 11, a limited displacement model where the debtor operates the business under the supervision of the insolvency representative or total displacement of the debtor management in favour of the insolvency representative.[15]

However, in contrast with Chapter 11, the EBL often does not specify in detail the mechanisms on disclosure issues and how the creditors and other stakeholders should participate in the negotiation process.[16] Due to the lacunae in the EBL, the Supreme People's Court (SPC), the highest judicial body in Mainland China, often has to supplement by promulgating judicial guidance or judicial interpretations, as well as conference minutes and opinions, for the lower courts to follow.[17] For instance, Article 75 of the EBL provides that during the period of automatic stay, enforcement of a secured creditor's security is suspended but the creditor may apply to the Court to restore the exercise of his/her rights if there is damage or depreciation of the secured assets. Unlike the US Bankruptcy Code,[18] Article 75 of the EBL does not provide details on the considerations that the Court should consider in determining whether to restore the rights, particularly if the secured assets are vital to the debtor's operations, and the consequences of the restoration. Instead, it is left to the 2019 conference minutes promulgated by the SPC to provide the details.[19] In the course of the discussions in the book, there are frequent references to these instruments.[20] The intermediate people's courts, which hear the EBL cases, are also proactive in having guidelines, such as the guidelines on pre-negotiated administrations.[21]

The EBL introduces a hybrid DIP and PIP model as both the debtor (if the debtor is in charge of managing the business and operations) and the administrator (if he/she is in charge of the business and operations) can propose the plan.[22] The debtor can initiate or petition for reorganisation even if it is not insolvent but 'apparently'

[15] *UNCITRAL Guide*, Recommendation 112.

[16] S Gao, 'Cramdown, reorganization bargaining and inefficient markets: The cases of the United States and China' (2021) 30 *International Insolvency Review* S5.

[17] Judicial interpretations have been issued by the SPC since 2017 and they are broadly equivalent to delegated subsidiary legislation in common law jurisdictions, and the SPC has the power to make, amend or abolish the rules that must be abided by all of the courts. See Organic Law of People's Courts of the People's Republic of China (adopted at the 2nd session of the Fifth National People's Congress on 1 July 1979, last revised and adopted at the 6th session of the Standing Committee of the 13th National People's Congress on 26 October 2018 [中国人民共和国人民法院组织法 (1979年7月1日第五届全国人民代表大会第二次会议通过 根据1983年9月2日第六届全国人民代表大会常务委员会第二次会议《关于修改〈中华人民共和国人民法院组织法〉的决定》第一次修正 根据1986年12月2日第六届全国人民代表大会常务委员会第十八次会议《关于修改〈中华人民共和国地方各级人民代表大会和地方各级人民政府组织法〉的决定》第二次修正 根据2006年10月31日第十届全国人民代表大会常务委员会第二十四次会议《关于修改〈中华人民共和国人民法院组织法〉的决定》第三次修正 2018年10月26日第十三届全国人民代表大会常务委员会第六次会议修订)].

[18] 11 USC § 361 (secured creditors may obtain relief from the automatic stay to protect against decline of the value of the security or obtain 'adequate protection' of their proprietary interests).

[19] Notice of the Supreme People's Court on Issuing the Minutes of the National Courts' Civil and Commercial Trial Work Conference, [2019] No 254, effective 8 November 2019 [最高人民法院关于印发《全国法院民商事审判工作会议纪要》的通知 [现行有效] （法〔2019〕254号）, Art 112.

[20] See ch 7, section 7.5.1. The Supreme People's Court has issued directives to clarify the operation of the EBL, strengthened the creditors' rights to information and introduced measures that lend legitimacy to existing practice.

[21] ch 7.

[22] EBL, Art 79, read with Art 80.

lacks the ability to pay its debts.[23] When the debtor or the administrator petitions for reorganisation and the court accepts the petition, an administrator is appointed immediately.[24] The debtor can subsequently apply to the court for DIP so that it can continue to manage the business and operations while in reorganisation, while the administrator supervises the process.[25]

In the 2019 conference minutes,[26] the SPC provided that the court may approve the debtor's DIP application if all of the following conditions are fulfilled:[27] (1) the governance mechanism of the debtor continues to function normally; (2) a DIP process is favourable for the debtor's continuance of operation; (3) the debtor has not hidden or improperly transferred its assets; and (4) the debtor has not acted contrary to the interests of the creditors. After the plan is proposed, the court convenes the first creditors' meeting, where creditors can vote on the plan in classes, comprising secured creditors, employees, tax claimants and other unsecured creditors.[28] The plan is binding if it is passed by a majority in number representing two-thirds or more of the unsecured debt in value.[29] If the creditors fail to approve the plan at the first creditors' meeting, the administrator can convene a second creditors' meeting. In the absence of approval again at the second creditors' meeting, the court can cram down the plan.[30] When the cram-down occurs, the priorities are in the following order: secured creditors; employees' claims; tax claims; and other unsecured creditors.[31] Except for the paucity of conditions of the cram-down power, there are substantial similarities with Chapter 11 in terms of the holding of creditors' meetings and approval thresholds. The Chinese courts also use various means to ensure consistency in the rulings of the lower courts. The concept of a choice between DIP and PIP (and its development) has a parallel to the (then) German Insolvency Code of 1999, which allows the court to order a DIP in theory, but this power is seldom exercised.[32]

In practice, there are several other issues facing the debtors in the operation in the EBL in its first decade. First, the petition must be accepted by the court before the reorganisation proceedings commence. Earlier accounts document that the courts often fail to accept the petitions, unless there is concurrence by the local government, and often successful acceptance of petitions are for often only either SOEs or listed companies.[33] Second, the courts have been quick to order a cram-down against the creditors' interests, particularly for listed company reorganisations, without necessarily articulating the reasons for the cram-down.[34] Third, as a socialist state, the

[23] EBL, Art 2.

[24] EBL, Art 13.

[25] EBL, Art 73.

[26] Notice of the Supreme People's Court on Issuing the Minutes of the National Courts' Civil and Commercial Trial Work Conference, [2019] No 254, effective 8 November 2019 [最高人民法院关于印发《全国法院民商事审判工作会议纪要》的通知 [现行有效] （法〔2019〕254号）].

[27] ibid, para 111.

[28] EBL, Art 62.

[29] EBL, Arts 84 and 86.

[30] EBL, Art 87.

[31] EBL, Art 87.

[32] G Hoher, 'ESUG: German for "Modernising Bankruptcy Law"', Eurofenix (Spring 2012) (reporting that the court orders DIP only in 2% of the cases).

[33] Mrockova (n 5) 79, fn 125. See also ch 7.

[34] ch 3. See also H Zhao, Government Intervention in the Reorganisation of Listed Companies in China (Cambridge, CUP, 2019) 202–09.

courts have often given priority to employee interests in view of local governments' concerns that bankruptcy and firm closures can lead to widespread unemployment and social unrest. Fourth, when liquidation groups are appointed as administrators, they include government members who consider non-market considerations in decision-making.[35] Fifth, despite the timelines stated in the EBL, it is documented that these timelines are not complied with.[36]

However, the institutions have also made substantial progress in recent years in promoting market reforms and improving the operation of the EBL, which is seen as an essential tool to enable an orderly exit for companies that fail. In particular, China has been concerned with the problem of 'zombie' companies, most of which are economically unviable SOEs that are only kept alive with government support. Since 2011, the rising non-performing loan ratio and special purpose loans for the commercial banks in China have had to be aggressively addressed, with the EBL being one of the toolkits to close unviable SOEs and other private enterprises. In addition to the judicial pronouncements by the SPC and publication of representative cases by the intermediate courts, the regulators have also published various regulations guiding market participants that reflect well-established practices in offshore bond restructurings, including the formation of creditor committees.[37]

When it comes to the types of restructuring that have been approved, considering the examples in Appendix A, they range from amending the term of the loan to extend payment of principal and interest, taking haircuts, debt-equity swaps and sale of the assets. New investors may also invest in the form of injecting cash or in kind, and the investment may take place over a period of time.[38]

2.2.2. India

Prior to the enactment of the IBC in 2016, India was a distinctly debtor-friendly regime. Enforcement of debts was a protracted affair. There were various estimates of the length of time for resolution, which could take up to 15 years.[39] Before the enactment of the Securitisation and Reconstruction of Financial Assets and Enforcement of Security Interest Act (SARFAESI) in 2002, other estimates were 10–12 years.[40] Enforcement of secured lending was also estimated to experience significant delays

[35] ch 6.

[36] Z Zhang, 'The Corporate Bankruptcy Substitute in China' (2019) 33 *Columbia Journal of Asian Law* 172.

[37] ch 4, section 4.4.1.2.

[38] In ST Pang Da Automobile Trade Limited's restructuring (see Appendix A), the creditors were to be repaid over six years, and only interest was payable over the first three years. The new investor received the controlling shareholder's shares for free and undertook to the company that if the profitability targets in the next three years were not met, it would pay the shortfall, which effectively meant that the creditors continued to take the risk that the new investor may fail to deliver on the shortfall. See ch 4, section 4.4.1.2.

[39] For an account on the difficulties in enforcement, see V Vig, 'Access to Collateral and Corporate Debt Structure: Evidence from a Natural Experiment' (2013) 68 *Journal of Finance* 881.

[40] L Viswanathan and Dhananjay Kumar, "India" in A Nassiri, *The Lending and Secured Finance Review*, 6th edn (London, The Law Reviews, 2020), available at www.cyrilshroff.com/wp-content/uploads/2020/07/India.pdf.

of five to seven years.[41] SARFAESI improved the ability of the banks and financial institutions to enforce on the security without having to invoke the judicial process. However, after the passage of SARFAESI, and even with the more optimistic assessment by the Indian Government, the estimated time period for recovery was over 4.3 years.[42]

While India, similar to other common law jurisdictions such as Hong Kong and Singapore, has the scheme of arrangement since the enactment of the Companies Act 1956,[43] the scheme of arrangement framework is rarely used to restructure debts because of inefficiencies in the court system and delays.[44] Instead, throughout the period 1980-2016, various attempts at insolvency law reform were made but were largely ineffective in assuring the restructuring of financially distressed but economically viable companies. In the 1980s, the Sick Industrial Companies (Special Provisions) Act 1985 (SICA) was enacted. In 1991, India liberalised its economy and moved away from central planning.[45] Several banking sector reforms followed, including the conferment on the statutory powers of the Securities and Exchange Board of India. Various attempts to improve the recovery to creditors followed, including the Recovery of Debts Due to Banks and Financial Institutions Act 1993 (RDDBFI), the Corporate Debt Restructuring framework introduced in 2001 guided by the Reserve Bank of India (RBI) and various schemes established under the Joint Lenders' Forum (JLF schemes) by the RBI between 2014 and 2016.[46]

SICA was intended to rescue financially distressed industrial companies through a DIP model under the supervision of the Board for Industrial and Financial Reconstruction. Non-industrial companies could be resolved with under other mechanisms, such as the scheme of arrangement or liquidation.[47] However, SICA was widely regarded as inefficient, in part because the courts routinely took it upon themselves to interpret the provisions in a manner that favoured corporate rescue of industrial companies so as to protect employees' jobs.[48] For instance, when the Board for Industrial and Financial Reconstruction recommended liquidation for a

[41] See R Rajan, 'A Hundred Small Steps: Report of the Committee on Financial Sector Reforms', Planning Commission, Government of India (2008) 168, available at faculty.iima.ac.in/~jrvarma/reports/Raghuram-Rajan/cfsr_all.pdf.

[42] Press Information Bureau, Government of India, 'India ranks 63 in World Bank's Doing Business Report' (24 October 2019), available at pib.gov.in/newsite/PrintRelease.aspx?relid=193994.

[43] The scheme of arrangement provisions are now found in Companies Act 2013.

[44] See ch 8.

[45] Armour and Lele, 'Law, Finance, and Politics' (2009).

[46] The Joint Lenders' Forum schemes include Strategic Debt Restructuring, Outside Strategic Debt Restructuring schemes and the Scheme for Strategic Structuring of Stressed Assets (S4A) and the Flexible Structuring of Existing Long Term Project Loans (5:25 Scheme). See Economic Times Bureau, 'RBI withdraws CDR, SDR, S4A, JLF schemes to restructure defaulted loans' (13 February 2018).

[46] K van Zwieten, 'Corporate Rescue in India: The Influence of the Courts' (2015) 15 *Journal of Corporate Law Studies* 1.

[47] U Varottil, 'The Scheme of Arrangement as a Debt Restructuring Tool in India: Problems and Prospects' (2018) 15 *European Company and Financial Law Review* 585.

[48] K van Zwieten, 'Corporate Rescue in India' (2015); Varottil, 'The Scheme of Arrangement as a Debt Restructuring Tool in India' (ibid); J Bhagwati, KM Shuheb and RR Bogathi, 'Can Asset Reconstruction Companies (ARCs) be Part of the Indian Debt Problem?' (Indian Council for Research on International Economic Relations, 2017), available at tile.loc.gov/storage-services/service/gdc/gdcovop/2018305088/2018305088.pdf.

particular firm and which would oblige the court to grant the winding-up order,[49] the court would order a stay of proceedings, adjourn hearings or simply not order the liquidation, so that the parties could explore further if there were other alternatives to rehabilitate the company.[50] Even when the board recommended revival of the company, the main complaint was the length of time that it took for its revival while the managers continue to be in charge (often eight–11 years), and the lenders could not enforce due to the moratorium in place.[51] SICA was eventually repealed in 2016.

When it was clear that SICA did not bring about the intended changes for restructuring companies, several other attempts followed. The Corporate Debt Restructuring framework, based on the London approach towards restructuring, involved a workout by financial institutions. While the Corporate Debt Restructuring framework was different from SICA in that the creditors would be in control of the process, in practice, the creditors' attempts to effect the workout were frustrated by the promoters.[52] On the enforcement side of the equation, India took steps to improve through the setting up of debt recovery tribunals and enactment of SARFAESI. Debt recovery tribunals were initially successful in improving the enforcement of secured debt outside of the court process, but they were soon bogged down by delays.[53] SARFAESI, as mentioned at the beginning of this section, was much more successful, and the evidence can be seen in the reduction of the NPA ratio following the passage of the legislation.[54]

All the earlier reforms relating to SICA, Corporate Debt Restructuring framework and the setting up of debt recovery tribunals, attracted two main criticisms. One was that the courts continued to adhere to a pro-rescue culture. Second, the promoters were widely criticised as stymieing the progress of the restructurings. However, the reforms were not seen as urgent until the mid-2010s. During the mid-2000s investment boom, several infrastructure projects commenced. Economic growth then was strong, and banks lent readily.[55] However, with the onset of the global financial crisis of 2008, exports dipped, and the infrastructural projects started to encounter several difficulties due to governmental delays and governance problems within the borrowers.[56] The sharp rise in NPLs in 2012/13 led to a refocus by the RBI on measures that were required to address them.

By 2015, in view of the recognition of the urgent difficulties that NPLs could threaten the stability of financial economy and hamper future growth, the Bankruptcy Law Reforms Committee submitted its report recommending that India required a completely new framework on resolution, rather than a piecemeal solution.[57] The report was the foundation of the setting up of the IBC.

[49] SICA, s 20 (as it then applied).
[50] van Zwieten (n 46).
[51] ibid. See ch 5, section 5.3.1.
[52] ch 3.
[53] Vig, 'Access to Collateral and Corporate Debt Structure' (2013). See R Rajan, 'A Hundred Small Steps' (2008).
[54] Vig (n 39). See ch 5 for the impact of SARFAESI on the NPA ratio.
[55] Rajan (n 5).
[56] ibid.
[57] The Bankruptcy Law Reform Committee was set up by the Ministry of Finance, Department of Economic Affairs in 2014. See Bankruptcy Law Reform Committee, 'Interim Report of the Bankruptcy Law Reform Committee' (2015), available at www.finmin.nic.in/sites/default/files/Interim_Report_BLRC_0.pdf.

The IBC sets up four key institutions: (1) the judicial authority that adjudicates on corporate insolvency, the National Company Law Tribunal (NCLT) (and dissatisfied litigants may appeal to the National Company Law Appellate Tribunal (NCLAT)); (2) the IBBI that oversees the licensing of insolvency professionals; (3) information utilities that are central depositories for the lenders containing information on the terms of the debtors' loans and the amount of debt that is in default; and (4) the Corporate Insolvency Resolution Process (CIRP). CIRP represents an important shift from a debtor-friendly to a creditor-friendly regime. Once the CIRP is admitted to the NCLT, the debtors' managers will be displaced and instead the debtors are administered by the insolvency practitioner (also known as the interim resolution professional) and supervised by the NCLT. The interim resolution professional handles the submission of claims, and the committee of creditors, comprising only of financial creditors, is constituted. The committee of creditors holds the first meeting and appoints the resolution professional as well as the valuer to determine the liquidation value. The resolution professional submits the information memorandum to the committee of creditors and issues an expression of interest. The resolution plan is negotiated and put before the committee of creditors for voting, and if passed by 66 per cent of the value of the debt held by the committee,[58] the resolution plan is submitted to the NCLT for approval.

The CIRP is a strict, time-bound process, requiring the matter to be resolved within 180 days with a single extension of another 90 days. The absolute deadline, including extensions and legal proceedings, is 330 days, whereupon the matter automatically goes to liquidation.[59] Membership of the NCLT comprises judicial and technical members, the latter of whom are not judges but have the requisite experience specified, including being chartered accountants.[60] The president of the NCLT and the chairperson for the NCLAT are the Judge of the High Court of at least five years and Judge of the Supreme Court or Chief Justice of the High Court, respectively.[61]

Under CIRP, those who are previously in control of the 'defaulting'[62] debtor or promoters, together with persons connected with them, cannot bid to reacquire the assets of the debtor within the IBC unless they first clear all outstanding defaults.[63] The CIRP resembles the UK administration in that it is a PIP model. However, as will be seen in chapter six, the resolution professional in the CIRP does not have the same powers as an English administrator in relation to the deployment of the assets, such as a sale. Creditors in India are required to bargain over both the issues of deployment and the distribution of the assets.

There were several initial teething problems with the CIRP. First, the lower courts were initially very keen to substantively review the decisions of the creditors'

[58] IBC, s 30(4).

[59] IBC, s 12. See also ch 8.

[60] Companies Act 2013, s 409.

[61] Companies Act 2013, ss 409–411.

[62] The ban is against a person who is, among others, a wilful defaulter pursuant to the RBI Guidelines issued under the Banking Regulation Act 1949 (India) or has an account classified as a non-performing asset by the RBI and at least one year has lapsed from the date of such classification. See IBC, s 29A.

[63] IBC, s 29A (introduced in 2017).

committee, which defeats the intention of the IBC to give effect to creditors' decisions.[64] In response, the Indian Parliament was quick to amend the legislation to deal with the problems as well as to address new issues that arose during the operation of the IBC. For example, after the decision of the NCLAT in *Essar Steel*, which surprisingly elevated the priority of the unsecured creditors to that of the secured creditors, the Supreme Court reversed the decision and separately, the IBC was amended in 2019 to restore the priorities of the creditors that would have applied had the debtor gone into liquidation.[65] The Supreme Court also took pains to emphasise the finality of the decisions of the creditors' committees on several occasions and most recently in *Pratap Technocrats v Monitoring Committee of Reliance Infratel*,[66] which made it clear that the NCLT cannot review the fairness of the decision of the committee of creditors.

Second, the proceedings took a long time to complete, past the statutory time-bound period.[67] The IBC was amended in 2019 to make it clear that the extended time-bound period of 330 days included the time taken for matters to be adjudicated. Further amendments followed, including the amendment in 2021 to introduce a pre-packaged framework that allows for an expedited process but only for micro, small and medium enterprises.[68] Third, the resolution professional, as a profession of insolvency practitioners, requires time to build capacity.[69] Fourth, the promoters litigated endlessly, particularly under section 29A of the IBC, with the result of causing delays.[70]

However, despite the initial problems, the IBC has brought fundamental change from a debtor-friendly to a creditor-friendly framework. Under the CIRP, as promoters cannot be the acquirer or remain in management (subject to limited exceptions such as when the CIRP is withdrawn), and the assets are sold to the bidder selected by the committee of creditors. Hence, unlike Chapter 11, the management does not remain post-restructuring. The IBC is undoubtedly regarded as a success in India. Figure 4.5 in chapter four shows the steady increase in the number of filings under the IBC from 2016 to 2019, which is the period prior to the implementation of the suspension of filings due to COVID-19. 1,943 filings were made in 2019/20 alone.[71] Recoveries under the IBC were dramatically improved compared with the previous recoveries under debt recovery tribunals and SARFAESI.[72] Prior to the discontinuation of the World Bank's 'Doing Business' reports,[73] India improved to 63rd position in 2020 from the 77th position in the previous year, and the improvements were

[64] ch 7.

[65] *Committee of Creditors of Essar Steel India Limited through Authorised Signatory v Satish Kumar Gupta & Ors* (hereinafter *Essar Steel*) Civil Appeal 8766-67 of 2019, [93]. See ch 4.

[66] *Pratap Technocrats (P) Ltd. & Ors. v Monitoring Committee of Reliance Infratel Limited* (Civil Appeal 676 of 2021).

[67] ch 8.

[68] Insolvency and Bankruptcy Code (Amendment) Ordinance 2021.

[69] ch 6.

[70] ch 3.

[71] ch 4, Figure 4.5.

[72] ch 5, Figure 5.3.

[73] World Bank, 'World Bank to Discontinue Doing Business Report' (16 September 2021), available at www.worldbank.org/en/news/statement/2021/09/16/world-bank-group-to-discontinue-doing-business-report.

demonstrated to result from, among others, the enactment of the IBC.[74] Further, confidence in the distressed loan market remains high in India; Debtwire recorded India as being the most active market for distressed loans in the Asia-Pacific (ex-Japan) in 2018 and 2019. While the distressed loan trades dipped in the last three-quarters of 2020 due to COVID-19, these trades rebounded in the first half of 2021, amounting to US$856 million and India dominating the Asia-Pacific market.[75] In 2018, with the high levels of NPLs, the RBI has tried to redress the problem by directing the financial institutions that are subject to RBI regulation to resolve the bad loans within six months, failing which the banks had to mandatorily refer the matter to the IBC.[76] After the mandatory direction was quashed by the Supreme Court of India,[77] the RBI issued the Prudential Framework for Resolution of Stressed Assets on 7 June 2019,[78] which puts in place incentives for the RBI-regulated entities to pursue out-of-court restructurings for large accounts (Rs 15 billion (US$202 million) and above) through consensual inter-creditor agreements, which carries the advantage of the regulatory treatment that the banks can invoke insofar as the restructuring of the NPLs is concerned.[79] However, the IBC continues to remain an important fall-back should the banks not invoke the framework.

2.3. ADVANCED JURISDICTIONS

In contrast to the emerging jurisdictions, the impetus for proposals on law reform in Hong Kong or Singapore has, until recently, primarily been the Asian financial crisis of 1997[80] and the global financial crisis of 2008. The most recent round of reforms in Singapore are, however, motivated by putting Singapore on the map as a hub for Asian restructurings.

2.3.1. Hong Kong

Hong Kong was a British colony from 1843 and only reunified with China in 1997. For much of its modern economic development, Hong Kong was regarded as

[74] World Bank, 'Doing Business 2020: Reforms Boost India's Business Climate Rankings; Among Top Ten Improvers for Third Straight Year' (24 October 2019), available at www.worldbank.org/en/news/press-release/2019/10/24/doing-business-india-top-10-improver-business-climate-ranking.

[75] Debtwire 1H/2021, 'Asia Pacific Distressed Loan Trading Report', copy on file with the author.

[76] Circular of 12 February 2018 introducing a revised framework for resolution of stressed assets by scheduled commercial banks and all Indian financial institutions.

[77] The Circular of 12 February 2018 was quashed by the Supreme Court of India via *Dharani Sugars and Chemicals Limited v Union of India* Transferred Case (Civil) No 66 of 2018 in Transfer Petition (Civil) No 1399 of 2018 (2 April 2019) on the ground of being ultra vires section 35AA of the Banking Regulation Act, 1949.

[78] Prudential Framework for Resolution of Stressed Assets, RBI/2018-19/203; DBR.No.BP.BC.45/21.04.048/2018-19.

[79] ibid.

[80] For a discussion on the impact of the Asian financial crisis on insolvency law in Asia, see OECD, *Insolvency Systems in Asia: An Efficiency Perspective* (Paris, OECD Publishing, 2001), available at doi.org/10.1787/9789264189539-en.

the icon of the laissez-faire economy.[81] English common law was introduced to Hong Kong, and in 1966 the Application of English Law Ordinance formalised the reception of English common law and rules of equity. When reunification took place on 1 July 1997, the Sino-British Joint Declaration of 1984 reached between Britain and China guaranteed the continuity of the existing legal system in Hong Kong. The Basic Law confirms the concept of 'one country, two systems', and Article 8 of the Basic Law provides that the laws previously enforced in Hong Kong, including the common law, rules of equity and ordinances, shall be maintained except for provisions that contravene the Basic Law.

Hong Kong first enacted the Companies Ordinance in 1865, which was modelled on the UK Companies Act of 1862. Subsequent amendments (and consolidations) between 1865 and 1986 were based on the legislation of UK companies applicable at the time, including the Companies Ordinance of 1932, which introduces the scheme of arrangement provisions (whose provisions were based on the UK Companies Act of 1929). These provisions are now in sections 673 and 674 of the Companies Ordinance, Cap 622.

Until the 1990s, Hong Kong restructurings largely followed the path of UK restructurings, with emphasis on consensual restructurings lead by the major commercial banks.[82] Early accounts of debt restructuring of large companies in the 1980s due the general downturn of the shipping industry were work-outs involving creditors, shareholders and new investors.[83] It was clear that the major banks in those times, such as Hongkong and Shanghai Banking Corporation, took the major lead in any work-out.[84] Tang argued that the reason for the support by the major commercial banks then, as compared with the later downturn during the Asian financial crisis of 1997, was the greater commitment shown to the survival of the companies by the founder shareholders in working out solutions, including contributing their own capital.[85] Even though there was no formal moratorium, restructuring took place due to the support of the creditor banks and largely on consensual basis, without having to use the cram-down provisions in the scheme of arrangement.[86] Hong Kong's insolvency regime in the 1980s was very much based on the UK's (then) creditor-friendly regime, which emphasised the realisation of assets rather than corporate rescue.[87] Even though the profile of the creditors have changed with the emergence of bond investors (as discussed in chapter four), Hong Kong's restructuring regime remains creditor-friendly.[88]

[81] See M Friedman, 'Asian values: right' (1997) 49 *National Review (New York)* 36. cf M Friedman, 'Hong Kong Wrong' *Wall St Journal* (6 October 2006).

[82] Tang, *Insolvency in China and Hong Kong* (2005) 342.

[83] ibid, 63-91. The early workouts included the restructuring of Hutchinson Whampoa Limited, Wah Kwong Shipping and Investment Company (Hong Kong) Limited and Orient Overseas Holdings Limited in the 1980s.

[84] ibid, 71.

[85] ibid, 71.

[86] ibid, 91; ELG Tyler, 'Insolvency Law in Hong Kong' in R Tomasic (ed), *Insolvency Law in East Asia* (Aldershot, Taylor & Francis, 2006) (on the lack of use of the scheme of arrangement).

[87] Tang (n 5) 431.

[88] See also *In the Matter of Trinity (Management Services Limited)* [2021] HKCFI 2207 (the court emphasised at para 5 that 'Hong Kong does not favour debtor in possession processes').

After the UK enacted the Insolvency Act of 1986, the Law Reform Commission of Hong Kong considered the matter in 1990.[89] At that time, it was thought that a corporate rescue framework was critical due to the deficiencies in the scheme framework as a rescue procedure in the mid-1980s.[90] There were three parts to the review: personal insolvency, corporate rescue and winding up. The provisions on personal insolvency proceeded first and were enacted via amendments to the Bankruptcy Ordinance in 1996.[91] In the same year, the Law Reform Commission published its report on corporate rescue and insolvent trading.[92] It recommended a provisional supervision framework that envisioned that the directors would initiate a rescue that would be supervised by a qualified accountant.[93] As explained later in this section, these attempts have yet to result in legislative reform.

After the publication of the Law Reform Commission report in 1996, the Asian financial crisis of 1997 hit the Asian economies adversely, bringing the lack of a formal corporate rescue regime to the forefront.[94] While there were no statistics on corporate rescue, the statistics on winding-up orders showed a steady increase between 1997 and 2002 before falling in 2003. Figure 2.1 shows the number of petitions filed and winding-up orders made. It was reported that there was an increase in companies seeking to restructure their debts.[95]

In 1998, the Hong Kong Association of Banks and the Hong Kong Monetary Authority issued guidelines on how banks should deal with customers in financial difficulty, encouraging a standstill, during which the parties could negotiate a restructuring plan.[96] The guidelines were based on the London approach, which only bound the banks; other creditors such as bondholders, employees and trade creditors can still proceed with enforcement actions.

Prior to 2006, when there was a lack of a stay of enforcement proceedings against a debtor, once a winding-up petition was filed against the company, the company would request the court to appoint a provisional liquidator (a qualified insolvency practitioner) if the debtor was incorporated in Hong Kong. Once the provisional liquidator was appointed, the management of the company was turned over to the provisional liquidator. With the appointment of the provisional liquidator, there is also a stay of proceedings under section 186 of the Companies (Winding Up and Miscellaneous Provisions) Ordinance.[97] The stay was helpful when indebted debtor companies began to do reverse takeovers to realise the value of their listing status, which was recognised as assets of the companies even though they were not reflected in the balance sheet.[98] In these transactions, a third-party investor would inject assets

[89] P Smart and CD Booth, 'Reforming Corporate Rescue Procedures in Hong Kong' (2001) 1 *Journal of Corporate Law Studies* 485.

[90] Tyler, 'Insolvency Law in Hong Kong' (2006).

[91] ibid.

[92] Law Reform Commission, 'Report on Corporate Rescue and Insolvent Trading' (Hong Kong, Government Printer, October 1996), available at www.hkreform.gov.hk/en/docs/rrescue-e.pdf.

[93] Smart and Booth, 'Reforming Corporate Rescue Procedures' (2001). See CZ Qu, 'Towards an Effective Scheme-Based Corporate Rescue System for Hong Kong' (2012) 12 *Journal of Corporate Law Studies* 85.

[94] Smart and Booth (n 89).

[95] ibid.

[96] ibid.

[97] Cap 32.

[98] *China Solar Energy* [2018] HKCFI 555, [39].

or cash into the company in return for shares.[99] A scheme of arrangement was then used for the debts of the creditors to be compromised, usually with a significant haircut. The courts had confirmed that the requisite approval of the shareholders will still be required even if the company is insolvent and the value of shares was zero.[100] As part of the approval process for the restructuring, the realisation of the listing status could be apportioned between the creditors and shareholders, though the courts indicated that the amount should be nominal for the shareholders.[101] These transactions involving the realisation of the listing status are quite different from the restructurings normally contemplated in DIP proceedings where management remains in place and a more sustainable debt structure is sought – in fact, in reverse takeovers, the management will be displaced by the new investor.

In 2006, a spanner was thrown in the works when the decision in *Re Legend International Resorts*[102] rendered the use of the provisional liquidation uncertain. In that case, the Court of Appeal held that it was impermissible to appoint provisional liquidators under the legislation principally for restructuring. The *Legend* litigation saga also threw into the spotlight the activities of the distressed funds in Hong Kong and the relative lessening of influence by the major banks in the major restructurings. A Morgan Stanley distressed fund purchased the debt of Legend, the debtor, from a financial institution and promptly applied for a winding-up petition of Legend. Legend was a Hong Kong company with assets in the Philippines. Subsequently Legend applied for a corporate rescue proceeding in the Philippines, which was objected to by Morgan Stanley.[103] In 2016, however, the Court clarified (in *Re China Solar Energy Holdings Ltd*[104]) that provisional liquidators can continue to be appointed if the company is insolvent and the assets are in jeopardy.

For companies that were not incorporated in Hong Kong, the insolvency practitioners started to use another adaptive device: the soft-touch liquidation process, appointing a provisional liquidator in the place of the incorporation of the company and subsequently having the provisional liquidator recognised in Hong Kong under a common law. *Z-Obee Holdings*[105] was the first case that recognised the use of the soft-touch liquidation of a Bermuda company listed on the Hong Kong Stock Exchange (SEHK), and this method of seeking recognition was followed by debtor companies in later cases.[106] In *Z-Obee Holdings* and in other cases, during the period of provisional liquidation, the SEHK would suspend the trading of the shares of the company and specify the conditions for such resumption to take place. Such a

[99] Tang (n 5) 426–427 (citing the 2000 restructuring proposal in Akai Holdings).

[100] *Re Albatronics (Far East) Ltd. (in liq)* [2001] 3 HKC 223. See also Tang (n 5) 160.

[101] Under the Companies Ordinance, Cap 32, ss 182 read with s 232, once the company is in liquidation, approval of the court is required for the transfer of the shares, and the court may impose conditions for such transfer: *Re Albatronics (Far East) Ltd. (in liq)* [2001] 3 HKC 223; *Re Yaohan Hong Kong Corp (in liq)* [2000] 4 HKC 488; *Re Rhine Holdings Ltd. (in liq)* [2000] 3 HKC 543.

[102] [2006] 2 HKLRD 192.

[103] Qu, 'Towards an Effective Scheme-Based Corporate Rescue System' (2012) fn 20.

[104] *Re China Solar Energy Holdings Ltd* HCCW 108/2015, [2016] HKCU 465 (CFI).

[105] *Re Z-Obee Holdings Limited* [2017] HKCFI 2204.

[106] eg *Hsin Chong Group Holdings Limited* [2019] HKCFI 805; *Agritrade Resources Ltd* [2020] 4 HKLRD 616; *Moody Technology Holdings Ltd* [2020] 2 HKLRD 187 and *FDG Electric Vehicles Ltd* [2020] 5 HKLRD 701.

soft-touch liquidation process is possible if the company is incorporated in Bermuda, the Cayman Islands or British Virgin Islands, as these jurisdictions are able to make such appointments in their respective company law.[107]

Figure 2.1 Winding-up petitions presented and ordered from 1997 to 2020

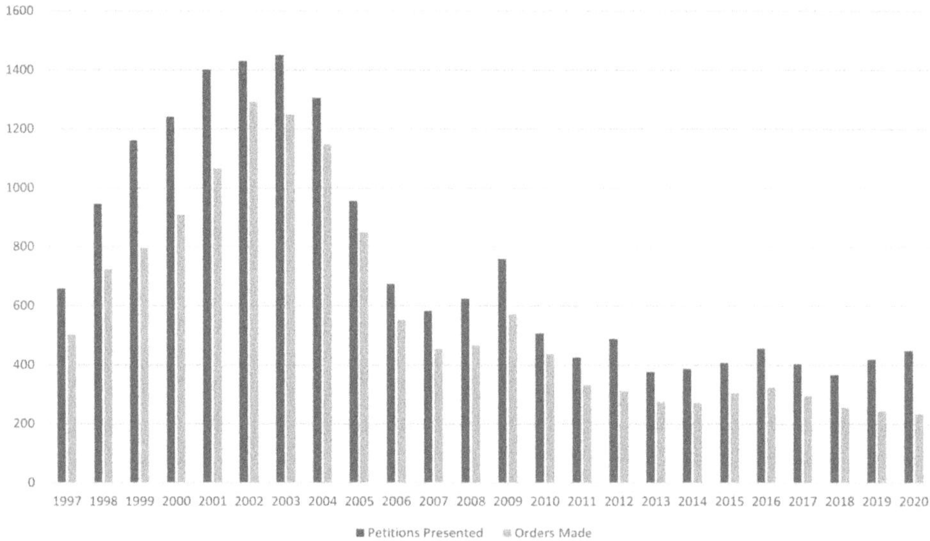

Source: Data collected from Official Receivers' Office, Hong Kong, available at www.oro.gov.hk/eng/statistics/compulsory_winding_up_and_bankruptcy/stat.php.

However, since 2015, debt restructuring of listed firms in Hong Kong began to face two headwinds. The first (and more recent) is that the SEHK made it more difficult for reverse takeovers to be effected in view of the various corporate governance scandals involving such transactions, which were perceived to be associated with the circumvention of the stringent listing criteria and lower disclosure requirements.[108] In October 2019, the listing rules were amended to considerably tighten the scrutiny of reverse takeovers and for the companies to be able to resume trading after the suspension.[109] For instance, in a reverse takeover, both the acquisition target and the enlarged group must meet the suitability requirements and achieve the profit requirements over the last three financial years.[110] For a distressed company that is proposing

[107] See *Re China Huiyan Juice Group Ltd* [2020] HKCFI 2940.

[108] SEHK listing rules, listing rule 14.06A.

[109] See Hong Kong Stock Exchange, 'Consultation Conclusions: Backdoor Listing, Continuous Listing Criteria and other Rule Amendments' (2019), available www.hkex.com.hk/-/media/HKEX-Market/News/Market-Consultations/2016-Present/June-2018-Backdoor-and-Continuing-Listing/Conclusions-(July-2019)/cp201806cc.pdf?la=en&hash=C0DD7A60622FE2C13EB380DAC231C07EC8953A2A&hash=C0DD7A60622FE2C13EB380DAC231C07EC8953A2A. See also Securities and Futures Commission, 'Statement on the SFC's approach to backdoor listings and shell activities' (26 July 2019), available at www.sfc.hk/en/News-and-announcements/Policy-statements-and-announcements/Statement-on-the-SFCs-approach-to-backdoor-listings-and-shell-activities.

[110] SEHK listing rules, listing rule 14.54.

to resume trading, it often will not meet the profitability requirement and thus, the market value for realisation of the listing status has dropped markedly.[111]

Second, as the economy in Mainland China begins to slow down due to the US–China trade war commencing in 2017, the Hong Kong courts have had to deal with restructuring cases that involve Hong Kong-listed companies (parent companies) whose operations are wholly or predominantly in Mainland China.[112] The parent companies are often not incorporated in Hong Kong,[113] and they would hold the PRC subsidiaries through one or more intermediary holding companies (intermediary companies) and the wholly owned foreign enterprise (WOFE). The parent companies have obtained financing from offshore bond issuances (usually with a view of the monies flowing back to the PRC subsidiaries), and the PRC subsidiaries would have borrowed from the Chinese banks (onshore banks). Repayment on the offshore bonds will depend on dividends or other cash flows from the PRC subsidiaries. Since 2000, for reasons not entirely clear, the SEHK allowed the listings of these foreign-incorporated companies with PRC subsidiaries. Perhaps with the benefit of hindsight, Harris J had described this state of affairs where the place of incorporation would assume jurisdiction if the companies ran into financial distress as not being something that was well considered by the regulators at the relevant time.[114]

These jurisdictional problems are now evident. When the PRC subsidiaries of the SEHK-listed company run into financial difficulties and try to restructure the debt, the complexity lies in navigating the restructuring for the onshore and offshore debts. Offshore creditors will be structurally subordinated to onshore creditors unless they have the benefit of security or guarantee by the PRC subsidiaries. Due to the limitations of Chinese companies being able to grant security directly to offshore creditors, in particular prior to May 2014, such security or guarantee would be rare. Prior to May 2014, security or guarantee to be granted by the WOFE or PRC subsidiaries to offshore lenders requires the approval of China's State Administration of Foreign Exchange, and such approval is not easy to obtain. Compounding the difficulties of the offshore creditors is that at the stage of onshore restructuring, offshore creditors have limited ability to exercise their shareholder rights (as shareholder of the WOFE) to influence the restructuring. To obtain ultimate control of the WOFE, the offshore creditors will have to, through liquidation, take possession of the shareholdings of parent companies and their intermediary holding companies and proceed to remove the directors and legal representative of the WOFE. However, it is by no means clear that the Chinese courts will recognise the appointment of the liquidators of the shareholder of the WOFE.[115] Further, if onshore restructuring of the onshore debt of the PRC subsidiaries takes place under the Chinese Enterprise Bankruptcy Law 2006 (EBL), offshore creditors (which would be expected to be subordinated creditors of

[111] eg *Re China Huiyuan Juice Group Ltd* [2020] HKCFI 2940.

[112] eg *Re China Huiyuan Juice Group Ltd* [2020] HKCFI 2940.

[113] More than 80% of the companies listed on the Hong Kong Stock Exchange are incorporated outside of Hong Kong. See WY Wan, C Chen and SH Goo, 'Public and Private Enforcement of Corporate and Securities Laws: An Empirical Comparison of Hong Kong and Singapore' (2019) 20 *European Business Organization Law Review* 319, fn 61.

[114] *Re Lamtex Holdings Limited* [2021] HKCFI 622, [34].

[115] See *Re China Huiyuan Juice Group Ltd* [2020] HKCFI 2940.

the PRC subsidiaries) may find themselves the subject of cram down under Article 87 of the EBL and hence have no recourse at all.[116]

There was some success in 2015/16 with the restructurings of the off-shore debt of these Hong Kong-listed companies. Kaisa and Winsway (both of which are listed in Appendix C) were incorporated offshore with assets in Mainland China and were listed on SEHK. Kaisa was a leading Chinese real estate property developer; its borrowings were made offshore (including bonds), and its PRC subsidiaries were borrowed onshore. Winsway provided coal for steelmakers in China. Winsway had onshore secured and unsecured bank borrowings and offshore bonds. In both instances, the offshore debts were restructured using schemes of arrangement in their respective places of incorporation and in Hong Kong. In both cases, US methods of bond restructurings are imported, such as the use of bond restructuring support agreements.[117]

However, with the changes to the listing rules and the fact that some of these companies might cease to be economically viable, the Hong Kong courts began to exercise more caution when the companies attempted to utilise the soft-touch liquidation to delay creditors' winding-up petitions brought in Hong Kong. In *Re Lerthai Group Limited*, a significant creditor petitioned for winding-up of the debtor. There was, according to the court, no real creditor support for the proposed restructuring, even though there was no opposition to the winding-up by other creditors. The court granted the winding-up petition.[118] In *Re Lamtex Holdings*,[119] similarly, the court did not believe that genuine and viable restructuring attempts were taking place, and there was lack of creditor support. In future cases, it is expected that recognition of these foreign provisional liquidators appointed on a soft-touch liquidation basis will be very limited and would not amount to a stay of winding-up proceedings in the absence of clear evidence of creditor support and genuine restructuring attempts.

Earlier in this section, I mentioned that the Hong Kong Government attempted to introduce legislation on corporate rescue after the publication of the Law Reform Commission of Hong Kong report in 1996. Two attempts were made in 2000 and 2001, which failed; what proved to be the downfall was the proposed treatment of the employee wages in that bill.[120] In particular, the procedure could not be invoked unless a premium was paid to the employees who were made redundant over their statutory entitlements under the Protection of Wages on the Insolvency Fund.[121] Later consultations took place in 2009/10 to address the economic fallout post-2008

[116] An example of the cram-down being exercised is Wuxi Suntech Co. Ltd; see ACW Tang and C Lam, 'INSOL International Case Study: Wuxi Suntech Co Ltd – The First PRC Reorganisation involving shareholders subject to Foreign Insolvency Proceedings, Case Study Number 7' (2016), copy available on file with author.

[117] WY Wan and C Watters, 'Mandatory Disclosure in Corporate Debt Restructuring via Schemes of Arrangement: A Comparative Approach' (2021) 30 *International Insolvency Review* S111.

[118] *Re Lerthai Group Limited* [2021] HKCFI 207.

[119] *Re Lamtex Holdings Ltd* [2021] HKCFI 622. See also *Re Trinity Management Services* [2021] HKCFI 2207.

[120] Smart and Booth (n 89).

[121] Qu (n 93).

global financial crisis, but did not lead to legislative change.[122] In light of the general economic downturn that began with the escalation of the US–China trade war in May 2019 and COVID-19, it remains to be seen whether the economy will rebound. The Hong Kong Government announced that the bill would be tabled in 2021,[123] but at the time of writing, the corporate rescue framework is still pending before the Legislative Council.

In summary, the history of Hong Kong's insolvency laws indicates a strong pro-creditor approach. The attempts in Hong Kong to introduce the corporate rescue bill have been motivated by the Asian financial crisis and the global financial crisis. While there is some move towards a slightly more pro-debtor stance, the proposed rescue framework remains pro-creditor because the rescue can only take place with the consent of the major secured creditor.[124] Even then, before the completion of the process of law reform, when the crises abated, they somewhat lessened the impetus for putting into place changes in the first place. While the restructuring framework has not fundamentally changed since the 1990s, the financial market has changed with the greater diversity in the kinds of creditors (and the lessening influence of the major commercial banks) and the types of debtors' operations. The profession had attempted to use adaptive devices to resolve the lack of the rescue framework, and the cases demonstrate the limitations in the adaptive devices available for restructuring.

2.3.2. Singapore

In contrast to Hong Kong, which is known for its laissez-faire economy, Singapore epitomises economic planning.[125] Before the 1960s, Singapore's economy was dominated by trade, and the legislation of the companies fell under the Companies Ordinance 1948, which included the schemes of arrangement provisions found in the UK Companies Act 1929.

After achieving independence first from Britain and subsequently Malaysia in 1965, Singapore enacted the Companies Act, Cap 50 of 1967, which was based on the Malaysian Companies Act of 1965 (and which was in turn based on the English companies legislation). The current provision on schemes of arrangement is found in section 210 of the Companies Act.[126]

English common law was received in Singapore via the Second Charter of Justice 1826 and formalised by the Application of English Law Act.[127] Thus, prior

[122] Financial Services and Treasury Bureau, 'Review of Corporate Rescue Procedure Legislative Proposals: Consultation Conclusions' (July 2010); Financial Services and Treasury Bureau, 'Consultation conclusions of improving corporate insolvency law and detailed proposals for introducing new statutory corporate rescue procedure' (2014).

[123] E Yiu, 'Hong Kong resurrects Chapter 11-style corporate rescue bill after 24-year hiatus as Singapore powers ahead with reforms' SCMP (12 March 2020).

[124] Legislative Council Secretariat, 'Updated background brief on the introduction of a statutory corporate rescue procedure and insolvent trading provisions in Hong Kong' (29 October 2020), available at www.legco.gov.hk/yr20-21/english/panels/fa/agenda/fa20201102.htm.

[125] See, eg, NMK Lam, *Government Intervention in the Economy: A Comparative Analysis of Singapore and Hong Kong* (2000) 20 *Public Administration and Development* 397.

[126] Companies Act, 2006 Rev Ed, Cap 50.

[127] Application of English Law Act, Cap 7A, 1994 rev edn.

to 1987, Singapore followed the English approach of a pro-creditor regime in which creditors have strong enforcement rights.[128] In particular, secured creditors are able to enforce against the security interests to the fullest extent under contract law.[129]

Between independence and 1984, the economy focused on export-led industrialisation and attracting multinational companies.[130] The first major recession came in 1985, led to the collapse of Pan-Electric Industries, resulting in the unprecedented closure of the Stock Exchange of Singapore for three days, and a number of corporate failures, including securities firms.[131] Urgent reforms were required to handle the crisis, and the prevailing view then was that consensual restructuring or the scheme of arrangement was insufficient.[132] In 1987, Parliament enacted the Companies (Amendment) Act 1987, which introduced the judicial management based on administration found in the UK Insolvency Act of 1986 (prior to its amendments via the Enterprise Act 2002).[133] Judicial management is a means for the court to appoint a qualified insolvency practitioner to take over the management of the company if one of the following objectives can be achieved: the survival of the company or the whole or part of its undertaking as a going concern; to obtain a scheme of arrangement; or to achieve a greater realisation of the company's assets than would be effected should the company be wound up. Once the judicial management order is filed, an automatic stay applies, and the judicial manager will attempt to achieve the stated purpose.[134] The process allows for the creditors to have a say on whether the judicial management should proceed early in the process (since the judicial manager must present his/her proposal to a meeting of creditors) within 60 days (which can be extended).[135] Any subsequent distribution of the assets requires a scheme of arrangement[136] or winding up.

Unfortunately, the judicial management, as it was originally enacted in 1987, was not regarded as a success, the majority of the appointments leading to liquidations.[137] This was attributed to the lack of motivation by the management of the debtor to work with the judicial manager and the complexity of the judicial management order.[138]

[128] See generally, J Lee, 'Is Singapore's Insolvency Regime Excessively Pro-creditor' (2003) 12 *International Insolvency Review* 37.

[129] For a discussion as to Singapore's insolvency law pre-2017, see generally, V Yeo and P Gan, 'Insolvency Law in Singapore' in Tomasic, *Insolvency Law in East Asia* (n 5). See also Lee, 'Singapore's Insolvency Regime' (2003).

[130] V Ooi and CH Tan, 'Singapore Company Law and the economy: reciprocal influence over 50 years' (2019) 27 *Asia Pacific Law Review* 14.

[131] ibid.

[132] See Lee (n 128) (citing the Economic Sub-Committee's recommendations in 1986 that the law needed to be changed so as to allow a viable business that was capable of making a contribution to the economy could be preserved for the benefit of employees and the community).

[133] See generally, CT Cheong, 'Judicial Management in Corporate Insolvency' (1988) 30 *Malaya Law Review* 259.

[134] Companies Act 2006 Rev edn, s 227C (repealed by IRDA and the provision is now in IRDA, s 96).

[135] Companies Act 2006 Rev edn, s 227N (repealed by IRDA and the provision is now in IRDA, s 99 read with s 107 where the time period is now 90 days).

[136] Companies Act 2006 Rev edn, s 227X (repealed by IRDA and the provision is now IRDA, s 117).

[137] See Lee (n 128). See 2013 Report, 82 (citing the statistic that between January 2001 and December 2010, out of the petitions for judicial management, 26% were successful, defined as emerging from judicial management and being financially viable).

[138] 2013 Report; see n 141 below.

The corporate insolvency framework remains pro-creditor, with only a slight shift to a pro-rescue stance.

The next economic recession occurred in 1997, arising from the Asian financial crisis.[139] In 1999, a major review of the companies' legislation and financial regulation was conducted to make a series of recommendations to include modernising company law and promoting a vibrant securities market that would lessen the reliance on bank borrowings. The Company Legislation and Framework Committee (CLFRC), appointed by the Ministry of Finance, the Attorney-General's Chambers and the Monetary Authority of Singapore undertook the review.[140] The published report covered, among others, insolvency laws and made a number of proposals, including the establishment of a separate omnibus legislation on corporate insolvency, improving corporate rescue and training for insolvency practitioners.

After its publication, Singapore began to implement the various wide-ranging recommendations pursuant to the CLFRC report. Singapore's Insolvency Law Review Committee, comprising insolvency practitioners, academics and representatives from the industry, was tasked to review Singapore's bankruptcy and corporate insolvency regimes, and published its reports in 2013 (*2013 Report*).[141] The Committee recommended a number of changes to both the schemes of arrangement and the judicial management process. Most of the Committee recommendations were accepted. However, in May 2015, before the recommendations were enacted, the Government appointed a separate Committee to Strengthen Singapore as an International Centre for Debt Restructuring (Restructuring Committee) to consider reforms that would specifically enhance Singapore's effectiveness as a centre for international debt restructuring. This was in response to the downturn in the shipping and commodities industries, which resulted in a number of insolvencies among companies with connections to Singapore, including Pacific Andes and Ezra. These companies eventually chose to restructure outside Singapore. For instance, in *Re Pacific Andes Resources Development*,[142] a company incorporated in Bermuda but listed on the Singapore Exchange defaulted on its bonds. The company's business activities were in Singapore, but its associated companies carried on substantial fishing businesses in Peru. The company commenced a filing for a moratorium in order to conduct a scheme of arrangement in 2016[143] but decided not to continue when the Singapore court declined to extend a worldwide moratorium to restrain enforcement actions by creditors against the company and its subsidiaries, holding among others that there

[139] KJ Ngiam, 'Coping with the Asian financial crisis: the Singapore experience' (Institute of Southeast Asian Studies, 2000).

[140] See Company Legislation and Regulatory Framework Committee, Report of the Company Legislation and Regulatory Framework Committee (CLRFC, October 2002), available at www.commonlii.org/sg/other/SGLRC/report/R14/14.html#Heading11.

[141] Insolvency Law Review Committee, 'Report of the Insolvency Law Review Committee: Final Report' (Ministry of Law, 2013), available at www.mlaw.gov.sg/content/dam/minlaw/corp/News/Revised%20Report%20of%20the%20Insolvency%20Law%20Review%20Committee.pdf (*2013 Report*).

[142] [2016] SGHC 210. See H Tjio, 'Restructuring the Bond Market in Singapore' (2019) 14 *Capital Markets Law Journal* 16.

[143] Companies Act, s 210(10) allows the court to grant a moratorium in aid of the scheme of arrangement but it is much narrower in scope than the automatic stay introduced pursuant to the 2017 reforms (see ch 8).

was no jurisdiction to grant such a worldwide moratorium against creditors subject to its jurisdiction.[144] The Government realised that there were a number of opportunities of debt restructuring and quickly convened the Restructuring Committee, which published its report in 2016 (*2016 Report*).[145]

The two earlier reviews led to the major change to the insolvency framework in 2017 by way of the Companies (Amendment) Act 2017 (the 2017 reforms). A further set of reforms took effect in the following year in 2018, to take into account the remaining recommendations of the *2013 Report*.

The 2017 reforms, distinctly influenced by Chapter 11, implemented a number of reforms to engraft new provisions in the scheme of arrangement framework.[146] The existing scheme framework in section 210 of the Companies Act mentioned above had remained; section 210 is based on the English scheme and had the same three-stage process for becoming effective.[147] The 2017 reforms, effected via Companies (Amendment) Act 2017, introduced a suite of reforms, which shifted the pro-creditor regime to one that is distinctly pro-debtor. In particular, the 2017 reforms introduced the automatic stay, the ability to have a cross-class cram-down, pre-pack schemes of arrangement and DIP financing. The DIP process was emphasised throughout the proceedings with the management being in charge and driving the restructuring.[148]

When the omnibus insolvency legislation, Insolvency, Dissolution and Restructuring Act 2018 (IRDA) came into force, the provisions in the Companies (Amendment) Act 2017 were moved to IRDA. Some minor changes were made to clarify provisions, such as clarifying that shareholders need not require their shares to be divested for the cram-down to be effected.[149] At the same time, changes were also made to the judicial management proceedings to introduce another avenue for the appointment of the judicial manager out of court, so long as they are supported by the holder of the floating charge over substantially the whole of the assets and by the majority of the creditors in number and in value.[150] *Ipso facto* clauses were prohibited,[151] and IRDA introduces a new wrongful trading regime.[152]

In terms of the impact of the 2017 reforms, there was a significant rise in the number of filings for the automatic stay of proceedings after the 2017 reforms.[153]

[144] [2016] SGHC 210, [29].

[145] Committee to Strengthen Singapore as an International Centre for Debt Restructuring, 'Report of the Committee' (Ministry of Law, 2016), available at www.mlaw.gov.sg/content/dam/minlaw/corp/News/Report%20of%20the%20Committee.pdf.

[146] G McCormack and WY Wan, 'Transplanting Chapter 11 of the US Bankruptcy Code into Singapore's Restructuring and Insolvency Laws: Opportunities and Challenges' (2019) 18 *Journal of Corporate Law Studies* 69.

[147] See ch 1. The three stages are: the leave of court to convene the meeting of creditors; the holding of the creditors' meeting to approve the scheme; and the court sanction.

[148] See McCormack and Wan, 'Transplanting Chapter 11' (2019).

[149] See ch 3; see generally, WY Wan, C Watters and G McCormack, 'Schemes of Arrangement in Singapore: Empirical and Comparative Analysis' (2020) 94 *American Bankruptcy Law Journal* 463.

[150] IRDA, s 94.

[151] IRDA, s 440.

[152] IRDA, s 239.

[153] Wan, Watters and McCormack, 'Schemes of Arrangement in Singapore' (2020) 149. See also ch 8.

There has been usage of the DIP financing and the pre-pack schemes of arrangement, but not the cross-class cram-down (see discussion in chapter three). One of the reasons for the latter could be that the threshold is high as it requires the approval of not just the majority in number and 75 per cent in value of the class, but also 75 per cent in value of all the debt.[154] The judicial management reforms do not appear to have a significant impact in respect of companies being able to emerge as financially viable businesses with the management remaining intact. In fact, the judicial management orders made in 2019 and 2020 for several large-scale business collapses have mostly ended up in winding-up and the liquidation sale of the business on a piecemeal basis, though this could be a function of the circumstances that have led to the companies' collapse, particularly if the creditors had lost the trust of the management due to alleged wrongdoing by the management or controlling shareholders.[155] This outcome is not surprising. If the creditors trust the management or treat the management as honest but unfortunate, the existing tools in the DIP will function very well to allow the DIP restructuring to occur. However, if the creditors do not trust the management, they are more likely to ask for judicial management, and it is hard to see how they would agree to allow the management to be in place post-restructuring.

2.4. CONCLUSION

This chapter outlines the history of modern restructuring laws in the four Asian jurisdictions and the impetus that has given rise to the reforms that have led to these laws being in place. It gives an account of the main features of each jurisdiction's modern restructuring law. It is clear that while the jurisdictions have either transplanted or are influenced by either the US or the UK approach to restructuring law, no one-size-fits-all regime is possible, given that the economics and institutional structures differ across the jurisdictions. This book seeks to address *how* these differences matter in the optimal design of each jurisdiction's restructuring laws. Together with chapter one, this chapter sets the foundation of the analysis in chapters three and four as to how frictions in shareholder–creditor, manager–creditor and creditor–creditor relationships have shaped the modern restructuring law, and how changes in these relationships will continue to lead to the evolvement and adaptation in practice by market professionals. The historical analysis also sets the background as to how bank

[154] IRDA, s 70. See also Wan, Watters and McCormack (n 149).

[155] The examples are Hyflux Limited, Agritrade International Limited and Hin Leong Trading Limited. Hyflux was converted from DIP to judicial management and was later wound up by the court. Hyflux, 'Appointment of Judicial Managers' (17 November 2020); 'Compulsory Liquidation and Appointment of Liquidators' (21 July 2021). See also Agritrade International which was put into judicial management and the judicial manager applied to wind up the company: see T Peck Gek, 'ZenRock, Agritrade face winding-up; Hontop put under JM' *Business Times* (14 September 2020). Likewise, Hin Leong was put into judicial management and ultimately wound up: see G Leong, 'Hin Leong Trading, once one of Asia's top oil traders, to be wound up' *Straits Times* (8 March 2021).

regulation influences the law and practice of restructuring law. Apart from the shareholders, creditors and management, the jurisdiction's institutions require involvement and oversight by the key independent gatekeepers in the restructuring process, and the benefits and limits of these institutions are included. The penultimate chapter explains the impact non-restructuring law has on the creditors' rights. The final chapter concludes with a summary of the propositions discussed in the book and offers thoughts on the prospects of reforms.

3

The Agency Costs of Manager–Creditor and Shareholder–Creditor Relationships in Restructuring

3.1. INTRODUCTION

CORPORATE RESTRUCTURING LAW aims to effectively reorganise debts of viable but otherwise financially distressed enterprises and allow non-viable companies to fail. Preserving the going-concern value will be a social benefit if that benefit exceeds the liquidation value of the debtor. In chapter one, I explained that the incentives of the various key stakeholders of a distressed firm, including its creditors, shareholders and managers, are often very different and at odds with one another. For instance, shareholders may wish to continue trading, in the hope that the company will turn around its fortune, even when there is doubt that the creditors will be paid. Hence, the goal of an effective regime is to minimise the agency costs of restructurings due to friction arising from the manager–creditor and shareholder–creditor relationships and different classes of creditors. This chapter addresses strategies to minimise agency costs arising from the manager–creditor and shareholder–creditor relationships in the debt restructuring of Asian companies.[1] For reasons explained below, given the concentration in shareholdings of Asian companies, it is appropriate to discuss in this same chapter the costs arising from manager–creditor and shareholder–creditor relationships as the managers are often appointed by the controlling shareholders.

The US Chapter 11, a debtor in possession (DIP) regime, is widely regarded as pro-debtor and pro-restructuring, and is highly flexible.[2] Chapter 11, the choice for large firm restructurings,[3] is designed to encourage efficient consensual bargaining by parties to maximise the debtor's assets and minimise the collection costs of creditors.[4]

[1] ch 1; see, eg TH Jackson, 'Bankruptcy, Non-Bankruptcy Entitlements, and the Creditors' Bargain' (1982) 91 *Yale Law Journal* 857; DG Baird, AJ Casey and RC Picker, 'The Bankruptcy Partition' (2018) 166 *University of Pennsylvania Law Review* 1675.

[2] T Eisenberg and S Sundgren, 'Is Chapter 11 Too Favorable to Debtors? Evidence from Abroad' (1997) 82 *Cornell Law Review* 1532; S Paterson, 'The Paradox of Alignment' (2016) (n 2).

[3] LM LoPucki and WC Whitford, 'Bargaining over Equity's Share in the Bankruptcy Reorganization of Large, Publicly Held Companies' (1990) 139 *University of Pennsylvania Law Review* 125.

[4] R Rasmussen, 'The Efficiency of Chapter 11' (1991) 8 *Bankruptcy Developments Journal* 319.

To this end, a price discovery of the restructuring plan by committees of creditors supported by a mandatory disclosure regime addresses the question of how assets are to be deployed. Creditors' or shareholders' hold-outs, or both, on how assets are to be distributed are addressed by the court's ability to impose a cram-down, either within-class or cross-class.[5] For the cross-class cram-down to be exercised, the absolute priority rule (APR) found in distributions in liquidation, that is, requiring that senior classes must be paid in full before junior classes can receive any payment in the absence of consent by the class in question, must be respected. In theory, shareholders of a company that is insolvent should be wiped out if the APR is strictly applied. Deviations from the APR are rare and judicially supervised.

In the UK, there are two possibilities for effecting a restructuring using a court-supervised process. The first is the traditional Part 26 of the Companies Act 2006 (Companies Act), which provides only for a within-class cram-down for the English schemes of arrangement. Effecting a de facto cross-class cram-down and squeezing out the junior creditors and shareholders is a more complex process, involving the twinning of the English scheme with administration under the Enterprise Act of 2002 in a pre-packed plan.[6] The English or English-modelled scheme is a DIP model but is classified as a secured creditor-in-control model in chapter one, as no restructuring can take place without the secured creditors' consent. The second is a recent innovation; since June 2020, a new Part 26A of the Companies Act allows for a restructuring plan where a cross-class cram-down is possible.

As explained in chapter one, each of the four Asian jurisdictions under study has adopted significant restructuring reforms based on the US/UK model. Hong Kong's scheme of arrangement draws on the UK case law on English schemes,[7] being a secured creditor-in-control model, though Hong Kong may be moving ahead with bankruptcy reforms that are likely to include a corporate rescue mechanism.[8] Under a secured creditor-in-control model, no restructuring is possible without the consent of the secured creditors. It is not possible to effect a pre-package plan using the scheme twinned with administration in Hong Kong due to the absence of an equivalent UK administration process. In the case of Singapore, prior to the enactment of the amendments to the company legislation and insolvency law framework in 2017, its regime was distinctly secured creditor-in-control model, that is similar to Hong Kong.[9] Following the 2017 reforms, Singapore's scheme of arrangement has shifted distinctly to a DIP model.[10]

Mainland China explicitly adopted Chapter 11 reforms in its restructuring framework, though with important local variations as to how the distribution of the

[5] ch 1; see TH Jackson, *The Logic and Limits of Bankruptcy Law* (Cambridge, MA, Harvard University Press, 1986) 216 (on the distinction between the deployment and distribution of assets): 'The groups, moreover, are negotiating distributional issues in a bilateral monopoly context, and any time this is done there is some danger that the distributional conflicts will interfere with the optimal deployment result.'

[6] See below, n 82 and accompanying text.

[7] In this book, the UK or English schemes refer to the schemes of arrangement under Pt 26 of the Companies Act 2006.

[8] E Yiu, 'Hong Kong resurrects Chapter 11-style corporate rescue bill after a 24-year hiatus as Singapore powers ahead with reforms' *South China Morning Post* (12 March 2020).

[9] See ch 1.

[10] See ch 2.

proceeds of the restructuring takes place, and in particular, in the application of the APR.[11] Mainland China adopts a hybrid of the DIP and practitioner in possession (PIP) model where either the administrator (if he/she is in charge of the management of the business or property) or the debtor (if it is in charge of the management of the business or property) can propose the plan. The debtor can continue to manage the business and operations whilst in reorganisation, with the approval of the court, whilst the administrator supervises the process.[12]

India enacted the Indian Insolvency and Bankruptcy Code (IBC) in 2016, and the solution in ensuring that the insolvency practitioner takes control of the assets is similar to the PIP model found in the UK's administration proceedings under the Enterprise Act 2002.[13] The issue of distribution of assets is a complex issue, and as discussed below, is determined by a modified form of the APR, including ensuring priority to secured creditors[14] and preventing promoter shareholders and their connected parties from reacquiring their assets unless they clear their outstanding debts, ensuring that the promoter ranks behind creditors.

However, whilst the Asian jurisdictions have transplanted the US/UK-style systems, the broader issue is whether transplantation is appropriate given the inherent agency costs that arise in the various stakeholder relationships are not identical to the US/UK. In this chapter, I examine the implications of the different ownership structures on the design of insolvency and restructuring laws. Concentrated shareholdings in Asian companies are far more prevalent, even among the publicly listed companies. In corporate governance literature, where high levels of insider ownership align management with the shareholders, the agency costs of conflicts between minority and controlling shareholders are well documented,[15] and there is an extensive and influential literature as to the appropriateness of the Anglo-American model of corporate governance and takeover regulation in insider-dominated economies.[16]

In insolvency and restructuring law, a set of similar (though not identical) myriad of issues arise. A strong DIP regime found in the US may not be appropriate where the management is appointed by the controlling shareholders and may not act in the creditors' interests. Yet to exclude controlling shareholders is often not optimal since they can be vital to the success of the restructuring, such as where they are significant creditors or provide financing or support, notwithstanding they may have been responsible for the debtor's state of affairs. This chapter focuses on how the US/UK insolvency and restructuring regimes address the direct agency costs posed by their

[11] See ch 2.

[12] EBL, Art 80. See ch 2.

[13] ch 2.

[14] ch 4.

[15] eg, see generally the following articles and the references therein: F Jiang and KA Kim, 'Corporate Governance in China: A Modern Perspective' (2014) 32 *Journal of Corporate Finance* 190 (for China); A Khosa, K Ahmed and D Henry, *Ownership Structure, Related-Party Transactions, and Firm Valuation: Evidence from Indian Business Groups* (Cambridge, CUP, 2019); C Chen, WY Wan and W Zhang, 'Board Independence as a Panacea to Tunneling? An Empirical Study of Related-Party Transactions in Hong Kong and Singapore' (2018) 15 *Journal of Empirical Legal Studies* 987 (for Singapore and Hong Kong); L Enriques, G Hertig, H Kanda and M Pargendler, 'Related-Party Transactions' in R Kraakman et al (eds), *The Anatomy of Corporate Law: A Comparative and Functional Approach*, 3rd edn (Oxford, OUP, 2017) 145.

[16] eg U Varottil and WY Wan, 'Hostile Takeover Regimes in Asia: A Comparative Approach' (2019) 15 *Berkeley Business Law Journal* 267 (and references therein).

ownership structures and how these strategies have limitations in the context of Asian companies. Issues of conflicts between different classes of creditors, such as senior and junior creditors, will be dealt with in chapter four.

A roadmap for this chapter is as follows: section 3.2 address one critical aspect of the institutional and organisational background relating to the shareholding structures of large companies in US/UK and Asia and the relevance to the insolvency and restructuring law and policy. Section 3.3 addresses the implications of these issues and how strategies in the US/UK are used to manage the conflicts that arise in the manager–creditor and shareholder–creditor relationships when the company is in financial distress. Section 3.4 addresses how the Asian jurisdictions address these conflicts in the context of financially distressed companies with controlling shareholders by using or adapting these strategies. Section 3.5 discusses measures that can enhance the restructuring framework in Asia. Section 3.6 concludes the chapter.

3.2. INSTITUTIONAL AND ORGANISATIONAL BACKGROUND

3.2.1. The US and the UK

The make-up of large company restructurings in the US and the UK has undergone significant changes in the last 30 years. In the 1990s, restructurings of large companies took place among publicly listed companies, which have wide dispersion in shareholding.[17] Conventional US/UK corporate law polices the excessive private benefits of control between the companies and management.[18] The existence of dispersed shareholding also has implications on the design of corporate insolvency and restructuring law. As highlighted in chapter one, Skeel, Armour and Cheffins have variously explained that the US model of DIP debt restructuring is co-related to the dispersed ownership and widely held debt, whilst the UK model of pro-creditor restructuring (at least in the 1990s) is co-related to its dispersed shareholding ownership but is concentrated in debt structure.[19]

Since the publication of their work, beginning from the 1990s, the capital markets in the US and the UK began to undergo significant changes. Private equity sponsors become very active in engaging in takeovers of publicly listed companies and

[17] See generally, S Paterson, 'Bargaining in Financial Restructuring: Market Norms, Legal Rights and Regulatory Standards' (2015) 14 *Journal of Corporate Law Studies* 333. For the literature on dispersion of shareholdings of publicly listed companies in the US and the UK, see generally, R La Porta, F Lopez-De-Silanes, A Shleifer and RW Vishny, 'Law and Finance' (1998) 106 *Journal of Political Economy* 1113; R La Porta, F Lopez-De-Silanes, A Shleifer and RW Vishny, 'Law and Finance' (1998) 106 *Journal of Political Economy* 1113; A Gurrea-Martínez, 'The Future of Reorganization Procedures in the Era of Pre-Insolvency Law' (2020) 21 *European Business Organizations Law Review* 829; A Cruz, A Medina and Y Tang, 'Owners of the World's Listed Companies' (2019) OECD Capital Market Series, available at oecd.org/corporate/ca/Owners-of-the-Worlds-Listed-Companies.pdf.

[18] See generally, R Kraakman et al, *The Anatomy of Corporate Law: A Comparative and Functional Approach*, 3rd edn (Oxford, OUP, 2017).

[19] DA Skeel, 'An Evolutionary Theory of Corporate Law and Corporate Bankruptcy' (1998) 51 *Vanderbilt Law Review* 1325; J Armour, BR Cheffins and DA Skeel, 'Corporate Ownership Structure and the Evolution of Bankruptcy Law: Lessons from the United Kingdom' (2002) 55 *Vanderbilt Law Review* 1699.

subsequently taking them private or acquiring other privately held companies.[20] The shareholding structures of these firms, ie portfolio companies, become concentrated after the buy-outs, and they are highly leveraged deals, which are financed with a mix of equity and junior debt provided by the private equity sponsors and senior debt arranged by bank lenders.[21] Management is also often given incentive in the form of equity to align their interests with the private equity funds. The investment horizon is limited in time (three to seven years), and the aim of the investment is to relist the company on a stock exchange or over a trade sale.[22] During the global financial crisis of 2008, these portfolio companies, which were highly leveraged, became highly susceptible to financial distress and had to be restructured.[23] The portfolio companies will have professional managers, and their compensation packages often include equity.[24]

3.2.2. Asia

In Asia, the make-up of companies that have undergone restructurings is vastly different. As a starting point, for the large publicly listed companies, shareholder concentration is the norm. Unlike the US,[25] concentration is often found in the hands of the state or families, as documented in the four jurisdictions under study: Singapore,[26] Hong Kong,[27] India[28] and Mainland China.[29] Controlling shareholders and managers are

[20] See generally, BR Cheffins and J Armour, 'The Eclipse of Private Equity' (2008) 33 *Delaware Journal of Corporate Law* 1, and the references therein.

[21] The amount of equity financing tends to be small compared with the debt financing because equity ranks behind debt. Various estimates in the market have provided that the debt financing constitutes 70–80% of the total funding costs: see eg Corporate Finance Institute, 'Leveraged Buyout' available at corporatefinanceinstitute.com/resources/knowledge/finance/leveraged-buyout-lbo/.

[22] See generally, S Beddow, D Carter and A Lewis, 'Private Equity Buyouts: An Overview' Practical Law for Companies, available at uk.practicallaw.thomsonreuters.com/6-518 0998?transitionType=Default&contextData=(sc.Default)&firstPage=true.

[23] See generally, Paterson, 'The Paradox of Alignment' (2016); S Paterson, *Corporate Reorganization Law and Forces of Change* (Oxford, OUP, 2020) 55–56, 147–48. In Paterson, 'The Paradox of Alignment' (2016) (n 2) the author identified 52 large or mid-size restructurings situations in the UK between 2008 and 2013, half of these situations involve portfolio companies.

[24] See Paterson, 'The Paradox of Alignment' (2016).

[25] cf CG Holderness, 'The Myth of a Diffused Ownership in the United States' (2009) 22 *Review of Financial Studies* 1377.

[26] For a recent empirical study on Singapore's shareholdings of publicly listed companies, see C Chen and WY Wan, 'Transnational Corporate Governance Codes: Lessons from Regulating Related Party Transactions in Hong Kong and Singapore' (2018) 36 *Chinese (Taiwan) Yearbook of International Law and Affairs* 56 (based on a sample of 25% of the companies that were listed on SGX during the 2009–15 period; the mean of shareholding interests of the largest beneficial holder was 40.7%).

[27] For a recent empirical study on Hong Kong, see Chen and Wan (ibid) (based on a sample of 25% of the companies that were listed on Stock Exchange of Hong Kong during 2009–15; the mean shareholding interests of the largest beneficial holder was 45.98%).

[28] See National Stock Exchange, India, including Ownership Tracker (January 2021) (showing that, as of September 2020, the average Indian promoter shareholding of companies on CNX Nifty (50-stock index representing about 66.2% of the free float market capitalisation of stocks listed on NSE), and CNX 500 (representing about 95.77% of the free float market capitalisation of stocks listed on NSE) is 39.8% and 34.8%, respectively).

[29] See F Jiang and KA Kim, 'Corporate Governance in China: A Modern Perspective' (2014) 32 *Journal of Corporate Finance* 190 (data showing that, as of 2012, for the non-financial firms listed on Shanghai

closely aligned in these jurisdictions, and managers may push forward incentives that favour the controlling shareholders. The concerns are not dissimilar to the situation when the company is solvent. In corporate governance literature, law and economics scholars have extensively debated on whether controlling shareholders can be beneficial or detrimental to companies.[30] Controlling shareholders raise significant agency costs between the controlling shareholders and the company when they transact with the company due to potential tunnelling;[31] however, they can be beneficial in that they are effective monitors of management and allow companies to access opportunities that would otherwise not be available to them.[32]

Again, unlike the US and the UK restructurings of large unlisted companies, which are private equity-owned portfolios (and where the drivers of these restructurings are driven by returns to the investors, and only sophisticated finance creditors are impacted), the incentives of the concentrated shareholders who are families or the state are vastly different. Thus, in restructuring law, the key question remains whether a DIP regime is appropriate in concentrated shareholding jurisdictions, even in jurisdictions such as Hong Kong and Singapore, which have a robust enforcement framework in place to curb abusive transactions.[33]

3.2.2.1. Hong Kong and Singapore: The Influence of Families as Shareholders

Concentrated shareholdings are dominant in Hong Kong and Singapore listed firms, held particularly in the hands of the state and the families. With reference to recent restructurings in both jurisdictions (2015–20) listed in Appendices C and D respectively, where there are controlling shareholders, these companies that underwent restructurings are family-controlled, rather than state-controlled firms.[34] Nevertheless, conflicts of interests are more pronounced than when creditors are also the controlling shareholders of the company, and it is proposed that the controlling shareholders continue to have a role post-reorganisation (and are not wiped out), even though the company is insolvent. Intuitively, if the company is insolvent, only the creditors should determine the future of the company and the shareholders should not have any say in the outcome of the restructuring.

and Shenzhen stock exchanges, the largest shareholder held on average 36.8% of the shareholding, and the five largest shareholders together held 53.2% of the shareholding). See also W Zhang et al, 'Mandatory Bids in China: You can Lead a Horse to Water, But You Can't Make Him Drink' (2021) 22 *European Business Organization Law Review* 351, who found that ownership of Chinese public companies had apparently become less concentrated in the past few years; eg, the average largest shareholding in Shenzhen Stock Exchange (SZSE) mainboard companies was found to be 34.26% in 2012, and 32.78% in 2017. Nevertheless, the concentration is still comparatively high, as viewed from the UK/US.

[30] eg ML Lemmon and KV Lins. 'Ownership Structure, Corporate Governance, and Firm Value: Evidence from the East Asian Financial Crisis' (2013) 58 *Journal of Finance* 1445. See also references in nn 26–29 above.

[31] eg ibid.

[32] ibid; see generally YL Cheung et al, 'Tunneling, Propping, and Expropriation: Evidence From Connected Party Transactions in Hong Kong' (2006) 82 *Journal of Financial Economics* 343.

[33] JKS Ho and RSY Chan, 'Is Debtor-in-Possession Viable in Hong Kong?' (2010) 39 *Common Law World Review* 204.

[34] See WY Wan and C Watters, 'Mandatory Disclosure in Corporate Debt Restructuring via Schemes of Arrangement: A Comparative Approach' (2021) 30 *International Insolvency Review* S111. For Hong Kong, all the companies that underwent restructuring via schemes in Appendix C have controlling shareholders.

However, the support of controlling shareholders may also be important as they may be required to contribute fresh financing or inject assets, or both, into the distressed enterprise. If the jurisdiction does not have an established framework for DIP financing, the realistic source of financing is often the existing shareholders or their affiliates, or both. In other cases, if the management of the company (appointed by the controlling shareholder) is regarded as having been instrumental to the previous success of the company or are regarded as being critical to the company post-restructuring, or both, a blanket ban on the continued involvement of the management may not be desirable.[35]

Whilst Hong Kong and Singapore have concentrated shareholdings, they present a contrast in how restructuring is dealt with. Hong Kong law remains creditor-friendly, whereas Singapore has moved significantly to a DIP model. Since 2017, the goal of Singapore is to be a restructuring hub and thus the law and policy has taken a distinctly different turn from Hong Kong.[36]

3.2.2.2. India: The Influence of Promoters

Prior to the enactment of the IBC in 2016, India's insolvency law was regarded as largely ineffective due to the powerful influence of the promoter shareholders. In fact, even with the IBC, the widespread belief in India is critical of promoter involvement in restructuring. According to a recent survey by Ernst and Young, promoters are still widely perceived as uncooperative with the resolution professionals unless they have provided personal guarantees (and hence their personal assets are at stake).[37] Prior to the restructuring regime that established the IBC, India had at its disposal the Sick Industrial Companies (Special Provisions) Act 1985 (SICA), the Corporate Debt Restructuring (CDR) framework introduced in 2001 and various schemes established under the Joint Lenders' Forum (JLF) by the Reserve Bank of India (RBI).[38] SICA was intended to rescue financially distressed industrial companies through a DIP model, under the supervision of the Board for Industrial and Financial Reconstruction. Non-industrial companies could be resolved with under other mechanisms in the Indian Companies Act, such as the scheme of arrangement or liquidation.[39]

[35] cf in the US, where the Small Business Reorganizations Act and the Coronavirus Aid, Relief and Economic Security (CARES) Act 2020 allow the owner to retain equity in the reorganised business. See ER Morrison and A Saavedra, 'Bankruptcy's Role in the COVID-19 Crisis' Columbia Law and Economics Working Paper No 624 (2020), available at ssrn.com/abstract=3567127.

[36] G McCormack and WY Wan, 'Transplanting Chapter 11 of the US Bankruptcy Code into Singapore's Restructuring and Insolvency Laws: Opportunities and Challenges' (2019) 18 *Journal of Corporate Law Studies* 69; see I Rajah, 'Enhancing Singapore as an International Centre for Debt Restructuring for Asia and Beyond' (2017), available at app.mlaw.gov.sg/files/NoteonDebtRestructuring.pdf; Committee to Strengthen Singapore as an International Centre for Debt Restructuring, 'Report of the Committee', available at www.mlaw.gov.sg/news/public-consultations/public-consultation-on-the-report-of-the-committee-to-strengthen.

[37] Ernst and Young, 'Evolving Landscape of Corporate Stress Resolution' (December 2019), copy on file with author.

[38] The Joint Lenders' Forum schemes include Strategic Debt Restructuring (SDR), Outside Strategic Debt Restructuring (OSDR) schemes and the Scheme for Strategic Structuring of Stressed Assets (S4A) and the Flexible Structuring of Existing Long Term Project Loans (5:25 Scheme). See Economic Times Bureau, 'RBI withdraws CDR, SDR, S4A, JLF schemes to restructure defaulted loans' (13 February 2018). See also K van Zwieten, 'Corporate Rescue in India: The Influence of the Courts' (2015) 15 *Journal of Corporate Law Studies* 1.

[39] U Varottil, 'The Scheme of Arrangement as a Debt Restructuring Tool in India: Problems and Prospects' (2018) 15 *European Company and Financial Law Review* 585.

SICA was widely regarded as inefficient, as promoters routinely frustrated the creditors' enforcement using moratorium to maintain control of their businesses, and was eventually repealed in 2016.[40] The CDR, based on the London approach towards restructuring, involves a workout by financial institutions. Even though the CDR is a creditor-driven process and strictly voluntary, scholars have been critical of it; successful restructurings are associated with equity brought in by promoters, and lenders face greater sacrifice than the promoters.[41] The JLF's schemes were eventually withdrawn after the passage of IBC and with the promulgation of the Prudential Framework for Resolution of Stressed Assets.[42]

The IBC introduces the Corporate Insolvency Resolution Process (CIRP), which represents an important shift in removing the power of the promoters and putting it into the hands of the committees of financial creditors. Once the CIRP is invoked, debtors' managers will be displaced and instead the debtor's business affairs will be administered by the insolvency practitioner (also known as resolution professional) and supervised by the NCLT. The resolution professional will solicit bids for the assets. Under CIRP, those who are previously in control of the 'defaulting'[43] debtor or promoters, together with persons connected with them, cannot bid to reacquire the assets of the debtor within the IBC unless they first clear all outstanding defaults.[44]

3.2.2.3. *Mainland China: The Influence of the State as a Shareholder*

A considerable body of literature on corporate governance in Mainland China highlights the issues that arise because of the high concentration of ownership of Chinese public companies by the state.[45] The dominant agency problem lies in the conflict between the controlling and minority shareholders. As of March 2021, the data on companies listed on the Shenzhen Stock Exchange and Shanghai Stock Exchange shows that approximately 28 per cent are state-owned enterprises (SOEs, either central SOEs[46] or local SOEs[47]). More than 80 per cent have at least one large shareholder (holding 20 per cent or more) and the average median shareholding of the largest controlling shareholder is 33 per cent as at 2018.[48]

[40] K van Zwieten, 'Corporate Rescue in India' (2015); Varottil (ibid).

[41] eg S Ghosh, 'Corporate Distress, Troubled Debt Restructurings and Equity Stripping' (2018) 8 *South Asian Journal of Business Studies* 105 (comparing the sacrifices incurred by lenders and promoters and concluding that the sacrifices by lenders, accounting for one-third of the restructured debt, outweigh the contributions or sacrifices made by promoters for a sample of Indian firms during 2002–13). cf Varottil (n 39) (arguing that CDR found favour with creditors). The CDR was revamped and brought under the Joint Lenders' Forum in 2015.

[42] Prudential Framework for Resolution of Stressed Assets, RBI/2018-19/203; DBR.No.BP.BC.45/21.04.048/2018-19.

[43] The ban is against a person who is, among others, a wilful defaulter pursuant to the RBI Guidelines issued under the Banking Regulation Act 1949 (India) or has an account classified as a non-performing asset by the RBI and at least a period of one year has lapsed from the date of such classification. See IBC, s 29A.

[44] IBC, s 29A (introduced in 2017).

[45] F Jiang and KA Kim, 'Corporate Governance in China: A Survey' (2020) 24 *Review of Finance* 733 (and references therein).

[46] For list of central SOEs, see Directory, State-owned Assets Supervision and Administrative Commission of the State Council, available at en.sasac.gov.cn/directory.html. Local SOEs are controlled by the local governments.

[47] Data from WIND database, as of 22 March 2021 (1,184 out of 4,232 companies, or 28%).

[48] Jiang and Kim, 'Corporate Governance in China' (2020).

In respect of the proportion of companies that issued onshore bonds and were in default between 2014 and 2020, SOEs (either central or local SOEs) constitute approximately 20.2 per cent of the total number of onshore bonds in default.[49] Figure 3.1 sets out the incidence and amounts of defaults in China's onshore bond market by SOEs and private enterprises. It shows that SOEs increasingly account for a significant share of bond defaults by number and volume in 2020.[50] In particular, in 2020, the default by China Yongcheng Coal and Electricity Holding Group, one of the largest provincial SOE in Henan, of its bonds indicated that the state is now more tolerant of defaults by SOEs.[51]

Figure 3.1 Number and amount of defaults in China's onshore bond market by SOEs and private enterprises

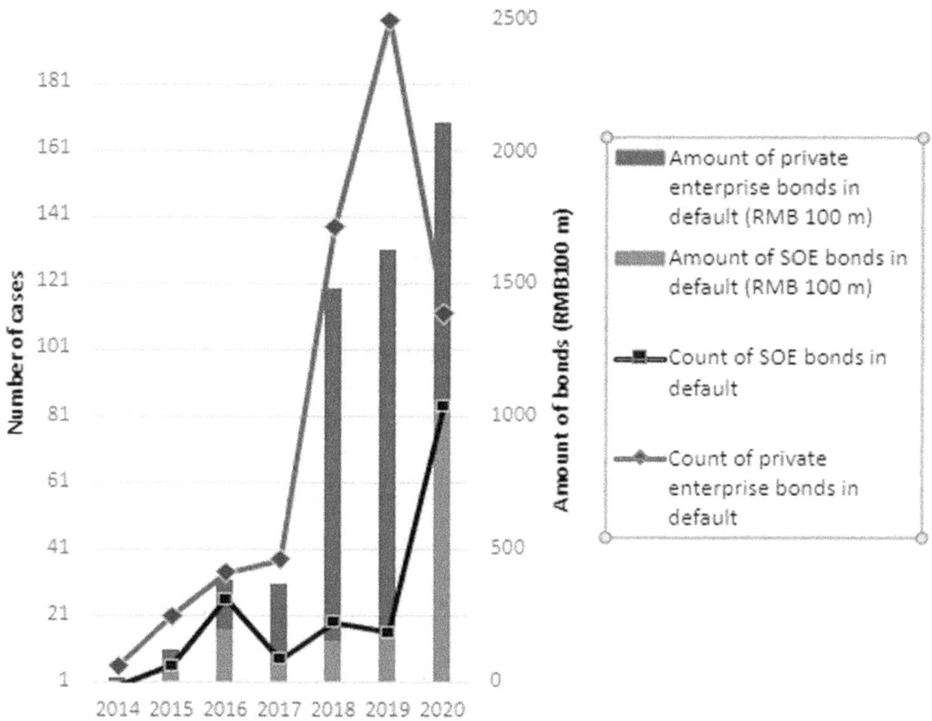

Source: Data extracted from WIND database for onshore bond defaults 2014–20 for SOEs and private enterprises. Onshore bond defaults only commenced in 2014.

[49] Data from WIND database for bond defaults 2014–20. The first onshore bond default occurred in 2014.

[50] SOE loans account for 57% of total corporate debt, or 72% of GDP in 2016. See WR Lam et al, 'Resolving China's Zombies: Tackling Debt and Raising Productivity' IMF Working Papers (2017) 177, available at www.imf.org/en/Publications/WP/Issues/2017/11/27/Resolving-China-Zombies-Tackling-Debt-and-Raising-Productivity-45432. There is an indication the percentages have been falling since 2016 but they remain significant. See International Monetary Fund, 'Selected Issues: People's Republic of China' IMF Country Report No 19/274 (August 2019).

[51] The Economist, 'No guarantees; China's bond market' *The Economist* (21 November 2020) 66.

Current literature on reorganisations in Mainland China has argued that when the state is a shareholder, such as with SOEs, the state has specific incentives that are not necessarily present in market restructurings. For example, Zhao argued that the reorganisation plans have been approved based on the special considerations of the state and local governments in favouring social stability and avoiding widespread unemployment.[52] Other scholars have documented similar observations.[53] However, the continued propping up of these SOEs may lead to the perpetuation of 'zombie' firms, which are kept alive as a result of government subsidies and preferential lines of credit, leading to the misallocation of resources.

3.3. STRATEGIES TO DEAL WITH AGENCY COSTS OF MANAGER–CREDITOR AND SHAREHOLDER–CREDITOR CONFLICTS IN ANGLO-AMERICAN RESTRUCTURINGS

3.3.1. The Hold-Out Problem

The longer an enterprise is engaged in restructuring, the costlier it is for creditors and debtor companies: financial creditors will lose out on the time value of money, and the company will incur underinvestment costs since managers are not inclined to pursue projects that are otherwise wealth-creating because any benefits will go to the creditors if the firm ends up in liquidation. The costs of professional advisers also increase. In the context of shareholder-equity relationship, the key to efficient restructuring is ensuring that lengthy and unreasonable hold-outs by individual creditors or shareholders do not occur. This is done on two levels: by determining how the assets should be deployed, and how they should be distributed.

3.3.1.1. Asset Deployment: Facilitating Bargaining through Reducing Information Asymmetry

In Chapter 11, the debtor has the exclusive right to propose a plan within the first 120 days.[54] The management is required to disclose information on the first day of filing, including first day declarations on the debtor's business affairs and events leading to the filing, followed by the schedule of assets and liabilities and its statement of financial affairs within 14 days of filing the petition.[55] It is also generally required that the debtor provides 'adequate information' that allows a 'hypothetical investor typical of the holders of claims or interests in the case' to make 'an informed judgement about the plan'.[56]

[52] H Zhao, *Government Intervention in the Reorganisation of Listed Companies in China* (Cambridge, CUP, 2019) 202.

[53] eg C Han, 'The Problem of Commercial Banks' Debt for Equity under the Insolvency Law' ['破产法视角下的商业银行债转股问题] (2017) 11 *Law Science* (法学) 58.

[54] 11 USC § 1121(b).

[55] Fed R Bankr P 1007(b).

[56] 11 USC §1125.

In the case of English schemes, company legislation does not prescribe the disclosure requirements; English case law has instead required debtors to disclose material information in the explanatory statement to enable creditors to make an informed decision as to how to exercise their votes in the scheme meeting. Of particular importance in recent English case law is identifying the appropriate comparable if the scheme of arrangement of the company does not succeed. The appropriate comparator is often the going concern sale of the company in administration, but can also be the value of the company if it is liquidated (also known as the liquidation analysis).[57] If there is no professional adviser's opinion, the directors' basis of their arrival of the appropriate comparator may be questioned. For example, in *Re Sunbird Business Services*, the directors of the company disclosed that the recovery upon liquidation is negligible, even though, on the face of the company's accounts, it had a positive total asset value. Snowden J found that, in such a case, a reasonable creditor could not reach an 'informed view' on whether the scheme was in his/her interest.[58] The company should also disclose the division of proposed returns pursuant to the scheme between the creditors and shareholders.[59]

The recent case law and practice demonstrates variation as to what the professional opinions attest to in the UK. In the case of House of Fraser (funding) PLC restructuring, the English High Court refused to accept evidence from KPMG regarding the liquidation analysis on a non-reliance basis.[60] In *Indah Kiat International Finance*,[61] where the fairness opinion was inherently contradictory on its face, Snowden J held that the fairness opinion should contain the full analysis on all alternatives and that it should be made clear in the opinion as to whether the authors of the fairness opinion would owe any duties to the scheme creditors.[62]

In short, UK/US law puts in place a mandatory disclosure framework, even though the details differ. Where financially distressed listed companies have dispersed shareholding structures, management would be expected to cooperate with the creditors since the creditors will be the new owners, post-reorganisation. However, there may be situations where management, who wish to entrench themselves, refuse to provide information to outside creditors or deliberately overvalue the company, or both. The threat of creditors taking over may not be credible since outside managers may not be readily found. Hence the disclosure framework operates mandatorily.

In the case of portfolio companies with concentrated shareholdings, and in particular when the management has equity in their compensation packages, there is a risk that the management of the distressed company will be biased towards the shareholders and are less likely to cooperate with the creditors.[63] The law on directors' duties to

[57] See *Re Sunbird Business Services* [2020] EWHC 2493 (Ch), [59]; *Re T&N Limited* (2006) EWHC 1447 (Ch), [82]; for an example of the professional opinion backing the liquidation analysis, see Noble Group Limited, Explanatory Statement in relation to Inter-conditional Schemes of Arrangement between Noble Group and the Scheme Creditors (17 October 2018) (copy on file with author).

[58] See *Re Sunbird Business Services* [2020] EWHC 2493, [81].

[59] See *Re Sunbird Business Services* [2020] EWHC 2493, [61]–[62].

[60] *Re House of Fraser (funding) PLC* [2018] EWHC 1906 (Ch).

[61] [2016] EWHC 246 (Ch).

[62] ibid, [78].

[63] Paterson, 'The Paradox of Alignment' (2016).

consider the creditors' interests will go towards mitigating against some of these risks, though the evidence has established that enforcement is often an issue.[64] However, the situation may not often be so clear-cut because if the restructuring envisages the retention of the professional management, they may then be more aligned with the creditors' interest. In any case, a mandatory disclosure framework will continue to be essential.

Scholars have suggested an alternative to the problem of information asymmetry; instead of compelling management to disclose, an auction process for the resolution of the debt is used that bypasses the requirement of judicial supervision of the bargaining process. For instance, Hart and his co-authors proposed that insiders and outsiders may place cash and non-cash offers for the assets of the firm.[65] All claims of the firm are transformed into a series of reorganisation rights. The rights are allocated to the most senior class of creditors, and the next most senior class of creditors can offer to purchase, in cash, the rights of the senior class of creditors in return of these rights. The holders of the reorganisation rights will vote on the best offer. A variant of the auction model is where the likely bidders are insiders and some creditors are willing to be paid ahead of other creditors, but at a larger discount.[66] In both auction models, there remains a firm commitment to honour the APR. However, this model still depends on the existence of inside bidders willing to bid for the assets.

3.3.1.2. Distribution: Eliminating or Reducing Creditor and Shareholder Hold-Outs through the APR

To mitigate the hold-outs by either or both junior creditors and shareholders, jurisdictions fix the order of priority from the outset, with the threat of the cross-class cram-down.[67] In Chapter 11, for the court to impose a cross-class cram-down, two tests must be satisfied: first, it must be fair and equitable, which is deemed to be satisfied if it adopts the APR; and, second, the plan should not 'discriminate unfairly'.[68] By adhering to both requirements for cram-down, they adequately reflect the risk/reward of each class of stakeholders.[69] Other requirements for a cram-down in the US include the 'best interests' test,[70] that is, creditors would receive at least the amount

[64] See Paterson. 'The Paradox of Alignment' (2016). For an overview on the case law relating directors' requirement to consider creditors' interests when the company is insolvent or in the zone of insolvency, see the discussion in ch 8, section 8.4.1. For the limitations on enforcement of directors' duties in the UK and US generally (and not limited to insolvency situations), see J Armour et al, 'Shareholder Protection and Stock Market Development: An Empirical Test of the Legal Origins Hypothesis' (2009) 6 *Journal of Empirical Legal Studies* 343.

[65] O Hart et al, 'Proposal for a New Bankruptcy Procedure in Emerging Markets' in RM Levich (ed), *Emerging Markets Capital Flows* (New York, Springer US, 1997) 401.

[66] See DB Hausch and S Ramachandran, 'Systemic Financial Distress and Auction-based Bankruptcy Reorganization' (2009) 18 *International Review of Economic and Finance* 366.

[67] E Warren, 'A Theory of Absolute Priority' (1992) 1 *Annual Survey of American Law* 9.

[68] US Bankruptcy Code, § 1129(b). See generally, DG Baird, 'Priority Matters: Absolute Priority, Relative Priority, and the Costs of Bankruptcy' (2017) 165 *University of Pennsylvania Law Review* 785; LA Bebchuk, 'Ex Ante Costs of Violating Absolute Priority in Bankruptcy' (2002) 57 *Journal of Finance* 445.

[69] See, eg BE Adler, 'Bankruptcy and Risk Allocation' (1992) 77 *Cornell Law Review* 439; A Schwartz, 'The Absolute Priority Rule and the Firm's Investment Policy' (1994) 72 *Washington University Law Quarterly* 1213.

[70] 11 USC § 1129(a)(7)(A)(ii).

to which they would be otherwise entitled in the liquidation. Secured creditors must also receive the indubitable equivalent value.

The APR requires further examination. Under the APR, before the court confirms a plan that one or more classes of stakeholders has rejected, members of each dissenting class must receive the full value of their claims before the members of a lower class receive or retain anything.[71] In the US, for large firm reorganisations, departures from APR under Chapter 11 are rare, though they exist, and are judicially supervised.[72] The rationale for the APR was reaffirmed and explained in *Czyzewski v Jevic Holding Corp*,[73] where the US Supreme Court held that the US Bankruptcy Code sets out a basic system of priority for distributing the insolvent debtor's estate. Departing from the APR in a within-class cram-down is possible, but such priority should be observed when seeking to cram-down the plan on an entire impaired class. (An impaired class is one if the plan would result in the holder altering the legal, equitable or contractual right to which it is entitled.[74]) In owner-manager firms in the US, there are also good reasons to respect the APR by incentivising the owner to maximise the success of the business (since he/she would not be paid unless the outside investors are paid first).[75] For an example of a departure from APR in the US and a recognition that a one-size-fits-all approach is impractical, the Small Business Reorganizations Act 2019 provides that, for small businesses, the court may confirm a plan with the debtor retaining equity if the projected disposable income for the next three to five years are used to make payments.[76]

Deviations to the APR can take several forms, such as not paying the senior creditors in full before paying the junior classes or even allowing the shareholders to retain the shares in an insolvent company. Within the APR and the US Bankruptcy Code, the US case law (such as *In re SPM Mfg Corp*[77]) has recognised deviations if the senior creditors have gifted the lower classes (and skipping immediate classes), though these cases may be doubted considering *Jevic Holdings*.

Whilst the APR reduces the hold-out problem, it does not bring with it zero costs. US legal scholars, such as Baird and Bernstein, have argued that APR is inefficient due to the inherent uncertainty in valuation of the enterprise seeking reorganisation.[78] In fact, valuation disputes are often significant.[79] Instead, a Relative Priority Rule (RPR) will better disincentivise creditors from insisting on absolute priority to frustrate

[71] 11 USC § 1129(b)(2)(A)–(C).

[72] LM LoPucki and WC Whitford, 'Bargaining over Equity's Share in the Bankruptcy Reorganization of Large, Publicly Held Companies' (1990) 139 *University of Pennsylvania Law Review* 125; cf S Lubben, 'The Overstated Absolute Priority Rule' (2016) 21 *Fordham Journal of Financial and Corporate Law* 581.

[73] 137 S Ct 973 (2017).

[74] 11 USC § 1124.

[75] DG Baird, 'Priority Matters: Absolute Priority, Relative Priority, and the Costs of Bankruptcy' (2017) 165 *University of Pennsylvania Law Review* 785.

[76] US Bankruptcy Code, § 1191. The limit to the debts of small business debt reorganisation is US$2,725,625, which is temporarily increased to US$7.5 million through the Coronavirus Aid, Relief, and Economic Security Act of 2020 and the extension is until 27 March 2022.

[77] 984 F 2d 1305 (1st Cir 1993).

[78] DG Baird and DS Bernstein, 'Absolute Priority, Valuation Uncertainty, and the Reorganization Bargain' (2006) 115 *Yale Law Journal* 1930.

[79] KM Ayotte and ER Morrison, 'Creditor Control and Conflict in Chapter 11' (2009) 1 *Journal of Legal Analysis* 511.

viable restructuring plans and reflects the re-contracting process between the shareholders (who have the ability to preserve the firm value) and debt-holders. However, there is no consensus on how an RPR should work. Baird and Bernstein proposed that the senior investor is provided with equity in the reorganised firm, and the junior investor gets a call option.[80] The exercise price of the call option is the amount owed to the senior investor plus a risk-adjusted return. If, say, within three years, the reorganised firm is such that the senior investor is able to recover in full, the junior investor will benefit as receiving the residual value. However, Baird and Bernstein's version of the RPR has not been adopted in the US, though it was proposed by the American Bankruptcy Institute.[81]

In the UK, there is no explicit cross-class cram-down provided in the company legislation for English schemes. It was not until the Corporate Insolvency and Governance Act 2020 was enacted that a cross-class cram-down was provided for. However, case law has developed such that the English scheme may be twinned with the administration and used to squeeze out shareholders (and junior creditors) in a pre-pack.[82] For the squeeze-out to take effect, determining where the value 'breaks' for the distressed company is critical. If the value 'breaks' at the creditors' debt, shareholders do not need to be consulted in the squeeze-out.[83] Thus, whilst the APR is not explicitly adopted in the legislation, the practical effect is that creditors will still be ranked ahead of the shareholders in the pre-pack sale.

3.3.2. Heightened Friction between Creditors and Shareholders

3.3.2.1. Settlement and Release Claims

Where the controlling shareholders are alleged to have caused the management to commit wrongdoings, creditors are in a conundrum. In such a case, if the jurisdiction has a DIP model, restructuring will often meet with resistance from creditors since the management was responsible for the state of affairs of the debtor. However, creditors may nevertheless prefer a restructuring (as opposed to liquidation) to maximise their recovery, and the only hope of a realistic rescue may be the controlling shareholders providing support to the company, such as injecting fresh funds or other assets. Inevitably, these controlling shareholders will ask for a release of their (and the managers') liabilities. In fact, the restructuring could not have happened without resolving the dispute at the same time.

A recent example in the UK can be seen in the 2018 restructuring of Noble Group Holdings Limited, where release clauses were used to release the management

[80] DG Baird and DS Bernstein, 'Absolute Priority, Valuation Uncertainty, and the Reorganization Bargain' (2006) 115 *Yale Law Journal* 1930.

[81] American Bankruptcy Institute, 'Commission to Study the Reform of Chapter 11: Final Report and Recommendations' (2012–14).

[82] *Re Bluebrook* [2009] EWHC 2114 (Ch). See also ch 4, section 4.3.2.

[83] See discussion in McCormack and Wan, 'Transplanting Chapter 11 of the US Bankruptcy Code' (2019).

(together with the advisers and underwriters).[84] However, if the court is quick to allow for such release, moral hazard costs may be generated; creditors may be wary of lending to enterprises since the controlling shareholders or directors who were seen to cause the enterprise to be in financial distress seem to get off lightly. Releases also mean that such parties will not face claims for alleged breaches of fiduciary duties or misconduct, which could have increased creditor recoveries.

The argument to allow a release is the strongest if it is a within-class cram-down, where the requisite majority of similarly situated creditors consented to the release in return for compensation; in such a case, it can be said that, given the requisite majority of creditors has agreed to the compensation for the release, there is no room for the dissenting creditors to object that the compensation is not a fair one. What if the release is non-consensual, such as being sought as part of the cram-down? In *Re Metromedia Fiber Network*,[85] the court held that third-party release can only be confirmed if the release is important to the success of the plan and that 'material contribution' by the person benefiting from the release to the debtor's estate as part of the restructuring is insufficient. Bankruptcy courts are recently paying attention to the issue of third-party releases. In the more recent case in *Re Midway Gold US*,[86] an exculpation clause intended to release, amongst others, directors of the debtor on conduct that did not arise out of the Chapter 11 proceedings was held to be too broad.

3.3.2.2. Related Party Debt

Equal treatment of all claims in the same class is vital in the US.[87] The exception of allowing unsecured claims below a certain threshold to be classified together is narrow.[88] The courts are also vigilant to ensure that debtors do not creatively classify claims to manipulate the cram-down requirements. The plan must provide claimants in the same class with the 'same treatment',[89] which case law has held that treating one set of creditors more favourably than the other members can occur if the treatment is not for the claim, but for the distinct rights or contributions from the favoured group.[90] 'Insiders'[91] may vote on the restructuring plan, but if it is proposed to cram-down the entire class of creditors, the impaired class that has accepted the plan must have been approved without reference to the insider.[92] If the insider sells the claim to a non-insider, the restriction on voting does not apply by reason only of the purchase of the claim.[93]

[84] Bloomberg, 'This Clause in Noble's restructuring Plan is Raising Concern' *The Business Times* (7 March 2018), stating that the scheme provides the 'full release of any and all other claims' that any senior creditor may have against Noble Group, its management, directors, advisers, agents and representatives in relation to its existing senior debt.

[85] 416 F 3d 136 (2005).

[86] 575 BR 475 (2017).

[87] 11 USC §1122(a).

[88] 11 USC §1122(b).

[89] 11 USC 1123(a)(4).

[90] *Re Peabody Energy Corporation* 933 F 3d 918 (2019).

[91] 11 USC §101(31)(B)(i)–(iii), which includes a person controlling the debtor company.

[92] 11 USC §1129(a)(10).

[93] *US Bank National Association v Village at Lakeridge LLC* 138 S Ct 960 (2018).

Likewise, in the UK schemes, equal treatment within the same class of creditors is required, and if it is not possible, claimants are separately classified even though they have the same priority in ranking. The mere fact that a party has a holding in more than one class of claims does not lead to separate classification.[94] At a minimum, however, there needs to be disclosure on the conflicts of interests that may be faced by directors in proposing the scheme in their capacity as directors and shareholders.[95] English law is cognisant that related party creditors may act in a way that strategically maximise their returns at the expense of other creditors. A particularly egregious example is found in *Indah Kiat International Finance*,[96] a scheme of arrangement that was attempted in the UK. In that case, after the company went into financial distress, there was suspicion that C, the creditor holding 28.2 per cent of the debt, was an affiliate of the debtor and had engineered the purchase of the debt to influence the outcome of the scheme of arrangement. Snowden J held that there should be stronger supporting evidence showing the independence of C, given the circumstantial evidence of its relationship to the family behind the debtor,[97] and suggested that C could not be in the same class of bonds that were held by the other creditors. Eventually, the debtor chose to restructure in Ireland, under a different process.

3.3.2.3. *Conflicted Pre-Packs and Sales to Controlling Shareholders*

Pre-packs can offer significant savings in the time that the company spends in restructuring; through the process of pre-pack, the company can enter confidential negotiations with buyers and agree on the restructuring plan – though it must satisfy the requirements of the applicable legislative regime – prior to formally filing for the relevant pre-insolvency proceeding or insolvency proceeding.

US and UK restructuring laws differ significantly on pre-packs. The US requires court approval of pre-packs because of the greater protection afforded to dissenting creditors.[98] However, the UK pre-pack does not require court approval; instead, prior to entering the administration, the company agrees with the secured lender for the sale of the assets, and the entire process is administered by the insolvency practitioner. UK pre-packs have been controversial because they often involve sales of businesses to the existing management team.[99]

[94] *Re Lehman Brothers International (Europe) (in administration)* [2018] EWHC 1980 (Ch).

[95] *Re Sunbird Business Services Ltd* [2020] EWHC 2493 (Ch).

[96] [2016] EWHC 246 (Ch). The scheme purported to release the debtor and its parent company liability pursuant to judgment entered into the US in favour of various plaintiffs in 2004 and 2006.

[97] Snowden J cited the earlier Bermudian Court judgment (*Fidelity Advisor Series VIII v APP China Group Ltd.* [2007] Bda LR 35) involving the other members of the family behind the *Indah Kiat* restructuring, where there was evidence that the controlling shareholders were connected with some of the creditors in voting for the scheme of arrangement.

[98] The US Bankruptcy Code allows for pre-packs: 11 USC § 1102(b)(1); 11 USC § 1121(a); 11 USC § 1126(b).

[99] See UK Insolvency Service, 'Graham Review into Pre-pack Administration' (16 June 2014), available at www.gov.uk/government/publications/graham-review-into-pre-pack-administration. See discussion on the creditor protection in UK pre-packs in ch 6, section 6.2.1.1.

3.4. ADDRESSING INFORMATION ASYMMETRY AND HOLD-OUT PROBLEMS IN ASIAN RESTRUCTURINGS

3.4.1. Process of Bargaining: Mandatory Disclosure Regime

As a prerequisite to efficiency in the bargaining process of restructuring, creditors need to have access to financial information on the debtor company to determine whether the going concern value of the company exceeds the value of the company's assets if sold at liquidation.[100] However, information disclosure is often costly to produce. Debtors may not be forthcoming with the information for fear that the creditors may utilise the information obtained whilst restructuring to benefit competitors. Promoters or controlling shareholders do not wish to lose control over the debtor companies. Compounding the problem is that the value that each creditor may obtain under the plan is often not determinable at the time of voting due to the uncertainty of the treatment of the reorganised firm, if they continue to have interests in the reorganised firm, such as through a debt-equity swap. The narrative on the transplantation of Chapter 11 shows that the transplantation is often not accompanied by the same degree of mandatory disclosure framework. I discuss now the examples of Singapore, Mainland China and India.

Singapore adopted the DIP model pursuant to 2017 reforms. However, the law on disclosure was not significantly changed and is still based on the law of disclosure on English schemes. In other words, the standards are set by the courts and tend to be piecemeal, rather than a prescriptive list of information that is to be disclosed. In a previous work, together with other authors, I highlighted that in Singapore the disclosure of the liquidation analysis, being the counter-factual if the schemes are unsuccessful, tends to be less than optimal.[101] Whilst there are distinct differences in which the disclosure regime has evolved in the US and UK, as Chapter 11 is regarded as a formal insolvency proceeding and, in the UK, a scheme of arrangement is a pre-insolvency proceeding, which can be invoked whether or not the company is insolvent, concerns still arise as to the quality and timing of the disclosure.

An illustrative example on the shortcomings of the disclosure regime in Singapore schemes is found in the Berau Coal Group restructuring. In late 2017, Berau Coal Group attempted its fourth round of scheme since 2015, even though the earlier schemes were either dismissed by the court for want of creditor support or withdrawn by the debtor, and the company had taken advantage of the earlier rounds of moratorium.[102] In this attempt, the creditors were unhappy at the absence of any financial statements post-2014 and challenged the convening of the scheme meeting. They argued that the company could be more profitable in 2018, given the rise in coal prices. The dispute over the proposed scheme culminated in the decision of *Pathfinder Strategic Credit LP v Empire Capital Resources (Pathfinder)*,[103] and the

[100] Chapter 11 requirements are discussed in the text accompanying nn 55–56.
[101] Wan and Watters, 'Mandatory Disclosure' (2021).
[102] *Re Empire Capital Resources Pte Ltd* [2018] SGHC 36.
[103] [2019] SGCA 29.

Singapore Court of Appeal held that, at the leave stage to convene scheme meeting, the company must disclose sufficient information to facilitate the courts' determination on a variety of issues, including those pertaining to the classification of creditors and the prospects of a successful reorganisation.[104] However, audited financial statements were not necessary. The requirements are lower than the requirements for the disclosures at the stage of the creditors' meeting, where the debtor company must show 'sufficient information to ensure that the creditors are able to exercise their voting rights meaningfully'.[105]

The decision highlights the reluctance of the court to impose on the directors to disclose financial statements in the early part of the DIP proceedings. Whilst it is understandable that the courts are reluctant to impose on the debtor the onerous obligation of coming up with a detailed restructuring plan early in the process (and incurring costs), it may mean that the creditors could be reluctant to be drawn to the negotiations at an early stage. In *Pathfinder*, given the repeated attempts by the debtor company to undertake restructuring, which did not seem to carry through to fruition,[106] creditors were also wary that the attempts are only to stave off the inevitable liquidation.

In Mainland China, where the Enterprise Bankruptcy Law 2006 (EBL) is based on Chapter 11, but the model is essentially a hybrid DIP/PIP model (as explained in chapter two), there is no equivalent of the mandatory disclosure regime in Chapter 11; the standards in which the court may confirm the plan under Articles 84–87 of the EBL are left largely open-ended.[107] The conditions of the cram-down are that the secured creditors must be given 'fair' compensation, and the secured interests must not be substantially impaired.[108] Given the lack of a compulsory method to compel the disclosure by the management of the debtor company,[109] creditors will not be able to efficiently bargain, an aspect that has been widely criticised in existing scholarship.[110]

In India, a PIP model, once the debtor goes into the CIRP process (as explained in section 3.2.2), the committee of creditors (COC) will decide on the issue of deployment of the assets of the debtor. Promoters are restricted from bidding for the assets[111]

[104] ibid, [50].

[105] ibid, [47].

[106] There were at least three previous applications to access court-supervised restructuring process under a scheme of arrangement or judicial management, or both. See *Pathfinder* [2019] SGCA 29, [15], and n 102 and accompanying text.

[107] In Notice of the Supreme People's Court on Issuing the Minutes of the National Court Work Conference on Bankruptcy Trials [最高人民法院印发《全国法院破产审判工作会议纪要》的通知], effective 4 March 2018, the SPC urges the courts to 'heighten communication' with administrators and debtors by directing them to analyse the reasons for plight of the debtors, to ensure success of the reorganisation plan: para 16. However, there are no specific items for disclosure.

[108] See text accompanying n 139.

[109] Provisions (III) of the Supreme People's Court on Several Issues concerning the Application of the Enterprise Bankruptcy Law of the People's Republic of China [Revised] Interpretation No 3 [2019] of the Supreme People's Court 最高人民法院关于适用《中华人民共和国企业破产法》若干问题的规定(三) [已被修订]（法释 [2019] 3号）('Judicial Interpretation III'), Art 10 allows for the creditors to apply to the court to obtain financial information of the debtor and minutes of creditors' meetings. However, the onus is on the creditors to make the application (as opposed to the debtor being obliged to disclose).

[110] eg S Gao and Q Wang, 'The U.S. Reorganization Regime in the Chinese Mirror: Legal Transplantation and Obstructed Efficiency' (2017) 91 *American Bankruptcy Law Journal* 139.

[111] See discussion in sections 3.2.2 and 3.4.2.3.

and face a real risk that they may lose control of the debtor. A large part of the delay to sanction a resolution plan is due to the challenges by promoters. For example, in the case of Essar Steel, the whole process took more than two years in part due to the challenges by the promoter, Ruia.[112] In Bhushan Power and Steel, Sanjay Singal, the promoter made an unsuccessful last-minute offer.[113] Promoters are often uncooperative in the CIRP process and regard a bidder for the assets as a hostile takeover bidder.[114] Enforcement against the promoters to obtain access to information is often non-existent or weak.[115]

In Mainland China and India, which are PIP and PIP-hybrid models respectively, the administrator or resolution professional will oversee the process of getting creditors' approval for the deployment of the assets in restructuring. This will, however, only partially mitigate the problem of information asymmetry between the creditors and the debtor. In companies with concentrated shareholdings, the challenge is that controlling shareholders lack the incentives to direct the management to cooperate with the administrator or his/her equivalent in respect of disclosure of financial information. Without access to information, it becomes challenging for the administrator or equivalent to maximise the value of the assets in a sale or other means to deploy the assets.

3.4.2. Distribution of Proceeds of Restructuring and the APR in Asia

Whilst the APR is central to Chapter 11, the APR is not the default rule in advanced economies that transplanted Chapter 11. For example, the recent European Union's default version of the priority rule under the European Union (EU) Restructuring Directive[116] is that of relative priority, that is, it only requires that the dissenting class is to be paid at least as favourable as the other classes with the same rank, and no class of lower rank is to be given better treatment. Even in the UK, under the Corporate Insolvency and Governance Act 2020, to carry out the new Part 26A plan, the cross-class cram-down does not require the APR to be complied with; it only requires that none of the members of the dissenting class would be worse off than they would be if the plan was not sanctioned (the appropriate comparator could include a going

[112] See nn 178–79 and accompanying text. The case was referred to the NCLT on 28 June 2017 and was approved by NCLT on 8 March 2019. It was finally resolved by the Supreme Court only on 15 November 2019, after appeals and other challenges. Source: Debtwire India.

[113] See below, n 252 and accompanying text. The case was referred to the NCLT on 26 July 2017, approved by the NCLT on 5 September 2019 and by the NCLAT on 17 February 2020. Source: Debtwire India.

[114] See eg Y Rana, 'Deconstructing Barriers', 'Speeding up Solvency: Bankruptcy Reform in India' (Columbia Business School Proceedings, 2019), available at www8.gsb.columbia.edu/chazen/sites/chazen/files/chazen_ibi_conference2019_summary_052019_v7.pdf?utm_source=newsletter&utm_campaign=cgi&utm_medium=email; see N Shika and U Shahi, 'Assessment of Corporate Insolvency and Resolution Timeline' IBBI, Indian Institute of Corporate Affairs RP 01/2021 (pointing out that a significant reason for the delay is the failure by the debtor to provide information).

[115] See ch 6.

[116] EU Restructuring Directive 2019/1023 of 20 June 2019. For discussion on the APR in the context of the Directive, see G McCormack, 'Absolute versus Relative Priority in the Context of the European Restructuring Directive' (2021) 64 *Canadian Business Law Journal* 197.

concern sale or where liquidation would take place).[117] In the sanction hearing of restructuring plans, the argument instead shifts to the appropriate comparator and the associated valuation of the company in determining where the value breaks.[118]

The benefits of the APR are high because the rule prevents restructuring plans that unduly favour the shareholders over the interests of the junior creditors; this ensures that the shareholders cannot hold out if they are out of money, thereby facilitating bargaining only amongst 'in the money' creditors. In restructuring law, scholars have argued that Chapter 11, which is a DIP regime, is inappropriate in concentrated shareholding jurisdictions, even in advance jurisdictions, such as Hong Kong, that has in place a robust enforcement framework to curb abusive transactions.[119] However, the costs of the APR are not zero. In jurisdictions with concentrated shareholdings, if the controlling shareholders cannot retain control in the debtor company or its business, they have no incentive to inject further resources into the business or to provide alternative (and more) viable plans for the problems of the company to be resolved at an early stage. Whilst most reorganisations consensually take place, bargaining ultimately takes place in the shadow of the law, which influences the outcomes of these bargains.[120]

Therefore, for large corporate enterprises that have concentrated shareholdings, adhering strictly to the APR is not often necessarily optimal nor practical. Whilst controlling shareholders raise significant agency costs between the controlling shareholders and the company when they transact with the company due to potential tunnelling, they can be beneficial in that they are effective monitors of management and allow companies to access opportunities that would otherwise not be available to them.[121]

In this section, I demonstrate the divergence in the application of the APR in practice in the four Asian jurisdictions. Although much of the focus of the scholarship in some jurisdictions (particularly Mainland China) is on the deviation of the APR, the existing scholarship does so in binary terms, that is, whether there is or is no deviation, without considering in detail the extent of the deviation and the price for which such deviation is obtained. To account for a fuller picture, I include the impact and influence of the shareholders on the outcome of the restructuring. Even in cases where the courts do not exercise the cram-down, bargaining among the creditors occurs under the shadow of the law, and the outcomes of such bargaining indicates how the creditors view the importance (or lack thereof) of shareholders.[122]

[117] The approval requirement is that of at least 75% by value of the class of creditors or shareholders that would receive a payment or have a genuine economic interest if the relevant alternative (such as the liquidation) was pursued. The courts have a general discretion to determine whether to approve the plan. See Companies Act 2006, Pt 26A. Recent decisions involving the exercise of cross-class cram-down such as *Re Virgin Active Holdings Limited* [2021] EWHC 1246 (Ch) did not impute the APR into Pt 26A plan.

[118] eg *Re Hurricane Energy Plc* [2021] EWHC 1759 (Ch). See also ch 7.

[119] JKS Ho and RSY Chan, 'Is Debtor-in-Possession Viable in Hong Kong?' (2010) 39 *Common Law World Review* 204.

[120] See DG Baird and DS Bernstein, 'Absolute Priority, Valuation Uncertainty, and the Reorganization Bargain' (2006) 115 *Yale Law Journal* 1930.

[121] eg Y Cheung, P Rau and A Stouraitis, 'Tunneling, Propping, and Expropriation: Evidence from Connected Party Transactions in Hong Kong' (2006) 82 *Journal of Financial Economics* 343.

[122] See n 120 above and accompanying text.

Singapore and Mainland China adopt the DIP model and hybrid DIP/PIP model, respectively, but they deviate from the APR in significant but different ways. India is a PIP model but represents an outlier: it completely bans resolution plans from promoters who are regarded to be in default from bidding for its assets, ostensibly to ensure that the promoters will not be able to repurchase the assets. Hong Kong is included in the study; even though a cross-class cram-down is not possible under the legislative framework, as the shareholders continue to have a say in the outcome of the restructuring that involves a debt-equity swap.

3.4.2.1. Singapore (DIP Model)

In Singapore, a within-class cram-down need not follow the APR.[123] For the cross-class cram-down, whilst the APR is explicitly adopted,[124] the Singaporean version does not require the shareholders to be divested of their shareholdings, unlike the US version of Chapter 11.[125] Initially, when the 2017 reforms were passed, there was some confusion as to whether the cram-down of shareholders required divestment of their shares (such as in the US), but the Singapore Parliament clarified that s 70 of the Insolvency, Restructuring and Dissolution Act 2018 was not intended to have such an effect.[126] Hence, there is no prospect of divesting the shares unless the shareholders individually consent[127] or are bound by a within-class cram-down (pursuant to the scheme). Whilst the reasons are not explicitly articulated by the Parliament, the justification of not adopting a strict APR is likely to be one of incentivising controlling shareholders to participate in the restructuring; such incentives will be insufficient if the controlling shareholders are unable to retain equity.[128] Similar to Chapter 11, the court must be satisfied that the scheme is 'fair and equitable' to dissenting creditors and does not 'discriminate unfairly' between two or more classes of creditors.[129]

However, unlike Chapter 11, shareholder approval continues to be required for the sale of businesses or the issuance of new shares, including a debt-equity swap.[130] Further, given the additional requirement that there must be an approval of 75 per cent by all creditors in value, effecting cross-class cram-downs in Singapore is difficult.[131] This may explain why there are no cases of cram-down being exercised in Singapore at time of writing.

[123] *Hitachi Plant Engineering & Construction v Eltraco International* [2003] SGCA 38 (holding that the *pari passu* rule does not apply to schemes of arrangement).

[124] IRDA, s 70.

[125] McCormack and Wan (n 36).

[126] IRDA, s 70(4).

[127] An example was the scheme of arrangement involving China Aviation Oil in 2005 where the controlling shareholder voluntarily gave up some of its shares as compensation to settle potential security law claims. See n 201 and accompanying text.

[128] McCormack and Wan (n 36).

[129] IRDA, s 70(3)(c).

[130] McCormack and Wan (n 36), citing Companies Act, s 160 (sale of substantially all of the assets of the company requires shareholder approval) and s 161 (advance approval of shareholders required for the issuance of new shares), Singapore Exchange's listing rules Ch 10 (requiring shareholder approval for substantial disposal of assets) and Singapore Code on Takeovers and Mergers (requiring shareholder approval to waive the mandatory takeover obligation, if pursuant to a debt-equity swap or injection of assets, a person ends up holding 30% or more of the issued shares of the company).

[131] IRDA, s 70(3).

In a previous work, together with others, I have argued that the empirical evidence is that controlling shareholders in Singapore restructurings often participate in the rescue in the form of injecting new assets or providing loans.[132] For example, in the case of the restructuring of SGX-listed Nam Cheong Limited in 2017 (post-2017 reforms), as part of the restructuring, the company were to fund the cash payments to the creditors by a rights issue, and its controlling shareholder (holding 51 per cent of the shares) undertook to subscribe for its entitlement to the rights shares (and thereby avoiding having the company to have an underwritten rights issue).[133] In the 2015 restructuring of SGX-listed PT Berlian Laju Tankers Tbk, amongst others, the controlling shareholders, the Surya parties, agreed to procure the investment of fresh equity into the company and provided an additional two per cent of their shares to unsecured creditors.[134] Given that Singapore's aspiration is to the regional restructuring hub for Asian restructurings, including companies headquartered in the region, and that Singapore is one of the fundraising jurisdictions for their bonds,[135] a strict APR is not likely to incentivise such companies to restructure in Singapore.

Given the incentives, the more pertinent question is not whether the APR be retained, but how significant this deviation can be tolerated. Based on the schemes of arrangement that are filed and completed between 2015 and 2020 for publicly listed companies, in six out of nine cases, the dilution of the existing shareholders is between 81 per cent and 100 per cent.[136] See Table 3.1. Given this relatively small deviation from the APR, it would suggest that the deviations are consistent with 'crumbs off the table' theory put forward by White[137] to allow the shareholders to receive a small incentive to vote in favour of the reorganisation (in the form of retention of their shareholdings).

Table 3.1 Schemes of arrangement for listed companies in Singapore (2015–20)
N = 9

Dilution to minority shareholders	Number of cases
0	1
0.1%–20%	0
21%–40%	0
41%–60%	0
61%–80%	2
81%–100%	6
Total	9

Source: Dataset extracted from Wan et al (2020) and updated to 31 December 2020. The list of cases in the dataset can be found in Appendix D. (I exclude the three cases in 2020 where the dilution information cannot be determined.)

[132] Wan and Watters (n 34).
[133] Nam Cheong, shareholders circular dated 27 July 2018, copy on file with author.
[134] PT Berlian Laju Tanker, shareholders circular dated 26 October 2015, copy on file with author.
[135] eg R Rahman, 'Indonesian Firms Prefer to Seek Funding from Debt Market' *Jakarta Post* (18 May 2020).
[136] cf WY Wan, C Watters and G McCormack, 'Schemes of Arrangement in Singapore: Empirical and Comparative Analysis' (2020) 94 *American Bankruptcy Law Journal* 463.
[137] MJ White, 'Measuring Deviations from the Absolute Priority Rule in Chapter 11 Bankruptcy' (1992) 2 *Journal of Legal Economics* 71.

3.4.2.2. Mainland China (Hybrid DIP and PIP Model)

Cram-down provisions are set out in Articles 84-87 of the EBL. A within-class cram-down takes place if more than half of the creditors representing two-thirds in value vote in favour of the reorganisation plan. If the requisite approval of a class is not obtained, the debtor or the administrator may consult the dissenting classes and take a second vote. If there is a negative second vote, the court may impose cram-down of an entire class.[138] The conditions of the cram-down are as follows: the secured creditors must be given 'fair' compensation, and the secured interests must not be substantially impaired;[139] wages and tax liabilities are paid;[140] 'common' creditors receive at least what they would receive in a liquidation;[141] the rights of the contributors are adjusted in a 'fair and impartial manner';[142] claimants in the same class are equally treated;[143] and the plan must be feasible.[144] Whilst there is no consensus as to whether Article 87 also additionally imports the APR as a condition of the cram-down (Lee[145] and Zhang[146] argued that Article 87 imports the APR, but Gao[147] argued that the APR is not formally part of Article 87), the APR should be an important tool of protection for the unsecured creditors.[148] What occurs in practice is that the courts hire third-party experts to value the company on a liquidation basis (and determine what the unsecured creditors will receive) before exercising the cram-down,[149] and the report is not made directly to the creditors though the creditors can apply to inspect.[150] As is the case of Singapore, shareholders' approval is required if it is proposed that their rights be adjusted,[151] though there is the possibility of the cram-down.

In prior studies, scholars have argued that departures from the APR in cram-downs is routine in Chinese restructurings, and are largely critical as being out of step with market-driven restructurings.[152] Zhang analysed the dataset of reorganisation of companies between 2007 and 2015 and argued that shareholders often retained their equity, whilst creditors only recovered a fraction of their claims, which is in violation of the APR.[153] He found that, out of 158 reorganisation cases filed between 2007 and 2015, where information is publicly available, 43.7 per cent (or 69) of the cases had

[138] EBL, Art 87. Under Art 88, if the court does not cram-down the plan and the plan is not approved by the creditors, the reorganisation automatically fails, and the debtor goes into liquidation.

[139] EBL, Art 87(1). There is no further guidance on what is regarded as fair compensation, such as in the Bankruptcy Code (US), 11 USC 1129, which defines fair compensation as, among others, the indubitably equivalent compensation.

[140] EBL, Art 87(2).

[141] EBL, Art 87(3).

[142] EBL, Art 87(4).

[143] EBL Art 87(5).

[144] EBL, Art 87 (6).

[145] E Lee, 'The Reorganization Process Under China's Corporate Bankruptcy System' (2011) 45 *The International Lawyer* 939.

[146] Z Zhang, *Corporate Reorganisations in China: An Empirical Analysis* (Cambridge, CUP, 2018).

[147] S Gao, 'Cramdown, reorganization bargaining and inefficient markets: The cases of the United States and China' (2021) 30 *International Insolvency Review* S5.

[148] eg Gao (ibid); Zhao, *Government Intervention* (2019).

[149] Gao (ibid) S15.

[150] This position was confirmed by discussions with insolvency practitioners active in Mainland China. See also ch 4, section 4.4.2.3.

[151] Judicial Interpretation III, Art 11.

[152] Zhang, *Corporate Reorganisations in China* (2018); Zhao, *Governmental Intervention* (2019).

[153] Zhang (ibid); Z Zhang, 'Corporate Reorganisations of Chinese Listed Companies: Winners and Losers' (2016) 16 *Journal of Corporate Law Studies* 101.

deviations from APR, which Zhang defined as where the shareholders retained equity in the new reorganised entity, whilst creditors took a haircut.[154] Of these 69 cases, 48 companies were publicly listed. Zhao analysed the reorganisation of listed companies during 2007–18 and found that 50 of 52 of the cases breached the APR (similarly defined by Zhang as shareholders retained some equity, whilst creditors took a haircut), and in 13 of 52 cases, cram-down was exercised.[155] Zhao similarly argued that the reorganisation plans have been approved based on the considerations of the state and local governments.[156] Other scholars have documented similar observations.[157]

Since 2009, the Supreme People's Court (SPC) has repeatedly emphasised that cram-down should be cautiously exercised.[158] As recently as 4 March 2018, in the Minutes of the National Court Work Conference on Bankruptcy Trials, the SPC imposes two further conditions for the cram-down: at least one of the classes has voted for the plan, and the dissenting votes in each class are entitled to not less than what they would have received under the liquidation.[159]

The SPC's second condition for the exercise of cram-down on the floor as to the distribution does not address the problem where there are disputes as to the valuation reached between the creditors and the administrators, and the problem is in turn compounded by the absence of a requirement to compel the administrators to disclose the methodology. Nevertheless, the judicial pronouncements give rise to two issues: first, have they led to a more circumspect exercise of judicial cram-down; and second, even if the cram-down is not utilised, do the shareholders divest or retain their shareholdings? To answer these questions, I hand-collected a dataset of listed company restructurings and companies involved in restructuring in bond defaults during 2015–19, which I obtained through various sources, including Debtwire Asia, WIND financial database, National Enterprise Bankruptcy Information Disclosure Platform (Disclosure Platform)[160] and other studies.[161] The list of these restructurings

[154] Zhang, *Corporate Reorganisations in China* (2018) 163.

[155] See also S Li and Z Zheng, *Law Review of Corporate Reorganization and Restructuring* 公司重整法律评论：上市公司重整专辑 vol 5 (Beijing, China Law Press 法律出版社, 2019).

[156] Zhao (n 52), 202.

[157] eg C Han (n 53) (observing that, for restructuring cases as of 2014, except for ST companies, which are companies marked as having special treatment on the Chinese stock exchanges and which serves as caution to investors, in debt for equity swaps, old existing shareholders continue to retain at least 70% of the equity, and the creditors, whose debt is swapped for equity, do not hold more than 30%).

[158] eg Opinions of the Supreme People's Court on Several Issues Concerning Correctly Trying Enterprise Bankruptcy Cases to Provide Judicial Protection for Maintaining the Order of Market Economy 最高人民法院关于正确审理企业破产案件为维护市场经济秩序提供司法保障若干问题的意见 (12 June 2009), promulgation [2009] 36. Other later promulgations and notices include Notice of the Supreme People's Court on the Summary of Minutes of the Symposium on the Trial of Cases concerning Bankruptcy Reorganisation of Listed Companies 最高人民法院印发《关于审理上市公司破产重整案件工作座谈会纪要》的通知 (29 October 2012), promulgation [2012] 261, and Supreme People's Court, *Status Reports* (18 October 2016).

[159] Notice of the Supreme People's Court on Issuing the Minutes of the National Court Work Conference on Bankruptcy Trials [最高人民法院印发《全国法院破产审判工作会议纪要》的通知], effective 4 March 2018, (para 18). Minutes of the Supreme People's Court are intended to achieve uniformity of practice in the lower courts.

[160] National Enterprise Bankruptcy Information Disclosure Platform, available at pccz.court.gov.cn/pcajxxw/index/xxwsy.

[161] eg S Li and Z Zheng, Law Review of Corporate Reorganization and Restructuring 公司重整法律评论：上市公司重整专辑 vol 5 (Beijing, China Law Press 法律出版社, 2019), has data on listed company reorganisations from 2011 to 2018.

is found in Appendix A, comprising a mix of SOE and non-SOE restructurings. The status of the restructurings is updated to 31 December 2020.

I find that the incidents of cram-down in the case of listed company reorganisations have decreased significantly from the earlier reorganisation cases (pre-2015) documented by Han,[162] Zhang[163] and Zhao.[164] For the 2015–19 period, there was only one case of cram-down for listed company reorganisation being exercised which occurred in 2015 (Guizhou Guochang Energy Holdings). However, existing shareholders of the insolvent companies often had to divest some or part of their shareholdings pursuant to the restructurings. Over the same period, one-third of the completed listed company reorganisations under the EBL involve controlling shareholders divesting all or part of their shares (seven of 21). For example, in the case of Shenzhen Xindu Hotel Co Ltd, which operated hotels in Shenzhen, the reorganisation plan that was approved by the Shenzhen Intermediate People's Court called for the repayment of debt to be funded by, among others, the distribution of 50 per cent of shares held by the controlling shareholders, Shenzhen Hanming Investment Co Ltd, to the new investors for no consideration.[165] The only explanation is that controlling shareholders were seen to be required to bear responsibility for the financial distress and hence would be expected to give up some or part of their shares to satisfy the creditors as part of the reorganisation. Hence, even if the cram-down does not operate as a matter of law, controlling shareholders would be expected to be partially wiped out after the reorganisation.

For the reorganisations of companies that issued bonds in Appendix A, Panel A, there is one case of cram-down exercised. In Dandong Port Group debt restructuring, also discussed in chapter four, which was approved in 2019, called for the debtor company, together with its affiliates, to be restructured into two different entities, where the allegedly profitable assets were transferred to one company (owned by the state-owned provincial entity) and the less profitable assets were transferred to another company and which was owned by the creditors.[166] The court crammed down the restructuring plan, notwithstanding the objections of the unsecured creditors.[167] In the longer term, it remains to be seen whether Dandong Port Group restructuring is an aberration. The other case details of restructurings listed in Appendix A, Panel A provide illustrative examples on restructuring involving controlling shareholders. For Bright Oceans Co Ltd, which is an unlisted company that is in default of its bonds, upon completion of the restructuring, the existing shareholders would transfer all their shares to the new investor, and the creditors would receive equity

[162] Han, '破产法视角下的商业银行债转股问题 (The Problem of Commercial Banks' Debt)' (2017).

[163] Zhang, 'Corporate Reorganisations of Chinese Listed Companies' (2016).

[164] Zhao (n 52).

[165] Reorganisation plan of Shenzhen Xindu Hotel Co Ltd, copy on file with author; see also announcement by Shenzhen Xindu Hotel Co Ltd dated 17 December 2015 stating that the court had approved the reorganisation plan.

[166] See T Dong, J Zhao and S Hong, 'China Port Defaulter's Bankruptcy Ruling Stirs Up a Storm' *Bloomberg News* (14 January 2020).

[167] Judgment of the Liaoning Intermediate People's Court on Dandong Port Group debt restructuring [辽宁省丹东市中级人民法院民事裁定书：关于批准丹东港集团重整草案的裁定 (2019) 辽06破2-5号], dated 31 December 2019.

in the debt–equity swap.[168] Thus, even though there was no exercise of the cram-down power, existing shareholders divested all their shares. In the 2019 reorganisation of Pang Da Automobile Trade Limited, the controlling shareholder of Pang Da, in accepting responsibility for the financial state of the company, transferred its shareholdings to the new investors for no consideration. In return, the investors promised the future net profits of Pang Da to be no less than a specified amount for 2020/21 or would be required to compensate the listed company in cash.[169]

Although much of the earlier scholarship in Mainland China has been critical of the manner in which the cram-down has been applied, I find that in recent practice, the balance is struck through the greater circumspection in the judicial use of the cram-down and the de facto adherence to the APR in non-cram down cases. However, the lack of clarity in the legislative safeguards in Article 87 of the EBL may leave the outside creditors with uncertainty in determining how the courts would view the restructuring plans and affect their decisions as to whether to trade their debt or loans.

3.4.2.3. *India (PIP Model)*

The IBC has a within-class creditor class cram-down provision; the plan is binding on all the financial creditors, including those who dissent, if a 66 per cent majority in value approves the resolution plan.[170] Cram-down of an entire class of operational creditors is possible.[171] The priority of the creditors, as outlined in chapter four, is to be determined by the committee of creditors.[172] Section 29A of the IBC prevents promoters from rebidding for their assets, whether such bids are at a discount or a premium.[173] The rationale is to prevent promoters to reacquire businesses cheaply and prejudice the financial creditors, and to prevent the perpetuation of the cycle of boom and bust.[174] This prohibition, which has survived constitutional challenge in the Indian Supreme Court,[175] applies even if the promoters have made the highest bid for the assets. In theory, promoters who wish to wrest back control of companies have to first settle their debt with the financial creditors, and the resolution applicant or debtor can then file to withdraw the CIRP.[176] However, it appears that promoters would still find a way to surface and buy the assets if they are willing to make

[168] Reorganisation Plan of Bright Oceans Co Ltd (2020), copy on file with author.

[169] Reorganisation Plan of Pang Da Automobile Trade (2019), copy on file with author.

[170] IBC, s 30(4).

[171] See discussion in ch 4.

[172] *Committee of Creditors of Essar Steel India v Satish Kumar Gupta* Civil Appeal No 8766-67 OF 2019 (SC), [56], [92].

[173] IBC, s 29A.

[174] Insolvency and Bankruptcy Board of India, 'The Report of the Bankruptcy Law Reforms Committee, Volume I: Rationale and Design' (November 2015) 13, available at ibbi.gov.in/BLRCReportVol1_04112015.pdf.

[175] *Swiss Ribbons Private Limited v Union of India* (2019) 4 SCC 17; S Rautray, 'Supreme Court Upholds Bankruptcy Code, Rejects Promoters' Challenges' *The Economic Times* (22 January 2019).

[176] Withdrawal of the CIRP can be made if 90% of the creditors agreed under IBC, s 12A. IBC, s 12A survived the constitutional challenge in *Swiss Ribbons v Union of India* (ibid), where the court held that 90% was a sufficiently high threshold. The provision was inserted by an amendment legislation in June 2018.

such settlement.[177] Section 29A of the IBC does not distinguish the circumstances in which the promoters are in default, whether due to market circumstances or their own default.[178]

The litigation of the high-profile case of Essar Steel illustrates the principles. Essar Steel entered CIRP in 2017. ArcelorMittal, one of the bidders, had to pay the dues of two defaulting firms that it (or its founder) has a stake in to become eligible to bid for Essar Steel.[179] The former promoter, Ruia, which previously made bids for Essar Steel but was ruled to be disqualified under section 29A, made a last-ditch attempt to submit a resolution plan to bid for the company after ArcelorMittal's successful bid and offered to pay 100 per cent of its debt, but was ultimately unsuccessful.[180]

The judicial tribunals and the Government are quick to close any possible loophole to section 29A of the IBC. Even if the promoters have also provided guarantees for the corporate debt, the National Company Law Appellate Tribunal (NCLAT) has ruled that promoters do not have subrogation rights in the restructuring and cannot step into the shoes of a creditor of a defaulting company to reimburse itself for payment made to the corporate debtor; the rationale is that the IBC is aimed at maximising the value of the corporate debtor's assets.[181] It is a clear signal that promoter shareholders would always rank behind the creditors. In November 2019, the Ministry of Corporate Affairs issued a series of regulations to strengthen the creditors' negotiation powers against the promoter shareholders;[182] assets of promoters who have given guarantees to corporate debtors can now be attached in the resolution process in the NCLT.[183] Previously, the guarantees can only be enforced in the Debt Recovery Tribunal under the Presidency Towns Insolvency Act of 1902, which entail extensive delays.

Nevertheless, section 29A of the IBC has come under criticism for not only generating litigation but also for the fact that the wide-ranging prohibition would bar many bidders, including promoters and their related persons, who could have made the bids at the most favourable prices.[184] Some issues remain outstanding: first, whilst

[177] An example is Sterling Biotech, where the promoters settled with the creditors and offered to purchase the assets at 64% discount, and the withdrawal was approved by National Company Law Appellate Tribunal (NCLAT).

[178] There is a relaxation for micro, small and medium-enterprises pursuant to the Micro, Small and Medium Enterprises Development Act of 2006, but this chapter focuses on the large company restructurings.

[179] *Committee of Creditors of Essar Steel India v Satish Kumar Gupta* Civil Appeal No 8766-67 OF 2019 (SC); *ArcelorMittal India Private Limited v. Satish Kumar Gupta* (2019) 2 SCC 1.

[180] T Bandyopadhyay, 'Bad debts to break: Challenges, achievements of Indian's insolvency law' *Business Standard* (20 February 2019). The committee of creditors chose AcelorMittal's bid, which was upheld by NCLT: 'Essar Steel: NCLT Junks Ruia's Plea' *The Hindu Times* (29 January 2019).

[181] *Lalit Mishra & Ors v Sharon Bio Medicine Ltd*, Company Appeal Insolvency no 164 of 2018 (holding that a guarantor cannot exercise rights of subrogation under the Indian Contracts Act).

[182] Insolvency and Bankruptcy (Application to Adjudicating Authority for Insolvency Resolution Process for Personal Guarantors to Corporate Debtors) Rules, 2019; The Insolvency and Bankruptcy (Application to Adjudicating Authority for Bankruptcy Process for Personal Guarantors to Corporate Debtors) Regulations, 2019. See Ministry of Corporate Affairs, Press Release, 'IBBI notifies Regulations for Insolvency Resolution and Bankruptcy Proceedings of Personal Guarantors to Corporate Debtors' (15 November 2019), available at pib.gov.in/Pressreleaseshare.aspx?PRID=1592517.

[183] J Rebello, 'Personal Guarantees May Aid Bad Loan Resolution' *Economic Times* (20 November 2019).

[184] Aside from Essar Steel, other high-profile cases that have challenged s 29A include the restructuring of Bhushan Power and Steel. See n 189 and accompanying text.

the disqualified promoter cannot use the backdoor manner to circumvent section 29A by being a proposer of a scheme of arrangement when the company goes into liquidation proceedings,[185] it remains unclear if the scheme of arrangement, which requires a majority in number representing 75 per cent in value, allows for present management and equity-holders to retain control post-scheme. Second, if the promoter proposes a settlement that makes an offer more favourable than the existing bids, can the COC reject the offer? The Supreme Court in *Swiss Ribbons* held that section 60 of the IBC allows the National Company Law Tribunal (NCLT) to set aside the decision of the COC if the decision is unjust.[186] In *Committee of Creditors of Essar Steel India v Satish Kumar Guptar (Essar Steel)*,[187] however, the COC's rejection of Ruia's bid was upheld by the NCLT, but this aspect of the decision was not directly addressed by the Supreme Court. Third, the litigation generated for the qualification of the bidder inevitably results in lengthy delays. For example, out of the nine completed CIRPs for large accounts that were directed by creditor banks to be initiated by the RBI,[188] at least six involved challenges to bidder disqualification.[189] In unreported findings, the average time taken up to completion for the 12 large accounts cases was 753 days (that is, nine of the 12 completed cases are listed in Panel A of Appendix B). In contrast, the average time taken for CIRP plans in the sample up to completion (the cases listed in Panel B of Appendix B) generally was 450 days.[190]

3.4.2.4. Hong Kong (Secured Creditor-in-Control Model)

In Hong Kong, there is no cross-class cram-down; only within-class cram-down is possible under a scheme of arrangement. Similar to Singapore, a debt-equity swap that involves issuance of shares will require shareholder approval,[191] and Table 3.2 shows the dilution to the minority shareholders in the cases in Appendix C.

In the case of a restructuring via a scheme of arrangement that involves the sale of the listing status, the courts have confirmed that the requisite approval of the

[185] Companies Act of 2013, s 230. See *Jindal Steel & Power Limited v Arun Kumar Jagatramka & Gujarat NRE Coke*, Company Appeal (AT) No 221 of 2018 (NCLAT holding that a petition for a scheme of arrangement under s 230 of the Companies Act of 1949 can be proposed whilst the company is in liquidation proceedings; however, a person disqualified under s 29A of the IBC cannot file an application for a scheme of arrangement), clarifying *SC Sekaran v Amit Gupta and Ors*, Company Appeal (AT) Nos 495 and 496 of 2019.

[186] *Swiss Ribbons v Union of India* [53]: 'Also under Section 60 of the Code, the committee of creditors do not have the last word on the subject. If the committee of creditors arbitrarily rejects either or both a just settlement and withdrawal claim, the NCLT and, thereafter, the NCLAT can always set aside such decision under Section 60 of the Code'.

[187] See n 179 above.

[188] In 2017, RBI had directed the resolution of 12 large accounts, which constituted 25% of the total non-performing assets of the banking system in India. The list is in Panel A, Appendix B. See 'RBI Lists 12 NPA Accounts For Insolvency Proceedings' *The Hindu Business Line* (12 January 2018), available at www.thehindubusinessline.com/money-and-banking/rbi-lists-12-npa-accounts-for-insolvency-proceedings/article9726354.ece.

[189] They are Electrosteel Steels Ltd, Bhushan Steel Ltd, Monnet Ispat & Energy Ltd, Essar Steel India Ltd, Bhushan Power & Steel and Jaypee Infratech Ltd.

[190] See also Insolvency and Bankruptcy Board of India, 'Insolvency and Bankruptcy News' (March 2021) (Table 6) where the average time for all of the CIRP cases approved up to March 2020 was 414 days.

[191] Companies Ordinance (Cap 622), s 141.

shareholders will still be required even if the company is insolvent and the value of shares is zero.[192] As part of the approval process for the restructuring, the apportionment of the sale of the listing status can be apportioned between the creditors and shareholders, though the courts indicated that the amount should be nominal for the shareholders.[193]

While the sample size of schemes in Table 3.2 is small, two of the eight involve existing controlling shareholder support, whether in the form of subscription of shares for the placements or debt-equity swap.[194]

Table 3.2 Schemes of arrangement for listed companies in Hong Kong (2015–20)

N = 8*

Dilution to minority shareholders	Number of cases
0	1
0.1%–20%	1
21%–40%	0
41%–60%	0
61%–80%	1
81%–100%	5
Total	8

Source: The list of cases in the dataset can be found in Appendix C. Information on dilution is obtained from the explanatory statements and shareholder circulars issued by the companies in question.

3.4.3. Heightened Conflicts in Asian Restructurings

3.4.3.1. Settlement and Release of Claims

As part of the restructuring, where controlling shareholders have injected cash or assets or otherwise supported the restructuring, they would ask for claims to be released against them and the directors (appointed by the controlling shareholders) to avoid claims of breaches of fiduciary duties or misconduct potentially hanging over post-restructuring. In the UK, the problem is addressed through imposing disclosure requirements on the debtor company so that the creditors are aware of these claims. However, as can be seen in Asia, disclosure has its limits.

[192] *Re Albatronics (Far East) Ltd (in liq)* [2001] 3 HKC 223.

[193] Under the Companies (Winding Up and Miscellaneous Provisions) Ordinance, Cap 32, s 182 read with s 232, once the company is in liquidation, approval of the court is required for the transfer of the shares, and the court may impose conditions for such transfer: *Re Albatronics (Far East) Ltd. (in liq)* [2001] 3 HKC 223; *Re Yaohan Hong Kong Corp Ltd (in liq)* [2000] 4 HKC 488; *Re Rhine Holdings Ltd. (in liq)* [2000] 3 HKC 543. As explained in chapter 2, in Hong Kong, in practice, the liquidators often combine provisional liquidation and scheme of arrangement to effect a restructuring; see also A Tang, *Insolvency in China and Hong Kong: A Practitioner's Perspective* (Hong Kong, Sweet & Maxwell Asia, 2005) 160.

[194] Restructurings of Mongolian Mining and Winsway Enterprises.

3.4.3.1.1. Singapore

In Singapore, where the cause of financial distress is perceived by creditors to be due to wrongdoing or fraud either or both by management and controlling shareholders or there are allegations of asset dissipation, there often will be significant opposition to the restructuring conducted via a DIP model. The concern is that where the management remains in charge, not only are there few incentives of examining past misconduct, but management may also seek to release potential liabilities. In many of these cases,[195] the creditors will request for judicial management, where the judicial manager (who is the insolvency practitioner appointed by the court) takes control of the assets and has the power and obligation to investigate prior wrongdoings of directors and scrutinise antecedent transactions.[196]

The problem is particularly acute in the situation where the alleged fraud is one of security mis-selling. In the high-profile but failed restructuring of Hyflux Ltd., the retail investors who were sold perpetual capital securities and preference shares (P&P holders) complained that they were misled into purchasing these securities without fully understanding that they are deeply subordinated securities that are worthless when the company is insolvent.[197] In the explanatory statement that set out the (then) proposed scheme of arrangement, between Hyflux and Utico, the proposed white knight, the P&P holders would, amongst others, receive deeply discounted haircut,[198] and their claims against the directors, including any mis-selling claims, would be released. Considering the ongoing investigations against Hyflux, creditors had serious concerns about such claims being swept under the carpet. Utico would have no incentive pursuing the claims since it was not harmed by the loss in value when the company went into financial distress. Ultimately, two and a half years after the first filing for a moratorium, judicial managers were appointed and the company was eventually wound up.[199]

There are exceptions, notably where the only prospect of a (realistic) rescue is for the existing controlling shareholders to remain in management while they provide

[195] eg recent high-profile judicial management orders include Hin Leong in 2020 (where the bank creditors cited strong distrust of the management of the companies when it appeared that the management had doctored the financial statements). See A Gabriel, 'High Court Grants Troubled Hin Leong Judicial Management' *Business Times* (27 April 2020).

[196] IRDA, s 99(3); IRDA, Pt 9.

[197] G Leong, 'More than 100 Hyflux Investors Protest at Hong Lim Park' *Straits Times* (31 March 2019), available at www.straitstimes.com/business/more-than-100-hyflux-investors-protest-at-hong-lim-park; Monetary Authority of Singapore, 'CAD, MAS and ACRA Commence Joint Investigation into Hyflux' (2 June 2020), available at www.mas.gov.sg/news/media-releases/2020/cad-mas-and-acra-commence-joint-investigation-into-hyflux.

[198] The maximum aggregate amount payable was capped at S$50 million, and the P&P holders were owed an aggregate of S$900 million. See Explanatory Statement of Hyflux Ltd. in respect of Proposal of Scheme of Arrangement pursuant to s 210(10) of the Companies Act dated 17 March 2020, copy on file with author. Securities Investors Association (Singapore) (SIAS), the association that represents the interests of retail investors including P&P holders, strenuously objected to the release. See SIAS, 'Press Statement: SIAS to hold independent briefings to Hyflux P&Ps' (12 March 2020), available at sias.org.sg/latest-updates/press-statement-sias-to-hold-independent-briefings-to-hyflux-pps. This proposed scheme of arrangement did not eventually materialise because of non-fulfilment of the conditions precedent.

[199] Hyflux, 'Appointment of Judicial Managers' (17 November 2020); 'Compulsory Liquidation and Appointment of Liquidators' (21 July 2021), available at www.sgx.com.

the requisite compensation in exchange for the releases. An illustrative example is the restructuring of China Aviation Oil (CAO) in 2005. CAO incurred losses of US$550 million arising from certain speculative derivative trading that was conducted by the company's employees without authority, and became insolvent. When CAO's parent company discovered the losses, and prior to the public announcement, it sold some of its CAO shares in the market whilst in possession of price-sensitive information related to the losses and on-lent the proceeds of the sale to CAO.[200] Such security trading would lead to, amongst others, civil liabilities to investors who had traded in the market pursuant to the securities legislation.[201] CAO and its directors also failed to disclose the losses in a timely manner, which was also actionable by investors under the same securities legislation. In the scheme of arrangement of CAO to compromise its debts, CAO's parent company agreed to transfer some of the shares that it would receive as part of the debt–equity swap to the minority shareholders and, in return, sought the release of liabilities to CAO, its directors and CAO's parent company by minority shareholders.[202]

3.4.3.2. *Favourable Treatment to Related Parties in Debt Restructuring*

Where the creditors are related parties of the debtor or are controlling shareholders (or their affiliates), should the restructuring framework prescribe a special rule, such as to exclude the votes of related parties? What if the debt is sold to third parties? Conversely, if the rescuers are controlling shareholders (or their affiliates), can they vote in their capacity as creditors and/or shareholders of the debtor?

3.4.3.2.1. Hong Kong and Singapore

In Hong Kong, three cases have discussed this issue, though there was no definitive conclusion in one. In *Re APP (Hong Kong) Limited*,[203] at the hearing to call for court meeting, the court held that, at the sanction stage, there may be discounting if interests differ. However, at the stage of hearing to call court meeting, the company only needed to show an arguable case that the votes will not be discounted. In a later case, in *Re KB (Asia) Ltd*,[204] the court discounted the family creditors' vote to zero on the grounds that they have special interests to promote the scheme. However, in the most recent case of *Re Century Sun International Limited*,[205] the court held that the mere

[200] Monetary Authority of Singapore, 'MAS Takes Civil Penalty Enforcement Action Against China Aviation Oil Holding Company for Insider Trading' (19 August 2005), on file with the author. See, generally, C Milhaupt and K Pistor, 'The China Aviation Oil Episode: Law and Development in China and Singapore' in D Kennedy and JE Stiglitz (eds), *Law and Economics with Chinese Characteristics: Institutions for Promoting Development in the Twenty-First Century* (Oxford Scholarship Online, 2013).

[201] Securities and Futures Act 2002 (Singapore).

[202] Monetary Authority of Singapore, MAS Takes Civil Penalty Enforcement Action Against China Aviation Oil Holding Company for Insider Trading (19 August 2005), on file with the author. See also Circular to Shareholders of China Aviation Oil (8 February 2006), copy on file with the author.

[203] [2005] 1 HKLRD 272.

[204] [2014] HKEC 1192.

[205] [2021] HKCFI 2928.

fact that the creditors included affiliates of the company should not prevent them from voting because the test should be focused on why the creditors should support the scheme, as opposed to why they should not. In other words, the test is whether the affiliated creditors' interests are so adverse to the rest of the class that they cannot be said to be representative of the rest of the creditors. On the facts, given that the scheme yielded a return of 30 per cent versus 14 per cent upon liquidation to the creditors, the independent creditors could not demonstrate that the affiliated creditors were motivated by other impermissible factors.

In Singapore, the issue has arisen in at least three cases in the last decade. The first is *TT International*, in which the Court of Appeal held that an option that was given to the two controlling shareholders (who were also creditors) to purchase certain redeemable convertible bonds and the shares arising from such conversion but not to the other creditors put these controlling shareholders in a different class from the other creditors. For the rearrangement of the debts, the related parties (who were creditors) were placed in the same class of creditors as the non-related party debts, but the Court held that their votes should be discounted.[206] For the creditors, which were wholly owned by the debtor, their votes would be discounted to zero. For creditors which were not wholly owned subsidiaries, it was held that partial discounting should take place. Such an approach would suggest that, in each case, the creditors who wish to admit their claims to proof must indicate not only the outstanding amounts but also the relationship between the creditors and the debtor companies for the scheme managers (and the courts) to decide how to apply the discounting.

But how much of the discount should be applied for related party debt? In a later case of *SK Engineering v Conchubar*,[207] the Court of Appeal (where four of the five judges were not in the coram that decided *TT International*), by way of dicta, expressed concerns with this approach:

> 67 From a broader perspective, it seems to us that the exercise of determining an appropriate partial discount is inevitably arbitrary and subjective, and not amenable to definitive guidance. This is hardly surprising, given the myriad fact situations in which a creditor may be found to be related to a scheme company in the context of voting on a scheme of arrangement. It seems to us to be a more principled and certain approach to wholly discount the votes of creditors once they are found to be related to the scheme company: if the position of a creditor is in any way tainted, it should follow that that creditor's votes on the scheme should be entirely disregarded.[208]

The third case which recently considered this issue is *Re DSG Asia Holdings Pte Ltd*.[209] In this case, companies within Design Studio Group Ltd (DSG) and its subsidiaries had related party debts which were assigned to Allington Advisory Pte Ltd (Allington), the white knight investor. The debtor then proceeded to implement a pre-packaged scheme of arrangement which involved a subsidiary company becoming a co-obligor of all of the debts owed by the group, with Allington voting alongside the unsecured

[206] *The Royal Bank of Scotland NV (formerly known as ABN Amro Bank NV) and others v TT International Ltd and another appeal* [2012] 2 SLR 213.
[207] [2017] SGCA 51.
[208] [2017] SGCA 51, [61].
[209] [2021] SGHC 209.

creditors. An unsecured creditor, OCBC Bank, objected on two principal grounds: that the debtor failed to disclose to creditors the price that the debts were transferred to Allington; and that Allington should not be in the same class as the other unsecured creditors as it was a white knight investor which would acquire a majority stake in DSG and provide emergency working capital. OCBC Bank succeeded on the two grounds. On the first ground, the High Court held that the price at which the related party debt was acquired was relevant to whether DSG orchestrated the sale to allow the related party debt to be voted. In relation to the second ground, it was held that Allington's proposed investment into DSG (and not the fact that it was a secured creditor) meant that its rights were so dissimilar with the other creditors' rights that its votes ought to be in a separate class. The court was conscious to ensure that the transfer of the related party debt was not a sham to get around the voting, indicating a far stricter approach towards the treatment of related party debt.

3.4.3.2.2. India

The position in India is complex and is finally settled. A resolution plan must be approved by the COC, with not less than 66 per cent of the majority voting shares of the financial creditors. Section 21 of the IBC provides that the COC comprises all the financial creditors, but a 'related party' to whom a corporate debtor owes a debt will not be able to vote.[210] 'Related party' is broadly defined to include a director, a person who can control the composition of the board and a person that holds 20 per cent or more of the debtor. Given the expansive definition, is it possible to circumvent this by transferring to a third party? Here, there is a difference in the case law on whether the non-related party can exercise the vote once a related party assigns the debt to a non-related party.[211] The matter was finally decided by the Supreme Court where it was held that the section 21 prohibition applies when the creditor is related at the time of filing of claim.[212] However, the Supreme Court also held that former related parties who divested their interests with the only intention of extricating from the related party status, and thereby frustrating a CIRP process, could not be part of the COC.[213] As is the case with Singapore, this case demonstrates the extent to which the Indian courts are vigilant against sham voting processes by related creditors.

3.4.3.3. The State as a Shareholder of Distressed Companies

3.4.3.3.1. Mainland China: Reorganisation of SOEs

In Mainland China, several of the restructurings of SOEs, including listed SOEs, have taken place through the assistance of the local or central government in getting other

[210] IBC, s 21.

[211] *Edelweiss Asset Reconstruction Company Limited v Synergies Dooray Automotive Ltd.*, Company Appeal (AT) (Insolvency) No 169 of 2017 (holding that the non-related party can vote on the resolution plan once there was assignment of debt to a non-related party); cf *Pankaj Yadav v. State Bank of India*, Company Appeal (AT) (Insolvency) No 28 of 2018 (holding that the status of the related party is not changed by the transfer to a non-related party).

[212] *Phoenix Arc Private Limited v Spade Financial Services Limited*, Civil Appeal 2842 of 2020 (decision delivered on 1 February 2020).

[213] ibid.

SOEs or Mainland lenders to inject capital or to merge with other financially healthy SOEs or their affiliates. Listed SOEs are likely to have significant employees and have a wide base of retail shareholders, and their collapse can result in social unrest.[214] The EBL has often been used as a process to facilitate such rescue,[215] and the more recent cases indicate continued government support. Notably, the EBL does not prohibit conflicted shareholders from voting on the reorganisation plan in state-led or state-sanctioned rescues.[216]

State support comes in various forms. The most straightforward is for the local government to lean on provincial SOE banks to continue to lend to the SOE debtor. In other cases, it involves the merger between the financially distressed SOEs with other SOEs or the injection of assets into the financially distressed SOEs. Taking the cases found in Panel B of Appendix A, Jiangsu Sainty Co Ltd (Sainty Marine) is an example of a corporate rescue by the state, involved the injection of assets by Jiangsu Trust into Sainty Marine in exchange for new shares.[217] Jiangsu Investment Guoxin and Sainty Marine are controlled by the Jiangsu State-owned Assets Oversight Committee. It was reported that Jiangsu Trust would otherwise have been unlikely to have its assets listed due to the regulatory requirements of the China Securities Regulatory Commission.[218] Another example is the reorganisation of Chongqing Iron & Steel Limited approved by the court in 2017.[219] The controlling shareholder Chongqing Iron & Steel (Group) Co Ltd agreed to transfer its shares to the new investor Chongqing Longevity Iron & Steel Co Ltd, which is itself controlled by the state-owned Assets Supervisory Management Committee (through China Baowu Steel Group Corporation Limited).[220]

As for bond restructurings, it is only recently that regulations are promulgated prohibiting conflicting creditors from voting.[221] The rate of default by SOEs (at 20.2 per cent as of 31 December 2020) is historically lower than that for private enterprises, but there is a clear trend that more SOEs will continue to default in the wake of the COVID-19 pandemic.[222] Referring to the successful restructurings of bonds issued by SOEs in Panel A of Appendix A, Dongbei Steel restructuring was widely regarded

[214] See nn 52–53 and accompanying text.

[215] On the political influence over reorganisations, see generally Zhang, *Corporate Reorganisations in China* (2018); Zhao (n 52).

[216] Zhang (ibid).

[217] *Reorganisation Plan for Sainty Marine* (2015), on file with author.

[218] X Zhan, 'Trust company listed after Twenty years [20年来江苏信托成首家借壳上市但不意味着开闸]' *Investor Journal Weekly* 投资者报 (12 December 2016), available at www.sohu.com/a/121278578_112589.

[219] *Reorganisation Plan for Chongqing Iron & Steel Limited* (2017), on file with author.

[220] ibid.

[221] China's Supreme People's Court (SPC) has issued minutes from the December 2019 forum between officials from the court, People's Bank of China, China Securities Regulatory Commission and National Development and Reform Commission, which emphasise that, in bondholders' meetings, issuers and related parties, and bondholders with conflicts of interests, should avoid voting in such resolutions. See Notice by the SPC on Issuing the Minutes of the National Courts Symposium on the Trial of Bond Disputes, dated 15 July 2020, 最高人民法院关于印发《全国法院审理债券纠纷案件座谈会纪要》的通知 [现行有效] （法 [2020] 185号）, para 15.

[222] Data from WIND database shows that for the first quarter of 2021, the number of bond defaults of SOEs is at least 34, which is greater than the total number of defaults for 2019 (19) and 2018 (16) respectively. See also Figure 3.1.

as a market-led restructuring involving a debt-equity swap for a SOE in the EBL process.[223] However, in Dandong Port Group debt restructuring, which was discussed above, the restructuring plan called for the debtor and affiliates to be restructured into two different entities, where the allegedly profitable assets were transferred to one company owned by an SOE, and the less profitable assets were transferred to another company owned by the creditors.[224] Even though the company was a private enterprise, likely due to the strategic importance of the port assets, the court crammed down the restructuring plan in favour of a merger with a SOE, notwithstanding the objections of the unsecured creditors.[225] The other SOE bond restructurings (Shenyang Machine Tool and its affiliates) involved bail-outs by another SOE.[226]

The examples given in Panel B of Appendix A do not include the unsuccessful restructuring attempts of SOE bond defaults. For example, for Guangxi Nonferrous, an SOE, the company was admitted to the reorganisation process under EBL by the Nanning court in 2016, and the court appointed the administrator team. The creditors failed to approve the restructuring plan after two creditors' meetings, but the Government did not intervene to provide any rescue.[227]

In summary, the experience of Chinese restructurings has been that central or local government has actively coordinated or rescued SOEs in industries which are viewed as being of strategic importance.[228] In at least one instance, the private enterprise in an industry of strategic importance is rescued by an SOE. Even until recently, the perception remained that some implicit state guarantee is associated with SOE lending, though the market recognises that not all distressed SOEs will receive state support.[229] In a bid to accelerate market reforms in recent years and to eliminate overcapacity in non-strategic areas, policy-makers in Mainland China have taken steps to remove zombie companies from the market through liquidation or to restructure them by merging with other SOEs or their affiliates. Interestingly, in this context, the EBL has been explicitly referenced as an important tool to achieve the means for such removal (and not only as a means of effecting corporate rescue).[230] In tandem,

[223] M Amstad and Z He, 'Chinese Bond Market and Interbank Market' (2019) NBER Working Paper 25549, available at www.nber.org/system/files/working_papers/w25549/w25549.pdf. See also SCMP Reporter, 'Xi Jinping's Debt-Relief Recipe: How China's Biggest Bond Defaulter Unloaded its Liabilities' *South China Morning Post* (14 October 2017) (reporting that a private steel maker took a 43% equity stake).

[224] Judgment of the Liaoning Intermediate People's Court on Dandong Port Group debt restructuring (31 December 2019) fn 167.

[225] See T Dong, J Zhao and S Hong, 'China Port Defaulter's Bankruptcy Ruling Stirs Up a Storm' (n 166).

[226] See *Reorganisation Plan of Shenyang Machine Tool (Group) Ltd* dated 28 October 2019, copy on file with author.

[227] See 'Inter-bank Market First Default' [如何看待银行间市场第一例破产清算], 云掌财经-债券理财, 26 September 2016, copy on file with author. See also Amstad and He, 'Chinese Bond Market' (2019) (n 223). The case is not listed in Appendix A as the restructuring plan was not confirmed by the court.

[228] See also Chief China Economist's Office of Hong Kong Exchanges and Clearing Limited, 'Credit Event of Offshore Chinese State-related Issuers and their Onshore Support' (2021).

[229] ibid.

[230] National Development and Reform Commission, 'Notice on Steps to Deal with Zombie Companies and Eliminate Over-Capacity' [关于进一步做好"僵尸企业"及去产能企业债务处置工作的通知]; National Development and Reform Commission, the China Securities Regulatory Commission, the Ministry of Human Resources and Social Security, and the Supreme Court, 'Reform Plan for Accelerating the Improvement of the Exit System for Market Participants【关于印发《加快完善市场主体退出制度改革方案》的通知; 发改财金】22 June 2019〔2019〕1104号.

the SPC has accelerated the setting up of specialist courts to handle the rising tide of defaults caused by the push towards removing zombie companies.[231] Thus, the current narrative is that the EBL is seen as an important process to achieve an orderly liquidation process and thus perform a signalling role to its commitment to market-based reforms.

The push towards market-oriented reforms can also be seen in the treatment of bond defaults. Figure 3.1 shows that the SOE bond defaults were relatively rare until 2018. (Privately owned enterprises (POEs) accounted for the majority of the bond defaults in 2015–19.) In 2018 and 2019, the SOE bond defaults were largely from SOEs that were in sectors that have excess capacity and do not carry systematic risks. However, in November 2020, the default by China Yongcheng Coal and Electricity Group Holdings, the largest provincial SOE in Henan, of its bonds signalled that the state was more tolerant of bond defaults and pushing a more market-oriented approach towards companies in financial distress.[232]

3.4.3.4. Pre-Packs

Only Singapore and China allow for pre-packs, and in both cases, the experiences are recent.[233] In 2021, India introduces the pre-pack in the IBC, but it applies to micro, small and medium-sized enterprises (MSMEs).[234] In India, the amendments follow from COVID-19 and the recommendation of the Law Reform Committee of the Insolvency Law Committee that pre-packs benefit MSMEs, given that the full-blown CIRP is cumbersome and the MSMEs may not survive the full resolution period.[235] In a pre-pack, the promoter continues to drive the process and ensures that the process is fair and transparent, subject to a number of safeguards. Likely due to concerns of the lack of transparency until the IBC filing and the fact that the process may be used by a connected party to make the purchase, the pre-pack regime is not extended more broadly to other companies. However, in principle, one way around is to utilise section 12A, which allows the CIRP to be withdrawn if there is 90 per cent approval of the creditors, enabling creditors and the debtor company to come to an arrangement, albeit negotiations take place after the commencement of the CIRP (rather than before, which is a feature of the pre-pack).[236]

The Singapore experience with pre-packs is still relatively nascent, given that the reforms that allow pre-packs came into force in 2017, and has thusfar not achieved

[231] eg H Xu, 'Setting the Tone for 2017 – The Central Economic Work Conference' *China and US Focus* (29 December 2016); National Development and Reform Commission, 'Notice on Steps to Deal with Zombie Companies and Eliminate Over-Capacity' [关于进一步做好"僵尸企业"及去产能企业债务处置工作的通知] (No. 1756 [2018]); S Li, 'The Insolvency of the "Zombie Enterprise" through the Insolvency System' 通过破产制度实现"僵尸企业"的破产出清' (2018) 23 *People's Forum* 人民论坛98, 98.

[232] 'No guarantees; China's bond market' *The Economist* (12 February 2020) 66.

[233] Hong Kong does not have a system of pre-packs and hence is not included in the discussion.

[234] Insolvency and Bankruptcy (Amendment) Ordinance 2021.

[235] Ministry of Corporate Affairs, 'Report of the Sub-committee of the Insolvency Law Committee on Pre-packaged Insolvency Resolution Process' (31 October 2020), available at ibbi.gov.in/uploads/resources/24c7fc03cdffff69960ce374416fa646.pdf.

[236] Above, n 177.

controversy in the same manner as in the UK. In an earlier work with others, I pointed out that pre-packs continue to require shareholders' approval for asset disposal or share issuance under the Companies Act, and additionally, in the case of listed companies, independent shareholders' approval is required under the Singapore Exchange listing rules and Singapore Code on Takeovers and Mergers.[237] At the time of writing, the cases in Appendix D in which the Singapore courts have approved the pre-packs did not involve sales to management or controlling shareholders.[238]

In Mainland China, reforms to permit pre-packs have been raised by the National Development and Reform Commission and other departments in 2018[239] and 2019.[240] However, there are reports that Chinese courts have allowed pre-pack reorganisations even prior to these reforms. Unlike the US version of the pre-pack, the Chinese administrator was appointed early at the pre-filing stage to negotiate with the creditors and to find investors prior to the acceptance of the case by the court.[241]

3.5. ENHANCING THE RESTRUCTURING REGIME: LESSONS AND IMPLICATIONS

How can the Asian jurisdictions improve their restructuring regime to achieve market-based outcomes and minimise agency costs? Each of the four Asian jurisdictions has reformed their restructuring laws by adopting the various forms of governance of DIP (Singapore), PIP (India) and a hybrid of the DIP/PIP model (Mainland China). Hong Kong firmly remains a secured creditor-in-control model. Each of the regimes has its advantages and disadvantages, and the jurisdictions have, to a varying extent, put in strategies to limit opportunistic behaviours through unreasonable hold-outs that harm senior lenders.

[237] Wan and McCormack (n 36). See n 130 and accompanying text.

[238] The six pre-packs in Appendix D are Hoe Leong Corporation, TT International, Asiatravel.com, Viking Offshore and Marine, Capital World Limited, and PT MNC Investama Tbk.

[239] Notice of the National Development and Reform Commission on Steps to Deal with Zombie Companies and Eliminate Over-Capacity (No 1756) [2018]) [关于进一步做好“僵尸企业”及去产能企业债务处置工作的通知 (发改财)金 [2018] 1756号); Notice of the Supreme People's Court on Issuing the Minutes of the National Court Work Conference on Bankruptcy Trials [最高人民法院印发《全国法院破产审判工作会议纪要》的通知], effective 4 March 2018, Art 22 (encouraging the courts to explore different routes to pre-packs).

[240] Notice of the Supreme People's Court on Issuing the Minutes of the National Courts' Civil and Commercial Trial Work Conference, [最高人民法院关于印发《全国法院民商事审判工作会议纪要》的通知 [现行有效] （法〔2019〕254号）] effective 8 November 2019 (explaining the transition from pre-packaged reorganisation to reorganisation proceedings).

[241] In the restructuring of Shenzhen Fuchang Electronic Technology in 2017, prior to the formal acceptance of the application, the court allowed pre-filing and designated an administrator to carry out negotiations with the creditors. Once the application was accepted, the reorganisation plan was tabled for voting. See Shenzhen Intermediate People's Court, Restructuring of Shenzhen Fuchang Electronic Technology [深圳市福昌电子技术有限公司破产重整案] (14 April 2017). DA Austin and C Lin, 'Bankruptcy with Chinese Characteristics: Insolvency Administration in the People's Republic of China' (2020) 94 *American Bankruptcy Law Journal* 85 identified another pre-pack case, which they called a 'pre-reform' case of Beijing Zhongxing Science and Technology, where the Beijing Intermediate People's Court approved the prepack reorganisation in 2017.

3.5.1. No One-Size-Fits-All Rule for APR and Cram-Down

In chapter seven, I argue that courts are often not good at sifting restructuring proposals that are purely opportunistic and which divert value away from the creditors to the shareholders or the ones that will be wealth-creating. Depending on the jurisdiction's past experiences with controlling shareholders and the circumstances surrounding financial distress, their continued involvement may or may not be positive regarding the future of the reorganised enterprise. Creditors are in the best place to make the decisions on the best proposals and how the controlling shareholders would continue to be involved. Hence, legal rules on priorities of distributions and conditions for cross-class cram-downs cannot uniform across all the jurisdictions to address the hold-out problems. Instead, what should be proposed is that, if controlling shareholders are given the opportunity to participate in the rescue, such opportunity must be countered by appropriate safeguards to the unconflicted creditors (explained below), and these creditors should be the ones deciding.

For instance, Singapore and Mainland China tolerate, to a certain extent, shareholders retaining their equity in the debtor company after the restructuring, notwithstanding that the debtor company is insolvent and 'out of money'. This may be the price for securing the success of the reorganisation. It is notable, though, that the lack of explicit safeguards in the Chinese legislation has meant that there is continued uncertainty as creditors and shareholders would find it difficult to predict the outcomes. The SPC's conditions for the exercise of cram-down, including the condition that creditors must receive not less than what they would have received in the liquidation, does not adequately address the problem when valuation disputes arise, and are in turn compounded by the absence of requirement to compel administrators to disclose the valuation methodology. One possibility of a safeguard is to have a range of acceptability of distributions to the creditors and shareholders and the satisfaction of the prerequisite for the cram-down to take place before the court can exercise the ability to cram-down. The other is Singapore's solution, which is to make the cram-down exceedingly difficult to utilise by requiring the consent of creditors holding 75 per cent in value of all debts.

3.5.2. The Example of Corporate Governance

Much of corporate and securities law deals with the proper protection and treatment of outside (minority) shareholders. The confidence of investors is vital to creating a vibrant securities market.[242] There should be no difference for treatment of minority

[242] There is a large body of work in and finance literature which suggests that the legal framework governing corporate governance has an important role in creating the conditions for economic growth in low- and middle-income countries (R La Porta et al, 'Law and Finance' (1998) 106 *Journal of Political Economy* 1113, R La Porta, F Lopez-de-Silanes and A Shleifer, 'The Economic Consequences of Legal Origins' (2008) 46 *Journal of Economic Literature* 285). Although the law and finance theory has been criticized (J Armour et al, 'Shareholder Protection and Stock Market Development: An Empirical Test of the Legal Origins Hypothesis' (2009) 6 *Journal of Empirical Legal Studies* 343; H Spamann, 'Antidirector Rights

outside creditors,[243] given the importance of deepening the capital markets in any jurisdiction. I suggest that future reforms borrow from the rich literature in corporate and security law on shareholding voting in dealing with related party transactions (RPTs) or conflicted transactions (including the release or settlement of claims against the controlling shareholders or directors). These transactions are dealt with through a combination of controlling the voting by controlling shareholders, mandatory disclosures and imposing duties on directors.

3.5.2.1. Controlling Participation by Controlling Shareholders

In this respect, there is a rich literature on the law of voting related to conflicts of interests faced by controlling shareholders and minority shareholders in shareholders' meetings found in RPTs. In Anglo-American corporate governance, companies may enter into agreements with controlling shareholders: these RPTs are not banned outright, but a number of strategies are used through robust mandatory disclosure, approval by independent directors, audit committee review and, in some cases, approval by independent financial advisers and by independent shareholders.[244] In the US, fiduciary duties are sometimes owed by controlling shareholders to minority shareholders in buyouts, but this is beyond the scope of this book.

In corporate and securities laws, the strategy to obtain the shareholder votes is that of majority of the minority, found for listed companies in Singapore,[245] Hong Kong,[246] India[247] and Mainland China.[248] Whilst there is no necessary convergence on how most of the minority voting work in each jurisdiction, the basic premise is that some controls are placed on the ability of controlling shareholder to vote.

First, controlling shareholders who try to manipulate the vote by acquiring debt post-financial distress or selling the debt to friendly parties should not form the same class of creditors as the others.[249] The Singaporean and Indian examples show that the courts are vigilant to ensure that the debt is not whitewashed so easily.[250]

Index Revisited' (2010) 23 *Review of Financial Studies* 467), the theory remains influential and the work by La Porta has been the endorsed by the World Bank in its 'Doing Business' reports (at least prior to their discontinuation).

[243] See MJ Roe and DA Skeel, 'Assessing the Chrysler Bankruptcy' (2010) 108 *Michigan Law Review* 727.

[244] See discussion and references in L Enriques et al, 'Related Party Transactions' in R Kraakman et al, *The Anatomy of Corporate Law: A Comparative and Functional Approach*, 3rd edn (Oxford, OUP, 2017).

[245] C Chen, WY Wan and W Zhang, 'Board Independence as a Panacea to Tunneling? An Empirical Study of Related-Party Transactions in Hong Kong and Singapore. Transactions in Hong Kong and Singapore' (2018) 15 *Journal of Empirical Legal Studies* 987.

[246] ibid.

[247] Companies Act, 2013, s 188(1). See generally, DW Puchniak and U Varottil, 'Related Party Transactions in Commonwealth Asia: Complicating the Comparative Paradigm' (2020) 17 *Berkeley Business Law Journal* 1.

[248] eg see Rules Governing Shenzhen Stock Exchange, Ch 10, s 2, available at www.szse.cn/www/English/rules/siteRule/P020201111614265071408.pdf; See generally, KS Kim, 'Related Party Transactions in East Asia' in L Enriques and T Troger (eds), The Law and Finance of Related Party Transactions (Cambridge, Cambridge University Press, 2019) ch 11.

[249] See also discussion on *Indah Kiat* (n 96) and accompanying text.

[250] See discussion in *DSG Asia* and *Phoenix Arc Private Limited v Spade Financial Services Limited*, above nn 209–12.

Second, alongside effective creditor committees and other independent third-party oversight mechanisms, the voting processes by the creditors becomes extremely important. When the company is insolvent and it is proposed that controlling shareholders (as creditors) are to be treated differently to other creditors, they should not be able to vote at creditors' meetings and hence should not be treated in the same way as other unsecured creditors. This is the situation in Singapore and Hong Kong, which utilise the schemes of arrangement as a debt restructuring tool, though Hong Kong has shown some departure from the strict position. Independent of the situation that involved shareholders, the SPC in Mainland China has recently prescribed the abstention of voting by conflicted bondholders for bondholder restructuring,[251] and there is no reason not to extend the abstention to other kinds of debt restructurings. In fact, I would go further and argue that controlling shareholders (who are also creditors) should not be permitted to vote at creditors' meetings. This is in fact the position in India where related parties (defined widely), at the time of filing, and those who aim to evade the prohibition, cannot vote.[252]

Third, should the courts go further and preventing them from bidding in the sale? India is at one extreme by not allowing promoters to bid for the assets in the reorganisation exercise even if they offer the highest price via an auction, thereby mitigating any conflict-of-interest problems (as well as eliminating the disclosure issues).[253] If the promoters are precluded from the exercise and the exercise is one that is creditor-driven, in theory, the incentives for non-disclosure of involvement of the related parties should be lessened. This, however, presents two problems: first, banning promoters and their associates is overinclusive; and, second, it generates considerable satellite litigation and partially defeats the purpose of speedy resolution, which was the original purpose of the IBC. For example, two high-profile cases were Bhushan Power and Steel[254] and Essar Steel,[255] both of which underwent resolution plans (that were approved), but the promoters continued to bring litigation.[256] Thus, the problem with not allowing promoters to bid in the asset purchase may overwhelm the cure. The better solution is to allow promoters as bidders, but subject to the affirmative vote of creditors.

Fourth, should shareholders be able to vote on the restructuring if the debtor is 'out of money'? Singapore and Hong Kong allow for shareholders to vote on the grounds if the restructuring involves a debt–equity swap or issuance of equity, and so does China under the EBL, though the latter has been criticised in the literature.[257] It is suggested that the better view is not to have a blanket prohibition on shareholder voting, as excluding the shareholders from the decision-making would disincentivise them completely from putting forward rescue proposals.

[251] See above, n 221.
[252] IBC, s 21. See above, section 3.4.3.2.
[253] IBC, s 29A. See above, section 3.4.2.3.
[254] *JSW Steel Ltd. v Mahender Kumar Khandelwal*, Company Appeal (AT) (Insolvency) No 957 of 2019.
[255] *Committee of Creditors of Essar Steel India through SBI v Satish Kumar Gupta* Company Appeal (AT) (Ins) No 242 of 2019.
[256] Above, nn 112–13 and accompanying text.
[257] Zhang, *Corporate Reorganisations in China* (2018) (n 146).

Fifth, what is the future of pre-packs in Asian restructurings? China's experiences with pre-packs will represent an interesting development to the future of restructuring law. Currently, one version of the pre-pack appears that the court may have oversight, given that a provisional administrator is appointed, though there could be out-of-court negotiations before the court accepts the bankruptcy petition.[258] Given the frequent complaints over the adequacy of disclosure processes, pre-packs may not work well, especially if the controlling shareholders are proposing for the sale of the distressed assets to themselves and if they have had long periods that they could have control over the business. The perceived lack of transparency may mean that pre-packs will still need to be subject to the oversight of the administrator, with ultimate judicial oversight.

3.5.2.2. Imposing Mandatory Disclosure of Debtors' Financial Information to Address Information Asymmetry

In restructurings, debtors have access to superior financial information. Asymmetric information is present in the case of DIP and PIP/DIP hybrid models, but the problem is exacerbated when there are controlling shareholders. Based on the experiences of India, Mainland China and Singapore, it is suggested that the legislation should prescribe the key financial information that would be regarded as essential and when the information must be disclosed to the creditors or the insolvency practitioner in the PIP model (or PIP/DIP model), and this should ideally take place as early as possible in the restructuring process. However, recourse to the courts is often an inefficient remedy; for instance, in India, the remedy of recourse is seldom used. There are benefits of having incentives to allow controlling shareholders to have some participation in the outcome of the restructuring, as argued in the preceding section, so as to incentivise them to work with the insolvency practitioners and creditors.

3.5.2.3. Duties of Directors

It is well established in Anglo-American corporate law, as well as the corporate law in Singapore, Hong Kong and India, that directors owe fiduciary duties to the company.[259] Chinese corporate law and securities regulation also prescribe duties owed by directors to the company.[260]

For large companies with dispersed shareholdings and are solvent, on traditional agency costs arguments, independent directors are appointed to provide a check on management. Where the company has controlling shareholders, there is a higher risk of opportunistic behaviour by controlling shareholders (who control the boards) vis-a-vis the minority shareholders. The solution reached in Anglo-American corporate

[258] See discussion in n 241 above. See also ch 7.

[259] For a discussion on fiduciary duties owed by directors in RPTs, see Puchniak and Varottil, 'Related Party Transactions in Commonwealth Asia' (2020).

[260] See, generally, strategies to regulate RPTs in East Asian countries: eg Kim, 'Related Party Transactions in East Asia' (2019) (n 248).

law (and applicable to Singapore, Hong Kong and India) and Mainland China is that, at least for listed companies, independent directors are appointed to safeguard the interests of the listed company in entering RPTs and conflicted transactions to mitigate controlling and minority shareholder conflicts.

When the company is in financial distress, the dynamics change. For large companies with dispersed shareholdings, traditional agency analysis is that directors may prefer shareholder interests to creditors and may enter transactions that destroy value in a gamble to resurrect or trade the company out of insolvency. English law responds by requiring directors' duties to consider the creditors' interests and wrongful trading rules.[261] Different issues arise for portfolio companies; due to the types of restructurings in the market that will provide directors with equity compensation in the newly reorganised company, directors may prefer to support the creditors' plan.[262]

For Asian companies with concentrated shareholdings, unless independent directors are sufficiently experienced to manage key aspects of restructurings, which would be relatively rare unless they happen to be insolvency practitioners. Hence, for jurisdictions with concentrated shareholdings that choose to move to a DIP or a hybrid DIP/PIP model, sufficient safeguards against such opportunistic behaviour are needed, and the scope of duties of directors will need to be reconsidered to manage the agency costs of shareholder–creditor conflicts. If the DIP model implemented does not come with hard timelines, which are policed stringently by the courts, there needs to be heightened scrutiny by the courts regarding the duties of the management as to the adequacy disclosures during the restructuring and their self-interests in ensuring that potential claims are swept under the market. It also needs to be recognised that there are limitations to such enforcement due to the general limitations on the enforcement of directors' duties in most parts of the world outside the US under general corporate law.[263]

3.5.2.4. *The State as a Shareholder in Reorganisations*

In section 3.4.3.3, I explained that the experience of many of the Chinese restructurings of bond defaults and financially distressed SOEs has been the function of the central or local government's coordination and bail-outs. These bail-outs could have taken place using processes outside the EBL, albeit imperfectly, such as the Government arranging emergency loans to the SOEs to repay the bondholders or creditors.[264] Quite apart from the inefficiencies of keeping zombie companies alive, there are at least two problems with the government bail-outs using the court-approved reorganisation in the EBL as a tool. First, the reorganisation process in the EBL will

[261] See, generally, L Gullifer and J Payne, *Corporate Finance Law: Principles and Policy*, 3rd edn (Oxford, Hart Publishing, 2020) 116.

[262] See Paterson, 'The Paradox of Alignment' (2016).

[263] See generally, discussion in ch 8, section 8.4. For a discussion on limitations of enforcement of directors' duties in corporate law, see Wan, Chen and Goo (n 125); R Huang and N Howson, *Enforcement of Corporate and Securities Law: China and the World* (Cambridge, Cambridge University Press, 2017).

[264] For example, in the bond default of Sichuan Coal Industry Group in 2016, the company borrowed from the state-owned Mainland banks to repay the creditors. However less than six months later, the company defaulted again. See Amstad and He (n 223).

not serve as a useful price discovery mechanism, as third-party bidders are unlikely to come forward if they know that the intention of the government is to preserve the business (and jobs) at all costs. Second, for the PIP/DIP hybrid model found in Mainland China, where the management theoretically plays an important role in the bankruptcy negotiations, it is unclear how management of SOEs will speedily work out a solution with the administrator, creditors and the Government (as financiers) within the bankruptcy forum as their (management's) interests are not aligned with the creditors'.[265] Being shut out of the capital market is less of a concern for SOEs than private enterprises. Hence, for the rescue to work, much of the work has to be done outside of management.

With the recent attempts to accelerate market reforms, the invoking of EBL is an important process to allow the reorganisation of companies that are economically viable, though in financial distress, and to achieve an orderly liquidation of companies that are unviable. For the EBL to be an effective restructuring tool, there needs to be compliance with good insolvency law practice to ensure an effective bargaining process to obtain price discovery and that priorities by adhered to, subject to well defined departures. A general low regard for the bargaining process and priorities may spill over to non-SOE restructurings. Hence, it is vital that future restructurings, including those of SOEs, would need to comply with market-based methods. Where there is government bail-out or state rescue due to the importance of these industries, this should be regarded as falling outside the EBL, lest the techniques unique to state bail-outs be replicated in non-bail-out situations.

3.6. CONCLUSION

When companies are in financial distress, manager–creditor and shareholder–creditor conflicts play out differently, depending on the ownership structures. The large restructurings in the US and UK used to be the listed companies with dispersed shareholdings, though in more recent times, the restructurings have involved portfolio companies whose shareholdings are the private equity funds. In contrast, the large restructurings of Asian companies are concentrated in the hands of families or the state, or both.

In the US/UK model, a DIP regime allows the management to drive the restructuring, and where shareholders are dispersed, management should work in the interests of creditors in determining how assets should be deployed. In portfolio firms where the management may be inclined to support the shareholders, their incentives remain firmly market driven. However, where shareholdings are concentrated in families as are found in Asian companies, a DIP regime will not work well if the creditors

[265] The attempted (but failed restructuring) of Guangxi Nonferrous was a case where several Chinese press articles reported that institutional creditors criticised the administrator for failing to engage with the creditors except only during the voting of the plan at the two creditors' meetings and the management of the company did not propose any practical plan. eg Shanghai Brilliance Credit Rating & Investors [上海新世纪资信评估投资服务有限公司], 'Criticism of Guangxi Nonferrous' [广西有色破产点评 – 研发部/何金中] 21 September 2016; JM Dai, 'Who is Directing the Reorganisation' [谁在主导破产重整] *World Economics* [世纪经济] (29 October 2016). See n 227 and accompanying text.

perceive the management or the controlling shareholders to have brought about the distressed situation. The appointment of an independent administrator is not the complete solution in a PIP or a hybrid PIP/DIP model if he/she is unable to obtain information from the controlling shareholders who are often unwilling to provide full disclosure. Yet, to shut out controlling shareholders, as attempted in India, may not be the appropriate remedy. As the cases of India and Mainland China demonstrate, controlling shareholders may sometimes even emerge as the highest bidders or are able to coordinate the rescue.

Turning to the question of distribution, shareholders rank after debt, and if the pre-bankruptcy entitles are strictly given effect, they should be wiped out. Yet, as the cases of Mainland China and Singapore demonstrate, wiping out their interests completely may be counterproductive if they are disincentivised to participate in the rescue. For these reasons, shareholders have been allowed to retain some of their equity in Mainland China Singapore, even though they are diluted in the process.

Based on the case studies of the four Asian jurisdictions, restructuring regimes will need to consider the potential inefficiencies by these different ownership structures in minimising agency costs.

4

The Agency and Coordination Costs of Creditor–Creditor Relationships in Restructuring

4.1. INTRODUCTION

In chapter one, I explained that restructuring law is concerned with maximising the debtor's estate and minimising wasteful rent-seeking conduct.[1] Chapter three dealt with minimising wasteful direct agency costs of the conflicts arising from the manager–creditor and shareholder–creditor relationships in Asian restructurings (by comparison with the Anglo-American restructurings), due to the differences in the make-up of shareholders. In this chapter, I address strategies to minimise the agency and coordination costs of hold-outs and majority creditor oppression arising from the heterogeneity of creditors in Anglo-American and Asian restructurings.

In chapter three, I explained that addressing hold-outs is done at two levels: first, developing how the assets should be deployed; and the second, determining how the assets should be distributed. The United States (US) Chapter 11 of the Bankruptcy Code 1978 is designed to address the collective problem of the various stakeholders. In relation to the former, the moratorium applies when the debtor makes the Chapter 11 filing, which encourages parties to the negotiation table to bargain consensually within specified parameters. In order to reduce unreasonable hold-outs, Chapter 11 fixes the order of priority by the absolute priority rule (APR). Under the APR, before the court confirms a plan that one or more classes of stakeholders has rejected, members of each dissenting class must receive the full value of their claims before the members of a lower class receive or retain anything.[2] The UK scheme of arrangement and the recent UK restructuring plan under Parts 26 and 26A of the Companies Act 2006 respectively similarly encourage consensual bargaining by creditors within the same class of creditors except that in the restructuring plan under Part 26A, there is the additional possibility of a cross-class cram-down if the relevant conditions are satisfied.[3] Even prior to the enactment of Part 26A of the Companies Act 2006,

[1] ch 2; see generally, DG Baird, AJ Casey and RC Picker, 'The Bankruptcy Partition' (2018) 166 *University of Pennsylvania Law Review* 1675.

[2] US Bankruptcy Code, § 1129(b)(2). See also ch 3.

[3] Companies Act 2006, Pt 26 (for schemes); Pt 26A (for restructuring plans).

practitioners have devised the method of twinning the UK scheme of arrangement with administration, which achieves a de facto cram-down of the junior classes of debt and equity that reflects the entitlements of the creditors and shareholders upon liquidation.[4] In the US Chapter 11, UK scheme of arrangement and UK restructuring plan, appropriate classification of the creditors is critical. Creditor committees, backed by mandatory information disclosure, are either required or widely utilised in practice.[5]

The legal strategies relating to controlling shareholder–creditor and manager–creditor relationships have some similarities in creditor–creditor relationships. However, there are important differences in the composition of the debtors whose debts are being restructured even within the Anglo-American regime, at least up until the 1990s. Chapter 11 is designed to address the financial and operational restructuring of the debtor and the debtor will negotiate with a small number of secured creditors, the creditors' committee representing the wide base of unsecured creditors and the shareholders.[6] In contrast, the UK schemes of arrangement are traditionally used widely in financial restructurings involving either banks or sophisticated finance creditors; operational debts could be, but are often not, subject of the schemes though there are recent exceptions.[7] Thus, concentrated debt structures will lower the coordination costs among creditors but it also means that the financial creditors are able to influence the managers in a dispersed ownership system. The UK Part 26A plan, in contrast, has been used for operational restructuring in the early cases, such as restructuring of tenancy agreements.[8] In both US and UK, the changes in the financial markets, including the rise of restructurings involving large unlisted companies which are private equity portfolios and the increasing activities of the distressed trading market, have also introduced changes to the practices to the restructuring practice.

In the four Asian jurisdictions which have transplanted insolvency and restructuring regimes that are based on the US/UK models, either the composition of the debt that is sought to be restructured, or the institutional background, is very different from the US/UK regime, and thus gives rise to the question as to the appropriate strategies to resolve the various creditor–creditor conflicts. In Mainland China, the Enterprise Bankruptcy Law 2006 (EBL) requires the restructuring of the entire balance sheet of the debtor and is thus closest to an outcome associated under Chapter 11. However, even though financial debt remains concentrated largely with the banks, there are often numerous small or non-financial creditors, and concerns of social stability arise if these creditors are subject to haircut. In India, the Indian Insolvency and Bankruptcy Code 2016 prioritises the resolution process in a strict time-bound manner, and a question arises as to whether it is justified to only allow the financial creditors to vote, which cuts down on the amount of time required to

[4] See ch 1 on the four gateways to restructuring in the UK: the scheme of arrangement; the restructuring plan; administration and company voluntary arrangement. For twinning of the scheme of arrangement and administration, see section 4.3.2 below.

[5] See section 4.3.1.2 below.

[6] D Skeel, 'Distorted Choice in Corporate Bankruptcy' (2020) 130 *Yale Law Journal* 366.

[7] eg *Re MAB Leasing Ltd* [2021] EWHC 379 (Ch); see also *All Scheme Limited* [2021] EWHC 1401 (Ch) (discussed below).

[8] *Re Virgin Active Holdings Limited* [2021] EWHC 1246 (Ch).

coordinate among the operational creditors. In Hong Kong and Singapore, unlike the UK, the English-origin schemes of arrangement are used to restructure both financial and operational debt. However, even among financial creditors, they are far from homogenous as compared with the UK. Due to a series of measures promoting the investments by retail or wealthy individual investors, these bondholders have a level of sophistication which is very different from the professional and institutional investors. Further, in all the jurisdictions, due to the concentration of shareholding outlined in chapter three, because some of the creditors may be related parties of the debtor or its controlling shareholders, they have a strong bias towards promoting the restructuring even if the debtor is no longer economically viable, raising the problem of agency costs that are similar to those found in shareholder–creditor relationships.

In this chapter, I address how the US and UK address the strategies that are used to reduce agency and coordination costs that arise as a result of creditor–creditor conflicts and how some of these strategies require changes when dealing with Asian restructurings. Agency costs arise where the interests of the majority of the creditors (the agent) diverge from the minority of the creditors (the principal) or where the interests of one class of creditors diverge from the other classes. As the number of creditors increases, there will also be an increase in the costs of coordination. Section 4.2 first sets out the institutional and organisational background of debt-holdings for large distressed company restructurings in the US and the UK, and the market adaptations. It then outlines the debt market in the four Asian jurisdictions and the state of the bond markets, with a focus on bonds issued by non-financial companies.[9] Section 4.3 outlines the strategies used in Anglo-American restructurings to reduce the agency and coordination costs arising from hold-outs. Section 4.4 outlines the strategies that are adapted from the Anglo-American restructurings in Asia and how they have limitations. Section 4.5 outlines suggestions for reform, and section 4.6 concludes.

In this book, I am not exploring the merits of whether to place certain types of statutory claims, including employee claims and taxation claims, ahead of the secured or unsecured creditors. Priority of statutory claims raises unique policy considerations outside of bankruptcy law. In discussing the Singapore position, I primarily refer to the scheme of arrangement. There is another gateway to the court-supervised restructuring via the judicial management (being a PIP model), as distinct from the scheme simpliciter (being a DIP model). As explained in chapter two, the judicial management is a process where the restructuring plan is proposed by the judicial manager, but the actual execution of the plan continues to require a scheme of arrangement.

4.2. INSTITUTIONAL AND ORGANISATIONAL BACKGROUND

4.2.1. The US and the UK

Chapter 11 was designed to address the collective action problem posed by widely scattered creditors: with the moratorium that applies when the debtor makes the filing for

[9] The discussion on bonds issued directly by governments or financial institutions is outside the scope of this book.

Chapter 11, creditors are incentivised to go to the negotiating table. When Chapter 11 was enacted in 1978, creditors mostly held the debt until maturity. However, two developments became significant in the late 1990s into the twenty-first century which significantly affected the practice of insolvency and restructuring law. The first, as documented in chapter one, was the rise of the private equity. Private equity uses leveraged loans in order to raise funds for acquiring private companies or privatising listed companies. In these situations, the shareholding structures of these firms become concentrated in the hands of the private equity firms and their sponsors, with a small slice of equity going to management. The repayment of these loans would be generated from the cash flows of the businesses whose companies are acquired. When the global financial crisis occurred in 2008, the firms which were heavily leveraged were directly impacted, ran into financial distress and had to be restructured.

The second was the rise of distressed debt trading. In response to market demand, distressed debt was driven by intermediaries repacking debt into instruments that are attractive to investors. Distressed debt makes it more difficult for a company seeking to restructure to identify the creditors for the purposes of the negotiation. Once the financial creditors are no longer the original bank lenders or bondholders, fragmentation in the interests of the financial creditors is inevitable given the diversity of their interests. Purchasers of the distressed debt or loan at a discount are motivated to achieve an outcome that promises a profit on the trade quickly; they are not necessarily motivated to wait for a process that allows the company to emerge as an independent going concern (as opposed to being sold or liquidated), even though this may fetch better returns in the long run. Alternatively, purchasers of distressed debt or loan may be motivated to hold up negotiations among creditors unless they receive other benefits and fees in exchange for agreeing to vote in advance of the meeting, even though it may heighten the risk of delay and that the firm may not successfully exit from reorganisation as a going concern.[10] Distressed debt-holders may also be motivated by the fact that they have taken positions in other classes of debt within the debtor's capital structure.[11]

Paterson argues that both these developments change the focus of reorganisation law from resolving the collective action problem to one which requires rapid deleveraging to prevent the financial distress from spreading to the operations of the company. In so doing, she argues that practitioners have to adapt Chapter 11 to allow for exchange offers (where the debtor exchanges the existing debt instruments with newly issued package of more sustainable debt securities that would meet the debtor's financial requirements), pre-packaged sales (where the bidder is selected prior to the filing) and going-concern sales,[12] as opposed to a reorganisation where the

[10] V Ivashina, B Iverson and DC Smith, 'The Ownership and Trading of Debt Claims in Chapter 11 Restructurings' (2016) 119 *Journal of Financial Economics* 316.

[11] S Paterson, *Corporate Reorganization Law and Forces of Change* (Oxford, OUP, 2020) ch 4. See also *In re Worldcom, Inc*, No 02-13533, 2002 WL 1732646 (Bank SDNY 22 July 22,2002) (a creditor on the creditors' committee had a US$400 million claim but was found to have hedged all but US$6.5 million and hence did not have an economic interest in the full amount).

[12] Paterson (ibid) ch 4.

management remains intact.[13] The impact of the concentration of debt arising from distressed trading on reorganisations have been documented by other scholars. For instance, Ivashina and his team have documented the concentration of ownership of claims through the debt-trading process in the course of Chapter 11 proceedings, which is a proxy for low-coordination friction. They find that higher concentration at the start of Chapter 11 is associated with faster bankruptcy resolution and higher likelihood of survival as an independent entity, but greater concentration during the course of Chapter 11 through claims trading leads to a greater likelihood of liquidation.[14]

In contrast, in the UK, the relationship between the banks and the debtor companies began to weaken when banks started to sell their debt in the distressed debt market. However, as compared to Chapter 11, an English scheme of arrangement adapts well to these changes as it originally developed as a means of restructuring of large financial creditors and the shift is now to restructure the debt held by sophisticated distressed debt investors. However, given the move towards including operational creditors in the restructuring, the concern should instead focus on how the scheme framework will develop to adapt to the changes.[15]

4.2.2. Asia

Prior to the Asian financial crisis of 1997, the Asian jurisdictions were reliant on bank debt as the dominant means of financing. In the aftermath of the Asian financial crisis, due to a series of tighter prudential regulation and stronger economic growth, bank asset quality has in general improved. The local currency bond markets have also been established to shift some of the corporates' reliance away from bank credit. However, despite the development of the local currency bond markets, bank credit remains the most important source of corporate financing, particularly for the emerging Asian jurisdictions. For illustrative examples within the private non-financial sectors, Table 4.1 shows the domestic bank credit to GDP, the total credit to GDP and the ratio of bank credit to total credit of the non-financial private sector in the four Asian jurisdictions respectively, in comparison to US and the UK, for 2019. As can be seen from Table 4.1, under the column 'Bank credit to total credit', the private sector in the four Asian jurisdictions very much continues to rely on domestic bank debt, as compared to the US/UK economies.[16]

In the last decade, bond markets in Asia have matured to compete with the corporates' sources of funding and to reduce the reliance on bank credit. The rest of this section explains how the bond markets have developed in the four Asian jurisdictions, which has profound implications for the law and practice of debt restructuring.

[13] eg HR Miller, 'The Changing Face of Chapter 11: A Reemergence of the Bankruptcy Judge as Producer, Director, and Sometimes Star of the Reorganization Passion Play' (1995) 69 *American Bankruptcy Law Journal* 431.

[14] Ivashina, Iverson and Smith, 'The Ownership and Trading of Debt Claims' (2016).

[15] Paterson, *Corporate Reorganization Law* (2020) ch 9.

[16] The bank credit does not take into account non-performing loans, which is discussed in ch 5.

Table 4.1 Bank and total credit to GDP for non-financial private sector

For the quarter ending 31 December 2019			
Jurisdictions	**Domestic bank credit to GDP (%)**	**Total credit to GDP (%)**	**Bank credit to total credit (%)**
China	165.7	205.6	80.59%
Hong Kong SAR	253.2	305.9*	82.77%
India	53	87	60.92%
Singapore	114.1	175.1	65.16%
UK	86.5	155.8	55.52%
US	51	150.3	33.93%

Source: Bank of International Settlements.

*For Hong Kong, the HKMA has clarified that the high total credit to GDP does not represent a complete reflection of the macro-prudential risk in Hong Kong, which is an international financial centre, because the credit is often extended to companies for their operations outside Hong Kong. See Y Liu, 'Monetary authority pushes back on warning that soaring private-sector debt in Hong Kong could lead to recession' SCMP (22 October 2020).

4.2.2.1. Mainland China

The onshore corporate bond market has increased exponentially since the late 1990s, and by 2019 Mainland China had the second largest bond market in the world after the US.[17] Figure 4.1 shows the size of the onshore bond market for companies since 1998. By 2020, the outstanding onshore debt securities market for non-financial companies was approximately US$4.026 trillion.[18] The offshore bond market has also taken off significantly since 2010 due to the low funding costs in US dollars.[19] As at November 2020, the offshore bond market for China was estimated to be US$752 million.[20] Chinese issuers can now issue bonds denominated in RMB (known as Panda Bonds) and foreign currency-denominated bonds.

It is difficult to estimate the aggregate of foreign investors' holdings in the bond market, which are issued and traded across the inter-bank market, stock exchanges and bank counters.[21] Based on the data from China Central Depository & Clearing Co, Ltd (CCDC), a depository for China Inter-bank Bond Market Direct (a scheme that allows foreign issuers to invest directly on the China Inter-bank Bond Market) and Bond Connect (a mutual access scheme that allows investors to invest in Mainland China),[22]

[17] HKEX, 'Credit Events of Offshore Chinese State-related Issuers and their Onshore Support' (2021).

[18] Data from CEIS, which is obtained from Bank of International Settlements. See Figure 4.1.

[19] Data from BIS: stats.bis.org/statx/srs/table/c3?c=CN&p=20204. The total onshore debt securities market (including government, financial and non-financial companies) was US$17.3 trillion.

[20] International Capital Market Association, 'The Internationalisation of the China Corporate Bond Market' (2021), available at www.icmagroup.org/News/news-in-brief/the-internationalization-of-the-china-corporate-bond-market-new-report-from-icma.

[21] Fitch Ratings, *China Corporate Bond Market Bluebook* (Beijing, A Fitch China Research Initiative Publication, 2019), available at your.fitch.group/rs/732-CKH-767/images/china-corporate-bond-market-blue-book_fitch_10083315.pdf.

[22] Bond Connect is a joint venture between HKEX and China Foreign Exchange Trade System. See www.chinabondconnect.com/en/About-Us/Company-Introduction.html.

the holdings by foreign investors are at US$1107.9 billion and US$140.6 billion respectively.[23]

The regulatory framework on corporate bonds rests in a number of authorities: the National Association of Financial Market Institutional Investors (NAFII) and the People's Bank of China regulate the inter-bank market, the National Development and Reform Commission regulates the issuance of enterprise bonds (which are bonds issued by the SOEs and local government financing vehicles) and China Securities Regulatory Commission (CSRC) regulates the company bond market.[24]

This background sets the scene for the offshore restructuring of the debts issued by the offshore vehicles of the Chinese companies which have defaulted in recent years, including Winsway, Kaisa, and more recently Peking University Founder Group.[25] Some of these offshore bond issues had support from the Chinese parent corporates, either in the form of guarantees (which are rare) or keepwell deeds (more common, and which are discussed below). While in many of these cases, the restructuring of the onshore companies occurred without reference to the offshore restructurings, some of the credit events which happened for offshore bonds were triggered by onshore defaults (such as China City Construction (International) in 2016 and Future Land in 2019).[26] The interaction between onshore and offshore restructuring is complex due to the legal structures in which the firms have raised funds offshore (which are discussed below).

Figure 4.1 Onshore bond market for Mainland China

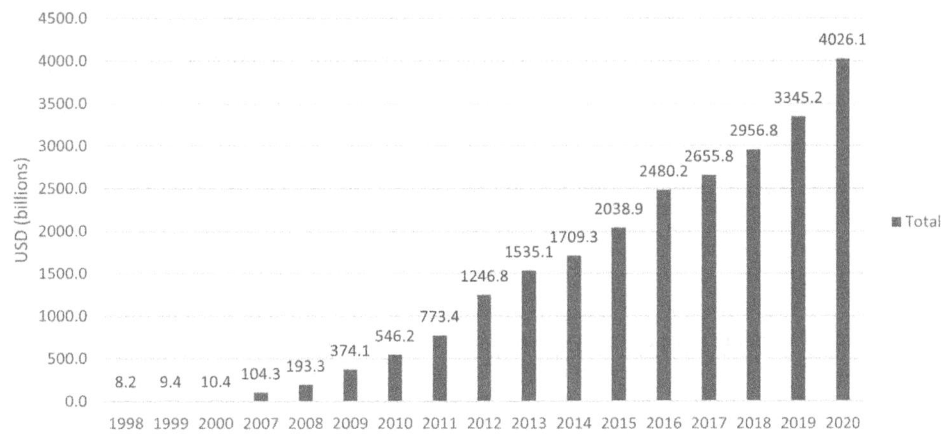

Source: Data collected from CEIC and People's Bank of China (issuance is in local currency converted to US$ for comparability).

[23] Figures as at 30 June 2021. Source: CEIC, obtained from CCDC.

[24] See W Shen, *Conceptualizing the Regulatory Thicket* (Abingdon, Routledge, 2021) ch 2.

[25] Fitch Ratings, 'Fitch China Bond Defaults' (10 October 2018) (for Winsway and Kaisa). For Peking University Founder Group, see E White, 'Foreign investors face critical legal test for $82bn in China bonds' Financial Times (8 April 2021).

[26] HKEX (n 17).

Historically, the use of the EBL to resolve onshore bond defaults has not been high. As explained below, the first bond default occurred in 2014.[27] Figure 4.2 shows the status of onshore bond defaults during the period 2015–19 in Mainland China. The status of these defaults is as at 31 December 2020. As can be seen in Figure 4.2, only a minority of the onshore bond defaults are resolved through the EBL in the court. In the vast majority of the cases, there is no repayment disclosed and often no other information is disclosed on the outstanding bonds. The reasons for the low usage of the EBL are explained further in chapter eight. However, it is expected with the recent rising onshore bond defaults (see Figure 3.1) and the number of onshore bond defaults announced in 2021,[28] together with the Chinese Government's pronouncement that the EBL is an important tool to resolve zombie companies, the EBL will assume in importance though it is likely that not all of the insolvencies will be resolved by the EBL.

Figure 4.2 Status of issuers of bonds in default as at 31 December 2020

N=144

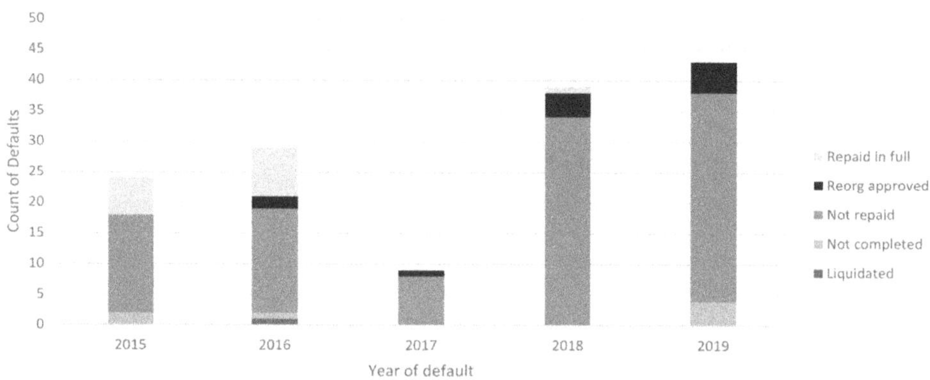

Source: Data collected from WIND; Fitch.

4.2.2.2. *India*

The Indian financial system has traditionally been bank-centric.[29] While the onshore bond market has a long history[30] and has grown considerably in the last decade (see Figure 4.3) due to various reforms to the regulatory framework,[31] bank credit is still traditionally more significant, comprising 61 per cent of the total available

[27] See n 60 below, and accompanying text.

[28] See White (n 25).

[29] S Sahoo, 'Financial Intermediation and Growth: Bank-Based Versus Market-Based Systems' (2014) 8 *Journal of Applied Economic Research* 93.

[30] See generally, R Rangotra, 'A Trend Analysis of Reforms in the Indian Bond Market' in H Chahal, J Jyoti and J Wirtz (eds), *Understanding the Role of Business Analytics* (Singapore, Springer, 2019) 65.

[31] eg P Neemey and N Sahay, 'Indian Corporate Bond Market: An Analysis of Growth and Impact of Macroeconomic Determinants' (2019) 23 *Vision* 244; S Thukral, S Sridhar and MS Joshi, 'Review of Factors Constraining the Development of Indian Corporate Bond Markets' (2015) 7 *Qualitative Research in Financial Markets* 429.

for credit (see Table 4.1). In terms of the significance of the corporate bond market, the amount issued constitutes less than five per cent of its gross domestic product (GDP) in each of the fiscal years between 2011 and 2020.[32] More than 95 per cent of the corporate debt is issued via private placements (to non-retail investors) with the balance issued to retail investors.[33] Corporate debt issuance is dominated by banks, insurance and financial companies.[34] In the offshore bond markets, also known as 'external commercial borrowings', Indian issuers may issue bonds denominated in rupee (known as 'Masala Bonds') and foreign currency ECB.[35]

As seen in Table 4.1, there remains room for Indian credit market to grow since the total credit to GDP ratio in India is 87 per cent for 2019, which is comparatively lower than the markets in Mainland China or the US/UK.[36] What has held back the credit market has been the presence of the non-performing loans, discussed in chapter five.

Figure 4.3 Onshore bond market for India

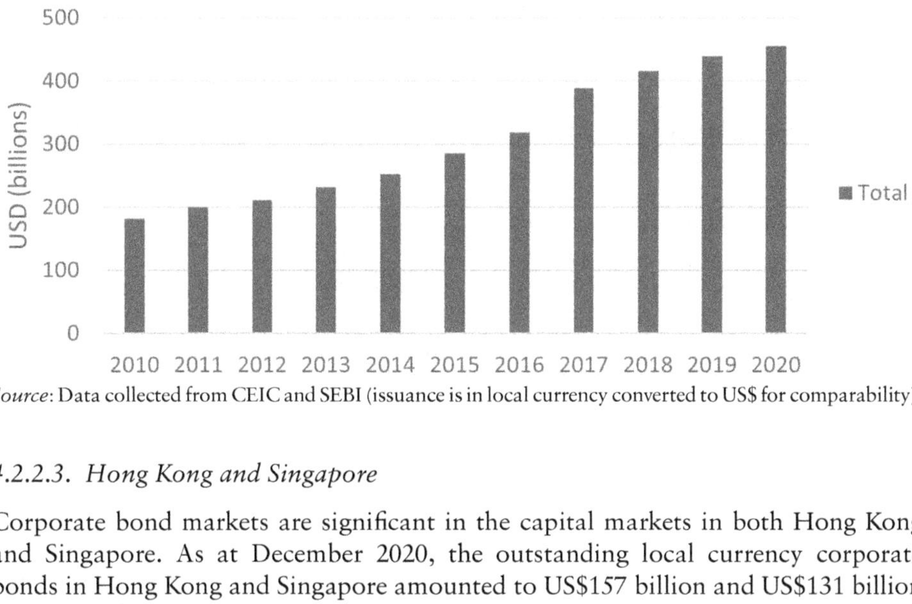

Source: Data collected from CEIC and SEBI (issuance is in local currency converted to US$ for comparability).

4.2.2.3. Hong Kong and Singapore

Corporate bond markets are significant in the capital markets in both Hong Kong and Singapore. As at December 2020, the outstanding local currency corporate bonds in Hong Kong and Singapore amounted to US$157 billion and US$131 billion respectively.[37] The total outstanding foreign currency bonds in Hong Kong and Singapore amounted to US$139.6 billion and US$88.36 billion respectively.[38] The increase in the bond issuance in the last decade has been pronounced, as seen in Figure 4.4.

[32] See CRISIL, *Yearbook on the Indian Debt Market 2021*, available at www.crisil.com/content/dam/crisil/events-tiles/bond-market/2021/bonds-that-build-a-nation/CRISIL-Yearbook-on-the-Indian-Debt-Market-2021.pdf.

[33] ibid (98% of the corporate debt is issued via private placements in fiscal year 2020).

[34] ibid. A list of the public issuances in recent years is set out by SEBI: www.sebi.gov.in/statistics/corporate-bonds/publicissuedata.html.

[35] RBI, 'RBI Announces the New External Commercial Borrowings (ECB) Framework' (2019), available at www.rbi.org.in/Scripts/BS_PressReleaseDisplay.aspx?prid=46031.

[36] Table 4.1.

[37] Singapore and Hong Kong bond data is obtained from asianbondsonline.adb.org.

[38] Bond data is obtained from Asian Bonds Online.

Figure 4.4 Corporate local and foreign currency bonds outstanding in Hong Kong and Singapore

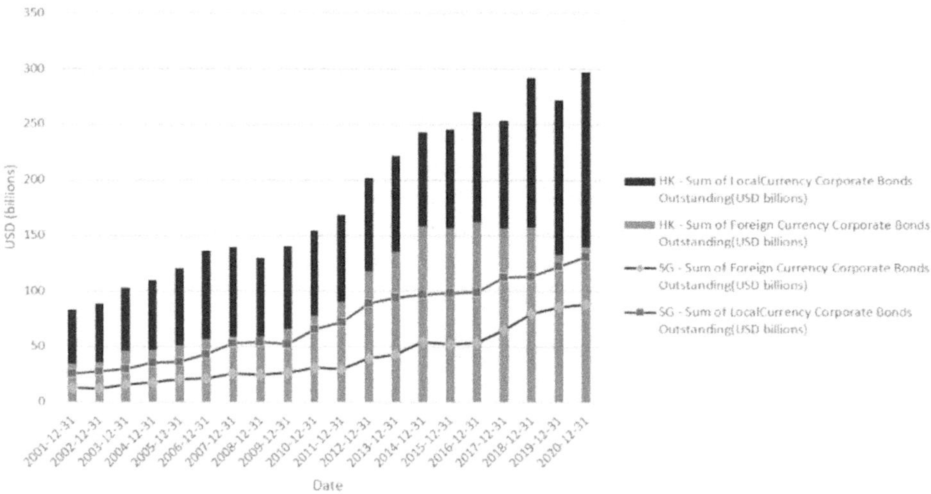

Source: Data collected from Asian Bonds Online (amounts outstanding in US$ for comparability), available at asianbondsonline.adb.org.

In 2019, in Singapore, the non-financial corporates accounted for the single largest group of issuances for local currency bonds, that is, 45.6 per cent of the issuance volume;[39] the proportion is lower for Hong Kong, which is at 19.1 per cent.[40]

With large companies in Hong Kong and Singapore now tapping into the bond market more aggressively, the dynamics are quite different when it comes to the restructuring of debts. The banks are often no longer the largest financial creditors, and the creditor base is considerably more diverse, with the inclusion of the bondholders. When it comes to the restructuring, the company faces a diverse composition of bondholders comprising not only institutional investors, but also distressed debt funds and wealthy investors, for the reasons explained in this section. Similar to the US and UK, this wider base of creditors has an impact on the manner in which restructuring of large companies takes place as negotiation takes place with a much wider group of investors.

4.2.2.3.1. Retail Holdings

In the last five years, there has been a rise in bonds held by retail investors and high-net-worth individuals in Singapore, and the Singapore courts had to consider the

[39] Financial institutions and government account for 31.7% and 22.7% respectively. Source: MAS, 'Singapore Corporate Debt Market Development 2020' (2020).

[40] Central government and government account for 80.4% and 0.50% respectively. Source: AsianBondsOnline, asianbondsonline.adb.org.

cases when the issuers of the bonds defaulted on their payment.[41] This did not happen by accident. In the decade following the Asian financial crisis of 1997, the bonds were still largely held by the wholesale market. When the global financial crisis hit in 2008, the governance weaknesses of several SGX-listed firms and, in particular, the S-Chips, which are the companies whose operations are located outside of Singapore but which have used the SGX as a venue of fund-raising, were exposed. In the aftermath of the scandals, and for a number of years thereafter, the equity markets in Singapore faced considerable challenges to stay vibrant due to the weak valuation and competition from regional markets, including Hong Kong, Shanghai and Shenzhen stock exchanges. The SGX remained active in the real estate investment trusts, but its equity capital market became less important.

In contrast, the bond markets grew quickly and the amounts raised in the bond markets quickly overtook the equity market.[42] In 2015, S$512 million (US$361 million) was raised in the IPO market, which was dwarfed by the S$26.68 billion (US$18.84 billion) raised for the corporate bond market.[43] Prior to 2015, the bonds were mostly issued in the whole-sale market sold to institutional investors which did not require a prospectus. In 2016, the Monetary Authority of Singapore granted exemptions to allow retail investors to participate in the retail offerings of issuers without issuers having to issue prospectuses, thereby drastically increasing of the appeal of issuers issuing bonds for the retail markets.[44] Under these exemptions, eligible issuers can offer bonds to retail investors in the secondary market after bonds have been listed on SGX for six months, also known as the 'seasoning period'. Eligible issuers which achieve certain credit ratings can also issue bonds to retail investors without a prospectus and without undergoing a seasoning period, if at least 20 per cent of the initial issuance is offered to professional and institutional investors. By 2017, it was reported that for the bonds denominated in Singapore dollars (which are more likely to be issued by Singapore issuers), private banking clients take up 21.6 per cent of the bonds as compared to 40.6 per cent of the financial institutions, indicating the relatively high proportion of these debts that have been sold to high net-worth individuals and that retail investors take up 5.1 per cent of these bonds issue.[45]

The problems began to manifest as early as 2016. Towards the end of that year, in view of the softening of commodity prices and downturn in the shipping industry, many shipping and commodity companies reported having to restructure their debts. Swiber Holdings Limited, a maritime services contractor, was the first to collapse with

[41] Bloomberg, 'Rich Singapore Investors Stuck as Local Bond Restructuring Drags' *Straits Times* (25 July 2017).

[42] See H Tjio, 'Restructuring the Bond Market in Singapore' (2019) 14 *Capital Markets Law Journal* 16.

[43] Statistics from the MAS Annual Report 2015/2016, G1, available at www.mas.gov.sg/annual_reports/annual20152016/Annual%20Report.pdf.

[44] Tjio, 'Restructuring the Bond Market in Singapore' (2019).

[45] MAS, 'Singapore Corporate Bond Market 2017' (2017), available at www.mas.gov.sg/-/media/MAS/News-and-Publications/Surveys/Debts/Singapore-Corporate-Debt-Market-Report-2017.pdf?la=en&hash=F6180C5FF32F54856C45A0A0903569B0860A843E.

liabilities of approximately US$1.6 billion, and went into judicial management.[46] By 2019, for bonds denominated in Singapore dollars, private banking clients took up a lower proportion of 23.4 per cent, financial institutions held 29 per cent, and retail investors held 4.7 per cent.[47] The slight fall in the debt held by retail investors could be explained by the fact that in 2017, calls were made to encourage issuers to get the bonds rated if they are sold to retail investors (which would have made the process more costly and fewer bonds were issued).

The relaxation of the sale of bonds to retail investors set the scene for debt restructurings in Singapore in 2018 onwards. In particular, Hyflux Ltd, a global water treatment plant and widely regarded as a home-grown unicorn, marketed its deeply subordinated debt, which comprised a mix of preference shares and perpetual capital securities, to the public, filed for moratorium in 2019. In the course of the protracted restructuring of Hyflux, it was reported that many of the investors of the deeply subordinated debt did not understand the nature of the instruments that they invested in.[48] In response, SGX has set up a working group to review the retail bonds regulatory framework, but the consultations had not yet been published as at December 2021.[49]

Like Singapore, Hong Kong had historically encouraged retail investors to invest in bond markets as alternative sources of investments from equity.[50] In Hong Kong, in the lead-up to the Lehman Brothers minibond saga, around HK$20 billion of products were sold through retail banks to 48,000 investors.[51] However, it is difficult to obtain data on the composition of holdings of the bonds in Hong Kong. Most of the corporate debt listed on HKSE that is issued by private sector companies is not sold to retail; as at January 2021, it was reported that only one first corporate bond has been marketed to retail.[52] In the same report, it states that only six unlisted corporate bonds have been marketed to retail since 2010.[53] In practice, however, while the

[46] A Gabriel, 'Singapore court gives green light for Swiber to be placed under JM' *Business Times* (8 October 2016).

[47] MAS, 'Singapore Corporate Bond Market 2019' available at www.mas.gov.sg/-/media/MAS/News-and-Publications/Surveys/Debts/Singapore-Corporate-Debt-Market-Development-2019.pdf?la=en&hash=B62FF66BD26D794562B5291D6693966C85F1DC55.

[48] eg Bloomberg, 'Rich Singapore Investors Stuck as Local Bond Restructuring Drags' *Straits Times* (25 July 2017); G Leong, 'More than 100 Hyflux Investors Protest at Hong Lim Park' *Straits Times* (31 March 2019); MAS, 'CAD, MAS and ACRA commence joint investigation into Hyflux' (2 June 2020), available at www.mas.gov.sg/news/media-releases/2020/cad-mas-and-acra-commence-joint-investigation-into-hyflux; see also R Hui, 'Miclyn Express Offshore Working with SIAS to Engage Bondholders' *The Business Times* (14 November 2017) (SIAS is an investor body representing retail investors in Singapore.).

[49] SGX, 'SGX Regco Forms Working Group to Review Retail Bonds Framework' (2 January 2020), available at links.sgx.com/FileOpen/20200102_SGX_RegCo_forms_working_group_to_review_retail_bonds_framework.ashx?App=Announcement&FileID=592104.

[50] See Legislative Council Panel on Financial Affairs, 'Development of the Retail Debt Market in Hong Kong' (7 January 2002), available at www.legco.gov.hk/yr01-02/english/panels/fa/papers/fa0107cb1-716-5e.pdf; see also 'Corporate Bond Issues Mark New Era for Hong Kong Retail Market' *International Financial Law Review* (November 2003).

[51] Hong Kong Monetary Authority, 'Report of the Hong Kong Monetary Authority on Issues Concerning the Distribution of Structured Products Connected to Lehman Group Companies' (2008) at para 2.2, available at www.hkma.gov.hk/media/eng/doc/other-information/lehman_report.pdf.

[52] Seewww.hkex.com.hk/News/News-Release/2019/190523news?sc_lang=en; see also Research Office of Legislative Council Secretariat, 'Fact Sheet: Bond Markets in Hong Kong and Singapore' (January 2021).

[53] ibid.

Hong Kong framework to restrict retail investors from largely investing in publicly traded debt (since little of such debt is marketed), there has been in recent restructurings a pattern of individual bond investors who invest in non-publicly traded debt.[54] The profile of these individuals appears to be high-net-worth Mainland investors who have invested in the debt of listed companies in Hong Kong (whose operating subsidiaries are in Mainland). While they are not necessarily retail investors, they are described by the court as 'ripe for exploitation',[55] do not appear to be properly advised as to their rights, and the directors give short shrift as to their interests, even though the company is in financial distress and ought to prioritise their interests over that of the shareholders.[56]

4.2.3. Distressed Debt and Loan Markets

The distressed debt and loan markets are alternatives that enable bondholders and lenders who do not wish to support the proposed restructuring to exit from their investment. As seen in the the preceding section, the rise of bond issuances in Hong Kong and Singapore has meant that in many cases when the bonds are restructured, the creditor banks no longer drive the restructurings, as was the case in the 1990s. In fact, many of the restructuring cases in Hong Kong involve the participation of distressed funds who have purchased the distressed bonds or loans. For instance, *Re Legend International Resorts Ltd*,[57] a Morgan Stanley distressed fund purchased the debt of Legend, the debtor, from a financial institution and promptly applied for a winding-up petition of Legend. Legend was a Hong Kong company with assets in the Philippines. Subsequently Legend applied for a corporate rescue proceeding in the Philippines which was objected to by Morgan Stanley.[58] Where restructurings involve debt which is widely held, insolvency lawyers and practitioner would import the practice of using restructuring support agreements (RSAs) found in the US and UK restructurings in order to obtain the agreement of some of the creditors ahead of the creditors' meeting.[59]

Trading in distressed onshore bonds in Mainland China and India, particularly by foreign distressed funds, is still in the early days. In Mainland China, onshore bond defaults are still relatively recent, with the first onshore bond default in 2014.[60]

[54] eg *Re Lamtex* [2021] HKCFI 1182; *Re China Bozza Development* [2021] HKCFI 1235.

[55] *Re China Bozza Development Holdings* [2021] HKCFI 1235, [22]. The indications are that these investors had subscribed to the bonds to fulfil the residency requirements in Hong Kong or to evade Mainland exchange controls, at [18].

[56] ibid.

[57] [2005] 3 HKLRD 16.

[58] C Qu, 'Towards an Effective Scheme-Based Corporate Rescue System for Hong Kong' (2012) 12 *Journal of Corporate Law Studies* 85, fn 20.

[59] WY Wan and C Watters, 'Mandatory Disclosure in Corporate Debt Restructuring via Schemes of Arrangement: A Comparative Approach' (2021) 30 *International Insolvency Review* S111.

[60] The first corporate default was Shanghai Chaori Solar Energy Science and Technology in 2014. See D Ren, 'Private Borrowers Bear the Brunt of China's Soaring Bond Defaults as Slowing Economy and Trade War put the Sequence on Finances' *South China Morning Post* (24 July 2019), available at www.scmp.com/business/companies/article/3019742/private-borrowers-bear-brunt-chinas-soaring-bond-defaults.

The secondary market for the trading of distressed bonds was introduced by CSRC in May 2019.[61] Likewise, it was only in July 2020 that SEBI permitted trading in defaulted debt securities.[62]

For distressed loan markets, investments in NPLs have a longer history. Foreign distressed funds have traditionally stayed away due to a combination of high entrance costs[63] and foreign exchange regulation. Foreign investors are estimated to purchase only four per cent of the total NPL portfolio by value in Mainland China.[64] In India, the exchange control laws have traditionally restricted investments on onshore lending by overseas distressed funds.[65] The indications, however, are that there are attractive opportunities in Mainland China and India. Both markets are emerging economies and have large markets of distressed loans; as at 2020, the volume of NPAs in Mainland China and India stood at US$503.5 billion and US$126.4 billion respectively.[66] While the regulatory framework either requires or incentivises the sale of the bank NPAs to the asset management companies, as further described in chapter five, foreign distressed funds have worked with these companies in India[67] and Mainland China.[68] The agency and coordination costs posed by asset management companies are discussed further in chapter five.

4.3. STRATEGIES TO DEAL WITH AGENCY AND COORDINATION COSTS OF CREDITOR–CREDITOR CONFLICTS IN ANGLO-AMERICAN RESTRUCTURINGS

Chapter 11 provides a framework for a 'structured' bargaining to take place among the creditors and the management of the debtor within specified parameters.[69] These negotiations relate to how the assets are deployed (or how the company is reorganised) and how the assets are to be distributed.[70] At the end of the negotiations, the management of the debtor company puts forward the plan and the creditors in similar classes will vote on the plan. The plan is binding if the majority in number and two-thirds in amount of vote in favour of the plan. Similarly, in the English scheme

[61] Moody's, 'China's New Distressed Bond Market to Boost Liquidity and allow for risk based trading' (31 May 2019), available at www.moodys.com/research/Moodys-Chinas-new-distressed-bond-market-to-boost-liquidity-and--PBC_1178611.

[62] D Mallick, 'SEBI move to allow trading in 'defaulted debt securities' is welcome' *HinduBusinessline* (13 July 2020), available at www.thehindubusinessline.com/opinion/sebi-move-to-allow-trading-in-defaulted-debt-securities-is-welcome/article32065894.ece.

[63] eg 'Fees Hinder Entry of Foreign Distressed Debt Funds – Report' *Regulation Asia* (18 February 2020) (transaction fees can be up to 15% of the deal value).

[64] Figures are from Deloitte LLP, 'Deleveraging Asia' Financial Advisory (2019).

[65] N Narayan, 'A Guide to Special Situations and Distressed Investments in India for International Investors' (2018) 8 *Emerging Markets Restructuring Journal* 1.

[66] Statistics obtained from CECIC databases and China Banking and Insurance Regulatory Commission (for China) and RBI Statistical Tables. Further details on the NPAs are found in ch 5, Figures 5.2 and 5.5.

[67] Narayan, 'A Guide to Special Situations' (n 65).

[68] C Miao and H Liu, 'China: Legal Avenues for Foreign Investors to Participate in China's NPL Market' *Mondaq; JunHe Law Office* (3 January 2017).

[69] O Hart, 'Incomplete Contracts and Control' (2017) 107 *American Economic Review* 1731. See below, section 4.3.1.1.

[70] ibid.

of arrangement and the Part 26A restructuring plan, the management of the debtor negotiates with the creditors as to both the deployment and distribution questions before the debtor proposes the scheme to its creditors. This section compares the similarities and differences in how both the US and the UK deal with the issues relating to deployment and distribution.

4.3.1. The Deployment Question

4.3.1.1. Giving the Company Breathing Space to Restructure; Automatic Stay and Ipso Facto *Restrictions*

The US Chapter 11 and UK schemes have significant differences in how the negotiations take place between the debtor and the creditors. When the debtor is negotiating with the creditors, Chapter 11 imposes a strong automatic stay or a moratorium on creditor claims and restrictions of the operation of *ipso facto* clauses in certain kinds of contracts. Upon filing of the bankruptcy petition, the debtor enjoys an automatic moratorium against all creditor actions and enforcement of security without leave of court, while its management has 120 days to exclusively formulate the plan.[71] Chapter 11 also restricts the ability of the debtor's counter-parties to contracts invoke *ipso facto* clauses, and the debtor may 'cherry pick' from among outstanding contracts, subject to certain limitations.[72] In fact, Jackson argues that the justification of bankruptcy law is the strong automatic stay which prevented creditors, including secured creditors, from racing to grab the assets from the debtor company.[73] Once creditors are prevented from grabbing the assets, creditors have the incentive to cooperate and bargain over how the assets could be put to the best use, whether it is a liquidation, a sale of assets or a reorganisation. The moratorium facilitates such negotiation. Closely related to the automatic stay is the ban on *ipso facto* clauses to prevent suppliers and trade creditors for relying on their otherwise strict legal rights in terminating contracts or imposing more onerous terms (such as acceleration of payment) on the ground of the reorganisation proceedings. However, *ipso facto* clauses can also be costly as they can trigger strategic defaults to rearrange contractual obligations that are otherwise not available outside of bankruptcy.[74]

In contrast, in the UK, prior to the Corporate Insolvency and Governance Act 2020 (CIGA), there was no automatic stay when debtor companies proposed to undertake schemes of arrangement. The reason is that schemes were primarily used to reorganise financial debt – there was no requirement for an automatic stay against legal action because the inter-creditor agreement among the creditors that are typically used are based on the London Loan Market Association, which contains the moratorium against a junior creditor or bondholder against enforcement actions.

[71] 11 USC §362(a).
[72] 11 USC §365(e) and §541(c).
[73] TH Jackson, 'Bankruptcy, Non-Bankruptcy Entitlements, and the Creditors' Bargain' (1982) 91 *Yale Law Journal* 857.
[74] K Delaney, *Strategic Bankruptcy: How Corporations and Creditors Use Chapter 11 to Their Advantage* (Berkeley, University of California Press, 1999).

Creditors who did not wish to support the reorganisation would have traded their bonds in the distressed debt market.[75]

The CIGA introduced a free-standing statutory moratorium for a company in financial distress, which is available upon making a filing with the court.[76] It provides to a company an initial breathing space of 20 business days and the directors may file for an extension of a further 20 business days. Any extension beyond 40 business days requires the consent of the company's pre-moratorium creditors or the court. The moratorium ends, among other circumstances, once the company enters into administration or liquidation, or if the scheme or plan is sanctioned. Interestingly, there is a capital market exemption to the moratorium which means that many companies that have tapped into the capital markets will not be able to use the exemption.[77]

Further, the CIGA restricts the use of *ipso facto* clauses in contracts for not only the essential supply provisions that were previously found in the Insolvency Act 1986[78] but also the contracts for the supply of goods and services, though there are exemptions.[79] When a company becomes subject to a relevant insolvency procedure, including the statutory moratorium and restructuring plan (but not the scheme of arrangement), the provisions apply to any clause in a contract for goods or services that automatically terminates the contract or entitles the supplier to terminate the contract upon the company being subject to an insolvency procedure.

Where the company enters into liquidation or administration within 12 weeks of the end of the moratorium, the moratorium debts and pre-moratorium debts payable during the moratorium will have priority in distribution ahead of the preferential creditors expense claims under paragraph 99 of Schedule B1 of the Insolvency Act 1986 and floating charge distributions in an administration.[80] The practical implication is that since the financial services debts are not subject of a payment holiday, they will obtain super-priority if the company goes into administration or insolvent liquidation commencing within 12 weeks after a moratorium. However, the debt which is accelerated during the moratorium will not be the subject of super-priority.[81]

4.3.1.2. Dealing with Information Asymmetry: Informational Rights in Negotiations

Under Chapter 11, the US Trustee (under the US Trustee Programme) appoints creditor committees which represent unsecured creditors' interests, usually comprising

[75] Paterson (n 11) 270. For a discussion on how the stay operates in London Loan Market Association's inter-creditor agreement, see generally, M Wolf, 'Benefits of Intercreditor Agreements in Cross-Border Restructurings' (2017) 5 *Norton Journal of Bankruptcy Law and Practice* 630.

[76] Insolvency Act 1986, Pt A1, Ch 2, ss A3–A4 (and for overseas companies see s A5). Part A1 was introduced by CIGA 2020, ss 1–6 and Schs 1–8.

[77] Insolvency Act 1986, Sch ZA1 paras 13–14. The moratorium cannot be invoked by a company if on the filing date it is a party to an agreement which is or forms part of a capital market arrangement, a party has incurred or expected to incur a debt of £10 million under the arrangement (during the life of the capital market arrangement) and the arrangement involves the issue of a capital market investment.

[78] Insolvency Act 1986, ss 233–223A.

[79] Insolvency Act 1986, s 233B. Financial services providers such as lenders are not subject to the *ipso facto* provisions; see the new s 233B(10) of the Insolvency Act 1986 inserting Sch 4ZZA.

[80] Insolvency Act 1986, s 174A.

[81] Insolvency Act 1986, s 174A(4) and (11).

members that represent seven to nine of the debtor's largest unsecured creditors.[82] Creditor committees receive access to the debtor's confidential information and negotiate with the company as to the reorganisation, with the objective of countering the collective inaction that otherwise may exist among the creditors.[83] Creditor committees are found to be associated in certain outcomes of the reorganisations though not necessarily increasing returns to the unsecured creditors.[84] For instance, cases with one single creditors' committee were more likely than cases with no committee or multiple committees to result in plans that lead to liquidation or sale of substantially of the debtor's assets.[85]

In the UK, while there is no formal requirement for creditor committees, in practice, a review of the judgments of the English courts hearing the applications for scheme meetings provides evidence that informal creditor committees among institutional creditors with shared common interests are formed, and they are often advised by legal advisors.[86] These informal creditor committees (also known as ad hoc creditor groups) will advance their sectòrial interests in their negotiations with the debtor company and other creditors.

4.3.1.3. Dealing with Restructuring Innovations

In both US and UK restructurings, to deal with the diverse base of creditors, insolvency practitioners have innovated by introducing the RSAs with creditor groups to improve the likelihood of success of the restructurings.[87] Prior to the creditors' meeting, a debtor may negotiate with certain creditors to enter into an RSA where they undertake to vote in favour of the proposed plan in return for receiving a consent fee or some other benefit of early commitment.[88] Such benefits also include backstop fees payable for underwriting new lending, advisor fees and work fees.[89] RSAs ensure that there is some degree of certainty that the restructuring plan will receive the requisite approval at the time of the scheme meeting.

[82] 11 USC § 1102; see generally MM Harner and J Marincic, 'Committee Capture? An Empirical Analysis of the Role of Creditors' Committees in Business Reorganizations' (2011) 64 *Vanderbilt Law Review* 749.

[83] ibid.

[84] ibid.

[85] ibid.

[86] For example, see *Re Telewest Communications Plc* [2004] EWHC 924 (Ch), where sterling bondholders representing 15% of the sterling bonds formed a committee to oppose the scheme of arrangement that proposed to convert the sterling claims into US dollars in accordance with the rate of exchange that was unfavourable to them; the company had proposed the scheme of arrangement comprising holders of sterling and US dollar bonds in a single class. In *Re Codere Finance II* [2020] EWHC 2441, an ad hoc committee of creditors holding 55% of the notes entered into a lock-up agreement with the company which provided for, among others, work fee (for the work done in the restructuring), backstop fee (conditional upon the scheme being implemented) and payment of the fees of the committee's legal and financial advisers.

[87] For the US, see generally DG Baird, 'Bankruptcy's Quiet Revolution' (2017) 91 *American Bankruptcy Law Journal* 593; EJ Janger and AJ Levitin, 'Badges of Opportunim: Principles for Policing Restructuring Support Agreements' (2018) 13 *Brooklyn Journal of Corporate* 169; DA Skeel, 'Taking Stock of Chapter 11' (2021) 71 *Syracuse Law Review* 931. For the UK, see, eg *Re Telewest Communications Plc* [2004] EWHC 924 (Ch); *Re Noble Group Ltd* [2018] EWHC 2911 (Ch).

[88] See eg *Re Telewest Communications Plc* [2004] EWHC 924 (Ch) [52].

[89] See eg *Re Codere Finance II (UK) Limited* [2020] EWHC 2441 (Ch).

However, RSAs are controversial. In addition to concerns as to the parity of information disclosed to all creditors,[90] RSAs also question the equality of treatment of creditors in view of the various fees that are payable only to the creditors signing the RSAs to lock up their support.[91] In the US, bankruptcy courts have upheld RSAs, including those that include signing fees.[92] In the UK, in *Re Noble Group*, the RSA had two types of fees payable to creditors that were parties to the RSA: (1) fees that compensate creditors for waiver of revolving credit facilities and work done pursuant to the scheme; these fees were payable irrespective of whether the scheme became effective and were thus regarded as payments 'made for legitimate reasons and be genuinely independent of the scheme and restructuring',[93] and (2) 'backstop fees', which were fees that compensate creditors for underwriting new financing required for the reorganised company's operational purposes, and thus were conditional upon the scheme becoming effective. For (2), the return to the participating creditors (relative to the outstanding amount) was not large enough to make a difference to a scheme creditor's decision to participate.[94] Even though the size of the combined fees for (1) and (2) was significant, Snowden J did not require these creditors to be separately classified, but the fees were required to be disclosed in the explanatory statement. However, more recent case law in UK has raised the concerns of work fees, expressed as a percentage of the notes that is payable to RSA participants pro rata their value of note-holdings and conditional upon holders with 75 per cent by value of the debt acceding to the lock-up, as being relevant to class composition.[95]

4.3.2. The Distribution Question

4.3.2.1. Dealing with Inter-Class Conflicts with the APR in Chapter 11

In chapter three, I explained that the creditor hold-outs are addressed with the threat of the court imposing a cross-class cram-down.[96] The two important conditions are that the plan must be fair and equitable, and that it must not discriminate unfairly. Taking the latter first, successful claims for unfair discrimination are rare in Chapter 11 plans. For instance, in *In re Breitburn Energy Partners LP*,[97] the court refused to confirm a Chapter 11 plan, ruling that the proposal 'unfairly discriminates' against retail bondholders that held US$44.6 million of the unsecured bond debt as they would be excluded from a rights offering of new equity in the one of the two reorganised firms (after the split) that was available only to accredited investors (comprising

[90] See *Re Sunbird Business Services Ltd* [2020] EWHC 2493 (Ch), which raises concerns on equality of information that is provided. Advanced information is often disclosed to the creditors who are likely to participate in the RSAs to enable an early commitment to vote in favour of the plan.

[91] Wan and Watters, 'Mandatory Disclosure' (2021).

[92] eg *Ad Hoc Committee of Non-consenting Creditors v Peabody Energy Corp* 933 F 3d 918 (8th Cir 2019). For a discussion on the case law on US RSAs, see Skeel, 'Taking Stock of Chapter 11' (2021).

[93] *Re Noble Group Ltd* [2018] EWHC 2911 (Ch) [132].

[94] ibid, [151]–[155].

[95] eg *Re Codere Finance II* (UK) Limited [2020] EWHC 2441 (Ch), [2020] EWHC 2683 (Ch).

[96] O Hart et al, 'A New Bankruptcy Procedure That Uses Multiple Auctions' (1997) 41 *European Economic Review* 461.

[97] 582 BR 321 (Bankr. SDNY 2018).

mostly hedge funds). With the rights offering, the accredited investors would recover more than twice what the retail bondholders would recover.[98]

In relation to the first criterion, for a plan to be fair and equitable, the APR must be complied with. As explained in chapter three, the APR is not without costs, and the disputes between creditors and shareholders often shift to disputes over valuation. Similar disputes arise between creditor conflicts; in fact, where the value 'breaks' in the class of debt is often contentious. US law explicitly draws the distinction between financial and economic distress.[99] Even if the basis of valuation is fixed at the outset (for example, valuing on the basis of a going-concern sale),[100] there remains a choice of established methodologies and assumptions that the valuer may utilise, and the results will depend on those choices. For example, the valuer may pick a discounted cash flow basis rather than using comparable transactions or comparable companies.

Thus, participants have different incentives to exploit the inherent uncertainty in valuation; in particular, senior creditors are incentivised to undervalue the business (and thus negotiating for receiving a larger share of the equity upside) and junior creditors are incentivised to overvalue the business. If the value 'breaks' at the senior tranches of debt, the junior claimants will be regarded as having no economic interest in the outcome of the restructuring. In the event that the restructured business ultimately turns out to be more valuable than all of the debt claims, the senior creditors would be able to keep the surplus.[101] While the court may be called upon to solve the valuation dispute, the court usually does not have any superior information compared to the parties, and inherent uncertainties will mean that the parties will try to avoid a valuation fight with the management team.

Many scholars have attempted to solve the valuation problem in Chapter 11. One view is that the junior creditors are to share in the potential upside in the future, through the 'redemption option value', as discussed by the American Bankruptcy Institute[102] and in chapter three of this book. Adler has suggested a take-it-or-leave-it approach, where, as part of the plan, the debtor makes an offer to the secured creditor. If the plan is rejected by the secured creditor, the collateral must be sold to a third party on the open market and the firm be liquidated. He argues that this approach

[98] ibid, 351.

[99] eg *United Airlines, Inc. v HSBC Bank USA, NA* 416 F 3d 609 (2005) 612–13: per Judge Frank H Easterbrook: 'Many provisions in the [US Bankruptcy Code], particularly those that deal with the treatment of secured credit, are designed to distinguish financial from economic distress. A firm that cannot meet its debts as they come due, but has a positive cash flow from current operations, is in financial but not economic distress. It is carrying too much debt, which can be written down in a reorganization. A firm with a negative cash flow, by contrast, is in economic distress, and liquidation may be the best option. In order to distinguish financial from economic distress, the [US Bankruptcy Code] effectively treats the date on which the bankruptcy begins as the creation of a new firm, unburdened by the debts of its predecessor.' See also G Andrade and SN Kaplan, 'How Costly Is Financial (Not Economic) Distress? Evidence From Highly Leveraged Transactions That Became Distressed' (1998) 53 *Journal of Finance* 1443.

[100] S Paterson, 'Bargaining in Financial Restructuring: Market Norms, Legal Rights and Regulatory Standards' (2015) 14 *Journal of Corporate Law Studies* 344.

[101] See generally, G Gilson, E Hotchkiss and R Ruback, 'Valuation of Bankrupt Firms' (2000) 13 *Review of Financial Studies* 43.

[102] American Bankruptcy Institute (2014), 'Commission to Study the Reform of Chapter 11: Final Report and Recommendations' (2012–14), Section VI.C.1 'Creditors' Rights to Reorganization Value and Redemption Option Value'.

ensures that secured creditors will retain their priority but are not in a position to extract further value from the debtor, and non-viable firms would liquidate promptly without going through a protracted process.[103] However, such an approach requires changes to US bankruptcy law.

Nevertheless, can explicit deviations from the APR ever be justified? From an *ex ante* perspective, deviations from the APR result in an overall increase in the costs of borrowing since senior lenders will adjust their prices to reflect the fact that the loans are now riskier if junior creditors and shareholders may get the value that would otherwise have gone to senior creditors.[104] Hence, deviations only occur in rare instances, if they enhance the overall value of the debtor. For example, trade creditors are able to claim priority ahead by arguing that they are critical vendors to the debtor, and enhance the debtor's overall value, benefiting all creditors.[105] More controversially, roll-up financing has been permitted, which is discussed below.

4.3.2.2. UK's Approach

In UK, cross-class cram-down is not provided for under the English scheme but de facto cram-down may take place using the scheme twinned with a pre-packaged administration. Under this process, the scheme is structured so that it is only necessary to obtain the approval of those classes of creditors who have an economic interest in the restructuring.[106] The administrator will propose a scheme of arrangement to compel the dissenting senior creditors of the company to 'roll over' their interests to a new company (newco), and then effect the sale of shares of the operating subsidiaries of the insolvent company to newco. The 'out of money' or junior creditors remain with the old company, which will not have any assets. In determining whether the creditors are in or out of money, the relevant perspective is where the valuation breaks using a counter-factual analysis, that is, what is the alternative if the scheme of arrangement is not approved, which is either a liquidation or, more commonly, a sale at a going concern by an administrator.[107] That is not the end of the debate, however, as it merely shifts to what should be regarded the market value of the assets, especially when the market value of the assets is depressed at the time of the purported valuation during the restructuring process.[108]

While the English scheme provisions in the Companies Act 2006 do not explicitly allow for a cram-down of dissenting classes, the practice and case law have made several adaptations. First when the scheme is twinned with administration, the sale of the debtor's assets can take place to a new entity and junior creditors of the debtor

[103] BE Adler, 'Game-Theoretic Bankruptcy Valuation' (2012) 41 *Journal of Legal Studies* 209.

[104] eg DG Baird, 'Priority Matters: Absolute Priority, Relative Priority, and the Costs of Bankruptcy' (2017) 165 *University of Pennsylvania Law Review* 785; AJ Casey, 'The Creditors' Bargain and Option-Preservation Priority in Chapter 11' (2011) 78 *University of Chicago Law Review* 759.

[105] *In re Kmart Corp* 359 F 3d 866 (7th Cir 2004).

[106] S Paterson, 'Bargaining in Financial Restructuring: Market Norms, Legal Rights and Regulatory Standards' (2014) 14 *Journal of Corporate Law Studies* 333. An example of the counter-factual being a liquidation was *Re Mytravel Group Plc* [2004] EWHC 2741 (Ch).

[107] Paterson (ibid).

[108] See eg *Re Bluebrook Ltd* [2009] EWHC 2114 (Ch).

company who have no economic interest in the outcome of the restructuring will not be able to vote and are effectively crammed down.[109] Second, the scheme is very flexible as the parties can pick and choose which classes of creditors are the subject of the scheme; recent restructurings have excluded trade suppliers and essential vendors as they are paid in full.[110]

Part 26A of the Companies Act 2006 allows for cross-class cram-down but without explicitly requiring the APR. In the first case involving a cross-class cram-down under Part 26A, *Re DeepOcean I UK Limited*,[111] in exercising the discretion for cross-class cramdown, the court considered such discretion to be an incremental amendment to the court's power, first established in *Re Tea Corporation*,[112] to cram-down the dissenting creditors within no economic interest, to now cram-down dissenting creditors with some economic value. On the facts, it was an appropriate case to exercise the cram-down as the dissenting class of creditors was in fact out of money in the counter-factual scenario where the scheme was not sanctioned. Further, the court also took into account that either all or a very substantial majority of the creditors in the other classes had approved the plan.

4.3.3. Creditor Protection in Cram-Downs

4.3.3.1. Classification

In chapter three, I dealt with the issues surrounding the conflicts of interests that may be faced by creditors who are also related parties of the debtor (through shareholdings). In this chapter, I look at dealing with creditors within the same class. There are three significant features to be highlighted: first, the kinds of creditors whose debt are being sought to be compromised; second, the nature of the debt that is being compromised; and third, whether the debtor company has the choice to select what kinds of debt that is compromised.

Whilst the distribution to the creditors and other stakeholders is important, consideration is just as important as the rules on classification. In Chapter 11, similar claims must be classified in the same class.[113] Small creditors who are paid in full can be in a separate class.[114] US Chapter 11 deals with restructuring of financial debt[115] and operational debt since Chapter 11 involves the restructuring of the whole firm. Similar to schemes, the US Bankruptcy Code provides that 'a plan may place any claim or interest in a particular class only if such claim or interest is substantially similar to the other claims or interests of such class'.[116]

[109] ch 3, section 3.3.1.2.

[110] *Re Virgin Atlantic* [2020] EWHC 2376 (Ch); *Sea Assets v PT Garuda* [2001] EWCA Civ 1696.

[111] [2021] EWHC 138 (Ch). In *Re Hurricane Energy Plc* [2021] EWHC 1759 (Ch), the court declined to exercise the cram-down, but this was in the context of determining that the appropriate comparator was not the one that was selected by the debtor. See also ch 8.

[112] [1904] 1 Ch 12.

[113] 11 USC §1122(a).

[114] 11 USC §1122(b).

[115] Paterson (n 11) 226–28.

[116] 11 USC § 1122(a).

In contrast to Chapter 11, English schemes of arrangement are traditionally used to reorganise or compromise financial debt only,[117] though recent restructurings in the wake of the COVID-19 pandemic have used schemes to compromise operational debt.[118] Further, the prospectus and registration rules for sales of securities have traditionally meant that retail investors do not participate in the bond markets directly. A recent exception is *Re All Scheme Limited*,[119] where the court declined to sanction the scheme of arrangement involving non-sophisticated claimants. All Scheme Limited was a special purpose vehicle set up by Amigo group, a subprime guarantor of loans provided to those unable to borrow from mainstream lenders. Amigo decided that it could not meet the claims of the redress creditors and filed for a scheme of arrangement, arguing that the alternative was imminent insolvency. Under the terms of the scheme, the redress creditors would receive payments from a fund set up to pay these creditors (representing an almost 90 per cent haircut) and shareholders of Amigo would retain their economic interests. The UK Financial Conduct Authority opposed the scheme, arguing that the compromise was not fair, challenging Amigo's assertion that the alternative was imminent insolvency, and the fact that shareholders would retain their economic interests. The court declined to sanction the scheme, even though it met the numerical threshold of creditor approval, on the ground that the disclosure in the explanatory statement were insufficient as it failed to discuss alternatives to imminent insolvency. Emphasis was made that the redress creditors were vulnerable.

Excluding the more recent exceptions, the English schemes are primarily used to restructure the debt of financial creditors that are sophisticated and have access to advisers. While there is somewhat extensive law on classification on creditors, the fundamental test is whether creditors are placed in the same class for the purposes of voting if their rights are not dissimilar such that they can be consulted together with a view to their common interests.[120] Substantive consideration of the classes is made at the first hearing since it allows for much greater certainty in the process.[121] If a creditor's position will improve or decline to such a different extent vis-a-vis other creditors because of the terms of the scheme (and not private interests) assessed against the appropriate comparator (in this case, an insolvent liquidation), then it would be placed in a different voting class. Further, in restructuring of financial debt, these debts are hardly ever disputed by creditors. Thus, the votes that are admitted for the purposes of the restructuring tend to be straightforward.

[117] J Payne, 'The Role of the Court in Debt Restructuring' (2018) 77 *Cambridge Law Journal* 124.

[118] See n 125 below.

[119] [2021] EWHC 1401 (Ch).

[120] *Sovereign Life Assurance Co v Dodd* [1892] 2 QB 573 (UK); *UDL Argos Engineering & Heavy Industries Co Ltd v Li Oi Lin* [2001] 3 HKLRD 634 (Hong Kong). See generally, J Payne, *Schemes of Arrangement: Theory, Structure and Operation* (Cambridge, CUP, 2014) ch 2. See also *Re Hawk Insurance Co Ltd* [2001] EWCA Civ 241; *Primacom Holding sGmbH v Credit Agricole* [2012] EWHC 164 (Ch); *Re New Look Secured Issuer plc* [2019] EWHC 960 (Ch).

[121] Practice Statement (Companies: Schemes of Arrangement under Part 26 and Part 26A of the Companies Act 2006), available at www.judiciary.uk/wp-content/uploads/2020/06/Schemes-Practice-Statement-FINAL-25-6-20-1.pdf. The Practice Statement replaces the Practice Statement (Companies: Schemes of Arrangement) [2002] 1 WLR 1345.

Once non-financial debt is involved, there are greater complexities. First, non-financial creditors such as trade suppliers and landlords are much more varied, and homogeneity within the class cannot be assumed. Second, in many situations, the debt may be disputed, raising questions as to the amount of debt that can be voted upon. While not provided in the legislation, English insolvency practitioners have dealt with this issue in a pragmatic manner; in *Re Noble Group*, the process was modelled on the procedure by which such claims were determined in the liquidation: the claims were assessed by a scheme administrator and if the claims are rejected, the creditors could refer their claims to an independent adjudicator whose decision is final and binding.[122]

Third, even if the operational debt is not disputed, the debtor may choose to target certain trade creditors to be paid in full in order to assure that the business would continue uninterrupted. In the English schemes, it is the prerogative of the company to determine to whom it wants to propose a compromise or arrangement, and can decide not to include certain creditors.[123] There are more recent cases where operational creditors would be bound by the scheme of arrangement, such as that occurred in the *Re Noble* restructuring.[124] Also, in *Re Virgin Atlantic*,[125] the restructuring plan was also used to comprise operational debt of some (though not all) of the trade creditors.

Fourth, the legislation or case law in US and the UK have ensure the catch-all protection to creditors. For instance, creditors in Chapter 11 are protected by 'best interests tests' and that the plan must not discriminate unfairly and has to be fair and equitable. The plan also needs to satisfy the conditions in §1129 of the US Bankruptcy Code. Generally, the secured creditor will be effectively protected by ensuring that it is entitled to full payment over time. In the UK, the court can decline to exercise its discretion to sanction the plan, as occurred in *All Scheme Limited*.

4.3.4. Existing Bank Creditor Providing New Finance

When the company faces financial distress, it may be hard to convince creditors (whether existing or new) to lend to the company. To incentivise the granting of new loans, some jurisdictions have granted priority to these new loans. Under Chapter 11, credit extended during the restructuring process has priority over existing unsecured debt and priority is automatic if the credit is granted in the ordinary course of course of business.[126] Priority can also be obtained over existing secured creditors in certain circumstances if the court sanctions it, notably where the company can show that it cannot obtain the loan without granting such security interest and the secured creditor is adequately protected against loss.[127]

[122] This process was adopted for Noble Group restructuring, due to the complexities involved as the claims included trading claims. See *Re Noble Group* [2018] EWHC 2911 (Ch), [8]–[9].

[123] See *Noble Group Limited* [2018] EWHC 2911 [28], affirming *SEA Assets v PT Garuda* [2001] EWCA Civ 1696; *Re SABMiller plc* [2016] EWHC 2153 (Ch).

[124] [2018] EWHC 2911 (Ch), [36].

[125] [2020] EWHC 2376 (Ch).

[126] US Bankruptcy Code, §364.

[127] US Bankruptcy Code, §364(d).

However, the granting of super-priority of new financing has its own costs as it may only serve as a means to transfer wealth from the existing creditors to the new creditors, without actually providing the means to enhance the debtor's overall financial position.[128] Super-priority financing granted in connection with a company in financial distress is not available in the UK.[129] The CIGA did not introduce the grant of super-security for loans due to concerns that it would result in the increase in the costs of debt.[130] McCormack argues that the effect of the CIGA is to encourage the existing financial creditors to continue to support the distressed company but does not encourage a new lender to come forward, given the lack of super-priority.[131]

More controversially, some existing bank creditors have been able to 'roll up' their pre-petition claims into new secured loans and prioritised loans. In a roll-up, an existing creditor protects its position (and any further capital advanced) by granting financing to debtor in possession regime (DIP financing) where the debtor is required to draw down to pay off some or all of the pre-petition debt. Thus, the pre-petition debt is rolled up into the post-petition debt, which elevates the creditor's pre-petition debt to post-petition secured claim with super-priority administrative expense status. US courts have granted such roll-ups where the debtor is unable to secure other financing, even though it allows some of the creditors to be treated differently from the other creditors.[132]

4.4. THE FEATURES OF ASIAN RESTRUCTURINGS

4.4.1. The Deployment Question

4.4.1.1. Giving the Company Breathing Space: Automatic Stays and Ipso Facto *Clauses*

Mainland China, India and Singapore provide for a stay while the debtor undergoes restructuring. However, only Singapore provides for an automatic stay that is similar to the US. The stay is not automatic in Mainland China or India.

[128] G Triantis, 'A Theory of the Regulation of Debtor-in-Possession Financing' (1993) 46 *Vanderbilt Law Review* 901.

[129] G McCormack, 'Business Restructuring Law in Europe: Making a Fresh Start' (2017) 17 *Journal of Corporate Law Studies* 167. See, however, G McCormack, 'Super-priority New Financing and Corporate Rescue' (2007) *Journal of Business Law* 701 (arguing that in the case of administration, a loan that is made by an administrator on behalf of the debtor may qualify as a 'sum payable in respect of a debt or liability arising out of a contract entered into by the former administrator or a predecessor' under the Insolvency Act 1986, Sch B1, para 99, and would then rank ahead of the administrator's remuneration and also ahead of the floating charge).

[130] UK Insolvency Service, 'Insolvency and Corporate Governance: Government Response' (August 2018), paras 5.177–5.186.

[131] G McCormack, 'Permanent Changes to the UK's Restructuring and Insolvency Laws in the Wake of COVID 19' INSOL International Special Report (2020).

[132] *In re Uno Restaurant Holdings Corporation, et al*, Ch 11 Case No 10-10209 (MG) (Bankr SDNY 20 January 2010); *In re Foamex International Inc, et al*, Ch 11 Case No 09-10560 (KJC) (Bankr D Del 18 February 2009); *In re Aleris International, Inc, et al*, Ch 11 Case No 09-10478 (BLS) (Bankr D Del 12 February 2009); *In re Tronox Incorporated, et al*, Ch 11 Case No 09-10156 (ALG) (Bankr SDNY 12 January 2009); and *In re Lyondell Chemical Company, et al*, Ch 11 Case No 09-10023 (REG) (Bankr SDNY 6 January 2009).

In Mainland China, EBL prescribes that a stay is triggered upon acceptance by the court, and the court has 15 days to decide whether to accept the bankruptcy case.[133] However, the stay does not necessarily continue until the end of the reorganisation, but the actions may resume when the administrator takes control of the estate.[134] It is possible to commence new actions against the debtor only if they are filed in the same court that has accepted the case.[135] Once the court accepts the bankruptcy application, enforcement or processes to preserve the assets including attachment, seizure and freezing against the debtor's assets will cease.[136] Secured creditors affected by the stay during the restructuring process may apply for relief.[137]

In India, under the IBC, the Corporate Insolvency Resolution Process (CIRP) has to be completed within 180 days of admission, which can be extended by a further 90 days by NCLT, and the maximum period in which the process must be completed is 330 days.[138] Once the CIRP is admitted, however, there is no automatic moratorium. Instead, NCLT will declare a moratorium in respect of the debtor, including, in respect of institution or continuation of proceedings and enforcement, if the court determines that there is payment default.[139] If the CIRP is rejected or not approved within the time-bound period, the NCLT shall order the liquidation of the company.[140] When the debtor is granted licences, permits or other concessions by the Indian Government in respect of its business, such grants cannot be terminated or suspended during the moratorium period.[141] Essential goods and services (defined as water, electricity, telecommunication services and information technology services to the extent they are not direct inputs to the output produced or supplied by the corporate debtor) cannot be stopped during the moratorium.[142] However, the IBC does not otherwise deal with the *ipso facto* clauses.[143]

Singapore has a strong automatic stay and is also the outlier among the Asian jurisdictions when it comes to invalidating *ipso facto* clauses. The conditions and the operation of the stay is further explained in chapter seven. As to *ipso facto* clauses, a party is restricted from exercising their rights to *ipso facto* clauses in terminating a

[133] EBL, Art 10. Liu and Wei (2017) criticised the requirement as giving the opportunity for the directors and management to divert assets during this period.

[134] EBL, Art 20.

[135] EBL, Art 21.

[136] Notice of the Supreme People's Court on Issuing the Minutes of the National Court Work Conference on Bankruptcy Trials, effective 4 March 2018 最高人民法院印发《全国法院破产审判工作会议纪要》的通知[现行有效]（法（2018）53号）paras 40–42; Notice of the Supreme People's Court on Issuing the Minutes of the National Courts' Civil and Commercial Trial Work Conference, effective 8 November 2019, 最高人民法院关于印发《全国法院民商事审判工作会议纪要》的通知[现行有效]（法（2019）254号）paras 109–10 (emphasising that tax authorities, public security bureaus and customs should comply).

[137] EBL, Art 75.

[138] IBC, s 12.

[139] ibid.

[140] IBC, s 33.

[141] IBC, s 14.

[142] IBC, s 14. The resolution professional gets to decide which goods services are critical to the operation of the company and those supply of goods or services cannot be terminated, suspended or interrupted unless there are unpaid dues during the period of the moratorium.

[143] In *Gujarat Urja Vikas Nigam Limited v Amit Gupta & Ors*. Civil Appeal No 9241 of 2019 (21 March 2021), the Supreme Court urged legislature to address the issue of the validity of *ipso facto* clauses, noting the gap in the legislation.

contract or exercising certain remedies upon the occurrence of contractually stipulated events by reason for the company's commencement of scheme of arrangement.[144] There is an exception if the operation of the restriction results in 'significant financial hardship' to the counter-party.[145] This exception is modelled on section 65.1(6) of the Canadian Bankruptcy and Insolvency Act.[146] The *ipso facto* restriction is consistent with Singapore's overall rationale of pushing forward a suite of pro-debtor reforms that would promote debt restructuring in the jurisdiction. As at the time of writing, there are no reported cases of how the Singapore court would exercise its discretion, though it is expected that Canadian position, which requires that the hardship must be demonstrated quantitatively, may be persuasive,[147] and that the court will balance the interests of the creditor claiming hardship versus the interests of the other general body of creditors.

In contrast, India, Mainland China and Hong Kong do not have legislation that limits the effectiveness of *ipso facto* clauses, except in the case of India; it only applies to the limited situation involving essential goods and services. The case for the *ipso facto* clauses in these jurisdictions is much less clear because there are complex trade-offs between making inroads into freedom of contract and promoting the overall objectives of the reorganisation. A regime that has a broad prohibition on *ipso facto* clauses coupled with the exception that the scope is to be determined by the courts may lead to excessive satellite litigation and also unequal treatment of the various creditors, even within the same class. For these reasons, it is suggested that jurisdictions be cautious about adopting the ban on *ipso facto* clauses.

In Hong Kong, the scheme of arrangement does not provide for an automatic stay. The insolvency practitioner profession has worked around this by seeking to appoint provisional liquidators to take advantage of the moratorium against the bringing and continuation of legal proceedings once the company goes into liquidation.[148] However, the appointment of the provisional liquidator does not stay the secured creditors' enforcement of their rights. While there is some initial doubt as to whether such an appointment of provisional liquidator in order to stay creditor actions is proper,[149] current case law indicates the court will appoint the provisional liquidator on the ground of asset preservation but, if necessary, restructuring powers will be given to enable them to carry out their duties.[150] Soft-touch foreign provisional

[144] Insolvency, Restructuring and Dissolution Act 2018 (IRDA), s 440. There are carve-outs from the application of s 440 to certain kinds of financial contracts under Insolvency, Restructuring and Dissolution (Prescribed Contracts under Section 440) Regulations 2020 (including derivatives, margin lending or securities contract).

[145] IRDA, s 440(4).

[146] Bankruptcy and Insolvency Act, RSC 1985, c B-3 (Canada).

[147] *Toronto-Dominion Bank v. Ty (Canada) Inc* (2003), 42 CBR (4th) 142, 2003 Carswell Ont 1371 (Ont SCJ). See also JP Sarra, J Payne and S Madaus, The Promise and Perils of Regulating Ipso Facto Clauses, *International Insolvency Review* (13 December 2021), available at onlinelibrary.wiley.com/doi/full/10.1002/iir.1446.

[148] Companies (Winding Up and Miscellaneous Provisions) Ordinance, Cap 32 (Hong Kong), ss 186, 192. See also ch 7, section 7.3.1.2.

[149] *Re Legend International Resorts* [2006] 2 HKLRD 192.

[150] *Re China Solar Energy Holdings Limited* [2018] HKCFI 555. See also CZ Qu, 'The Court's Power to Appoint Provisional Liquidators to Carry Out Rescue Roles: Rethinking Legend' (2019) 28 *International Insolvency Review* 86.

liquidation has also been recognised at common law; in a soft-touch liquidation, the debtor management seeks to appoint provisional liquidators in the place of incorporation of the debtor for the sole purpose of restructuring, and then seek a recognition in Hong Kong. Chapter seven discusses how courts have been treating the soft-touch provisional liquidation in practice. In summary, in recent cases, courts have granted only limited recognition of the appointment of such soft-touch liquidators in the absence of evidence that the debtor is actually attempting a viable restructuring, and have not allowed the appointment to stay winding-up proceedings in Hong Kong.[151]

4.4.1.2. *Information Asymmetry and Creditors' Decision-Making*

In all four jurisdictions, the restructuring framework, as in the Anglo-American approaches, requires creditors to negotiate how they want the reorganised firm to emerge; that is, the deployment of the assets and the decision-making is collective in nature. In Mainland China and India, while the creditors would need to ultimately approve the plan by the requisite majority, both have elements of the PIP models and the insolvency practitioner plays an important role in formulating or proposing the plan. The legislative framework in the DIP model in the Singapore schemes of arrangement does not have a similar role for the insolvency practitioner. In Hong Kong, the practical effect is that secured creditor would need to consent before the scheme takes place for the unsecured creditors. If a moratorium is desired to protect the assets, the company will have to be put into provisional liquidation, where the insolvency practitioner displaces the board of directors. However, the evidence shows that negotiations are often not efficient in the four jurisdictions because of the asymmetry of information between the creditors and the debtor.

4.4.1.2.1. Mainland China

EBL does not impose the informational disclosure requirements by the debtor nor specify a minimum notice period pursuant to which the creditors receive a copy of the plan. For example, the valuer's report on the liquidation value is not disclosed with the plan.[152] Even when the reorganisation plan contemplates a rescue involving significant execution risks, the plan does not disclose the risks in any amount of detail. For instance, in the Pang Da restructuring (see Panel B, Appendix A) where it was contemplated that the new investors promised the future net profits of Pang Da to be no less than a specified amount for 2020/21 or would be required to compensate the listed company in cash,[153] there was no disclosure as to whether such compensation was realistic. In fact, the implementation of the restructuring plan ran into difficulties almost right after the court's approval when the investors did not acquire 4.99 per cent shareholding as promised.[154]

[151] *Re FDG Electric Vehicles Limited* [2020] HKCFI 2931. See ch 7.

[152] See below, n 212 and accompanying text.

[153] Reorganisation Plan of Pang Da Automobile Trade (2019), copy on file with author.

[154] See G Fei Chan, '[RMB]7 billion promise may not be fulfilled', EEC (18 December 2020), available at www.eeo.com.cn/2020/1218/447377.shtml. Eventually the acquisition of the shares was made but the identity of the new investors changed and there was uncertainty if the profit targets could be met.

Creditors have frequently complained about receiving the reorganisation plan only on the eve of the meeting, or a lack of consultation.[155] In fact, the EBL does not contemplate the company or its administrator being required to consult the creditors prior to voting; thus, there is no conspicuous requirement for the bargaining to take place prior to the first round. Under Article 87 of the EBL (the cram-down provision), if parties cannot reach an agreement in the first round of voting, then the proposer can negotiate with the dissenting creditors with a view of reaching an agreement. If an agreement cannot be reached the proposer may then ask for the court to cram-down the plan.[156] One obvious advantage, at least on the books, is that the process is a quick one, compared with the Indian IBC where the committee of creditors (comprising financial creditors) will negotiate how the assets are to be deployed (such as a sale). Thus, the EBL anticipates that if the restructuring is not approved after the two creditors' meeting, the company goes into liquidation.[157]

Creditors' committees are prescribed under the EBL[158] but it appears that they do not have significant powers in the same way as their counterpart in US Chapter 11. For instance, while the creditors' committee reports to the creditors' meeting, they are usually appointed only in liquidation cases.[159] However, there are signs that matters are changing. In December 2020, CBIRC issued new guidelines which call for the establishment of creditor committees comprising not less than three financial institutions who are creditors, including banks, insurance institutions and broker-dealers.[160] Institutional creditors should join the committee, and major decisions require the approval of a majority in number of the committee members that represent more than two-thirds of the total financial claims and not less than half of the total unsecured debt.[161] The introduction of the requirements on the holding of the unsecured debt is an improvement from the previous 2016 guidelines, which only require the approval of a majority in number presenting two-thirds of the total financial claims. Zombie companies and companies which have evaded debts should not be restructured.[162]

[155] eg in the case of Guangxi Nonferrous, the company was admitted to the reorganisation process under EBL by the Nanning court in 2016 and the court appointed the administrator team. However, the bondholders complained that the administrator did not consult them on the restructuring plan except at the two creditors' meetings, and did not seek to apply for an extension of time for the sale when the court-imposed deadline expired. See 'Inter-bank Market First Default' *Yunzhangcaijin* [如何看待银行间市场第一例破产清算], 云掌财经-债券理财 (26 September 2016), copy on file with author.

[156] See also S Gao, 'Cramdown, reorganization bargaining and inefficient markets: The cases of the United States and China' (2021) 30 *International Insolvency Review* S5. See also discussion above, n 210 and accompanying text.

[157] In the case of Guangxi Nonferrous, the creditors failed to approve after the failure to obtain approval after the two creditors' meetings. See n 155. However, in practice, the timelines may be longer. See discussion in ch 7.

[158] EBL, Art 67.

[159] DA Austin and C Lin, 'Bankruptcy with Chinese Characteristics: Insolvency Administration in the People's Republic of China' (2020) 94 *American Bankruptcy Law Journal* 104.

[160] Notice by the China Banking and Insurance Regulatory Commission, the National Development and Reform Commission, the People's Bank of China, and the China Securities Regulatory Commission of Issuing the Work Procedures of Financial Institutional Creditors' Committees [Effective] No. 57 [2020] [中国银保监会、发展改革委、中国人民银行、中国证监会关于印发金融机构债权人委员会工作规程的通知（银保监发[2020]57号）], effective 28 December 2020.

[161] ibid, Art 10.

[162] ibid, Art 12.

4.4.1.2.2. India

Financial creditors decide on the deployment of the assets of the debtor; however, resolution professionals solicit and examine the plans that are submitted by the resolution applicants. Resolution professionals do not have the power of sale without the approval of the committee creditors, and committees have historically favoured the use of Swiss challenge, though in a recent instance, the court did not accepted the argument that the Swiss challenge method was mandatory.[163] The IBC does not prescribe the content of the resolution plan. Instead, the committee of creditors will have to bargain to determine the deployment and distribution of the assets. The role of the committee of creditors has been the subject of controversies.

For instance, in the reorganisation of Sharon Bio-Medicine,[164] Peters Beck & Partners were bondholders of the foreign currency convertible bond, and were also the successful bidders for the company.[165] These bondholders contributed 28 per cent of the vote and had voted for the resolution plan.[166]

In the *Essar Steel* litigation, the Supreme Court of India overturned the decision of the NCLAT, holding that the committee of creditors does not owe fiduciary duties to maximise the recovery under the IBC, even at the expense of the members' own interests.[167] The Supreme Court clarified that it was open for the committee of creditors to negotiate with the resolution applicant, and in its determination of which of the bid by the resolution applicant should be approved, the committee can take into account not only the financial terms, but also the proposed allocation among the secured, unsecured, financial and operational creditors.[168] In other words, the committee has the discretion to decide on the distribution of the proceeds so long as its objectives are to maximise the value of the assets of the debtor and adequately balances the interests of all stakeholders.[169]

But how far should the role of the committee of creditors to maximise the debtor's asset values be pushed? For example, is the role of the committee to maximise the recovery in engagements with the bidder, including being able to extend the deadline for the bidding? In the CIRP of Dewan Housing Finance Corporation, India's first CIRP process involving a non-bank financial company,[170] there were four bidders by the deadline for the bids: Oaktree (a US distressed fund); Piramal (an Indian family-controlled conglomerate); Housing Finance; and SC Lowry. The creditors were due to

[163] The Swiss challenge method is used for government tendering process to facilitate the awarding of contract in the second round of bidding to the highest bidder. See *Saket Tex Dye Private Limited* v *Kailash T Shah* MA 705/2020 in CP 1981(IB)/MB/2019.

[164] The order was made by the National Company Law Tribunal: see *Peter Beck & Partners v Sharon Bio Medicine Limited* [2018] 1 IBJ 254 (NCLT).

[165] See S Mehta, 'Conflict of Interest in Resolution Plans may Erode IBC Credibility' *The Economic Times* (5 July 2018), available at economictimes.indiatimes.com/industry/banking/finance/banking/conflict-of-interest-in-resolution-plans-may-erode-ibc-credibility/articleshow/64849092.cms?from=mdr, arguing that the plan was skewed in favour of the unsecured creditors because there was minimal haircut and they could retain the equity upside while the secured creditors have to experience a substantial haircut).

[166] ibid.

[167] *Committee of Creditors of Essar Steel India Limited through Authorised Signatory v Satish Kumar Gupta & Ors* (hereinafter *Essar Steel*) Civil Appeal 8766-67 of 2019, [93].

[168] ibid, [56].

[169] ibid, [92]–[93].

[170] The IBC was expanded to cover such financial firms in November 2019.

vote on the winning bid. However, Adani Group decided to submit a late bid, on the ground that the bidders failed to fully value the company. Eventually, the committee of creditors allowed for the bidding process to be reopened and Oaktree and Piramal submitting rival bids, with Piramal being declared the winning bidder, notwithstanding that Oaktree put in yet another late bid.[171] While creditors cannot object to the committee of creditors trying to maximise its value, the problem with allowing the bidding process to be reopened meant that no bidder would be willing to put forward its best bid at the outset, thereby prolonging the process right up to the statutory deadline for the plan to be put in place for CIRP.[172]

Further, unlike many jurisdictions, such as the US, in assessing the 'best interests' of the creditors test in approving the plan, the NCLT does not have the authority to analyse or evaluate the commercial decision of the committee of creditors in voting for a particular resolution plan or to reject the plan by dissenting creditors.[173] It can only investigate based on the limited procedural grounds set out in section 61(3) of IBC.[174]

The point left open in *Essar Steel* that the committee of creditors is to balance the interests of the various competing stakeholders left a potential loophole of future challenges appears now to be addressed in *Pratap Technocrats (P) Ltd v Monitoring Committee of Reliance Infratel Limited*,[175] where the court held that there can be no review of the committee of creditors' decision.

4.4.1.2.3. Singapore and Hong Kong

I explained above that until recently English schemes of arrangement typically only involved sophisticated financial creditors and investors.[176] The concentration of the bank creditors gave way in the 1990s to concentration among the private equity fund sponsors. However, in Singapore[177] and Hong Kong,[178] trade creditors routinely have their debts compromised in the scheme of arrangement. The debt markets have also evolved, particularly in the last decade, with an increasing number of companies tapping the bond markets. Further, debt that is held by creditors in Singapore and Hong Kong is widely held to include not only bank creditors and bondholders, but also retail investors (Singapore) or wealthy individual investors (Hong Kong).

[171] B Parkin and S Findlay, 'India bankruptcy law faces vital test with DHFL creditor vote' *Financial Times* (14 January 2021); see also 'DHFL Bidding: CoC Declares Piramal as Successful Bidder' *Business Today* (21 January 2021).

[172] This is 180 days, with extension to 270 days; see n 138 above and accompanying text.

[173] *Sashidhar v Indian Overseas Bank & Ors* Civil Appeal 10673 of 2018 (Supreme Court, 5 February 2019).

[174] These grounds are limited to the situations such as where the plan is contrary to Indian law or there is material irregularity in the conduct of the CIRP, and does not include the merits of the plan.

[175] *Pratap Technocrats (P) Ltd & Ors v Monitoring Committee of Reliance Infratel Limited* Civil Appeal 676 of 2021.

[176] J Payne, 'The Role of the Court in Debt Restructuring' (2018) 77 *Cambridge Law Journal* 124.

[177] For Singapore, eg, see the restructuring of TT International (whose creditors included suppliers and other service providers) in *Re TT International* [2012] 2 SLR 213; see generally, WY Wan, C Watters and G McCormack, 'Schemes of Arrangement in Singapore: Empirical and Comparative Analysis' (2020) 94 *American Bankruptcy Law Journal* 463.

[178] For Hong Kong, eg, see *Re 3D-Gold Jewellery Holdings Ltd* [2009] HKEC 1104, read together with 'Explanatory Statement of 3D-Gold Jewellery Holdings Ltd' (9 April 2009) (copy on file with author), disclosing the list of participating creditors that include suppliers; see *Re Lehman Brothers Securities Asia Ltd (in liquidation)* [2017] HKCFI 204, [2017] 2 HKLRD 871, HCMP 2266/2016 (judgment setting out the profile of the scheme creditors that include suppliers).

Given that English case law has developed disclosure around schemes involving financial creditors, the question arises as to whether they need to be changed when we are dealing with non-financial creditors.

4.4.2. Distribution of Assets

On the issue of distribution, the departure from the APR model in US Chapter 11 is more pronounced in Asian restructurings for Mainland China, India and Singapore. These differences lie in: (1) differential treatment of operational creditors and financial creditors (within the same class of unsecured creditors); (2) treatment of small creditors (within the same class of unsecured creditors); (3) cramming down junior creditors without strictly following the APR (inter-class conflicts); and (4) disenfranchising operating creditors where their debts are disputed.

4.4.2.1. Differential Treatment of Operational Creditors and Financial Creditors

4.4.2.1.1. India: Operational Creditors Cannot Vote

Under the IBC, only financial creditors can vote on the restructuring.[179] While operational creditors can file the CIRP, they do not have any say on outcome of the CIRP, though they are bound by the plan. Unlike English schemes where certain critical operational creditors are usually excluded from the scheme but with the intention that the creditors will be able to recover in full,[180] under the IBC, it is clear that the operational creditors are *not* intended to be paid in full as a matter of course. In fact, prior to the 2019, IBC allowed them minimal distributions that are not less than what they receive in a liquidation.[181] This was changed in the 2019 reforms and operational creditors' position were improved by requiring that they receive not less than the amount they would receive in a liquidation or the amount they would receive if the proceeds from the resolution plan were distributed on the same basis as in a liquidation, whichever is higher.[182]

The issue as to the priority of distributions following pre-bankruptcy entitlements has a somewhat chequered history, though the position is much improved now. In *Essar Steel*, the National Company Law Appellate Tribunal (NCLAT) held the decision to treat the secured creditors and the operational creditors in accordance with the likely payouts in liquidation as discriminatory, arbitrary and inequitable, and that there should be no difference in treating the financial creditors and operating creditors,[183] creating widespread alarm in the lending market. However, the Supreme Court overturned the decision, restoring the right of the committee of creditors to determine that secured creditors have priority.[184] In the meantime, amendments were made

[179] IBC, s 21. In *Swiss Ribbons v Union Bank of India* (2019) 4 SCC 17, the Supreme Court held that the treating the operational creditors differently from the financial creditors was not unconstitutional. See also A Casey and B Zaveri, 'Is the IBC unfair to operational creditors?' *Business Standard* (7 August 2019).

[180] See discussion on *Virgin Atlantic* [2020] EWHC 2376 (Ch) at n 110 (and accompanying text).

[181] IBC, s 30(2) (pre-amendment).

[182] IBC, s 30(2).

[183] See *Committee of Creditors of Essar Steel v Satish Kumar Gupta & Ors* Civil Appeal No 8766-67 of 2019 (Supreme Court referring to the NCLAT decision at [5]).

[184] *Committee of Creditors of Essar Steel v Satish Kumar Gupta & Ors* Civil Appeal No 8766-67 of 2019.

to section 30(2) of the IBC to similar effect. Section 30(4) of the IBC requires the committee of creditors to consider, among others, the 'feasibility and viability' and the distribution waterfall before approving the plan. While there is some uncertainty whether these requirement of feasibility and viability are independent requirements, the Supreme Court has held that it is for the committee of creditors to determine what amounts to feasibility and viability in its commercial wisdom, which is not subject to review.[185]

While there are merits in not getting bogged down in notifying all the trade creditors, which can number several thousand or more, the problem with only focusing on the financial restructuring is that it does not adequately take into account the fact that operational creditors are often critical to the lifeline of ensuring that the business continues. Also, while the company is in restructuring, service providers are reluctant to deal with the debtor,[186] and excluding operational creditors will only serve to exacerbate the problem. Nevertheless, the apparent unfairness to operational creditors did not seem to dampen the operational creditors' willingness to file the CIRP. Figure 4.5 shows that between 1 April 2017 and 31 March 2020, consistently more operational unsecured creditors invoked the CIRP process than the financial creditors. One explanation for this is that operational creditors, particularly critical vendors, are not completely helpless as they can still negotiate for better distribution with the threat of withdrawing their services.

Figure 4.5 Number of CIRPs filed

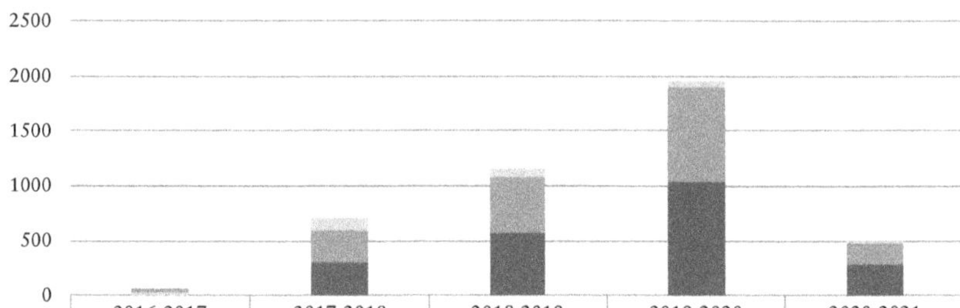

	2016-2017	2017-2018	2018-2019	2019-2020	2020-2021
Corporate debtors	22	110	71	41	21
Financial creditors	8	285	514	870	188
Operational creditors	7	310	567	1032	290

Operational creditors   Financial creditors   Corporate debtors

Source: Data collected from IBBI, Insolvency and Bankruptcy News, July to September 2020 and January to March 2021, available at www.ibbi.gov.in. The number of filings in 2020–21 is lower due to the suspension of the filings under the IBC between 25 March 2020 to 24 March 2021 in view of the COVID-19 situation.[187]

[185] *India Resurgence ARC Private Limited v Amit Metaliks Limited* Civil Appeal No 1700 of 2021.

[186] A Waghmare, 'Systemic change: Hits and misses of India's bankruptcy reforms code" *Business Standard* (5 February 2020).

[187] Insolvency and Bankruptcy Code (Amendment) Ordinance, 2020 effective 5 June 2020 (applies to defaults occurring after 25 March 2020).

An alternative (or complementary) explanation for the invocation by operational creditors can be the success of using the CIRP to recover their debt. Prior to the IBC, recovery of the debt sat at around 26 per cent[188] and the time period for recovery was over 4.3 years.[189] The cost of the recovery was nine per cent.[190] After the enactment of the IBC, as of 31 March 2019, the reported figures showed that the average recovery rate was 48.2 per cent for financial creditors and between 42 per cent[191] to 48.3 per cent[192] for operational creditors. The time taken improved to 1.6 years.[193] Chapter eight further discusses the implication of the improved recovery time-table that the IBC poses in the context of general enforcement of contracts.

Where the state is an operational creditor, there may be other ways in which operational creditors can put pressure on the distribution of the proceeds. In the CIRP involving Aircel, a telecommunications company, the question was whether its spectrum licence granted under the Department of Telecommunications (DOT), which was its most valuable asset, was an asset that could be sold to the new purchaser in the resolution plan.[194] In that case, Aircel also owed substantial fees to DOT, and the DOT had objected to the sale.[195] While it was presented ostensibly as a dispute over the value ascribed to the licence, it has been argued that DOT's objection was due to the fact that, as an operational creditor, it would rank behind the financial creditors and could only recover a portion of its dues.[196]

However, non-adjusting creditors such as tort victims will be vulnerable under section 53 of IBC (since they are not financial creditors and cannot vote). They rank below financial creditors and are unable to negotiate for better distribution because unlike employees and trade creditors who can threaten the company by withholding services, they have no bargaining power.

4.4.2.1.2. Mainland China: Operational Creditors are More Readily Able to Exit in Cash

In recent reorganisations in Mainland China, debtors differentiate between financial and non-financial creditors in their respective recoveries. See Table 4.2 on the

[188] D Mondal, 'How IBC helped improve India's ease of doing business rankings' (24 October 2019), available at www.businesstoday.in/latest/economy-politics/story/how-ibc-helped-improve-india-ease-of-doing-business-rankings-235937-2019-10-24.

[189] Press Information Bureau, Government of India, 'India ranks63 in World Bank's Doing Business Report' (24 October 2019), available at pib.gov.in/newsite/PrintRelease.aspx?relid=193994.

[190] Mondal (n 188).

[191] AR Palepu, 'Operational Creditors Recover 42% Of Claims Under IBC, Says ICRA', Bloomberg (19 June 2019), available at www.bloombergquint.com/business/operational-creditors-recover-42-of-claims-under-ibc-says-icra.

[192] 'Operational creditors benefit equally from IBC: IBBI' *Economic Times* (9 March 2019), available at economictimes.indiatimes.com/industry/banking/finance/banking/operational-creditors-benefits-equally-from-ibc-ibbi/articleshow/68338344.cms?utm_source=contentofinterest&utm_medium=text&utm_campaign=cppst.

[193] Mondal (n 188).

[194] *Union of India v Vijaykumar V Iyer* Company Appeal (AT) (Insolvency) No 733 of 2020.

[195] ibid. The NCLAT held that the spectrum rights were an asset but could not be transferred unless the dues were first paid. As at the time of writing, the case is on appeal before the Supreme Court.

[196] A Handa, 'An Analysis of the corporate insolvency resolution process as a route for acquisitions in India' (2020) 29 *International Insolvency Review* 234.

companies in Appendix A. (The other companies in Appendix A did not disclose differentiated treatment.) The most pronounced difference is the preference for a larger proportion of cash repayments to non-financial creditors, as compared to the financial creditors. In the reorganisation of Yunnan Yunwei Company Limited (2015), for debts exceeding RMB300,000, the financial unsecured creditors will receive 30 per cent, out of which six per cent of the debts exceeding RMB300,000 is payable in cash and 24 per cent in the form of debt-equity swap at an issue price of RMB7.55 per share. The non-financial unsecured creditors receive 30 per cent in cash.[197] Likewise, for Fushun Special Steel Co (2018),[198] the operational creditors are paid 70 per cent in cash over seven years (with the remainder by way of debt-equity swap), while the financial creditors are paid 28 per cent in cash over 10 years (with the remainder by way of debt-equity swap).

Table 4.2 Differential treatment of financial versus non-financial creditors

Name of issuer (English)	Differential treatment
Yunnan Yunwei Company Ltd	For financial creditors whose debt is above RMB300,000, recovery is 30% out of which 6% in cash, 24% in the form of stock in the debt-equity swap; for non-financial creditors whose debt is above RMB300,000, recovery is 30% in cash
Sichuan Liutianhua Company Ltd	Financial creditors whose debt is above RMB100,000 receive debt-equity swap. Non-financial creditors can select either debt-equity swap or cash of 60%
Fushun Special Steel Co	Operational creditors whose debt is above RMB500,000 may elect to be repaid in instalments, enter into debt-equity swap; or receive haircut. Financial creditors are partly repaid within 10 years and the balance by way of debt-equity swap
ST XGMA Machinery Company Limited	Difference in the amounts payable to financial and non-financial creditors with non-financial creditors receiving a higher payout in the initial years
Shenyang Machine Tool (Group) Co Ltd	Debt-equity swap option available for financial creditors, but not for non-financial creditors

Sources: Reorganisation plans of the companies concerned.

Recent restructurings, however, demonstrate that some of the assumptions in treating financial and non-financial creditors (where it is assumed that financial creditors are banks or large institutional investors) may not always hold. For instance, in the restructuring of HNA Group, there are 60,000 of retail investors, mainly employees, who have invested in the wealth-management products and have filed claims.[199]

[197] Reorganisation plan of Yunan Yunwei (2015), copy on file with author.

[198] Reorganisation plan of Fushun Special Steel Co (2018), copy on file with author.

[199] J Wang J and N Yu, 'Bankrupt HNA Group Struggles to Repay 60,000 Retail Investors' *Caixin Global* (20 July 2021), available at www.caixinglobal.com/2021-07-20/bankrupt-hna-group-struggles-to-repay-60000-retail-investors-101742371.html.

4.4.2.2. Preferential Treatment of Small Creditors

4.4.2.2.1. Mainland China

One distinctive feature of Chinese reorganisations is that smaller claimants are not treated the same as the larger claimants, even within the same class. Based on the data on the listed companies that underwent (and completed) their restructuring from 2015 to 2019, found in Appendix A, there is stark deviation for the small debt-holders. In all but two of the completed restructurings in the dataset for 2015–19, the Chinese courts allowed the small holders of debt below the specified threshold (ranging from RMB50,000–1,200,000) to be repaid in full and in cash; the other larger debt-holders are required to swap their credit for equity. See Table 4.3 below.

The differential treatment for the financial versus non-financial creditors can be explained on the ground that for the non-financial creditors, which normally comprise the suppliers and other operational creditors, there are good reasons to provide more favourable treatment so that they are incentivised to continue their contractual relationships to the debtors. Also, given that their debts are usually less than the financial debt, the proposal is more feasible for the debtor to accept. However, unlike US Chapter 11, which requires the small creditors to be treated in a separate class,[200] small creditors are in the same class as the other creditors.

Table 4.3 Differential treatment of small debt-holders

Name of issuer (English)	Differences in treatment for small creditors
Jiangsu Sainty Marine Co Ltd	Creditors with debt less than RMB300,000 are paid in full; creditors owing over RMB300,000 receive cash of 10.56%; balance debt–equity swap
Guizhou Guochang Energy Holding (Group) Co Ltd	N/A
Shenzhen Xindu Hotel Co Ltd	Creditors with debt of less than RMB200,000 paid in full; the rest are paid 60%
Yunnan Yunwei Company Ltd	Creditors with debt of less than RMB300,000 are paid in full; above RMB300,000 for financial creditor, recovery is 30% out of which 6% in cash, 24% in stock; above RMB 300,000 for non-financial creditor, 30% recovery in full
Chuanhua Co, Ltd	Creditors with debt of less than RMB1 milllion repaid in full; the rest receive 50%
Sichuan Liutianhua Company Ltd	Creditors with debt of less than RMB100,000 recover in full; above RMB100,000 financial creditors get debt–equity swap; non-financial creditors choose between debt–equity or cash of 60%

(continued)

[200] 11 USC 1122(b). See n 114 and accompanying text.

Table 4.1 *(Continued)*

Name of issuer (English)	Differences in treatment for small creditors
Liuzhou Chemical Industry Co Ltd	Creditors with debt of less than RMB200,000 paid in full; between RMB200,000 to RMB1 million, creditors get 50% in cash; above RMB1,000,000, creditors receive debt–equity swap
Chongqing Iron and Steel Company Ltd	Creditors with debt of less than RMB500,000 paid in full; those above RMB500,000 receive debt–equity swap
Fushun Special Steel Co	Creditors with debt of less than RMB500,000 paid in full; those above RMB500,000, various options given, including repay in instalments, debt–equity swap or haircut
Yinyi Co, Ltd	Creditors with debt of less than RMB1.2 million repaid in full; those above over RMB1.2 million converted into equity
Qinghai Salt Lake Industry Co Ltd	Creditors with debt of less than RMB500,000 are repaid in cash. For higher amounts, creditors can choose debt–equity swap or repayment in instalments
ST XGMA Machinery Company Limited	Creditors with debt of less than RMB500,000 paid in full; balance is recoverable by way of debt–equity swap
Lotus Health Group Company	Creditors with debt of less than RMB100,000 paid in full; balance is recoverable at 17.48%
Shenyang Machine Tool(Group) Co Ltd	Creditors with debt of less than RMB500,000 paid in full; balance is recoverable by way of debt–equity swap
DEA General Aviation Holding	Creditors with debt of less than RMB500,000 paid in full; exceeding RMB500,000, receive 85% in cash
Ningxia Zhongyin Cashmere Limited	Creditors with debt of less than RMB500,000 paid in full; balance is recoverable by way of debt–equity swap
Shenzhen Feima International Supply Chain Co Ltd	N/A
Liyuan Precision Manufacturing	Creditors with debt of less than RMB100,000 paid in full; balance is recoverable by way of debt–equity swap
Chenzhou City Jingui Silver Industry Co Ltd	Creditors with debt of less than RMB200,000 paid in full; more than RMB200,000 have recovery rate of 46.09% (in the form of a combination of cash and shares).
Pang Da Automobile Trade Limited	Creditors of less than RMB500,000 paid in full; balance is recoverable by way of debt–equity swap
Shanxi J&R Optimum Energy Co, Ltd (now Baoli New Energy Technology)	Creditors of less than RMB50,000 paid in full, balance is recoverable by way of debt–equity swap

Sources: Reorganisation plans of the companies concerned.

This finding on the treatment of small unsecured debtors is consistent with Zhang in respect of corporate restructurings during the pre-2015 reorganisations.[201] The motivation appears to be twofold: first, the administrator is incentivised to achieve the numerical majority among the creditors for the plan to be approved and, hence, propose a scheme that the unsecured small debtors will in all likelihood accept. Second, the favourable payouts to the small debtors would avoid social unrest that may happen if the small debtholders are unhappy with any haircut.[202] The findings are also consistent with earlier studies on restructurings in Mainland China that document that debtors' interest to achieve numerical majority in number; for example, in the restructuring of Shanghai Worldbest Co Ltd, the first reorganisation of a central SOE listed on Shanghai Stock Exchange, related companies of Shanghai Worldbest, who are also its creditors, negotiated with the smaller creditors to purchase their debt in exchange for them voting in favour of the reorganisation.[203]

4.4.2.2.2. Hong Kong and Singapore

With sophisticated creditors of large companies, but with the possible exception of distressed debt investors who acquired the debt after the company becomes financially distressed, creditors and debtors often want to restructure quickly if the company remains economically viable. Debtors will want to reduce their own transaction costs and ensure that financial distress does not become operational distress. Institutional financial creditors will minimise the loss due to the time value of money and will have the resources to hire advisors in the negotiations. However, once non-sophisticated debt investors enter, they are highly fragmented and often unable to afford meaningful representations in the negotiations in demanding for quality information in order to assess their position. The Hyflux incident demonstrates that retail investors are very much worse off than the institutional investors.[204] Financial creditors have no incentive to treat the retail investors fairly since they are subordinated creditors and sit at the lower end of the priority ladder. These subordinate investors are not operational creditors where financial creditors may have some incentives to treat them fairly if they would like the firm to be reorganised and kept alive. In Hong Kong, *Re China Bozza Development Holdings Limited*[205] and *Re Lamtex Holdings Ltd*[206] suggested the directors of the financially distressed companies did not seriously consider their obligations to the individual bondholders, but instead prioritised the interests of the shareholders over the creditors when it came to the process of restructuring.

Thus, in the English schemes of arrangement, which until recently typically only involved financial sophisticated creditors and investors, appears not to fit well in a

[201] Z Zhang, *Corporate Reorganisations in China: An Empirical Analysis* (Cambridge, CUP, 2018) 131–35.

[202] ibid.

[203] INSOL International, *Shanghai Worldbest Co Ltd, Case Study Series* -5 (2011).

[204] See n 48 and accompanying text. See Bloomberg, 'Rich Singapore Investors Stuck as Local Bond Restructuring Drags' *Straits Times* (25 July 2017). Many UK schemes only involve financial creditors. See also Wan and Watters (n 59).

[205] *Re China Bozza Development Holdings Ltd* [2021] HKCFI 1235. See n 54 and accompanying text.

[206] *Re Lamtex Holdings Ltd* [2021] HKCFI 622. See also ch 2.

regime with many dispersed creditors.[207] In Singapore[208] and Hong Kong,[209] trade creditors routinely have their debts compromised in the schemes of arrangement. Further, debt that is held by creditors in Singapore and Hong Kong is widely held to include not only financial creditors but also retail investors. However, unlike the position reached in Mainland China, small creditors and retail investors in Singapore and Hong Kong are often put in the same class of creditors as the other unsecured creditors.

Given the vulnerability of the non-sophisticated creditors, and in light of the findings in chapter three that debtors are often reluctant to disclose information early, the suggestion is that more aggressive consideration by the courts will be required when it comes to non-sophisticated creditors to ensure that they receive information as to the restructuring early in the process. In Singapore, the court has the opportunity to consider the request by the creditors on provision of information at the stage of extension of moratorium. In chapter seven, I discuss how the conditions of the moratorium should be imposed as to information requests. Likewise, in Hong Kong, at the stage of the application of recognition of soft-touch provisional liquidation or adjournment of winding-up proceedings, there needs to be aggressive screening of non-viable companies and stalling tactics by the management.

4.4.2.3. *Inter-Class Conflicts: Departing from the APR*

Mainland China and India do not have an explicit APR. This has led to several problems in practice when the creditors negotiate over the distribution.

4.4.2.3.1. Mainland China

Unlike US Chapter 11, which lists other requirements for cram-down such as the best interests of the creditors test, and the APR being satisfied, Article 87 does not have the APR. Instead, the safeguards are more limited: (1) secured creditors shall receive payment up to the value of the relevant security and receive fair compensation for any delay in receiving their payment, unless they agree with the plan proposal;[210] (2) common creditors cannot receive less than what they receive in a liquidation; (3) rights of contributors are adjusted fairly; and (4) the business plan is feasible. For (1), there is no criteria on how the valuation of secured asset in question takes place so in the event of under-valuation by the plan proposer (or the debtor company), the secured creditor may be prejudiced. Valuation is a significant problem. Chinese courts

[207] Payne, 'The Role of the Court' (2018) 124.

[208] For Singapore, eg, see the restructuring of TT International (whose creditors included suppliers and other service providers) in *Re TT International* [2012] 2 SLR 213; see generally, Wan, Watters and McCormack, 'Schemes of Arrangement in Singapore' (2020) 463.

[209] For Hong Kong, eg, see *Re 3D-Gold Jewellery Holdings Ltd* [2009] HKEC 1104, read together with Explanatory Statement of 3D-Gold Jewellery Holdings Ltd (9 April 2009) (copy on file with author), disclosing the list of participating creditors that include suppliers; see *Re Lehman Brothers Securities Asia Ltd (in liquidation)* [2017] HKCFI 204, [2017] 2 HKLRD 871; HCMP 2266/2016 (judgment setting out the profile of the scheme creditors that include suppliers).

[210] EBL, Art 87(1).

hire third-party experts to assess the liquidation value of the debtor.[211] The report of the valuer is not disclosed with the reorganisation plan, but creditors may separately request permission from the court to inspect the report.[212]

However, the value of the debtor company does not take into account the listing status, which in itself could be very valuable, but whose value is not reflected in the financial statements and whose value is also speculative since it would depend on how much other purchasers are willing to pay in light of the existing queues to be listed and whether the purchaser can obtain approval to use the shell status to effect back-door listing.[213] If the listing status ends up being sold for value, the unsecured creditors do not receive the value since the listing status is not an asset listed in the financial statements.[214]

While the courts are able to exercise the power of cram-down, there were comparatively fewer cram-down cases for listed companies under the EBL during 2015–19 compared to the immediately preceding period; there was one case for listed company restructuring,[215] as compared with four out of 19 during 2010–14 (21 per cent).[216]

The more recent case of Dandong Port Group debt restructuring, which was approved in 2019, represented somewhat of a setback. In that case, the restructuring plan called for the debtor company, together with its affiliates, to be restructured into two different entities, with the allegedly profitable assets transferred to one company (owned by the state-owned provincial entity) and the less profitable assets transferred to another company that was owned by the creditors.[217] The court crammed down the restructuring plan, notwithstanding the objections of the unsecured creditors.[218] Other cases in which cram-downs have been imposed for unlisted onshore companies (outside our dataset) have also been heavily criticised.[219] In the longer term, it remains to be seen whether Dandong Port Group restructuring is an aberration.

[211] Gao, 'Cramdown, reorganization bargaining and inefficient markets' (2021).

[212] This is based on the conversations with insolvency practitioners active in Mainland China.

[213] See Y Xie, '"Shell company" Shares Plunge as China Tightens Back-door Listing Approvals' *South China Morning Post* (20 June 2016).

[214] See Gao (n 156), raising the example of ST Jincheng, where the cram-down took place in the context of the value of the company's assets (excluding the listing status) being very much less than the outstanding claims, but it turned out that the listing status was sold for RMB3.46 billion. Much of the value was distributed to the controlling shareholder.

[215] ch 3, section 3.4.2.2.

[216] Data for 2010–14 is obtained from H Zhao, *Government Intervention in the Reorganisation of Listed Companies in China* (Cambridge, CUP, 2019) and S Li and Z Zheng, *Law Review of Corporate Reorganization and Restructuring* [公司重整法律评论：上市公司重整专辑] vol 5 (Beijing, China Law Press [法律出版社], 2019).

[217] See Bloomberg, 'China Port Defaulter's Bankruptcy Ruling Stirs Up a Storm' *Bloomberg News* (14 January 2020).

[218] Judgment of the Dandong Intermediate People's Court on Dandong Port Group debt restructuring [辽宁省丹东市中级人民法院民事裁定书：关于批准丹东港集团重整草案的裁定 (2019) 辽06破2-5号], dated 31 December 2019.

[219] In 2015–19, but outside of the sample in Appendix A (which comprises listed companies and corporate onshore bond defaults), there is another high-profile case involving cram-down exercised by the court in the subsidiaries of LDK Solar in 2016. The court crammed down the bank creditors who voted against the plan on the ground that they would receive only 14.75% return as part of the reorganisation; however, pursuant to the cram-down, ironically, these creditors' return would fall to 6.62%. See Sina Finance, 'Jiangxi LDK's Reorganisation Plan Crammed Down by the Court' [江西赛维重整计划被法院强裁 12 家债权银行成冤大头]' *Sina Finance* (October 2016). For criticism of the LDK restructuring, see S Li, 'Reforms to the Chinese EBL [李曙光:改革和完善我国破产重整中的关键制度]' *Chinaform.net*

4.4.2.3.2. India

In the *Essar Steel* litigation, the Supreme Court held that it is for the financial creditors to decide on how the assets are to be deployed.[220] However, the Supreme Court also held that the objectives of the committee of creditors are to maximise the value of the debtors' assets.[221] As outlined above, it is by no means clear as to how the committee of creditors can so act when its members are not independent but represent their own interests, though the scope of challenge is reduced in more recent cases.[222]

There is one further limitation in the IBC relating to dissenting financial creditors, which is designed to provide a stick to the hold-out financial creditors. Section 30(2) of the IBC provides that dissenting financial creditors shall receive at least the amount that would have been received if the liquidation value had been distributed in accordance with section 53 (the waterfall mechanism for distribution in the event of a liquidation).[223] It would appear that the court will uphold a committee of creditors' decision, even if the result is one in which a financial creditor receives a lower payout than what that they would receive upon liquidation under section 53.[224] In *DBS Bank Ltd v Shailendra Ajmera (Resolution Professional of Ruchi Soya Industries Limited)*,[225] the committee of creditors approved a resolution plan which treated the secured creditors (including DBS Bank) equally prior to section 30(2) of the IBC coming into force. DBS Bank argued that its security was worth 90 per cent of its claim (had the company been liquidated), but the committee of creditors approved a plan that would entitle it to receive only 49 per cent. DBS Bank dissented at the vote of the committee of creditors. Nevertheless, the NCLAT upheld the resolution plan and, interestingly, held that even if section 30(2) of the IBC had applied, DBS Bank was not entitled to receive more funds as a dissenting creditor just to get better treatment over the other lenders.[226] The advantage of this approach is that the courts will not have to review each decision of the committee of creditors, but it raises the question as to whether the financial creditors can be said to be truly in the same class if the value of their collateral differs significantly from one another.

4.4.2.4. *Operational Creditors and their Disputed Debts*

The English scheme of arrangement has several disadvantages from the perspective of operational creditors who have disputed debts with the company. When the existence

(20 November 2019), available at www.chinareform.net/index.php?m=content&c=index&a=show&catid=29&id=34835.

[220] *Essar Steel*, nn 167-69 above, and accompanying text.

[221] ibid.

[222] ibid.

[223] IBC, s 30(2).

[224] See the Supreme Court of India in its recent judgment in the matter of *Maharashtra Seamless Steel Ltd v Padmanabhan Venkatesh & Ors*, Civil Appeal No 4242 of 2019, upheld the primacy of 'commercial wisdom' of the committee of creditors and held that there is no requirement in s 30(2) that amounts payable must be higher than the liquidation value of the debtor.

[225] Company Appeal (AT) (Insolvency) No 788 of 2019.

[226] ibid.

and/or amount of the debt is disputed, how much should the company admit for the purposes of voting at the scheme meeting? What if the disputed debts are large enough to block the scheme or would swing the outcome of the scheme meeting? It is often not practical to require the matter to be litigated and concluded prior to the scheme meeting.

This problem arose in Hong Kong, Singapore and India. In *Re UDL Argos Engineering & Heavy Industries Co*,[227] involving a scheme of arrangement of the debtor, N argued that it was a creditor under a guarantee issued in respect of a construction contract entered into between N and the debtor's subsidiaries. The subsidiaries disputed liability and asserted a cross-claim against N. The Court of First Instance held that if the disputed claim has commenced arbitration, the company should need to wait for arbitral award (and presumably this should apply to litigation).[228] However, on the facts of the case, proceedings had not yet commenced. The company disputed liability, and rejected the claims in whole for voting purposes in the scheme of arrangement.[229] The Court held that as there were no *mala fides* on the part of the company, the company could reject the claims on the ground that these disputed claims were not claims that could allow the company to bring a winding-up petition.

However, a different approach was taken in Singapore. In *Royal Bank of Scotland v TT International*,[230] the Court of Appeal had to consider the creditors of disputed debts who held the swing votes. TT International was listed on the Singapore Exchange and was in the business of trading and distributing consumer electronic products. The global financial crisis of 2008 hit the business very badly and it ran into serious financial difficulties, owing significant sums to a number of bank creditors as well as its contractors. The company proposed a scheme of arrangement involving a combination of reverse Dutch auction, repayment over an extended period and conversion to equity. The chairperson of the scheme meeting, who was also the proposed scheme manager, N, made several judgement calls in admitting certain debts for the purposes of voting at the scheme meeting and rejecting the rest. The scheme was voted and approved by a slim majority just over the 75 per cent approval threshold and sanctioned by the High Court.

However, there are certain unusual features of the scheme meeting; for instance, the creditors were not provided with the list of scheme creditors and the quantum of claim for the purposes of voting prior to the vote. Instead, even after the vote took place, N was still adjudicating the proofs of debt and the report of the scheme meeting took place more than two months after the date of the scheme meeting.[231] N later separately appointed special accountants to review the assessment of the proof of debts, which concurred that there were reasonable grounds for N's decisions. The steps that were taken can be contrasted with the later UK case of Noble Group restructuring where the adjudication by the assessor occurred prior to the vote.[232]

[227] [2000] HKCFI 1568. The matter went on appeal but on different points: [2001] 3 HKLRD 634.
[228] [2000] HKCFI 1568, [38].
[229] ibid, [41].
[230] [2012] 2 SLR 213.
[231] ibid, [96].
[232] See n 122 above and accompanying text.

On appeal to the Court of Appeal, one of the bank creditors argued that where the disputed debt had the prospect of swinging the outcome of the vote, the disputed debt should be excluded. Ho Lee, the debtor's main contractor, submitted a claim of S$84.56 million (which Ho Lee argued represented damages payable to sub-contractors and suppliers as a result of the debtor's termination of the construction contract) and loss of profits due to the termination of contract. N admitted only S$22.77 million on the basis that there was insufficient documentary evidence. Ho Lee had voted against the scheme. Ho Lee argued that during the two-month period between the scheme meeting and the confirmation of the results, N would have known how each creditor voted but not how much the claim was admitted, giving N 'perfect foresight' when it came to adjudicating the claims submitted for voting.[233]

The Court of Appeal held that the decisions of N were matters that could be adjudicated by the court, and held that the damages claim was not supportable (since there was in fact no claim against Ho Lee), but Ho Lee could claim for the loss of profits, by reference to an objective criteria: (1) the average of Ho Lee's profits (on a percentage basis) in three of its largest contracts in the last two years; and (2) apply that percentage to the contract with the debtor.

After the enactment of IRDA, Parliament opted for an independent assessor to adjudicate the dispute between the opposing creditor and the chairperson of the meeting on the proof of debt.[234] A person who disagrees with the decision of the independent assessor can file an application to the court.[235] The independent assessor's remuneration is borne by the opposing creditor, though the court can depart from the default rule.[236]

Similar issues arose in India, where several operational creditors made claims to the resolution professional in *Essar Steel*, which were disputed by the company.[237] The resolution professional admitted the claims on the notional value of INR1. However, the NCLAT had instead adjudicated on these claims on the merits, and allowed them to be admitted. On appeal, the Supreme Court clarified that the jurisdiction of the resolution professionals is limited to the verification and collation of the claims, and not the adjudication of these claims, and set aside the admission of these disputed claims. More pertinently, the Supreme Court held that the successful resolution applicants would be able to acquire the assets free from the prior claims (including the disputed claims). The implication is that the operational creditors would not be able to bring their actions for recovery thereafter.

4.4.2.5. *Vulnerable/Non-Adjusting Creditors*

The most difficult situation deals with the case of the vulnerable or non-adjusting creditor, such as tort victims. In regimes where restructuring only takes place among

[233] At [98].

[234] IRDA, s 68(9), read with Insolvency, Restructuring and Dissolution (Corporate Insolvency and Restructuring) Rules 2020, r 44.

[235] ibid, r 46.

[236] Insolvency, Restructuring and Dissolution (Proofs of Debt in Schemes of Arrangement) Regulation 2020, r 6.

[237] *Committee of Creditors of Essar Steel India Limited (through authorized signatory) v Satish Kumar Gupta and Others* (2020) 8 SCC 531, [67].

the financial creditors but binds the operational creditors (such as India), the non-adjusting creditors are the most vulnerable. As is the case under Anglo-American regimes, these are not persons who are in a strong bargaining position with the debtor. However, more generally, should tort victims be given the highest priorities? Adler and Capkun have argued that when companies are in financial distress or are declining, management is incentivised to use secured credit to finance their operations, creating externalities for the non-adjusting creditors, and hence the latter should be prioritised, even ahead of the secured creditors.[238]

Further, if the debtor proposes to enter into a settlement agreement with the non-adjusting creditors in a bid to resolve the uncertainty required to resolve large-scale claims that threaten the survival of the business, there is the added complexity in evaluating whether the release of these claims is made with the full disclosure of relevant information.[239]

4.5. ENHANCING THE RESTRUCTURING REGIME IN ASIA: LESSONS AND IMPLICATIONS

4.5.1. The Advantages and Limits of the APR and Equal Treatment

In chapter three, I argued that there are good reasons for deviations from the absolute priority rule (APR), which allows for the equity retention due to the peculiar agency costs arising from shareholder–creditor conflicts. In jurisdictions with companies that have controlling shareholders who are families or the state, it is necessary for the modification of the APR to incentivise new investment or a rescue of otherwise economically viable companies by controlling shareholders. In the case of *cross-class* creditor–creditor conflicts, however, I would argue a strict adherence to the APR regime where a cross-class cram-down of *creditors* is effected. Strong justifications will be required for departure from this rule.

True, there are good reasons to think that some of the deviations to the APR may facilitate the ability of the creditors to reach a conclusion to the bargain due to uncertainties as to valuation. However, bargaining remains a costly process and the costs of bargaining can be better utilised for other socially useful functions. When the decision is made to sell the assets and the choice is between various bidders, there is no reason for the creditors to bargain for their entitlements; instead, it is much more straightforward for creditors to receive the distributions in accordance with the pre-bankruptcy waterfall. Otherwise, potential unfairness as to the distribution (that is, who gets what) means that the courts will be required to police the distribution, generating satellite litigation or uncertainty. The following are illustrative examples.

In India, a number of disputes in the case law centre around who is a financial creditor and the priority of the secured versus unsecured creditors. In the former,

[238] BE Adler and V Capkun, 'Debt-Equity Conflict and the Incidence of Secured Credit' (2019) 62 *Journal of Law & Economics* 551.

[239] Wan, Watters and McCormack (n 177) (on the case study of a large-scale settlement scheme involving securities law violations in Singapore).

conceptually, other than banks and non-bank financial companies, it is not always clear whether a lender should be properly regarded as a financial or operational creditor. For instance, there was considerable litigation as to whether a financial creditor includes a home-buyer, though the issue was finally settled with the enactment of the Indian Insolvency and Bankruptcy Code (Second Amendment Act) 2018 in favour of the home-buyer.[240] Nevertheless, it is not obvious how the home-buyer should be represented on the committee of creditors when they constitute hundreds of thousands of real estate developer failures. In the *Essar Steel* litigation, the Supreme Court (and legislature) reached the result that would have held the parties to their pre-bankruptcy waterfall entitlement. Yet, instead of a hard rule requiring the creditors to distribute in accordance with such entitlement, the Supreme Court instead required the committee of creditors to take into account the proposed allocation to the various classes of creditors and balance the interests of the various stakeholders. While this appears to put in place a creditor protection mechanism, the committee is never the right party to do so, particularly when its members are not dispassionate and are on the committee to protect their own interests. The better view is that the creditors only determine the issue of deployment of assets, and not determine how the assets are to be distributed. The latter question should be determined based on the creditors' pre-bankruptcy waterfall entitlements.

When it comes to within-class creditor conflicts, I would argue in support of treating all creditors within the same class equally. If a departure is proposed, strong justifications are required on the grounds that the outcome is better off for the creditors as a whole. For instance, small creditors can be paid off in full; the reason is not because their votes should count but because it is expedient not to involve them in the bargaining process and thereby will save overall costs of restructuring. The key point is that classification, even within the class of secured creditors, will need to be carefully determined. Hence, in India, I argue that contrary to *DBS Bank Ltd v Shailendra Ajmera (Resolution Professional of Ruchi Soya Industries Limited)*, financial creditors with different recoveries of the collateral should not be put in the same class for their entire debt.

In Mainland China, until recently, the lack of a formal structured negotiation in the creditors' process, including the fact that creditors' committees are not institutionalised, has led to the administrator not consulting the creditors prior to holding the vote. Yet, all unsecured creditors are put in the same class, even though in certain situations, there is differential treatment of the financial and non-financial creditors, as shown in the cases in Table 4.2 above. One can argue that the approach is not objectionable if financial creditors are treated differently because they acquiesced to take greater risks of the debt–equity swap because they are in a better position to bear the risks as compared to the non-financial creditors. However, given the increasing complexity of restructurings and where financial creditors include retail investors, the assumption that they are better risk-bearers does not always hold. A more principled approach is to disallow the differentiated treatment if the creditors are to be grouped

[240] See discussion in *Jaypee Kensington Boulevard Apartments Welfare Association & Ors v NBCC (India) Ltd & Ors* Civil Appeal No 3395 of 2020.

in the same class unless justifications can be demonstrated that would overall lead to the facilitation of the process.

Deviations of priority require court oversight, and with the judicial resources at a scarcity, it is often not the most appropriate forum of determining whether these deviations are justifiable. Hence, it is more efficient to leave the issue of bargaining over the deployment of the assets to creditors only (without the court policing the outcome of the bargain unless there is a defect in the process of bargaining).

There remain three final questions for insisting the adherence to the APR in inter-class creditor conflicts and equal treatment for creditors in the same class. First, is the treatment fair to subordinated creditors? If the proposed framework is accepted, subordinated creditors will be worse off since they rank above shareholders, yet do not have a say over the outcome (given that my argument is that any limited exception to the APR is for controlling shareholders whose support may be required for the restructuring). One counter-argument is that if the subordinated investors, *ex ante*, know that this is the outcome, it would have been priced into the debt. In Singapore, the Hyflux demonstrates the vulnerability of the retail subordinated investors or individual wealthy but unsophisticated investors, but this is more of a solution that needs to be targeted at educating this group of investors who may not fully understand the nature of their investment.[241]

Second, how about unsecured bank creditors who wish to roll up their pre-petition debt (and thus are able move up the priority chain in comparison with other creditors in the same class)? Roll-up financing is arguably only possible in Singapore among the four Asian jurisdictions. In theory, the judges can examine the DIP financing (including roll-up financing) and reject those that are problematic as merely transfers of wealth, as opposed to adding value to the debtor.[242] However, the introduction of judicial discretion into the process may not be beneficial, particularly if there is no established market for DIP financing in order to determine whether a DIP loan is uncompetitive or whether such DIP financing merely exacerbates the disparity of treatment among the creditors (that is, between those willing to grant the roll-up and those that are not). These considerations weigh against allowing roll-up financing, given the evidence that the benefits of such financing are often not clear.

Finally, on non-adjusting creditors, including tort victims, adherence to the APR would put them in a vulnerable position as unsecured creditors since they rank behind the secured creditors and are unable to offer to roll up the debt (which is the case for the unsecured bank creditors). Settlement claims with this group is often plagued with disclosure challenges as to what would constitute sufficient information for them to make a decision. Given that the key goal of restructuring law is to minimise the transaction costs of the restructuring, allowing these claims to jump ahead (as argued by Adler and Capkun, 2019) would disincentivise the debtor companies from filing for restructuring early to resolve the problems.

[241] See above, n 49 and accompanying text.
[242] See above, n 128.

4.5.2. Reducing the Costs of Negotiation Among Creditors

If the above suggestion is accepted, creditors will focus their bargain over deployment of assets, as opposed to distribution. In the creditors' structured negotiation, given the scarcity of judicial resources, the involvement of the court should not be the only or main means of supervising the process of bargaining. Instead, the approach should be to focus on willingness of creditors to enter into good faith bargaining process of Asian restructurings can be enhanced in the following areas: (1) institutionalising the committee of creditors and incentivising them to negotiate in good faith; and (2) having an automatic stay and restricting the use of *ipso facto* clauses.

4.5.2.1. Incentivising Good Faith Negotiations of Creditors

The presence of large numbers of creditors will make the bargaining process difficult. Thus, the creditors' committee serves as an important bridge between the creditors and the debtor company. Mainland China regulatory frameworks provide for the committee of creditors in bond restructurings[243] as well as committees of financial creditors in large non-financial enterprises.[244]

However, institutionalising the committee of creditors is not the end of the process. The key is to incentivise creditors to negotiate in good faith; section 4.3 above identifies two main obstacles in inter-class creditor and within-class conflicts which may lead to delay in reaching the agreed outcomes: the presence of asymmetric information; and conflicts of interests. Asymmetric information leads to parties making low-ball offers which are then rejected, leading to delays. Conflicts of interest leads to a creditor rejecting an otherwise optimal proposal because of his/her private interests (such as being creditors in a different class) dictate a different proposal that would allow a greater capture of the remaining assets. Conflicts of interest can arise when the secured creditor, who is over-secured, prefers a liquidation and a fire-sale, even if such sale is substantially below the market price.

In relation to asymmetric information, chapter three argues that the debtor should be obliged to disclose early in the process relevant information to the committee of creditors. This enables the creditors to negotiate based on the baseline information.

However, other conflicts of interests pose greater challenges. Asian jurisdictions have used several tools to mitigate the conflicts of interests. One tool, also commonly used in the US/UK, is the use of abstention of voting if it is proposed that that not all creditors within the same class are treated equally. In Mainland China, the bond restructuring framework prescribed by the SPC requires the abstention of voting by conflicted bondholders for bondholder restructuring, though this framework is only

[243] Notice of the Supreme People's Court on Issuing the Minutes of the National Courts' Civil and Commercial Trial Work Conference [2019] No 254, effective 8 November 2019. 最高人民法院关于印发《全国法院民商事审判工作会议纪要》的通知 [现行有效] (法（2019）254号).

[244] Notice by the China Banking and Insurance Regulatory Commission, the National Development and Reform Commission, the People's Bank of China, and the China Securities Regulatory Commission of Issuing the Work Procedures of Financial Institutional Creditors' Committees [Effective] No 57 [2020], [中国银保监会、发展改革委、中国人民银行、中国证监会关于印发金融机构债权人委员会工作规程的通知（银保监发[2020]57号）], effective 28 December 2020.

specific to bond restructurings.[245] The broader question in the preceding section is whether the special treatment accorded to small creditors and non-financial creditors should continue. It is argued that the former can be allowed given the coordination costs in obtaining the consent, but the latter is difficult to justify as there are more restructurings involving retail financial investors.

Another tool that is currently being debated in India is the IBBI proposal for a code of conduct for the committee of creditors to ensure the accountability of their decisions and transparency in the process.[246] While the code of conduct has laudable aims, in light of the various complaints that the committee of creditors may not have acted in good faith,[247] it is not clear how such code is enforceable, and also there is the potential for generating satellite litigation.

Insofar as there are disputed claims faced by the debtor (often from the operational creditors rather than financial creditors), there should be a mechanism to deal with such claims in jurisdictions if these claims would be wiped out as an outcome of the restructuring (as is the case in India), even if the mechanism is not perfect. Even if these claims do not constitute the swing vote, depriving the operational creditors will put them at a very large disadvantage. The solution in Singapore of an independent assessor, albeit for the purposes of the proof of claim, can be adapted as a form of summary procedure.

Other ways to address within-class conflicts include imposing a duty on the part of the committee of creditors to act in a fiduciary capacity or a more watered-down duty to maximise the sale of the assets, the latter of which was suggested in India in *Essar Steel*. However, for the reasons mentioned in section 4.4.1, such a duty is fraught with difficulties as to scope and enforcement. The alternative is for the courts to police the bargain, such as that used in the US in assessing the best interests of the creditors. However, if the priority of the restructuring framework is to resolve the bad debt speedily, it is likely that the assessment will not meet the objective. Reorganisation is often better used when judicial discretion is minimised, particularly in jurisdictions where judicial time is scarce.

Finally, I would argue that RSAs need to be scrutinised, not only for concerns over unequal disclosure, but also as backdoor means to obtain increased payouts. Again, in jurisdictions where judicial time is scarce, it does not appear to be a good reason to uphold RSAs if the sole purpose is only to counteract hold-out behaviour. The better view, it is submitted, is to draw a bright-line rule to permit small fees only.

Overall, the better approach to deal with within-class conflicts of interests is for proper classification of creditors and for conflicted creditors to abstain from voting at the creditors' meetings.

[245] Notice of the Supreme People's Court on Issuing the Minutes of the National Courts' Civil and Commercial Trial Work Conference, [2019] No 254, effective 8 November 2019 最高人民法院关于印发《全国法院民商事审判工作会议纪要》的通知 [现行有效] （法 2019） 254号), para 15. There is no corresponding requirement to abstain for the large restructurings of financial creditors in No 57 [2020], ibid.

[246] IBBI, Discussion Paper (21 August 2021), available at ibbi.gov.in/Discussionpaper-CIRP-27Aug2021.pdf.

[247] ibid. The questionable behaviour of the committee of creditors (comprising financial creditors) outlined included, among others, colluding with ineligible promoters, improper payments to the professional fees of lenders, and pressurising the resolution professional to make distributions.

4.5.2.2. *Automatic Stay and* Ipso Facto *Clauses*

In jurisdictions with concentrated debt structures, the need for the automatic stay is less acute as that found in jurisdictions with dispersed debt structures, given that it is relatively easy for the creditors to coordinate and agree to a stay while the debtor formulates a rescue plan. One could argue that, in India and Mainland China, if bank debt continues to dominate the restructuring, a stay may not be so critical. However, in all the Asian jurisdictions which have or aspire to have public bond markets where the creditor base is considerably more diverse, it becomes imperative to design a process that will minimise coordination costs among creditors and a stay of proceedings is essential.

Further, where the dominant debt structure is that of secured debt, an automatic stay that applies to all debt, including secured debt, becomes even more critical. When senior creditors are over-secured and are likely to be repaid in full, research have shown that the insolvency firm is more likely to be sold even at very low prices.[248]

However, there needs to be strict limits on the automatic stays. In chapter seven, I discuss the data on the length of the stays that have been approved by the courts and how judicial limits should be placed on the length of such stays.

As to the validity of *ipso facto* clauses, as highlighted by UNCITRAL and World Bank,[249] *ipso facto* clauses do raise complex issues on the tension between upholding the parties' contractual bargain and ensuring that the debtor's business is able to continue during the period of restructuring. These issues are more complex than those relating to the automatic stay. The ban on *ipso facto* clauses will shift the incentives of the parties in different ways. The ability of the debtor to reject executory contracts in a restructuring can incentivise the debtor management to enter into strategic defaults to disclaim trade union or other organised labour contracts,[250] and reorganisations are costly exercises.

4.5.3. Recent Developments in Onshore and Offshore Restructuring

Hong Kong and Mainland Chinese restructurings often involve considerations of cross-border insolvency and restructuring, and the conflict between the offshore and the onshore creditors. As explained in chapter two, companies listed on Hong Kong Stock Exchange and often not incorporated in Hong Kong but in Cayman Islands, Bermuda or British Virgin Islands.[251] These companies would have raised funds in Hong Kong and the proceeds are used by operating subsidiaries in Mainland China.

[248] KM Ayotte and ER Morrison, 'Creditor Control and Conflict in Chapter 11' (2009) 1 *The Journal of Legal Analysis* 511.

[249] UNCITRAL, 'UNCITRAL Legislative Guide on Insolvency Law', available at uncitral.un.org/sites/uncitral.un.org/files/mediadocuments/uncitral/en/05-80722_ebook.pdf. The UNITRAL Guide was created with the objective that it would be used as a reference by national authorities and legislative bodies when preparing new laws and regulations or reviewing the adequacy of existing laws and regulations; World Bank, 'Principles for Effective Insolvency and Creditor/Debtor Regimes' (2016), available at pubdocs.worldbank.org/en/919511468425523509/ICR-Principles-Insolvency-CreditorDebtor-Regimes-2016.pdf.

[250] Delaney, *Strategic Bankruptcy* (1999).

[251] See *Re China Huiyuan Juice Group Limited* [2020] HKCFI 2940.

In fact, Hong Kong investments represents the largest foreign investment in Mainland China.[252] If the operating subsidiaries in Mainland China did not provide guarantees directly to the offshore creditors,[253] these loans would usually be supported by a charge over the wholly owned foreign enterprise (WOFE) that has shares in the subsidiaries.[254] In such cases, generally, the offshore creditors of the listed company have little hope to participate in the onshore recovery because they will be structurally subordinated to the creditors of the onshore debt (being shareholders upon liquidation of the WOFE), and even if they can obtain control of WOFE, they will face considerable obstacles in removing directors of the operating subsidiaries and seizing control of the assets of these subsidiaries under Chinese law.[255] Thus, when the group runs into financial difficulties, the onshore and offshore restructurings will take place separately (either in parallel or sequentially), such as the restructurings LDK Solar Ltd, Kaisa and Asian Aluminum,[256] and it has been reported that in most of these cases, the offshore recovery is worse than the onshore recovery.[257]

More recent controversies have involved the use of keepwell deeds as credit enhancement for the bonds issued by subsidiaries of PRC companies. As the PRC companies could not issue guarantees directly as credit support for the offshore debt for the monies to be used onshore due to foreign exchange laws, a keepwell structure is used as a closest substitute.[258] In a keepwell structure, an offshore issuer issues the bonds and its onshore parent, the provider, issues the keepwell deed to the offshore issuer or the offshore guarantor (which may not be an operating company) if there is one. The monies are on-lent to the PRC parent. The keepwell deed is a strongly worded letter of comfort by the provider, which also contains an equity purchase undertaking and defined obligations to maintain the subsidiary issuer's financial well-being, and provides an avenue for the provider to disburse funds offshore for bond repayment. Breach of the keepwell deed does not allow for a direct legal action against the keepwell provider by bondholders, and the enforcement of the keepwell deeds is often unclear. The precedent for enforcement was partly tested by the *CEFC Shanghai Investment* case, where the bondholders sued the offshore vehicle in

[252] Trade and Industry Department, available at www.tid.gov.hk/english/aboutus/publications/factsheet/china.html.

[253] eg prior to July 2014, approval of State Administration of Foreign Exchange of the PRC (SAFE) was required for an onshore entity to grant a guarantee to offshore financial creditors. Since 2014, onshore companies may provide guarantees for offshore debt, but this was subject to a restriction that the funds must be used offshore. See State Administration of Foreign Exchange of the PRC (SAFE), 'Notice of the State Administration of Foreign Exchange on Issuing the Provisions on the Foreign Exchange Administration of Cross-border Guarantees No 29' [2014] Circular of the SAFE on Releasing the Provisions on Foreign Exchange Administration for Cross-border Guarantees (Huifa No 29 [2014]) [国家外汇管理局关于发布《跨境担保外汇管理规定》的通知] (汇发 [2014] 29号) (12 May 2014).

[254] D McCahill and A Tracy, 'Restructuring Offshore PRC Debt' (Skadden, 2015).

[255] D Kidd and J Warboys, 'Extracting Value for Offshore Creditors Either Side of the Chinese Wall: Restructuring PRC Financing Structures' (2016) *Journal of International Banking and Financial Law* 299a, available at www.lexisnexis.co.uk/blog/docs/default-source/loan-ranger-documents/extracting-value.pdf.

[256] Source: Fitch Ratings, 'China Corporate Bond Defaults' (2018), available at cdn.roxhillmedia.com/production/email/attachment/690001_700000/Bond%20defaults.pdf.

[257] ibid.

[258] The approval of SAFE was required for the guarantee to be given by a Chinese enterprise. See White (n 25).

Hong Kong, obtained default judgment and proceeded to cause the offshore vehicle to enforce the judgment in the Shanghai court successfully.[259] This would pave the way for the claims of to be admitted in the bankruptcy of the keepwell provider.

However, in the recent Peking University Founder Group restructuring, which also concerned the use of keepwell deed, the bankruptcy administrator refused to admit the US$1.7 billion claims of the bondholders of its keepwell-backed bonds.[260] The success in *CEFC Shanghai Investment* is limited as no other court has yet to follow the case it is not clear if future Chinese courts may regard this form of enforcement as a violation of public policy given that keepwell deeds are designed to evade the foreign exchange requirements. The recent mutual recognition and assistance to insolvency proceedings framework between Mainland China and Hong Kong[261] cannot provide any assistance in such cases if the keepwell deeds are found to violate public policy.

The use of keepwell deeds is becoming a challenge for bankruptcy reorganisation. One could argue that these non-retail bondholders knew or ought to know about the risks of enforcing keepwell deeds, which are detailed in the offering memorandum. However, in the longer term, it seems inimical to efficiency that the onshore and offshore restructuring takes place in parallel but separately, if the original intention is for some kind of credit enhancement to be obtained from the parent company in connection with the issuance of bonds.

4.6. CONCLUSION

Although the statutory frameworks in the English scheme of arrangement and Chapter 11 have not changed dramatically in the last two decades, the practice of restructuring has certainly adapted in light of market changes in the UK and the US. These adaptions mean that there is a shift in paradigm as to how assets should be deployed and how distributions should be made. Some of the practices, such as RSAs and DIP financing, have emerged or evolved respectively. Just as there is a shift in paradigm in Anglo-American restructuring practice, the rules that were transplanted into Asian jurisdictions often have to be adapted in light of the differences in the composition of creditors and institutional environments in order to reduce the frictions arising from creditor–creditor relationships. Concerns as to social unrest, the

[259] Shanghai Financial Court, 'Decision of the Court on Keepwell Deed' (16 November 2020), 上海金融法院涉"维好协议"香港特别行政区法院判决在内地申请认可和执行的认定标准—时和全球投资基金SPC-时和价值投资基金申请认可和执行香港特别行政区法院民事判决; P Sito, 'Shanghai Court's Nod to Hong Kong Ruling on Keepwell Clause Bodes Well for Offshore Creditors of Defaulting Chinese Bonds' *South China Morning Post* (9 December 2020). Recognition was given pursuant to the Arrangement on Reciprocal Recognition and Enforcement of Judgments in Civil and Commercial Matters between the Courts of the Mainland and of the HKSAR pursuant to the Choice of Court Agreements between Parties Concerned.

[260] See White (n 25).

[261] HK Government, 'HKSAR and Mainland Sign Record of Meeting Concerning Mutual Recognition of and Assistance to Insolvency Proceedings' (15 May 2021); see also Department of Justice, 'The Supreme People's Court's Opinion on Taking Forward a Pilot Measure in relation to the Recognition of and Assistance to Insolvency Proceedings in the Hong Kong Special Administrative Region' (14 May 2021), available at www.doj.gov.hk/en/mainland_and_macao/pdf/RRECCJ_opinion_en_tc.pdf.

requirement to deal with the resolution speedily in a time-bound manner, and the presence of non-sophisticated investors and operational creditors may mean that the solutions used in the US and UK may need to be adjusted. While the much-discussed tools present in the US and the UK, the automatic stay, the operation of the cram-down and the restriction on invoking *ipso facto* clauses (in the case of the US) allow the debtor to establish a forum for the creditors to bargain, but the trade-offs of including and modifying these tools must be carefully considered.

5

Managing Non-Performing Loans and their Impact on Agency and Coordination Costs in Two Emerging Jurisdictions

5.1. INTRODUCTION

THIS CHAPTER FOCUSES on important variations to the agency and coordination costs arising in jurisdictions which have to deal with high levels of banks' non-performing loans (NPLs).[1] In chapters three and four, I argued that the shareholder–creditor and creditor–creditor relationships generate agency and coordination costs, which vary in accordance with the differences in the shareholding structures and the composition of the creditors respectively. In particular, in chapter four, I argued that in the restructurings involving related party creditors, non-sophisticated creditors or non-adjusting/weakly adjusted creditors in Asia, the respective incentives and ability to assert their rights among these creditors are very different from the traditional financial creditors. In that chapter, bank creditors are assumed to seek maximisation of the value of their assets in restructuring proceedings.

However, where a jurisdiction's NPLs are unacceptably high, banking regulators have to intervene to ensure the stability of the country's banking market; high levels of NPLs depress credit growth, impede recovery and do not allow assets to be put to productive use.[2] In dealing with NPLs, it is well established that reforms to the insolvency and restructuring law framework for such resolution is important.[3] However, it is also clear that insolvency law reforms, by themselves, are not the complete cure. Certainly, banking crises in the last three decades, including the savings and loans crisis in the United States (US) in the 1980s, the Asian financial crisis in 1997 and the global financial crisis in 2008, have meant that advanced and emerging jurisdictions

[1] In this chapter, the terms 'non-performing loans' (NPLs) and 'non-performing assets' (NPAs) are used interchangeably.

[2] VV Acharya et al, 'Real Effects of the Sovereign Debt Crisis in Europe: Evidence from Syndicated Loans' (2018) 31 *Review of Financial Studies* 2855; S Aiyar et al, 'A Strategy for Resolving Europe's Problem Loan' (2015) IMF Staff Discussion Note 15/19.

[3] JC Bricongne et al, *Macroeconomic Relevance of Insolvency Frameworks in a High-Debt Context: An EU Perspective* (European Commission Discussion Paper 32, 2016).

must use other measures, including less favourable bank provisioning for NPLs, requiring the offloading of the NPLs, bank bail-outs or bail-ins, tax measures and accounting rules.[4] In requiring banks to off-load their NPLs, two measures are prominent: using asset management companies (AMCs) or their equivalents to acquire the NPLs (and thus taking the NPLs off the balance sheet of the banks); and developing an active distressed loan market for NPLs.

In this chapter, I argue that the analysis of the standard agency and transaction costs in restructuring proceedings must further consider the use of AMCs as a means to resolve NPLs. In theory, AMCs and a distressed debt market can reduce the coordination costs in at least two ways. First, by mandating the banks to sell the NPLs only to the AMCs in the primary market, the AMCs can more easily aggregate debt, reduce the time that is required for the negotiations with the debtor, and potentially reach faster resolutions for the NPLs. AMCs may also use a larger variety of resolution strategies, including agreeing to longer pay-offs, supplying management expertise to the debtor, providing rescue financing to enable projects to be completed and effecting mergers with other companies that AMCs have stakes in. These strategies may not be open to banks due to their regulatory requirements. Second, the relationship between the lender and the debtor changes as the new lender has acquired the NPLs. If the reason for the NPL problem is that the banks are not sufficiently disciplined to clean up the NPLs, AMCs or the subsequent secondary purchasers of the NPLs should instil the discipline in maximising recoveries, particularly if NPLs are acquired on market terms and these purchasers have to account for their own stakeholders.

However, the assumption that AMCs will always seek to maximise their overall recoveries in restructuring proceedings should be reassessed in light of the interlinked ownership structures of the banks and AMCs and the regulatory objectives of the AMCs, thus raising agency costs. In the case of the former, if both the banks and the AMCs are also state-owned or state-controlled, AMCs may demand generous terms or non-market terms for the restructuring. In the case of the latter, if the AMCs are not permitted to run the business but to only resolve the debt, they may end up merely being parking vehicles for the debt and would not be incentivised to turn around the business through the contribution of their expertise such as the provision of management. In such a case, AMCs become highly inefficient as they only increase the overall transaction costs of participating in the distressed debt market. I then discuss the implications of the two jurisdictions' attempts to develop active distressed NPL markets on restructuring outcomes.

I draw upon the case studies of Mainland China and India in addressing NPLs as both jurisdictions have used AMCs (in this paper, the Chinese AMCs are known as CAMCs) and asset reconstruction companies (ARCs) respectively to purchase corporate NPLs from the state-owned banks. In particular, for India, one of the key methods to resolve the NPLs, acquired from ARCs, is the use of the judicial process of Corporate Insolvency Resolution Process (CIRP) under the Indian Insolvency and Bankruptcy Code 2006 (IBC). Both jurisdictions have attempted, to varying levels of success, to liberalise the market for distressed assets to foreign investors. They offer

[4] ibid, 13.

contrasting perspectives. In both jurisdictions, the state-owned banks are dominant. However, in India, the active ARCs are privately sponsored (at least until recently),[5] whereas in Mainland China, the Chinese AMCs (CAMCs) are mostly state-owned or state-controlled. At the debtor's side, the majority of the NPLs to be resolved are loans to SOEs for Mainland China, potentially exacerbating the agency costs of conflicts of interests. India also has a vibrant market for the institutional trading of distressed loans, whereas China is making inroads to allow the wider retail public to invest in distressed NPL market.

Due to space constraints, the focus of this chapter is on the interaction of measures to deal with NPLs and insolvency law and policy, and I exclude other prudential methods of dealing with NPLs, such as measures to recapitalise banks (except insofar as they explain the incentives of the AMCs), special insolvency and resolution proceedings that pertain to banks only or special measures of resolution outside of the insolvency processes.

In this chapter, section 5.2 first addresses the institutional and organisational background for using AMCs as debt aggregation vehicles and developing active markets for distressed assets for resolving NPLs. Section 5.3 addresses the NPL situations in India and Mainland China. Section 5.4 discusses how both jurisdictions have used AMCs to resolve NPLs and the variations in transaction costs incurred by the use of AMCs. Section 5.5 addresses how both jurisdictions have developed the secondary markets for distressed assets and the impact on restructuring outcomes. Section 5.6 concludes the chapter with lessons and implications for managing NPLs, particularly with the influx of foreign investment.

5.2. INSTITUTIONAL AND ORGANISATIONAL BACKGROUND IN THE INTERNATIONAL CONTEXT FOR RESOLVING NPLs

5.2.1. AMCs as Debt Aggregation Vehicles

Globally, the experience of banking crises in the last 30 years has driven the use of AMCs and other debt aggregation vehicles as key policy tools to effect the transfers of the bad debt or loans from the banks in order to bring the NPL ratios to manageable levels (along with tightening of the prudential policies in respect to the granting of loans and write-downs).[6] After the transfers, these vehicles then seek to either restructure the loan or proceed to affect the sale of the assets, which may occur within or outside the formal insolvency proceedings. The premise is that AMCs are better placed to resolve these NPLs (such as through higher recovery rates over the lifetime of the loans) than the original lending banks and to stabilise the banking sectors.[7]

In addition, the benefits of the AMCs include the fact that AMCs would develop in-house expertise on debt resolution, and they can take advantage of the benefits

[5] In 2021, the state-sponsored bad bank, the National Asset Reconstruction Company Ltd, was set up. See B Beniwal, 'India to Give New Bad Bank [US]$4.2 Billion Sovereign Guarantee' Bloomberg (16 September 2021).

[6] See generally, European Commission, 'Commission Staff working Document: AMC Blueprint Com' (2018) 133, 1-81.

[7] ibid.

of economies of scale in aggregating debt and coordinating with numerous creditors. AMCs can be publicly or privately funded, although existing regulations even in advanced jurisdictions, such as those in the European Union (EU), often contemplate that substantial state aid is required. The EU has developed a blueprint in March 2018 to provide practical guidance for Member States when considering the design and set-up of public sector AMCs.[8]

5.2.2. Developing the Market for Distressed Assets

In chapter four, I discussed the impact of distressed debt markets on US and UK bankruptcy law practice. The distressed debt market in the US has been active since the 1990s.[9] On one estimate, the total value of distressed and defaulted debt as of 30 June 2019 was US$773 billion.[10] Banks and other creditors which are not willing to hold debt that is in default can sell their debt to distressed debt players. Bankruptcy scholars have been divided over the impact of the distressed debt players in the reorganisation process. One view is that once debt becomes concentrated in the hands of a few players (including distressed debt players), there would be fewer creditors to negotiate with, thereby accelerating the restructuring process. Recent research on US data has demonstrated that higher debt concentration at the commencement of Chapter 11 is more likely to lead to the filing of prearranged bankruptcy claims, in order to move through the process quickly and to emerge from the other side as an ongoing concern.[11] A contrasting view distressed trading gives rise to other transaction costs, such as coordination costs. The debtor has to identify the new creditors to start the negotiation, which may keep changing in the course of the restructuring.[12] The incentives of the new creditors, as opposed to the original lenders, may not often be clear-cut. If these new creditors who are distressed funds had purchased the bonds from the market at a steep discount, their interests are not the same as with the other creditors who have loaned the debtor directly. Further, if the distressed funds hold different positions in the debt structures (for example, they may hold both senior and junior debt), their interests conflict with the other creditors within the same class. These creditors may thus hold out unnecessarily or misjudge the responses to the complex debt structure.[13]

[8] ibid.

[9] See also S Paterson, *Corporate Reorganization Law and Forces of Change* (Oxford, OUP, 2020) ch 4.

[10] EI Altman and R Benhenni, 'The Anatomy of Distressed Debt Markets' (2019) 11 *Annual Review of Financial Economics* 21.

[11] V Ivashina, B Iverson and DC Smith, 'The Ownership and Trading of Debt Claims in Chapter 11 Restructurings' (2016) 119 *Journal of Financial Economics* 316 (arguing that activist investors play an important role in consolidating the claims in the bankruptcy process; cf JA Ellias, 'Bankruptcy Claims Trading' (2018) 15 *Journal of Empirical Legal Studies* 772 (arguing that the activist group of investors tend to enter into purchases of debt early in the process and hence have a lesser impact).

[12] Ivashina, Iverson and Smith (ibid); Paterson, *Corporate Reorganization Law* (2020) 92; F Tung, 'Confirmation and Claims Trading' (1996) 90 *Northwestern University Law Review* 1684.

[13] WW Bratton and AJ Levitin, 'The New Bond Workouts' (2018) 166 *University of Pennsylvania Law Review* 1597.

5.3. INSTITUTIONAL BACKGROUND TO NPLs IN INDIA AND MAINLAND CHINA

5.3.1. India

Figure 5.1 presents the gross NPA ratios of all of the scheduled commercial banks from 1998 to 2020.[14] To provide the context of the ratios, Figure 5.2 presents the volume of the NPLs for the same period. Similar to many emerging jurisdictions, while there have been some inroads to developing an active bond market, India remains highly depends on secured debt and bank borrowings.[15] However, while India is a former British colony has a common law jurisdiction and has strong creditor rights in its books, until the enactment of Securitisation and Reconstruction of Financial Assets and Enforcement of Securities Interest Act 2002 (SARFAESI), the only process for enforcing a debt was the filing of a civil suit according to the Civil Procedure Code, which was very lengthy and which can take as long as 15 years.[16] Other estimates are 10 to 12 years.[17] Enforcement of secured lending is also estimated to experience significant delays of five to seven years.[18] Extrajudicial enforcement of secured debt, such as through the appointment of receivers that is commonly used in UK, was not available.

Since the 1980s, various attempts have been made to improve the debt enforcement framework. In 1985, the Sick Industrial Companies (Special Provisions) Act 1985 (SICA) was introduced to sift out viable industrial companies (which had been in existence for at least five years but had accumulated losses that were equivalent to its entire net worth) to be evaluated by the Board of Industrial and Financial Reconstruction.[19] However, by most accounts, SICA was a failure, due to the length of time for a company to be revived (eight to 11 years),[20] and the fact that very few companies that were revived under SICA actually later went on to be successful companies.[21]

Later attempts followed, including the setting up of debt recovery tribunals (DRTs)[22] pursuant to Recovery of Debts Due to Banks and Financial Institutions Act 1993 and the passage of the SARFAESI in 2002. For the former, the recovery officers of the DRT may directly enforce by attaching property of the defaulting borrower

[14] The scheduled commercial banks are those included under the Second Schedule of the Reserve Bank of India Act 1934 and are regulated by the RBI. They include state-owned banks, private sector banks and foreign banks.

[15] S Sahoo, 'Financial Intermediation and Growth: Bank-Based Versus Market-Based Systems' (2014) 8 *Margin: The Journal of Applied Economic Research* 93. See also ch 4.

[16] For an account, see V Vig, 'Access to Collateral and Corporate Debt Structure: Evidence from a Natural Experiment' (2013) 68 *Journal of Finance* 881.

[17] L Viswanathan and Dhananjay Kumar, 'India' in A Nassiri, *The Lending and Secured Finance Review*, 6th edn (London, The Law Reviews, 2020), available at www.cyrilshroff.com/wp-content/uploads/2020/07/India.pdf.

[18] See R Rajan, 'A Hundred Small Steps: Report of the Committee on Financial Sector Reforms', Planning Commission, Government of India (2008) 168, available at faculty.iima.ac.in/~jrvarma/reports/Raghuram-Rajan/cfsr_all.pdf. R Rajan was the Governor of the Reserve Bank of India.

[19] SICA, s 3(o).

[20] K van Zwieten, 'Corporate Rescue in India: The Influence of the Courts' (2015) 15 *Journal of Corporate Law Studies* 1.

[21] ibid.

[22] Debt Recovery Tribunals Act 1993. Specialised tribunals were established for the recovery of loans by banks and financial institutions without having to follow the Civil Procedure Code.

to secure payment without having to follow the Civil Procedure Code.[23] The most important legislation which improves the position of the banks is SARFAESI, which allowed banks and certain financial institutions, to enforce secured assets of a firm that defaulted directly without having to go through the judicial process,[24] though enforcement is not open to other non-financial creditors.[25] SARFAESI also introduced the ARCs as a means of resolving the debt of the financial institutions.[26]

In 2002, the Reserve Bank of India (RBI) also introduced the corporate debt restructuring mechanism, in which lenders can jointly agree to the restructuring of distressed corporations if their lending exposure to the company exceeds INR100 million. The process is initiated by the creditors or debtors with support from the bank or financial institution.[27] Corporate debt restructuring is entirely voluntary, and the restructuring process is a contractual arrangement.

The earlier measures and the SARFAESI have had some success; for instance, as shown in Figure 5.1, the NPL ratio of the public sector banks was reduced from 10.4 per cent (in 2002) to 7.2 per cent (in 2004).[28] Net NPAs, being the difference between the addition of new NPAs and the recovery of NPAs in the year improved as well.[29] However, the improvements between 2002 to 2008 began to be eroded after the global financial crisis of 2008. With the slowdown in the economy, the stoppage of several infrastructure projects and delays in land acquisition, the NPL ratio started to rise sharply from 2011 (see Figure 5.1).[30] It was clear that the existing institutions were not adequate to deal with the rising NPLs. DRTs continued to have a large backlog.[31] More drastic measures were needed.

In 2014, the RBI made it mandatory for domestic lending banks and financial institutions of the borrower to form the Joint Lender's Forum (JLF) if the exposure was at least INR1 billion and the borrower has unpaid overdue debts to the creditors for over 30 days.[32] In 2015, the RBI introduced the Strategic Debt Restructuring Scheme to help financial institutions recover NPLs by taking over distressed assets and imposing stricter guidelines on asset quality review for banks under the JLF. Under this scheme, banks were required to recognise restructured loans as non-performing. The JLF gave its consortium members the option to convert the debt to equity if the consortium had more than 51 per cent of the debts of the borrower, though the consortium was required

[23] Recovery of Debt Due to Banks and Financial Institutions Act 1993.

[24] SARFAESI applies to enforcement by banks and post-2016, it also applies to certain kinds of non-bank financial companies (NBFC). Since 2016, the Indian Central Government has tweaked the criterion for NBFCs using SARFAESI. For empirical studies on SARFAESI and DRTs, see also Vig, 'Access to Collateral and Corporate Debt Structure' (2013); S Visaria, 'Legal Reform and Loan Repayment: The Microeconomic Impact of Debt Recovery Tribunals in India' (2009) 1 *American Economic Journal: Applied Economics* 59.

[25] For example, a mutual fund which holds bonds cannot utilise SARFAESI.

[26] See section 5.4.1.

[27] ibid.

[28] Figure 5.1. A list of public sector banks is found at RBI, 'List of Scheduled Commercial Banks', available at m.rbi.org.in/scripts/bs_viewcontent.aspx?Id=3657.

[29] Vig (n 16).

[30] J Bhagwati, KM Shuheb and RR Bogathi, 'Can Asset Reconstruction Companies be Part of the Indian Debt Problem?' Working Paper No 338, Indian Council for Research on International Economic Relations, available at tile.loc.gov/storage-services/service/gdc/gdcovop/2018305088/2018305088.pdf.

[31] As of the end of 2014, approximately 60,000 cases involving RS3.74 trillion (US$56 billion) in bank loans were pending: see V Nair, 'Pending Cases Pile Up at Debt Recovery Tribunals' *Live Mint* (28 August 2015).

[32] Bhagwati, Shuheb and Bogathi (n 30).

to divest the shareholding within 18 months.[33] The revision in the asset quality review guidelines resulted in the sharp increase in the NPA ratios from 4.6 per cent of the gross advances in March 2015 to 11.5 per cent of the gross advances in March 2018.[34]

Most of the problems with the NPAs lie within the state-owned banks in India. For instance, the NPA ratio among public sector banks is almost twice that among private and foreign banks.[35]

Figure 5.1 NPL ratios in India

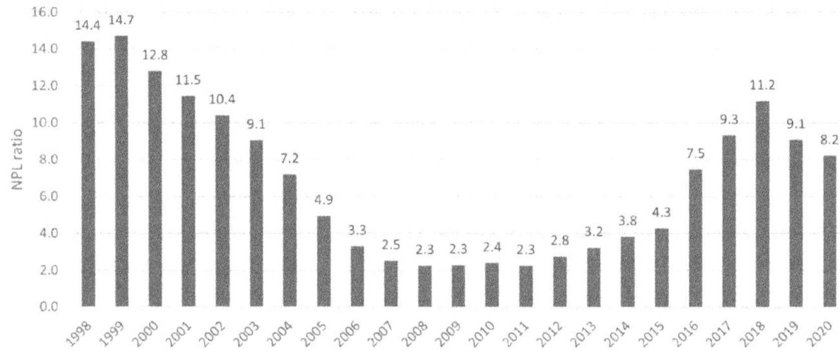

Source: Data collected from CEIC and RBI Statistical Tables.

The IBC was introduced in 2016, establishing the Corporate Insolvency and Resolution Process (CIRP) for resolving companies within 180 days, which can be extended to 270 days. The IBC was later amended to provide that the aggregate period for the resolution (including the time taken in court proceedings) was 330 days 2019.[36] In the initial year of the implementation, the banks were hesitant to initiate the IBC proceedings.[37] To increase the use of the IBC, in May 2017, the RBI was empowered to initiate proceedings under the IBC by way of an amendment to the Banking Regulation Act 1948. The RBI did not hesitate to use these new powers. In June 2017, the RBI compelled banks to initiate IBC proceedings against the 12 large defaulters (see Panel A of Appendix B) that account for 25 per cent of the total NPL.[38] Within the same year, the RBI issued a second list of 28 cases, which comprised 15 per cent of the banks' NPLs, to be resolved by the end of December 2017.[39]

[33] ibid.

[34] 'Scheduled Banks Healthier Now as gross NPA ratio dips in FY19' *Hindu Business Line* (9 June 2019), available at www.thehindubusinessline.com/money-and-banking/scheduled-banks-healthier-now-as-gross-npa-ratio-dips-in-fy19/article27704992.ece.

[35] RBI discloses the NPA ratios for public sector banks (PSBs) and private sector banks (PVBs). For the gross NPA as a percentage of gross advances, the ratios are 10.3% and 5.5% (for 2019/20) and 11.6% and 5.3% (for 2018/19). See m.rbi.org.in/Scripts/PublicationsView.aspx?id=20270 (Table IV. 11).

[36] Insolvency and Bankruptcy Code (Amendment) Act 2019, No 26 of 2019.

[37] INSOL International, 'The New Insolvency and Bankruptcy Code in India: Impact of the Distressed Debt Market' (April 2018), INSOL International Technical Series Issue No 39).

[38] V Nair, 'Why RBI Picked These 12 Accounts For Insolvency Action: BQ Explains' Bloomberg Quint (17 June 2017). These 12 accounts made up of nearly 25% of the total amount of all NPAs at that time (amounting to RS7.7 lakh crones or US$180 billion) of Indian banks.

[39] V Nair, 'Four Years On, Did RBI's IBC Gamble With 40 Large Defaulters Work? Bloomberg Quint (14 June 2021).

Figure 5.2 Size of non-performing loans in India

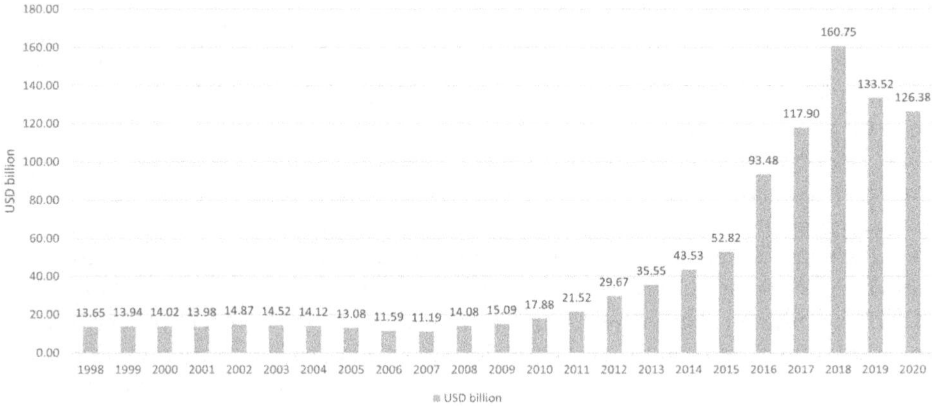

Source: Data collected from CEIC and RBI Statistical Tables.

The recovery rates under the IBC improved significantly in 2018 and 2019, as compared with 2017 (see Figure 5.3), to an average of approximately 46 per cent. Figure 5.3 presents the recovery rates for NPAs through the DRTs, SARFAESI and IBC. The sharp increase in the number of cases resolved under the IBC is demonstrated from 2018 onwards.

Figure 5.3 Recovery of NPAs through various channels

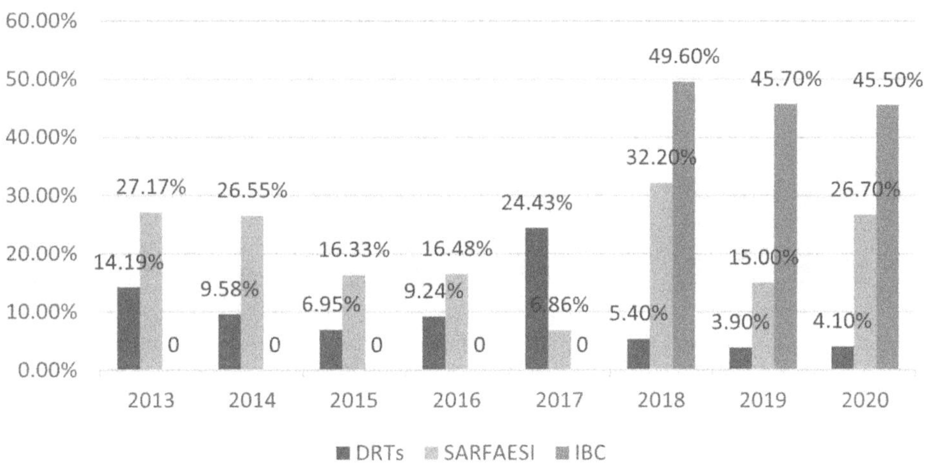

Sources: Data collected from RBI Statistical Tables Relating to Banks for the years that ended in 31 March 2013 through 31 March 2017 and RBI, 'Reports of Trend and Progress of Banking in India for 2019/2020', available at www.rbi.org.in.

5.3.2. Mainland China

Although NPL ratios have been historically low in the last decade for Mainland China, it should be noted that the NPL ratio is viewed in conjunction with the special mention loans, in which borrowers are still able to service the loans but repayment may be affected by other factors.[40] The clear trend in Figure 5.4 indicates that the NPL ratio has been increasing since 2013. One may argue that the relative apparent small increase in the NPL ratio between 2016 and 2020 (1.75 to 1.90) should be viewed positively; however, it should be noted that in addition to the ratio, the actual volume of the overall lending has increased. At the end of 2016 and 2020, the amount of NPAs stood at RMB2.19 trillion (US$330.3 billion) and RMB 3.47 trillion (US$503.5 billion), respectively,[41] representing an increase of 58 per cent between the two timeframes. See Figure 5.5. Figure 5.6 shows that special mention loans reached a high level in March 2020 (though the proportion of special mention loans has been decreasing since March 2018).

As a further illustrative example of the current severity of NPL problem, the amount of NPLs disposed of by the commercial banks between 2017 and 2020 was RMB 8.8 trillion (US$1,340 billion), which is equivalent to the total value of NPLs disposed of for the period of 2005–16.[42] It is expected that in the aftermath of COVID-19, the amount of NPLs to be disposed of in 2021 and 2022 will increase.[43]

Figure 5.4 NPA ratios in China (%)

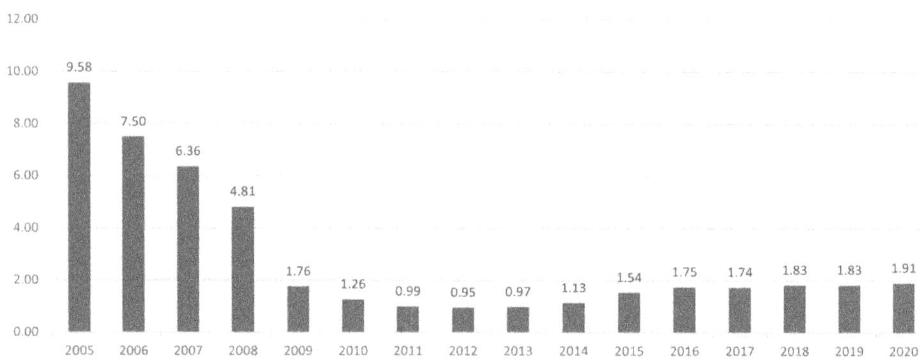

Sources: Data collected from CEIC and China Banking and Insurance Regulatory Commission.

[40] People's Bank of China, Notice of the People's Bank of China on Guidance on Provisioning for Loan Losses [中国人民银行关于印发《银行贷款损失准备计提指引》的通知 (银发[2002] 98号)], effective 1 January 2002. See P Baudino, J Orlandi and R Zamil, 'FSI Insights on Policy implementation No 7: The Identification and Measurement of Nonperforming Assets: A Cross-Country Comparison' (Bank For International Settlements, 2018).

[41] Figures are obtained from the CEIC database on NPLs (source from CBIRC). See, generally, F Tang, 'China's Top Banking Regulator Sees Surge of Bad Loans in 2021 as Effects of Coronavirus Bite' *South China Morning Post* (3 March 2021), available at www.scmp.com/economy/china-economy/article/3123785/chinas-top-banking-regulator-sees-surge-bad-loans-2021.

[42] See Tang (ibid).

[43] ibid.

Figure 5.5 Size of NPLs in Mainland China

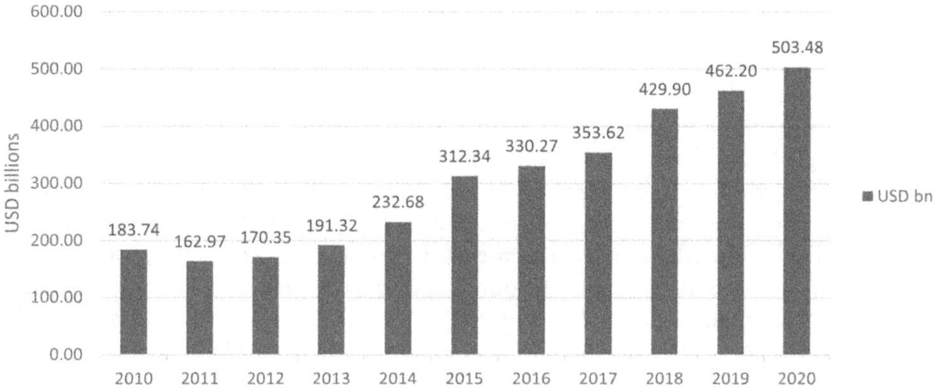

Sources: Data collected from CEIC database; China Banking and Insurance Regulatory Commission.

Figure 5.6 Special mention loans for commercial banks in China

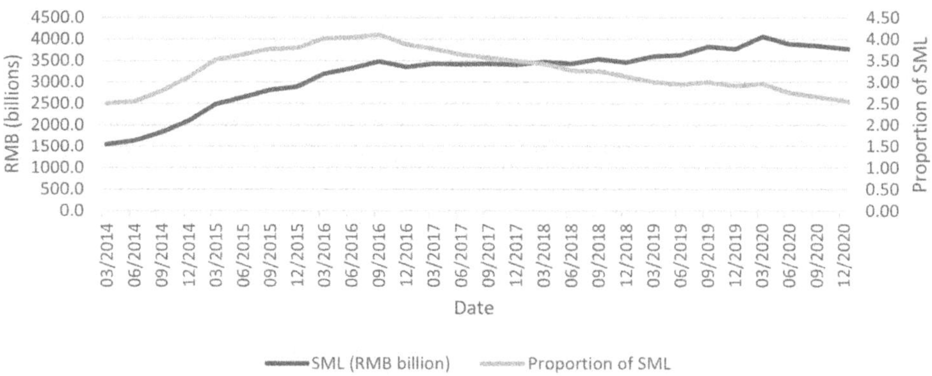

Sources: Data collected from CEIC and China Banking and Insurance Regulatory Commission.

5.4. AMCs AND VARIATIONS TO AGENCY AND COORDINATION COSTS IN RESTRUCTURING

In theory, AMCs should develop their own professional capabilities to distinguish between financial stress and economic stress, and to evaluate the feasibility and viability of the restructuring plans. By acquiring and thereby aggregating the debt from the banks early, they would have the power to influence the vote at the creditor committees. However, as can be seen in the following discussion, the objectives of the AMCs are often not necessarily aligned with value maximisation of recoveries.

5.4.1. AMCs in India

In conjunction with the passage of SARFAESI, ARCs fall within the purview of the RBI and were formed for the purpose of asset reconstruction or securitisation.[44] Initially, banks can only sell their NPAs to ARCs, though this was liberalised in 2016 to allow sales to non-banking financial companies and other financial institutions.[45] ARCs are not the magic bullet to mop up all of the NPAs, as RBI data shows that only 10 per cent of the NPAs of the banks are sold to ARCs in 2019, with the remaining NPAs remaining unresolved or through other means such as SARFAESI and IBC.[46] Among the NPAs sold to the ARCs, private sector banks dominate the sales (at approximately 65 per cent of the total sales) and the public sector banks are at less than five per cent in 2019.[47] Nevertheless, the amounts of NPAs that the ARCs have acquired have been steadily increasing, reaching 4,31,339 crore (US$58 billion) in March 2020.[48]

There are at least three main ways by which ARCs can acquire the NPLs. First, ARCs acquire a proportion of the NPA portfolio, with the balance being held by the selling bank in the form of security receipts.[49] Security receipts are liquid instruments and can be traded. Second, ARCs acquire, in cash, the entire NPA portfolio.[50] Third, ARCs work with the promoters, and the latter purchase the NPA portfolio directly from the banks via a one-time settlement. ARCs then restructure the loan together with the promoters.

The choices that ARCs make on debt aggregation are influenced by several historical regulatory factors. While ARCs are privately sponsored, it wasn't until 2017 that more incentives were put in place to encourage a clean break from the original bank lender after the NPLs are sold to the ARCs. Before 2017, ARCs purchased the NPLs from the banks via cash upfront (15 per cent of the NPLs) and banks were issued security receipts for the balance of 85 per cent; the security receipts were redeemable over five to eight years (the period during which the ARCs will resolve the NPLs). In terms of recovery, banks will recover their share of proceeds of 85 per cent and make provisions on the security receipts.[51] In fact, prior to August 2014, ARCs only needed to retain five per cent of the value of the NPLs purchased. However, it has been proven inadequate to incentivise the ARCs to engage in the resolution of the

[44] SARFAESI Act 2002, s 2.

[45] RBI, 'Guidelines on Sales of Stressed Assets by Banks', RBI/2016-17/56 (2016), available at rbi.org.in/Scripts/BS_CircularIndexDisplay.aspx?Id=10588. However, the task force set up by RBI noted that sales to other banks are not as active as sales to ARCs. See RBI, 'Report of the Task Force on the Development of Secondary Market for Corporate Loans' (2019) 3, available at https://www.rbi.org.in/Scripts/PublicationReportDetails.aspx?UrlPage=&ID=940.

[46] RBI, 'Reports of Trend and Progress of Banking in India for 2019/2020', available at rbi.org.in/scripts/PublicationsView.aspx?Id=20270#TIV.14 (Chart IV.20).

[47] ibid.

[48] ibid.

[49] N Narayanan 'Distressed Debt Investing in India – The Use of Debt Aggregation Vehicles' (2016) 2 *Emerging Markets Restructuring Journal* 6.

[50] Deloitte LLP, 'Asset Reconstruction Companies: Tax and Regulatory Framework' Debriefs (2019), available at www2.deloitte.com/content/dam/Deloitte/in/Documents/tax/in-tax-asset-reconstruction-companies-tax-regulatory-framework-noexp.pdf.

[51] M Salian, 'NPA resolution: Banks go for all cash sale of stressed assets' *Financial Express* (5 December 2018), available at www.financialexpress.com/market/poor-security-receipt-redemptions-banks-go-for-all-cash-npa-sales-2/1403641.

distressed assets,[52] and the minimum value required to retain the value of the NPLs was increased to 15 per cent in 2014.

In 2017, higher provisioning requirements were imposed for the banks retaining more than 50 per cent of the security receipts (which was eventually lowered to 10 per cent); in other words, the banks must make provision for the loans sold as if these loans were still on the books if they retain more than the applicable threshold of the security receipts.[53] Consequently, this creates incentives for banks to sell their loans outright for cash without subscription of the security receipts, even at a large discount, to take the NPAs off the books. Figure 5.7 presents the trend of the sum of the security receipts held by banks, ARCs, foreign institutional investors (FIIs) and qualified institutional buyers. Figure 5.8 demonstrates that the foreign investors have been increasing their shares in the holding of the security receipts and the banks have been decreasing in the share of holding security receipts.

Figure 5.7 NPAs acquired and security receipts subscribed

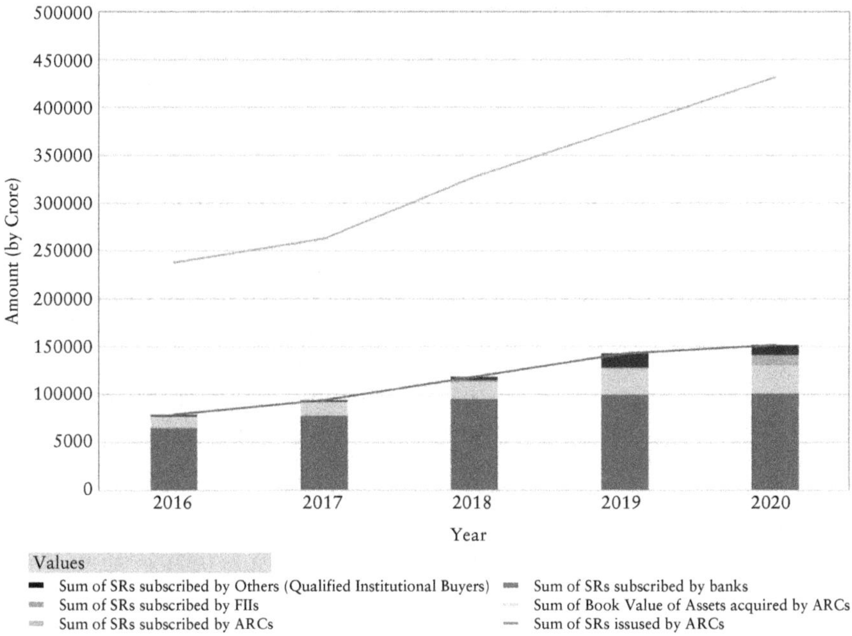

Source: Data collected from the RBI Report on the Trends and Progress of Banking in 2017/18 and 2019/20. FIIs refer to foreign institutional investors.

In terms of the mode of acquisition, the ARCs normally acquire the NPA portfolio from the banks via the Swiss challenge system.[54] Debt that is 60 days past the default

[52] ARCs also obtain management fees of up to 1.5% (see Bhagwati, Shuheb and Bogathi (n 30)).

[53] B Shritama, 'New Asset Reconstruction Committee: Banks likely to ask RBI to relax norm' *Financial Express* (4 February 2021), available at www.financialexpress.com/industry/banking-finance/new-asset-reconstruction-committee-banks-likely-to-ask-rbi-to-relax-norms/2187450.

[54] RBI, 'Guidelines on Sale of Stressed Assets by Banks' (n 45). Under the Swiss challenge system, in the first round of bids, the highest bid becomes the base bid. In the second round, all bidders, including the

Figure 5.8 Security receipts subscribed by parties

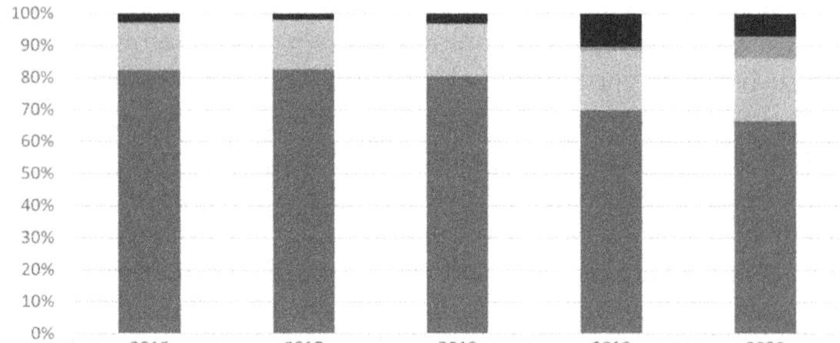

	2016	2017	2018	2019	2020
% of SRs subscribed by Others (Qualified Institutional Buyers)	2.75%	1.92%	3.06%	10.42%	7.07%
% of SRs subscribed by FIIs	0.41%	0.35%	0.43%	1.18%	6.85%
% SRs subscribed by ARCs	14.43%	15.08%	15.99%	18.53%	19.44%
% of SRs subscribed by banks	82.41%	82.68%	80.52%	69.87%	66.65%

% of SRs subscribed by banks; % SRs subscribed by ARCs; % of SRs subscribed by FIIs; % of SRs subscribed by Others (Qualified Institutional Buyers)

Source: Data collected from the RBI Report on the Trends and Progress of Banking in 2017/18 and 2019/20. FIIs refer to foreign institutional investors.

stage is eligible for acquisition by ARCs.[55] As with the bank creditors, ARCs may enforce on the NPL and the security under SARFAESI without having to turn to the courts;[56] such enforcement is possible once an ARC aggregates 60 per cent of the debt.[57] It should be noted that the advantage of obtaining enforcement via SARFAESI is lost once the matter undergoes the CIRP process as the moratorium will take place. The IBC is expressed to prevail over other legislation, including SARFAESI.[58]

Once the ARCs aggregate the debt through purchases, there are a range of strategies that they may use in connection with the resolution. They may swap the debt for equity in the reorganisation pursuant to the IBC, change the management and then make a profit out of the equity upside when the business cycle improves and the better-managed business is sold after a few years. Alternatively, they may enforce their rights by taking legal proceedings in court but only if the debt is acquired before the debtor undergoes the CIRP process.

Insofar as the IBC is concerned, the coordination costs are impacted by the emergence of the ARCs and the change from hold to maturity to ARCs in at least two ways. First, the IBC process requires negotiation among the financial creditors, and once there is a transition from the original lenders to the new purchasers of the loans, including ARCs, different frictions may arise. The next section explores how different transaction costs arise from the use of ARCs.

highest bidder in the first round, may place a counter-bid and the highest counter-bidder in the second round will succeed. For a description of the Swiss challenge, see IBBI, Discussion Paper (21 August 2021), available at ibbi.gov.in/Discussionpaper-CIRP-27Aug2021.pdf. See also *Saket Tex Dye Private Limited v Kailash T Shah* MA 705/2020 in CP 1981(IB)/MB/2019.

[55] ibid.

[56] SARFAESI, s 13.

[57] SARFAESI, s 13.

[58] IBC, s 238.

Second, the constraints of ARCs may also give rise to frictions. ARCs are created by SARFAESI and are tightly regulated. For instance, SARFAESI stipulates that ARCs are to undertake the role of asset reconstruction or securitisation;[59] SARFAESI does not stipulate that ARCs may pay cash for fresh equity of the borrower, though it can obtain equity through debt–equity swap as part of the resolution plan. As a result, RBI has interpreted the role of the ARCs narrowly and does not allow the ARC to be a resolution applicant bidding for ownership of the distressed assets.[60] These prohibitions have caused difficulties to the ARCs and their investors, as explained in the next section.

5.4.1.1. ARCs and IBC Process

In theory, if the ARCs can aggregate the NPL early, they are able to influence the negotiation processes either at the time or shortly after the debtor undergoes the CIRP process, thereby avoiding a lengthy protraction of the proceedings and the consequent destruction of the value. Bank creditors who do not wish to wait for the outcome of the CIRP could also sell their debt to the ARCs. To ascertain the influence of the ARCs on the outcomes of the CIRP process, I collected data from Debtwire on the sales of the single loan trades on NPLs by the banks between 2017 and March 2021, including the dates of the commencement of CIRPs, the dates when the transactions took place, and the identities of selling banks and the end buyers. I have adopted the classifications of selling banks (whether they are public sector, private sector and foreign banks) and end buyers (whether they are ARCs, banks or other entities) used by the RBI.[61] The focus is the end buyers being ARCs which, in any event, constitute 80 per cent of the total buyers in the dataset. Data collection is possible as sales by banks need to be conducted through an auction process, which will involve some degree of publicity.[62]

There are limitations on the dataset as the data is based on single-loan trades only (and not the entire NPL portfolios, if any) and only contains trades of loans of the large distressed Indian debtors undergoing the CIRP process.[63] However, in terms of the distribution of the ARCs, the top four ARCs (by size of the NPLs purchased) in the dataset broadly reflect the activeness of the major ARCs in the market by the size of the security receipts held as of 31 March 2019 that is reported by RBI.[64] Figure 5.9 presents a scatterplot of the number of days when the sale of the NPLs occurred before or after the commencement of the CIRP (row 0 refers to the date of commencement of the CIRP).

[59] SARFAESI, s 2(1).

[60] 'Aircel Resolution Plan; RBI Issues Notice to UVARACL, Asks to Explain Flouted Norms' *Business Today* (21 November 2020). RBI reasoned that such bids would be inconsistent with SARFAESI. Under SARFAESI, ARCs can only conduct securitisation and asset reconstruction.

[61] Reserve Bank of India, 'List of Asset Reconstruction Companies Registered with RBI' (as at 31 January 2021), available at www.rbi.org.in.

[62] RBI, 'Guidelines on Sale of Stressed Assets by Banks' (n 45).

[63] In ch 1, I define large companies that are those whose financial debts are at least INR100 million. I assume that for the sale of NPLs to ARCs, only debts of large companies are relevant.

[64] RBI, 'Report of the Task Force' (n 45) (showing the security receipts held by the top five ARCs, namely, Edelweiss Asset Reconstruction Company Limited, JM Financial Asset Reconstruction Company Limited, Asset Reconstruction Company (India) Ltd, Asset Care Enterprise Ltd and Phoenix ARC Pvt Ltd).

Figure 5.9 shows that in an overwhelming number of cases, the majority of the bank creditors sell their NPLs to ARCs *after* the debtors undergo the CIRP process, indicating that the original lending banks would first have to undertake the filing of the petition under the IBC. These original lending banks would have been under the moratorium when the CIRP commences and would not have been able to enforce the debt using SARFAESI. Unless they exit the loans through sales, the defaulted loans will have to be dealt with under the CIRP process.

Figure 5.9 also shows that for more recent trades, sales of the NPLs (and thus debt aggregation) to ARCs occur earlier in the CIRP process (see the time trend in Figure 5.9). This, also reflects, in part, the fact that the RBI requires the bank to recognise default after 30 days in 2019, though the trend has commenced even before the said year.[65]

As mentioned above, the RBI data shows that private sector banks sell a much larger proportion of their NPLs to ARCs compared with the public sector banks.[66] Furthermore, I compared the stages at which the sales take place when the debtor is undergoing the CIRP. Figure 5.10 is a box–whisker chart showing the comparison; I found that on average, among banks, public sector banks also wait the longest in the CIRP process before they sell their loans to the ARCs, as compared with the private sector banks and foreign banks in India. Thus, the evidence suggests that public sector banks are more reluctant to sell their NPLs to ARCs, and when they do, they do so later in the day, preferring to undergo the CIRP process. There is a need for further research on the reasons for the wait, eg the quality of NPLs or the preference to deal with the NPLs in-house, such as through direct enforcement or the CIRP process.

Figure 5.9 Time period in which single loan trades to ARCs take place before or after commencement of CIRP

N = 70

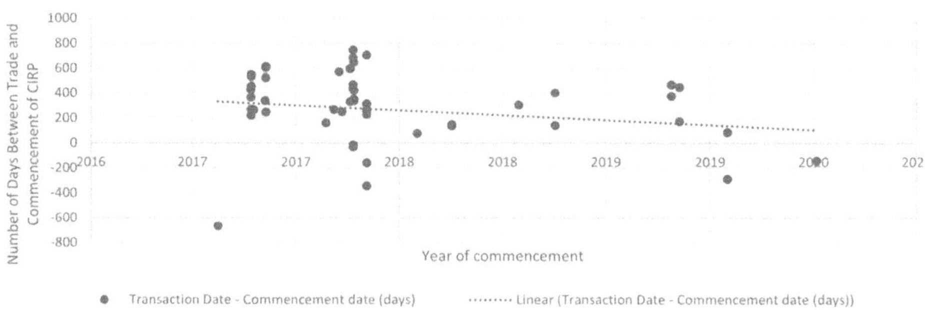

Sources: Data collected from Debtwire (for single-loan trades of NPLs, 2017–20); only single-loan trades to ARCs are included.

[65] RBI, 'Prudential Framework for Resolution of Stressed Assets' (7 June 2019), available at www.rbi.org.in/Scripts/NotificationUser.aspx?Id=11580.

[66] See discussion in n 46 and accompanying text.

Figure 5.10 Time for sale of NPLs by classification of seller
N = 92

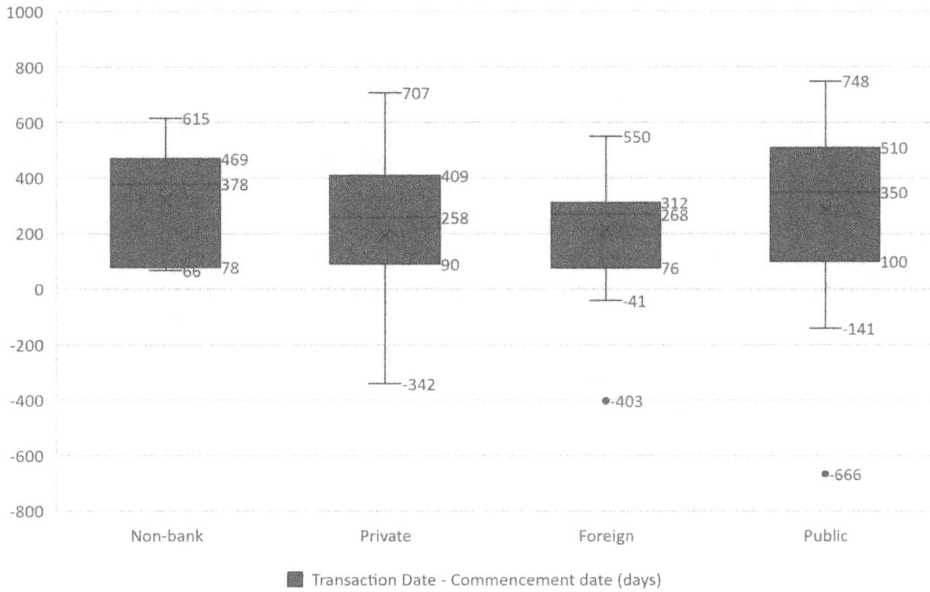

Source: Data collected from Debtwire (for sales of NPLs relating to the debtors, 2017–20); only transactions involving sales of NPLs are included. 'Non-bank', 'Private', 'foreign' and 'public' refer to sales by non-bank financial companies, private sector banks, foreign banks and public sector banks respectively.

5.4.1.2. ARCs and Coordination Costs in India

5.4.1.2.1. ARCs' Incentives to Resolve NPLs

Traditional bankruptcy policy assumes that lenders will maximise the value of their assets in the reorganisation process. When the original lenders sell the NPLs to the ARCs, the new creditors do not have the same information as the original lenders. However, such disadvantages should theoretically be outweighed by the advantages as ARCs face greater incentives and competence to resolve the NPLs quickly, maximising recovery for the creditors and minimising value destruction. However, the validity of the assumption of ARCs maximising value will depend on two factors. The first is the price at which the ARCs acquire the NPLs and consequently, how much ARCs have 'skin in the game' to effect the resolution. The second is the ownership structure of the selling bank lenders and the ARC buyers.

For the first factor relating to the price at which ARCs acquire the NPLs, the original lenders normally run the Swiss challenge system for price discovery, mitigating any perception of collusion between the banks, ARCs and the debtors.[67] The RBI has clearly stated that its objective is to have ARCs to achieve more 'skin in the game' through a series of measures aimed at increasing the cash

[67] Bhagwati, Shuheb and Bogathi (n 30); RBI, 'Guidelines on Sale of Stressed Assets by Banks' (n 45).

component payable for the NPLs.[68] Figure 5.8 demonstrates that foreign institutional investors (FIIs) have increased their investments in the security receipts between 2016 and 2020.

However, as is the case of sales by original lenders, the downside is that the ARCs, as subsequent purchasers, will not have the same information on the debtor as the original lenders.[69] For the purposes of the acquisition, ARCs will have to incur costs to do due diligence and value the assets. The disparity of information will be reflected in the price the ARCs are willing to pay, especially if the collateral is not readily marketable.

For the second factor, as mentioned above, many of the problems relating to the NPLs lie in the state-owned public sector banks.[70] Unlike the Chinese asset management companies which are state-owned or state-controlled, as discussed below, the active ARCs are privately sponsored. Out of the 29 ARCs in India, Table 5.1 presents the shareholding ownership of the top five ARCs by volume of NPLs purchased (where the top five is identified based on the Debtwire data), all of which are sponsored by private sector banks or privately held financial companies, rather than by the public sector banks. The national bad bank that would be co-owned by the public and private sector was only set up in 2021.[71] Hence, in theory, it would be expected that ARCs would be motivated by maximising the recoveries. However, in practice, the regulation of the ARCs has not been aligned to promote maximisation of recoveries.

Table 5.1 Shareholdings of asset reconstruction companies

Name of ARCs	Single largest shareholder	Classification of ARCs
Assets Care and Reconstruction Enterprise	SSG Capital Management (49%)	Privately sponsored
Phoenix ARC	Kotak Mahindra (49%)	Privately sponsored
Reliance ARC	Reliance Capital (49%)	Privately sponsored
Edelweiss ARC	Various Edelweiss Financial entities (49%)	Privately sponsored
JM Financial ARC	JM Financial (49%)	Privately sponsored

Sources of shareholding: Data collected from Orbis and Capital IQ (as of April 2021).

5.4.1.2.2. Conflicting Regulatory Goals of Role of ARCs

ARCs are regulated under SARFAESI, and there is a separate framework for the IBC overseen by the IBBI. The interests of the regulators are not always in agreement. SARFAESI's goal is for the ARCs to play an important role in the resolution of

[68] See nn 51-52 and accompanying text.
[69] F Tung, 'Confirmation and Claims Trading' (1996) 90 *Northwestern University Law Review* 1684.
[70] See n 35 and accompanying text.
[71] V Beniwal, 'India to Give New Bad Bank [US]$4.2 Billion Sovereign Guarantee' Bloomberg (16 September 2021).

the debt. However, several legacy issues continue to linger. First, as outlined above, historically, there is no necessarily clean break between the ARC and original lending bank even after the sale. Banks can subscribe for the security receipts originated by the ARCs. This often reduces the incentives of the ARCs to proactively resolve the loans. Second, conceptually, the role of the ARCs is often unclear. Can ARCs own equity in the business or are they merely confined to holding debt (or debt converted into equity)? If they are only debt-holders, how can they be incentivised to turn the business around?

On the second issue, the Aircel controversy is a prime example of the RBI disqualifying the resolution applicant, UV Asset Reconstruction Company (an ARC), from bidding for Aircel, on the ground that the bid by the ARC did not conform to SARFAESI's or RBI's guidelines on ARCs,[72] and that the role of the ARC is only to undertake asset securitisation or asset reconstruction.[73] The CIRP process under the IBC requires the resolution applicant to bid for the business as a whole and not as merely parts of the assets of the company. By definition, however, ARCs will not have a role in the liquidation process (since they are only to undertake asset securitisation and reconstruction), hence are often not appropriate to bid for the business as a whole.

5.4.1.2.3. Types of NPLs

The types of NPLs in India also pose challenge for the ARCs to resolve. Taking the examples of successful resolutions in the US, the Resolution Trust Companies were successful in resolving the NPLs arising from the savings and loans crisis in the 1980s. However, as experienced by the US, the resolution has been dominated by real-estate NPLs.[74] Real-estate NPLs are relatively easier to dispose as they can be repackaged and securitised or sold on a bulk basis.[75] Also, the requirement to retain the management is often not critical if the real estate is disposed of.

In the case of India, however, the NPLs concentrate not only on real estate but also manufacturing. Figure 5.11 demonstrates that among the firms admitted to CIRPs, manufacturing dominates, followed by real estate, renting and related business activities.

In terms of the single acquisition of the NPLs by ARCs only, Figure 5.12 shows that ARCs continue to prefer acquiring manufacturing NPLs (reflected as industrial products and services) followed by printing and consumer products. Thus, the nature of the NPLs may mean that the success of the resolution of the ARCs may take longer than that observed in the US and other Western markets.

[72] D Sengupta and S Shukla, 'Aircel Resolution Plan: RBI warns UVARCL' *Economic Times Telecom.com* (21 November 2020), available at telecom.economictimes.indiatimes.com/news/aircel-resolution-plan-rbi-warns-uvarcl/79333696. See n 60 and accompanying text.

[73] ibid.

[74] D Klingebiel, 'The Use of Asset Management Companies in the Resolution of Banking Crises Cross-Country Experiences' (February 2000), available at ssrn.com/abstract=282518.

[75] ibid.

Figure 5.11 Sector distribution of CIRPS admitted 2016–20
N = 4,139

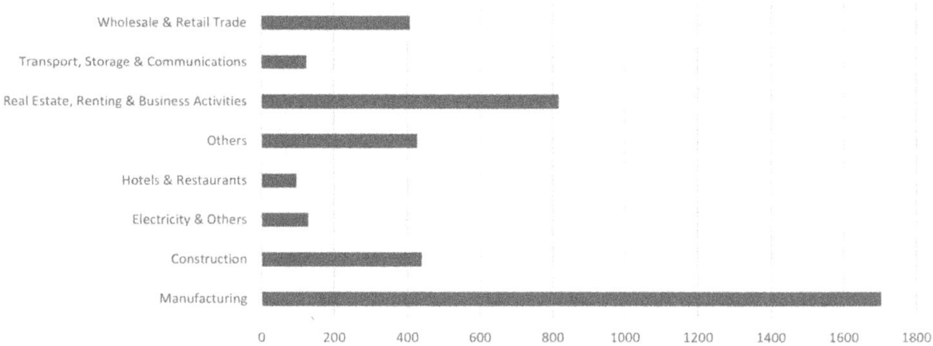

Source: Data collected from IBBI Newsletter (October–December 2020), available at ibbi.gov.in/publication.

Figure 5.12 Number of single NPL sales to ARCs by sector
N = 80 (ARCs as buyers only)

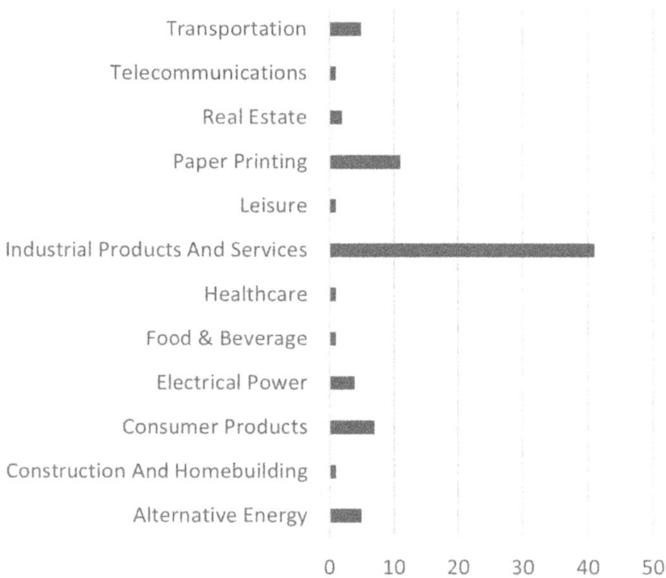

Sources: Data collected form Debtwire (only where the sales of the NPLs are made to ARCs).

5.4.2. CAMCs in China

5.4.2.1. *History of CAMCs*

The role of the CAMCs in the resolution of the NPLs has to be understood in the context of China's banking reforms. In 1979, China began a series of economic reforms to gradually open up the economy to market measures, known as socialist market economy. Between 1979 to the mid-1980s, the People's Bank of China was established as the central bank and four state-owned banks were restructured and established, namely, the Bank of China (BOC), Agricultural Bank of China (ABC), China Construction Bank (CCB) and Industrial and Commercial Bank of China (ICBC), which were the main sources of funding of the SOEs in the decades that followed.[76]

In 1993, another set of financial reforms introduced more market-oriented policies. The Government set up three policy banks – China Development Bank, Export–Import Bank of China and Agricultural Development Bank of China – to separate policy lending from commercial lending to be undertaken by the four state-owned banks.[77] However, lending to SOEs continued and by the time the Asian financial crisis of 1997 commenced, it was estimated that the lending by the NPLs of the four state-owned commercial banks to the SOEs amounted to 20-25 per cent of the country's GDP.[78] This lending amount created large systemic risks and the NPL crisis.[79]

In response to the NPL crisis, CAMCs were established in response, both to ensure the stability in the financial system and also to accelerate the reforms to the SOEs, which were loss-making and running on subsidies from the state.[80] The development of CAMCs can be divided into four phases: 1999–2003 (the policy phase), 2004–09 (the transition phase), 2010–17 (the commercialisation phase) and 2018 to date.[81] In the late 1990s, reference was drawn from the international experience in handling the various distressed assets, including the Resolution Trust Corporation, which used to resolve the savings and loan crisis in the 1980s by the US Government. In 1999, four CAMCs – China Cinda Asset Management (Cinda), China Huarong Asset

[76] K Okazaki, 'Banking Reform System in China' RAND Security Research Division (2007), available at www.rand.org/content/dam/rand/pubs/occasional_papers/2007/RAND_OP194.pdf. Most of these banks were set up much earlier but were restructured in light of the economic reforms.

[77] K Pistor, L Guo and C Zhou, 'The Hybridization of Chinese's Financial System' in BL Liebman and CJ Milhaupt (eds), *Regulating the Visible Hand: The Institutional Implications of Chinese State Capitalism* (Oxford, OUP, 2015) 353.

[78] YK Mo, 'A review of recent banking reforms' in BIS Monetary and Economic Department, *Strengthening the Banking System in China: Issues and Experiences* (Basel, 1999) 75, available at www.bis.org/publ/plcy07.pdf. The author states that many market participants believed that the actual numbers were higher, if international accounting standards were applied.

[79] ibid.

[80] ibid.

[81] cf S Ho and T Marois, 'China's Asset Management Companies as State Spatial–Temporal Strategy' (2019) 239 *China Quarterly* 728, which divided in assessment into three phases (1999-2003, 2003-09 and 2009 onwards). See, generally, Global Offering, 'China Cinda Asset Management Co Ltd' ('Cinda Prospectus') (28 November 2013), copy on file with author (this was used in connection with the listing of Cinda on Stock Exchange of Hong Kong (SEHK) describing the phases and evolution of CAMCs). A similar history can be seen for Huarong: see Global Offering, 'China Huarong Asset Management Co Ltd' ('Huarong Prospectus') (16 October 2015), copy on file with author.

Management (Huarong), China Orient Asset Management (Orient) and China Great Wall Asset Management (Great Wall) (collectively the national CAMCs) – were set up to purchase the NPLs from the four state-owned commercial banks.[82] The CAMCs were initially funded by capital injection from the Ministry of Finance of RMB10 billion to each CAMC, by central bank financing of RMB570 billion and by the issuance of 10-year bonds that were implicitly guaranteed by the state.[83] Approximately RMB1.4 trillion of NPLs was acquired by the four national AMCs at face value.[84]

During this policy phase, the national CAMCs acquired all the NPLs from the state-owned banks, which were regarded as pre-1996 lending when the state-owned bank banks were directed to make loans to companies that were deemed to require state support.[85] After 1996, these banks were relieved of these responsibilities, which were reassigned to the three designated policy banks.

It was during this phase that the national AMCs managed the NPLs acquired in accordance with the set, predetermined cash recovery ratio and expense ratio.[86] The state-owned banks were compensated for the loans, either in the form of reduction of their claims to the central bank or the banks subscribed for the 10-year bonds issued to the AMC, implicitly guaranteed by the state.[87] The bonds were meant to mature in 2009. As described below, the bonds were eventually extended under different circumstances.

The second stage commenced in 2004 with the promulgation of the Administrative Measures on Risk Management for Certain Businesses of AMCs,[88] which incorporated some element of market competition when the CAMCs acquired the NPLs through auctions but over-seen by MoF, PBOC and China Banking Regulatory Commission (CBRC).[89]

The process of acquisition of the distressed assets from the state-owned commercial banks by CAMCs enabled these banks to list on stock exchanges in the next few years.[90] For example, for Bank of Communications (BOCOM), loans with principal

[82] G Ma and BSC Fung, 'China's Asset Management Corporations' BIS Working Papers No 115 (2002), available at www.bis.org/publ/work115.pdf. Each of the big four CAMCs was paired up with a state-owned bank (China Orient with Bank of China, Great Wall with Agricultural Bank of China, Cinda with China Construction Bank and Huarong with Industrial and Commercial Bank of China).

[83] Ma and Fung (ibid); see also J Li, 'Non-Performing Loans and Asset Management Companies in China: Legal and Regulatory Challenges for Achieving Effective Debt Resolution and Recovery' (2013) 1 *PKU Transnational Law Review* 85 (citing references in nn 31 and 39). The bonds were not expressed to be guaranteed by the state, but the existing literature points to some implicit guarantee. See Ma and Fung (ibid).

[84] Pistor, Guo and Zhou, 'The Hybridization of Chinese's Financial System' (2015). However, Ma and Fung (ibid) estimated that the volume was much higher at RMB3.4 trillion (US$410 billion) or 42% of the total outstanding NPLs that were transferred to the big four CAMCs.

[85] Ma and Fung (ibid).

[86] ibid.

[87] ibid.

[88] Notice of the Ministry of Finance about Issuing the Measures for the Administration of the Asset Disposal of Financial Asset Management Companies (Revision) No 41 (20 April 2004) [财政部关于印发《金融资产管理公司资产处置管理办法(修订)》的通知].

[89] See Li, 'Non-Performing Loans and Asset Management Companies in China' (2013). CBRC was merged with the insurance regulator to form CBIRC in 2018.

[90] On the listing of the state-owned banks, see, generally, PB McGuinness and K Keasey, 'The Listing of Chinese State-Owned Banks and Their Path to Banking and Ownership Reform' (2010) 201 *China Quarterly* 125.

value exceeding RMB53 billion were sold to Cinda for a nearly 60 per cent discount.[91] CCB also sold its NPLs to Cinda at a 50 per cent discount prior to its IPO.[92] Between 2005 and 2007, BOCOM, CCB, BOC, China Merchants Bank, ICBC and China CITIC Bank were listed on the Hong Kong and Shanghai stock exchanges. ABC was listed in 2010.[93] Between 2004 and 2006 (first quarter), the year-to-date cash recovery ratio for all of the four CAMCs has ranged from 20 per cent to 21 per cent.[94] However, there is a range over the recoveries: during the same period, Cinda has been an outlier in the cash recoveries (of consistently achieving over 30 per cent), but Great Wall has achieved consistently only around 10 per cent.[95]

Towards the end of the transition phase, in 2008, the national CAMCs were required to record their policy and commercial businesses on separate accounts and assumed the losses on their commercial acquisition and disposal of distressed assets independently.[96] The NPA ratio fell from 9.58 (2005) to 1.76 (2009) (Figure 5.4). It is not clear whether the causal reasons for the fall in the NPA ratio are the effectiveness of the NPL disposals or the strong GDP growth between 2005 and 2009 which led to the market value of the collateral increasing (11.4 per cent in 2005 and 9.4 per cent in 2009).

Towards the start of the commercialisation phase in 2010, national CAMCs began to diversify into other kinds of businesses, including brokerages, trust companies, banking, real estate and insurance.[97] Unlike the original intention of sunsetting the AMCs after 10 years, the CAMCs instead grew in size. By 2010, the CAMCs had diversified into providing other financial services,[98] and the strategy was focused on attracting foreign strategic investors.[99] To raise external capital, two of the national CAMCs – Cinda and Huarong – were listed on the Hong Kong Stock Exchange in 2013 and 2015, respectively.

What then became of the bonds that were issued in 1999? In 2004–05, the Ministry of Finance explicitly provided financial support for the repayment of the interest and principal sums, particularly for Cinda and Huarong.[100] In 2009, MoF directed that the existing bonds be extended for another 20 years, and MoF would continue to provide the support during this period.[101] In 2010 and 2012, respectively, Cinda and Huarong underwent restructuring. They each established a jointly managed fund, funded by enterprise income taxes payable by Cinda (with CCB) and Huarong (with ICBC) respectively, to manage the repayment of the principal of the bonds that were removed from the balance sheet.[102]

[91] ibid.
[92] ibid.
[93] ibid.
[94] Source is from CEIC, which draws its statistics from China Banking Regulatory Commission 2004–06.
[95] ibid.
[96] Cinda Prospectus, 161.
[97] Ho and Marois, 'China's Asset Management Companies' (2019).
[98] ibid.
[99] For example, the strategic investors of Cinda included UBS and Standard Chartered Bank. See Cinda Prospectus, 26. Strategic investors of Huarong included Pincus, Khazanah and Goldman Sachs. See Huarong Prospectus, 179.
[100] Cinda Prospectus, 161; Huarong Prospectus, 182.
[101] ibid.
[102] The source of funding is 'enterprise income taxes payable by CCB [China Construction Bank] and Cinda during the life of the jointly managed fund and other capital allocated by the MOF': Cinda Prospectus, 161; similar arrangements are found for Huarong; Huarong Prospectus, 182.

However, in the first half of the commercialisation phase, it was clear that there were mounting signs of instability in the financial system. The global financial crisis in 2008 resulted in a massive stimulus package and fuelled speculative activities that became apparent a few years later.[103] In 2012, MOF and CBRC undertook a series of reforms to revive the NPL market, including the licensing of provincial CAMCs.[104]

In 2014, the NPA ratio started to increase after experiencing a downward trend from 2005 to 2012. The number of special-mention loans also increased sharply from 2014 to 2020 (see Figure 5.6). In 2016 and 2018, the State Council issued various guidelines[105] to move towards debt–equity swaps as a strategy to reduce the high amount of corporate debt. Unlike the previous exercise in 1999, zombie firms are explicitly prohibited from participating in the debt–equity swap.[106] If the companies undergo such swaps, the arrangements should occur on commercial terms[107] and the swaps are extended not only to the NPLs but also to performing and special-mention loans.[108] However, as banks are unable to directly swap their loans for equity, they can only do so via certain implementing intermediaries,[109] which then prompted the five largest commercial banks to set up asset investment companies.[110]

Asset investment companies are not licensed as CAMCs but are set up to acquire the debt of the banks, and asset investment companies can raise funds from qualified private investors, such as private equity.[111] In respect of the debt that is acquired (which is not confined only to NPLs), asset investment companies specialise in debt-to-equity conversion and disposal, as well as investment and capital raising.[112] It was reported that the asset investment companies had signed 254 swap agreements, representing

[103] Ho and Marois (n 81).

[104] MOF and the China Bank Regulatory Commission (CBRC), 'Administrative Measures for Bulk Transfer of Non-Performing Assets of Financial Enterprises' (January 2012).

[105] See State Council, 'Opinions on Vigorously, Steadily and Properly Reducing Corporate Leverage Ratios' [国务院关于积极稳妥降低 企业杠杆率的意见国发] (22 September 2016); National Development and Reform Commission, 'Notice on the Specific Policy Issues Concerning the Implementation of the Market-Oriented Debt-to-Equity Swaps of Banks' [国家发展改革委、人民银行、财政部等关于市场化银行债权转股权实施中有关具体政策问题的通知 [现行有效] (2018) 15 (19 January 2018).

[106] Opinions of the State Council on Vigorously, Steadily and Properly Reducing Corporate Leverage Ratios [Effective] (No 54 [2016] of the State Council) 国务院关于积极稳妥降低企业杠杆率的意见[现行有效] (国发[2016] 54号) (see ibid).

[107] ibid.

[108] National Development and Reform Commission, 'Notice' (n 105).

[109] They include the banks' subordinate implementation institutions, financial asset management companies, state-owned capital investment and operation companies and insurance asset management institutions. See National Development and Reform Commission (n 105) para VI.

[110] C Zhang, 'More Chinese banks set up own bad-loan asset management companies' *South China Morning Post* (20 October 2016). The five banks are ICBC, ABC, BOC, CCB and BOCOM: see China Local Asset Management Companies Industry, 'China's Local Asset Management Companies White Paper 2020' [中国地方资产管理行业白皮书] (August 2020), available at news.alphalio.cn/PDF/%E4%B8%AD%E5%9B%BD%E5%9C%B0%E6%96%B9%E8%B5%84%E4%BA%A7%E7%AE%A1%E7%90%86%E8%A1%8C%E4%B8%9A%E7%99%BD%E7%9A%AE%E4%B9%A6%EF%BC%882019%EF%BC%89-2020.8-123%E9%A1%B5.pdf.

[111] X Jiang, 'Banks to Set Up Investment Plans Using Debt-to-Equity Swaps' *China Daily* (13 May 2020). The regulatory authority is CBIRC, and the applicable guidelines to asset investment companies are set out in Notice on Measures Relating to the Asset Management Business of Financial Assets Investment Companies [关于金融资产投资公司开展资管理业务有关事项的通知] (No 12 [2020] CBIRC).

[112] 'White Paper 2020' (n 110).

44 per cent of the swap value (RMB 400 billion of the total value of RMB 909.5 billion) by the end of April 2019.[113]

In 2012, the MoF and CBRC allowed the establishment of local or provincial asset management companies in order to participate in the acquisition and disposal of NPLs within their respective provinces.[114] Between 2017 and 2019, more than 50 local or provincial CAMCs were created to purchase bad debt from the local banks in their provinces.[115] As of August 2020, there were 57 local CAMCs distributed across almost all of the provinces and autonomous regions in Mainland China, out of which 76 per cent are owned or controlled by the state (including local governments) and the rest are owned or controlled by private individuals.[116] Local CAMCs have their own advantages as they have closer relationships with the provincial banks (selling the NPLs) and are able to more effectively conduct due diligence on the underlying NPLs and reach pricing more effectively.[117] Provincial banks are incentivised to work with the local CAMCs as they have little bargaining power with the national CAMCs.[118]

During the commercialisation phase, between 2013 to 2018, the four national CAMCs embarked aggressively beyond Mainland China and raised a combined US$100 billion from the debt markets.[119] In particular, Huarong expanded the most aggressively and often purchasing securities from companies that are not necessarily in financial distress.[120] By 2015, its international assets increased by more than 300 per cent.[121] However, following the corruption conviction of Lai Xiaomin, the former chairman of Huarong, in 2018, the regulators began to clamp down on AMCs and required them to divest their non-core business and focus on their core business, that is, the resolution of the NPLs.[122] The national CAMCs promptly complied.[123] The failure of the three Chinese banks in 2019, namely Baoshang Bank, Bank of Jinzhou and Hengfeng Bank, with massive losses to the creditors, also indicated the end of any implicit government guarantee to the banking institutions.[124] In 2020, a fifth

[113] T Huang, 'Tracking China's Debt-to-Equity Swap Program: 'Great Cry and Little Wool' Peterson Institute of International Economics (Washington DC, 24 June 2019), available at www.piie.com/blogs/china-economic-watch/tracking-chinas-debt-equity-swap-program-great-cry-and-little-wool.

[114] See W Shen, *Conceptualising the Regulatory Thicket, China's Financial Markets: After the Global Financial Crisis* (Abingdon, Routledge, 2021) 35.

[115] A Trivedi, 'China Spins a Trade-deal Trap in Bad Debt Market' Bloomberg (17 January 2020).

[116] 'White Paper 2020' (n 110).

[117] P Lei, Y Luo and J Bian, 'The Evolution of Local AMCs'[当前中国地方AMC高质量发展路径研究] [2020] *Southwest Finance* 69.

[118] ibid.

[119] T Hale and E White, 'Pressure Builds to Resolve Fate of Chinese Bad Debt Manager Huarong' *Financial Times* (29 June 2021).

[120] ibid.

[121] ibid.

[122] M Luo and Y Quan, 'Corrupt Bad Bank Chief Was 'Enemy Within,' Watchdogs Say' *Caixin Global* (21 January 2021).

[123] eg Huarong, 2018 Annual Results Announcements of China Huarong (stressing that Huarong would embrace 'two returns' policy where it will focus on its core NPL business and sound internal control system (copy on file with author); China Great Wall International Holdings IV Limited, the affiliate of Great Wall AMC, offering circular dated 24 July 2019 (indicating that Great Wall AMC would pursue the 'dual return' strategy, that is, 'return to onshore, return to core distressed investment business').

[124] See also People's Bank of China, 'Financial Stability Report 2019', available at http://www.centerforfinancialstability.org/fsr/chn_fsr_201911.pdf.

AMC, China Galaxy Investment Management, also state-owned, was established.[125] Its performance remains to be seen.

5.4.2.2. *How CAMCs Manage Distressed Loans*

In general, CAMCs have several advantages compared with other investors of distressed debt. Commercial banks must sell the portfolios of NPLs to the AMCs and not directly to investors, though there are certain relaxations in respect to NPLs that are sold singly or in pairs, including sales to asset investment companies.[126] Sales involving three or more corporate loans must still be conducted by AMCs.[127]

In managing NPLs that are acquired, the CAMCs use a variety of resolution strategies, including packaging and reselling of the NPLs, encouraging the creditors to agree to the revision of the terms of the debt including discounting the pay-offs and longer pay-offs, debt-to-equity swaps, sale of collateral to repay the loans, litigation to enforce loans and sale of the NPLs to third parties.[128] CAMCs can also provide financing in the form of 'mutual benefit claims', which are commonly used in the case of real estate developer restructurings.[129] In such a case, CAMCs jointly finance the construction of the final phase of the buildings, enabling the debtor to complete the sales of the units (and the debtor can then receive the payment from the purchasers for repayment as mutual benefits claims which have priority over the other unsecured creditors).[130] In addition to the acquisition of the NPLs, CAMCs may also acquire voting control of the equity of distressed debtor (and hence control of the underlying assets).[131] In terms of expertise, CAMCs contribute personnel to be in management and in particular, for local CAMCS, serve as local conduit in negotiations with the local governments.[132] However, national CAMCs have limitations on their own leverage. Conversely, local AMCs have limited means to raise funds by bonds and other issues, and they will not be able to absorb all of the NPLs.

[125] S Zhang, 'China Adds a Fifth Bad-debt Manager to Prepare for Decade-high Dud Loans as Covid-19 Weighs on Banks and Borrowers' *South China Morning Post* (18 December 2020).

[126] CBIRC, 'Circular of the General Office of the CBIRC on the Pilot Work of NPL transfers' (2021).

[127] CBRC, 'Relevant Questions Regarding CBRC Measures on Commercial Banks Transferring Loans to Social Investors' No 24 (2009) 银监会《中国银监会办公厅关于商业银行向社会投资者转让贷款债权法律效力有关问题的批复》[2009] 24号.

[128] RL Neyens et al, 'The Successful Asset Management Companies' in M Pomerleano and W Shaw (eds), *Corporate Restructuring: Lessons From Experience*, 1st edn (Washington DC, World Bank, 2005). See also Cinda Prospectus.

[129] 'Mutual benefit' claims are payments that generally benefit all creditors and thus paid from the bankruptcy estate at any time. This concept is rather similar to the US concept of an administrative expense. See EBL Arts 42-43.

[130] X Guo, 'Huang Yun: AMCs and Reorganisations' [黄云：新形势下金融资产管理公司参与破产重整的难点及对策] *Zifeng* (1 April 2019).

[131] T Hu, Z Lu and Q Chen, 'A Study of Cinda Asset Management's Restructuring of Guangdong Jiaye Group' [房地产企业破产重整动因与重组经济后果 – – 以信达资产重组嘉粤集团为例] (2021) China Real Estate [中國房地] 21 (describing Cinda's acquisition of debt and indirect voting control of Jiaye Group, a real estate conglomerate).

[132] eg LS Chen, 'Asset management companies participating in restructuring regimes' [金融资产管理公司参与困难企业重组实践] (2015) 10 *Zhejiang Finance* [浙江金融] 15.

5.4.3. Variations to the Agency Costs of CAMCs in China

There are many advantages of the use of CAMCs to resolve the NPLs as opposed to leaving it to the original creditor banks. These are documented extensively.[133] First, since 1999, CAMCs (particularly the national CAMCs) have been building up strong teams of professionals to deal with the resolution of NPLs.[134] Second, by acquiring and aggregating debt from various creditors, they are also able to control the voting in the creditor meetings during the reorganisation processes, including whether to vote in favour of resolution plans.[135] Third, albeit an unintended consequence of setting up CAMCs, pursuant to debt–equity swaps, the CAMCs end up being shareholders of SOEs in several strategic industries, thereby enabling the state to continue to assert control over the SOEs.[136]

However, the use of CAMCs has several agency costs, which are described below.

5.4.3.1. CAMCs as Market Entities in Times of Market Volatility

The success of CAMCs is evaluated in their enhanced capacity to resolve the NPLs (as distinct from them residing with the banks), whose record can only be assessed realistically from 2010 onwards when the national CAMCs completed their transition into market-oriented commercial entities. However, CAMCs still face legacy issues on implicit guarantees. CAMCs historically have been set up to perform social functions, such as enabling the state-owned banks to be relieved of the NPLs on their books in 1999, and were meant to last 10 years.

As demonstrated in the preceding section, during the policy and the transition phases, CAMCs benefited from the implicit guarantee from the state in respect to the bonds that were issued by the CAMCs, which were supposed to end by 2009 but were allowed to roll over after 2010. After 2010, it was clear that the acquisition of NPLs could only be achieved on commercial terms and at market prices (including via auctions). However, at least for Huarong and Cinda, the bonds continued to roll over for another 10 years pending the completion of the alternative joint funding arrangement.

Meanwhile, for the five large commercial banks, MoF and/or Central Huijin Investment Co Ltd (a subsidiary of MOF) are the shareholders of each of BOC, ABC, CCB, ICBC and BOCOM.[137] Other scholars have observed that MoF, by implicitly guaranteeing the repayment of the bonds to the five largest commercial banks, are fully integrated and that the state bears the ultimate risks and costs.[138]

Proponents of the CAMCs can point to two metrics for evaluation. One is that the NPA ratios for the domestic banks had in fact improved after the setting up of the CAMCs: the NPA ratio fell from 9.58 (2005) to 1.76 (2009) (Figure 5.4).

[133] eg Ho and Marois (n 81).
[134] Li (n 83); Guo, 'Huang Yun' (2019).
[135] ibid.
[136] Ho and Marois (n 81).
[137] Source: CapitalIQ. Central Huijin Investment Co Ltd has the largest equity interests in each of the five banks.
[138] R Chen, 'Legal Informality and Human Capital Development in China' in BL Liebman and CJ Milhaupt (eds), *Regulating the Visible Hand: The Institutional Implications of Chinese State Capitalism*, 1st edn (Oxford, OUP, 2016) 151.

However, the role of the CAMCs in such a fall is unclear since this reduction was coupled with strong GDP growth between 2005 and 2009 (11.4 per cent in 2005 and 9.4 per cent in 2009).

The second is that CAMCs successfully transitioned to market governance: Huarong and Cinda have been successfully listed on the Hong Kong Stock Exchange. During the course of listing, they have attracted several institutional foreign investors. Since the mid-2010s, Great Wall and Orient have regularly tapped into the international bond market for fundraising.[139] However, it is not clear whether the initial success can be attributable to their improved performance in resolving the NPLs or the existence of the implicit guarantee from the state.[140]

In chapter three, I discussed the role of the state as a shareholder of the SOEs, which have been in default of their loans or public debt. The experience is that central or local governments have actively coordinated or rescued SOEs, but such coordination or rescue has been less prominent in the last five years in the push towards market reforms.[141] Nevertheless, CAMCs play a unique role in ensuring the stability of the banking sector. Huarong is a cautionary tale in which a listed CAMC, which was the largest CAMC by total assets as of the end of 2018,[142] was forced by the regulators to scale back its activities to focus on distressed asset management. In 2020 and 2021, Huarong's high-yield debt experienced great volatility because there were some doubts in the market as to whether Huarong was able to pay its outstanding bonds. At the time of writing, it was not clear whether the state would bail out Huarong.

In addition to the implicit guarantee of the banks, it is widely believed that national CAMCs benefit from funding on favourable terms from state-owned commercial banks owing to their policy role; these banks are incentivised to make loans to the AMCs, which in turn purchase their NPLs.[143] Thus, CAMCs may not have the same incentives to manage the NPLs prudently as other commercial entities if they benefit from the implicit state support.

5.4.3.2. *Managing Conflicts of Interests by CAMCs*

CAMCs are state-controlled entities, and a high proportion (55 per cent) of the corporate NPLs is still estimated SOE loans.[144] MoF has the major control of the four CAMCs. Table 5.2 presents the largest shareholding of each of the national CAMCs.

In theory, an asset management company structure will decouple any close relationship between the original lender and debtor. For both the original lender and SOEs, such a decoupling should be viewed favourably by market-oriented commentators. Once the loan is transferred to an asset management company as the new creditor, it should demand the maximisation of the asset recoveries from the defaulting SOEs.

[139] eg recent offerings include bond offerings in August 2020 and November 2020 by Great Wall group and Orient group respectively. Copies of offering memoranda are with author.

[140] See Pistor, Guo and Zhou (n 77) 353.

[141] See ch 3.

[142] Fitch Ratings, China Huarong Asset Management (16 December 2019).

[143] eg, ibid.

[144] D Lipton, 'IMF First Deputy Managing Director speaking at: 'Rebalancing China: International Lessons in Corporate Debt' IMF China Economic Society Conference On Sustainable Development in China and the World (11 June 2016).

Likewise, the state, as a shareholder of the CAMCs, would demand for maximisation of the recovery of the NPLs, whether through liquidation or restructuring. However, the incentives are not so clear-cut if the CAMCs continue to be state-owned or state-controlled; the state, as a shareholder of the defaulting SOE, would want generous restructuring terms that benefit it as a shareholder as opposed to maximising recovery in its capacity as a creditor.

Table 5.2 Shareholding of national Chinese asset management companies

CAMC	Single largest shareholder	Listing status
Orient	MOF (71.6%)	Non-listed
Great Wall	MOF (73.5%)	Non-listed
Cinda	MOF (58%)	Listed
Huarong	MOF (57%)	Listed
China Galaxy Asset Management	China Galaxy Financial Holdings (SOE) (65%)	Non-listed

Source: Data collected from Wind database (as of December 2020) and SCMP (for China Galaxy).

5.4.3.3. Fragmentation of the CAMC Industry in Mainland China

There are currently four national CAMCs (with the fifth being set up) and 57 local CAMCs (as at August 2020).[145] CAMCs are regulated by CBIRC. Local CAMCs and big four CAMCs are regulated differently, with the local CAMCs being restricted from purchasing NPLs other than those from their province, though local CAMCs can sell these NPLs outside their province.[146] Local CAMCs do not enjoy the advantages of national CAMCs in terms of access to loans or loans on favourable terms from financial institutions, but they have the advantages of closer relationships with the local governments, the expertise in the relevant industry and ability to tap into local contacts to attract investors.[147]

5.4.3.4. The Dominance of Manufacturing and Wholesale/Retail NPLs

As in the case of India (see Figure 5.11), the NPLs in China are not concentrated in real estate. Figure 5.13 presents the NPL ratio by industry for the commercial banks for the period between 2006 and 2019. Manufacturing and wholesale/retail trade dominate the NPLs as compared with real estate. Manufacturing NPLs are more challenging to restructure[148] than real estate NPLs due to the need for management to be retained or replaced. Some support can be seen from Figure 5.14, which shows the profiles of the distressed debt assets of the two national CAMCs, where their real

[145] 'White Paper 2020' (n 110).

[146] MOF and the China Bank Regulatory Commission (CBRC), 'Administrative Measures for Bulk Transfer of Non-Performing Assets of Financial Enterprises' (January 2012).

[147] X Wu and X Wu, 'The Development of Asset Management Companies in the Pandemic' [疫情下不良资产管理行业发展趋势] (2020) 4 *Shandong Finance* [山东国资] 13.

[148] ibid.

estate NPL portfolios constitute a much more significant proportion of the NPLs acquired, which suggest that they regard real estate NPLs as having more likelihood of reaching successful resolution.[149]

Figure 5.13 NPLs of commercial banks by top five industries

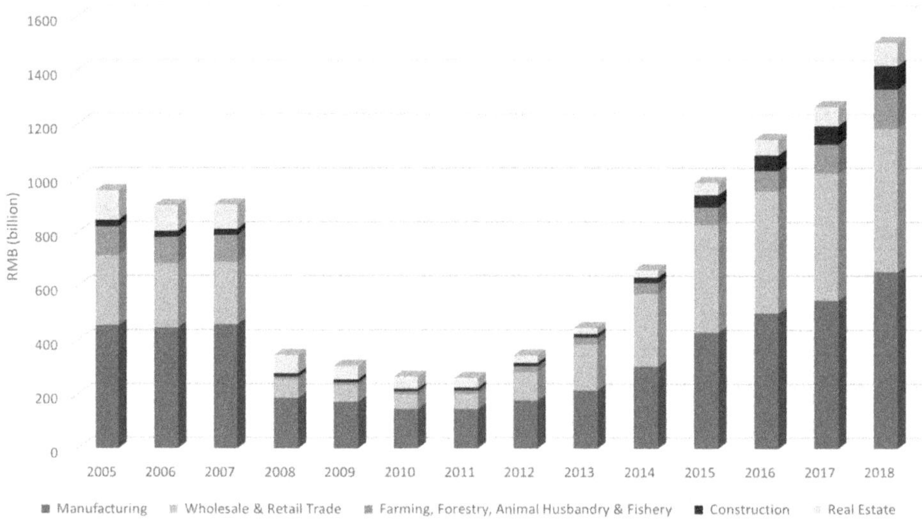

Source: Data collected from CEIC.

Figure 5.14 Risk concentration of distressed assets of Cinda and Huarong

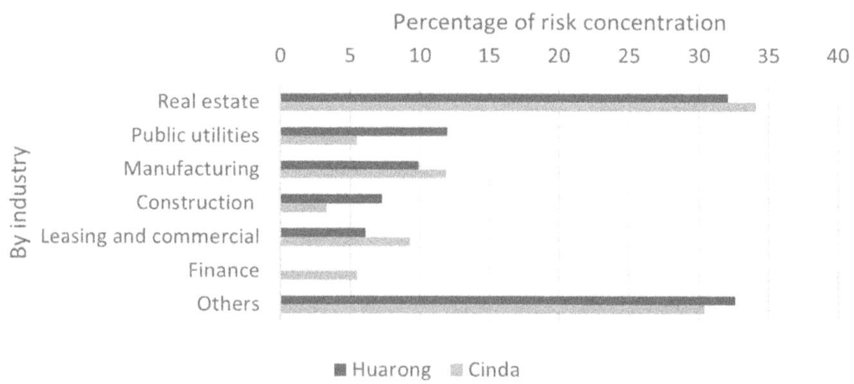

Source: Data collected from the annual report of Cinda as of 31 December 2020 and interim results of Huarong as of 30 June 2020.

[149] As Great Wall and Orient are not listed, comparable information is not available.

5.5. DEVELOPING ACTIVE DISTRESSED LOAN MARKETS IN INDIA AND MAINLAND CHINA

India and Mainland China have recognised the importance of having active distressed loan and debt markets, particularly to encourage foreign investors to invest in the NPLs and to enable holders of distressed debt to exit. Unlike the US and the UK, where distressed loan and debt trading takes place as a result of the shifts in the markets towards portfolio trading techniques rather than regulatory changes,[150] the banking or securities regulators in India and Mainland China have been proactive in developing active distressed loan and debt markets. Such development is seen as critical because it is recognised that the AMCs will not have the financial capacity to resolve the staggering amount of NPLs in the relevant jurisdiction. With an active market for distressed loan, the avenues of taking the NPLs off the books of the banks increase. Distressed funds can acquire the loans from the banks or from the AMCs and later use various tools like debt enforcement or the insolvency and restructuring laws to realise the maximum value.

5.5.1. India

The market for distressed loans has been active in India in recent times, as can be seen from the number of single-loan trades in Figure 5.9. Figure 5.7 also demonstrates that the absolute sum of the book value of NPAs acquired have shown a steady increase during 2016–20. There are three reasons for great interest in acquiring NPAs. First, there is a very large pipeline of distressed loans for acquisition; there is approximately US$126.4 billion of NPAs in banking as of 31 March 2020.[151] Of this figure, the NPAs attributable to corporate borrowers represent 70 per cent.[152] Second, India has an emerging economy, with a number of opportunities for certain sectors of the distressed assets to be turned around with the appropriate management and expertise. Third, the IBC has been a major contributor to the resolution of distressed debt by providing a time-bound process that provides some degree of predictability for recovery and is thus favoured by distressed funds.[153] Chapter eight describes how the IBC has dramatically contributed to the recovery by creditors as compared with the judicial process of debt enforcement. Distressed debt investors are unlikely to be keen in investing in NPAs if the timeline for enforcement of the debt is extremely unpredictable.

[150] Paterson (n 9).

[151] RBI, 'Operations and Performance of Commercial Banks' in Report on Trend and Progress in Banking in India 2019/2020, available at https://rbi.org.in/Scripts/PublicationsView.aspx?id=20270. See also Figure 5.2.

[152] CRISIL, 'Bolstering ARCs: Focus on Quicker Resolutions and Co-investor Model Among Imperatives' (August 2019).

[153] N Narayanan, 'A Guide to Special Situations and Distressed Investments in India for International Investors' (2018) 8 *Emerging Markets Restructuring Journal* 1, available at www.clearygottlieb.com/-/media/files/emrj-materials/issue-8-winter-2018_2019/aguide1-pdf.pdf.

Nevertheless, the channels of NPL disposal continue to remain limited in India. First, as noted by the RBI, trades of NPLs are only to other ARCs and other lenders on an ad hoc basis.[154] The RBI has recently made several recommendations to develop secondary loan and debt markets,[155] and in July 2020, Securities and Exchange Board of India, the securities regulator, permitted trading in defaulted debt securities.[156] Second, due to the restrictions on direct foreign investment in India,[157] foreign investors are limited in the manner of investment of NPLs: one common method is to acquire security receipts issued by the ARCs that have acquired the NPLs.[158] Alternatively, foreign investors could invest up to 100 per cent of the equity in ARCs.[159] However, even though the ARCs are open to foreign investors, the lack of clarity as to regulation of the scope of activities of the ARC will need to be clarified by RBI in order to incentivise such participation.

If a vibrant secondary loan and/or debt market takes place beyond the ARCs, and the regulatory conditions incentivise the banks to get the NPLs off the books, the widespread trading of the distressed debt will have important repercussions on how the debt restructuring will occur in India. Currently, under the IBC, only financial creditors are represented on the committee of creditors and drawing reference from the US and UK experience, it would be expected that the coordination costs among the creditors will increase due not only to divergence in the interests of the original financial creditors and new financial creditors but also the likelihood that there are now significantly more new creditors beyond the ARCs. However, given that the new financial creditors comprise not only ARCs but also other players which are not bound by the RBI requirements, these new players can have more flexibility in serving as resolution applicants. In such a case, it is worth revisiting the question of whether the committee of creditors should be allowed to determine both the questions of deployment and distribution of assets and instead only allow them to determine the deployment question.[160] The question is how much the various creditors should receive is determined by the APR, with perhaps some flexibility for deviation involving shareholders.

[154] RBI, 'Reserve Bank of India Constitutes Task Force on the Development of Secondary Market for Corporate Loans' Press Release (29 May 2019), available at www.rbi.org.in/Scripts/BS_PressReleaseDisplay.aspx?prid=47155.

[155] RBI, 'Report of the Task Force on the Development of Secondary Market for Corporate Loans' (2019), available at rbidocs.rbi.org.in/rdocs//PublicationReport/Pdfs/DSMCLOANSBB7C3EDF738D4038B734E909AC054D68.PDF.

[156] D Mallick, 'SEBI move to allow trading in 'defaulted debt securities' is welcome' *HinduBusinessline* (13 July 2020), available at www.thehindubusinessline.com/opinion/sebi-move-to-allow-trading-in-defaulted-debt-securities-is-welcome/article32065894.ece.

[157] RBI allows funds to buy secondary debt directly, but debt must be external commercial borrowings (ECBs) (ie foreign loans) and few loans are ECB. Other methods include direct lending of INR to non-bank financial companies (NBFCs) (but the investor will need to invest in the NBFC) and direct lending of INR via alternative investment funds which invest in debt securities.

[158] Narayanan, 'A Guide to Special Situations' (2018).

[159] The investor must satisfy certain fitness requirements if he/she holds above 10% of the equity in the ARC. See Narayanan, 'Distressed Debt Investing in India' (2016).

[160] See also ch 4, section 4.5.1.

5.5.2. Mainland China

Mainland China has a large amount of NPLs for disposal, which has grown steadily in the last few years.[161] In 2020, the value of NPLs disposed amounted to RMB3.02 trillion (US$466.6 billion), which represents a sharp increase from RMB2.3 trillion (US$333 billion) in 2019 and RMB1.9 trillion (US$275.5 billion) in 2018.[162] The disposals here refer to write-downs, debt–equity swaps and transfers to third parties. Ascertaining a breakdown of the data between the disposal in the primary and secondary debt market is challenging, but data from Deloitte has estimated that in 2018, the primary market for the sale of NPLs was approximately RMB488 billion (US$70.8 billion), and the secondary market was approximately RMB383 billion (US$55.5 billion).[163] In the primary market, the national and provincial CAMCs constitute 74 per cent and 19 per cent of the total buyers of NPLs by volume.[164] In respect to the secondary market for the trading of the NPLs, local investors purchased 62 per cent of the NPLs by volume, followed by CAMCs (34 per cent) and foreign investors (four per cent).[165]

Historically, the Chinese regulators have instituted programmes and channels in attempts to improve the primary and secondary trading of the NPLs and in attracting foreign investors into the NPL market.[166] Even as early as 2001, Morgan Stanley and Goldman Sachs participated in the disposal of NPLs by Huarong, with a total book value of US$1.5 billion.[167] Until 2006, which was then the original deadline for the CAMCs to dispose the NPL portfolios, various structures were used to dispose of NPLs to foreign investors, either in return for cash or equity interests.[168] CAMCs also established joint ventures with foreign investors with the CAMCs' contribution to the joint ventures taking the form of NPL portfolios.[169] In 2020, phase 1 of the trade deal between the US and China (the Economic and Trade Agreement) allows for US financial services firms to apply for licences to set up AMCs. These foreign-owned AMCs can purchase distressed debt from the banks directly without having to purchase from the national or provincial AMCs.[170]

[161] Deloitte LLP, 'Deleveraging Asia' Financial Advisory (2019), available at www2.deloitte.com/content/dam/Deloitte/sg/Documents/finance/sea-fa-restructuring-services-deleveraging-asia-2019.pdf.

[162] CGTN, '2020: Chinese banks dispose $467b in non-performing assets' *CGTN* (22 January 2021), availableatnews.cgtn.com/news/2021-01-22/2020-Chinese-banks-dispose-467-bln-in-non-performing-assets-XggBVOE492/index.html#:~:text=China's%20banking%20sector%20disposed%203.02,(CBIRC)%20said%20on%20Friday; China Banking News Editor, 'China Disposed of 2 Trillion Yuan in Bad Loans in 2019: CBIRC' *China Banking News* (13 January 2020) available at www.chinabankingnews.com/2020/01/13/china-disposed-of-2-trillion-yuan-in-bad-loans-in-2019-cbirc; Shorevest, 'China Debt Dynamics: Dealing With a Coming Surge in Nonperforming Loans' (2020) available at shorevest.com/wp-content/uploads/2020/11/20.-ShoreVest-China-Debt-Dynamics-Dealing-With-a-Coming-Surge-in-Nonperforming-Loans.pdf.

[163] Deloitte LLP (n 161).

[164] ibid.

[165] ibid.

[166] eg C Miao and H Liu, 'China: Legal Avenues for Foreign Investors to Participate in China's NPL Market' Mondaq, JunHe Law Office (3 January 2017), available at www.mondaq.com/china/international-trade-investment/557088/legal-avenues-for-foreign-investors-to-participate-in-china39s-npl-market.

[167] RL Neyens et al, 'The Successful Asset Management Companies' in M Pomerleano and W Shaw (eds), *Corporate Restructuring: Lessons From Experience*, 1st edn (Washington, DC, World Bank, 2005).

[168] Miao and Liu, 'China: Legal Avenues' (2017).

[169] ibid.

[170] The first foreign-owned AMC was set up by Oaktree Capital. See Finews Asia, 'A Surprise Inclusion in the Phase one U.S.-China Trade Deal, Oaktree Capital Management becomes the first foreign beneficiary

However, notwithstanding these avenues, there are several difficulties for foreign institutional investors to participate in the distressed loan market in China, including the high professional costs,[171] lack of easy access to the court processes, difficulties in finding local purchasers for the underlying assets, and difficulties in negotiations with other local stakeholders.[172] Other factors that could discourage investment include the low usage of the Enterprise Bankruptcy Law 2006 (which is discussed in chapter eight) and the length of time in the legal system enforcing loans (estimated by analysts to take 18 to 36 months).[173]

Further, at the regulatory level, in the primary market, banks are required to sell the portfolios of NPLs to the CAMCs; investors are unable to purchase the NPLs directly from banks unless the purchases are in respect of less than three portfolios. Unlike retail NPLs, it is relatively less common for corporate NPLs to be packaged into asset-backed securities for sale to investors due to their more complex requirements for due diligence as corporate NPLs are often secured.[174] CAMCs tend to decentralise the NPL sales at the relevant branches rather than at the headquarter level, requiring the buyers (particularly foreign buyers) to build local relationships if they are sourcing the portfolios across provinces.[175]

In more recent years, more channels of disposal of NPLs have been added. In addition to the direct sales of NPLs, banks and also CAMCs can also dispose NPLs[176] by selling them online on the financial asset exchanges to the public, though this constituted a small portion of the overall NPLs sold in Mainland China.[177] In 2018, the State Administration of Foreign Exchange (SAFE) allowed commercial banks to sell NPLs privately to foreign investors through Shenzhen Qianhai Financial Assets Exchange (SQFAE).[178] Similar arrangement was made for Guangdong Financial Assets Exchange.[179]

of liberalized access to the mainland's distressed debt market' (19 February 2020), available at www.finews.asia/finance/31031-oaktree-capital-china-s-first-foreign-wholly-owned-bad-loan-manager.

[171] N Somasundaram, 'High costs hold back foreign funds from investing in Chinese debt' *Nikkei Asian Review* (17 February 2020), available at asia.nikkei.com/Business/Finance/High-costs-hold-back-foreign-funds-from-investing-in-Chinese-debt (pointing out that fees for accountants and lawyers can add 15% to value of the transactions).

[172] See Shorevest (n 162).

[173] ibid. The estimates are very large in view of the diversity in economic development among the various provinces in Mainland China. See, however, the World Bank *Doing Business 2020* rankings which give the average time as 16.5 months for 2020 for the major cities of Shanghai and Beijing (available at www.doingbusiness.org/en/doingbusiness). See also ch 7 discussing the length of time in enforcing contracts.

[174] Shorevest (n 162).

[175] PwC, 'The Chinese NPL Market in 2020', available at www.pwccn.com/en/deals/publications/the-chinese-npl-market-in-2020.pdf.

[176] NPLs involving national security or sensitive information and certain private loans involving individual loans cannot be sold on the platform.

[177] An estimate by Marco Polo puts the volume of loans as RMB90.4 billion in the fourth quarter of 2017. See D McMahon, 'Financial Asset Exchanges: Auctioning Bad Loans to the Masses' *Marco Polo* (2018), available at macropolo.org/cleanup_analysis/financial-asset-exchanges-auctioning-bad-loans-to-the-masses. In comparison, Cinda was willing to sell RMB124.1 billion during the same period.

[178] SAFE, 'Notice regarding the Establishment of a Pilot Program by SAFE's Shenzhen Branch for the Cross-border Transfer of NPLs' (HuiFu (2017) No 24) (《国家外汇管理局关于深圳市分局开展辖区内银行不良资产跨境转让试点业务有关事项的批复》(汇复 [2017] 24 号)).

[179] White & Case, 'Developments on the Chinese NPL Market' (9 November 2018), available at www.jdsupra.com/legalnews/developments-in-the-chinese-npl-market-46283.

Other innovations for the disposal of NPLs to retail investors include various online platforms, including Taobao,[180] which is managed by Alibaba and JD.com.[181] Judicial auctions in respect to the collateral that is to be disposed are also carried out over five online platforms, namely, JD.com, People's Court Litigation Assets Network,[182] Public Auction,[183] the China Association of Auctioneers[184] and Taobao. In comparison with financial asset exchanges, Taobao has been more attractive to CAMCs for selling their NPLs in the secondary market (as compared with the banks).[185] In theory, by broadening the avenues through which the NPLs may be sold to the public via open and transparent auctions, the price transparency of the NPLs will be improved, because potential investors can compute the internal rate of return with the bids. However, with the exception of Taobao, it is often difficult to obtain data on the price of the NPLs that are sold.[186] Other criticisms of the online auction platform include information asymmetry between the debtor and the purchasers of the NPLs, the suitability of NPL purchases by retail investors and challenges in regulating the platforms.[187]

Insofar as restructurings are concerned, the availability of alternative ways to dispose NPLs in the market and in particular, the presence of foreign investors on the distressed debt market, would lead to more market-based methods to resolve the NPLs. However, the opposing force is that there will be greater fragmentation of the creditors, since the NPLs are not concentrated in the hands of the original lenders or the CAMCs. Clarifications over the scope of the APR becomes important to avoid hold-outs. As is the case of India, this is likely to increase the coordination costs of the creditors when it comes to the reorganisation of the debt. The ability to commence pre-negotiated or pre-packaged sales prior to bankruptcy filing will assume greater importance.[188]

5.6. CONCLUSION, LESSONS AND IMPLICATIONS FOR MANAGING NPLs

Addressing the NPL problems in India and in Mainland China necessitates not only the legal framework for debt enforcement, reorganisation and restructuring, but also the utilisation of several tools at the disposal of banking regulators, particularly the use of ARCs/AMCs and their functional equivalents to acquire and restructure the NPLs as well as deepening the market for distressed assets. As both jurisdictions are emerging markets, investors may take the benefit of considerable upside if they

[180] www.taobao.com.

[181] www.jd.com.

[182] www.rmfysszc.gov.cn.

[183] www.gpai.net.

[184] www.caa123.org.cn.

[185] D McMahon, 'Taobao Bad Loan Auctions: What online Prices Reveal about the NPL Market' Marco Polo (2019), available at macropolo.org/cleanup_analysis/taobao-bad-loan-china-data.

[186] ibid.

[187] See generally, LJ He and M Yuan, 'Research on Internet platforms and NPL disposal' [互联网+"背景下不良资产业务模式创新研究] (2015) 7 *Internet Finance* [特别聚焦·互联网金融], available at www.ixueshu.com/document/679a46508972abf18921a81bbdd55229318947a18e7f9386.html.

[188] ch 7, section 7.5.3 discusses the Chinese experiments with the pre-packs.

successfully turn around the distressed businesses. According to some accounts indicated in this chapter, while ARCs and AMCs will not be able to resolve all of the NPLs in the two jurisdictions, they remain important regulatory tools.

5.6.1. Incentivising CAMCs/ARCs

Thus far, the review of the agency and coordination costs of CAMCs and ARCs indicates the progressive manner in which the regulators have demanded more 'skin in the game' and more market-oriented ways of dealing with the NPLs, particularly in the last decade. In India, since August 2014, ARCs were required to retain some of the risks in the distressed debt that was sold and thus had to hold 15 per cent in the distressed assets which cannot be sub-contracted out. In Mainland China, foreign investment limits in the AMCs were lifted in 2018, though all of the national CAMCs were still controlled by the state. The regulators have also experimented in the ways to liberalise the NPL market to allow the setting up of local CAMCs and to allow various innovative exchanges for the sale of the NPLs.

Ultimately, the key to the success of the CAMCs/ARCs in the ecosystem of NPLs is that the ARCs/AMCs should acquire and resolve NPLs on a commercial basis and must not extract rent by being mere parking vehicles for the distressed debt. Thus, CAMCs/ARCs should add value in resolving the debt through enforcement of the debt through the courts or restructuring and should adopt market-oriented ways to acquire and dispose of the loan at market prices. However, several agency and coordination costs remain, which may have impacted the debt of the secondary markets. In India, the active ARCs are privately sponsored and not state-owned in nature and theoretically do not face the problems of implicit state guarantee. Further, due to the presence of foreign investors taking equity stakes the ARCs or bidding jointly with the ARCs, the distressed loan market in India is more market-oriented. However, the data on the transactions of single-loan NPLs show that the incentives of the state-owned banks still are to sell the NPLs later than the private sector banks even after the debtor is insolvent (having commenced the CIPR process). Often, the earlier the ARCs can get into the reorganisation process, the earlier the ARCs can provide stability and can negotiate with the various stakeholders. There is often no clean break from the original banks after the sale of the NPLs and the original banks continue to participate in the form of subscription to the security receipts.

In China, the large commercial banks and national AMCs are state-owned, and the latter have, in the past, served as policy goals for state-owned commercial banks to dispose of the NPLs. The majority of the NPLs are also SOE loans. It is unclear whether the implicit guarantees available to the national CAMCs and the SOEs will continue, making it challenging for investors to determine whether to invest in the CAMCs or their joint ventures that are set up to deal with NPLs. The volume of single-trade NPL activity in the secondary loan market is not as active as that of India.[189]

[189] Debtwire, Distressed Loan Trades for 4Q2020, 2H 2019 and 4Q2018.

5.6.2. Future of the CAMC/ARC Model and Distressed Loan Markets

Several recent developments will shape the future of the CAMCs/ARCs. First, the role of ARCs in India has been rapidly evolving. The broader question is what should be the role of ARCs? Is it one of debt resolution only, or owning and running the business of the distressed debtor? The former, which is the current model and is tightly regulated by the RBI, limits the potential of the ARCs.

The second relates to the make-up of the distressed loan market. In both jurisdictions, manufacturing NPLs dominate among the corporate NPLs, rather than the real estate NPLs found in the US. However, in the case of Mainland China, real estate is the leading distressed debt investment of the two national CAMCs, being Cinda and Huarong. The landscape suggests that some policy shifts may be required to deepen the attractiveness of the NPL market not only for distressed real estate but also in other types of sectors such as manufacturing, where the identity of the management team required to run the business is important.

5.7. POSTSCRIPT

In late 2021, when the manuscript for this book was being edited, the RBI published the report of the Committee to Review the Working of Asset Reconstruction Companies, which the RBI had convened to make recommendations on, among other matters, improving the legal and regulatory framework of the ARCs.[190] In particular, the Committee highlighted that the performance of the ARCs could be improved. For instance, the redemption of the security receipts issued by ARCs (which is a proxy for recovery for their holders) has been dismal and the acquisition costs of the NPAs by ARCs have been at inflated rates. For the financial years 2004 through to 2013, and 2014 through to 2021, the average redemption amount of the security receipts to the book value of the NPAs acquired was 14.3 per cent and 10.4 per cent respectively.[191] Further, 80 per cent of the recovery by the ARCs did not go towards optimising recovery of the debtor's businesses.[192] The Committee has made a number of comprehensive recommendations which better align the incentives of the ARCs, both in respect of maximising recovery of the stressed financial assets and facilitating the revival of the debtors' businesses. Many of these recommendations are discussed in this chapter, including incentivising selling banks to sell the NPAs at an earlier stage and allowing ARCs to have a broader role in the restructuring, such as the ability to acquire the debtor's equity and to act as resolution applicants.

[190] RBI, 'Report of the Committee to Review the Working of Asset Reconstruction Companies' (September 2021).

[191] ibid, 33.

[192] ibid, 5.

6

Insolvency Practitioners as Gatekeeper Intermediaries

6.1. INTRODUCTION

IN THIS CHAPTER, I focus on the role of insolvency practitioners (IPs) as gatekeeper intermediaries between the company and its creditors in court-supervised restructurings. The term 'gatekeeper' describes outside professionals providing services without which the transaction cannot be completed.[1] This would be relevant in the practitioner in possession (PIP) models, such as the United Kingdom (UK)) administration, the Indian corporate insolvency resolution process (CIRP) and the Singapore judicial management, as well as hybrid debtor in possession (DIP) and PIP model, such as the Chinese reorganisation process under the Enterprise Bankruptcy Law 2006 (EBL). In PIP or hybrid PIP proceedings, an IP, as an intermediary, would replace the functions of the board of directors, and his/her appointment (and discharge of duties) is subject to court approval and oversight. In some jurisdictions, where restructuring is part of the insolvency procedure, the IP is required to bring actions to reverse fraudulent transfers, unfair preferences or terminate unfavourable contracts.

Although English schemes of arrangement and restructuring plans under Parts 26 and 26A of the Companies Act 2006 do not have any statutory roles for the IP, I include in the discussion the role of the scheme managers in Singapore, as they have a statutory role and are held accountable to creditors by case law.[2] In Hong Kong, I include the discussion on the role of the IP appointed by the Hong Kong court as a provisional liquidator while recognising that a provisional liquidator is appointed not only for the purpose of restructuring, but for other purposes such as the safeguarding of the debtor's assets.[3] I exclude the purely advisory relationship between the professional and his/her creditor client as the professional does not serve as a gatekeeper

[1] See RH Kraakman, 'Gatekeepers: The Anatomy of a Third-Party Enforcement Strategy' (1986) 2 *Journal of Law, Economics, & Organization* 53; JC Coffee, 'Gatekeeper Failure and Reform: The Challenge of Fashioning Relevant Reforms' (2004) 84 *Boston University Law Review* 301.

[2] Insolvency, Restructuring and Dissolution Act 2018, Pt 5. See discussion below, section 6.2.2.1. A scheme manager does not need to be a licensed IP.

[3] See ch 1 generally. Excluded in the discussion is the role of the soft-touch provisional liquidator as that is appointed pursuant to the court of the offshore jurisdiction since it remains a DIP proceeding and the provisional liquidator has no statutory role in Hong Kong. See ch 1, section 1.5.4.1.

intermediary.[4] Thus, bankruptcy attorneys appointed to carry out Chapter 11 reorganisations are excluded as the debtor appoints its professional advisers accountable only to their appointer.[5] I also exclude the assessment of the effectiveness of non-judicial government agencies, such as the Insolvency and Bankruptcy Board of India (IBBI) or the US Trustee under the US Trustee Programme, a component of the US Department of Justice.

As intermediaries, IPs play several valuable roles. In this chapter, I focus on two key roles: (1) collecting information and managing the business of the financially distressed company while the company is undergoing restructuring; and (2) devising and implementing rescue strategies.[6] Both roles are essential in preventing value destruction of the debtor prior to its exit from the restructuring. Unlike DIP proceedings, where management drives the restructuring and may not be objective in their assessment of the viability of the debtor company, IPs, as independent professionals, objectively evaluate the viability of the debtor and often the competence and honesty of the management. In discharging their duties, they pledge their reputational capital by acting independently and in the interests of the creditors as a whole. It is important for IPs, particularly those in PIP regimes, to be seen as not favouring either the debtor management or any particular creditor.

Nonetheless, for various reasons, an IP may not always be counted upon as an independent or effective intermediary on whom to rely. First, IPs are often experience conflicts of interest and may prioritise the interests of particular parties over those of other stakeholders. Second, IPs are ineffective if they are unable to gather the requisite information or work with the existing stakeholders to manage the business in the interim (thereby failing to prevent value destruction) or are unable to devise rescue strategies even for economically viable companies (and lead to premature liquidation). The IP is unable to secure the management's cooperation because the management is displaced by the IP and is unable to negotiate effectively with a diverse set of creditors.[7]

To limit opportunistic behaviour and increase accountability (particularly in emerging markets), the regulatory framework responds with various controls in terms of appointments, fee arrangements and professional body oversight, which are over and above the oversight by creditors. A licensing regime for IPs is created for India and Singapore. Regulation of conflicts of interests and fees, supplemented by judicial oversight, features prominently as well, in all the jurisdictions. However, when it comes to restructuring, unlike an insolvent liquidation, the focus of which is to sell the assets to recover the value to the creditors and distribution of the assets, which is

[4] See the discussion in ch 3 and WY Wan and C Watters, 'Mandatory Disclosure in Corporate Debt Restructuring via Schemes of Arrangement: A Comparative Approach' (2021) 30 *International Insolvency Review* S111 generally on RSAs.

[5] For a discussion on professional fees in Chapter 11 proceedings, see L LoPucki and JW Doherty, 'The Determinants of Professional Fees in Large Bankruptcy Reorganization Cases' (2004) 1 *Journal of Empirical Legal Studies* 111.

[6] V Finch, 'Corporate Rescue: a Game of Three Halves' (2012) 32 *Legal Studies* 302.

[7] J Dickfos, 'The Costs and Benefits of Regulating the Market for Corporate Insolvency Practitioner Remuneration' (2015) 25 *International Insolvency Review* 56.

normally but not always in accordance with the set order of relative pre-bankruptcy priorities, matters are much more complex. Restructuring often involves having to deal with the whole of the company's finances to determine the best option, and it is often not possible to assess whether the IPs should be able to charge the fees they demand. Overly prescriptive rules of conflicts of interests may sacrifice competence for independence.

Although a large body of literature has examined the theoretical issues and empirical evidence on IPs as intermediaries in the UK, such as Armour and Mokal,[8] Finch,[9] Armour et al[10] and Wheeler,[11] there is comparatively less discussion on the role of the intermediaries in the restructurings in the four Asian jurisdictions. This chapter fills the gap. It discusses how the professional advisers generate their own agency costs because of structural ineffectiveness and conflicts of interests and how these costs can be controlled or managed to maximise the preservation of the debtor's estate in the restructuring process. In recommending reforms to deal with conflicts of interests, this chapter also partly draws from the discussion in the theoretical literature on professionals as gatekeepers in other roles when it comes to their incentives and appropriate responses.[12]

This chapter analyses externalities and agency costs differently to chapters three, four and five. For one thing, the discussion on Anglo-American literature in this chapter does not focus on the US position because creditor negotiations in Chapter 11 take place using creditor committees that are given wide-ranging powers to investigate and even to reject the Chapter 11 plan proposed in the absence of satisfactory disclosures. The creditor committee has the fiduciary duties to represent the unsecured creditors as a whole,[13] but the advisers appointed by the committee do not perform intermediary functions. In the plan of reorganisation under Chapter 11, the debtor, with the assistance of the financial advisers, may prepare the hypothetical Chapter 7 liquidation analysis if the plan is not approved through persuading the court that the proposed plan satisfies the 'best interests of creditors' test. However, the advisers do not give their opinions to the creditors in the disclosure statements.[14] Instead, the relevant comparator here will be the UK administration under the Enterprise Act 2002. The UK scheme of arrangement and restructuring plans are excluded because the IP does not displace the directors; also, neither provides for a statutory power of investigation, and there is no power to challenge an unfair preference or an

[8] J Armour and RJ Mokal, 'Reforming the Governance of Corporate Rescue: the Enterprise Act 2002' (2005) 1 *Lloyd's Maritime and Commercial Law Quarterly* 28.

[9] V Finch, 'Insolvency Practitioners: Avenues of Accountability' (2012) 8 *Journal of Business Law* 645.

[10] J Armour, A Hsu and A Walters, 'The Impact of the Enterprise Act 2002 on Realisations and Costs in Corporate Rescue Proceedings: A Report Prepared for the Insolvency Service' (December 2006).

[11] S Wheeler, 'Capital Fractionalized: the role of insolvency practitioners in asset distribution' in M Cain and CB Harrington (eds), *Lawyers in a Postmodern World* (Buckingham, Open University Press, 1994).

[12] eg Coffee, 'Gatekeeper Failure and Reform' (2004); I Fletcher, 'UK Corporate Rescue: Recent developments – Changes to Administrative Receivership, Administration and Company Voluntary Arrangements – the Insolvency Act 2000, the White Paper 2001, and the Enterprise Act 2002' (2002) 5 *European Business Organization Law Review* 119 (the role of IPs in the context of company voluntary arrangements).

[13] DG Baird and RK Rasmussen, 'Anti-bankruptcy' (2009) 119 *Yale Law Journal* 648.

[14] Author's perusal of disclosure statements of Chapter 11 plans in recent restructurings.

undervalued transaction.[15] Instead I include the UK administration which may be invoked either in court or out of court.[16]

6.2. ROLE OF INSOLVENCY PRACTITIONERS: A COMPARATIVE PERSPECTIVE

6.2.1. The PIP Model

In PIP regimes, where IPs displace managers to various degrees, there is a need to ensure the accountability of the IPs to creditors or stakeholders with claims to the assets of the company. As is the case with solvent companies, the directors are accountable to the company, and the shareholders' meetings are the means of holding such directors accountable.

6.2.1.1. UK Administration

The Enterprise Act 2002 introduced the administration procedure as a mechanism of corporate rescue. The primary objective is to rescue the company as a going concern.[17] However, the legislation prescribes two other objectives, which are the achievement of a better result for the company's creditors as a whole than would be likely if the company were wound up[18] and the realisation of some or all of the company's property to distribute to one or more secured or preferential creditors.[19]

Administration can be invoked after a formal hearing by a court order or an out-of-court process filed by the holder of a floating charge or by the company.[20] Once the company is put into administration, the administrator, a qualified IP, displaces the board of directors. The administrator has powers to manage the business affairs of a company[21] and negotiates and presents the plan for the creditors to approve. Although bank creditors may control or have a significant influence over the choice of administrator and his/her appointment, once appointed, the administrator is an officer to the court[22] and owes duties to all the creditors as a whole.[23] He/she has wide-ranging powers to carry out investigations and sets aside unfair preferences and undervalue transactions.[24]

[15] J Payne, *Schemes of Arrangement: Theory Structure and Operation* (Cambridge, CUP, 2014), 231 (explaining that the scheme of arrangement is not an insolvency procedure). However, in *Re Gategroup Guarantee Limited* [2021] EWHC 304 (Ch), the High Court of England and Wales recently held that the Pt 26A restructuring plan is an insolvency procedure which falls within the insolvency exception under the Lugano Convention.

[16] Insolvency Act 1986, Sch B1. See generally, Payne (ibid) 196–97; Armour and Mokal, 'Reforming the Governance of Corporate Rescue' (2005).

[17] Insolvency Act 1986, Sch B1, para 3(1)(a).

[18] Insolvency Act 1986, Sch B1, para 3(1)(b).

[19] Insolvency Act 1986, Sch B1, para 3(1)(c).

[20] Insolvency Act 1986, Sch B1, paras 11 and 14.

[21] Insolvency Act 1986, Sch B1, para 59.

[22] Insolvency Act 1986, Sch B1, para 5.

[23] Insolvency Act 1986, Sch B1, para 3.

[24] Insolvency Act 1986, ss 238 and 239.

In exercising his/her powers, the administrator must seek the approval of unsecured creditors with regard to the proposed plan.[25] Secured creditors continue to retain significant rights in the administration, including insisting on non-interference with charged assets notwithstanding the moratorium.[26] The approval of unsecured creditors is not required if the administrator thinks that the company is solvent; there are insufficient assets to distribute to the unsecured creditors or if the objectives of administration cannot be satisfied.[27] An important power that the administrator has is the ability to enter into a pre-packed sale of the underlying business, which has become increasingly popular in the past two decades. For instance, major companies have been put into administration, including Johnston Press plc[28] and Debenhams plc,[29] with a view towards effecting pre-pack sales. Under the pre-pack, the company is put into administration, and its business or assets are immediately sold by the administrator under a sale arranged before formal administration, without the agreement of the unsecured creditors or consent of the court.[30] If the administration is twinned with a scheme of arrangement, the out-of-money junior creditors and shareholders can be crammed down.[31] There are special disclosure rules and approval requirements that apply if the sale is to a 'connected person',[32] pursuant to Administration (Restrictions on Disposal, etc to Connected Persons) Regulations 2021.[33] Pre-packs where the sales are made to the existing management even prior to the previously mentioned regulations could possibly be abused. Therefore, the current Statement of Insolvency Practice 16, introduced by the Insolvency Practitioner Association, imposes certain minimum disclosure obligations on IPs in pre-packs and independent valuations, upon failure of which regulatory action may be taken against the IPs.[34]

Administrators may charge hourly rates, fixed fees or fees based on the value of the assets.[35] Either the court or creditors' committees (as the case may be) fix the fees.[36] At the end of administration, the company is liquidated, and its assets are distributed in accordance with the liquidation waterfall.[37]

[25] Insolvency Act 1986, Sch B1, para 49.

[26] Insolvency Act 1986, Sch B1, para 73.

[27] Insolvency Act 1986, Sch B1, para 52.

[28] M Garrahan and P Wells, 'Johnston Press agrees administration deal with lenders' *Financial Times* (17 November 2018).

[29] FT Reporters, 'Debenhams in Administration: a Timeline' *Financial Times* (10 April 2019).

[30] See *DKLL Solicitors v HMRC* [2007] EWHC 2067 (Ch); Payne, *Schemes of Arrangement* (2014), ch 5 generally. Secured and preferential creditors must consent to the CVA for the CVA to be binding on them.

[31] See ch 4, section 4.3.2.2.

[32] Insolvency Act 1986, s 435 read with para 60A of Sch B1.

[33] The current regulations are found in Administration (Restrictions on Disposal etc to Connected Persons) Regulations 2021 (SI 2021/427).

[34] Insolvency Practitioner Association, 'Statement of Insolvency Practice 16' (SIP 16) (2015). Earlier versions were introduced by Association of Business Recovery Professionals.

[35] Insolvency Rules 1986 (SI 1986/1925), as amended.

[36] Insolvency Rules 1986, rr 2.47–2.49.

[37] There may be cases the court is prepared to sanction distribution without a winding up. See, eg, *Re Lehman Brothers Europe Ltd* [2017] EWHC 2031 (Ch).

Decisions of the administrator are subject to challenge under the Insolvency Act 1986 by a creditor or member upon unfair harm being inflicted to his/her interests,[38] but the courts give the administrator wide discretion to exercise his/her powers.[39]

While the UK administration is distinctly PIP, developments since the onset of COVID-19 pandemic show that the market practitioners are using a 'light-touch' administration, where the administrator allows the management to exercise some of these powers while the administrator continues to have oversight.[40] This development is understandable as COVID-19 pandemic was unexpected and the financial distress experienced by many of the firms is not due to management fraud or incompetence but to extraneous factors which are not readily foreseeable.

6.2.1.2. Hybrid PIP and DIP Model: Mainland China

Under the EBL, the debtor or the creditors may file the petition in the courts if the debtor is unable to pay its debts.[41] Once the bankruptcy petition is accepted by the courts, an administrator is appointed to oversee the case.[42] However, the debtor's management may remain in control of the property and manage the business with the court's approval.[43]

Local courts publish the list of qualified law firms and accounting firms that are eligible to act as administrators.[44] Depending on the province, the appointment of the administrator may be held through random or competitive bids, and the courts often have a significant influence over the manner of appointment. Commentators have observed that appointment is consistent with the view of professionalising administrators.[45] Competitive bids are required for bankruptcies of banks, securities companies, insurance companies, finance companies and companies that have a great impact in society and complex matters.[46] Different courts set out their competitive bidding processes. For instance, the Shenzhen Intermediate Court invokes a competitive tender process evaluated by its review committee.[47] The Zhejiang High Court

[38] Insolvency Act, Sch B1, para 74. See also Armour and Mokal (n 8).

[39] See eg *Four Private Investment Funds v Lomas and others* [2009] 1 BCLC 161; *Re Charnley Davies Ltd (No 2)* [1990] BCLC 760; *In re Meem* [2017] WLR(D) 718 *and Lehman Bros Australia Ltd v MacNamara and others* [2020] 3 WLR 147.

[40] eg *Re Debenhams Retail Ltd (in administration)* [2020] EWHC 921 (Ch) 20; *Re Debenhams Retail Ltd (in administration)* [2020] EWCA Civ 600 (the company goes into administration under a light-touch procedure that allows the management of the company to stabilise the business during the period of uncertainty resulting from COVID-19).

[41] EBL, Arts 2 and 7.

[42] EBL, Art 13.

[43] EBL, Art 73.

[44] S Steele et al, 'Trends and Developments in Chinese Insolvency Law: The First Decade of the PRC Enterprise Bankruptcy Law' (2018) 66 *American Journal of Comparative Law* 669.

[45] ibid.

[46] SPC, Provisions of the Supreme People's Court on Designating the Administrator during the Trial of Enterprise Bankruptcy Cases [关于审理企业破产案件指定管理人的规定], Judicial Interpretation No 8 [2007] Art 21.

[47] S Li and Z Zheng, *Law Review of Corporate Reorganization and Restructuring* [公司重整法律评论：上市公司重整专辑] vol 5 (Beijing, China Law Press [法律出版社], 2019) (in Chinese) 279.

selects through a combination of shortlisting eligible administrators, after invitation for qualified persons to bid, and ultimately random selection from the shortlist.[48] The Zhejiang High Court also allows for selection outside of the province.[49]

An administrator may be a 'social intermediary' or a 'liquidation team'.[50] The former refers to a law firm, accounting firm or a bankruptcy liquidation firm and can include an individual affiliated to the aforementioned.[51] In practice, social intermediary administrators are often law firms.[52] Liquidation teams comprise government officials who will depend on the industry and the location of the debtor, officers from People's Bank of China, lawyers and accountants.[53] The Supreme People's Court provides that the liquidation team is an exception rather than the rule, such as where the laws expressly require such appointment, with a catch-all that the court will appoint a liquidation team when deems it proper to do so.[54] However, the requirement is apparently not met in practice.[55] In the dataset of reorganisations of listed companies in Appendix A, Panel B, in 10 out of 21 cases, liquidation teams with government officials were, in fact, appointed.[56] The rest were social intermediary agencies, which were mostly law firms. In the dataset in Appendix A, Panel B, liquidation teams are often appointed for SOE restructurings but are also sometimes appointed for private enterprise restructuring, suggesting that if the enterprises are sufficiently large or significant to the local economy and their failures can result in widespread social instability, the local government would be involved.[57] In fact, in the list of typical EBL cases issued by the Supreme People's Court in 2018 and 2020, whether for SOEs or privately owned enterprises, the role of the local government is often emphasised in the coordination process with lenders, investors or other government departments, particularly in respect of resettling the workers.[58]

The administrator is subject to supervision by the creditors' committees, and he/she reports to the court.[59] Although not explicitly stated in the EBL, the administrator

[48] Steele et al, 'Trends and Developments in Chinese Insolvency Law' (2018).

[49] ibid.

[50] EBL, Art 24.

[51] EBL, Art 24. However, an individual without an affiliation to a firm or organisation cannot be appointed.

[52] Li and Zheng, *Law Review of Corporate Reorganization and Restructuring* (2019) 271.

[53] ibid, 267. Recent observations suggest that at least in certain regions such as Zhejiang, the appointment of government-led liquidation teams is being phased out: Steele et al (n 44).

[54] Provisions of the SPC on Designating the Administrator during the Trial of Enterprise Bankruptcy Cases, issued on 12 April 2007 [关于审理企业破产案件指定管理人的规定], Arts 18–19.

[55] H Zhao, *Government Intervention in the Reorganisation of Listed Companies in China* (Cambridge, CUP, 2019) 178.

[56] In comparison, Zhao (ibid), found that more than 75% of the 53 listed reorganisations (as at October 2018) have had liquidation team appointments.

[57] See also Y Ren, *A comparative study of the corporate bankruptcy reorganization law of the US and China* (The Hague, Netherlands/Portland, Eleven International Publishing, 2012) 169, observing that if the debtor is an SOE, the Government will always control the liquidation team through the appointment of relevant government officials since the officials are in the best position to deal with widespread unemployment, and they can instruct affiliated creditors (such as state-owned financial institutions) to agree to a haircut and to obtain new financing. However, these findings relate to restructurings in the first six years post-EBL.

[58] See Typical of EBL Cases issued by the SPC (2018) and (2020) [全国法院审理破产典型案例], available at pccz.court.gov.cn/pcajxxw/pcdxal/dxal.

[59] EBL, Art 23.

owes duties to the creditors and the court.[60] EBL requires that the administrators be disinterested in the case.[61] Once appointed, the administrator is in charge of managing the property and business operations unless otherwise ordered by the court.[62] Either the administrator or the debtor formulates a plan for creditors, depending on who is in charge of managing the business.[63] (The creditors do not propose the plan.) Compensation of the administrator is based on scaled fees, depending on the value of the debtor's property recovered by unsecured creditors and subject to the final approval of the court.[64] Unlike the US's and UK's restructuring regimes, where the debtor's estate would be expected to pay the costs of the creditors' professional fees upon successful restructuring, the creditors bear their own fees.[65] The administrator has the power to take actions to reverse fraudulent transfers[66] and void preferences.[67] He/she has the power to affirm or disclaim executory contracts.[68]

6.2.1.3. PIP Models: India and Singapore

I next discuss two other variants of the PIP models under the IBC in India and judicial management in Singapore.

6.2.1.3.1. India – Resolution Professional

The IBC provides for the IPs,[69] the interim resolution professional (interim RP) and the resolution professional (RP), to play a central role in the process. The IBBI, as the regulator of IPs, has spearheaded many efforts in professionalising IPs through the administration of mandatory courses and licensing exams.[70] Upon an CIRP application being admitted, the court appoints the interim RP who is vested with the powers of the board of directors.[71] The power includes amending existing contracts,[72] but the exercise of other powers requires the approval of the creditors.[73] During the moratorium period, RPs can decide on which goods and services are critical to the operation of the company, and the supply of those goods and services cannot be terminated,

[60] EBL, Art 27 provides that the duties must be discharged faithfully.

[61] EBL, Art 24.

[62] EBL, Art 73.

[63] EBL, Art 80.

[64] Supreme People's Court Regulations on Determination of Bankruptcy Administrator Compensation No 129 [2007] of the Supreme People's Court.最高人民法院关于执行《最高人民法院审理企业破产案件指定管理人的规定》、《最高人民法院审理企业破产案件确定管理人报酬的规定》几个问题的通知(2007年4月12日　法明传[2007] 129号).

[65] DA Austin and C Lin, 'Bankruptcy with Chinese Characteristics: Insolvency Administration in the People's Republic of China' (2020) 94 *American Bankruptcy Law Journal* 85.

[66] EBL, Art 32.

[67] EBL, Art 33.

[68] EBL, Art 18.

[69] IBC, s 3(19).

[70] IBBI, 'Insolvency Professional: the Key to Resolution Information Brochure', available at www.ibbi.gov.in/uploads/whatsnew/2021-04-13-163323-pt2ei-a56e6e185a5c5b7e8c7355f7a68f612f.pdf.

[71] IBC, s 17.

[72] IBC, s 20(2).

[73] IBC, s 28.

suspended or interrupted unless there are unpaid dues.[74] RPs (including those who are formerly interim RPs) are appointed by the committee of creditors at the first creditors' meeting, with a 66 per cent majority approval.[75] RPs are licensed by IBBI and are aided by information utilities, which are licensed repositories of information relating to the debtor. RPs adhere to a code of conduct and are independent of the debtor.[76] RPs are subject to various disclosure requirements pertaining to conflicts of interests to the committee of creditors.[77]

RPs can appoint their own professional advisers who are often essential if complex businesses are involved.[78] Valuers appointed by the RPs are also required to be independent.[79] Fees of the RPs are approved by the committee of creditors.[80] As is the case with UK administrators, RPs are required to investigate avoidable transactions.[81]

However, RPs, unlike UK administrators, do not have the power of sale of assets without creditor approval. The role of the RP is to collate and verify creditor claims, prepare the contents of an information memorandum to solicit bids, solicit bids for resolution plans and present their findings to the committee of creditors for the latter to approve.[82] In running the bidding process, the method used is normally that of the Swiss challenge[83] although the courts have not mandated that method in every case. In practice, RPs do not prepare or negotiate resolution plans, which are left to the resolution applicants and the creditors directly.[84] The committee of creditors, comprising financial creditors, decides on the deployment of the assets (eg who to sell the assets to) and the distribution of the proceeds.[85] Once approved, the RP presents the plan to the NCLT for approval.

[74] IBC, s 14. This was introduced by an amendment legislation to the IBC in 2019.

[75] IBC, s 22(2).

[76] Insolvency and Bankruptcy Board of India (Insolvency Resolution Process for Corporate Persons) Regulations, 2016 (CIRP Regulations), reg 3, which prohibits a RP taking up assignments where any of his/her relatives, or any of the partners or directors of the insolvency professional entity in which he/she is a partner/director, are in any way connected to the insolvent company or any of its related parties. See also Insolvency and Bankruptcy Board of India (Insolvency Professionals) Regulations 2016 (which has a Code of Conduct applicable to the RPs).

[77] IBBI and International Finance Corporation, 'Understanding the IBC', available at www.ibbi.gov.in/uploads/whatsnew/e42fddce80e99d28b683a7e21c81110e.pdf; IBBI, 'Circular Disclosures by Insolvency Professionals and other Professionals appointed by Insolvency Professionals conducting Resolution Processes' (12 January 2018), available at ibbi.gov.in//webadmin/pdf/legalframwork/2018/Jan/Disclosures-Circular-12.01.2018%20(1)-1_2018-01-16%2018:26:45.pdf.

[78] Insolvency and Bankruptcy Board of India (Insolvency Professionals) Regulations 2016, First Schedule, Code of Conduct, para 25 (the RP must ensure that his/her fees and fees of advisers engaged by him/her are reasonable).

[79] CIRP Regulations, reg 27.

[80] CIRP Regulations, reg 34.

[81] IBC, s 25.

[82] IBC, s 25. In *Essar Steel*, the Supreme Court clarified that the RP does not have to determine whether the resolution plan contravenes applicable law but only needs to present the findings to the committee of creditors.

[83] The Swiss challenge method is used for government tendering process to facilitate the awarding of contract in the second round of bidding to the highest bidder. See *Saket Tex Dye Private Limited v Kailash T Shah* MA 705/2020 in CP 1981(IB)/MB/2019.

[84] D Kumar and G Sundaresh, 'Insolvency Professionals Under India's New Insolvency Regime' (2018) 8 *Emerging Markets Restructuring Journal* 1.

[85] See ch 1 on the discussion on the issues of both deployment and distribution.

The RP's fees are fixed by the committee of creditors and constitute insolvency process resolution costs that have priority in the distribution.[86] The fees are required to be 'reasonable'.[87] Success fees (alongside fixed fees) charged by RPs (or advisers appointed by the RPs) have been reported in case law and in proceedings before the disciplinary proceedings of IBBI, and the NCLT has reviewed the fees for reasonableness even if the fees have been approved by the committee of creditors.[88] Reviews of fees are distinct from the decisions of the committee of creditors that relate to the approval of the plan where only a light-touch review is generally used[89] because fees are not regarded as a business decision exclusively within the commercial purview of the committee of creditors.[90] The discussion on court oversight of fees is further detailed in chapter seven.

6.2.1.3.2. Singapore Judicial Manager

Judicial management was the functional equivalent of the original UK administration order procedure as introduced by Insolvency Act 1986 until the Enterprise Act 2002 substantially revised it by allowing an administrator appointed out of court either by the debtor company or by a general secured creditor.[91] The judicial management regime was revised as part of the 2017 insolvency reforms in Singapore to make Singapore a restructuring hub.[92] In the current judicial management regime, which applies only to insolvent companies, the judicial manager can be appointed by the court[93] or out of court (by the creditors).[94] The purpose is to achieve one of the objectives, ie to secure the survival of the company as a whole in order to implement a scheme of arrangement or a more advantageous method of realising assets.[95] The secured creditor can nominate its choice of judicial manager but does not have an absolute veto power over the appointment.[96] In general, the court grants the judicial management order when the preeminent creditor(s) support it.[97]

[86] IBC, s 30 read with CIRP Regulations, reg 34.

[87] IBC, s 208(2). The IBBI and Society of Insolvency Practitioners of India listed their views of reasonableness: see IBBI, 'Circular on Fee and other Expenses incurred for CIRP' (June 2018), available at www.ibbi.gov.in/webadmin/pdf/whatsnew/2018/Jun/Circular%20on%20Fee%20and%20other%20Expenses%20incurred%20for%20CIRP%20[June%202018]_2018-06-18%2014:06:58.pdf.

[88] See eg *Ashok Commercial Enterprises v Ariisto Developers Pvt. Ltd* MA NO 391 OF 2020 (NCLT); IBBI Disciplinary Committee, order dated 5 March 2021, available at ibbi.gov.in/uploads/order/99021d25ea6922dc843d3c792ef85443.pdf.

[89] The NCLT does not have the authority to analyse or evaluate the commercial decision of the committee of creditors in voting for a particular resolution plan or to reject the plan by dissenting creditors. See *Sashidhar v Indian Overseas Bank* (Supreme Court, 5 February 2019). See ch 4, section 4.4.1.2. However, see also ch 7 (discussing the role of the courts criticising the larger haircut in recent cases).

[90] ibid.

[91] IRDA, Pt 7.

[92] G McCormack and WY Wan, 'Transplanting Chapter 11 of the US Bankruptcy Code into Singapore's Restructuring and Insolvency Laws: Opportunities and Challenges' (2019) 19 *Journal of Corporate Law Studies* 69. See also ch 2.

[93] IRDA, s 91.

[94] IRDA, s 94.

[95] IRDA, s 89.

[96] IRDA, s 91(3).

[97] *Re KS Energy Ltd and another matter* [2020] SGHC 198.

Once appointed, as is the case with the UK administrators, the duties are owed to the creditors as a whole.[98]

Unlike the scheme of arrangement, the judicial manager reports to the court and drives the structuring. The judicial manager prepares a proposal that would enable the company to achieve the purposes of restructuring and obtains creditors' approval before proceeding to obtain creditors' approval for implementation.[99] However, although the judicial manager has the power to deal with the assets of the company,[100] he/she still needs to table a statement of proposal for the majority of the creditors to approve within 90 days (unless extended).[101] If a pre-pack is desired, the Singapore version still requires evidence of creditor approval.[102] In any event, the debtor company must enter into a scheme of arrangement for the debts of the company to be adjusted such that it is binding on the creditors or class of creditors.[103] As is the case with the liquidator, the judicial manager has the power to challenge antecedent transactions, such as unfair preferences and undervalue transactions,[104] and is able to secure a third-party funding agreement to pursue these actions.[105] He/she has the power to disclaim onerous contracts, subject to setting aside by the court.[106] When a company enters judicial management, it operates as a temporary stay of proceedings.[107]

Similar to the UK, it is possible for the creditor or residual claimants to challenge the judicial manager's decision on the grounds of unfair prejudice.[108] Considerable weight is still given to the judicial manager. In a recent case, the court declined to intervene in the judicial manager's decision to implement a sale of assets (which were the shares of the operating subsidiaries) to a company that was connected with a former director, as opposed to a competing bidder that was favoured by the shareholder.[109] The court reasoned that even though the competing bidder was willing to offer a higher price, its completion was less certain and would have taken a longer time.[110]

6.2.1.3.3. Key Differences in the PIP Regimes

The Singapore judicial manager or the RP in India have two significant differences with the UK administrator. First, unlike the UK administrator, the Singapore judicial

[98] IRDA, s 89(2).

[99] IRDA, s 107.

[100] IRDA, s 99, read with First Sch.

[101] Discussions with Singapore insolvency lawyers confirmed that the power of sale is seldom used in the absence of the approval of the creditors as to the judicial managers' statement of proposal.

[102] IRDA, s 71.

[103] IRDA, s 107 read with s 117. For a discussion on the relationship between judicial management and schemes, see EB Lee, 'Insolvency Law' (2003) 4 *Singapore Academic of Law Annual Review of Singapore Cases* 263.

[104] IRDA, Pt 9.

[105] IRDA, s 99, read with First Schedule, para (f).

[106] IRDA, ss 230 and 232.

[107] IRDA, s 96(4).

[108] IRDA, s 115.

[109] *Re HTL International Holdings Pte Ltd* [2021] SGHC 86 (considering the predecessor provision to IRDA, s 115). The decision was upheld on appeal in *Yihua Lifestyle Technology Co, Ltd and another v HTL International Holdings Pte Ltd and others* [2021] SGCA 87.

[110] *Re HTL International Holdings Pte Ltd* [2021] SGHC 86 (holding that to intervene, the conduct must be 'plainly wrongful conduct, has been conspicuously unfair or has been perverse' at [43]).

manager or the RP in India does not normally exercise (or in the case of India, does not have) the power to enter into a sale of assets or substantially all of the assets without prior creditor approval.[111] Neither does the pre-pack route available in Singapore allow for an independent power of sale.[112] The implication is that in the deployment question, the creditors must still bargain among themselves and with the IP in Singapore's judicial management system and in the Indian CIRP. Second, unlike the UK administration where the proceeds are distributed based on the liquidation waterfall, the creditors in Singapore's judicial management and the Indian CIRP need to bargain over the distribution of proceeds.

Generally, the administrator's powers are most extensive in Mainland China in the EBL when compared with other regimes such as those in India and Singapore. The administrator has the power to affirm or disclaim executory contracts, and such a power is not subject to the court's approval.[113] However, given that judicial oversight by the administrator is extensive because the appointment and remuneration of the administrator are made by the court, the administrator is likely to have sought directions of the court.[114]

6.2.2. Schemes of Arrangement with Insolvency Practitioner Having a Statutory or an Intermediary Role

6.2.2.1. Singapore

In Singapore, even before the 2017 reforms, the scheme of arrangement did not require that a formal insolvency practitioner be appointed. However, the practice, which has continued after the 2017 reforms, has been to appoint a financial adviser (also known as a turnaround specialist) or an insolvency practitioner, who is later appointed by the court as the scheme manager when the scheme is sanctioned. The choice of scheme manager is one that the major creditors have informally supported. Prior to court sanction, the proposed scheme manager administers the proofs of claims and determines the eligibility of voting. After the scheme is sanctioned, he/she administers the scheme, and the powers are derived from the scheme. Because the scheme is between the company and its creditors and not with the scheme manager, the scheme manager covenants to the company to administer the scheme.[115] The proposed scheme manager or another financial adviser may also give advice to the creditors on recovery pursuant to liquidation analysis, that is, the value received by the creditors upon liquidation if the scheme is not approved. This value is disclosed in the explanatory statement

[111] See n 100 and accompanying text. While IRDA, s 99(6) allows for the power of sale, the Singapore judicial manager is required to put the statement of proposal before the creditors within 90 days under IRDA, s 107. In practice, discussions with the insolvency lawyers and practitioners indicated that the power of sale is very seldom exercised in the absence of creditor approval.

[112] IRDA, s 71.

[113] EBL, Art 18.

[114] See ch 7.

[115] See Payne (n 15) 234 on the English practice.

although it is not the practice in Singapore to include the entire liquidation analysis prepared by the proposed scheme manager.[116]

As the scheme of arrangement is not an insolvency proceeding, unlike the judicial manager, the scheme manager, before or after his/her appointment, is not tasked to make an independent investigation on the prior transaction avoidance or wrongdoing. There is wide latitude on the role of the proposed scheme manager. When a financial adviser is appointed by the company to conduct restructuring through a scheme in Singapore, he/she acts more as an investment bank or financial adviser rather than as an intermediary. This is evident in some (but not all) cases where the adviser is paid a success fee or the adviser receives compensation in equity of the debtor (thereby taking the upside) rather than cash.[117] *TT International* (discussed below) involved the proposed scheme manager who had a success fee with the debtor company.[118] The case prompted judicial pronouncements on the role of the scheme manager, indicating concerns that the scheme manager may stray too far into the realm of acting solely for the debtor without regard to the creditors' interests.[119]

When Parliament had the opportunity to consider making wide-ranging reforms to the insolvency framework in 2018,[120] the role of the scheme manager was codified in IRDA but not the duties. Under IRDA, the scheme manager is not required to be a licensed insolvency practitioner, unlike a liquidator; this continues to leave the door open for the scheme manager to act more as an investment bank or financial adviser than as an intermediary.[121]

6.2.2.2. *Hong Kong*

Prior to *Re Legend International Resorts*,[122] provisional liquidation was widely used as a tool for the debtor to obtain a stay on enforcement proceedings while the debtor undertook a scheme of arrangement.[123] Once provisional liquidators are appointed, the directors' powers immediately cease. In chapter one, I explained the limitations placed on the use of provisional liquidation as a tool for implementing restructuring posed by *Re Legend International Resorts*, and these limitations were softened in *Re China Solar Energy Holdings Ltd*.[124] The current situation is that it

[116] Wan and Watters, 'Mandatory Disclosure in Corporate Debt Restructuring' (2021).

[117] WY Wan, C Watters and G McCormack, 'Schemes of Arrangement in Singapore: Empirical and Comparative Analysis' (2020) 94 *American Bankruptcy Law Journal* 463.

[118] See n143 below.

[119] ibid.

[120] Ch 2.

[121] IRDA, s 47. See also Ministry of Law, Licensing and Regulatory Regime under IRDA, available at https://www.mlaw.gov.sg/files/IRDA-Annex-B-Licensing-Regime.pdf.

[122] [2006] 2 HKLRD 192.

[123] Companies (Miscellaneous Provisions and Winding Up) Ordinance, Cap 32, s 186. See also SHC Lo and CZ Qu, *Law of Companies in Hong Kong* (Hong Kong, Sweet Maxwell/Thomson Reuters, 2018) ch 19.

[124] [2016] HKCU 465; *Re China Solar Energy Holdings Ltd* [2017] 2 HKLRD 1074; *Re China Solar Energy Holdings Ltd* [2018] HKCFI 555. See CZ Qu, 'The Court's Power to Appoint Provisional Liquidators to Carry Out Rescue Roles: Rethinking Legend' (2019) 28 *International Insolvency Review* 86. See also ch 2.

is possible to appoint provisional liquidators if the company is insolvent so long as the assets are in jeopardy, even if one of the reasons for the appointment is to effect a restructuring.[125]

When it comes to the fee arrangements, IPs engaged by debtors are generally paid on an hourly basis, whether they are involved in restructuring or liquidation work, in Hong Kong.[126] In some cases, there could be a success element, on top of the hourly rate, pegged to the successful restructuring of the debtor and its survival for an agreed period.[127] However, there remains the issue that fee arrangements are often not transparent to the creditors. When liquidators (or provisional liquidators) are appointed, Hong Kong courts do not regard fees as a matter to be decided purely by the debtor and the liquidators.[128] In *Re Da Yu Financial Holdings Ltd*,[129] a court found that the one-line disclosure of the restructuring fees of the IPs and the legal advisers (without the associated breakdown) was not adequate. The court made it clear that if the fees were disproportionately large when compared with creditor recovery, the broader question would be one of whether the scheme was pursued for the benefit of the creditors as a whole.

Da Yu Financial Holdings takes place in the context of a peculiar feature not found in Singapore that the listing status is the only asset of value of the distressed firm. Listing status is not recorded on the company's balance sheet, but the proceeds of the listing status can be used, either wholly or partially, to repay the creditors and the costs of the restructuring. In *Da Yu Financial*, the company, which was listed but was suspended from trading, acquired assets from the white knight investor who received shares through a reverse takeover. The investor subscribed for the shares in cash. The cash was used to pay the professional fees incurred and the creditors who had the debts compromised in the scheme of arrangement (and took a haircut). Thus, the court expressed concern that if the entire cost of the restructuring was consumed by the cash amount being made available, rendering there being very little benefit for the creditors who took more than a 95 per cent haircut. The scheme of arrangement was sanctioned but on the condition that the costs of the restructuring be taxed.

6.3. THE GOVERNANCE OF INTERMEDIARIES: ACCOUNTABILITY, CONFLICTS OF INTEREST AND EFFECTIVENESS

As outlined in section 6.1, IPs perform two essential roles: (1) collecting information and managing the business of the financially distressed company; and (2) devising

[125] ibid.

[126] Interviews with various insolvency practitioners in Hong Kong. This is the case even for schemes of arrangement where there is no requirement for the fees to be subject to review by the courts.

[127] ibid.

[128] See also *Re Rhine Holdings Ltd* HCCW 510/1998 (this was a case where liquidators were appointed and were getting the approval of the Hong Kong court for a transfer of shares pursuant to a scheme of arrangement to be sanctioned offshore).

[129] [2019] HKCFI 2531.

and implementing rescue strategies. The former is essential for preventing value destruction of the debtor prior to its exit from restructuring. Unlike DIP proceedings, where the management drives the restructuring (and may not be objective in their assessment on the viability of the debtor company), IPs, as independent professionals, objectively evaluate the viability of the debtor, and often the competence and honesty of the management. In discharging their duties, IPs effectively pledge their reputational capital and would not rationally sacrifice their reputation in a transaction for a relatively modest fee. IPs are also very visible, and league tables (such as Debtwire) track advisory mandates and the size of these mandates.

Nonetheless, reliance on the IP as the gatekeeper intermediary might be misplaced for various reasons. First, there could be lack of accountability of IPs, which means a lack of incentive not to behave badly. Second, IPs may be induced to breach their duties. Such inducement can arise because of their close relationships with selected creditor banks (due to being repeat players in PIP proceedings) or fee arrangements that unduly favour the debtor's management over the creditors'.

Third, the IP may not be effective. Unlike a solvent company that is incentivised to cooperate with the gatekeeper intermediaries employed (such as auditors), the incentives are not present in financially distressed situations and may, in fact, be counterproductive. IPs may be ineffective as they are unable to gather the requisite information and/or to manage the business (thereby failing to prevent value destruction) or devise viable rescue strategies (and lead to premature liquidation). The management, which is partly or wholly displaced by the IP, might not be willing to disclose requisite information. Creditor banks may still control the cash flow during the process and be unwilling to allow expenditures to enable control of trading or new financing that rank *pari passu* or trump their priorities. The state of the lending market might mean that the IP cannot rely on his/her repeat player status to negotiate only with repeat player creditor banks. He/she has to negotiate with much more diverse and varied lenders, including institutions that purchased bonds at market when the company was solvent and distressed debt traders who acquire the debt after the company goes into distress. The outsized fees of IPs can also trigger criticism by the creditors, particularly where creditors take severe haircuts and it is not clear whether the advisers added value, although it is recognised that professional advisers must be remunerated fairly to attract and retain the best.[130]

6.3.1. Appointment and Accountability

In theory, IPs are appointed on the basis of their experience and reputation, built up over several years and over several transactions, such that they will not risk their professional reputation over a relatively small fee. The mechanism of the creditors' meetings is the means of holding the IPs accountable. In the UK, owing

[130] Dickfos, 'The Costs and Benefits of Regulating the Market' (2015).

to the process of appointment that is outlined above, creditor banks retain some influence in the choice of administrator through their own tender panel systems.[131] However, such influence is limited if there is greater divergence in the creditors' profile and there is no single largest creditor bank.[132] Once they are appointed, the Insolvency Act 1986 places direct duties on the administrators to act in the interests of the creditors as a whole. The administrator, as an officer of the court, is accountable to the court.[133] Administrators can be disciplined by their professional bodies.[134]

Among the four Asian jurisdictions, the Chinese courts have taken the somewhat unusual method of professionalising the appointment of the administrators through random or competitive bids. The selection of the administrator rests entirely on the court so as to ensure independence and fairness. To address the requirements of complex listed-company restructurings, a separate set of criteria based on depth of expertise is used by the courts as random selection may lack the requisite expertise.[135]

The challenge is that for an administrator to function effectively, independence is a necessary but insufficient condition. Competence and the ability to canvass support by the relevant stakeholders is critical. In Mainland China, the difficulty with the law on the books is that if the administrator is not one who is recommended by the majority of the creditors, he/she may not have the relevant financial information provided by the banks, and banks may not trust his/her judgements on the proposed rescue strategies. Further, if the debtor is an SOE, social stability, the stability of the financial sector and tax revenues would inevitably be important factors,[136] and the random appointment of professional advisers is not optimal to achieve good outcomes. In these cases, if the state implements a corporate rescue through either direct injection of assets, a bail-out or coordinate the rescue,[137] the support of the state is crucial, and the role of the administrator tends to be distorted in the process. The cases in Appendix A, discussed in chapter three, indicate that state support of restructuring can be implemented in various manners, including steering state-owned banks to lend to the borrower, a merger of the debtor with other SOEs or injection of cash or assets by other SOEs.

Thus, particularly in the earlier years of the EBL (2007–14), legal and finance scholars documented the high degree of governmental involvement in the reorganisation

[131] Armour and Mokal (n 8).

[132] ibid.

[133] See above, n 22.

[134] V Finch, 'Corporate Rescue' (2012); Armour and Mokal (n 8). The professional bodies are recognised are the Institute of Chartered Accountants in England and Wales (ICAEW), Institute of Chartered Accountants in Ireland; Institute of Chartered Accountants in Scotland; and Insolvency Practitioners Association. See Insolvency Service, 'Recognised Professional Bodies', available at www.gov.uk/government/publications/insolvency-practitioners-recognised-professional-bodies/recognised-professional-bodies.

[135] Li and Zheng (n 47) 277–78.

[136] See ch 3. See eg Zhao, *Government Intervention* (2019); Austin and Lin, 'Bankruptcy with Chinese Characteristics' (2020).

[137] See ch 3, section 3.4.3.3 (state rescue in listed company and bond restructuring).

process, using the channel of liquidation teams.[138] Government officials serve as members of liquidation teams, appointed as administrators. In addition, Zhao also reported that municipal governments form informal interim groups and propose their list of candidates (who are lawyers or accountants) to the courts, which is contrary to promulgations by the SPC that the appointment of liquidation teams should be rarely permitted.[139]

Oversight by the courts over administrators also plays an important role in ensuring accountability. For example, in the Rules Governing Bankruptcy Administrators promulgated by the Shenzhen Intermediate People's Court,[140] there is a high degree of supervision by the court over the administrators. The rules prescribe the timelines wherein administrators must deliver the requisite reports to the court. Prior to the first creditors' meeting, the administrator cannot carry out acts that significantly affect the creditors and the decision of the administrator for the company to continue trading; the court's approval is required. New financing raised by the administrator also requires the court's approval. The reorganisation plan formulated by the debtor must be submitted by the administrator to the court, together with his/her opinion on feasibility, prior to the creditors' meeting.[141] These rules reinforce the fact that the IPs' accountability under the EBL is to the court, rather than to the creditors.

A high degree of supervision means that valuable court time is consumed in managing the cases closely. This supervision process may work in the earlier years immediately after the promulgation, but greater devolvement should be made to the administrators once the expertise is developed.

6.3.2. Fee Arrangements

6.3.2.1. The Rise of the Financial Adviser/Investment Bank in Restructuring Work

At least two issues with fee arrangements of the IPs can distort their independence and incentives to act in the interest of the debtor's creditors. First, when the company is insolvent, the company's appointment of advisers and the associated costs are paid out of the money that would otherwise go to the creditors. Second, fee arrangements can induce behaviours in IPs that are not necessarily consistent with maximising creditors' welfare as a whole. In particular, fee arrangement transparency and the incentives of IPs feature prominently where IPs seek to act more akin to financial advisers than as insolvency practitioners. In Singapore, the remuneration of IPs in schemes of arrangement is more varied in that it includes fixed-rate fees and success-based fees.[142] Fees may also be paid in the form of equity in the debtor company in Singapore.

[138] Zhao (n 55). See also Y He, L Xu and RP McIver, 'How Does Political Connection Affect Firm Financial Distress and Resolution in China?' (2019) 51 *Applied Economics* 2770.

[139] Zhao (n 55) 182.

[140] Shenzhen Intermediate People's Court, Rules Governing Bankruptcy Administrators【深圳市中级人法院破产案件管理人工作规范】(2015), available at www.szcourt.gov.cn/type/187/1.

[141] ibid.

[142] Wan, Watters and McCormack, 'Schemes of Arrangement in Singapore' (2020).

In TT International's 2009 restructuring,[143] the creditors of the debtor company argued that they were caught by surprise at the fee arrangement entered into by the company and the insolvency practitioner (who was later appointed as the scheme manager), which had a success fee that was a percentage of the debt waived, written off or extinguished pursuant to the scheme. This was rather unusual as this fee favoured the *debtor* because the more the debt was written off, the more the IP would be paid (as opposed to the more the debt was recovered, the more the IP would be paid by creditors). At its conclusion, owing to a number of factors, including non-disclosure of the fee arrangement to the creditors, the Court of Appeal ordered that the fee be based on the time costs with an uplift. The amount eventually awarded was substantially less than the success fee claimed.[144] In a recent scheme involving Hyflux Limited, subsequently placed under judicial management,[145] some of the creditors objected to the S$25 million success fee payable by the debtor company to the proposed scheme manager (who was the same firm as TT International's 2009 restructuring) on the grounds that it was disproportionately large when compared with the recovery had the scheme was successful.[146] This time round, the proposed scheme manager disclosed the fees to the creditors.

Notwithstanding the fact that disclosures of fee arrangement are required, a more fundamental problem is the role of the proposed scheme manager as an intermediary and its fee arrangement. In Singapore, it is not uncommon for the adviser to contract for a success fee in return for bringing in white knights for the corporate rescue as in the case of *TT International*. With a success fee, it is most likely that he/she will take all necessary steps to secure the creditors' approval, including expediting the process over the creditors' objections. In *TT International*, before IRDA came into force, some unsecured creditors argued that their proofs of debt were unfairly rejected, which prevented them from exercising their votes to the extent that they thought they could.[147] The Court of Appeal laid down several guidelines on the duties expected of the proposed scheme manager as well as the duties after the scheme is sanctioned.[148] The court held that the proposed scheme manager owes a duty of good faith to the company and creditors as a whole.[149] He/she has a quasi-judicial role and owes a duty, in adjudicating the proof of debts for the purposes of voting at the scheme, to be objective, independent, fair and impartial.[150]

[143] *TT International Ltd* [2012] SGCA 9.

[144] *See nTan Corporate Advisory Pte Ltd v TT International Ltd* [2018] SGCA 69.

[145] See G Leong, 'Embattled Firm Hyflux Comes Under Judicial Management' *Straits Times* (17 November 2020).

[146] The holders of the perpetual securities and preference shares would receive SG$50 million, but had invested SG$900 million. See F Lam, 'Hyflux says nTan Fees 'Fully Justified', Terms from Utico "Best Possible"' *Business Times* (5 March 2020).

[147] *TT International* (n 143) (one of the contractors, whose project could not continue, argued that its claims should not be rejected). See also ch 4.

[148] WY Wan, 'Recent Developments in Schemes of Arrangement in Singapore: Classification of Creditors and Scheme Manager's Conflicts of Interest' (2013) *Journal of Business Law* 552.

[149] *TT International* (n 143), [74].

[150] *TT International* (n 143), [76].

Upon sanction of the scheme, he/she has fiduciary duties to the company in administering the scheme.[151]

The imposition of duties of good faith (pre-sanction) and fiduciary duties (post-sanction) is stark because in *TT International*, the scheme manager faced an intractable conflict of interest; 'if he successfully resuscitates the company, he is remunerated, inter alia, for managing the scheme and reviving the company'.[152] Yet, the chances of company survival meant that creditors would be expected to incur major haircuts. Although IRDA now clarifies the procedure related to the proofs of debt in a scheme of arrangement,[153] it would appear that the duties imposed on *TT International* remain good law.

In India, as mentioned above, success fees have been reported to be utilised by the RPs or advisers appointed by the RPs (but whose expenses will also have priority), and these fees are reviewable by the courts. Even though success fees are linked to the recovery of the overall debt and do not pose the kind of conflicts of interests faced in *TT International*, the concern remains that these fees pose other kinds of conflicts. RPs are incentivised to favour particular financial creditors (since the creditors bargain on not only deployment but also the distribution).[154] RPs are also incentivised to bring in white knights or other bidders as resolution applicants; in themselves, they are not objectionable, but incentive arrangements also induce IPs to favour external bidders (particularly funds or other players that give the RPs repeat work).

If restructuring entails only financial and sophisticated creditors, there is less objection to financial advisers with success fee arrangements once appropriate disclosures are made and acquiesced by these creditors. These creditors would have their own advisers and would be able to assess whether the benefits of hiring the particular financial adviser or IP as resolution professional outweigh the downside of conflicts of interests. However, the objection applies in full force where non-sophisticated financial creditors are involved, such as the case of home-buyers.[155]

6.3.3. Conflicts of Interest

In a PIP model or hybrid PIP-DIP model, it is critical that the IP is (and be seen as) independent of the debtor and its management. In jurisdictions where the insolvency infrastructure or ecosystem is in a relatively nascent stage, it is not uncommon for there to be a shortage of competent insolvency professionals. Because of the small

[151] *TT International* (n 143), [76].

[152] Wan, 'Recent Developments in Schemes of Arrangement in Singapore' (2013).

[153] IRDA, s 68.

[154] These arguments were raised in the disciplinary proceedings against a RP who had appointed an adviser based on a success fee arrangement: IBBI Disciplinary Committee, order dated 5 March 2021, available at ibbi.gov.in/uploads/order/99021d25ea6922dc843d3c792ef85443.pdf.

[155] See discussion in *Jaypee Kensington Boulevard Apartments Welfare Association & Ors. v NBCC (India) Ltd & Ors* Civil Appeal No 3395 of 2020.

numbers of law firms or accounting firms that have the requisite expertise, as well as the small number of creditor banks, many of these practitioners would have ongoing relationships with the creditor banks.[156] IPs could also have ongoing relationships with repeat player bidders (such as distressed funds).

In India, while the CIRP allows RPs to have considerable discretion to run the sale process, the issue of independence of the RP has been raised on several occasions before the courts.[157] For instance, professional advisers advising the RP who was soliciting bids were also acting for one of the bidders.[158] In another case, it was held that even if the RP is otherwise eligible, the RP can nevertheless be disqualified if there is an apparent bias.[159] The courts have criticised RPs who attempt to reverse the decisions of the committees of creditors after they are taken, which would have affected the reputation of the RPs concerned.[160] Recently, the professional bodies have decided to deal with issues of conflicts of interests through codes of conduct, though it is too early to tell if these codes of conduct are effective.[161]

6.3.4. Effectiveness of the Insolvency Practitioner

6.3.4.1. India

Prior to the IBC, the restructuring regime was largely debtor-driven, given the difficulties faced by creditors in enforcing their debts in the courts and the paucity of self-help remedies.[162] When the CIRP was introduced, the fundamental change to the regime was that IPs (being the RPs) displace the board of directors upon their appointment.

Once the court accepts the debtor into the CIRP, the interim RP takes over the management of the company, and directors and officers of the company are required to report to and provide access to documents to the interim RP.[163] It is critical for the RP to be able to keep operations of a company going so that a sale can take place as a going concern. Under the IBC, promoters are required to extend assistance to the interim RP.[164] However, enforcement is often weak, and recent research demonstrates that only a small minority of RPs seek recourse from the

[156] cf Finch, 'Insolvency Practitioners' (2012) (arguing that the banks and the IPs would be familiar with each other).

[157] *State Bank of India v Ram Dev International Ltd*, Company Appeal (AT) (Insolvency) No 302 of 2018; *State Bank of India vs M/s Metenere Ltd Company* Appeal (AT) (Insolvency) No 76 of 2020.

[158] A Handa, 'An Analysis of the Corporate Insolvency Resolution Process as A Route for Acquisitions' (2020) 29 *International Insolvency Review* 234.

[159] *State Bank of India v Ram Dev International Ltd*, Company Appeal (AT) (Insolvency) No 302 of 2018 (the only basis of disqualification was that RP was an ex-employee of one of the creditor banks).

[160] Kumar and Sundaresh, 'Insolvency Professionals' (2018).

[161] eg IBBI and UK Government, 'Handbook on Ethics for Insolvency Professionals: Ethical and Regulatory Framework' (March 2021), available at www.ibbi.gov.in/uploads/whatsnew/0ab3ccba77975af cd9eb7ac679154de8.pdf (India).

[162] ch 2.

[163] IBC, s 17.

[164] IBC, s 19.

courts to enforce disclosure.[165] Promoters are still widely perceived as uncooperative with the RPs unless there are cases where personal guarantees are provided (and where their personal assets are at stake).[166] Because promoters are not allowed to be resolution applicants under section 29A of the IBC, they have no incentive to cooperate with RPs.

As mentioned in section 6.2.1.3, RPs in the CIRP does not have powers as extensive as those the administrator in the UK has in the sale.[167] Unlike the administrator in the UK, the RP does not have the power of sale over the assets of the debtor without the creditors' approval. Instead, in respect of sale, the RP is appointed to solicit bids, do due diligence on the resolution applicant's resolution plan and submit the plan to the creditors. It is for the creditors to determine to whom the sale should be made. RPs also admit and process claims. RPs are not in a position to offer representations and warranties on behalf of the debtor.[168] In a recent *Essar Steel* case, a challenge arose as to whether the resolution applicant was disqualified under section 29A from making a bid.[169] (The IBC disqualifies the resolution applicant from bidding for the assets under section 29A among others if he/she has been a wilful defaulter (see chapter three). The Supreme Court held that it was not the role of the RP to determine whether the bid contravened section 29A.[170]

In response to complaints of delays, although the CIRP is time-bound, the IBC was amended in 2019 to impose an absolute deadline for the conclusion of the CIRP, including time spent in litigation.[171] RPs now have to comply with stricter timelines, the time-bound nature is often not carried out in practice (see chapter seven).

6.3.4.2. *Singapore*

Judicial managers must be licensed IPs.[172] Judicial managers displace the board of directors and can exercise all the powers of the directors conferred under the IRDA, Companies Act and the constitution of the company.[173] It is a requirement of directors to submit information on the company's financial affairs to the judicial manager, and failure to do so is an offence.[174]

[165] S Neeti and S Urvashi, 'Assessment of Corporate Insolvency and Resolution Timeline' IBBI, Indian Institute of Corporate Affairs RP 01/2021 (3% in the sample under survey).

[166] Ernst and Young, 'Evolving Landscape of Corporate Stress Resolution' (December 2019), copy on file with author. See eg Y Rana, 'Deconstructing Barriers' in 'Speeding up Solvency: Bankruptcy Reform in India' (Columbia Business School Proceedings, 2019) 8, available at www8.gsb.columbia.edu/chazen/sites/chazen/files/chazen_ibi_conference2019_summary_052019_v7.pdf?utm_source=newsletter&utm_campaign=cgi&utm_medium=email; see S Neeti and S Urvashi, 'Assessment of Corporate Insolvency and Resolution Timeline' IBBI, Indian Institute of Corporate Affairs RP 01/2021 (pointing out that a significant reason for the delay is the failure by the debtor to provide information).

[167] *Committee of Creditors of Essar Steel India Limited v Satish Kumar Gupta* (Supreme Court of India) Civil Appeal No. 8766-67 OF 2019 (hereafter *Essar Steel*), [27].

[168] Kumar and Sundaresh (n 84).

[169] *ArcelorMittal India Private Limited v Satish Kumar Gupta & Others* (Supreme Court of India) Civil Appeal No 9582 OF 2018.

[170] ibid.

[171] IBC, s 12.

[172] IRDA, s 47.

[173] IRDA, s 99.

[174] IRDA, s 106.

Judicial management has not been regarded as a resounding success in that it has not resulted in the successful rehabilitation of many companies, but it is not obsolete because it provides an opportunity to explore the viability of a company when creditors lack confidence in the management.[175] In addition, it provides an avenue for the judicial manager to investigate antecedent transactions of the management. The key challenges instead lie in the judicial managers lacking the expertise and the experience to run the business.[176] However, as the judicial manager appointments would have been generally recommended or supported by the creditor banks,[177] and as the creditor banks would have information regarding the quality of the management and the finances, the judicial manager would be able to form some degree of judgement on the management team. Recently, a number of high-profile cases have entered judicial management in the wake of the decline in oil and commodity prices, turmoil in the shipping industry or allegations of management misconduct.[178]

6.3.4.3. Mainland China

Excluding the distorting effects of the state on administrators that are liquidation groups, are the administrators under the EBL in fact effective?[179] The evidence is somewhat mixed even though the EBL confers extensive powers on the administrator.[180] Austin and Lin reported that on the basis of their interviews, management would frequently cooperate with the administrator, providing feedback on the plan and business operations.[181] However, another scholar conducted interviews with practitioners and others in the profession and found that in practice, administrators failed to carry out their duties diligently for reasons ranging from lack of resources, the administrators being seldom held liable to account to the courts for their failures, and direct and indirect state influence over the work of the administrators through local governments.[182] As Mainland China is moving towards market-oriented reforms,[183] one of the first issues that need to be addressed is the re-examination of the role of the state in the appointment of administrators and in their decision-making exercise.

[175] Insolvency Law Reform Committee, 'Report of the Insolvency Law Review Committee: Final Report' (Ministry of Law, 2013), available at www.mlaw.gov.sg/files/news/announcements/2013/10/ReportoftheInsolvencyLawReviewCommittee.pdf.

[176] ibid, 85.

[177] IRDA, s 91(3). The applicant petitions to the court with a nomination of the judicial manager; if the applicant is the company, the appointment must have majority creditor support and if the applicant has a floating charge over the entire taking, the court will nominate the applicant's choice unless the appointment was not appropriate.

[178] Swiber, Hyflux, Hin Leong (the background is set out in *Ocean Tankers (Pte Ltd) v Rajah & Tann* Originating Summons No 666 of 2020 (Summons No 4317 of 2020).

[179] eg Ren, *A Comparative Study* (2012); H Zhao (n 55).

[180] See section 6.2.1.2 above.

[181] DA Austin and C Lin, 'Bankruptcy with Chinese Characteristics: Insolvency Administration in the People's Republic of China' (2020) 94 *American Bankruptcy Law Journal* 85.

[182] N Mrockova, *Corporate Bankruptcy Law in China: Principles, Limitations and Options for Reform* (Oxford, Hart Publishing, 2021) 150.

[183] See discussion in ch 2.

6.4. LESSONS, IMPLICATIONS AND OPTIONS FOR REFORM IN ASIAN JURISDICTIONS

6.4.1. Reconceptualising the Role of the Insolvency Practitioner

Table 6.1 Role of the IP in PIP regimes

Intermediaries	UK: administrator	Singapore: judicial manager	Mainland China: administrator	India: resolution professional
Role of IP in determining deployment	High: IP can decide on deployment, with or without approval of creditors)	Medium: JM prepares a plan; creditors vote on the plan	Medium: debtor or administrator prepares a plan; creditors vote on the plan	Low: debtor or resolution applicant prepares a plan; financial creditors negotiate with the resolution applicant directly
Role of IP in determining distribution	None: distribution upon end of administration and winding up are in accordance with relative pre-bankruptcy entitlements	Low: distribution is subject to scheme of arrangement; creditors vote on the scheme of arrangement, which does not have a hard absolute priority rule	Low: distribution subject to statutory priorities; creditors decide on distribution, subject to the statutory priorities; there is no hard absolute priority rule	Low: financial creditors to vote on how to distribute to financial and operational creditors

To examine the areas of improvement, the proper role of the IP must be conceptualised vis-a-vis the creditors and the courts. Table 6.1 provides a taxonomy of the role of the IP in PIP and hybrid DIP/PIP regimes in determining the twin questions of deployment and distribution. (See also Table 1.1 for the explanation of the continuum of manager control or creditor control of the debt restructuring system.) Only the UK administrator can decide on deployment without reference to the creditors. However, on the question of distribution of proceeds in the UK administration, the creditors do not bargain over the distribution, which is determined solely in accordance with the relative pre-bankruptcy entitlements (when the company is liquidated upon the exit of administration or, exceptionally, before that).[184] However, the Singapore judicial manager and the Chinese administrator have a more active role over the future of the debtor in that the relevant IP would negotiate with the creditors bargaining over the deployment, and in the case of Mainland China, the IP would give his/her opinion to the courts. By contrast, the RP or the administrator in India does not have the

[184] See n 37 above and accompanying text.

power of sale, nor does the RP bargain with the resolution applicant as a matter of practice,[185] and any sale requires the creditors (or financial creditors in India) to vote.

When it comes to distribution, Singapore and Mainland China do not have a hard absolute priority rule (see chapter three); this means that the creditors and the shareholders are incentivised to bargain over the entitlements on distribution. Likewise, in India, because of *Essar Steel*, where the Supreme Court held that the court would generally respect the decision of the committee of creditors regarding their decision over the allocation of the distribution (subject to certain limits in section 30(2) as to the floor of distribution[186]), financial creditors would be expected to bargain over the distribution of the proceeds.[187]

Theoretically, a high degree of trust in the IP as an intermediary to act in his/her commercial judgement (and an absence of litigation challenging the IP's decision-making) and the absence of any allegation of conflicts of interest on the part of the IP, the UK approach towards the pre-pack administration sale is the fastest way of resolving the restructuring. The longer a company spends on restructuring, the more likely it is to incur transaction costs and have potentially value destruction, leading to greater difficulties if the debtor is ultimately sold. In particular, if the creditor base is large and diverse (such as where there are outstanding bonds), the negotiations between the creditors can turn out to be protracted.

If the IP has the power of sale in the pre-pack, then he/she only needs to negotiate with the secured creditors (assuming the valuation breaks at secured debt, an issue that could be a thorny one) and the buyer. The unsecured creditors would not have a say until after the pre-pack is agreed upon, and the creditors will not delay matters by bargaining over the entitlements. Of course, speed comes with disadvantages. One is that the pre-pack sale through administration is not likely to maximise value for the unsecured creditors because it is not likely that the administrator will do an extensive market check (which may drive down the value of the business further), drawing criticism that the pre-pack is really there only to benefit the secured creditors.[188] The larger concern is that if there is fraud or misconduct on the part of the management, there is really no incentive for the IP to investigate once the secured creditors are paid in full unless the unsecured creditors or other junior stakeholders are willing to fund the litigation by the IPs.

In contrast to the English approach, in Singapore, India and Mainland China, IPs do not have such powers when it comes to the deployment question; the creditors would be expected to bargain over this question. Judicial oversight varies in each jurisdiction, with case law in Singapore and India demonstrating that the courts are unlikely to intervene in the commercial decisions reached by the committee of creditors. Even with the introduction of pre-packs, the reforms are gradual in nature.

[185] See n 84 above and accompanying text.

[186] ch 4, n 182 (and accompanying text).

[187] ch 4, section 4.4.1.2. There is one limitation: the IBC further provides that dissenting financial creditors and operational creditors shall receive at least the amount that would have been received if the liquidation value had been distributed in accordance with s 53 (which is the waterfall mechanism for distribution in the event of a liquidation), whichever is higher.

[188] See generally, AJ Walters, 'Statutory Erosion of Secured Creditors' Rights: Some Insights from the United Kingdom' (2015) 2015 *University of Illinois Law Review* 543.

For instance, both the Chinese version and the Singapore versions of pre-pack are more akin to pre-negotiated sales prior to the filing (rather than pre-packs in the US/UK manner).[189] The Indian pre-packs currently only apply to micro, small and medium-sized enterprises.[190] Even then, it requires consent of the creditors and the court, albeit within a tighter timeframe.[191] Further delays due to the bargaining process over entitlements would be expected for these jurisdictions as they do not have hard absolute priority rule.

6.4.1.1. *Devolving Power of Sale to the IP*

In India, in view of the experience of the debtor-driven model pre-IBC,[192] the legislature might be reluctant to give RPs significant power over the deployment issue (as the RPs could be influenced by the debtor) as evidenced from the recent amendments to allow pre-packs for the micro, small and medium-sized enterprises. The problem is also exacerbated by concerns (not unwarranted) over promoters, deemed to have contributed to the failure of debtors through mismanagement or misconduct, who continue to attempt to acquire the assets in the cheap (using the CIRP). However, there are indications that more power would be devolved to the decision-making of RPs and committee of creditors. More powers were granted to RPs in 2019 in order for them to deal with contracts of essential goods and services so as to ensure that the company continues its operations.[193]

Consequent to the resolution under CIRP is executed through a sale to the most favourable bidder, RPs do not need to judge the competence of the existing management team whose retention is up to the bidder. Further, promoters are disqualified from participating. Hence, there are good reasons why RPs should be conferred the power of sale of the assets without creditors' approval and/or court approval. Without the prior consent of creditors in the sale, the restructuring can avoid hold-out behaviour by creditors.

Should the same power of sale be recommended for Singapore's judicial management and the Chinese administration? It is not suggested because in these two jurisdictions, one of the options as to the outcome could be that the existing management remains in the debtor (an option that is not possible for the CIRP). In such a case, the IP may be subject to capture by the debtor, particularly if the proposition is that of a sale to a connected party. Hence, creditors' approval to the sale should still be the norm.

One remaining question is the valuation of the assets that is the subject matter of the sale by the IP. The IP relies on the professional judgement of the valuer to determine where the value breaks or may conduct an auction (such as the Swiss challenge). In the former, the IP may appoint more than one valuer although care must be taken

[189] See ch 3.
[190] ch 3, section 3.4.3.4.
[191] Insolvency and Bankruptcy (Amendment) Ordinance 2021.
[192] ch 2.
[193] IBC, s 14.

not to run down the assets of the company (which works against preserving the value of the company). As in all cases of valuation, a range of methodologies can be used by the valuer.

6.4.1.2. *Reducing Judicial Oversight Over IPs*

Ultimately, if the direction is for the IP to have greater power with respect to deployment, it is critical for the IPs to have a high professional standing, preserve their independence, account to the body of creditors, and ensure that their work is not impeded by failing to have effective access to information on the debtor. In chapter three, I explained that the restructuring framework should incentivise the management to work with the IPs, particularly in jurisdictions where controlled companies dominate. IPs need to be incentivised to investigate antecedent transactions. RPs in India have been criticised for not having done sufficiently to investigate antecedent improper related-party transactions even if they have the requisite forensic evidence.[194]

Equally, in unconflicted situations, in market-based restructurings, there are good reasons why IPs should be primarily accountable to the creditors; once they run a transparent process to effect a sale of the assets, their commercial decisions in managing the companies and forming the restructuring are capable of challenge only in exceptional situations. Where judicial time is scarce, requiring each decision to be approved by the courts would result in delay. Often, the decisions are commercial decisions, and for the reasons outlined in chapter seven, the creditors, as opposed to the courts, are in the best position to determine what to do with their assets.

6.4.2. Reforms Addressing the Insolvency Practitioner's Conflicts of Interest

In determining the regulatory responses, an established line of literature exists that studies conflicts of interests faced by gatekeeper intermediaries (such as auditors) who focus on four options: providing greater oversight, precluding conflicts of interest, seeking greater independence for the gatekeeper and enhancing the liabilities framework.[195] A prime example is the response to the regulation of auditors after the Enron and Worldcom scandals; in these cases, the Sarbanes-Oxley Act 2002 was enacted to include greater oversight over the auditors by creating a new body, the Public Company Accounting Oversight Board, prohibiting auditors from undertaking non-audit-fee work and increased scrutiny over the auditors[196] In this section, I consider how responses to gatekeeper failure in capital markets law can be applied to restructuring law.

[194] A Waghmare, 'Systemic change: Hits and misses of India's bankruptcy reforms code' *Business Standard* (5 February 2020).
[195] Coffee (n 1).
[196] ibid.

6.4.2.1. *Greater Oversight by Stakeholders*

IPs account to the creditors, the courts, applicable professional bodies and, in India, the regulator (IBBI). An important issue is whether the collective oversight of the IPs is sufficient. A process that is seen as transparent, and in which the IP has acted even-handedly, leads to greater success, obtains buy-in and reduces transaction costs. All the various bodies for accountability have their own benefits and limitations. In the UK, the ability to challenge the administrator's decisions is limited by the costs of such challenges and the latitude given to the administrators under the Insolvency Act 1986.[197] For the reasons explained in chapter seven, close court supervision is often not the optimal solution in jurisdictions where demands on judicial time are the greatest, and it would limit the speed at which these decisions should be made. Regulation by professional bodies requires these bodies to be willing to enforce standards of conduct. A new regulator can be created to monitor conflicts, but for it to be effective, there needs to be high degree of buy-in from the professional bodies, and enforcement must be backed by effective sanctions.

6.4.2.2. *Precluding Conflicts of Interests and Maximising IP Independence*

The trend towards conflict of interests by gatekeepers is to preclude the possibility of direct conflicts or to remove situations where conflicts may occur. In situations where the depth of talent among the IPs is still nascent, such preclusion can be unduly restrictive in terms of the choice of IPs that are available.

6.4.2.3. *Enhancing Gatekeeper Liabilities*

One method to ensure greater compliance by IPs to avoid conflicts of interests is to enhance liabilities through public or private enforcement. However, this method can be counterproductive as it can have a chilling effect on the part of the IPs and drive up the costs of the services to make up for the liability risks. Given that the IP exercises considerable discretion in determining how to exercise his/her powers, to make it easier for liabilities to be imposed, the IP will be more risk-averse and concurrently incur greater compliance costs in ensuring appropriate documentation of their decision-making.

6.4.2.4. *Assessment of Options*

IPs, as professionals, have their reputations on the line when they accept appointments. On balance, the role of the IPs to ensure the integrity of the outcomes of restructuring cannot purely be left to regulation by the professional bodies. The IPs face potentially conflicting responsibilities and incentives to prioritise certain sets of interests of particular stakeholders. The least interventionist approach is to require the IPs to declare their conflicts of interests to creditors and for the creditors to

[197] Insolvency Act 1986, Sch B1, para 3. See n 38 above and accompanying text.

endorse or recommend the appointments. However, this kind of intervention may not be sufficient if the disclosures in the market are on generalised terms[198] and if the creditors do not fully comprehend the extent of conflicts of interests.

Further, when left to market regulation, the evidence seen in Singapore and India is that professionals, ostensibly in gatekeeping roles, have been willing to act as financial advisers and take success fees. Thus, there is a case for more interventionist approaches. In jurisdictions where the IPs are still in a state of professionalising, a bright-line rule is more preferable, lest valuable judicial time is taken up in determining whether the conflicts of interests are well mitigated. The bright-line rule includes prohibiting appointments in specified situations, such as those who have offered professional services to the company within a period prior to restructuring because there would be questions raised as to whether they are able to act in the interests of the creditors as a whole. The success fee of the IPs should be carefully regulated for the reasons set out in section 6.2.2.1 above. Even if the success fee is based on the recovery of debts, these fee arrangements incentivise the IPs to favour certain creditors over others (such as where the creditors are pursuing the loan-to-own strategies) in a bid to complete a transaction as opposed to maximising the value of the returns for all.

However, should take care not to be overly prescriptive about the remuneration of the IP, or the arrangements may lead to perverse incentives. For example, in Mainland China, where compensation is on scaled fees, commentators have pointed out inadequacies of the compensation model of administrators. For instance, at the higher end of the value of the assets, where the cases are likely more complex, the administrators have no incentive to do the work to maximise recovery because the percentage of recovery at the highest levels is capped.[199] Further, the remuneration plan is voted by creditors at the first creditors' meeting that occurs shortly after the acceptance of the case but before the start of the substantial amount of work, and it is not straightforward to estimate the scale of work required.[200] A fixed fee or time-based billing will work better provided there is capacity for judicial oversight in ensuring that the fees based on time-cost are not disproportionate to the work rendered.

6.5. CONCLUSION

The role of the IP is central to the PIP and the associated variants to the PIP regimes. IPs are accountable to the body of creditors, and to be effective, they are required to be both competent and independent. I have argued that the key focus of oversight should look at the benefits and costs of granting more autonomy and judicial oversight. This involves looking at the appointment, remuneration, accountability and

[198] eg, if the IP merely discloses the basis that the IP, in the course of its business, acts for a number of clients including clients who may have conflicting interests with the matter at hand, such disclosure does not generally assist the creditors to assess the particular conflict of interest at hand.

[199] Where the amount to be distributed is above RMB500 million, the administrator's remuneration is capped at 0.5% of the value distributed. See Steele (n 44).

[200] Steele (n 44).

independence. The practice of the IP also has to be dynamic in view of the changes in the composition of creditors and the evolving judicial attitude towards its role in overseeing IPs.

The main point is not to set forth a definitive generic regulatory response to the different DIP and PIP regimes, but to demonstrate that the regulatory response is necessary for IPs in the PIP and hybrid PIP/DIP regime and to highlight considerations that should structure that response by addressing the need for an effective and independent IP process. Some of this oversight may even need to extend to DIP regimes in light of the evolving practice of IPs. Without such a response, there is a real risk that with the economic incentives, IPs act more akin to financial advisers or investment banks than as intermediaries between the debtor and the creditors.

7

Role of the Courts in Court-Supervised Restructurings

7.1. INTRODUCTION

IN THIS CHAPTER, I analyse the role that the courts in the US/UK and the four Asian jurisdictions have played in court-supervised debt restructurings. Existing accounts of Chapter 11 have emphasised not only the efficiency of the law but also the central importance of institutions and, in this case, the roles of the highly efficient judiciary in reaching optimal outcomes. Other scholars have also indicated that the US ecosystem depends on the highly competent bankruptcy judges, sophisticated advisers and a strong US trustee programme for ensuring that economically viable companies are rescued within reasonable timeframes.

A functioning and efficient restructuring regime requires predictability, certainty and speed, all of which would reduce transaction costs of restructuring and, above all, sift out companies that are capable of being rescued from those that are not economically viable. In terms of the ex post benefits, creditors and shareholders requires predictability and speed so that they know the range wherein they bargain over the expected recoveries, when they would receive the pay-outs, and whether they should exit their investments and not engage in unnecessary hold-outs. In the same vein, investors who are considering investing in the debt or equity of financially distressed companies will also need to predict the outcomes of the restructurings in determining whether and how to invest.

In comparative law scholarship regarding optimal bankruptcy law design, Ayotte and Yun have argued that bankruptcy judges and bankruptcy law play a key role in solving the twin problems of incomplete debt contracts (that are inevitable in contracting) and the imperfect enforcement of contracts.[1] For the reorganised entity to be restructured into a going concern, they argue that high judicial expertise is required to make decisions on several disputes between the creditors and the management – including the right of secured creditors to enforce against the collateral and on confirmation of the plan – and that in the absence of such expertise, a creditor-friendly model is preferred.[2] However, in the last decade, for many of the

[1] K Ayotte and H Yun, 'Matching Bankruptcy Laws to Legal Environments' (2007) 25 *Journal of Law, Economics & Organization* 2.

[2] ibid.

reasons listed in chapter one, several jurisdictions have implemented variants of the US Chapter 11 provisions or the UK scheme of arrangement. In particular, inherent in the legal transplantation has been to give the courts the central role to oversee the process of court-supervised restructurings. These reforms are made while judicial capacity is being developed, rather than after it is built. The difficulties faced by Mainland China and India on their paths towards insolvency reforms have been attributed to the absence of high judicial expertise in handling insolvencies.[3] In response, both jurisdictions have boosted judicial capacity by introducing specialised bankruptcy courts or tribunals to handle these cases in the last decade.[4] Singapore and Hong Kong have not introduced specialised insolvency courts though in Singapore, there is the introduction of specialised commercial lists of judges, including for hearing insolvency cases.[5]

However, when one considers the range of opportunistic (and inefficient) behaviours that can be engaged by various market participants, increasing judicial expertise will not be, in itself, the panacea because even the most well-trained judges may have difficulty in distinguishing between opportunistic and non-opportunistic behaviour except in the most egregious cases. For instance, the debtor's management may be seeking to prolong a business past its viability while ostensibly seeking a rescue through running a prolonged sale process. Even the most well-trained judge cannot advise on a proposal that is not tabled before him/her.

By analysing the range of circumstances that the courts are required to decide in different scenarios, we understand the comparative advantages and limitations that judges face. The analysis reviews that common law courts in Asia are adept at balancing the need for certainty and predictability with flexibility in using restructuring law to device solutions. While Mainland China has a civil law system, the system also allows considerable room for the judges to similarly adapt their approaches to achieve the balance. However, a bottoms-up analysis reveals that the specific ways wherein agency and coordination costs are created or exacerbated by market participants and differences in national policy goals law mean that there are limitations to leave the balancing exercises solely to the judges.

In this chapter, I evaluate how the courts have exercised their discretion in adjudicating on two important features of restructuring practice in reaching the balance between certainty and predictability versus flexibility: the automatic stay or moratorium and the substantive fairness of the final plans in the US/UK and as compared with the four Asian jurisdictions. The chapter does not deal with the expertise and competence on the part of the judges that has been discussed elsewhere.[6] Rather, the focus is on how judicial discretion has been exercised. The exercise yields a

[3] B Li and J Ponticelli, 'Going Bankrupt in China' (2020) PBCSF-NIFR Research Paper, available at ssrn.com/abstract=3251570; K van Zwieten, 'Corporate Rescue in India: The Influence of the Courts' (2015) 15 *Journal of Corporate Law Studies* 1.

[4] Li and Ponticelli (ibid). India has the NCLTs to handle CIRP cases. See ch 2.

[5] D Lim, 'Singapore Law Watch: Bankruptcy and Insolvency', available at www.singaporelawwatch.sg/About-Singapore-Law/Commercial-Law/ch-30-bankruptcy-and-insolvency.

[6] For a discussion on the judicial expertise of Chinese judiciary in administering the EBL, see N Mrockova, *Corporate Bankruptcy Law in China: Principles, Limitations and Options for Reform* (Oxford, Hart Publishing, 2021) 142–45.

comparative analysis of the strengths and limitations of the role of the courts. I then address how these strengths can be undermined (or limitations magnified) in dealing with the agency and coordination costs of restructurings identified in chapters three, four and five as well as the national goals of restructuring. In considering the UK, I consider only the scheme of arrangement, and not administration, as the administrator has considerable power to trade freely and to dispose the business or assets without having to obtain the consent of the court.[7]

The roadmap is as follows. In section 7.2, I compare the exercise of judicial discretion in the US and the UK. In the US Chapter 11, judges give a lot of leeway in favour of management to choose whether and how to reorganise.[8] Prior to the introduction of the moratorium under the Corporate Insolvency and Governance Act 2020 (CIGA) in the UK, judges are more removed as they hear the cases only at the time of leave to convene the scheme meeting, when significant work has been done. In both jurisdictions, the courts generally uphold the creditors' decision on the substantive outcomes of the plan except when it comes to resolving valuation disputes. However, in the UK appears to be a rising number of recent cases where dissenting creditors or shareholders have pushed back against the debtor's choice of comparator in the event that the scheme or restructuring plan is not approved.

In section 7.3, I examine the common law Asian jurisdictions. All the three jurisdictions involve the courts hearing the application for stay of proceedings. The approach of the common law judges indicates that the courts are more willing to give significant leeway in favour of management in deciding how to effect the rescue, but with intervention in obvious egregious cases of abuse. When it comes to substantive decisions, as also demonstrated in chapters three and four, for Hong Kong and Singapore, the courts generally uphold decisions of within-class creditors with properly constituted classes, but the approach towards the treatment of conflicted creditors remains somewhat unclear. In India, the judicial attitude among the lower courts has been to read in the discretion to review the plan for fairness and equity, though this discretion has been progressively curtailed by the legislative amendments to the Indian Insolvency and Bankruptcy Code 2016 (IBC) and Supreme Court decisions that held that the National Company Law Tribunal (NCLT), the tribunal hearing IBC cases, must give effect to committee of creditors decisions with little room to depart otherwise. The IBC also bans promoters from being resolution applicants.

In section 7.4, I argue that comparison among the common law Asian jurisdictions (and with the US/UK) reveals the following lessons and implications. First, the mode of regulation is as important as the substance of regulation. In the absence of bright line rules imposed by legislation, the courts in common law jurisdictions are willing to allow the management to drive the restructuring and give the debtor the benefit of the doubt that it is asking for stay of proceedings (or extension). Second, opportunistic behaviour arises from agency and coordination costs arising from the shareholder – creditor and creditor – creditor conflicts that may be curtailed by legislation but will carry with it inflexibility and other costs. Third, while the broad goal

[7] See ch 6, section 6.2.1.1.

[8] G Triantis, 'The Interplay Between Liquidation and Reorganization in Bankruptcy: The Role of Screens, Gatekeepers, and Guillotines' (1996) 16 *International Review of Law and Economics* 101.

of each jurisdiction is to create an efficient restructuring framework that is certain and predictable (thereby reducing transaction costs), the states also have different priorities which factor into the question of how much of the regulation occurs via judicial discretion and bright-line rules. Singapore's avowed goal is to create a restructuring hub, and the legislation that gives the debtor management access to significant restructuring tools (and incentives to file) is an important and significant step in that direction. While there is no similar push in Hong Kong, the lack of a formal pre-insolvency procedure in Hong Kong has led to various adaptive devices being used, but all of which depends on court oversight. In India, the model of limited judicial challenge of the committee of creditor decisions is well under way, but the progressive shift towards curtailing judicial discretion, driven by a need to resolve the stability of the banking sector, will ultimately mean a loss of flexibility.

In section 7.5, I turn to Mainland China. Mainland China is dealt with differently from the common law Asian jurisdictions due to the history of governmental involvement in restructurings of large companies. I argue that the discretion given to the judges under the Enterprise Bankruptcy Law 2006 (EBL) is very wide, but the courts have used various adaptive devices to address certainty and predictability through judicial pronouncements. The courts have also experimented with the use of pre-negotiation reorganisations to shorten the time for resolution. Section 7.6 concludes.

7.2. LEGISLATIVE FRAMEWORK AND JUDICIAL DISCRETION IN THE US AND THE UK: STRENGTHS AND LIMITATIONS

I now focus on the two most critical aspects in corporate restructuring law: (1) the approval of the extension of the moratorium, together with the conditions that are imposed and orders for disclosure; and (2) confirmation of the plan or the sanction of the scheme of arrangement. A review will show that the US and the UK approaches diverge for the moratorium, but are much closer in respect of dealing with plan confirmations, in line with takeover law, which is closely related to corporate restructuring law since management can also lose control of the company in favour of outsiders.

7.2.1. The Moratorium

The availability of the statutory moratorium is one of the core features of any debtor in possession (DIP) proceeding. The moratorium allows the halt of all efforts to seek repayment from the debtor and gives the borrower breathing space to discuss the exit plan with key stakeholders, usually through liquidation, sale or reorganisation.[9] The appropriate length of the moratorium is often contentious. If too much time is allowed, there is a high risk of destruction of value by the existing debtor management. However, if too little time is given, the restructuring does not stand a reasonable

[9] See TH Jackson, *The Logic and Limits of Bankruptcy Law* (Cambridge, MA, Harvard University Press, 1986) 16–17.

chance of success or maximising recovery for the creditors. As the courts are not involved in the negotiations prior to the plan being proposed, or even up to the time of the plan confirmation or sanction, the courts can only determine on the evidence assessed whether the moratorium will facilitate a genuine restructuring as opposed to merely delaying the inevitable. Thus, the courts have to balance the question of the length of the moratorium carefully in the applications.

7.2.1.1. *United States*

In the US, once the petition is filed, there is an automatic worldwide moratorium on proceedings against the debtor.[10] The moratorium applies until the restructuring plan is confirmed (or dismissed), or until the stay is lifted upon application by a party.[11] There is also the possibility to apply for relief against the say.[12] The debtor has the exclusive right to file a Chapter 11 plan for a period of 120 days, and the debtor has 180 days to solicit acceptance for a plan filed within the 120 days.[13] The 120- or 180-day period can be extended 'with cause', and scholars have criticised the lengthy delays due to the almost unlimited exclusivity periods that were granted to the debtor.[14] In 2005, the Bankruptcy Abuse Prevention and Consumer Protection Act (BAPCHA) was enacted to set the upper thresholds of the period of 18 and 20 months, respectively.[15] The result of the amendment was a sharp reduction in the period the matter spent in bankruptcy (the mean period for traditional bankruptcies reduced from 634 to 430 days, a reduction of 32 per cent), and there was a significant increase in pre-packaged and pre-negotiated bankruptcies, where the terms of the sale are negotiated by creditors prior to the filing of the petition, though there could be unintended consequences of a higher proportion of refiling.[16]

For more recent cases I extracted a sample of large companies (assets totalling at least US$100 million) that filed for Chapter 11 and exited with approved reorganisation plans for the five-year period between 2016 and 2020 from the UCLA–LoPucki Bankruptcy Research Database. The final sample (after excluding cases where the financial data are not available and excluding financial institutions, depository and insurance companies) consisted of 151 cases, out of which were 40 pre-packs. The duration of each case was calculated as the number of days between the date of filing and date of plan confirmation. The average duration was 182 days for the traditional Chapter 11 filings (free-falls) and 55 days for the pre-packed filings. Figure 7.1 shows the distribution of all the cases, demonstrating that with very few outliers, most of the cases are completed within 365 days (or 12 months).

[10] 11 USC §362.
[11] 11 USC §362.
[12] 11 USC §361.
[13] 11 USC §1121.
[14] See references in F Teloni, 'Chapter 11 Duration, Preplanned Cases and Refiling Rates: An Empirical Analysis in the Post-BAPCPA Era' (2015) 23 *American Bankruptcy Institute Law Review* 571.
[15] 11 USC§1121(d).
[16] Teloni, 'Chapter 11 Duration' (2015) (based on a study of large companies entering Chapter 11 with more than US$100 million in assets).

Figure 7.1 Distribution of the number of days in Chapter 11

N = 151

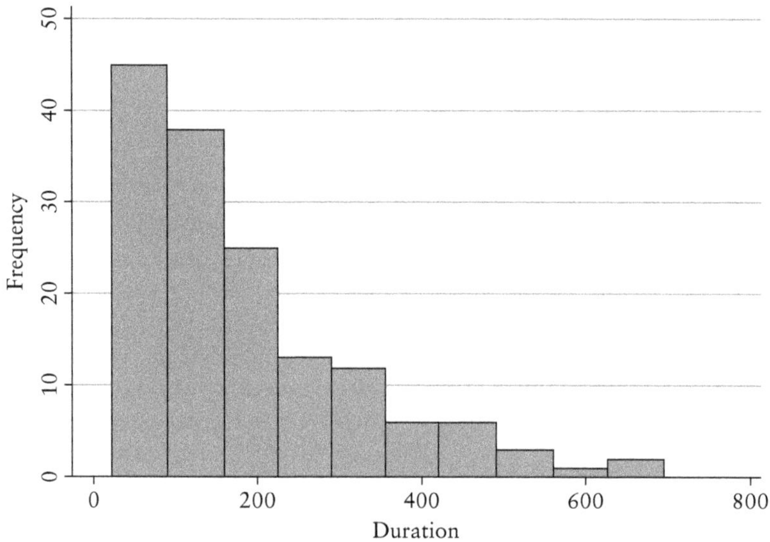

Source: Data collected from UCLA–LoPucki Bankruptcy Research Database, available at lopucki.law.ucla.edu.

The history of BAPCHA is an example of the use of legislation to curb the periods spent in Chapter 11 (where the moratorium will be expected to apply), thereby reducing the prospect of abuse. When it comes to obtaining information from the debtor management, in Chapter 11 proceedings, the schedule of assets and liabilities and its statement of financial affairs are required to be filed within 14 days of filing the petition, in addition to the 'first day' declarations on the debtor's business affairs and events leading to the filing.[17]

One final note on Chapter 11 is that recent scholarship has reported with the rise of the secured debt since the 2000s (particularly after the amendment to the Uniform Commercial Code that clarifies the taking of secured debt); this has led to an increase in restructuring in Chapter 11 via a section 363 sale to financial creditors, as opposed to a reorganisation.[18] In a section 363 sale, which is common among debtors whose asserts are fully secured, the financial creditors (secured creditors) form a special purpose vehicle (SPV) and make a credit bid for the company. The assets of the company are sold to the SPV. The characteristic of the section 363 sale is the speed at which the sale occurs, because only consent of the secured creditors is required and valuation disputes are often non-existent as the assets are valued on the basis of an auction. Whether the increase in section 363 sales is good or not has been the subject of debate in the scholarship. It has been argued that with the accompanying rise of

[17] Fed R Bankr P 1007(b).

[18] eg HR Miller, 'The Changing Face of Chapter 11: A Reemergence of the Bankruptcy Judge as Producer, Director, and Sometimes Star of the Reorganization Passion Play' (1995) 69 *American Bankruptcy Law Journal* 431.

distressed trading, there is less of an objection to a section 363 sale that is largely a financial restructuring involving only financial creditors, and does not impact weakly adjusting creditors.[19]

7.2.1.2. United Kingdom

In the UK, until CIGA was enacted, there was no independent standalone moratorium that could be relied upon by the debtor. UK schemes are not traditionally categorised as insolvency proceedings, and a statutory moratorium was absent. Scholars and the practitioners have argued that the moratorium is unnecessary given the focus on financial restructuring.[20] For the first time, CIGA introduces a free-standing moratorium into Part A1 of Insolvency Act 1986 (Part A1 moratorium), if among other requirements, it results in the rescue of the company as a going concern, but it is important to note that the moratorium is limited in scope. For example, it does not extend to staying enforcement actions by financial creditors.[21] Thus, the primary stay of enforcement is really targeted at the operational creditors, including landlords. The initial period of moratorium is 20 business days, though it can be extended; without creditor consent, the moratorium is extended a further 20 business days, and with creditor consent, it can be extended up to a year.[22] The moratorium is overseen by an insolvency practitioner who can bring the moratorium to an end if he/she considers that the company is not financially viable or if critical debts are not paid.[23] It is still too early to determine whether the moratorium leads to a fundamental change in the restructuring law and practice.

7.2.2. Plan Confirmation or Sanction of the Scheme of Arrangement

7.2.2.1. US Approach

In chapter three, I discussed the operation and conditions of the cram-down in Chapter 11; the US Bankruptcy Code provides that if a restructuring plan has to cram-down on a dissenting class of creditors, one of the conditions that it should satisfy is that it does not unfairly discriminate, and is fair and equitable to each dissenting class.[24] Generally, the absolute priority rule (APR) is given effect to, except that a small degree of exceptions is permitted. The US courts scrutinise the plan carefully in assessing the appropriate alternative to the plan, and that is where valuation disputes are brought to the fore. Unlike the UK approach discussed below, the US method is to

[19] S Paterson, Corporate Reorganization Law and Forces of Change (Oxford, OUP, 2020) 236–38.

[20] See ch 4, section 4.3.1.1 (the inter-creditor agreement among the creditors that are typically used in the UK is based on the London Loan Market Association, which contains the moratorium against a junior creditor or bondholder against enforcement actions. Creditors who do not wish to support the reorganisation would have traded their bonds in the distressed debt market).

[21] Insolvency Act 1986, Pt A1, Sch ZA2.

[22] Insolvency Act 1986, Pt A1, ss 9(2) and 12.

[23] Insolvency Act 1986, Pt A1, s 38.

[24] 11 USC §1129.

approach the company's valuation not from the perspective of going-concern value but on non-market basis (such as discounted cash-flow method or comparable pricing and private equity valuation), with the threat of the bankruptcy judge imposing his/her value if parties are unable to agree.[25] The reason for the non-market valuation is that valuation obtained in the downturn market is unlikely to represent the value at which the debtor's assets can be put to the best use. The threat of the judicial valuation (which is often uncertain) often forces the parties to agree. In fact, Baird and Bernstein have argued that the reason for departure from the absolute priority rule is not due to the bias of judges, but the inherent uncertainty over valuation.[26]

7.2.2.2. UK Approach

In the English scheme of arrangement, there are two stages where the application is placed before the court: the stage of the leave to convene the scheme meeting; and the sanction stage.[27] It is well established that at the first stage, the court will grant leave if there is sufficient general support by the creditors and the proposed division of creditors appears to be correct.[28] The fairness of the scheme and class composition is finally determined at the court sanction stage.[29] The court is concerned to ensure that creditors make an informed decision on the outcome of the vote. The key protection to creditors in a within-class cram-down is used through classification, where only the rights and not interests are relevant in grouping creditors into classes. The court ensures that no undue rights are given to minorities by not requiring excessive classification.[30]

Small departures from the equality of treatment of similarly situated creditors are tolerated, as can be seen in the fact that payment of consent fees to creditors that sign up to restructuring support agreements (RSAs) has not been held to fracture the classes.[31] However, in more recent times, more aggressive fees have been seen in the market. These fees include bridge financing (to be provided by the creditors), work fees granted to the ad hoc committee of creditors, backstop fees to underwrite to provision of new facilities that are conditional upon the success of the scheme and advisers' fees.[32] While the courts have not held these fees to fracture the class, care should be taken to ensure that the fees are either justifiable commercially and/or not for an unduly large amount.

In the absence of inadequacy of disclosures, while the case law has emphasised that the courts are duty bound to examine the terms of the scheme as to whether the

[25] S Paterson, 'Rethinking the Corporate Bankruptcy Theory in the Twenty-first Century' (2016) 36 *Oxford Journal of Legal Studies* 697, 719.

[26] DG Baird and DS Bernstein, 'Absolute Priority, Valuation Uncertainty, and the Reorganization Bargain' (2006) 115 *Yale Law Journal* 1930.

[27] J Payne, 'The Role of the Court in Debt Restructuring' (2018) 77 *CLJ* 124.

[28] *Re Savoy Hotel Ltd* [1981] Ch 351.

[29] *Re Hawk Insurance Co Ltd* [2001] EWCA Civ 241.

[30] J Payne, *Schemes of Arrangement: Theory, Structure and Operation* (Cambridge, CUP, 2014) 200–01.

[31] WY Wan and C Watters, 'Mandatory Disclosure in Corporate Debt Restructuring via Schemes of Arrangement: A Comparative Approach' (2021) 30 *International Insolvency Review* S111, discussing *Re Noble Group Limited* [2018] EWHC 3092 (Ch).

[32] *Re Codere Finance II (UK) Limited* [2020] EWHC 2683 (Ch); *Re Swissport Fuelling Ltd* [2020] EWHC 1499.

scheme was 'fair' and not rubber-stamp the creditors' decision,[33] the English courts rarely refuse to sanction schemes in the face of the outcome of a properly convened meeting of a class of creditors and in the absence of allegations of non-disclosure. There is one exception: where on the face of the evidence, the debtor management's assessment as to what should be regarded as the correct comparator[34] (also known as the best alternative if the scheme is not approved) is unsupported. The comparator is critical as the creditors are asked to approve the scheme, and they need to know what would be an alternative recovery if the scheme is not approved. Unlike the US approach, the comparator that is used is often the going-concern sale (though other approaches can be used); in other words, the question is whether the creditors would be worse off than if an auction is held.[35]

Recent examples of such intervention occurred in *Re Sunbird Business Services Limited*[36] and *Re All Scheme Limited*,[37] where the court disagreed with the debtor's version of the comparator. In *Re Sunbird Business*, Snowden J emphasised that there was no professional adviser's opinion and the opinion of the management that liquidation was the appropriate comparator was not consistent with the accounts on record showing that the company was still solvent. In *All Scheme Limited*, it was emphasised that the creditors, who were the customers of a sub-prime lender, were unsophisticated and particularly vulnerable and were presented a misleading picture that imminent liquidation was at hand, which was not necessarily the case as the company could be restructured. Further, the Financial Conduct Authority, which regulates financial services firms and financial markets, objected to the compromise.

CIGA introduced the flexible Part 26A plan, which allows for a cross-class cram-down. Recent cases have established that the case law established for Part 26 schemes will be applicable, subject to the special provision on the cross-class cram-down.[38] It was indicated in *Re Virgin Atlantic Plc*[39] and in *Re Hurricane Energy Plc*[40] that the dispute often turns on the appropriate valuation placed on the assets and liabilities of the debtor. In exercising the discretion to cram-down, the court will need to balance the interests of not having a prolonged process against the interests of the class of stakeholders who are proposed to be crammed down (and who faced difficulties in challenging the plan proponents on the comparator).[41] In *Hurricane Energy*, the bondholders argued that the company was cash-flow insolvent as it was unable to pay its debt falling due in 13 months. Notwithstanding that the bondholders had approved the plan by the requisite majority, the shareholders objected to being crammed down

[33] See generally, *Re Noble Group Limited* [2018] EWHC 3092 (Ch), [2018] EWHC 2911 (Ch).

[34] *Re Hawk Insurance Co Ltd* [2001] EWCA Civ 241.

[35] eg J Payne, 'Debt Restructuring in English Law: Lessons from the US and the Need for Reform (2014) *LQR* 282, 302–05; S Paterson, 'Bargaining in Financial Restructuring – Market Norms, Legal Rights and Regulatory Standards' (2014) 14 *Journal of Corporate Law Studies* 333, 364–68.

[36] [2020] EWHC 2493 (Ch).

[37] [2021] EWHC 1401 (Ch).

[38] In exercising the cross-class cram-down, there are two conditions: (1) the court is satisfied that the dissenting class would not be worse off than they would be in the relevant alternative; and (2) the compromise is agreed by 75% in value of the creditors present and voting who would receive a payment or has a genuine economic interest in the company. See Companies Act 2006, s 901G(2)–(5).

[39] [2020] EWHC 2376 (Ch).

[40] [2021] EWHC 1759 (Ch).

[41] ibid [49].

(and left with a five per cent equity stake), on the ground that the shareholders are not out of the money. In this case, the court held that the relevant alternative was not imminent insolvent liquidation of the company but that the company would continue to trade at least for a further year. Because there was a realistic prospect that the company could continue to trade profitably and discharge its obligations to the bondholders, the court found that the shareholders were better off retaining all of the equity as opposed to giving up all of the equity in return for only five per cent.[42]

7.2.3. Analysis

In restructuring cases, due to the courts only deciding on cases as they come up, the judges are not involved in the decision-making by the creditors. Even in the US, with respect to the management of Chapter 11 cases, the original intention of US Bankruptcy Code 1978 was described as shifting the bulk of the administrative role of the bankruptcy judges to the US Trustee Programme.[43] While bankruptcy judges have access to broad powers given under section 105 of the US Bankruptcy Code to actively manage the cases through the holding of status conferences and issuing case-management orders, in practice, not all are obliged to actively monitor the bankruptcy processes.[44]

As compared to the US bankruptcy judges, English judges are even more removed in schemes of arrangement or restructuring plans as they only hear the case to convene the meetings and to sanction the schemes or plans, unless a moratorium is sought, which is not expected to be routine given the limited scope of the moratorium. As the English judges do not have investigative powers, unless there is a challenge or the scheme demonstrates clearly contradictory evidence, it is likely the scheme will be passed.

The approach of the courts in the common-law world is not surprising. I draw from the regulation of a closely related field of regulating hostile takeovers, which is similar to restructuring as both result in outcomes where management may lose control of the company in favour of outsiders.[45] For hostile takeovers, at least in the 1980s, there is a line of influential scholarship first led by Armour and Skeel,[46] who argue that judge-made laws tend to give a much greater leeway to directors and management to determine what they regard as the best interests of the firms in hostile takeover disputes, even though there is an obvious conflict between the interests of the management and shareholders in these situations.[47] Judge-made laws depend on the parties

[42] ibid [125].

[43] See Miller, 'The Changing Face of Chapter 11' (1995); HR Miller, 'Chapter 11 Reorganization Cases and the Delaware Myth' (2002) 55 *Vanderbilt Law Review* 1987; BA Markell, 'Lawyers, Judges and Unwritten Rules' (2020) 36 *Emory Bankruptcy Developments Journal* 719.

[44] BA Markell, 'Lawyers, Judges and Unwritten Rules' (2020) 36 *Emory Bankruptcy Developments Journal* 719; DL Dick, 'The Chapter 11 Efficiency Fallacy' (2013) 2013 *Brigham Young University Law Review* 759; cf Miller (n 18).

[45] Triantis, 'The Interplay Between Liquidation and Reorganization in Bankruptcy' (1996).

[46] J Armour and DA Skeel, 'Who Writes the Rules for Hostile Takeovers, and Why? – The Peculiar Divergence of U.S. and U.K. Takeover Regulation' (2007) 95 *Georgetown Law Journal* 1727; J Armour, J Jacobs and C Milhaupt, 'The Evolution of Hostile Takeover Regimes in Developed and Emerging Markets: An Analytical Framework' (2011) 52 *Harvard International Law Journal* 219.

[47] For the references to the line of debate on hostile takeovers, see U Varottil and WY Wan, 'Hostile Takeover Regimes in Asia: A Comparative Approach' (2019) 15 *Berkeley Business Law Journal* 267.

bringing the cases, which would be the target board directors, represented by counsel who argue these cases and who are often repeat players. Analysing the contrasting approaches between the UK and the US, they argue that the UK's self-regulatory takeover regime and aggressive lobbying by strong institutional shareholders have resulted in a pro-shareholder regime that limits the ability of the directors to take defensive measures. In contrast, US courts serve as arbiters of takeover disputes – where the directors and management are the ones who will file in the courts and who argue for greater leeway in giving them the right to determine what they regard as the interests of the firm.[48] Since the 2000s, however, the role of the US courts has been reduced in takeovers in view of other reasons, ie that there are now other powerful monitoring devices to check the excesses of directorial behaviour in corporate governance, including the fact that independent directors are becoming more powerful, and the rise of institutional shareholder monitoring.[49] Their conclusion was also buttressed by their analysis of the common law in the era of pre-takeover code in the UK,[50] where the judges gave leeway to what the directors thought to be in the legitimate interest of the company, even if this amounted to a frustration of a bona fide bid.

Similarly, in the case of US Chapter 11 cases, given that it is often the debtor who files for Chapter 11 and the management that supplies the arguments for the viability of the reorganised firms, it is not surprising that the courts give leeway to decisions of the management in determining whether the debtor is capable of being rescued.

Recent case law shows more reluctance by the English judges to approve the schemes and restructuring plans in the face of significant opposition from junior creditors and shareholders. This could partially be attributed to the fact that the English judge lacks the US trustee or some other independent party to independently verify some of the claims that are raised and, in particular, relating to the correct comparator. As discussed in chapter six, in schemes of arrangement and Part 26A restructuring plans, there is no statutory role of the financial adviser typically appointed by the company to assist in the restructuring.

7.3. LEGISLATIVE FRAMEWORK AND JUDICIAL DISCRETION IN ASIA

In all of the four jurisdictions, as is the case in the US and UK, often the most significant aspects of restructuring law have been shaped by judges. While the legislature may formulate hard rules that allow little variation for judicial discretion (such as the ban on promoters serving as resolution applicants in India),[51] in practice, there remain situations that are sufficiently open-textured where even well-trained judges are often not able to identify parties that act opportunistically. Yet, the legislation often does not give guidance on how the discretion should be exercised, while the

[48] *Unocal Corp v Mesa Petroleum Co*, 493 A 2d 946, 958 (Del 1985); *Revlon, Inc v MacAndrews & Forbes Holdings, Inc*, 506 A 2d 173, 184 (Del 1985).

[49] RS Thomas and SD Solomon 'The Rise and Fall of Delaware's Takeover Standards' in RS Thomas and SD Solomon (eds), *The Corporate Contract in Changing Times* (Chicago, University of Chicago Press. 2019).

[50] Armour and Skeel, 'Who Writes the Rules' (2007); the City Code on Takeovers and Mergers (UK) came into force in 1968. See the Takeover Panel, 'Takeover Code', available at www.thetakeoverpanel.org.uk/the-code/download-code.

[51] ch 3.

courts are conscious of the need for certainty and predictability in developing the restructuring framework (both of which are essential for reducing ex post and *ex ante* transaction costs).

In this section, I argue that in restructuring law in common law Asian jurisdictions, there is a pro-debtor tendency to allow the management *to manage the process while the company undergoes reorganisation*. This tendency arises because it is often not possible to tell whether the debtor is viable unless the situation is egregious. However, when it comes to the question of plan confirmation, the creditors' decision is normally given effect to. Finally, I deal with the question of rescue financing.

7.3.1. Moratorium and Conditions

Singapore,[52] Hong Kong and India are common law jurisdictions that have addressed the issue relating to stay of proceedings, although in very different ways.

7.3.1.1. Singapore

In Singapore, prior to the insolvency law reforms of 2017, debtors could obtain a limited stay of proceedings while the scheme of arrangement was being effected.[53] However, the scope of the stay is limited and the 2017 reforms, included in Insolvency, Restructuring and Dissolution Act 2008 (IRDA), significantly strengthen the moratorium period.[54] The period is 30 days upon filing, with the ability to ask for extension prior to the expiry of the moratorium.[55] The moratorium has extra-territorial effect, which may apply to any person in Singapore or within the jurisdiction of the Singapore court, and the application must be made specifically to the court.[56] The moratorium is wide-ranging covers the stay of proceedings against the company as well as enforcement of security interests.[57] In *IM Skagen SE*, it was held that the evidence for extension is either in the form of the scheme of arrangement that is proposed together with evidence of creditor support or if the company intends to propose the scheme (but the scheme is not yet ready), the company needs to show creditor support for the moratorium and importance of the same, with description of the proposed scheme of arrangement to enable the court to determine its feasibility.[58] In a recent unreported decision, the High Court turned down the application on the moratorium, doubting the feasibility of the plan and noting that the debtor waited close to a year after financial distress commenced to apply for a moratorium.[59]

[52] For an overall discussion on the scope of the Singapore moratorium, see WY Wan, C Watters and G McCormack, 'Schemes of Arrangement in Singapore: Empirical and Comparative Analysis' (2020) 94 *American Bankruptcy Law Journal* 463.

[53] Companies Act 2006, s 210(10).

[54] See also Wan, Watters and McCormack, 'Schemes of Arrangement in Singapore' (2020).

[55] IRDA, ss 64–66. The moratorium can be made for the stay of proceeding against the debtor as well as its subsidiary and holding company. See also *Pathfinder Strategic Credit LP v Empire Capital Resources* [2019] SGCA 29.

[56] IRDA, s 65(5). *Re IM Skaugen SE* [2018] SGHC 259, [86].

[57] IRDA, ss 64–65.

[58] *Re IM Skaugen SE* [2018] SGHC 259.

[59] *Re Kobian Pte Ltd* HC/OS 1269/2020, unreported. The grounds of the decision are described by Allen and Gledhill, 'The requirements of feasibility for moratorium applications under Insolvency

Since the enactment of the 2017 reforms, together with others, I previously reported that the moratorium was very well utilised. For example, the number of filings made for the moratorium in support of restructuring in the one year after the strengthened moratorium has increased (in comparison with the immediately preceding period).[60]

Extensions of the moratoria are typically for a period of between three and six months (and can be extended),[61] with various conditions including the submission of financial statements and valuation reports.[62] Even if a major (but not majority) creditor objects to the moratorium, it is not necessarily fatal as the restructuring is still in the early days and the creditors may ultimately change their mind if alternatives are presented.[63] The full effects of the 2017 reforms are still in their early days, though there have been criticisms of two high profile cases of listed company restructurings where the stay has been extended on multiple occasions. For example, in the Hyflux restructuring, the cumulative extension was 2.5 years before an order for judicial management was made.[64] In Pacific Radiance's restructuring, the moratorium for certain companies within the group was on 12 June 2018 and the debtor announced the updated restructuring plan on 30 June 2021 (three years later).[65] As of 30 September 2021, the debtor's moratorium had yet to end. Possibly with a view to address some of these issues, the Singapore Supreme Court introduced the Guide for the Conduct of Applications for Moratoria under Sections 64 and 65 of the Insolvency, Restructuring and Dissolution Act 2018,[66] which require the debtor to set out a list of milestones for the restructuring and undertakings to file the application for the scheme of arrangement meeting to be held. The requirements as to the proposed scheme of arrangement or intention to propose a scheme of arrangement, as set out in the earlier decision of *IM v Skaugen*, were reiterated.[67]

On the whole, for the sanctioned schemes, I refer to the dataset of companies in Appendix D between 2015 and 2020 (which excludes schemes under judicial management), the average length of time that the companies were in the scheme process was 270 days (or nine months). This is in line with the World Bank report,

Restructuring Dissolution Act' (18 March 2021), available at www.allenandgledhill.com/sg/perspectives/articles/17893/sgkh-the-requirement-of-feasibility-for-moratorium-applications-under-the-new-insolvency-restructuring-and-dissolution-act.

[60] Wan, Watters and McCormack (n 52) (Table 6: an increase from 24 to 29 filings in the one year pre- and post-23 May 2017), the date on which the legislation came into force.

[61] eg see *Re IM Skaugen SE* [2018] SGHC 259; see also restructuring of Miclyn Express Offshore, 'Update to Stakeholders' (6 December 2018), available at www.meogroup.com/wp-content/uploads/2018/12/MEOL-Update-to-Stakeholders-6-Dec-2018.pdf; Hyflux (the moratorium was extended several times and the total period was approximately 2.5 years); see Hyflux, 'Hyflux Put Under Judicial Management; Founder Olivia Lum Loses Control Over Firm' *Strait Times* (16 November 2020).

[62] IRDA, s 64(6); see also *Re IM Skaugen SE* [2018] SGHC 259.

[63] *Re IM Skaugen SE* [2018] SGHC 259.

[64] See n 61 (Hyflux).

[65] Pacific Radiance Ltd, 'Update on Restructuring – Principal Terms of Debt Restructuring' (30 June 2021); Pacific Radiance Ltd, 'Application for Extension of Moratoria' (17 September 2021), announcements available at www.sgx.com.

[66] Supreme Court, 'Guide for the Conduct of Applications for Moratoria under Sections 64 and 65 of the Insolvency, Restructuring and Dissolution Act 2018' (21 February 2021), available at www.supremecourt.gov.sg/legal-professional/rc-012021---issuance-of-the-guide-for-the-conduct-of-applications-for-moratoria-under-sections-64-and-65-of-the-insolvency--restructuring-and-dissolution-act-2018.

[67] See above, nn 58–63.

Doing Business 2020, in which the average time between default and recovery of assets in Singapore insolvency cases was 9.6 months.

While there are obvious advantages in granting broad discretionary powers to the judges in determining how long the moratorium should be granted, the question arises as to the conditions that should be imposed alongside the extension. One issue that frequently arises in practice is the extent to which should creditors receive the key financial information of the company early in the proceedings. It is unlikely to be an issue for the bank creditors, who would probably receive the information in the regular review as part of the terms of the loan, but it would be for the less connected creditors, such as bondholders. Provision of information can be costly to prepare, while the debtor management is busy trying to effect a rescue. At the same time, the lack of information can be seriously concerning on the part of the creditors to support the restructuring exercise. In chapter four, I highlighted that in *Pathfinder Strategic Credit LP v Empire Capital Resources* (*Pathfinder*), the Singapore Court of Appeal clarified that a lower standard applies for leave to convene a meeting of creditors (and a higher standard after leave is granted to permit creditors the meaningful exercise of their voting rights).[68] By holding that the disclosure only needs to be a lower standard to convene a meeting of creditors, it follows that considerable leeway is in fact given to the debtor management to determine what to disclose at earlier stages of the proceedings.

Finally, one major factor that is likely to play a much more important role is the use of pre-packs in schemes of arrangement under section 71 of IRDA. Pre-packs were introduced by the 2017 reforms, streamlining the process by removing the requirement of the meeting of the creditors called by the court as long as the debtor can show that if a meeting is called, the requisite number of creditors will be passed. It differs from the UK pre-packs as court approval is required in view of the greater protection afforded to dissenting creditors. There is evidence of its widespread use – in Appendix D, six of the nine cases of schemes of arrangement (after the passage of the 2017 reforms) involved the use of pre-packs.

7.3.1.2. Hong Kong

Hong Kong lacks a formal moratorium in the legislation as there is no formal rescue legislation. In theory, its approach towards schemes of arrangement should be closest to the English scheme as the court will only consider the matter at the stage of the leave of court to convene the scheme meeting and at the sanction stages. However, the market participants were innovative in finding adaptive tools. Initially, beginning with the Asian financial crisis of 1998, provisional liquidation was used,[69] but the decision in *Re Legend International Resorts Ltd*[70] put a stop to that when the Court of Appeal held that it was impermissible to appoint provisional liquidators under

[68] Pathfinder Strategic Credit LP v Empire Capital [2019] SGCA 29, [50].

[69] Once the winding-up petition is filed, there is a stay on proceedings under the Companies (Winding up and Miscellaneous Provisions) Ordinance, s 186. A history of the use of provisional liquidation is described by Harris J in *Re China Bozza Development Holdings* [2021] HKCFI 1235. See also ch 2.

[70] [2006] 2 HKLRD 192.

the legislation principally for restructuring.[71] A decade later, the court clarified that provisional liquidators can continue to be appointed if the company is insolvent and the assets are in fact in jeopardy.[72]

The appointment of provisional liquidators triggers an automatic stay of legal proceedings against the debtor[73] but does not stop the secured creditors from enforcing their security since such enforcement can take place without court proceedings. In the meantime, the debtor who wishes to conduct a restructuring would have to persuade the court and the other creditors to adjourn the winding-up petition. The problem is that creditors may object, not necessarily because they do not believe that the company is viable, but for their own private reasons. Hence, market participants have adapted using other innovative ways to obtain a de facto moratorium that have been given judicial recognition.[74] In a series of cases beginning with *Z-Obee*,[75] the court allowed the use of the soft-touch provisional liquidation procedure for companies that are incorporated in offshore jurisdictions to effect a DIP restructuring procedure, if that is allowed in those jurisdictions.[76] In particular, as more than 80 per cent of the companies listed in Hong Kong are incorporated in the Cayman Islands, Bermuda or the British Virgin Islands, appointing a provisional liquidator and getting him/her recognised in Hong Kong became an attractive option.[77] The recognition is important as Hong Kong is the place of listing of these companies and the assets are also located in Hong Kong. Recognition is done under common law in Hong Kong, and Hong Kong is not party to the United Nations Commission on International Trade Law (UNCITRAL) Model Law on Cross-border Insolvency,[78] and the debtor will often ask for active assistance such as the adjournment of the winding-up petition. Such assistance is granted if there is a viable proposal and evidence of creditor support that would allow the threshold to be met.[79] All the company restructurings in Appendix C, with the exception of Hsin Chong Aster Building Services Limited, involve companies incorporated outside of Hong Kong.

However, in recent cases, it appears that the soft-touch process may have been misused to delay winding-up proceedings taken in Hong Kong to the creditors' detriment.[80] In two recent cases, the judge stressed that it was essential that creditor

[71] Companies (Winding Up and Miscellaneous Provisions) Ordinance, Cap 32, s 193 sets out the appointment of the provisional liquidator.

[72] See *China Solar Energy Holdings Ltd* [2016] HKCU 465; see discussion in ch 4, section 4.4.1.

[73] Companies (Winding Up and Miscellaneous Provisions) Ordinance, Cap 32, s 186.

[74] See discussion in ch 4, section 4.4.1.

[75] [2018] 1 HKLRD 165.

[76] For recent examples as to the exercise of the appointments of soft-touch or light-touch provisional liquidation in Bermuda of a company that also sought a moratorium order in Singapore, see *Re Agritrade Resources Limited* [2020] SC (Bda) 28 Com (17 June 2020), available at www.gov.bm/sites/default/files/Final-Draft-Judgment-2020-No.-150-civ.-In-the-Matter-of-Agritrade-Resources-Limited-with-Citation.pdf.

[77] The Stock Exchange of Hong Kong does not automatically suspend the trading of the shares if the company is in soft-touch liquidation, unlike the case where the petition for winding up is filed against the company in Hong Kong. This was confirmed by interviews with insolvency practitioners.

[78] The UNCITRAL Model Law on Cross-Border Insolvency was conceived with the aim to grant foreign courts relief by providing a consistent framework for countries to obtain recognition of foreign insolvency proceedings. See generally, G McCormack and WY Wan, 'The UNCITRAL Model Law on Cross-Border Insolvency Comes of Age: New Times or New Paradigms' (2019) 54 *Texas International Law Journal* 273.

[79] *Li Yiqing v Lamtex Holdings Ltd* [2021] HKCFI 622.

[80] *Re FDG Electric Vehicles Limited* [2020] HKCFI 2931.

support be in place for a genuine restructuring or the court would not allow an adjournment of the winding-up proceedings in Hong Kong, notwithstanding that the provisional liquidator is recognised.[81] In *China Bozza Development Holdings*, the creditors were individuals (probably high-net-worth individuals) who loaned money at low interest rates to the company, and they were not consulted when the provisional liquidator was appointed.[82] In *Re Victory City*, the debtor largely ignored the requests by the creditor banks for additional information over the sudden appointment of the joint provisional liquidators, expressed to be for the purpose of restructuring, in the foreign court.[83] (At the time of writing, Hong Kong is proposing a corporate rescue bill to be tabled before Legislative Council that will have a moratorium, but this is an out-of-court process.[84])

The experience shows that the market participants regard moratorium to be critical to the restructuring process, but it also shows that the process can be subject to abuse to the detriment of the creditors. These incidents are not easy to detect, except in egregious cases such as when there is a complete lack of creditor consultation and a long period between the date of the presentation of the winding-up petition and the application for soft-touch liquidation. Additionally, the recent cases indicate that the debtors lack urgency and are likely to be prompted only by the stock exchange's delisting timetable. Furthermore, case law is necessarily reactive, as the court can only hold that the process should be curtailed when brought to its attention.

7.3.1.3. India

Under the IBC, after the debtor is admitted in the Corporate Insolvency Resolution Process (CIRP) process by the court, the court orders a moratorium against enforcement of proceedings (including the secured creditors' ability to enforce their security rights) until completion of the process or liquidation.[85] Under the IBC, when it is first enacted, the CIRP must be concluded within a maximum of 180 days within the date of commencement, with a maximum one-time extension from 90 days. Extensions require the majority approval of the majority of creditors. The date of commencement is the date of appointment of the interim resolution processional. Due to the fact that many cases exceeded this 270-day limit due to litigation brought by the debtor's creditors as well as resolution applicants, in 2019, the IBC was amended to provide that the CIRP must be completed within 330 days from the date of commencement date, including extensions granted as well as legal proceedings.[86] Once the period is reached, the debtor must proceed to liquidation.

It appears unlikely that the period of 330 days can be realistically adhered to, even considering that the initial lengthy delays are due to the fact that the market

[81] *Re China Bozza Development Holdings Ltd* [2021] HKCFI 1235; *Re Victory City International Holdings Ltd* [2021] HKCFI 1370.

[82] ibid.

[83] *Re Victory City International Holdings Ltd* [2021] HKCFI 1370, [17].

[84] See ch 9.

[85] IBC, ss 13 and 14.

[86] Insolvency and Bankruptcy Code (Amendment) Act 2019, No 26 of 2019.

participants are getting familiar with the IBC and litigating on points of law that were uncertain. The Insolvency and Bankruptcy Board of India (IBBI) data shows that between 1 April 2020 and 31 March 2021, the average time for completion of CIRP was 536 days,[87] and 1,264 of the 4,541 (or 27.8 per cent) cases admitted to CIRP exceeded 270 days.[88]

The review of the case law shows that the courts do not impose a bright-line rule, notwithstanding the absolute language of the IBC as to the time-bound nature of the CIRP. In *Essar Steel India v Satish Kumar Gupta*,[89] the Supreme Court held that while the time in CIRP must ordinarily be completed within 330 days, if it can be shown that 'only a short period' is left for completion of the process beyond 330 days, it would be in the 'interest of all stakeholders that the corporate debtor be put back on its feet instead of being sent into liquidation' and that the time taken in legal proceedings is largely due to factors owing to which the fault cannot be ascribed to the litigants, the extension will be granted in exceptional circumstances.[90] To compare the time spent in CIRP for the various processes, in addition to the cases in Appendix B, Panel B, I analysed the data of all of the outcomes of the large cases, that is, those with financial liabilities that exceed INR100 million (US$1.3 million), that are concluded between 2016 and 2020. This expanded number of cases comprise those that are dismissed, liquidated, resolved or withdrawn. Figure 7.2 shows the average number of days that are taken in each case from the time of filing to the following outcomes: dismissal, liquidation, resolution or withdrawal, and demonstrates that those involving the approval of the resolution plans, on average, take the longest. Figure 7.3 shows the distribution of the duration for cases where the resolution plans are approved (ie those in Appendix B, Panel B). It shows that the 330-day period is often not complied with.

Figure 7.2 Average time spent in CIRP

N=233 cases

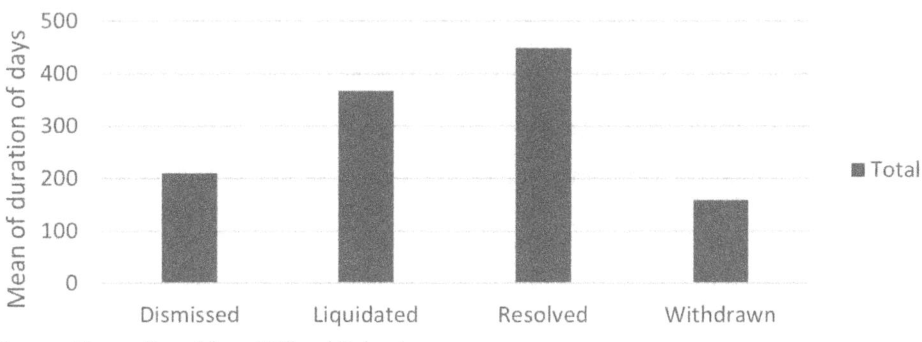

Sources: Data collected from IBBI and Debtwire.

[87] IBBI (March 2021), Table 6. Prior to 1 April 2020, the average time of completion was 414 days. The increase could be attributed to the disruptions caused by COVID-19.

[88] IBBI, 'Discussion Paper' (27 August 2021).

[89] *Essar Steel India v Satish Kumar Gupta* Civil Appeal No 8766-67 of 2019.

[90] ibid [79].

Figure 7.3 Distribution of the number of days spent in CIRP 2016–21 where resolution plans are approved

N=154 cases

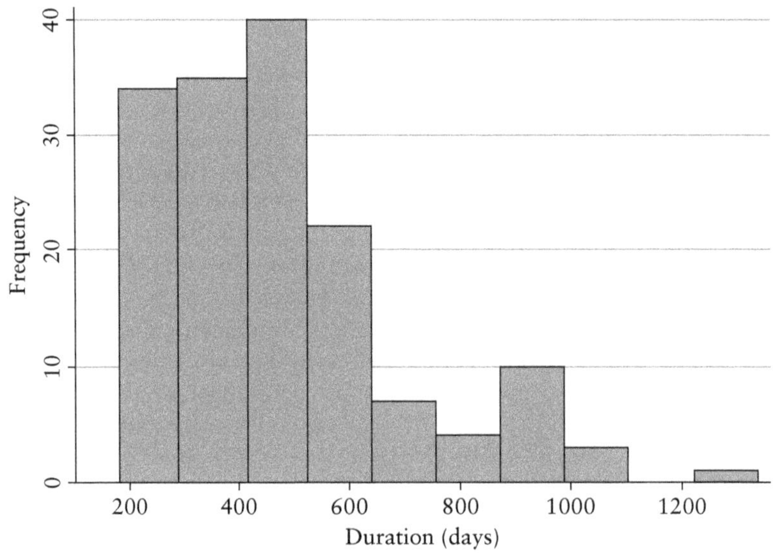

Source: Data collected from IBBI and Debtwire.

Quite apart from the time that the case requires to be litigated in the courts, another cause of the delay is that the resolution professional takes a long time to prepare the expression of interest and organise the due diligence process as there is also no incentive to cooperate with the resolution professional. The obvious implication is that the creditors often receive information very late in the day.[91]

7.3.2. Sanction of the Scheme

7.3.2.1. Singapore and Hong Kong

Broadly, the Singapore[92] and Hong Kong[93] courts have followed the English approach when dealing with within-class cram-down of creditors, and in the case of Hong Kong, the treatment of the restructuring support agreements (RSAs) where the consent fees given to the creditors who signed up for lock-ups did not fracture the classes of creditors.[94] In chapter three, I discussed the general wariness of the Singapore

[91] See N Shikha and U Shahi, 'Assessment of Corporate Insolvency and Resolution Timeline' IBBI, Indian Institute of Corporate Affairs RP 01/2021, available at ibbi.gov.in/uploads/publication/2021-02-12-154823-p3xwo-8b78d9548a60a756e4c71d49368def03.pdf.

[92] *Re TT International Ltd* [2012] SGCA 9.

[93] *Re UDL Argos Engineering & Heavy Industries* [2000] HKCFI 1568, [2001] 3 HKLRD 634.

[94] The treatment of RSAs has been discussed in *Re Winsway Enterprises Holdings Ltd* [2016] HKCFI 1915; *Re Kaisa Group Holdings Ltd* [2016] HKCU 2765; *Re Mongolian Mining Corporation* [2018] HKCU 3109; and *Re China Singyes Solar Technologies Holdings* [2020] HKCU 548; and in Wan and Watters, 'Mandatory Disclosure in Corporate Debt Restructuring' (2021).

courts in scrutinising that the class composition is properly formed, particularly in light of possible undue influence from related party creditors, which is in line with the English approaches in *Re Indah Kiat*[95] and *Re Sunbird*.[96] This can be seen in *TT International*'s earlier restructuring where the Court of Appeal held that related party creditors should be discounted based on their shareholdings, though the approach is controversial and doubt is cast in *SK Engineering v Conchubar*.[97]

The cross-class cram-down in Singapore permits the cram-down against entire dissenting class, but the court must be satisfied that the scheme does not 'discriminate unfairly' between classes of creditors and is 'fair and equitable to each dissenting class'.[98] The scheme must be approved by at least one class of creditors and by a majority in number representing at least three-quarters of value of all of the claims subject to the scheme.[99] In determining whether the scheme is fair and equitable to the dissenting class, the creditor must receive an amount not less than what is estimated to be received in the likely alternative scenario (had the scheme not been binding) and the APR is satisfied.[100] In chapter three, I explained that the Singaporean version of the APR is not identical with the APR as applied in Chapter 11, notably because it does not require that the shareholders be wiped out, even if the company is insolvent. As argued in chapter four, the discretion offered to the court as to determining the valuation of the company (which is necessary to determine the recoveries in the alternative scenario) can lead to significant disputes. There is yet no case of a cross-class cram-down to be exercised at time of writing.

7.3.2.2. India

The Indian Supreme Court has, on a number of the occasions, held that under sections 30(2) and 31 of the IBC, the role of the NCLT is not to adjudicate on the merits of the resolution plan, and its jurisdiction is limited to ensuring that the requisite threshold of financial creditors has approved the plan;[101] in other words, there is no scope to substitute the decision of the committee of creditors. If there is any shortcoming, the tribunal can only send the case back to the committee of creditors for reconsideration.[102] Despite the absolute clarity of the Supreme Court decision, the NCLT has on several occasions questioned the commercial wisdom of the decisions of the committee of creditors. Even as recently as 2021, in *Re Videocon Industries*,[103] the NCLT expressed unease at the 96 per cent haircut to all the creditors, and that the resolution applicant only had to pay 8.8 per cent of the total plan value (which was close to the liquidation value), and even then, the amount was payable over six years.

[95] [2016] EWHC 246 (Ch). See ch 3, section 3.3.2.2.
[96] [2020] EWHC 2493 (Ch). See ch 3, section 3.3.2.2.
[97] [2017] SGCA 51. See ch 3, section 3.4.3.2.
[98] See ch 3, section 3.4.2.1.
[99] ibid.
[100] ibid.
[101] eg *Sashidhar v Indian Overseas Bank* (Civil Appeal No 10673/2018); *Committee of Creditors of Essar Steel* (Civil Appeal No 8766-67 of 2019).
[102] ibid.
[103] *Re Videocon Industries Ltd* IA 196 of 2021.

As at the time of writing, the National Company Law Appellate Tribunal (NCLAT) – the appellate court to which the decisions of the NCLT are appealed – has stayed the order, pending an appeal.[104] However, it appears that an appeal is futile, because the Supreme Court reiterated in *Pratap Technocrats (P) Ltd & Ors v Monitoring Committee of Reliance Infratel Limited* that there is no jurisdiction of the NCLT to examine the fairness of the resolution plan.[105] Additionally, the Supreme Court has held that even if the resolution plan provides for a pay-out to a dissenting creditor that is lower than the liquidation value but the plan is approved by the committee of creditors, it is not open for the NCLT to set aside the plan.[106]

7.3.3. Rescue Financing

Finally, the question is how the jurisdiction's legal regime should address rescue financing or DIP financing, which may serve a tool to provide liquidity while the company is undergoing reorganisation or when the company exits from reorganisation.[107] DIP financing is well established in US bankruptcy law, where the providers of DIP financing may be existing secured creditors or new lenders, and is a tool by creditors to exert control over the reorganisation process; in any event the courts have to approve the rescue financing if what is proposed is to elevate the priority of the new lenders.[108] In chapter four, I discussed the conflicts that are faced between the existing lenders who are willing to grant further financing during the period of reorganisation or thereafter (and seeking to elevate their priority status) and those which are not willing to grant such financing and may find themselves relegated in terms of priority. In this section, I deal with the desirability of incentivising new lenders to grant post-petition financing, including during the restructuring process and enabling the company to exit. The continuation of viable businesses until the sale or reorganisation may only happen if the business receives financing from the lenders to cover the costs of administering the reorganisation and operating costs.

Legislation is required to give post-petition financing priority over the pre-petition lenders in the absence of consent by the pre-petition lenders. Traditionally, the justifications of rescue financing to be granted priority over existing creditors rest on the fact that the debtor would otherwise not be able to obtain the financing and that such financing would put the creditors in a better position when the company exits the restructuring than without the DIP financing.[109] Hence the approval of a

[104] *Bank of Maharashtra v Videocon Industries* (Company Appeal (AT) (Ins) No 503 of 2021.

[105] *Pratap Technocrats (P) Ltd & Ors v Monitoring Committee of Reliance Infratel Limited* (Civil Appeal 676 of 2021).

[106] See ch 4, section 4.4.2.3.

[107] K Ayotte and DA Skeel 'Bankruptcy Law as a Liquidity Provider' (2013) 80 *University of Chicago Law Review*1557.

[108] eg 11 USC § 364(d). See also K Ayotte and ER Morrison, 'Creditor Control and Conflict in Chapter 11' (2009) 1 *Journal of Legal Analysis* 511 (63% of the providers of DIP loans are existing lenders that have provided pre-revolving credit facilities).

[109] Ayotte and Skeel, 'Bankruptcy Law as a Liquidity Provider' (2013).

third-party adjudicator, such as the court, will be required to make the determinations. For instance, it may be beneficial for the company to borrow from a lender to fulfil a lucrative contract (such as completion of the construction of the buildings) so that the company can then be paid for the work, and the lender is only prepared to lend to an insolvent debtor if it gets priority over the existing claims. However, the court will need to make the determination.

Currently, among the four Asian jurisdictions, only Singapore allows for a Chapter 11-style priority in post-petition financing. Mainland China allows for super-priority status only in the limited circumstances set out below. India requires the consent of the creditors (though the consent need not be unanimous, as explained below.) Hong Kong, similar to the UK, does not have a DIP financing framework,[110] so the status of new financing will need to be contractually agreed between the parties.[111]

In Singapore, the 2017 reforms first introduced the concept of super-priority status for new financing;[112] unlike in India where the commercial case for raising interim financing is decided solely by the committee of creditors, in Singapore court approval is required. There are two conditions: (1) the credit must be otherwise unavailable; and (2) the financing must be necessary to enable the debtor to continue as a going concern. Adequate protection is required if it is proposed to grant super-priority over the secured creditors.[113] The number of cases where super-priority financing by *new lenders* has been ruled to be available by the courts has been limited, though there are promising signs. The first reported case of super-priority financing was granted in April 2019 to Asiatravel.com.[114] Asiatravel.com Holdings, a company listed on Catalist,[115] planned to restructure its debts via a scheme of arrangement and obtained the court's approval for super-priority financing to be granted by an investor in the form of a loan comprising cash and in-kind injection; upon approvals for the restructuring (including the sanction of the court and shareholder approval), the investor would be repaid in the form of shares. If the approvals were not forthcoming, the investor would be repaid in cash in accordance with the super-priority order. Asiatravel.com applied for, and was granted, super-priority again in 2020.[116] Another

[110] The UK Corporate Insolvency and Governance Act 2020 did not introduce a DIP financing regime; see Department for Business, Energy & Industrial Strategy, 'Insolvency and Corporate Governance, Government Response' (26 August 2018).

[111] For the position in the UK, see S Paterson, *Corporate Reorganization Law and Forces of Change* (Oxford, OUP, 2020) 241.

[112] IRDA, s 67. See generally G McCormack and WY Wan, 'Transplanting Chapter 11 of the US Bankruptcy Code into Singapore's Restructuring and Insolvency Laws: Opportunities and Challenges' (2019) 19 *Journal of Corporate Law Studies* 69.

[113] McCormack and Wan (ibid).

[114] See Asiatravel.com, 'Update on the outcome of the hearing for applications under s 211B and 211E of the Companies Act' (9 April 2019), and Asiatravel.com, 'Monthly update pursuant to rule 704(22) of the Singapore Exchange Securities Trading Limited's Listing Manual Section B: Rules of Catalist–Super Priority Financing Agreement' (10 June 2019), both available at www.sgx.com.

[115] Catalist is the second board of the Singapore Exchange, the first being the Mainboard.

[116] Asiatravel.com, 'Update on the Outcome of the Application to Court for Sanction and Approval of the Scheme of Arrangement and Super-priority Rescue financing under section 211E of the Companies Act' (1 February 2021), available at www.sgx.com.

kind of super-priority financing that has been allowed by the courts is roll-up financing, granted to existing pre-petition creditors that would protect the priority position of pre-filing debt.[117]

In India, the secured creditors have a lot of influence in the CIRP process; consistent with such influence, a resolution professional may raise interim finance but only with the consent of the committee of creditors (with the approval threshold set at 66 per cent of the voting shares).[118] Under the IBC, interim finance, defined as being raised by the resolution professional during the insolvency resolution period,[119] is categorised as insolvency resolution process costs,[120] and is accorded in highest priority during CIRP.[121] To further incentivise the lenders, the IBC provides that in the event the company proceeds to liquidation, interest that is payable on interim finance, for a period of 12 months or for the period from the commencement of liquidation until repayment, is conferred the status of liquidation costs, whichever is earlier.[122] Practitioners have pointed out, however, that interim financing is likely to be provided only by non-bank providers since Indian banks are reluctant to lend further to distressed companies.[123] However, new non-bank lenders (such as distressed funds) may be willing to advance rescue financing, particularly for borrowers who are unable to borrow outside of bankruptcy.

In China, the EBL introduces post-petition financing which allows the administrator or the debtor in possession to borrow loans to fund the continuing operations and to have them ranked as administrative expenses, which have priority over other pre-petition unsecured loans. If there are unencumbered assets, the administrator can take a charge over those assets for carrying on the business.[124] These two options are often not attractive due to the limited nature of the former and it is unlikely that the debtor has many unsecured assets left for the latter.

7.4. LESSONS AND IMPLICATIONS

Even if there is high judicial competence in hearing restructuring cases, the above discussion gives rise to the following lessons and implications. First, common law

[117] In *Re Design Studio Group Ltd* [2020] SGHC 148, the Singapore High Court approved a somewhat controversial application under what is now s 67 of IRDA for the roll-up of the new DIP loan into the existing pre-petition secured loan.

[118] IBC, s 28(1).

[119] IBC, s 5(15). The insolvency resolution process period is defined as 180 days beginning from the insolvency commencement date (being the date the CIRP is admitted by the NCLT) and ending on the 180th day.

[120] IBC, s 5(13)(a).

[121] IBC, s 30(2)(a), read with s 5(13)(a).

[122] Insolvency and Bankruptcy Board of India (Liquidation Process) (Amendment) Regulations, 2018.

[123] S Ho and SK Banerjee, 'Indian Bankruptcy Code – How Does It Compare' (2018) 8 *Emerging Markets Restructuring Journal*, available at www.clearygottlieb.com/-/media/files/emrj-materials/issue-8-winter-2018_2019/indian-bankruptcy-codehow-does-it-compare-pdf.pdf.

[124] See EBL, Arts 42 and 75. See also Provisions (III) of the Supreme People's Court on Several Issues concerning the Application of the Enterprise Bankruptcy Law of the People's Republic of China [Revised] Interpretation No 3 [2019] of the Supreme People's Court 最高人民法院关于适用《中华人民共和国企业破产法》若干问题的规定(三) [已被修订]（法释 [2019] 3号）, Art 2. Cf Mrockova, *Corporate Bankruptcy Law in China* (2021) 81.

courts tend to give the benefit of doubt to the debtor management's opinion that the enterprise could be rescued, at least early in the process. This exacerbates the agency costs when management of the debtor is not aligned with the creditors' interests, such as where the management is also appointed by controlling shareholders. Second, there are many possibilities of valuation of the distressed firm, and there is inherent uncertainty involved, leading to coordination costs and the question as to the extent to which the plan can be imposed on dissenting creditors. Even the best judges will face conflicting opinions on valuation. The problem is exacerbated by specific agency costs posed by not only related party creditors but also where the creditors are not homogenous. Third, states' views on the goals of bankruptcy differ, and this would have an implication on the outcomes.

7.4.1. Leeway to Debtor's Management

It can be seen from the preceding sections that when the common law courts determine whether to grant a stay (or to extend the stay) of proceedings or moratorium, considerable leeway is given to the decisions of debtor management in determining the viability of the proposed scheme or restructuring plan, unless the exceptions apply. If there is particularly egregious conduct on the part of management or the plan has no reasonable prospect of success (such as where creditors convincingly allege fraud on the part of management[125] or where the majority creditors expressly indicate their refusal of support), the extension of the stay (or associated proceedings) will be refused. The approach is expected as it is always difficult to assess the viability of the success of the debtor's reorganisation at the early stage. As others have noted, the development of common law depends on the cases that are brought before the courts, and the development depends on the debtors' counsel.

In Singapore, at the first stage for application of the extension of the moratorium, the courts often grant the first extension except in extreme egregious cases such as where the debtor took no steps to enter into discussions with the creditors until very late in the day *Re Kobian* (Singapore).[126] The courts recognise that time is required for the debtor to consider the prospects and prepare a plan for reorganisation. In Hong Kong, the courts have historically granted the stay of winding up in connection with recognition of soft-touch provisional liquidation proceedings, though there is more recent some push back in *Re China Bozza* and later cases where there was no evidence of discussion with the creditors at all. The implicit suggestions appear to be that the common law courts in Asia are reluctant to pronounce on the non-viability of the prospect of restructuring, at least not during the initial few months, unless it is clear that the debtor has no plan or the plan has no prospect of success.

In India, the average length of the cases resolved is outside the legislatively mandated timeframe. The position is consistent with the fact that judges are often

[125] R Khasawneh and A Daga, 'Banks Accuse Singapore Commodity Trade Agritrade of 'Massive' Fraud' Reuters (6 March 2020); H Leong, 'Banks in Crossfire as PwC Plays Hardball', *Lloyd's List* (26 June 2020).

[126] See n 59 above.

not able to tell which are the cases when the debtor management has little interest in the outcome but is stalling for time unless it is very late in the day.

Considerable leeway is also granted to the debtor in determining when to disclose information to the creditors prior to obtaining the sanction of the scheme in Singapore, as can be seen in *Pathfinder*.[127] Again, information production is costly, and the court has to balance between the costs of ordering early disclosure that may not have the requisite benefits and the prospect of the creditors reaching a decision. If the management does not have incentive in providing as much information as possible at the early stage to the creditors, giving leeway to the debtor can lead to a waste of time and unnecessary delay (and consequent value destruction). Additionally, without an independent intermediary's investigation, there is often little avenue for the court to investigate whether the debtor's argument of viability is credible except in the most extreme cases.

7.4.2. Cram-Down of Dissenting Creditors and Valuation

Once the matter reaches sanction or confirmation, the common law courts approach the matter differently from pre-confirmation. The courts will rigorously review the disclosures to the creditors in determining whether sanction will be granted, and the courts will be slow to depart from the decision of the creditors in properly constituted classes. For schemes of arrangement in Hong Kong and Singapore, as in the UK, the legislation has prescribed how to cram-down dissenting creditors. Generally, for within-class cram-downs, the case law is broadly similar to the UK except in two respects.

First, the treatment of related party creditors differs across jurisdictions. The recent Hong Kong decision has allowed the votes to be counted, and the Singapore appellate court had indicated a measure of partial discounting, but the approach was doubted in a later case. As for India, the matter was settled by the Supreme Court that gave effect to the legislation (and extended) to mean that related parties at the time of filing could not vote. In chapter three, I made a case for how the voting of related party creditors should be treated as if related parties are voting in related party transactions.[128] Second, unlike in the UK where the relevant comparator is a going-concern sale, the alternative comparator in the Hong Kong and Singapore schemes of arrangement is usually the liquidation value, an explanation for which might be that there is no equivalent of an administration to allow for the going concern sale.

For the cross-class cram-down in Singapore, I explained in chapter three that the APR operates differently from Chapter 11 since the shareholders are not compulsorily divested. A valuation expert could be appointed to assist the court in determining the amount that a creditor would receive in the comparator scenario – that is, if the scheme is not approved – though it is not specified whether the valuation is on the

[127] See n 68 above.
[128] ch 3, section 3.5.2.1.

basis of an auction or non-market methodology.[129] In India, the cram-down on operational creditors means that they have less protection,[130] and it is the committee of financial creditors that makes the determination as to the distribution for both financial and operational creditors.

However, in the three common law jurisdictions, there is often no effective enforcement on breach of disclosure requirements by the debtor to the creditors. In the schemes of arrangement, the worst that can occur to the debtor company is that at the sanction stage, the court will not sanction the scheme or may require the revote to be taken (permissible in Singapore).[131] In theory, even if the scheme has been approved, and the court can subsequently unravel the scheme, though it is almost never ordered due to the prejudice to the creditors.[132] The professional advisers may also be criticised by the court, and if there is misconduct by the insolvency practitioner, their fees can be set aside in favour of an alternative arrangement or face discipline. However, there are no sanctions against the directors save for disqualification or in the unlikely event that the liquidator is willing to bring an action against the director for conduct during the restructuring process.

7.4.3. Rescue Financing

In principle, there are good reasons to make available legislatively the tool of rescue financing since this is hard to achieve without the consent of the existing lenders – but the challenge lies in the conditions for such financing to be approved. In particular, existing banks and financial institutions that have outstanding loans with the debtor will be particularly concerned if their pre-bankruptcy security interest is impacted with the grant of rescue financing. For these reasons, India and Mainland China are more circumspect in allowing for rescue financing. In the case of India, if the pre-CIRP secured lenders agree to other lenders to grant the financing, there can be no objection. In Mainland China, priority for rescue financing is limited to administrative expenses, but not to priming of secured debt.

If the courts are solely tasked with the gatekeeping function of approving post-petitioning financing to have priority as administrative expenses or even super-priority over the existing secured creditors, the difficulty is that the courts are usually not in a position to determine whether the rescue financing is only a means of transferring wealth from creditors to DIP lenders. Unless the jurisdiction has a strong DIP financing ecosystem, it is also difficult to evaluate whether the terms of the DIP loan are in fact competitive. For these reasons, priority or super-priority given for rescue financing has to be approached in a circumspect manner.

[129] IRDA, s 70(5).

[130] The only condition is that the operational creditors receive not less than the amount they would receive in a liquidation or the amount they would receive if the proceeds from the resolution plan were distributed on the same basis as in a liquidation, whichever is higher. See ch 4, section 4.4.2.1.

[131] IRDA, s 69.

[132] eg *Re TT International* [2012] SGCA 53.

7.4.4. The Choice and Objectives of Regulation

7.4.4.1. Promoting a Restructuring Hub: Singapore

Singapore's avowed goal is to create a restructuring hub for international companies, and in particular, Asian companies prompted the 2017 reforms.[133] The 2017 reforms, designed to give the debtor management access to significant restructuring tools (and incentives to file), are important steps in that direction. Less prescriptive and more open-textured rules are favoured as they can consider a wide range of situations that arise. However, given management–creditor and creditor–creditor frictions, certain stakeholders are incentivised to act opportunistically, and it is often not possible to tell when such behaviour occurs except in the most egregious cases. Chapters three and four demonstrate that the worst affected parties are often the creditors who face opportunistic behaviour by shareholders and retail or non-sophisticated creditors.

To address the issue of the need to incentivise debtors companies to pursue restructuring more vigorously upon filing, one possibility to tweak the system is to require the appointment of an insolvency practitioner if the extension of the moratorium that is being sought exceeds six months from the date of filing and the restructuring has not reached the stage of a scheme of arrangement being proposed to the creditors; the insolvency practitioner can then assist the court in evaluating the information on the debtor and can report to the court and other stakeholders. The procedure still remains DIP (as distinct from the judicial management, which is a practitioner in possession (PIP)), but the insolvency practitioner can investigate whether the claims of the debtor as to viability are within the realm of reasonableness. Conditions ought to be imposed on the debtor to release key financial information and prospects to the creditors early in the process (such as within the first three months), and the failure to do so indicates the non-viability of the plan or the likely inability to garner creditor support. Revealing the financial information and prospects to the creditors early will also facilitate the auction of the assets.[134]

7.4.4.2. Creditor Protection: Hong Kong

In the absence of a formal rescue legislation in Hong Kong, the market participants who wish to obtain a stay of proceedings while negotiating the terms of the restructuring currently rely on provisional liquidation, or if a DIP procedure is desired which is coupled with a stay of proceedings, the appointment of soft-touch liquidators in overseas jurisdictions based on the place of incorporation (and getting that appointment recognised in Hong Kong), to obtain an adjournment of winding-up proceedings brought against the debtor. In Hong Kong, the places of incorporation of listed companies are located in the British Virgin Islands, Cayman Islands and Bermuda; these have been described as 'letterbox jurisdiction[s]'[135] as the companies conduct no substantive business activities in those jurisdictions, but they are chosen as

[133] McCormack and Wan, 'Transplanting Chapter 11' (2019).

[134] Triantis (n 8).

[135] *Li Yiqing v Lamtex Holdings Ltd* [2021] HKCFI 622 [1]9. See also discussion in ch 2, section 2.3.1.

places of incorporation for tax and other reasons. The debtor's management seeks to appoint a soft-touch provisional liquidator in the relevant place of incorporation, and then to apply to the court for a recognition of such appointment in Hong Kong, where the debtor has assets, at common law. Hong Kong is not a party to the UNCITRAL Model Law and does not have legislation that specifically pertains to the cross-border recognition of such appointments.

The case law makes it clear that the screening process pursuant to the recognition of the soft-touch liquidation process in Hong Kong is rigorous.[136] Even if the debtors argue that they are in the process of restructuring, winding-up petitions will not be stayed for debtors that are not viable or for which there is a lack of creditor support, and they will proceed to liquidation. At the stage of recognition of the provisional liquidation in Hong Kong, to adjourn the winding-up petition, the debtor must show that it has creditor support, which means that advanced discussions must have occurred with the creditors. This is understandable as there are limited means for the court to incentivise the debtor to pursue restructuring efforts speedily in the recognition of the foreign soft-touch liquidation order. In addition, the use of soft-touch liquidation reduces the role of the Hong Kong courts in the management of insolvency, even where Hong Kong is the centre of main interest (COMI). This may be to the detriment of creditors who have lent to the foreign company that has listed in Hong Kong.[137] Hence, there is a case to facilitate the parties to restructure in Hong Kong, which would be the place of COMI of most of its listed companies and also to implement restructuring plans particularly when the creditors are based in Hong Kong and are familiar with the domestic restructuring regime.

Enforcement of directors' duties in Hong Kong is largely within the public enforcement.[138] Retail and non-sophisticated creditors would be in a vulnerable position in the face of directors who prioritise the shareholders' interests and do not act in the interests of the creditors notwithstanding the insolvency as they are often not in a position to fund actions against the errant directors.

Restructuring fees are scrutinised by the Hong Kong courts. In a recent case, the court criticised the professional advisers for advising the company to pursue a soft-touch liquidation in place of its incorporation, even when there is no creditor support and it is unlikely that any of the assets of the company will be realised for the benefit of its creditors.[139] The major assets of the company were shares in Mainland subsidiaries whose assets were already charged to onshore creditors and are unlikely to be available for the creditors of the company. In *Re China Oil Gangran Energy Group Holdings Ltd*,[140] Harris J opined that there was no reason to propose the scheme of arrangement at the place of incorporation, with parallel proceedings in Hong Kong, given that the debts were governed by Hong Kong law and the assets were in Hong Kong.

[136] See discussion in ch 2, section 2.3.1.

[137] See also *Re China Huiyuan Juice Group Limited* [2020] HKCFI 2940.

[138] WY Wan, C Chen and SH Goo, 'Public and Private Enforcement of Corporate and Securities Laws: An Empirical Comparison of Hong Kong and Singapore' (2019) 20 *European Business Organization Law Review* 319.

[139] *Re China Bozza Development Holdings Ltd* [2021] HKCFI 1235.

[140] [2021] HKCFI 1592.

7.4.4.3. Certainty and Predictability versus Flexibility: India

Apart from the objectives of modernising its insolvency laws, and improving the image of doing business, the IBC has been transformational in moving from a debtor-friendly jurisdiction to a PIP regime and is seen as an important tool in tackling India's non-performing loans (NPL) problem. The IBC has been credited with the improvement of India on the World Bank's *Doing Business 2020* rankings[141] and in particular compelling a change in the culture of the promoters of distressed firms to one where they would be more willing to negotiate the settlement of the debts[142] and leading to far greater certainty and predictability for creditors. The evolvement of an active distressed loan market is also the result of the IBC because the secondary purchasers now have an avenue for debt resolution.

Despite the clarity in the legislation, the evidence shows that the judiciary had originally treated the rules in the IBC as flexible, rather than hard-bound, and capable of substantive review if the court does not believe that the distribution is fair or equitable. Challenges of the decisions of the committee of creditors and the resolution applicants had led to the delay in completion of the CIRP proceedings; the most serious threat was the decision of the NCLAT in *Essar Steel*,[143] which held that the operational creditors should be treated in the same manner as the financial creditors and reallocated the distribution of the proceeds among the creditor classes. Fortunately, the Supreme Court set the decision aside, making it clear that the decision of the committee of creditors was final, and that their proposed distribution in accordance with the priority waterfall pre-insolvency was not arbitrary or capricious.[144] The IBC was amended in 2019 to clarify the position.[145]

History shows that the NCLT and the NCLAT tend to review the merits of the decision-making of the committee of creditors, which undermines some of the gains of the IBC in promoting a certain and predictability regime for the creditors. The likelihood of such challenges should subside after the Supreme Court decision in *Essar Steel*, though it does not appear that unhappy creditors would stop trying to reverse the decisions of the committee of creditors.[146] However, it now appears that the pendulum may have swung far to the other side when it comes to non-interference with the committee of creditors decisions; in *DBS Bank Ltd v Ruchi Soya Industries Ltd*,[147] discussed in chapter four, the NCLAT refused to depart from the committee of creditors' decision that had voted for treating all secured creditors equally without having regard to the economic interests of their security interest; this had the effect of causing one of the secured (dissenting) creditors to receive much less than what it

[141] World Bank, *Doing Business 2020* (Economy Profile: India), available at www.doingbusiness.org/en/reports/global-reports/doing-business-2020.

[142] See eg UR Patel (Governor), 'Resolution of Stressed Assets: Towards the Endgame: Inaugural Session of the National Conference on Insolvency and Bankruptcy: Changing Paradigm' (19 August 2017), available at https://m.rbi.org.in/Scripts/BS_SpeechesView.aspx?Id=1044.

[143] *Committee of Creditors of Essar Steel India Limited through Authorised Signatory v Satish Kumar Gupta & Ors* (2019) Civil Appeal 8766-67 of 2019 [93].

[144] ibid.

[145] IBC, s 30(2).

[146] See eg *Re Videocon Industries Ltd* IA 196 of 2021.

[147] Company Appeal (AT) (Insolvency) No 788 of 2019.

would otherwise have received had the matter gone to liquidation. It remains to be seen whether this decision would be upheld on appeal to the Supreme Court.

One remaining point is the time-bound nature of the proceedings; the Supreme Court in *Essar Steel* left the issue on the time-bound nature of the IBC open as to whether the time-bound nature of the IBC was in fact as absolute as the legislation suggests, holding that it is still possible to extend beyond 330 days.

7.5. THE EXPERIENCE OF MAINLAND CHINA

The EBL borrows extensively from, among other countries, Chapter 11 and the UK administration,[148] with the inclusion of 'Chinese characteristics'. Article 1 of the EBL explicitly refers to not only safeguarding the interests of creditors and debtors but also 'maintaining the order of the socialist market economy'. The EBL calls for a hybrid PIP and DIP process of restructuring and allows for the broad open-ended rules as to how the court confirms the plan.[149] (For instance, the conditions that specify for cram-down in Article 87 do not require that at least one impaired class has voted for the plan or that there is compliance with the APR.[150]) Apart from the specific directive to give priority to secured creditors, employee interests and other preferential creditors that require them ahead of unsecured creditors,[151] and that unsecured creditors are paid at least the liquidation value, there is little guidance as to the extent for the courts to exercise the cram-down, including whether they may take into account non-market considerations to promote the goals of a socialist market economy in decision-making.[152]

However, the open-textured rules have allowed considerable leeway in how the courts have exercised their discretion to implement the EBL in line with the shifts to emphasise national priorities. In the previous account of the first decade of the EBL (2007–14), scholars have criticised the judiciary for refusing to accept petitions under the EBL (thereby preventing the commencement of restructuring and the triggering of the automatic stay) and for exercising cram-down liberally in the restructurings of listed companies, and effecting distributional goals (notably in favour of employees and bias towards rescue) that are at odds with market-based methods. Scholars were also critical of the courts considering the maintenance of social order in the decision-making, particularly when it comes to the rescue of large state-owned enterprises (SOEs).

Since 2015, for reasons set out in chapters two and five, including the slowdown in the Chinese economy and the pressing need to resolve zombie companies, the EBL is now regarded as an important market-based tool to clean up insolvent companies and

[148] L Qi, 'The Corporate Reorganization Regime under China's New Enterprise Bankruptcy Law' (2008) 19 *International Insolvency Review* 13, 16.

[149] EBL, Art 87.

[150] ch 3, section 3.4.2.2.

[151] EBL, Arts 6, 82.

[152] Art 87. Elsewhere, the EBL refers to the prioritisation of employee interests ahead of unsecured creditors in Art 6. See also ch 3, section 3.4.2.2.

to rescue financially distressed but viable firms. A series of judicial pronouncements (described below) followed, with emphasis of effecting rescues and liquidations using market-based solutions. The recent minutes promulgated by the Supreme People's Court (SPC) in November 2019 have made it clear that the courts could no longer reject hearing the petition on grounds of potential social instability, which had been the excuse used previously.[153] After 2015, cross-class cram-downs became rarer.[154] While shareholders are not wiped out, various adaptive devices are used, including the fact that controlling shareholders (who would be wiped out in a strict application of the APR) are expected to give up some or all of their shares. Nevertheless, without an explicit APR, there is evidence of benefits being accrued to the shareholders at the expense of the creditors. For instance, in listed company reorganisations, the listing status of the listed companies in Mainland China is valuable but is not an asset that is reflected on the balance sheet. Scholars have documented that the value of the listing status (which is not reflected in the balance sheet) is not considered in the restructuring, but controlling shareholders have monetised the value to their benefit, to the detriment of the creditors.[155] In Hong Kong, which has a similar problem in that the listing status is a valuable asset, the courts have put a limit as to how much of it can be used to accrue to the shareholders.

However, even if the cram-down is not exercised, the threat of cram-down is normally a driver of the parties' willingness to settle. Outside of an explicit cram-down, the EBL does not specify that the courts will need to review the fairness of the plans or even that the unsecured creditors receive the liquidation value.[156] All this suggest that a market-based solution will mean giving effect to the creditors' bargain, though the plan proposers see the value in giving more to the small unsecured creditors and non-financial creditors.

The EBL is also silent on the disclosures that are required, and a perusal of the reorganisation plans for Panel B, Appendix A restructurings reveal a lack of information on the debtor's financial position. The plans do not usually reveal the estimation of the liquidation or break-up value (much less how the liquidation value is arrived at).[157] If a merger with another entity is the objective of the restructuring, there is little explanation as to the choice of the entity to be merged (that is often in the same industry and that could be subject to similar or enhanced risk factors if the cause of the distress is a general downturn in the industry). Where debt–equity swaps are employed, there is also little explanation as to the basis on which the swap ratios are arrived at, nor is there information to assess the value of the debt–equity swap.

[153] See the Notice of the Supreme People's Court on Issuing the Minutes of the National Courts' Civil and Commercial Trial Work Conference, effective 8 November 2019 (Arts 107 and 108). In the earlier years, it is widely documented that the court will not accept the petitions unless the local government supports the restructuring.

[154] ch 3, section 3.4.2.2 (references).

[155] See S Gao, 'Cramdown, reorganization bargaining and inefficient markets: The cases of the United States and China' (2020) 30 *International Insolvency Review* S5 (giving the example of the restructuring of ST Jincheng in 2015).

[156] The requirements of the feasibility and payment of at least the liquidation value only apply if the court is exercising its cram-down function. See also Gao (ibid).

[157] See Gao (ibid).

When the plans refer to the minimum profitability levels that the new investors have promised to achieve under their (new) management,[158] presumably to assure the creditors that the repayment in the extended period is viable, there is minimal disclosure to assess how these profitability levels would be achieved through an operational restructuring. This may not be critical for the large bank creditors who are likely to have the information on the debtors and their management anyway (and would make their own assessment as to the viability), and the smaller creditors do not normally have the options to receive equity in lieu of their debt, but it raises questions as to the transparency of the process, particularly for the bondholders.

The reality is that governmental intervention, whether in the form of coordination or bail-outs, is likely to persist in the restructuring of large financially distressed companies. In the typical EBL cases issued by the SPC for 2018 and 2020, the role of the local government is often emphasised.[159] The process of intervention is not monotonic but can take several forms, including procuring the provision of lending or infusion of capital from other non-financially distressed SOEs or SOE banks, and coordination to effect mergers, consolidations and divestments. An additional layer of complexity arises where the creditor is not the original lender, such as when the asset management companies (that are state-owned) have acquired the loan, discussed in chapter five.

In the background of governmental intervention, the key question is how the EBL can be enforced to provide an adequate means of corporate rescue of economically viable companies. In this regard, the courts, together with the other regulators, have attempted to introduce some degree of certainty and predictability.

7.5.1. Improving Certainty and Predictability of Plan Approval through Judicial Pronouncements

The SPC has been very proactive in issuing judicial interpretations relating to plan confirmations that are not binding on lower courts but that are followed as a matter of practice by the lower courts. Unlike common law countries whose pronouncements that are issued are largely relating to practice directions, the SPC issues issued directives that have clarified the operation of the EBL,[160] strengthened the creditors' rights to information[161] and introduced measures that lend legitimacy to existing practice.[162] Other applicable regulators have also issued directions to improve the

[158] eg Pang Da Automobile (2019) restructuring, on file with author.

[159] List of Typical of EBL Cases issued by the SPC for the years 2018 and 2020, [全国法院审理破产典型案例] available at pccz.court.gov.cn/pcajxxw/pcdxal/dxal.

[160] eg SPC Minutes of the National Court Work Conference on Bankruptcy Trials in 2018 imposed conditions on the ability to cram-down dissenting classes. See ch 3, section 3.4.2.2.

[161] eg SPC, Judicial Interpretation III to address how creditors may obtain information on the administration's report, and the debtor's financial and operational information and in the absence of such disclosure, the creditors may make an application to the court (March 2019).

[162] In November 2019, the SPC issued Minutes of the National Courts' Civil and Commercial Trial Work Conference, effective 8 November 2019 (November 2019 Minutes) [最高人民法院关于印发《全国法院民

disclosure of information to creditors, including one by the China Banking and Insurance Regulatory Commission (CBIRC) calling for the establishment of creditor committees.[163] This guidance will enhance the ability of the creditors to make an informed decision. With greater transparency, the market will be able to assess how closely the restructurings occur in accordance with market-based principles, which will enhance predictability and certainty to the process.

7.5.2. Addressing the Length of Time in Restructuring and Moratorium

The EBL prescribes for a six-month period to propose the reorganisation plan and a three-month extension by the court.[164] If the plan is not submitted within the specified time, the court can terminate the proceedings, and the company goes into liquidation.[165] In chapter four, I explained that, in theory, the EBL is a quick process because there are only two chances for the administrator to place the plan before the creditors. After the first round, if the creditors do not approve by the requisite majority, the proposer negotiates with the creditors to reach an agreement at the second round. If an agreement cannot be reached, the proposer asks the court to cram-down. Otherwise, the debtor goes into liquidation.

In determining the length of time that companies spend in restructuring under the EBL, there are very limited data. An empirical study by Li and Ponticelli found that in the sample of 152 reorganisation cases in their sample between 2016 and 2020, the average time between the time the petition was accepted to the time the case was closed was 445 days.[166] Another financial data source states that the average number of days spent in in-court restructuring is 679.[167] Other scholars have documented significant delays beyond the nine-month period prescribed in the EBL.[168]

Figure 7.4 shows the length of time that the listed company cases in Panel B of Appendix A (2015–19) spent in restructuring, with a mean of 241 days or eight months. It is difficult to draw the conclusion that the reduced time spent is due only to the increased efficiencies in the court system in more recent years. An alternative (supplementary) explanation is that pre-filing closed-door negotiations in listed company reorganisations occur among the key creditors (likely under some degree of governmental influence), which reduced the length of the time spent in the court process.[169]

商事审判工作会议纪要》的通知 [现行有效] （法〔2019〕254号）, Art 115, explained how pre-packs could be used within the framework of the EBL.

[163] ch 3, section 3.4.1.2.

[164] EBL, Art 79.

[165] ibid.

[166] Li and Ponticelli, 'Going Bankrupt in China' (2020) (Table 6).

[167] E White, 'China Courts Take Centre Stage as Defaults Share Bonds Landscape' *Financial Times* (25 August 2021), available at www.ft.com/content/b19e4f40-b4c3-4f0e-8609-76706bc7657f, quoting S&P.

[168] Mrockova (n 6) 147.

[169] ibid, 183.

Figure 7.4 Length of time Chinese listed companies spent in restructuring in court

N = 21

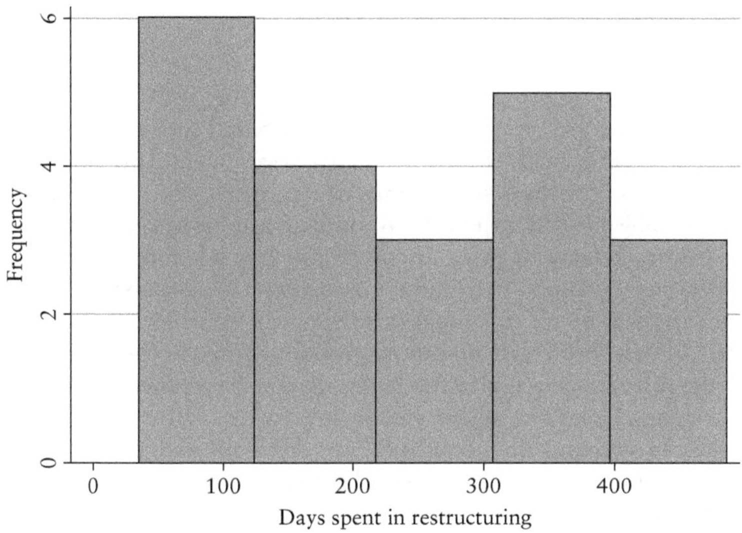

Source: Data collected from the reorganisation plans of debtors listed in Panel B, Appendix A.

Certainly, when one looks at the evidence on onshore bond restructurings (where the creditors are more diverse than bank creditors), the moratorium may not be as significant a tool as compared to the bond restructurings in the US/UK. The petition under the EBL is often not filed immediately after the first default by the debtor to take advantage of the moratorium, which indicates that the parties prefer to attempt a solution outside of the EBL. For illustrative purposes, I take the recent 2021 high-profile complex restructuring of Peking University Founder Group that was approved by the court in 581 days (19 months)[170] from the date of first default in December 2019, which is regarded by the market as an example of government-coordinated but market-based outcome.[171] The petition was only filed in July 2020, the court accepted the petition in the same month, and the approval of the plan occurred in July 2021 (approximately 13 months).[172] Similarly, in restructuring of Dalian Machine Tools, the first default of the bonds occurred in October 2016, and the petition was only accepted in November 2017,[173] with the approval transpiring in April 2019. In other restructurings in Panel A of Appendix A, the plans were approved in periods ranging

[170] White, 'China Courts Take Centre Stage' (25 August 2021).

[171] Reference is made to the date of default rather than the date that the petition is filed or accepted because the companies do not often disclose the date on which the petition is accepted by the courts. One obvious limitation with the data in assessing the time period of the court's involvement is that while default may have taken place, the parties attempted out-of-court restructuring before in-court restructuring (and hence delay the filing of the petition).

[172] Sources: Wind and Debtwire.

[173] The date that the petition was filed is not available.

from five to 29 months from the date of first default, and in many of these cases, the petition was not filed within six months of the date of first default.[174]

7.5.3. Analysis and the Future of Pre-Packs

The transition to the use of the EBL as a market-based tool to resolve insolvencies remains a work in progress. It is clear that active governmental involvement and coordination will remain for the restructurings of large companies and. In chapter four, I suggest that using the EBL to effect bail-outs of zombie firms is often problematic because it neither achieves a price discovery process, nor reflects upholding of the creditors' decision-making. There is also no clarity on the distributional goals. Where there are reasons for rescue, it is suggested that such rescue mechanism should occur outside the EBL lest they create unwanted precedents for all types of restructuring.

Where the restructuring is effected under market-based methods pursuant to the EBL, history shows that the courts can repurpose the EBL to fit these goals. The challenge lies in creating the conditions for certainty and predictability because the presence of governmental involvement clearly impacts the ultimate form the rescue will occur. However, even for governmental-coordinated or governmental-led restructuring, much can be done to improve the process, including the quality of the disclosures in the plans and the supervision of the administrators to achieve these goals.

While there is uncertainty in the EBL as to whether pre-pack reorganisations are in fact permitted,[175] the courts have allowed pre-negotiated reorganisations where the administrator was appointed early at the pre-filing stage to negotiate with the creditors and to find investors prior to the acceptance of the case by the court.[176] After the endorsement by the SPC,[177] many bankruptcy courts, including Shenzhen and Beijing, have issued guidance on pre-packs and experimented with various approaches such as pre-registration of bankruptcy applications and ways wherein the courts can support such efforts.[178] The benefits of the pre-negotiated reorganisations are the shortening of time that the company spends in restructuring though court and creditor approvals are still required.

[174] Sources: Wind and Debtwire.

[175] EBL, Art 73.

[176] In the restructuring of Shenzhen Fuchang Electronic Technology in 2017, prior to the formal acceptance of the application, the court allowed pre-filing and designated an administrator to carry out negotiations with the creditors. Once the application was accepted, the reorganisation plan was tabled for voting. See Shenzhen Intermediate People's Court, 'Restructuring of Shenzhen Fuchang Electronic Technology' [深圳市福昌电子技术有限公司破产重整案】 (14 April 2017), available at www.yunqingsuan.com/news/detail/13065 (in Chinese); DA Austin and C Lin, 'Bankruptcy with Chinese Characteristics: Insolvency Administration in the People's Republic of China' (2020) 94 *American Bankruptcy Law Journal* 85 identified another pre-pack case, which they called a 'pre-reform' case of Beijing Zhongxing Science and Technology, where the Beijing Intermediate People's Court approved the pre-pack reorganisation in 2017.

[177] November 2019 Minutes.

[178] eg Beijing No. One Intermediate People's Court, Beijing's Bankruptcy Courts Trial Cases [北京市第一中级人民法院关于印发【北京破产法庭破产重整案件办理规范（试行）】 的通知]，北一中法【2019】 437 号；Shenzhen Intermediate People's Court, Shenzhen's Bankruptcy Courts Trial cases (*Shenzhen Prepack Rules*) [深圳市中级人民法院审理企业重整案件的工作指引（试行）] (2019 年3月14 日本院审判委员会民事执行专业委员会2019 年第3 次会议讨论通过).

For instance, the Shenzhen bankruptcy court rules provide that the pre-negotiated reorganisation takes three months, with liberty to extend for one more month. However, the types of companies that are targeted appear to be quite different from the UK's pre-packs, which are often targeted at debtors with few secured creditors, and the terms of the sale are negotiated between the administrator and the creditors with the buyer. For instance, in Shenzhen, the rules of court provide that the pre-negotiated reorganisation of target companies should have any one of the following characteristics: (1) more than 500 employees, (2) more than 200 creditors, (3) more than 100 upstream and downstream industrial chain enterprises; and (4) operations which would result in major production, operational or social instability if there is direct entry to reorganisation.[179] Thus, it appears that the target users are the larger enterprises and the pre-negotiation administrator who will reach an agreement with the creditors prior to filing, aided by a limited stay during this period of pre-negotiation.[180] As discussed in chapter three, section 3.5.2.1, particular care should be taken if the controlling shareholders are proposing the sale of the distressed assets to themselves, due to allegations of lack of transparency. The oversight of the administrator and the judiciary will still be required.

7.6. CONCLUSION

This chapter examined, on a comparative basis, how the courts have enforced the restructuring regimes in the US/UK and the four Asian jurisdictions. US bankruptcy scholars have argued for the central importance of the moratorium on all creditor action, so that the company has the time to breathe and a plan can be formulated for the company to be restructured or sold. For the moratorium, the US courts have given a lot of leeway for the management to drive the restructuring. The moratorium against a stay of proceedings has been exported as part of the key legislative reforms in Singapore, Mainland China and India, but with different levels of judicial discretion being permitted. Singapore is the closest to the Chapter 11 model in that the courts have allowed considerable leeway to management, and this chapter suggests a further screening process where lengthy periods of moratorium are sought, particularly given the agency conflicts between the management/shareholders and creditors. The Indian IBC attempts to put upper thresholds on the length of the moratorium in response to the judiciary's holding that the time-bound period is not necessarily absolute. In Mainland China, the moratorium is available but does not appear to be a critical part of the restructuring process. Even though Hong Kong does not have a formal moratorium, the courts have recognised the moratorium through the soft-touch liquidation, but with aggressive screening to avoid situations of abuse.

When confirming the plan, all the jurisdictions place importance on the creditors' decision as different as to the courts' outer limits of the power to review the decisions of the creditors when the cram-down is exercised. As creditors are not homogenous

[179] Shenzhen Prepack Rules, r 28.
[180] Shenzhen Prepack Rules, r 33.

and their composition differs in various jurisdictions, the limits of their involvement are also tested. It is clear that none of the jurisdictions is in favour of the reduced involvement of the courts. At the same time, giving effect to national goals also has an impact, as can be seen in Mainland China, where considerable protection was given to employees. Even then, there is a growing recognition that restructuring law should not unduly interfere with the rights of secured and unsecured creditors, with the consequences of undermining certainty and predictability. It is also clear that the developments in restructuring law in the four Asian jurisdictions will continue.

8

Relationship between Restructuring Law, Enforcing Contracts and Directors' Duties

8.1. INTRODUCTION

IN CHAPTER ONE, I discussed the manager-in-control (or debtor-in-possession), practitioner-in-control and secured creditor-in-control models of debt restructuring. In a secured creditor-in-control model, the creditor can petition for liquidation or foreclose on the security relatively expeditiously and quickly. In particular, in such a regime, there is no possibility of staying enforcement actions by secured creditors without their consent while the debtor is embarking on the restructuring exercise. In a manager-in-control model, the management of the debtor drives the restructuring process, usually with the assistance of an automatic or discretionary grant of a stay of proceedings. In a practitioner-in-control model, it is the insolvency practitioner that drives the restructuring process.

Chapters three through seven examine the agency and coordination costs that are involved among the market participants in debt restructurings and how law and policy have responded to these costs. Chapters three and four focus on the agency costs of shareholder–creditor relationships and the agency and coordination costs of creditor–creditor relationships. Chapter five discusses how some of these costs are exacerbated or mitigated when asset management companies are required by banking regulation to purchase non-performing loans from domestic banks to stabilise the banking system, using Mainland China and India as case studies. Chapters six and seven discuss the roles of independent gatekeepers and courts respectively in the restructuring process and the extent to which they are in the best position to constrain the agency and coordination costs given their strengths and limitations.

In this chapter, I discuss the impact of the legal regime relating to enforcing creditor rights on restructuring law. A related issue is how managers of financially distressed companies may be incentivised to file to invoke the insolvency and restructuring regime early so that there are options available before the financial distress impacts the operations of the company.

The former issue relating to how a creditor can easily and expeditiously enforce its contractual right has an important impact on the outcome of restructuring law. For instance, in jurisdictions where enforcement of debt or security is weak or non-existent, the debtor protection features in restructuring law will only render the bankruptcy system more inefficient by exacerbating the coordination costs between the senior and junior creditors.[1] Similarly, if secured creditors cannot easily enforce their security interests, the debtor enjoys a de facto moratorium on enforcement of the security interests, rendering it an extremely debtor-friendly regime.[2] Restructuring law may also potentially worsen the overall transaction costs of restructuring given the state diverting resources that are required for the process to be invoked, including the appointment of insolvency practitioners and judicial time, even if the only possible outcome is a sale on a break-up value. I argue that in India the difficulties in enforcement of debt have made the Insolvency and Bankruptcy Code (IBC) the de facto forum for operational creditors to enforce their debts, but have likely led to the ramping up of demand on scarce judicial capacity and time.

If secured creditors are in a worse position post-restructuring than they would have been had they enforced their security, either because value destruction has occurred or there is excessive interference in the priority of rights, the system will discourage secured creditors from participating in the restructuring process. An example is the case of Mainland China where debt enforcement is good (and on par with several advanced jurisdictions) but there is little demand for the use of the Enterprise Bankruptcy Law 2006 (EBL). In this chapter, I argue that the reasons have to do with the design of the EBL, which benefits certain preferential groups of creditors (ie employees), but secured creditors appear to lack adequate protection under the EBL, which leads their hesitation to use or participate in the EBL process.

The second question relates to what encourages the parties to invoke insolvency and restructuring law. In all systems, there is every reason to encourage the debtor company to address restructuring early, particularly if operational restructuring is urgently required. Even if financial restructuring (and not operational restructuring) is required, addressing the problem early can prevent the spread of financial distress to the operations. To this end, a corporate law that presents directors with carrots to file for insolvency (and to address problems) early and sticks (liabilities or consequences for the directors if the company continues trading while being insolvent) – which are important tools – is proposed. In jurisdictions where such carrots and sticks are not present or where the threat of enforcement is not a credible one, having the best restructuring toolkit will not be useful. In Asia, public enforcement of directors' duties has always been significantly more prominent than private enforcement, and I argue that this has a detrimental impact on the willingness of the directors to act early.

This chapter is organised as follows. Section 8.2 discusses how debts are enforced under general law and how it compares with the restructuring framework in that jurisdiction. Particularly, I discuss the position of secured creditors. Section 8.3 analyses how the jurisdiction's contract enforcement system impacts the agency and coordination costs of restructuring. Section 8.4 discusses what incentives can be put in place for the debtor to file or commence insolvency processes promptly. Section 8.5 concludes.

[1] S Djankov et al, 'Debt Enforcement around the World' (2008) 116 *Journal of Political Economy* 1105.

[2] See generally, ER Morrison, 'Bankruptcy's Rarity: An Essay on Small Business Bankruptcy in the United States' (2008) 5 *European Company and Financial Law Review* 172.

8.2. IMPACT OF ENFORCING CREDITOR RIGHTS ON RESTRUCTURING LAW

8.2.1. Enforcement of Debts and Resolving Insolvency

Insolvency and restructuring law exist in the broader institutional framework on the general enforcement of debts (and security). In advanced jurisdictions, the underlying assumption is that of an efficient creditor enforcement of debts through the court system and self-help remedies (for secured debts).[3] Hence, if reorganisation attempts fail, the creditors have alternative remedies in enforcing their debts, including liquidating the company and repossessing the collateral for secured claims. Furthermore, advanced jurisdictions have mechanisms outside of insolvency law, including regulations governing directors' duties generally, constraining tunnelling through related party transactions, fraudulent transfers and illegal payments by the companies to their shareholders. These processes collectively ensure the protection of creditors from the debtor disposing of property or otherwise putting it out of reach from the creditors.

In the US, the moratorium, which is an important part of the toolkit in Chapter 11, automatically stays enforcement (thereby tying the hands of the secured creditor) while the debtor works out a plan. The moratorium serves as an important incentive for the managers to file earlier when the debtor can still be salvaged,[4] and also for the creditors and the debtor to come to the negotiation table. Secured creditors in the restructuring will have a high degree of certainty of recovery of their loan subject to costs of proceedings (assuming that the value of security is covered by the loan). They only have their enforcement delayed, and there are monitoring processes to enable the secured creditors to apply for relief if the debtor management engages in value destruction of the secured assets. Additionally, outside of the Bankruptcy Code, state laws relating to fraudulent conveyance[5] and restrictions on payments of dividends by the debtor to the shareholders[6] regulate dispositions of property by the debtor. Therefore, in theory, secured creditors should have fewer reasons to object to a filing under Chapter 11 if they feel that they are adequately protected.

Nevertheless, where enforcement under general law is weak or non-existent, or when the outcomes to the secured creditors under the formal insolvency and restructuring law are extremely unfavourable, it distorts the incentives of the market participants in using either contract enforcement or insolvency proceedings. India and Mainland China respectively rank 163rd and fifth in contract enforcement and have relatively well-developed insolvency laws, ranking 52nd and 51st on the resolving insolvency index, respectively. The reason for the stark difference in the ranking on contract enforcement is that it takes 1,445 days to enforce a contract in India in

[3] cf ZR Azar, 'Bankruptcy Policy: An Empirical Investigation of 50 Jurisdictions Worldwide' (2008) 82 *American Bankruptcy Law Journal* 407 (who argues that the efficiency depends on both creditor enforcement and observing pre-bankruptcy entitlements).

[4] E Warren, 'Bankruptcy Policy-Making in an Imperfect World' (1993) 92 *Michigan Law Review* 336.

[5] eg New York's Uniform Voidable Transactions Act; see PM Guffy 'Exempt No More: How New York's Uniform Fraudulent Conveyance Act Threatens Exemptions in Bankruptcy' (2015) 80 *Brooklyn Law Review* 1123.

[6] eg Delaware General Corporations Law, s 173.

comparison with 496 days in Mainland China. However, in terms of the rate of recovery to secured creditors, these creditors in Mainland China fare much worse under the EBL than under general law on enforcement of contracts. See Figure 8.1, which presents the World Bank's 'Doing Business 2020' report on two metrics: length of time to enforce a debt; and the recovery rate for the secured debt. Figure 8.1 also presents the same metrics for Singapore and Hong Kong, as well as the US and the UK.

On 16 September 2021, the World Bank decided to discontinue the 'Doing Business' reports in light of data irregularities found in certain of the jurisdictions including Mainland China and in respect of the rankings in 'Doing Business 2018'.[7] However, I have included the data here on enforcement of contracts and resolving insolvency in Mainland China given the comparability of information across jurisdictions and the fact that the irregularities identified did not include data relating to enforcing contracts or resolving insolvency but to 'Starting A Business', 'Legal Rights – Getting Credit' and 'Paying Taxes'.[8] Also, for Mainland China, insofar as the metrics of enforcing contracts or resolving insolvency, the time for enforcement and resolving insolvency, as well as the recovery rate in each of the two situations, has remained largely similar since 'Doing Business 2016', and the reports prior to 'Doing Business 2018' were not found to contain data irregularities.[9]

It is the thesis of this chapter that the interaction of time taken and the recovery rates in the enforcement of contractual rights could result in differences in usage of the formal insolvency and restructuring law, as shown in Figures 8.2 and 8.3.

Figure 8.1 Enforcement of contracts and resolving insolvency

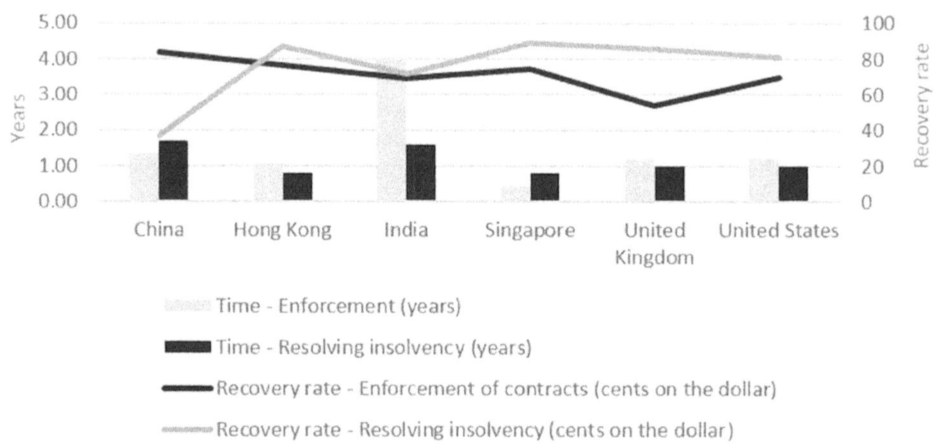

Source: Data collected from World Bank's 'Doing Business 2020' report (recovery rate on enforcement of contracts is assumed to be the claim amount less costs). 'Recovery rate' refers to recovery on the secured debt.

[7] World Bank, 'World Bank to Discontinue Doing Business Report' (16 September 2021), available at www.worldbank.org/en/news/statement/2009/21/16/world-bank-group-to-discontinue-doing-business-report.

[8] RC Machen et al, 'Investigation of Data Irregularities in *Doing Business 2018 and Doing Business 2020* – Investigation Findings and Report to the Board of Executive Directors' (Wilmerhale, 15 September

There are some limitations to the data presented in Figure 8.1. First, the World Bank's 'Doing Business 2020' report on recovery rates for resolving insolvency does not distinguish between informal renegotiation, formal liquidation, scheme of arrangement, going concern sale or sale on a break-up basis. However, the recovery rates in the report are largely comparable with the findings in Davydenko and Franks,[10] where the median recovery for senior lenders for formal liquidation is 82 per cent (the UK), and 70 per cent (the US) (in the case of the US, citing Gupton, Gates and Carty).[11] Second, the data on enforcement of contracts presented in Figure 8.1 does not take into account the fact that recovery may not be possible if directors are not effectively prevented under the applicable law from disposing property prior to the transfer of the rights to the property to the creditors through breach of directors' duties, fraudulent conveyance, illegal dividend payments and other substitutes.

8.2.2. Usage of Formal Insolvency and Restructuring Law

Figure 8.2 presents the frequency at which companies invoke formal insolvency and restructuring laws over the estimated number of active companies registered in the jurisdiction in 2019 for Mainland China, India, the US and the UK. It suggests that the usage for the formal insolvency and restructuring law is much lower in Mainland China, based on the number of registered companies, which is consistent with existing account.[12]

Figure 8.2 Usage of formal insolvency and restructuring law

Sources of data given below.[13]

2021) 1–16, available at thedocs.worldbank.org/en/doc/84a922cc9273b7b120d49ad3b9e9d3f9-0090012021/original/DB-Investigation-Findings-and-Report-to-the-Board-of-Executive-Directors-September-15-2021.pdf.

[9] Data from World Bank: www.doingbusiness.org/en/doingbusiness.

[10] SA Davydenko and JR Franks 'Do Bankruptcy Codes Matter? A Study of Defaults in France, Germany, and the U.K.' (2008) 63 *Journal of Finance* 565.

[11] G Gupton, D Gates and LV Carty, 'Bank-Loan Loss Given Default' (2000) Moody's Investors Service, Global Credit Research 69–92, available at fs.1473.cn/236363a1-2c6b-487e-9dc1-7aa9f216acba.pdf.

Figure 8.3 presents the percentage of winding-up or bankruptcy petitions leading to liquidation over company exits, demonstrating how often the insolvency framework was used in the four Asian jurisdictions and the US in 2019 to effect company exits. (In contrast to Figure 8.2, Figure 8.3 focuses only petitions that lead to liquidations.) In comparing India and Mainland China, as in Figure 8.2, debtor companies that invoke the IBC in India account for a larger proportion of company exits compared to the EBL in Mainland China. In Hong Kong and Singapore, in comparing the number of petitions for compulsory winding up over the company exits, Singapore shows a higher proportion, but the number of company exits for Hong Kong companies is approximately six times that of Singapore.

There are certain limitations to Figures 8.2 and 8.3 as the data collected is based on the sources accompanying the figures and may not necessary be comparable across the jurisdictions. However, the two figures paint a broad picture on the relative use of the insolvency and restructuring laws in the jurisdictions concerned.

Figure 8.3 Bankruptcy petitions (leading to liquidation) over company exits

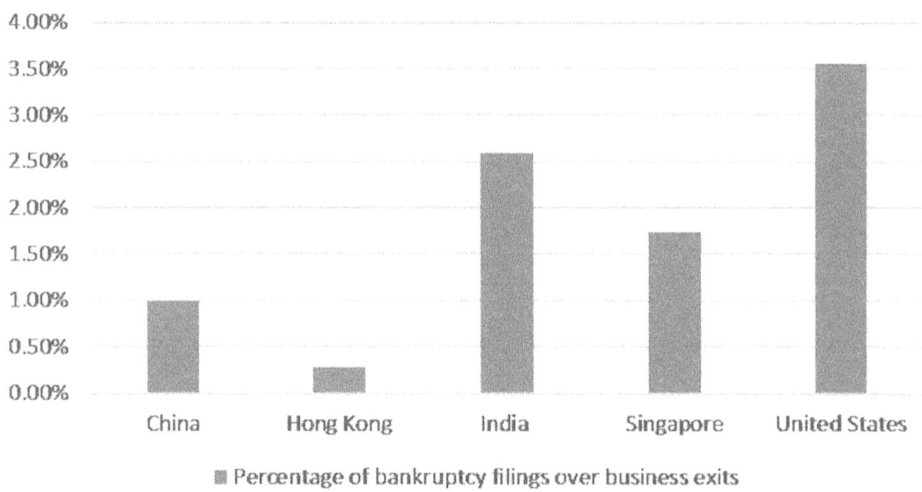

Sources of data given below.[14]

[12] eg N Mrockova, *Corporate Bankruptcy Law in China: Principles, Limitations and Options for Reform* (Oxford, Hart Publishing, 2021) 188–91.

[13] For Mainland China, the data on the number of applications for liquidation (強制清算) and bankruptcy (破产) in 2019 is obtained from the *Supreme People's Court Gazette [中华人民共和国最高人民法院公报. 北京]: 该办公厅* (2020). For India, the data are based on the number of CIRP filings for the year ending 31 March 2020, obtained from IBBI (India), available at www.ibbi.gov.in. For the US, the data on the business filings under US Chapter 7 (leading to liquidation) and Chapter 11 are obtained from US Courts for 2019, available at www.uscourts.gov/services-forms/bankruptcy/bankruptcy-basics/chapter-11-bankruptcy-basics. For the UK, the data on the usage of the formal insolvency and restructuring law (being the compulsory liquidations, creditors' voluntary winding up, administration and company voluntary arrangements) are obtained from UK Insolvency Service (2019 data), available at assets.publishing.service.gov.uk/government/uploads/system/uploads/attachment_data/file/861187/Commentary_-_Company_Insolvency_Statistics_Q4_2019.pdf. There is no centralised data of the use of schemes of arrangement; Debtwire data disclose an average of 11 filings per year between 2015 and 2020, even though the data only captures the large companies where the debt is US$100 million or more (including foreign-incorporated or registered companies). However, it is unlikely that schemes are used by small

8.2.2.1. India

India highly depends on secured debt and bank borrowings.[15] The World Bank's 'Principles for Effective Insolvency and Creditor/Debtor Rights' emphasises that the ability to enforce on the collateral granted in connection with secured lending is fundamental. However, although India is a common law jurisdiction and has strong creditor rights in its books, creditors face several challenges in speedy enforcement of their debt. Even for secured creditors, historically, there is no equivalent of enforcement outside of the court process (such as the appointment of receivers to effect a mortgagee sale outside the court process in the UK). Until the enactment of SARFAESI, a civil suit for judgment takes somewhere between 10 and 15 years[16] or 10 and 12 years.[17] Enforcement of secured lending is also estimated to experience significant delays of five to seven years.[18]

With the enactment of SARFAESI, the enforcement of secured debt by banks and financial institutions improved dramatically. Banks and financial institutions can proceed to enforcement without court intervention by giving 60 days' notice if the debt has been outstanding for more than six months.[19] However, SARFAESI applies only to secured debt and, even then, only to banks and financial institutions, not to other creditors. Based on World Bank's 'Doing Business 2020', it takes 1,445 days

companies and I use the estimate of 11 filings in 2019. In all the four jurisdictions, data on the estimated number of active registered companies in the relevant jurisdiction are drawn from Statista, a subscription database. Data on Singapore and Hong Kong is not included due to the non-availability of comprehensive data on creditors' voluntary winding up or schemes of arrangement.

[14] Data on bankruptcy orders over company exits for Mainland China are obtained from H Tao, 'Promote the Better Implementation of Bankruptcy Law' [依法推动企业破产制度更好实施] *People's Daily* [人民日报] (13 August 2021) (setting out the findings by the inspection team appointed by the Standing Committee of the National People's Congress for 2020), available at www.npc.gov.cn/npc/c30834/202108/d3fd86d9bd794fd8a779525566602085.shtml. For Hong Kong, the data on compulsory winding-up petitions and company exits are obtained from the Registry of Companies (Hong Kong) for 2019, available at www.cr.gov.hk/en/publication/fact-stat/statistics/dissolution.htm. For India, data on CIRP filings are obtained from IBBI (for the year ending 31 March 2020) and data on firm closures are obtained from the reports published by the Ministry of Corporate Affairs, Monthly Information Bulletin on Corporate Sector, available at mca.gov.in/content/mca/global/en/data-and-reports/reports/monthly-information-bulletin.html. For Singapore, the data on compulsory winding-up petitions and company exits for 2019 are obtained respectively from Ministry of Law, available at io.mlaw.gov.sg/files/CompaniesLiquidation.pdf and Accounting and Corporate Regulatory Authority, available at www.acra.gov.sg/training-and-resources/facts-and-figures/business-registry-statistics. For the US, data on bankruptcy filings under Chapter 7 (which lead to liquidation) and firm closures are obtained from LD Crane et al (2021) 'Business Exit During the COVID-19 Pandemic: Non Traditional Measures in Historical Context,' Finance and Economics Discussion Series 2020-089r1. Washington: Board of Governors of the Federal Reserve System, available at doi.org/10.17016/FEDS.2020.089r1. (For UK, the data on orders made for compulsory winding-up petitions and company exits are obtained Office of National Statistics (UK), available at www.ons.gov.uk/businessindustryandtrade/business/activitysizeandlocation, which shows that the number of orders made for compulsory liquidation over company exits is 0.93%. However, the data relates to the orders that are made, rather than to filings for winding-up petitions, and are not directly comparable with the other jurisdictions in Figure 8.3). Thus, the UK is excluded from the figure.

[15] See ch 5.

[16] For an account, see V Vig, 'Access to Collateral and Corporate Debt Structure: Evidence from a Natural Experiment' (2013) 68 *Journal of Finance* 881.

[17] See ch 5.

[18] See R Rajan, *A Hundred Small Steps: Report of the Committee on Financial Sector Reforms* (New Delhi, Planning Commission, Government of India, SAGE Publications India, 2008) 168, available at faculty.iima.ac.in/~jrvarma/reports/Raghuram-Rajan/cfsr_all.pdf.

[19] ibid, for a discussion on some of the areas in which SARFAESI has not worked so well.

(four years) to enforce a contract (including the trial to judgment and enforcement), and the costs of enforcing are 31 per cent.[20]

These difficulties in enforcing debts, particularly unsecured debt, have a far-reaching impact on restructuring law. In principle, if a jurisdiction's enforcement of debt is functional, expectedly, secured creditors are less likely to invoke any court-supervised resolution process than debtors (assuming the process is open for both creditors and debtors to commence proceedings). The reason is that secured bank creditors may be subject to a moratorium in the resolution process and are less likely to favour the reorganisation process (which results in the delay of their enforcement). Therefore, the resolution process will have to mediate the conflict between the secured and the unsecured creditors/shareholders, as discussed in chapter four.

Based on 'Doing Business 2020', the IBC has been a game-changer in that the time for resolving insolvency is now 1.6 years, representing a substantial reduction from 4.3 years in 2019. (Though the IBC was enacted in 2016, there was a time lag for the effects to become apparent.) It is the financial and operational creditors that have been the chief proponents of the use of the resolution process under the IBC (see Figure 4.5). There is much impetus to use the IBC, which is a time-bound process, considering that CIRP is meant to be completed in 330 days from the commencement date, including any extension and time taken in legal proceedings concerning the resolution process of the debtor, failing which the case ends up mandatorily in liquidation.[21] Based on the IBBI data, as of 31 March 2020, the number of filings by financial creditors (who are more likely to be secured creditors) and/or operational creditors outweigh the number of filings by the debtors. See the breakdown in Figure 4.5.

Figure 5.3 shows the recovery rates for the bank creditors using the DRT, SARFAESI and IBC. IBC shows recovery rates of 45.5 per cent and 45.7 per cent in 2020 and 2019 respectively for the bank creditors, which is considerably higher when compared with the DRT and the SARFAESI. For financial and operational creditors, the data show a similar picture of higher recovery. Prior to the impact of the IBC being felt, the average recovery of the debt (by all creditors) was approximately 26 per cent[22] and the time period for recovery was over 4.3 years.[23] The cost of the recovery was nine per cent.[24] Since the enactment of the IBC, as of 31 March 2019, various reports have put the figure of the average recovery rate was 48.2 per cent for financial creditors and between 42 per cent[25] and 48.3 per cent[26] for operational creditors. The average

[20] World Bank, *Doing Business 2020*.

[21] IBC, s 12 (the upper threshold of 330 days was introduced by the Insolvency and Bankruptcy Code (Amendment Ordinance) Act 2019).

[22] D Mondal, 'How IBC Helped Improve India's Ease of Doing Business Rankings' *BusinessToday* (24 October 2019).

[23] Press Information Bureau, Government of India, 'India Ranks 63 in World Bank's Doing Business Report – India Improves Rank by 14 Positions' (24 October 2019), available at pib.gov.in/newsite/PrintRelease.aspx?relid=193994.

[24] D Mondal, 'IBC' (2019). See also Press Information Bureau, Government of India (ibid).

[25] AR Palepu, 'Operational Creditors Recover 42% Of Claims Under IBC, Says ICRA' Bloomberg (19 June 2019), available at www.bloombergquint.com/business/operational-creditors-recover-42-of-claims-under-ibc-says-icra.

[26] *Economic Times*, 'Operational Creditors Benefit Equally from IBC: IBBI' (9 March 2019), available at economictimes.indiatimes.com/industry/banking/finance/banking/operational-creditors-benefits-equally-from-ibc-ibbi/articleshow/68338344.cms?utm_source=contentofinterest&utm_medium=text&utm_campaign=cppst.

time taken was 1.6 years though the cost of the resolution was not changed.[27] More broadly, the recovery rate on secured debt in Mumbai and Delhi, the major financial cities in India, is 71.6 per cent, which is a large improvement from the prior year at 26.5 per cent, as the impact of the IBC begins to be felt.[28] In terms of the number of cases that are filed under the IBC, excluding the filings for 2021 (because of the suspension of the IBC due to the COVID-19 pandemic), Figure 4.4 shows a steady increase in filings under the CIRP since 2017 (except for the year 2020/21 because of the suspension of the IBC).[29]

As a rough and ready measure, Figure 8.2 shows that for the year ended March 2020, the number of CIRPs[30] amounts to approximately 0.15 per cent of the total registered active companies in India.[31] The usage of the CIRP for resolving insolvency is higher than China's filings under the EBL, though lower than the US and the UK.[32] The usage of insolvency and restructuring law is approximately 0.28 per cent and 0.43 per cent in the US and the UK, respectively (Figure 8.2).

Hence, generally, it would be significantly faster to resolve a matter under the IBC than using general contract law. Although operational creditors are crammed down in the IBC and have no say over the question of how assets are to be deployed or the distribution of these assets,[33] the data in the preceding paragraph shows that operational creditors favour the use of the IBC.

Despite the success of the IBC, there remain two major challenges in improving recovery rates. The first is that creditors are now incentivised to use the resolution proceedings in the IBC as a substitute to debt enforcement or foreclosure of security. The heavy utilisation of the IBC is likely to overload the courts and put pressure on judicial capacity and time. Presently, the legislative deadline of 330 days appears to be unrealistic (see chapter seven). Thus, an appropriate solution has to be an aggressive screening process to ensure that cases that are unsuitable for resolution should proceed to liquidation without delay. Otherwise, the current CIRP process will mandatorily require that a market check be made for all debtors that are resolution applicants (with the associated timelines). Yet, for every case resolved under the IBC, four cases end up in liquidation, which means that there is significant investment of time which does not lead to a successful resolution.[34] Second, since creditors do not have the effective option of enforcement of the debt under general law, it is even more important for the moratorium imposed under CIRP to be strictly time-bound. Otherwise, the agency costs between creditors and shareholders are even

[27] World Bank, *Doing Business 2020*. Press Information Bureau, Government of India (n 23).

[28] World Bank (n 27).

[29] Insolvency and Bankruptcy Code (Amendment) Ordinance, 2020 effective 5 June 2020 (applies to defaults occurring after 25 March 2020).

[30] 1,943 CIRPs commenced in 2020.

[31] There are 1.26 million active companies limited by shares in India as at March 2020. Source: Statista, available at www.statista.com/statistics/1008330/india-number-of-registered-active-companies-by-type.

[32] For China, see Mrockova, *Corporate Bankruptcy Law in China* (2021) 190.

[33] ch4.

[34] N Shika and U Shahi, 'Assessment of Corporate Insolvency and Resolution Timeline' RP 01/2021, available at ibbi.gov.in/uploads/publication/2021-02-12-154823-p3xwo-8b78d9548a60a756e4c71d49368def03.pdf.

more pronounced under the IBC if the creditors, who are already facing a de facto moratorium because of difficulties in enforcement, face difficulties in recovery under the IBC.

Future reforms will need to address general civil enforcement in India so that the creditors are not specifically incentivised to invoke the IBC as a tool for the collection of debts. For completeness, I would mention that although India had the modern scheme of arrangement framework since the Companies Act 1956, the scheme framework is seldom utilised as a tool for debt restructuring.[35] The reasons range from the availability of the IBC, and prior to the IBC, the availability of alternative methods of out-of-court restructurings have been favoured including SARFAESI, Recovery of Debts Due to Banks and Financial Institutions Act 1993 and the various schemes introduced under the Joint Lenders Forum (before they were repealed). The scheme of arrangements was viewed as cumbersome and costly. The alternative methods have limitations as set out in chapter two, but they were seen as more favourable by the banks particularly in the case of the RBI frameworks because there was clarity over the treatment of stressed assets by the RBI.[36]

8.2.2.2. Mainland China

China presents a different problem. The enforcement of contracts in economically important cities is comparable with economically advanced jurisdictions in the last decade. For enforcement of contracts, the variations within China are inevitably very large given the differences in economic development across the country. Historically, the process of formal enforcement of security rights in the 1980s and 1990s has been described as expensive and cumbersome,[37] and that informal enforcement matters more than formal enforcement.[38] However, as China's economic development took off in the 2000s, formal enforcement and protection of property rights improved significantly.[39] On the basis of the World Bank's 'Doing Business 2020' report, it takes an average of 496 days (1.4 years) in Shanghai and Beijing the two most developed cities in China,[40] which compares favourably with the US (444 days) and the UK (437 days) and the cost of enforcement is at 16.2 per cent, which is lower than US (30.5 per cent) and UK (45.7 per cent). In the literature, lenders and academics

[35] U Varottil, 'The Scheme of Arrangement as a Debt Restructuring Tool in India: Problems and Prospects' (2018) 15 *European Company and Financial Law Review* 586.

[36] See also N Shikha and U Shahi, *Policy Inputs on Report on Subcommittee on Pre-packs: Centre for Insolvency and Bankruptcy, Indian Institute of Corporate Affairs* (2021), copy on file with author.

[37] M Williams, H Lu and CA Ong, *Secured Finance Law in China and Hong Kong* (Cambridge/New York, CUP, 2010) 363.

[38] See G Yu and H Zhang, 'Adaptive Efficiency and Financial Development in China: The Role of Contracts and Contractual Enforcement' (2008) 11 *Journal of International Economic Law* 459; cf M Trebilcock and J Leng, 'The Role of Formal Contract Law and Enforcement in Economic Development' (2006) 92 *Virginia Law Review* 1517.

[39] G Yu, 'Contract enforcement in China: Theory and Evidence' in G Yu (ed), *Rethinking Law and Development*, (London, Routledge, 2013) 63–91.

[40] Other scholars have pointed out the disparities in the difficulties of contract enforcement in different parts of China based on stages of economic development. eg see X He, 'A Tale of Two Chinese Courts: Economic Development and Contract Enforcement' (2012) 39 *Journal of Law and Society* 384.

have estimated that the time taken for the whole process is closer to 24–36 months,[41] although this remains an estimate, and there are variations across different courts and economic conditions in which the courts operate.

Security in China is traditionally in the form of the pledge over movable properties (including account receivables) and mortgage over real property, plant and machinery. Only the mortgage allows the mortgagor to remain in possession and enjoyment of the property that is secured, and is thus the most important form of security.[42] Although the enactment of the Property Law in 2007 represented an advancement for the creditors to be able to enforce their secured loans more easily,[43] there remains no right of self-help foreclosure of security equivalent to that which exists at common law. Enforcement through a mortgage must be taken only through local courts, which ordinarily involves the creditors suing the debtor, obtaining judgment and then taking enforcement action, whereupon the court will order an auction for the sale of the charged assets.[44] Extrajudicial sale is possible, thereby shortening the process significantly, if there is an agreement between the parties as to the value of the security.[45]

However, the relative ease in enforcing contracts does not, in itself, explain the low use of the EBL. To explore this further, I compare the outcomes of enforcement of contracts and restructuring proceedings; I draw from the data from the World Bank's 'Doing Business 2020' (concerning the recovery of secured debt) and also the data on resolution of onshore public bond defaults for unsecured debt. Public bond defaults are chosen because of the availability of data, the fact that most of the public bonds are not secured and the issuers of public onshore debt are large companies, which is the focus of this book.[46] When a debtor defaults on the bonds, in theory to resolve the default, the creditor or debtor can either attempt an out-of-court restructuring or a restructuring under the EBL, failing which the issuer goes into liquidation.[47] Unlike in the US where bond defaults are also dealt with by exchange offers, exchange offers are relatively uncommon in China. It was only in 2020 that China had its first exchange offer for an issuer that announced that it may not be able to pay on its maturity date.[48] Using the data on onshore bond defaults to illustrate how and

[41] Shorevest, 'China Debt Dynamics: Dealing With a Coming Surge in Nonperforming Loans' (2020) 4 Shorevest International Finance Center; W Shen, *Conceptualising the Regulatory Thicket, China's Financial Markets: After the Global Financial Crisis* (Abingdon, Routledge, 2021).

[42] See generally, L Wang, 'the Law of Secured Transactions in China: Comparison and Future Reform' in L Gullifer and D Neo (eds), *Secured Transactions Law in Asia: Principles, Perspectives and Reform* (Oxford, Hart Publishing, 2021); Williams, Lu and Ong, *Secured Finance Law* (2010).

[43] Williams, Lu and Ong (n 37) 368 (the mortgagee does not need to file a full action and is able to request the court to order the auction or sale, but such request must be made within the limitation period).

[44] There are other methods of debt collection which are not legal. See Shen, *Conceptualising the Regulatory Thicket* (2021) 33.

[45] Williams, Lu and Ong (n 37) 368.

[46] Information on publicly traded bonds is found on WIND and other subscription databases.

[47] There is no concept of voluntary liquidation in Mainland China and all liquidation cases must be administered by the courts. See X Wang, Y Xu and ACW Tang, 'PRC Enterprise Bankruptcy Law and Practice in China: 2007 to a Record-Breaking 2017' INSOL International Special Report (2018).

[48] Beijing Sound Environmental Engineering Co, Ltd, a water and sewage treatment facility manufacturer and operator. See Fitch Ratings, 'Non-Rating Action Commentary – China's First Onshore Bond Exchange Improves Restructuring Path' (16 March 2020), available at www.fitchratings.com/research/corporate-finance/china-first-onshore-bond-exchange-improves-restructuring-path-16-03-2020.

when reorganisations under the EBL are used, Figure 4.2 shows that, out of the 144 bond defaults between 2016 and 2019, by the end of 2020: (1) only 13.8 per cent had entered into EBL reorganisation, out of which 8.3 per cent of the bond defaults were resolved under the EBL; (2) only 10 per cent of the bond defaults were fully repaid; and (3) four per cent were in the process of undergoing reorganisation under the EBL (and were not completed). For most defaults, the bonds were not repaid and either there was no information (as there was no judicial proceeding being taken up) or there had been no meaningful progress towards resolution (including liquidation).

The data on public bond defaults and the low usage of the EBL are consistent with the overall narrative on the low usage of the EBL. It is widely documented that usage of the EBL is low, whether it is for restructuring or liquidation.[49] However, since 2015, the Central government has promoted the EBL as an important tool to effect market-based reforms, allow assets to be put to the most productive use and eliminate 'zombie' firms.[50] Figure 8.4 presents the bankruptcy cases that have been accepted for hearing by the courts since 2007; it can be seen that more cases are accepted for hearing since 2016, likely because of the acceleration of the setting-up of specialist courts from 2016 onwards.[51] The number of filings under the EBL is likely to increase in 2021 and 2022 given the fall-out from the COVID-19 pandemic and the repeated lock-downs. However, it is widely believed that even with the increased number of acceptances of the EBL cases by the courts, it is still a fraction of the insolvencies of companies that could be, but are not, resolved by the EBL. The number of bankruptcy filings represents approximately 0.04 per cent of the registered companies as of 2019 (see Figure 8.2).[52]

There are several reasons for the documented low use of the EBL.[53] First, creditors perceive the recovery to be low under the EBL. Based on the 'Doing Business 2020' data, the estimated recovery for secured debt in insolvency proceedings in Beijing and Shanghai is a low 36.9 per cent, when compared with, say, Hong Kong's 87.2 per cent. The low recovery of secured debt in insolvency proceedings,[54] despite the relative efficiency of the courts (496 days), cannot be solely explained by the high costs of proceedings. Although the costs of recovery are somewhat higher at 22 per cent than Hong Kong's (five per cent), it does not account for less than half recovery. The more likely explanations are that, notwithstanding the secured debt, priority to the proceeds has gone to employees post-default, particularly for the larger companies with a significant number of employees concentrated in a location, notwithstanding

[49] Mrockova (n 12) ch 5.

[50] ch 3, section 3.4.3.3.

[51] B Li and J Ponticelli, 'Going Bankrupt in China' PBCSF-NIFR Research Paper (2020), available at ssrn.com/abstract=3251570.

[52] See also Z Zhang, 'The Corporate Bankruptcy Substitute in China' (2019) 33 *Columbia Journal of Asian Law* 172, references in fn 18 (suggesting that if the number of insolvencies is estimated to be 1% of the total number of enterprises as at 2017, the number of insolvencies would be approximately 290,723; instead of 0.03% as was in 2017).

[53] eg Zhang (ibid); Mrockova (n 12) ch 5.

[54] Secured creditors are entitled to apply to the court for relief from the stay of proceedings during the period of automatic stay: EBL, Art 75. It has been argued that the scope of relief is unclear. A Godwin, 'Lengthy Stay the Impact of the PRC Enterprise Bankruptcy Law on the Rights of Secured Creditors' (2007) 30 *University of New South Wales Law Journal* 755.

Article 87 of the EBL, which ranks employees' claims after secured creditors.[55] In chapter four, I explained that small creditors and, in some cases, non-financial creditors, are treated differently from the financial creditors in terms of the cash recovery rate. It has been documented that local governments prioritise social stability and preservation of jobs and hence are willing to actively intervene to subordinate the secured creditors' interests.[56] The average recovery rate of less than 50 per cent shows that secured creditors would be motivated to resolve the matter outside the EBL where possible.

Second, notwithstanding Article 10 of the EBL that obliges the courts to accept or reject the petition within 15 days, the courts would only accept the bankruptcy petition filing if the local government supported the petition (but would not explicitly reject the balance).[57] The acceptance rate was historically a fraction compared with the number of applications filed.[58] This disparity discourages creditors from filing under the EBL.

Third, Zhang has argued that between 1998 and 2015, the courts have used the fair distribution or *pari passu* payment principle in judgment execution as a form to seeking equality of treatment among creditors who are enforcing against the corporate debtor.[59] This fair distribution was a convenient substitute to restructuring or liquidation due to the difficulties in invoking the EBL. Although the fair distribution was abolished by the Supreme People's Court in 2015, he argued that the procedure persists in certain cases, though with less intensity.

In the case of bondholders, I suggest that the EBL is not the preferred mode of resolution because bond-holders hold out for potentially more favourable results in out-of-court restructuring. For onshore bond defaults, the average recovery rate for bond-holders (which would usually be unsecured) in the EBL process is reported to be 23.7 per cent.[60] The more pressing problem is not just the low recovery rate.[61] Even if the recovery rate is low, but there is certainty as to how the claims will be dealt with in EBL, unsecured creditors can choose to effect an out-of-court restructuring if they reach a deal outside the courtroom under the shadow of expected recovery.

In the dataset, however, the range of variation of recovery is very wide; in the dataset of bonds in default between 2015 and 2019 (which is discussed in the text accompanying Figure 4.2), in unreported findings, approximately 10 per cent (15 out of 144) of the issuers in bond default (comprising a mix of SOEs and non-SOEs) had their principal and/or interest repaid in full without going through the court-supervised reorganisation process.[62] In many cases, as highlighted in chapter four, the

[55] B Li and J Ponticelli, 'Going Bankrupt in China' (2020).

[56] ibid.

[57] J Fan, J Huang and N Zhu, 'Institutions, Ownership Structures, and Distress Resolution in China' (2013) 23 *Journal of Corporate Finance* 71. See also Wang, Xu and Tang, 'PRC Enterprise Bankruptcy Law and Practice in China' (2018); Zhang, 'The Corporate Bankruptcy Substitute in China' (n 52).

[58] ibid.

[59] Zhang (n 52).

[60] E White, 'China's Courts Take Centre Stage as Defaults Shake $17tn Bond Market' *Financial Times* (24 August 2021), available at www.ftchinese.com/interactive/46668/en?exclusive. The source of the power is pursuant to the SPC, Judicial Notice on Judgment Execution issued on 8 July 1998, effective 8 July 1998.

[61] Mrockova (n 12) ch 5.

[62] See discussion accompanying text in ch 4, Figure 4.2.

bonds are not repaid at all and there is no progress towards resolution. Hence, if the parties fail to reach an agreement in the reorganisation, unsecured creditors may then see little incentive to enforce against the debtor by filing for bankruptcy or liquidation of the debtor, because they rank after the secured creditors and employees (unless they are small creditors or non-financial creditors, as discussed in chapter four). By the time that it is clear that there is no prospect of an out-of-court settlement, considerable value destruction has taken place such that the expenses of liquidation outweigh any recovery.[63] The unpredictability as to whether there is governmental support makes it difficult to predict which are the ones that are likely to receive support and which are not. This is the case even with the recent emphasis on market-oriented reforms, since many of the listed firms after 2015 were rescued with governmental coordination or other forms of support.[64]

The environment that the creditors in Mainland China find themselves in is very different from the typical Chapter 11 reorganisations in the US where the security interests of the secured creditors are protected in the reorganisation through the fair and equitable test,[65] thereby ensuring that they will receive the collateral value. In the US, it is usually the debtor or the unsecured creditors who are incentivised to enter into Chapter 11 to obtain better outcomes. In Mainland China, secured creditors are incentivised to race to enforce their security; the unsecured creditors (except the small creditors and non-financial creditors) prefer to wait for an out-of-court restructuring outcome and, by the time the matter goes into the EBL, it may be very late in the day.

In summary, there are several reasons for the low use of the EBL, apart from the initial reluctance of the courts to accept the bankruptcy petitions. First, the secured creditors are not incentivised to the invoke the EBL since they would be financially better off if they race to first obtain a judgment against the debtor and execute the judgment (given the efficiency of the legal system for enforcing debt) before the debtor enters into EBL proceedings; otherwise, not only are they subject to the moratorium, which provides a stay of proceedings, but their recovery is also substantially lowered. Second, unsecured financial creditors hesitate to use the EBL because of the inherent unpredictability of the process. Reaching deals outside of the EBL is difficult if the resolution regime is unpredictable. When no deal can be struck, the delay in filings may have already destroyed value.[66]

8.2.2.3. Hong Kong and Singapore

Figure 8.1 shows the relative effectiveness of the recovery of debts using general law and insolvency and restructuring law. Hong Kong and Singapore have efficient legal systems for enforcing contracts and security interests, and their situations are more

[63] During enforcement of the debt against the debtor, the court can convert the case to one of bankruptcy under the EBL. Zhang reported that this process is, however, seldom used. See Zhang (n 52).

[64] See ch 7.

[65] 11 USC 1129(b).

[66] For a discussion on how late filings destroy value in the US context, see BE Adler, V Capkun and LA Weiss, 'Value Destruction in Chapter 11' (2013) 29 *Journal of Law, Economics and Organization* 461.

Figure 8.4 Number of bankruptcy cases accepted by the Chinese courts

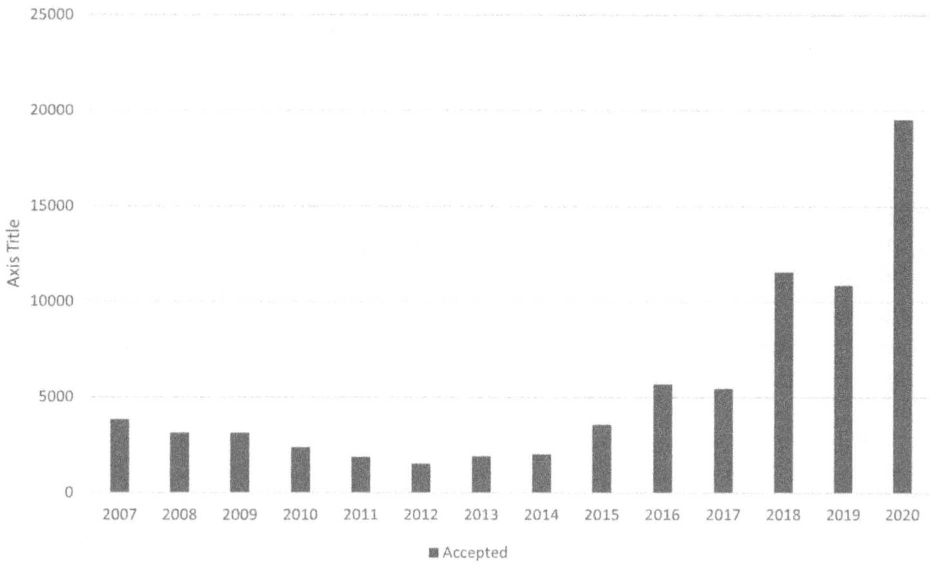

Sources: Data collected from X Wang, Y Xu and A Tang, 'PRC Enterprise Bankruptcy Law and Practice in China: 2007 to a Record-Breaking 2017' INSOL International Special Report (2018); *Supreme People's Court Gazette [中华人民共和国最高人民法院公报.北京]: 该办公厅*

similar to those in the UK. Both jurisdictions also have corporate law legislation (outside of insolvency) that disincentivises the disposal of property against the reach of creditors, which includes restrictions on payments of dividends in the absence of profits,[67] directors' duties to ensure that they act in the interest of the company (which encompass interests of the creditors in the zone of insolvency)[68] and legislation or applicable stock exchange rules on tunnelling through related party transactions.[69]

Thus, it is not surprising that the recovery rate for both jurisdictions under general law and under the insolvency framework is broadly similar (see Figure 8.1). For secured creditors in both jurisdictions, the World Bank's data on *Doing Business 2020* shows that the recovery in insolvency proceedings largely preserves their collateral value (Hong Kong's 87.2 per cent and Singapore's 88.7 per cent). In terms of contract enforcement, the average time for Hong Kong is longer (385 days) than that for Singapore (164 days). Nevertheless, the percentage of the claim that is spent on enforcement is approximately the same for Hong Kong (23.6 per cent) and Singapore's (25.8 per cent).[70] Thus, it is not surprising that the recovery by secured creditors

[67] Companies Act Cap 50 rev edn (Singapore), s 403; Companies Ordinance Cap 622 (Hong Kong), ss 297–98.

[68] *Re China Bozza Development Holding* [2021] HKCFI 1235.

[69] C Chen, WY Wan and W Zhang, 'Board Independence as a Panacea to Tunneling? An Empirical Study of Related-Party Transactions in Hong Kong and Singapore' (2018) 154 *Journal of Empirical Legal Studies* 987.

[70] Figures from World Bank Doing Business 2020. The percentage of the claim that is spent on enforcement is the aggregate of the attorney fees, court fees and enforcement fees.

for both jurisdictions through insolvency proceedings is similar to that of the UK (85.4 per cent) and the US (81 per cent). Contract enforcement for both jurisdictions is shorter than in the UK (437 days) and the US (444 days), and the costs are lower than in the UK (45.7 per cent) and the US (30.5 per cent).

8.3. ANALYSIS

The enforcement of creditors' rights is as important as having a good system of law in the books on contracts and property rights. A robust system of enforcement of creditors' rights and insolvency and restructuring law will imply that the secured creditors are protected in either case ahead of the unsecured creditors and the shareholders. If the company enters into restructuring proceedings, the secured creditors cannot enforce immediately, but are protected from the deterioration of the security value.

The balance of the agency and coordination costs between the secured and unsecured creditors/shareholders or between the creditors and shareholders can be altered by a weak contract enforcement system, which will affect the incentives of the various parties to utilise the restructuring law. A weak enforcement system (and a comparatively more efficient resolving insolvency legislation) incentivises both secured and unsecured creditors to become involved in the restructuring process, as has been the experience in India.

Further reforms to the IBC, notably on the time-bound nature of the IBC, are impossible to achieve without taking into account the fact that it is utilised to compensate for the shortcomings in state law. For instance, there are good reasons to extend the use of pre-negotiated or pre-packs, which are currently not only available to the smaller companies,[71] but also to larger ones. Taking advantage of the statutory time-bound period for pre-negotiated sales and the reduction in judicial time demands, secured and unsecured creditors are generally better off in such a system.

Nonetheless, if reorganisation or liquidation processes result in a worse outcome for secured creditors, it leads to a race to get to judgment (and enforce) first, because secured creditors benefit from a better outcome with lower costs. The race to judgment is the situation in Mainland China. As for the unsecured creditors, only small and trade creditors will be incentivised to use the EBL (as they recover in full), but they may not do so because of other reasons such as the upfront payment of costs to instruct advisers. Unsecured financial creditors (such as the bond-holders) delay filing because they are aiming for an out-of-court restructuring; as an overall result, eventually, the financial distress may have spread to the operations, and the restructuring will take place too late in the day, and they will not bother to put the company into liquidation. This hypothesis is supported by the low usage of the EBL and, more specifically, by several issuers of defaulted public debt that appear to be in limbo (and not utilise the EBL).

[71] Insolvency and Bankruptcy Code (Amendment) Ordinance 2021 (introducing pre-packs for micro, small and medium-size firms).

The low usage of the EBL also carries other implications. Existing scholarship has pointed out the widespread tunnelling by controlling shareholders[72] and that enforcement is largely public rather than private.[73] If the EBL is not invoked, the lack of orderly distribution of the assets, avoidable transactions (such as transactions at an undervalue, security for past consideration, waivers of claims, and preferential payments) will not be investigated by the administrator.[74] Hence, the EBL remains an important way to preserve value for creditors, and the key focus on any future reforms to the EBL to encourage greater use should be to reconsider the recovery that is given to the creditors and shareholders. Certainty and predictability are critical to incentivise the creditors and debtor to utilise the EBL, as well as to protect the general security interests of the secured creditors.

8.4. DIRECTORS' DUTIES AND INCENTIVES TO INVOKE OR USE RESTRUCTURING LAW

8.4.1. Why should Incentives to Commence Insolvency Proceedings Matter?

More generally, looking at the tools that incentivise the use of insolvency and restructuring law, we have thus far examined the incentives or 'carrots' available to debtors and creditors to benefit from the tools and the tool kit. This section looks at some of the other tools that exist to compel or nudge the debtor to utilise the insolvency or restructuring framework early. The earlier the firm invokes the insolvency and restructuring process, the more likely it is that the firm can be rescued, which leads to savings on transaction costs.[75] Even as we look at the incentives of putting the companies into the insolvency or restructuring framework (such as a DIP regime that enables directors or shareholders to enjoy the benefits of being in charge of restructuring), such incentives are also costly to the creditor group as a whole because they may trigger strategic default by the debtor for the benefit of its controlling shareholders or managers in cases where a DIP filing is unnecessary but is triggered to solve mass tort liabilities or to rearrange labour contracts to reduce costs.[76] As such, the solution is not to make the DIP too attractive; instead, there must be some 'stick' for the managers who delay unduly invoking of the formal process. If the company is not able to operate the assets efficiently, the failure to put the firm quickly into such a process (and thereby redeploy the assets either under new management or elsewhere) is economically inefficient and

[72] HW Hu and P Sun, 'What Determines the Severity of Tunneling in China?' (2019) 36 *Asia Pacific Journal of Management* 161.

[73] eg LH Haß, S Johan and MA Müller, 'The Effectiveness of Public Enforcement: Evidence from the Resolution of Tunneling in China' (2016) 134 *Journal of Business Ethics* 649.

[74] EBL, Arts 31, 33, 34.

[75] See eg P Povel, 'Optimal Soft or Tough Bankruptcy Procedures' (1999) 15 *Journal of Law Economics and Organization* 659.

[76] K Delaney, *Strategic Bankruptcy: How Corporations and Creditors Use Chapter 11 to Their Advantage* (Berkeley, University of California Press, 1999). See also DG Baird and TH Jackson, 'Corporate Reorganizations and the Treatment of Diverse Ownership Interests: A Comment on Adequate Protection of Secured Creditors in Bankruptcy' (1984) 51 *University of Chicago Law Review* 97, 101 (arguing that rule changes in bankruptcy should not induce a creditor to seek bankruptcy to access benefits to him/her personally regardless of costs or benefits to the investor group as a whole).

should be discouraged.[77] Mechanisms used by jurisdictions include the obligation on the part of directors to file for insolvency and putting in place an insolvent trading framework.

Considering the disincentives imposed on the directors, it is important to consider the duties that they are subject to outside of insolvency law. Where the regime in the jurisdiction does not actively enforce directors' duties to consider the interests of creditors when the company is in the zone of insolvency (or where the content of such duties is relatively thin), whether the balance of incentives and disincentives in the toolbox are sufficient must be considered to assure that the directors do not unnecessarily delay triggering the insolvency or restructuring regime. At the same time, any mechanism will also need to ensure that directors can continue to trade, within limits, and not push the company prematurely into insolvency.

This section addresses managerial incentives and disincentives to *commence* insolvency proceedings. I first compare the position in the US and the UK. In these two jurisdictions, the debtor is not obliged to file for bankruptcy or its equivalent.[78] However, there are several differences. In the UK, when companies are in the zone of insolvency, directors' duties shift such that they have to consider the interests of the creditors when making decisions as to whether to continue trading and not primarily the interests of shareholders.[79] In contrast, in the US (Delaware), the shift does not occur until actual insolvency; a solvent company that is operating in the zone of insolvency continues to discharge the duties to the company and its shareholders.[80]

The content of the duties and mode of enforcement are not identical. In the UK, the directors are directly responsible to consider the interests of the creditors as a whole when the company is insolvent or in the zone of insolvency; failure to do so is a breach of the duty, which is enforceable, usually initiated by the liquidator or administrator (in administration) of the company.[81] In the US, under the Delaware law, which is the law of incorporation of 50 per cent of the listed companies in the US, when the company is insolvent, there is a duty owed to the residual claimants by the directors; the creditors do not have a direct cause of action against the directors but can bring a derivative claim on behalf of the corporation.[82] However, what is crucial in both jurisdictions is the enforcement. In the US, when the corporation goes into a bankruptcy filing, the trustee in bankruptcy takes action to enforce the estate's claims against the director for failing to perform his/her duties.[83]

[77] MJ White, 'The Costs of Corporate Bankruptcy: A US-European Comparison' in JS Bhandar and LA Weiss (eds), *Corporate Bankruptcy: Economic and Legal Perspectives* (Cambridge, CUP, 1996).

[78] White (ibid).

[79] *BTI 2014 LLC v Sequana SA & others* [2019] EWCA Civ 112 (holding that the directors should consider the interests of the creditors when the directors know or ought to have known that the company is or is likely to become unable to repay its debts).

[80] *North American Catholic Educational Programming Foundation, Inc v Gheewalla* 930 A 2d 92, 101–02 (Del 2007).

[81] Companies Act 2006, s 172(3), codifying the common law. Common law decisions include *West Mercia Safetywear v Dodd* [1988] BCLC 250. See generally, A Keay, 'The Shifting of Directors' Duties in the Vicinity of Insolvency' (2015) 24 *International Insolvency Review* 140; K van Zwieten, 'Director Liability in Insolvency and Its Vicinity' (2018) 38 *OJLS* 382.

[82] n 80.

[83] J Armour et al, 'Private Enforcement of Corporate Law: An Empirical Comparison of the United Kingdom and the United States' (2009) 6 *Journal of Empirical Legal Studies* 687.

In the UK, private enforcement of the directors' duties by the liquidator is rare and other weaker substitutes such as directorial disqualification exist.[84] However, UK insolvency legislation imposes personal liability on directors who cause the companies to continue to trade while the directors have the requisite knowledge that there is no reasonable prospect of avoiding insolvent liquidation or administration.[85] At this stage, if directors do not in fact put the company into an insolvency process, they may be personally liable to contribute to the amount by which the company's assets are depleted by reason for continuation in trading beyond the point at which there was no reasonable prospect the company would avoid going into insolvent liquidation.[86] A director can avoid civil liability by demonstrating that he/she took all of the steps he/she should have taken to minimise potential loss to the company's creditors. Wrongful trading is viewed as being more effective than the fraudulent trading law, which is also a criminal offence.[87] Although there have been criticisms that wrongful trading did not achieve its intended objective of successfully penalising the errant director because of other difficulties in bringing the actions,[88] the provision does serve as a deterrence. By contrast, the US does not have an equivalent provision and is probably explicable through the more robust enforcement of the general directors' duties.[89]

8.4.2. Incentives in Asia

In each of the four Asian jurisdictions under consideration, the incentives and disincentives for the directors of the debtors to initiate the restructuring regime differ significantly. In Hong Kong, a company finds it arduous to invoke a corporate rescue because of a lack of a formal rescue framework. The company may propose a scheme of arrangement to the creditors as part of the restructuring. During the period of time when the company is in financial distress, given the lack of insolvent trading laws in Hong Kong, importantly, the duties of directors will be in accordance with the common law (which includes considering creditors' interests[90]) and if provisional liquidators are appointed, the duties are enforceable by the provisional liquidators. Misfeasance for summary breach of duty is also available as a remedy for breach of directors' duties.[91] Although litigation funding is available for the liquidator to file proceedings in insolvency cases, it will only be effective where large sums of money are at stake and the litigation funder is willing to fund the action.[92] The effect is that private enforcement of directors' duties (in failing to consider creditors' interests) is rare. This is not an unusual phenomenon in Hong Kong. Elsewhere, I have argued

[84] ibid. Directors may be disqualified under the Company Directors Disqualification Act 1986.

[85] Insolvency Act, s 214.

[86] ibid.

[87] Insolvency Act 1986, s 213.

[88] See generally, Keay (n 81).

[89] MJ White, 'The Costs of Corporate Bankruptcy: A US-European Comparison' in JS Bhandar and LA Weiss (eds), *Corporate Bankruptcy: Economic and Legal Perspectives* (Cambridge, CUP, 1996).

[90] *Re China Bozza Development Holdings Ltd* [2021] HKCFI 1235.

[91] Companies (Winding Up and Miscellaneous Provisions) Ordinance, s 276.

[92] *Re Cyberworks Audio Video Technology Ltd* [2010] 2 HKLRD 1137.

that the public regulators, such as the Securities and Futures Commission, under sections 213 and/or 214 of the Securities and Futures Ordinance (SFO), are principally responsible for enforcing directors' duties for (solvent) publicly listed companies.[93] When such enforcement occurs successfully (at least when the company is solvent), the directors are obliged to compensate the company for breach of duty (for the benefit of the shareholders) and are also liable to be disqualified.[94] Private enforcement of directors' duties is very rare (in the case of solvent companies).[95]

Arguably, sections 213 and 214 of the SFO, conversely, may not be of much assistance if the breach of directors' duties is attributable to the failure to consider creditors' interests (as opposed to shareholders' interests). Fraudulent trading provisions exist, which made such trading a criminal offence,[96] do not serve as an effective deterrent as there is hardly any prosecution under such provision.[97] As part of the introduction of the proposed corporate rescue and provisional supervision framework,[98] insolvent trading laws based on the Australian position of insolvent trading are also proposed.[99] The way it works is that the proposed insolvent trading laws serve as a safeguard when a firm's directors continue to trade while the company is undergoing restructuring under the corporate rescue framework.[100] Nevertheless, outside of this framework, if there are reforms to include rescue provisions such as a moratorium (as argued in chapter nine), careful consideration should be given to how to incentivise directors to apply these provisions early.

In Singapore, the Insolvency, Restructuring and Dissolution Act 2018 introduces wrongful trading,[101] which occurs when the company, when insolvent, incurs debt or other liabilities without reasonable prospect of meeting them in full or incurs such liabilities when it has no reasonable prospect of meeting in full and that resulted in the company becoming insolvent. It departs from the previous law that imposes civil liability only if the individual has been convicted of a criminal offence.[102] Under IRDA, a person (including a director or a party to the wrongful trading) is

[93] See Securities and Futures Ordinance, Cap 571. See also WY Wan, C Chen and SH Goo, 'Public and Private Enforcement of Corporate and Securities Laws: An Empirical Comparison of Hong Kong and Singapore' (2019) 20 *European Business Organization Law Review* 319.

[94] ibid.

[95] ibid.

[96] Companies (Winding Up and Miscellaneous Provisions) Ordinance, s 275.

[97] A search on the judgments with Hong Kong Legal Information Institute and LexisNexis did not reveal any prosecution under the provision.

[98] See discussion in WY Wan, 'Should Hong Kong Reform Its Insolvency Law in Times of COVID-19?' (2021) *Company Lawyer* 133. See also sections 1.5.3 and 9.2.3.

[99] For the Australian position on insolvent trading, see S Steel, I Ramsay and M Webster 'Insolvency law reform in Australia and Singapore: Directors' liability for insolvent trading and wrongful trading' (2019) 28 *International Insolvency Review* 363. The Australian Government is undergoing a review on the insolvent trading provisions when the company is undergoing restructuring. See Australian Government, Treasury, 'Review of the Insolvent Trading Safe Habour: Consultation Paper' (2021).

[100] See SHC Lo, 'Proposal for Insolvent Trading Laws in Hong Kong: A Comparative Analysis' (2020) 7 *Journal of International and Comparative Law* 229.

[101] IRDA, s 239.

[102] Companies Act, 2006 rev edn, s 339(3) read with s 340(2) (repealed). See Insolvency Law Reform Committee, 'Report of the Insolvency Law Review Committee: Final Report' (Ministry of Law, 2013) 201,

personally liable for all of the debts of the company if he/she knew the company was trading wrongfully or, as an officer of the company, should have known it was doing so. This action can be enforced by the judicial manager, liquidator or creditor (with leave of the judicial manager, liquidator or the court).[103] This provision also criminalises wrongful trading. The objective is for the directors to address the financial distress early and put the company into the insolvency and restructuring regime. Wrongful trading, which can be enforced privately, is essential here as there is no public enforcement of directors' duties in Singapore. Otherwise, the only way to enforce directors' duties is through private enforcement conducted by liquidators.[104]

In India, the overwhelming initiation of the filings under the CIRP is done by creditors (see Figure 4.5). As explained in section 8.2, the phenomenon can be explained by the fact that creditors utilise the CIRP as a form of substitute to recover the debts. Section 66 of the IBC introduces the regime of fraudulent and insolvent trading but is not likely to be the driver for the promoters or management of the debtor to invoke the CIRP. Nevertheless, if the proposal is for India to scale down reliance on the IBC as a debt recovery tool, consideration must be given to how to get the directors to address the problem early.

In Mainland China, the EBL is under-used by creditors for the reasons highlighted in section 8.2, which include the lack of predictability and uncertainty. There is no specific requirement for directors to file for bankruptcy when the company is insolvent. For limited liability companies, shareholders are obliged to put the company to liquidation, if the company is dissolved without liquidation or liquidation is yet to be completed and the assets are insufficient to pay the debts.[105] Directors and shareholders in joint-stock limited companies are also obliged to put the company into liquidation within a specified deadline, and such duty is triggered upon various events, including where the company's business licence is revoked (which may occur within or outside the company's insolvency).[106] Given the large numbers of companies that are dissolved without undergoing liquidation, the requirement to file is likely to be under-enforced in practice.[107]

There are no separate directors' duties that govern directors in the zone of insolvency, nor do they owe duties to creditors.[108] On a more general point, the duties of directors of listed companies and SOEs are enforced largely through public enforcement,[109] which is limited by budgetary constraints. If it is not proposed that company law be changed to include the consideration of creditors' interests by directors, it is

pointed out that the Committee was not aware of any civil proceedings brought under s 340(2) or criminal prosecution.

[103] IRDA, s 239.

[104] Wan, Chen and Goo, 'Public and Private Enforcement' (2019).

[105] EBL, Art 7.

[106] Company Law 2013, Art 183. Roughly speaking, small and medium enterprises are limited liability companies and larger firms with dispersed ownership are joint stock limited companies.

[107] Only 1% for the company exits are attributable to bankruptcy (see Figure 8.3).

[108] Company Law 2013, Art 20.

[109] See J Wang, 'The Political Logic of Corporate Governance in China's State-Owned Enterprises' (2014) 47 *Cornell International Law Journal* 631.

urged that future amendments to the EBL and/or supplementation by the equivalent of a wrongful trading provision should take into account such consideration.[110]

8.5. CONCLUSION

In determining how to proceed with insolvency and restructuring law reform, a jurisdiction will need to consider the broader context of the institutional framework and other laws, including the enforcement of the debt (and security) and corporate governance. In chapter two, I discuss how India and Mainland China are historically debtor-friendly given the weak formal enforcement of debt prior to the enactment of their modern insolvency laws. However, although Mainland China has improved the formal enforcement framework (making the regime more creditor-friendly), the EBL remains under-utilised. In India, formal enforcement remains challenging and the IBC becomes the default instrument by creditors to collect on the claim. If the IBC is not going to be overwhelmed with handling a large increase in workload, the framework on general contract enforcement should also be considered.

Finally, this chapter argues that there must be incentives to commence insolvency and restructuring proceedings when a company is in financial distress, which can be found in insolvency and restructuring law and in other areas such as corporate law.

[110] See also C Wei, J Zhao and G McCormack, 'Evolutionary Traditions and Corporate Law: the Effectiveness and Development of Liquidation Duty in China' (2019) 27 *Asia Pacific Law Review* 149; C Wei and Y Chen, 'The Predicament of Bank Creditors in Chinese Bankruptcy and the Way Out' (2018) 27 *International Insolvency Review* 110.

9

Restructuring Law, Implications for Reform and Conclusion

9.1. INTRODUCTION

RESTRUCTURING LAW PLAYS an essential role in enabling the market to rescue financially distressed but economically viable companies and enabling those which are unviable to be able to exit expeditiously. It is critical to minimise the transaction costs and, in particular, the agency and coordination costs that arise from the market participants. The four Asian jurisdictions draw much of their restructuring laws as well as recent reforms from the United States (US) and the United Kingdom (UK), and it is important to understand how their solutions have addressed or mitigated these costs and whether these solutions are appropriate in Asia. In particular, the composition of the market participants and their institutional backgrounds are very different. Thus, while there is some degree of formal convergence of restructuring law, there is far more divergence functionally.

It is a central argument of this book that the optimal design of restructuring law must take into account the following, which are not present to the same as extent as in the US and the UK: (1) the interaction between concentrated shareholdings and widely held debt; (2) the incentives of the state in resolving non-performing loans; (3) the benefits and limitations of the independent gatekeepers, being the insolvency practitioners and the courts; and (4) the interaction among restructuring law and enforcing contracts and duties of directors of financially distressed firms.

In this chapter, I discuss the approach of the book and the implications on either adopting or modifying the various restructuring tools for each Asian jurisdiction. The focus is only on the large firms, so the considerations specific to small and medium-size companies will be left for another day. I also discuss the trends and future prospects of reform. My analysis has shown the starkly different agency and coordination costs, institutional backgrounds and practices that will require continuous consideration as to the adequacy of the toolkits of restructuring law in the four Asian jurisdictions, even if they are transplants from the US and the UK. Just as in the US and the UK where practitioners have adapted the tools of the restructuring framework to deal with changes in the marketplace, Asian jurisdictions will also have to find new ways to address the changes as jurisdictions shift their focus to new objectives of restructuring law.

As the US seeks to influence the rest of the world on the goals of Chapter 11 through UNCITRAL's Legislative Guide on Insolvency Law and until recently, the World Bank's *Doing Business* reports (since discontinued), this book demonstrates the original Chapter 11 policy goals and tools are not necessarily suitable for everyone. Chapter 11, when formulated, deals with dispersed a shareholding model with widely held debt of a company that is seeking a restructuring. Even the English scheme of arrangement works best with a dispersed shareholding model and dealing only with financial debt. Change in the marketplace over the last two decades have resulted in adaptions by market players in Chapter 11 and the English scheme of arrangement. Thus, what is required is a detailed analysis on how restructuring law interacts with corporate governance, various non-insolvency rules and national goals. Where tools are absent from the toolkit or inadequate, careful consideration needs to be made as to what are the uses of the tools and how they can solve problems in the context of specific institutional backgrounds and national goals without exacerbating existing problems. Such an approach will be more useful than transplanting laws wholesale that would have addressed US problems (and also satisfy the World Bank's *Doing Business* reports) but which are otherwise not solving the problem at hand. None of the debtor in possession (DIP), the practitioner in possession (PIP), and the secured creditor-in-control models or variants thereof is an inherently more suitable model. Instead, what is more critical is the usefulness of the particular tools and how such tools would be used by market professionals in the particular jurisdiction.

At the time of writing, the world is still grappling with the COVID-19 pandemic, and it looks as if the economic downturn will be prolonged and recovery long-drawn. While all four Asian jurisdictions have used economic policies to support hard-hit industries, employment and continuation of credit facilities, and in certain cases also enact insolvency law reforms to better support businesses, this chapter will not discuss the temporary reforms that apply during the pandemic, but the more permanent reforms that arise out of the crisis.

Section 9.2 summarises the various conclusions of this book into seven propositions as each jurisdiction determines its optimal framework for restructuring law. Reference is made to four particular tools: the moratorium and the associated *ipso facto* clauses, the cross-class cram-down, pre-negotiated or pre-pack restructurings and rescue financing. Section 9.3 discusses the future prospects of each jurisdiction's restructuring regime and the major pressing problems that will require reforms to the law and practice of the restructuring framework. Section 9.4 concludes.

9.2. SEVEN PROPOSITIONS IN THIS BOOK

Proposition 1: To minimise agency costs in shareholder–creditor or manager–creditor relationships in restructurings of firms with controlling shareholders, a DIP or DIP-hybrid regime should: (1) enforce disclosure of information to creditors; (2) restrict the voting by controlling shareholders (who are also creditors) over the outcome of the restructuring in creditors' meetings; (3) conduct the valuation of the firm in a transparent manner; and (4) effectively enforce directors' duties to take into account creditors' interests (see proposition 7).

None of the DIP, PIP, secured creditor-in-control model or variants thereof is inherently the most suitable restructuring regime to minimise the agency costs (and in particular, the agency costs arising from the shareholder–creditor or manager–creditor conflict) for a jurisdiction with controlling shareholders. Instead, what is required is an analysis as to the benefits and trade-offs in having a particular regime, together with an analysis of the specific tools in the restructuring toolkit. In the Anglo-American tradition, shareholders' interests should become irrelevant when the company becomes insolvent, and instead attention should be given to the creditors' interests; the DIP regime is not necessarily a good fit if the manager (appointed by the controlling shareholders) drives the restructuring. However, what this book demonstrates is that the support of the controlling shareholders may often be critical in the outcome of the restructurings. The controlling shareholders in Asia are different from the controlling shareholders found in the restructurings of the large firms which are held by private equity portfolios (and who appoint professional managers) in the US/UK over the last two decades. The professional managers have equity in their compensation and may be offered retention post-restructuring (and hence may have their interests more aligned to creditors). In contrast, controlling shareholders in Asia are mostly held by families or the state. Controlling shareholders (in the form of families) may often contribute their personal assets to demonstrate their belief and sincerity to the creditors, or that their presence is critical to the company post-restructurings, such as in the Hong Kong restructurings in the 1980s and in Singapore schemes of arrangement. When the state is a controlling shareholder (eg Mainland China), the state is able to mobilise the support of other state-owned entities or resources to effect the restructuring, such as procuring lending by other state-owned banks and mergers of SOEs.

However, controlling shareholders can also have an undue influence over the restructuring outcome even when the company is insolvent (and where only the creditors' interests should prevail) in a number of ways. First, controlling shareholders are not incentivised to disclose information if they are not participants in the restructuring. Outside creditors face significant information asymmetry. India is a particular glaring example of promoters having been seen to stymie restructurings prior to the enactment of the IBC. Even under the IBC, the promoters are seen as uncooperative in disclosing information and thereby causing delay and have often tried to purchase the assets at a discount, notwithstanding the ban under section 29A of the IBC. Second, controlling shareholders, who are also creditors, may exercise their votes to support the restructuring in a way consistent with their interests, that are not consistent with the creditors as a whole. For example, they may cast their votes represented by their related party debt-holdings in favour of the restructuring or vote to release claims against themselves or directors appointed them in respect of past misconduct.

Consequently, Mainland China, India and Hong Kong have not embraced the DIP regime unreservedly. Thus, if it is desired to move to a DIP or a manager-in-control regime, the key is to ensure that companies exit restructurings speedily (whether with a plan or liquidation), thereby minimising destruction of value when the company is in the restructuring process. To these ends, creditors will need to have access to the debtor's financial information, which is often not forthcoming in controlled firms, where the management (appointed by controlling shareholders) do not view their interests as being aligned to the creditors. In a DIP regime, it is critical for there to be an avenue for the creditors to obtain a minimum set of information early in the process so that they can form an assessment as to the economic viability of the debtor before being able to take steps to terminate the restructuring attempts. Confidence can be built if creditors see that their interests are protected through voting restrictions by the controlling shareholders (who are also creditors). These controls can be drawn from the rich literature on corporate governance: (1) controlling shareholders who manipulate the vote by purchasing debt should not be in the same class; (2) controlling shareholders who are also creditors and are treated differently should not be in the same class as other creditors; and (3) having a limited means to allow the shareholders to have a say in the outcome. A valuation is also required so that creditors can determine the alternatives to the restructuring. The point as to valuation comes up in Proposition 2 below.

Proposition 2: If it is desired for a cross-class cram-down to reduce hold-out behaviour by junior creditors and shareholders, there is no one-size-fits-all rule as to the conditions pursuant to which this may be exercised. In particular, the absolute priority rule (APR) that is used in the US Chapter 11 imposes costs in jurisdictions with controlling shareholders. However, there is considerably less justification to depart from the APR to cram-down junior creditors (as distinct from shareholders).

There are several benefits to having a cross-class cram-down to reduce hold-out behaviour. However, any restructuring tool that is proposed to be introduced or modified must be carefully examined as to the benefits and trade-offs that would apply in the particular jurisdiction. This Proposition and Proposition 3 deal with the various restructuring tools.

A cross-class cram-down regime has the benefits of overcoming hold-out junior creditors and shareholders which unduly delay the completion of the restructuring and preventing the distribution of the assets of the debtor. In order to exercise the cross-class cram-down, US Chapter 11 imposes, among others, the following requirements: adherence to APR; that the plan does not discriminate unfairly and the plan is in the 'best interests' of creditors. However, an APR that crams down controlling shareholders will leave shareholders disincentivised to work towards the restructuring, and their support may often be required in the circumstances set out in Proposition 1. It should be noted that even if the cram-down is not actually utilised, the creditors and shareholders bargain under the shadow of the law.

Thus, it is not surprising that jurisdictions with the ability to cram down classes of dissenting creditors, such as Singapore, Mainland China and India, do not adhere to the US version of the APR. The Singaporean version of the APR has more stringent requirements on creditor approval (as compared to Chapter 11) and allows the controlling shareholders to have a right to vote on the restructuring if the restructuring involves a debt–equity swap or any kind of issuance of shares. The Mainland Chinese version does not explicitly require the APR though the Supreme People's Court has repeatedly emphasised that cram-downs should be sparingly exercised, and in 2018 imposed further conditions on how the cram-down powers are to be exercised, that is, at least one of the classes has voted for the plan, and the dissenting votes in each class are entitled to not less than what they would have received under the liquidation. The Chinese experience show that cram-downs which were much more common among listed company reorganisations pre-2015 decreased significantly after 2015. There are also other ways to effect a de facto cram-down through the controlling shareholders transferring their shares to the new investors for no consideration (even though they are not wiped out in a cram-down). India allows for the cram-down of the operational creditors by financial creditors, subject to the dissenting financial creditors and operational creditors receiving at least the amount that would have been received in liquidation.

In selecting the appropriate conditions for cram-down, instead of the strict APR, it is more realistic to determine the margins in which the deviation from the APR can be tolerated. If the deviations are not material, it should be seen as the price for seeking the approval of the parties as to the restructuring plan. Viewed in this light, there are good reasons to allow small deviations from the APR when what is sought is to cram-down shareholders. However, there are few justifications to allow deviation from the APR when it comes to the cram-down of junior creditors who do not contribute in the same way as controlling shareholders.

Valuation is the key to the exercise of the cram-down powers since the creditors and valuation is an inherently controversial exercise, and different valuers can come to different conclusions, even if the same methodologies are used. Even between the US and the UK, different valuation methods are used, with the UK using the market-based method (being the going-concern sale or the liquidation analysis depending on the appropriate comparator if the plan does not succeed) and the US using the standard valuation methodologies (such as the discounted cash flow methodology). Further, there is variation as to what the valuers attest in respect of the valuation and whether the valuation report is made available to creditors (in Singapore and Mainland China, the valuation report in the context of schemes of arrangement and the plan respectively is not automatically included in the documents to creditors). If the assumptions and methodologies are not made available, there is little basis for creditors to challenge the valuation. Thus, it is critical that the process as to how the valuation is to be arranged be clarified and be made available to creditors.

Proposition 3: When dealing with widely held debt and a restructuring that implicates a wide range of creditors:

(A) In within-class cram-downs, the restructuring regime should ensure that only creditors within the same class should be treated equally and deviations must be strongly justified. As in the case of Proposition 2, it is important that creditors receive information in a timely manner and the committee of creditors be properly institutionalised. It is not proposed that fiduciary or equivalent duties are imposed on the creditors to ensure that they maximise the value of the assets or in some other manner.

Following from Proposition 2, Proposition 3 deals with the main restructuring tools that jurisdictions have adopted or are considering to adopt in their framework. Chapter four demonstrates that in the absence of specific and mandatory rules, the debtor companies in Asian jurisdictions are often reluctant to disclose material financial information to the creditors early in the process. This information asymmetry impacts the weakly adjusting creditors, and leads to the signal that outside creditors are not sufficiently protected in the restructuring regime.

When it comes to voting and the formulation of correct classes, this is admittedly the most controversial as can be seen in the divergence among the four Asian jurisdictions. Singapore schemes of arrangement require that creditors whose rights are the same (even if the interests differ) be put in the same class. The debtor is free to conduct schemes of arrangement that exclude operational or trade creditors who continue to be paid in full and who continue to supply the goods. However, the others show more variation, and non-adjusting creditors and retail unsecured investors are often vulnerable since unless they are trade creditors they cannot negotiate for better distribution. Even in Hong Kong, which adheres to the English approach that creditors whose rights (and not interests) are the same should be put in the same class, the courts have tolerated some deviation from equality of treatment. For instance, restructuring support agreements that pay a small amount of consent fee to certain creditors only has been as not to fracture the class. In Mainland China, differential treatment of small creditors and non-financial creditors has been sanctioned by the courts. In India, the decision of the requisite majority of the committee of creditors (comprising financial creditors) will be binding, even if the creditors determine the same treatment for all financial creditors without regard for the relative value of their collateral, and the dissenting creditor cannot then recover more under the liquidation value. The Indian regime also places the non-adjusting creditors in a vulnerable position.

There are good reasons to require that only creditors whose rights are similar be in the same class for the purposes of voting. If there is any departure, the justifications must be on the basis that it is more efficient to do so. For example, it can be argued that small creditors should be paid in full because it is more expedient not to include them in the bargaining process. In the case of India, if the financial creditors have different recoveries based on the value of the collateral, they should not be placed class for the entire debt. There should not be differentiation between financial and non-financial creditors as the differentiation will only shift the debate as to who is a financial creditor. Restructuring support agreements that allow for payments of additional fees may be allowed so long as they are for relatively small amounts, and a bright-line rule should be drawn. To require the courts to determine in each case whether the additional fees will fracture the class will be costly.

In addition, to impose fiduciary duties on creditors to exercise their votes in a certain manner is not recommended as it can only lead to confusion and more satellite litigation. For the same reasons, is it not recommended that there be a positive duty on the part of the creditors to maximise the value of the assets.

(B) A stay of proceedings is important to bring the creditors together to negotiate over the outcome of the restructuring. However, if it is desired to have an automatic stay, it needs to be implemented under the following conditions: (1) the regime effectively enforces directors' duties to take into account creditors' interests (see Proposition 7); and (2) there is close monitoring over the automatic stay (whether through a PIP, mandatory disclosure regime, enhanced court scrutiny or the time-bound nature of

the stay). The ban on ipso facto *clauses, however, is much more complex and the trade-offs need to be carefully examined.*

Where there is a diversity of creditors and the restructuring implicates not only the financial but also the operational creditors, and where even the financial creditors are not homogenous, it becomes challenging for the creditors to agree on a resolution plan. As such, the value of a stay of proceedings enables all the creditors to come to the negotiation table. However, for the stay to work effectively, without it merely being a means to delay creditors' enforcement, the following issues needs to be addressed in the framework: (1) whether the debtor and/or creditor can access the stay mechanism; (2) the duration of the stay; and (3) the oversight of the stay.

The experience of the Asian jurisdictions which have the stay reveal the following lessons. First, if the debtor can access the stay mechanism and remains in possession, the stay operates in effect as a DIP proceeding. In Hong Kong, the experiment to adapt the process of the soft-touch liquidation process for companies incorporated in offshore jurisdictions in order to recognise these proceedings with a view of obtaining a stay of proceedings (in Hong Kong) has unfortunately led to abuses. In some cases that have been decided by the courts, the management does not utilise the stay to propose a viable restructuring plan but instead as a means to delay the winding-up petition. The problem is also compounded by the fact that directors' duty to take into account creditors' interests are often under-enforced in Hong Kong. In Singapore, two restructuring attempts after the 2017 reforms resulted in lengthy stays (exceeding two years) through repeated applications for extension of the moratorium by the debtor. It is clear that the framework is laudable to promote restructuring, but the parties may lack the urgency to resolve the matter speedily, so safeguards need to be put in place to disincentivise the debtor from dragging its feet.

Second, even if there is close monitoring through an insolvency practitioner, the stay needs to be strictly time-bound and enforced. In India, the drafting or the IBC made it clear that it was strictly time-bound but even then, the courts have allowed for extensions. In general, if the matter is left to the common law courts to determine the length of the stay, the courts do have a pro-debtor tendency to manage the process while the company undergoes reorganisation because it is often not possible to tell whether the debtor is viable unless the situation clearly indicates that the debtor is stalling for time. The data for Chinese restructurings also show that the time spent in restructuring exceeds the nine-month period set out in the restructuring law. Hence there needs to be strict limits on the stay.

Ipso facto clauses are more complex, and to allow the ban on *ipso facto* clauses may promote of the objectives of reorganisation but undermine freedom of contract. Any decision to address *ipso facto* clauses will need to be carefully considered in light of the trade-offs and may further exacerbate concerns over delays posed by these challenges.

(C) Rescue financing is an important restructuring tool-kit for the debtor to address its under-investment problem, but the decision to allow rescue financing to receive any kind of elevated priority must be tailored to the problem and not merely amount to a transfer of wealth from the creditors to the DIP lender.

As to rescue financing, prima facie, there are several benefits in introducing a new method of pre-petition financing. For example, in Singapore and Hong Kong where secured debt that is taken often comprises the fixed charge over tangible assets and floating charges over the entire undertaking, it is unlikely that many assets will be left unencumbered for which the debtor is able to raise further financing to run its operations. Likewise, in Mainland China, given that the secured debt is likely to include a charge over the property and the receivables, and it is unlikely that many assets will be left unencumbered. Yet, if a project is stalled but is commercially viable and only a small loan is required to complete the project, it makes commercial sense for the debtor to access such loan. A firm which is in financial distress and cannot raise further debt will have to forego profitable opportunities, also known as the under-investment problem.

In the absence of legislation introducing priority to post-petition loans, the elevation of the priority of such loans will require the consent of the existing creditors and, in particular, the secured creditors, if priming is sought. If the lenders comprise a small number of bank lenders only, it is relatively easy to negotiate with the lenders to convince them as to the merits of granting priority for new money. It is far more difficult to negotiate with a large group of syndicated lenders and with large numbers of bondholders.

Rescue or DIP financing comes in several forms, ranging from priming of secured debt to granting priority ahead of the unsecured debts or as an administrative expense. Thus far, based on the limited Singapore experience, which provides for a rescue financing regime closest to Chapter 11, the lender may get priority by lending on a roll-up basis. The difficulty with roll-up financing is that it elevates the priority of existing creditors who are willing to provide such finance, but it does not otherwise solve the debtor's under-investment problem. In addition, if there is no established market for such financing, it is difficult to judge whether the rescue financing in question is obtained on the most favourable terms. Rescue financing is also likely to adversely impact the non-adjusting creditors, who are unable to offer roll-up financing. For these reasons, India and Mainland China allow for DIP financing but in much more limited circumstances. Nevertheless, rescue financing is in itself a useful tool when operational restructuring is required and is used beyond roll-up financing.

Proposition 4: Where the jurisdiction is addressing high levels of non-performing loans (NPLs) that threaten the stability of the banking sector, the use of asset management companies or equivalent and the development of distressed debt markets generate their own separate agency and coordination costs which need to be minimised for market-based restructuring to take place.

In India and China, one of the solutions to deal with the jurisdiction's high NPL is to use asset reconstruction companies (in India) or asset management companies (in Mainland China) to purchase the NPLs from the banks and to restructure the debt. By concentrating the financial debt at an early stage, presumably to one which has the expertise and has its own timeframe to resolve the NPL, the coordination costs among the creditors should theoretically reduce. However, the Indian experience has been that various incentives have to be put in place to incentivise the asset-reconstruction companies to actually resolve the NPLs. The sale of the NPLs, particularly for public sector banks, normally take place well after the corporate insolvency resolution process (CIRP) commences, which does not suggest that they play a significant role early in the process, though there are indications that the regulatory pressure from the RBI has pushed for earlier disposals.

The regulatory framework of asset management companies can generate their own constraints that give rise to frictions. For instance, in India, the asset resolution companies cannot be resolution applicants and bid for the assets. Also, the NPLs in both China and India concentrate on a wide variety of assets including manufacturing and not merely real estate, which make the resolutions more challenging since assets that are restructured comprise not only the real estate (where management is less relevant) but manufacturing plants, which require competent management.

The ownership structures of the asset management companies, which are private ownership in India (except for the recent bad bank set up in 2021) and state ownership in Mainland China, will also impact on the outcome of the resolution of these NPLs. In Mainland China, the asset management companies themselves, being state-owned, face legacy issues on implicit guarantees. The financial distress that is currently facing China Huarong and the uncertainty as to whether there is a state bail-out symbolises the pervasive impact of the implicit guarantees, even as China is transitioning into a market economy. These asset management companies can also take advantage of the fact that they can get loans favourably, which raise the question as to whether they have incentives to manage the NPLs prudently.

Proposition 5: Insolvency practitioners serve important reputation intermediary roles between the debtor and the creditors, but their roles can be undermined by lack of accountability, conflicts of interest, or failure to obtain information from the debtor. In certain cases, such as when the insolvency profession is being established, there is a case for a bright-line rule over the appointments that they can undertake.

In PIP or hybrid regimes, the insolvency practitioners play important reputation intermediary roles between the company and its creditors in the restructuring. The insolvency practitioner plays a role in the rescue strategies, through formulating or putting the plan before the creditors for their determination, and facilitates the negotiations among the creditors over the distribution of the assets. The scale of involvement will depend on the regime, including whether there is a power of sale of the assets granted to the insolvency practitioner or a hard APR, which will require the creditors to bargain over not only the deployment of assets, but also the distribution.

However, the effectiveness of the insolvency practitioner may be undermined by lack of accountability to the creditors, conflicts of interests or plainly being unable to carry out his/her tasks due to the non-cooperation by the debtor. In particular, irrespective of how the insolvency practitioners are appointed by the court, primary accountability has to be to the creditors. To mitigate the conflict of interests, there is a case for a more interventionist approach. Where the insolvency practitioners are in the state of professionalising, a bright-line rule is preferable, including the prohibition of appointments where they have previously acted for the debtor, the prohibition of success fees of the kind that set them at odds with the creditors' interests, and arrangements that favour particular creditors' interests over others. Non-cooperation will have to be dealt with through incentivising the management to work with the insolvency practitioners. If these issues can be addressed and mitigated, other improvements may be able to take place to devolve greater power to the insolvency practitioner, including the power to effect sale of the assets to non-related parties, which will greatly reduce the amount of time that the debtor spends in restructuring.

Proposition 6: The regime in placing the court as a final gatekeeper over the outcome of the restructuring will have to balance between certainty/predictability and flexibility. This balancing act includes placing strict limits on the length of the proceedings (and often the length of the moratorium), and allowing adaptive devices by market participants when faced with the lacunae in the restructuring framework.

Assuming that there is high judicial competence in hearing restructuring cases, the role of the court will be to balance between certainty and predictability in the outcome (often giving effect to creditors' decisions in the absence of procedural defects), whilst offering some flexibility in dealing with situations that cannot be resolved with bright-line rules. Courts have handled judicial innovations including restructuring support agreements and have been adept in ensuring that class compositions are used to ensure that minority creditors are not trampled over. However, there remain certain limitations in the court as the final gatekeeper over the outcome of the restructuring. Common law courts in Singapore, India and Hong Kong (at least in earlier cases) tend to give the benefit of doubt to the debtor management in determining how the restructuring would take place, which includes giving them leeway over their requests for the stay and extensions. Care needs to be taken to ensure that there is no abuse. When the plan is being confirmed, the courts give effect to the creditors' decision, but vigilance is required when related party creditors seek to influence the outcome of the votes. In Mainland China, the practice of the courts similarly shows their ability in adapting to new innovations, such as pre-packaged or pre-negotiated restructurings. As the national goals of the national restructuring law changes to one that is far more market-driven, the courts have also demonstrated that they can pivot to such changes through the use of guiding principles.

Proposition 7: The choice of the jurisdiction's optimal insolvency and restructuring regime will depend on the enforcement of contractual rights and enforcement of directors' duties in corporate law.

Finally, any reform to the jurisdiction's insolvency and restructuring regime can only take place alongside consideration as to its enforcement of contractual rights and directors' duties. If the restructuring regime is used as a substitute for debt collection, a major concern will be that it then uses up scarce judicial time and allows for delays. It also modifies the coordination and agency costs between the secured and unsecured creditors and between the creditors and shareholders. Likewise, if entrance into the insolvency and restructuring regime leads to a substantially less favourable outcome for secured creditors than enforcement (as appears to be the case for Mainland China), the secured creditors are less likely to support the use of the restructuring regime.

More generally, there are benefits in the directors of debtor companies addressing the problems early. There is a limit in making the restructuring regime favourable to the debtor, and consideration needs to be given to the best 'stick' with which to nudge or compel the directors to invoke the process early. This 'stick' lies in the form of the enforcement of directors' duties; when the company is in financial distress, directors should consider the interests of the creditors. The lack of effective enforcement of directors' duties at varying levels will likewise create a shortage of incentives for the debtor to invoke the restructuring process early.

9.3. FUTURE PROSPECTS FOR REFORM IN THE ASIAN JURISDICTIONS

In this section, I discuss the prospects of the main areas of reform that are discussed in the current debates in the four Asian jurisdictions as well as the suggestions for how the restructuring framework may be improved.

9.3.1. Mainland China

The EBL remains a work in progress. Much has been achieved since it came into force in 2007, and the EBL has been adapted through the years as Mainland China shifts in its economic policies and priorities and as the markets change. Given that the reorganisation regime in the EBL is a transplant from Chapter 11 (albeit with modifications), the existing literature has a tendency to look to the US to resolve any problems. As this book demonstrates, Chapter 11 mitigates the agency and coordination costs between shareholder–creditor and creditor–creditor conflicts, and these costs are very different outside the US. This book has been written at a time of significant policy shifts towards increasing the usage of the EBL and adopting market-based methods for restructuring, especially in the highly visible onshore bond market. At the time of writing, consultations are ongoing for reforms to the EBL which are stated to be tabled in 2021 pursuant to the legislative plan.[1] The Standing Committee of the National People's Congress organised an inspection team in the first half of 2021 to study the practice of bankruptcy in certain provinces and made several findings as to bankruptcy law in practice, similar to those outlined in this book, including the low usage of the EBL, the relatively long process of bankruptcy proceedings and the antecedent costs involved.[2]

Based on the reports mentioned in the paragraph above, it is expected that market-based reforms will increasingly provide the exits for financially distressed companies (including SOEs) and to dispose NPAs in an orderly manner. The mounting levels of bond defaults and non-performing assets (NPAs) will provide the

[1] X Guan and D Peng, 'Promoting Bankruptcy Work to Ensure Development' [依法推进企业破产工作 助力高质量发展] *Zhongguorenda* [中国人大] (8 September 2021).

[2] H Tao, 'Promote the Better Implementation of Bankruptcy Law' [依法推动企业破产制度更好实施] *People's Daily* [人民日报] (13 August 2021) (setting out the summary of study by the inspection team appointed by the Standing Committee of the National People's Congress).

impetus for their management through market-based methods.[3] The amount of onshore bonds in default (excluding those that have been extended) has gone up from RMB156.5 billion (US$25 billion) in 2019 to RMB175.8 billion (US$28 billion) in 2020.[4] In the first half of 2021 alone, the value of bonds in default was RMB116 billion (US$18 billion). These figures are much larger than the defaults in 2016, where the aggregate amount was RMB38.9 billion (US$6 billion). COVID-19 will continue to have an adverse impact on the defaults; while Mainland China may have controlled the pandemic well, there remains repeated outbreaks and the need for lock-downs which will adversely impact businesses. Thus, the pursuit of market-based reforms to the EBL is more urgent than ever.

In terms of reforms, the more urgent priorities will be to increase the usage of the EBL and to better utilise the array of tools for debt restructuring and managing exits of unviable companies through a combination of out-of-court restructuring and the EBL. In both situations, increasing certainty and predictability in the outcomes of the EBL process is critical, and this will require giving substantive content to the scope of the duties that the market participants are under, given the relative brevity of the EBL provisions. At the same time, it would be a mistake to assume that the Chapter 11 solutions will work if transplanted into Mainland China. Much will turn on the bottoms-up analysis of why the problems have arisen and how each tool in the bankruptcy toolkit can be utilised to address the problem.

In giving effect to certainty and predictability as to the outcomes and improving the governance of restructuring, this book argues that there are six main areas that need to be addressed. First, the involvement of the state in the reorganisation process, whether directly in the form of providing rescue or through the administrator (also known as liquidation groups), has to be clarified. Assuming the hybrid PIP/PIP regime is retained, it is suggested that such bail-outs and rescues take place outside the EBL. A related issue is the disposal of the NPLs to the asset management companies being required to take place on market principles. Second, the process of obtaining creditors' approval for the deployment of assets, including class composition, abstention of voting and disclosure regimes to the creditors needs to be strengthened. Third, the conditions for which cram-down (and the associated APR) will need to be enforced, which closely ties in with how assets of the debtor should be valued.

Fourth, as the insolvency practitioners become more professionalised, the selection of the administrator should be based on market principles. Fifth, time-bound reorganisation proceedings will also aid in the certainty of the process. Sixth, if it is desired that the management of the company drives the process of restructuring where there is no fraud, there needs to be enforcement of directors' duties to take into account the interests of the creditors. If it is not desired to amend the corporate governance framework, there needs to be some deterrent to ensure that the directors carry out their duties through a wrongful trading regime.

[3] P Murugaboopathy and A Galbraith, 'China's corporate bond defaults touch a record high' Bloomberg (9 July 2021).

[4] Data from WIND database.

9.3.2. India

As at 1 October 2021, the IBC has been in operation for five years. There is no question that the IBC constitutes an enormous game-changer in the restructuring landscape, both in terms of improving recovery to creditors and changing the behaviour of the promoters. The huge improvement of India in the now defunct World Bank rankings on resolving insolvency has been celebrated in India. Parliament has been very responsive by amending the IBC on six occasions in the last five years. In August 2021, the Standing Committee on Finance published the 'Report on Implementation of Insolvency and Bankruptcy Code – Pitfalls and Solutions' (2021 Report),[5] which was presented to Lok Sabha and Rajya Sabha, the lower and upper houses of India's Parliament respectively on 3 August 2021. The 2021 report contains an outline of the achievements of the IBC and the required reforms to ensure that the goals of the IBC continue to be met.

First, there was considerable concern over the low recovery rates by financial creditors with haircuts in certain cases as much as 95 per cent,[6] and the delay in the resolution of the cases beyond 180 days (more than 71 per cent). It was suggested that there should be benchmark on the haircut. Second, there should be a code of conduct for the committee of creditors to ensure the accountability of their decisions and transparency in the process. Third, reforms are required to enforce the timelines set out in the IBC, including the admission of cases, strictly prohibiting post-bid bidders to emerge and reducing the constant litigation. Fourth, there should be some flexibility to allow the resolution applicants to bid for selected assets, as opposed to the entire business. Fifth, there should be self-regulation of resolution professionals, as is the case for chartered accountants.

All the reforms mentioned in the preceding paragraph, except for the self-regulation of resolution professionals, are controversial and relate to matters that are discussed in the earlier chapters of the book. First, it is not clear how the benchmark of the haircut will be useful in constraining the floor of haircut tolerated in the various types of restructuring. While the recoveries of secured creditors were previously published by the World Bank's *Doing Business* reports, it is not clear that setting a hard benchmark has any benefit. At best, it could reflect that creditors were anticipating one or more of the following if the creditors vote for a high haircut: the high costs of the restructuring process (indicating high transaction costs); loss in time value of money due to prolonged delay; or even a recognition that the financial creditors have failed to have been prudent in their lending. It is not clear why creditors, who act in accordance with their own interests, would vote for a high haircut unless they do not believe that they would have a better outcome in a liquidation. Second, the proposed

[5] Standing Committee on Finance, 'Report on the Implementation of Insolvency and Bankruptcy Code – Pitfalls and Solutions' (2021), available at www.ibbi.gov.in/uploads/whatsnew/fc8fd95f0816ac-c5b6ab9e64c0a892ac.pdf.

[6] It is not entirely clear from the report as to which are the types of cases that result in the haircut of 95%, but it appears that there is considerable range of haircut since the IBBI data shows an average of 48.2% recovery for financial creditors for 2019. See ch 4, section 4.4.2.1.

code of conduct for creditors is now published by IBBI.[7] While the code of conduct has laudable aims, in light of the various complaints that the committee of creditors may not have acted in good faith,[8] it is not clear how such a code is enforceable or that it would not lead to unnecessary litigation.

Third, delays in the resolution have posed to be a significant problem. However, the problems do not only lie in the three identified areas, namely, admission of cases, post-bid resolution applicant conduct and constant litigation. In the earlier chapters, the book identifies several other causes of delays. They include the high number of attempts by promoters to reassert control over the process and their failure to cooperate with the resolution professional. Promoters litigate frequently and if they refuse to cooperate with the resolution professional, they are often not taken to task. Further, the lower courts sometimes do not uphold the decision of the committee of creditors and necessitating an appeal, leading to a lack of certainty and predictability. The role of the asset reconstruction companies, which have until recently been privately sponsored, also need to be clarified since they constitute likely resolution applicants.[9] With the new addition of the 'bad bank' that is backed by the state to resolve the NPAs in India,[10] the role of the asset reconstruction companies becomes even more significant.

Beyond the 2021 Report, given India's history with promoters, it seems unlikely that there would be any pivot to a DIP regime. However, it is suggested that some reconsideration be given to the ban under section 29A on promoters from bidding for the assets as the current system does not incentivise the promoters to work with the resolution professionals, unless they have themselves given personal guarantees and their assets are personally at risks. If it is not proposed to make any change and promoters continue to be barred, there is a case for expediting the process to allow the committee of creditors to determine only the issue of deployment, and the distribution of the assets should follow the APR.

Finally, on the role of the committee of creditors, the intention is to afford them the ultimate decision-making process, subject to judicial review only as to the process. Creditors will focus on their recovery and will value speed and certainty. However, the incentives of the creditors that make decisions are not perfect since they will favour their own interests rather than the interests of the creditors as a whole. There is less objection if the financial creditors are in similar positions so that they can sensibly consult with one another – the approach taken in the schemes of arrangement. However, even on their economic interests alone (and excluding extraneous interests such as cross-holdings in other classes of debt), the financial creditors differ. Secured creditors who find that their security is undervalued vote alongside with creditors

[7] See also IBBI, Discussion Paper (21 August 2021), available at ibbi.gov.in/Discussionpaper-CIRP-27Aug2021.pdf.

[8] ibid. The questionable behaviour of the committee of creditors (comprising financial creditors) outlined included, among others, colluding with ineligible promoters, improper payments to the professional fees of lenders, and pressurising the resolution professional to make distributions.

[9] RBI has now published a separate set of recommendations on the asset reconstruction companies. See Postscript to ch 5 (discussing RBI, 'Report of the Committee to Review the Working of Asset Reconstruction Companies' (September 2021)).

[10] B Beniwal, 'India to Give New Bad Bank $4.2 Billion Sovereign Guarantee' Bloomberg (16 September 2021).

who are over-collaterised. The financial creditors are in no way obliged to consider the interests of operational creditors' who are subject to cram-down. The result is that if the committee of creditors, by the majority, decides not to consider the differences in how much security covers the debt, the dissenting secured creditors will not be able to take the liquidation value as a fall-back. Also, financial creditors are also able to cram down the operational creditors, and only limited safeguards are given to the operational creditors, a point that was raised in the representation by the Federation of Micro and Small & Medium Enterprises in the 2021 Report, but not directly addressed in the recommendations. These are unlikely to be matters that can be resolved by a code of conduct for creditors.

9.3.3. Hong Kong

At the time of writing, the proposed provisional supervision and corporate rescue bill, first raised in 1996, is intended to be tabled before the Legislative Council.[11] The draft bill has not been made publicly available and the discussions in this section will be based on the published proposals submitted by the Financial Services and Treasury Bureau to the Legislative Council.[12] The bill has a long and chequered history, and has previously met resistance at several levels, including from the labour unions. Nevertheless, even if the bill is passed, the restructuring framework remains primarily an out-of-court process and the tools that are available under the framework are limited, given that only the company can propose the entry into the corporate rescue and the consent of the major secured creditor is required for the rescue. The bill also proposes an insolvent trading framework that coexists with the proposed provisional supervision and corporate rescue, addressing the concern of the directors as to whether they can continue trading while restructuring takes place.[13]

In the absence of a formal rescue framework, outside of an out-of-court restructuring regime, the primary tool is the scheme of arrangement, which is modelled after the English scheme of arrangement. Insolvency practitioners have adapted to the lack of a moratorium or breathing space through either putting companies into provisional liquidation under the Companies (Winding Up and Miscellaneous Provisions) Ordinance[14] (if they are Hong Kong companies) or through the soft-touch liquidation process (if they are companies incorporated in the offshore jurisdictions) and seeking the recognition orders in Hong Kong. Neither model is perfect in addressing the lack of a formal moratorium in the legislation. The case law has held that provisional liquidation cannot be used solely for restructuring, though there is some relaxation of the rule if the assets are in jeopardy (which are the traditional grounds

[11] Financial Services and Treasury Bureau, 2020, 'Legislative Council, Panel on Financial Affairs, Legislative Proposals of the Companies (Corporate Rescue Bill) and Annex: Companies (Corporate Rescue) Bill: Details of Major Legislative Proposals', available at www.legco.gov.hk/yr20-21/english/panels/fa/papers/fa20201102cb1-48-3-e.pdf.

[12] ibid.

[13] SHC Lo, 'Proposal For Insolvent Trading Laws in Hong Kong: A Comparative Analysis' (2020) 7 *Journal of International and Comparative Law* 229.

[14] Cap 32.

for seeking a provisional liquidation order),[15] and recent cases indicate that the courts are more wary of using soft-touch liquidation to delay the enforcement of a debt in Hong Kong.[16]

Otherwise, in the absence of a statutory moratorium, the debtor has to seek a standstill contractually, which can be time-consuming from the debtor management's perspective, as the management seeks to negotiate with each and every creditor. A standstill is not practical when there are several creditors whose interests diverge greatly. As argued in chapter two, since the 2000s, as is the case in the UK, distressed funds became active in Hong Kong and their approach towards restructuring diverges from the banks, which are repeat players. In the mid-2010s, the large-scale restructurings of many debtors, including Kaisa, Winsway and Mongolian Mining, involved bondholders. The US practice of bond restructuring, such as the use of restructuring support agreements, has been imported to Hong Kong, and the bondholders who are in a better bargaining position would demand for the various consent fees and work fees demanded in exchange for restructuring support.

Further, the current approach provides neither carrots nor sticks to incentivise directors of the debtor (or their controlling shareholders) to seek help early in the process. More generally, if restructuring tools are added, creditors will need to be assured that the debtor will be safeguarded from directors or controlling shareholders that seek to gamble on resurrection or engage in tunnelling.

With changes in the financial markets and the diversification of debt-holdings, and the imperfect substitutes to a formal moratorium, it is increasingly clear that a lack of a moratorium will be a major impediment. Even if Hong Kong chooses to continue in its secured creditor-friendly approach, a statutory moratorium will be useful, but there needs to be controls to ensure that the moratorium is strictly time-bound (so as not to have unduly long moratoriums), and/or mandating disclosure of financial information. No doubt certain types of companies have appeared before the Hong Kong courts that are not suitable for a moratorium. In the case where capital that is raised in Hong Kong but entirely used for operating subsidiaries outside of Hong Kong (and particularly in Mainland China), these may not be good reasons for a restructuring. The offshore creditors are structurally subordinated to the creditors of the operating subsidiaries and are unlikely to be able to recover from these assets. As Harris J puts it in *China Bozza Development Holdings*, what is sought in these cases is merely the realisation of listing status for the benefit of the new investor in exchange for the new investor repaying some of the debt, and these are not cases for which the moratorium is suitable.[17]

Finally, in genuine cases of financial and operational restructurings, there is some indication that these companies, while having their listing or operations in Hong Kong, may seek to change the centre of main interest (COMI) to seek a restructuring in the UK or the US (depending on the law governing the underlying debt), such

[15] *Re Legend International Resorts* [2006] 2 HKLRD 192; *Re China Solar Energy* [2016] HKCU 465; *Re China Solar Energy Holdings Ltd* [2017] 2 HKLRD 1074; *Re China Solar Energy Holdings Ltd* [2018] HKCU 938.

[16] See discussion in ch 7, section 7.3.1.2.

[17] *Re China Bozza Development Holdings Ltd* [2021] HKCFI 1235.

as the restructuring of Noble Group in 2018. The reasons for forum shopping are often complex. However, there are in fact good reasons for the restructurings of these companies to take place in Hong Kong, which is the place of fundraising, the COMI and where the creditors are familiar with Hong Kong. It is the fundamental premise of UNCITRAL Model Law for Cross-border Insolvency (though it is noted that Hong Kong is not a signatory) that the COMI should govern questions relating to the distribution of the assets. Hence it is important for the existing restructuring framework in Hong Kong to be modernised to include some of the essential tools such as a moratorium.

Insofar as the cross-class cram-down or pre-packs are concerned, these tools are more difficult to implement in jurisdictions with concentrated shareholdings. As the Singapore example demonstrates, there may be good reasons not to insist on the US version of absolute priority rule in cross-class cram-downs. Pre-packs or pre-negotiated restructurings will exacerbate the agency costs between shareholders and creditors if the assets are sold to the original controlling shareholders.

9.3.4. Singapore

The 2017 reforms have introduced important changes to the restructuring landscape. The reforms have been carefully adapted from the restructuring practice in the US and the UK. Further tweaks continue to occur. For instance, in 2020, IRDA was amended to introduce a temporary simplified debt restructuring programme for micro, small and medium enterprises (MSMEs) to address the fall-out from COVID-19, where only one application to the court is required instead of two, and a lower threshold (two-thirds in value) is put in place.[18]

The data discussed in chapter seven shows that the 2017 reforms relating to the stay of proceedings filed in connection with the scheme of arrangement and the pre-packaged schemes of arrangement have had higher usage as compared with the other reforms. As at the time of writing, there no case of a cross-class cram-down and there are not many applications yet for priority treatment under the rescue financing. While the implementation of the 2017 reforms may have raised some areas of uncertainty or implementation challenges, Parliament and the courts are quick to address these issues, including making the clarificatory changes when the 2017 reforms, first enacted via amendments to the Companies Act 2006, were migrated to the omnibus insolvency framework in IRDA. The courts have also issued guidance in case law relating to the applications for extension of moratorium and a guide. Even though the debtor is required to show evidence of creditor support (where the scheme is proposed) or support for the moratorium (if there is intention to propose the scheme), and presumably the creditors would demand for information prior to giving support, the case law demonstrates that debtors are unwilling to disclose their information early in the process, even at the stage of leave to convene scheme meeting. What will merit reconsidering is tweaks to the system, including a robust external monitoring to require directors to take into account the interest of the creditors during the period of the

[18] Insolvency, Dissolution and Restructuring (Amendment) Act 2020.

stay and requiring early disclosure of information as to debtor so that the creditors can quickly determine whether the proposal is viable. As to the former, one possibility is to have the insolvency practitioner appointed by the creditors to monitor the stay and to make regular reports to the creditors.

One of the reasons for the lack of use of the cross-class cram-down could lie in the approval threshold, which not only requires the approval of a class of creditors but also a super-majority of 75 per cent in value of all of the claims. As the Chapter 11 reforms to the scheme of arrangement gain wider acceptance in Singapore, it may be time to relax this super-majority requirement, while retaining the rest of the safeguards, including its version of the APR and non-discrimination test.

Finally, in advancing towards the goal of becoming a restructuring hub, there are merits in building an infrastructure that will attract distressed fund investment and other lenders willing to lend in wider circumstances to companies in financial distress, and where it makes commercial sense. In situations where the assets of the debtors are fully secured, there are no free assets, and the debtor has a large number of creditors, obtaining consent is often very costly. The framework for according priority for rescue financing is an important tool, particularly since the schemes of arrangement in Singapore implicate not only financial but also operational restructuring. However, in the implementation that relies on judicial oversight, it is critical that the conferment of the elevated priority of the new financing must demonstrably solve the under-investment problem of the debtor.

9.4. CONCLUSION

The aim of the book is to set out a framework of analysing the restructuring laws in four economically significant Asian jurisdictions which have recently either reformed or are considering reforming, their corporate restructuring laws to promote regimes conducive to restructuring financially distressed but otherwise economically viable companies. These jurisdictions continue to adhere to a framework that requires the courts' approval but draw references from Chapter 11 of the Bankruptcy Code 1978 in the US and/or the schemes of arrangement in the UK. However, the institutional and market structures are very different in Asia; in particular, Asia has far higher concentration in shareholdings among listed firms, including holdings by families and the state, and a different composition of creditors. This book explains how, notwithstanding the legal transplantation, corporate restructuring laws in the four Asian jurisdictions have adapted and evolved due to the frictions in the manager–creditor, shareholder–creditor and creditor–creditor relationships, and the role of the state in resolving non-performing loans and financial distress of state-owned enterprises which are listed or which issue public debt. In particular, the financial markets are also undergoing a number of changes, with greater diversity of debt-holdings and the institutional make-up of the creditors. Mainland China and India are grappling with high levels of NPAs, which need to be resolved to ensure stability in prudential lending, and restructuring laws can provide some, though not all, of the tools. The gatekeepers, being the insolvency practitioners and the courts, have also adapted and evolved alongside the changes in the financial markets. More changes are likely to be expected as economies deal with the fall-out from COVID-19. While the wave of insolvency filings has not sky-rocked in the four Asian jurisdictions, likely as a result of the economic policies that each of the jurisdictions have put in place to cushion the support and protect jobs, ensure access to financing and liquidity, and in certain instances, restrict the filing of insolvency petitions, it is anticipated that restructurings we will see in the next few years will be complex, both financially and operationally. Any further reforms must address fundamental issues of corporate governance, bank regulation and enforcing contractual rights and directors' duties in practice.

Finally, the contrast and the solutions adopted in the four Asian jurisdictions have considerable relevance for emerging jurisdictions, not only in Asia, but in other parts of the world where shareholding concentration remains the norm. Reformers often assume that the Anglo-American approach (which is in itself divergent) is the way to manage bankruptcy reforms, and reforms are often driven by the now discontinued World Bank *Doing Business* rankings. This book demonstrates that the US and the UK approaches are not invariably the best strategies as they were first designed with dispersed shareholdings in mind and in a different institutional context. Even then, the approaches have to be adapted in view of changes in the financial markets. The story of modern restructuring law reform is not that different from the Asian stories – as national objectives change, so the approaches towards restructuring laws will need to change. Reformers and lawmakers need to understand that reforms to adopt specific tools must consider the benefits and trade-offs specific to the jurisdiction.

Appendices

APPENDIX A

Panel A

Listed Mainland China onshore corporate bond defaults 2015–19 with completed reorganisations

Name of issuer (in English)	Name of issuer (short form, in Chinese)	Year of first default	Status of issuer
Dalian Machine Tool Group Co, Ltd	大连机床集团	2016	Non-SOE
Dongbei Special Steel Group Co, Ltd	东北特殊钢集团	2016	SOE
Dandong Port Group Co, Ltd	丹东港集团	2017	Non-SOE
Shandong Jinmao Textile Chemicals Co, Ltd	金茂纺织	2018	Non-SOE
Shandong Sea Group Co, Ltd	大海集团	2018	Non-SOE
Bright Oceans Co, Ltd	亿阳集团	2018	Non-SOE
Qinghai Salt Lake Industry Co, Ltd (also listed company)	青海盐湖	2019	SOE
Shenyang Machine Tool Co Ltd (also listed company)	**沈机股份**	2019	SOE
Shenyang Machine Tool (Group) Co, Ltd	沈机床	2019	SOE
Pang Da Automobile Trade Co, Ltd (also a listed company)	庞大	2019	Non-SOE
Shandong Shengtong Group Co, Ltd	胜通集团	2019	Non-SOE
Yinyi Co Ltd	银亿股份	2019	Non-SOE

Sources: Data collected from WIND database (as of 1 January 2021), Disclosure Platform; Fitch Bond Data, 2019 (Fitch Ratings, 'China Corporate Bond Market Blue Book'), available at www.fitchratings.com/research/corporate-finance/china-corporate-bond-market-blue-book-03-11-2019.

Panel B

Listed Mainland China company reorganisations 2015–19

Name of issuer (English)	Name of Issuer (short form, in Chinese)	Year of filing	Status of issuer
Jiangsu Sainty Marine Co Ltd	舜船	2015	SOE
Guizhou Guochang Energy Holding (Group) Co Ltd	新亿	2015	Non-SOE
Shenzhen Xindu Hotel Co Ltd	新都	2015	Non-SOE
Yunnan Yunwei Company Ltd	云维	2016	SOE
Chuanhua Co Ltd	川化	2016	SOE
Sichuan Liutianhua Company Ltd	天化	2017	SOE
Liuzhou Chemical Industry Co Ltd	柳化	2017	SOE
Chongqing Iron and Steel Company Ltd	重钢	2017	SOE
Fushun Special Steel Co	抚顺特钢	2018	Non-SOE
Ningxia Zhongyin Cashmere Limited	中绒	2018	Non-SOE
Shanxi J&R Optimum Energy Co Ltd (now Baoli New Energy Technology)	坚瑞沃能	2018	Non-SOE
Yinyi Co Ltd	银亿	2019	Non-SOE
Qinghai Salt Lake Industry Co Ltd	盐湖	2019	SOE
ST XGMA Machinery Company Limited	厦工	2019	SOE
Lotus Health Group Company	莲花	2019	Non-SOE
Shenyang Machine Tool (Group) Co Ltd	沈机	2019	SOE
DEA General Aviation Holding	德奥	2019	Non-SOE
Shenzhen Feiman International Supply Chain Co Ltd	飞马	2019	Non-SOE
Liyuan Precision Manufacturing	利源	2019	Non-SOE
Chenzhou City Jingui Silver Industry Co Ltd	金贵	2019	SOE
Pang Da Automobile Trade Limited	庞大	2019	Non-SOE

Sources: Data collected from WIND and National Enterprise Bankruptcy Information Disclosure Platform, available at pccz.court.gov.cn/pcajxxw/index/xxwsy.

APPENDIX B

Panel A

12 large accounts initiated by banks as directed by RBI in 2017

Debtors	Status
Essar Steel India Limited	Resolved
Monnet Ispat & Energy Ltd	Resolved
Bhushan Steel Limited	Resolved
Alok Industries Limited	Resolved
Electrosteel Steels Limited	Resolved
Jyoti Structures Limited	Resolved
Bhushan Power and Steel Limited	Resolved
Jaypee Infratech Limited	Resolved
Amtek Auto Limited	Resolved
Era Infra Engineering Ltd	Under CIRP
Lanco Infratech Limited	Under liquidation
ABG Shipyard Ltd	Under liquidation

Source: Data collected from IBBI newsletter (September to December 2020) (status as at 31 December 2020), available at ibbi.gov.in/publication and Debtwire.

Panel B

CIRPS resolved as at 31 March 2021

Debtors	Completion year
Chhaparia Industries Pvt Ltd	2017
Hotel Gaudavan Pvt Ltd	2017
Shirdi Industries Limited	2017
Sree Metaliks Limited	2017
Synergies – Dooray Automotive Limited	2017
West Bengal Essential Commodities Supply Corporation Limited	2017
Admiron Life Sciences Pvt Ltd	2018
Arcee Ispat Udyog Ltd	2018
Assam Company India Limited	2018
Basai Steels and Power Pvt Ltd	2018
Bhadravathi Balaji Oil Palms Ltd	2018
Bhushan Steel Limited	2018

(continued)

(Continued)

Debtors	Completion year
Binani Cement Limited	2018
BJN Hotels Ltd	2018
Burn Standard Company Ltd	2018
Concord Hospitality Pvt Ltd	2018
Datre Corporation Ltd	2018
Divya Jyoti Sponge Iron Pvt Ltd	2018
Dooteriah & Kalej Valley Tea Estate Pvt Ltd	2018
Electrosteel Steels Limited	2018
Frontline Printers Pvt Ltd	2018
Garg Inox Ltd	2018
Haldia Coke and Chemicals Pvt Ltd	2018
Jalan Intercontinental Hotels Pvt Ltd	2018
Kalptaru Alloys Pvt Ltd	2018
Kalyanpur Cements Ltd	2018
Keti Highway Developers Pvt Ltd	2018
Kitply Industries Ltd	2018
Kohinoor CTNL Infrastructure Company Pvt Ltd	2018
Malabar Hotels Pvt Ltd	2018
Mandhana Industries Limited	2018
Manor Floatel Ltd	2018
Marmagoa Steel Limited	2018
MBL Infrastructure Limited	2018
Mohan Aromatics Pvt Ltd	2018
Monnet Ispat & Energy Ltd	2018
MOR Farms Pvt Ltd	2018
NSR Steels Pvt Ltd	2018
Nutri First Agro International Pvt Ltd	2018
Orissa Manganese & Minerals Limited	2018
Palogix Infrastructure Pvt Ltd	2018
Paragon Steels Pvt Ltd.	2018
Quality Rice Exports Pvt Ltd	2018
Quantum Ltd	2018
Raj Oil Mills Ltd	2018
Rajpur Hydro Power Pvt Ltd	2018
Rave Scans Pvt Ltd	2018
Recorders and Medicare Systems Pvt Ltd	2018

(continued)

(Continued)

Debtors	Completion year
Rishi Ganga Power Corporation Ltd	2018
S M M Steel Re-Rolling Mills Pvt Ltd	2018
Southern Cooling Tower Pvt Ltd	2018
Stesalit Ltd	2018
Sun Paper Mill Ltd	2018
The Sirpur Paper Mills Ltd	2018
Trinity Auto Components Ltd	2018
Universal Power Tranformers Pvt Ltd	2018
Vangal Amman Health Services Ltd	2018
Ved Cellulose Ltd	2018
Wig Associates Pvt Ltd	2018
Yashraaj Ethanoll Processing Pvt Ltd	2018
A&I Hospitality Private Limited	2019
Adhunik Alloys & Power Limited	2019
Albus India Limited	2019
Allied Strips Limited	2019
Ambey Constructech Pvt Ltd	2019
Ambey Iron Pvt Limited	2019
Amit Spinning Industries Ltd	2019
AML Steel and Power Ltd	2019
Anand Distilleries Pvt Ltd	2019
Apex Drugs Ltd	2019
Applied Electro Magnetics Pvt Ltd	2019
ARGL Limited	2019
Aristo Texcon Pvt Ltd	2019
Aryavart Chemicals Pvt Ltd	2019
Asis Plywood Limited	2019
Aster Building Solutions Pvt Ltd	2019
BCIL Red Earth Developers India Pvt Ltd	2019
BCIL Zed Ria Properties Private Limited	2019
Beans and More Hospitality Pvt Ltd	2019
Bhushan Energy Limited	2019
BSR Diagnostics Ltd	2019
Calyx Chemicals & Pharmaceuticals Ltd	2019
Dadi Impex Pvt Ltd	2019
Deccan Chronicle Holdings Limited	2019

(continued)

(Continued)

Debtors	Completion year
EMC Limited	2019
EPC Constructions India Private Limited	2019
Essar Steel India Limited	2019
Fenace Auto Ltd	2019
Fort Gloster Industries Limited	2019
Fortune Pharma Pvt Ltd	2019
Indus Fila Limited	2019
IVRCL Limited	2019
Jaihind Infra Tech Projects Private Limited	2019
Jyoti Structures Limited	2019
Khandoba Prasanna Sakhar Karkhana Ltd	2019
Lanco Teesta Hydro Power Limited	2019
Maharashtra Shetkari Sugar Limited	2019
Maiyas Beverages and Foods Private Limited	2019
Marsons Ltd	2019
Maruti Koatsu Cylinders Ltd	2019
Maxim Infrastructure & Real Estate Private Limited	2019
Merchem Limited	2019
MIC Electronics Ltd	2019
Miditech Pvt Ltd	2019
Murli Industries Ltd	2019
Naachair Paper Boards Pvt Ltd	2019
Network Industries Limited	2019
Olive Lifescience Pvt Ltd	2019
Paramshakti Steels Limited	2019
Pro Minerals Private Limited	2019
Rainbow Papers Limited	2019
Ramsarup Industries Limited	2019
Ruchi Soya Industries Limited	2019
Sai Wardha Power Generation Limited	2019
Say India Jewellers Pvt Ltd	2019
Scotts Garments Limited	2019
Sevenhills Healthcare Private Limited	2019
Shaifali Rolls Limited	2019
Sharon Bio-Medicine Limited	2019
Shrid Metal Technologies Private Limited	2019

(continued)

(Continued)

Debtors	Completion year
Solidaire India Limited	2019
SPS Steels Rolling Mills Limited	2019
Sri Srivathsa Paper Mills Ltd	2019
Star Agro Marine Exports Private Limited	2019
Subburaj Spinning Mills Pvt Ltd	2019
Sunil Ispat & Power Ltd	2019
Swadisht Oil Pvt Ltd	2019
Tiffins Barytes Asbestos & Paints Ltd	2019
United India Shoe Corporation Private Limited	2019
Uttam Strips Limited	2019
Vardhman Industries Ltd	2019
Vidharbha Iron and Steel Corporation Limited	2019
Vishwakarma Real Estate & Constructions Pvt Ltd	2019
Viz Infra Consultants Private Limited	2019
A Power Himalayas Ltd	2020
Adhunik Metaliks Limited	2020
Alok Industries Limited	2020
Amtek Auto Limited	2020
Cosmic Ferro Alloys Ltd	2020
Ferro Alloys Corporation Limited	2020
GVR Infra Projects Limited	2020
Haryana Steel & Alloys Limited	2020
Jaypee Infratech Limited	2020
JEKPL Private Limited	2020
Noble Explochem Limited	2020
Orchid Pharma Limited	2020
PRC International Hotels Pvt Ltd	2020
SRS Meditech Limited	2020
United Seamless Tubulaar Pvt Ltd	2020
Zion Steel Limited	2020
Bhushan Power and Steel Limited	2021
Dighi Port Limited	2021
Uttam Galva Metallics	2021
Uttam Value Steels Limited	2021

Sources: Data collected from IBBI newsletters 2016–21, available at ibbi.gov.in/publication; NCLT and NCLAT judgments, Debtwire.

APPENDIX C

Hong Kong schemes of arrangement 2015–20

Company	Year of commencement of filing
Da Yu Financial Holdings Limited	2015
Kaisa Group Holdings Limited	2016
Winsway Enterprises Holdings	2016
Mongolian Mining Corporation	2017
China Singyes Solar Technologies Holdings Limited	2019
China Lumena New Materials Corp	2019
Union Asia Enterprise Limited	2019
Hsin Chong Aster Building Services	2020

Sources: Hong Kong case law, filings from SEHK; Perfect Information; information agents for bond restructurings.

APPENDIX D

Singapore schemes of arrangement 2015–20

Company	Year of commencement of filing
Swee Hong Limited	2015
Serrano Limited	2016
Jason Holdings Limited	2016
Nam Cheong Limited (formerly Eagle Brand Holdings Limited)	2017
Hoe Leong Corporation Limited	2017
Marco Polo Marine Ltd	2017
Serrano Limited	2018
TT International Limited	2019
Capital World Limited	2020
Asiatravel.com	2020
Viking Offshore and Marine	2020
PT MNC Investama Tbk	2020

Source: Dataset of cases for 2015–19 are obtained from the dataset in WY Wan, C Watters and G McCormack, 'Schemes of Arrangement in Singapore: Empirical and Comparative Analysis' (2020) 94 *American Bankruptcy Law Journal* 463; cases in 2020 obtained from filings from Singapore Exchange, Perfect Information, press articles.

Bibliography

Acharya, VV, Eisert, T, Eufinger, C and Hirsch, C, 'Real Effects of the Sovereign Debt Crisis in Europe: Evidence from Syndicated Loans' (2018) 31 *The Review of Financial Studies* 2855.

Adler, BE, 'Bankruptcy and Risk Allocation' (1992) 77 *Cornell Law Review* 439.

—— 'Game-Theoretic Bankruptcy Valuation' (2012) 41 *The Journal of Legal Studies* 209.

Adler, BE and Capkun, V, 'Debt-Equity Conflict and the Incidence of Secured Credit' (2019) 62 *The Journal of Law & Economics* 551.

Adler, BE, Capkun, V and Weiss, LA, 'Value Destruction in Chapter 11' (2013) 29 *The Journal of Law, Economics and Organization* 461.

Aghion, P, Hart, O and Moore, J 'The economics of bankruptcy reform' (1992) 8 *Journal of Law Economics and Organization* 523.

Aiyar, S, Bergthaler, W, Garrido, JM, Ilyina, A, Jobst, A, Kang, KH, D, Kovtun, Liu, Y, Monaghan D and Moretti, M, 'A Strategy for Resolving Europe's Problem Loan' [2015] IMF Staff Discussion Note 15/19, Washington: International Monetary Fund.

Allen & Gledhill, 'The Requirements of Feasibility for Moratorium Applications Under Insolvency Restructuring Dissolution Act' (18 March 2021), available at www.allenandgledhill.com/sg/publication/articles/17894/the-requirement-of-feasibility-for-moratorium-applications-under-the-new-insolvency-restructuring-and-dissolution-act.

Altman, EI, 'A Further Empirical Investigation of the Bankruptcy Cost Question' (1984) 39 *The Journal of Finance* 1067.

Altman, EI and Benhenni, R, 'The Anatomy of Distressed Debt Markets' (2019) 11 *Annual Review of Financial Economics* 21.

American Bankruptcy Institute, 'Commission to Study the Reform of Chapter 11: Final Report and Recommendations' (2012–14).

Amstad, M and He, Z, 'Chinese Bond Market and Interbank Market' [2019] NBER Working Paper 25549.

Andrade, G and Kaplan, SN, 'How Costly Is Financial (Not Economic) Distress? Evidence From Highly Leveraged Transactions That Became Distressed' (1998) 53 *Journal of Finance* 1443.

Armour, J and Lele, P, 'Law, Finance, and Politics: The Case of India' (2009) 43 *Law & Society Review* 491.

Armour, J and Mokal, RJ, 'Reforming the Governance of Corporate Rescue: the Enterprise Act 2002' (2005) 1 *Lloyd's Maritime and Commercial Law Quarterly* 28.

Armour, J and Skeel, DA, 'Who Writes the Rules for Hostile Takeovers, and Why? – The Peculiar Divergence of U.S. and U.K. Takeover Regulation' (2007) 95 *The Georgetown Law Journal* 1727.

Armour, J, Black, B, Cheffins, B and Nolan, R, 'Private Enforcement of Corporate Law: An Empirical Comparison of the United Kingdom and the United States' (2008) 6 *Journal of Empirical Legal Studies* 687.

Armour, J, Cheffins, BR, Skeel, DA, 'Corporate Ownership Structure and the Evolution of Bankruptcy Law: Lessons from the United Kingdom' (2002) 55 *Vanderbilt Law Review* 1699.

Armour, J, Deakin, S, Sarkar, P, Mathias, S and Singh, A, 'Shareholder Protection and Stock Market Development: An Empirical Test of the Legal Origins Hypothesis' (2009) 6 *Journal of Empirical Legal Studies* 343.

Armour, J, Hertig, G and Kanda, H, 'Transaction with Creditors' in R Kraakman, J Armour, P Davies, L Enriques, H Hansmann, G Hertig, K Hopt, H Kanda, M Pargendler, W Ringe and E Rock, *The Anatomy of Corporate Law: A Comparative and Functional Approach*, 3rd edn (Oxford, OUP, 2017) 109.

Armour, J, Hsu, A and Walters, A, 'The Impact of the Enterprise Act 2002 on Realisations and Costs in Corporate Rescue Proceedings: A Report Prepared for the Insolvency Service' (December 2006).

Armour, J, Jacobs, J and Milhaupt, C, 'The Evolution of Hostile Takeover Regimes in Developed and Emerging Markets: An Analytical Framework' (2011) 52 *Harvard International Law Journal* 219.

Austin, DA and Lin, C, 'Bankruptcy with Chinese Characteristics: Insolvency Administration in the People's Republic of China' (2020) 94 *American Bankruptcy Law Journal* 85.

Australian Government, Treasury, 'Review of the Insolvent Trading Safe Habour: Consultation Paper' (2021).

Ayotte, K and Yun, H, 'Matching Bankruptcy Laws to Legal Environments' (2007) 25 *Journal of Law, Economics & Organization* 2.

Ayotte, KM and Morrison, ER, 'Creditor Control and Conflict in Chapter 11' (2009) 1 *The Journal of Legal Analysis* 511.

Azar, ZR, 'Bankruptcy Policy: An Empirical Investigation of 50 Jurisdictions Worldwide' (2008) 82 *The American Bankruptcy Law Journal* 407.

Baird, DG, 'Bankruptcy's Quiet Revolution' (2017) 91 *The American Bankruptcy Law Journal* 593.

—— 'Loss Distribution, Forum Shopping, and Bankruptcy: A Reply to Warren' (1987) 54 *The University of Chicago Law Review* 815.

—— 'Priority Matters: Absolute Priority, Relative Priority, and the Costs of Bankruptcy' (2017) 165 *University of Pennsylvania Law Review* 785.

—— 'The Uneasy Case for Corporate Reorganizations' (1986) 15 *Journal of Legal Studies* 127.

Baird, DG and Bernstein, DS, 'Absolute Priority, Valuation Uncertainty, and the Reorganization Bargain' (2006) 115 *The Yale Law Journal* 1930.

Baird, DG and Jackson, TH, 'Corporate Reorganizations and the Treatment of Diverse Ownership Interests: A Comment on Adequate Protection of Secured Creditors in Bankruptcy' (1984) 51 *The University of Chicago Law Review* 97.

Baird, DG and Rasmussen, RK, 'Anti-bankruptcy' (2009) 119 *Yale Law Journal* 648.

—— 'The End of Bankruptcy' (2002) 55 *Stanford Law Review* 751.

Baird, DG, Casey, AJ and Picker, RC, 'The Bankruptcy Partition' (2018) 166 *University of Pennsylvania Law Review* 1675.

Bandyopadhyay, T, 'Bad Debts to Break: Challenges, Achievements of Indian's Insolvency Law' *Business Standard* (20 February 2019).

Baudino, P, Orlandi, J and Zamil, R, 'FSI Insights on Policy implementation No 7: The Identification and Measurement of Nonperforming Assets: A Cross-Country Comparison' (Bank For International Settlements, 2018).

Bebchuk, LA, 'A new approach to corporate reorganizations' (1988) 101 *Harvard Law Review* 775.

—— 'Ex Ante Costs of Violating Absolute Priority in Bankruptcy' (2002) 57 *The Journal of Finance* 445.

Beddow, S, Carter, D and Lewis, A, 'Private Equity Buyouts: An Overview' Practical Law for Companies, available at uk.practicallaw.thomsonreuters.com/6-518 0998?transitionType=Default&contextData=(sc.Default)&firstPage=true.

Beniwal, V, 'India to Give New Bad Bank $4.2 Billion Sovereign Guarantee' Bloomberg (16 September 2021), available at www.bloomberg.com/news/articles/2021-09-16/india-to-give-new-bad-bank-4-2-billion-sovereign-guarantee.

Berkovitch, E, and Israel R, 'Optimal Bankruptcy Laws across Different Economic Systems' (1999) 12 *Review of Financial Studies* 347.

Bhagwati, J, Shuheb, KM and Bogathi, RR, 'Can Asset Reconstruction Companies (ARCs) be Part of the Indian Debt Problem?' (2007) Working Paper 338, Indian Council for Research on International Economic Relations, available at tile.loc.gov/storage-services/service/gdc/gdcovop/2018305088/2018305088.pdf

Block-Lieb, S and Halliday, TC, 'Harmonization And Modernization In UNCITRAL's Legislative Guide On Insolvency Law' (2007), available at papers.ssrn.com/sol3/papers.cfm?abstract_id=965710#.

Bloomberg, 'China Port Defaulter's Bankruptcy Ruling Stirs Up a Storm' *Bloomberg News* (14 January 2020),

—— 'Rich Singapore Investors Stuck as Local Bond Restructuring Drags' *Straits Times* (reprinting from Bloomberg) (25 July 2017).

—— 'This Clause in Noble's Restructuring Plan is Raising Concern' *The Business Times* (7 March 2018).

Bradley, M and Rosenzweig, M, 'The Untenable Case for Chapter 11' (1992) 101 *Yale Law Journal* 1043.

Bratton, WW and Levitin, AJ, 'The New Bond Workouts' (2018) *166 University of Pennsylvania Law Review* 1597.

Bricongne, JC, Demertzis, M, Pont'uch, P and Turrini, A, 'Macroeconomic Relevance of Insolvency Frameworks in a High-Debt Context: An EU Perspective' (European Commission Discussion Paper 32, 2016) available at ec.europa.eu/info/publications/economy-finance/macroeconomic-relevance-insolvency-frameworks-high-debt-context-eu-perspective_en.

Brumagim A and Wu, X, 'An Examination of Cross-Cultural Differences in Attitudes towards Risk: Testing Prospect Theory in the People's Republic of China' (2005) 13 *Multinational Business Review* 67.

Business Today.In, 'DHFL Bidding: CoC Declares Piramal as Successful Bidder' *Business Today* (21 January 2021).

Bussel, D, 'The Problem with Preferences' (2014) 100 *Iowa Law Review Bulletin* 11.

Calomiris, CW, Klingebiel, D and Laeven, L, 'Seven Ways to Deal with a Financial Crisis: Cross-Country Experience and Policy Implications' (2012) 24 *Journal of Applied Corporate Finance* 8.

Casey, AJ, 'The Creditors' Bargain and Option-Preservation Priority in Chapter 11' (2011) 78 *University of Chicago Law Review* 759.

Casey, AJ and Zaveri, B, 'Is the IBC unfair to operational creditors?' *Business Standard* (7 August 2019).

CGTN, '2020: Chinese banks dispose $467b in non-performing assets' *CGTN* (22 January 2021).

Chatterjee, S, Shaikh, G and Zaveri, B, 'An Empirical Analysis of the Early Days of the Insolvency and Bankruptcy Code, 2016' (2018) 30 *National Law School of India Review* 89.

Cheffins, BR and Armour, J, 'The Eclipse of Private Equity' (2008) 33 *Delaware Journal of Corporate Law* 1.

Chen, C and Wan, WY, 'Transnational Corporate Governance Codes: Lessons from Regulating Related Party Transactions in Hong Kong and Singapore' (2018) 36 *Chinese (Taiwan) Yearbook of International Law and Affairs* 56.

Chen, C, Wan, WY and Zhang, W, 'Board Independence as a Panacea to Tunneling? An Empirical Study of Related-Party Transactions in Hong Kong and Singapore. Transactions in Hong Kong and Singapore' (2018) 15 *Journal of Empirical Legal Studies* 987.

Chen, LS, 'Asset Management Companies Participating in Restructuring Regimes' [金融资产管理公司参与困难企业重组实践] (2015) 10 *Zhejiang Finance* [浙江金融] 15.

Chen, R, 'Legal Informality and Human Capital Development in China' in BL Liebman and CJ Milhaupt (eds), *Regulating the Visible Hand: The Institutional Implications of Chinese State Capitalism* (Oxford, OUP, 2016) 151–74.

Cheng, C, 'Are the Chinese Really More Risk Averse? A Cross-Cultural Comparison of the Risk-Return Relationship' (2009) 20 *Journal of Global Business Management* 37.

Cheung, Y, Rau, P and Stouraitis, A, 'Tunneling, Propping, and Expropriation: Evidence from Connected Party Transactions in Hong Kong' (2006) 82 *Journal of Financial Economics* 343.

Chief China Economist's Office of Hong Kong Exchanges and Clearing Limited, 'Credit Event of Offshore Chinese State-related Issuers and their Onshore Support' (January 2021), available at www.hkex.com.hk/-/media/HKEX-Market/News/Research-Reports/HKEx-Research-Papers/2021/CCEO_BondDefault_202101_e.pdf?la=en.

China Banking News Editor, 'China Disposed of 2 Trillion Yuan in Bad Loans in 2019: CBIRC' *China Banking News* (13 January 2020).

China Local Asset Management Companies Industry, 'China's Local Asset Management Companies White Paper 2020' [中国地方资产管理行业白皮书] (August 2020), available at news.alphalio.cn/PDF/%E4%B8%AD%E5%9B%BD%E5%9C%B0%E6%96%B9%E8%B5%84%E4%BA%A7%E7%AE%A1%E7%90%86%E8%A1%8C%E4%B8%9A%E7%99%BD%E7%9A%AE%E4%B9%A6%EF%BC%882019%EF%BC%89-2020.8-123%E9%A1%B5.pdf.

Choong, TC, 'Judicial Management in Corporate Insolvency' (1988) 30 *Malaya Law Review* 259.

Claesens, S, Djankov, S and Mody, A (eds), Resolution of Financial Distress: An International Perspective on the Design of Bankruptcy Laws (World Bank Publications, 2001).

Coffee, JC, 'Gatekeeper Failure and Reform: The Challenge of Fashioning Relevant Reforms' (2004) 84 *Boston University Law Review* 301.

'Corporate Bond Issues Mark New Era for Hong Kong Retail Market' [2003] *International Financial Law Review* 1.

Courts and Tribunals Judiciary, 'Practice Statement (Companies: Schemes of Arrangement under Part 26 and Part 26A of the Companies Act 2006)', available at www.judiciary.uk/publications/practice-statement-companies-schemes-of-arrangement-under-part-26-and-part-26a-of-the-companies-act-2006.

Crane, LD, Decker, RA, Flaaen, A, Hamins-Puertolas, A and Kurz, C, 'Business Exit During the COVID-19 Pandemic: Non Traditional Measures in Historical Context', Finance and Economics Discussion Series 2020-089r1 (Board of Governors of the Federal Reserve System, 2021), available at doi.org/10.17016/FEDS.2020.089r1.

Cruz, A, Medina, A and Tang, Y, 'Owners of the World's Listed Companies' [2019] OECD Capital Market Series.

Dai, JM, 'Who is Directing the Reorganisation' [谁在主导破产重整] World Economics [世纪经济] (29 October 2016), available at m.21jingji.com/article/20161029/37ef03923ac6e9b5a13fbec0b988f7c6.html (in Chinese).

Davydenko, SA and Franks, JR, 'Do Bankruptcy Codes Matter? A Study of Defaults in France, Germany, and the U.K.' (2008) 63 *The Journal of Finance* 565.

Delaney, K, *Strategic Bankruptcy: How Corporations and Creditors Use Chapter 11 to Their Advantage* (Berkeley, University of California Press, 1999).

Deloitte LLP, 'Asset Reconstruction Companies: Tax and Regulatory Framework' (2019) Debriefs, available at www2.deloitte.com/content/dam/Deloitte/in/Documents/tax/in-tax-asset-reconstruction-companies-tax-regulatory-framework-noexp.pdf.

'Deleveraging Asia', Financial Advisory (2019), available at www2.deloitte.com/content/dam/Deloitte/sg/Documents/finance/sea-fa-restructuring-services-deleveraging-asia-2019.pdf.

—— 'Deleveraging Europe' Financial Advisory (2019), available at www2.deloitte.com/content/dam/Deloitte/uk/Documents/corporate-finance/deloitte-uk-deleveraging-europe-2019.pdf.

Department for Business, Energy & Industrial Strategy (UK), 'Insolvency and Corporate Governance, Government Response' (26 August 2018).

Department Of Justice, 'The Supreme People's Court's Opinion on Taking Forward a Pilot Measure in relation to the Recognition of and Assistance to Insolvency Proceedings in the Hong Kong Special Administrative Region' (14 May 2021), available at www.doj.gov.hk/en/mainland_and_macao/pdf/RRECCJ_opinion_en_tc.pdf.

Dick, DL, 'The Chapter 11 Efficiency Fallacy' (2013) 2013 *Brigham Young University Law Review* 759.

Dickfos, J, 'The Costs and Benefits of Regulating the Market for Corporate Insolvency Practitioner Remuneration' (2015) 25 *International Insolvency Review* 56.

Djankov, S, Hart, O, McLiesh, C and Shleifer, A, 'Debt Enforcement around the World' (2008) 116 *The Journal of Political Economy* 1105.

Dong, T, Zhao, J and Hong, S, 'China Port Defaulter's Bankruptcy Ruling Stirs Up a Storm' *Bloomberg News* (14 January 2020).

Economic Times, 'Operational Creditors Benefit Equally from IBC: IBBI' (9 March 2019), available at economictimes.indiatimes.com/industry/banking/finance/banking/operational-creditors-benefits-equally-from-ibc-ibbi/articleshow/68338344.cms?utm_source=contentofinterest&utm_medium=text&utm_campaign=cppst.

Economic Times Bureau, 'RBI Withdraws CDR, SDR, S4A, JLF Schemes to Restructure Defaulted Loans' (13 February 2018).

Eisenberg, T and Sundgren, S, 'Is Chapter 11 Too Favorable to Debtors? Evidence from Abroad' (1997) 82 *Cornell Law Review* 1532.

Ellias, JA, 'Bankruptcy Claims Trading' (2018) 15 *Journal of Empirical Legal Studies* 772.

Enriques, L, Hertig, G, Kanda, H and Pargendler, M, 'Related Party Transactions' in R Kraakman et al (eds), *The Anatomy of Corporate Law: A Comparative and Functional Approach*, 3rd edn (Oxford, OUP, 2017).

Ernst and Young, 'Evolving Landscape of Corporate Stress Resolution' (December 2019), copy on file with author.

'Essar Steel: NCLT Junks Ruia's Plea' *The Hindu Times* (29 January 2019).

European Commission, 'Commission Staff Working Document: AMC Blueprint' Com (2018) 133, 1–81.

Fan, J, Huang, J and Zhu, N, 'Institutions, Ownership Structures, and Distress Resolution in China' (2013) 23 *Journal of Corporate Finance* 71.

Financial Services and Treasury Bureau, 'Review of Corporate Rescue Procedure Legislative Proposals: Consultation Conclusions' (July 2010), available at www.oro.gov.hk/pdf/eng/announcements/consultation_papers/review_of_corporate_rescue_procedure_legislative_proposals2.pdf.

Financial Services and Treasury Bureau, 'Consultation conclusions of improving corporate insolvency law and detailed proposals for introducing new statutory corporate rescue procedure' (2014), available at www.fstb.gov.hk/fsb/ppr/consult/doc/impcill_consult_conclusion_e.pdf

—— 'Legislative Council, Panel on Financial Affairs, Legislative Proposals of the Companies (Corporate Rescue Bill) and Annex: Companies (Corporate Rescue) Bill: Details of Major Legislative Proposals' (2020) available at www.legco.gov.hk/yr20-21/english/panels/fa/papers/fa20201102cb1-48-3-e.pdf.

Finews Asia, 'A Surprise Inclusion in the Phase one U.S.-China Trade Deal, Oaktree Capital Management Becomes the First Foreign Beneficiary of Liberalized Access to the Mainland's Distressed Debt Market' *Finews.asia* (19 February 2020).

Finch, V, 'Corporate Rescue: a Game of Three Halves' (2012) 32 *Legal Studies* 302.

—— 'Insolvency Practitioners: Avenues of Accountability' (2012) 8 *Journal of Business Law* 645.

Fitch Ratings, 'China Corporate Bond Market Blue Book' (Beijing, A Fitch China Research Initiative Publication, 2019), available at your.fitch.group/rs/732-CKH-767/images/china-corporate-bond-market-blue-book_fitch_10083315.pdf.

—— 'Fitch China Bond Defaults' (10 October 2018).

—— 'Non-Rating Action Commentary – China's First Onshore Bond Exchange Improves Restructuring Path' (16 March 2020), available at www.fitchratings.com/research/corporate-finance/china-first-onshore-bond-exchange-improves-restructuring-path-16-03-2020.

Fletcher, I, 'UK Corporate Rescue: Recent developments – Changes to Administrative Receivership, Administration and Company Voluntary Arrangements – the Insolvency Act 2000, the White Paper 2001, and the Enterprise Act 2002' (2002) 5 *European Business Organization Law Review* 119.

Franks, JR and Torous, W, 'An Empirical Investigation of U.S. Firms in Reorganization' (1989) 44 *The Journal of Finance* 747.

Friedman, M, 'Asian Values: Right' (1997) 49 *National Review (New York)* 36.

—— 'Hong Kong Wrong' *Wall Street Journal* (6 October 2006), available www.wsj.com/articles/SB116009800068684505.

FT Reporters, 'Debenhams in Administration: a Timeline' *Financial Times* (10 April 2019).

Gabriel, A, 'High Court Grants Troubled Hin Leong Judicial Management' *Business Times* (27 April 2020).

—— 'Singapore court gives green light for Swiber to be placed under JM' *Business Times* (8 October 2016).

Gao, S, 'Cramdown, reorganization bargaining and inefficient markets: The cases of the United States and China' [2021] 30 *International Insolvency Review* S5.

Gao, S and Wang, Q, 'The U.S. Reorganization Regime in the Chinese Mirror: Legal Transplantation and Obstructed Efficiency' (2017) 91 *American Bankruptcy Law Journal* 139.

Garrahan, M and Wells, P, 'Johnston Press Agrees Administration Deal with Lenders' *Financial Times* (17 November 2018).

Ghosh, S, 'Corporate Distress, Troubled Debt Restructurings and Equity Stripping' (2018) 8 *South Asian Journal of Business Studies* 105.

Gilson, G, Hotchkiss, E and Ruback, R, 'Valuation of Bankrupt Firms' (2000) 13 *Review of Financial Studies* 43.

Godwin, A, 'Lengthy Stay the Impact of the PRC Enterprise Bankruptcy Law on the Rights of Secured Creditors' (2007) 30 *University of New South Wales Law Journal* 755.

Government of India, Ministry of Corporate Affairs, 'Report of the Sub-committee of the Insolvency Law Committee on Pre-packaged Insolvency Resolution Process' (31 October 2020), available at ibbi.gov.in/uploads/whatsnew/34f5c5b6fb00a97dc4ab752a798d9ce3.pdf.

Gotberg, BE, 'Conflicting Preferences in Business Bankruptcy: The Need for Different Rules in Different Chapters' (2014) 100 *Iowa Law Review* 51.

Guan, X and Peng, D, 'Promoting Bankruptcy Work to Ensure Development' [依法推进企业破产工作 助力高质量发展] *Zhongguorenda* [中国人大] (8 September 2021), available at 依法推进企业破产工作 助力高质量发展_中国人大网 (npc.gov.cn).

Guffy, PM, 'Exempt No More: How New York's Uniform Fraudulent Conveyance Act Threaten Exemptions in bankruptcy' (2015) 80 *Brooklyn Law Review* 1123.

Gullifer, L and Payne, J, *Corporate Finance Law: Principles and Policy*, 3rd edn (Oxford, Hart Publishing, 2020).

Guo X, 'Huang Yun [AMC specialist]: AMCs and Reorganisations' [黄云：新形势下金融资产管理公司参与破产重整的难点及对策] *Zifeng* (1 April 2019).

Gupton, G, Gates, D and Carty, LV, 'Bank – Loan Loss Given Default' (2000) Moody's Investors Service, Global Credit Research 69-92, available at fs.1473.cn/236363a1-2c6b-487e-9dc1-7aa9f216acba.pdf.

Gurrea-Martínez, A, 'The Future of Reorganization Procedures in the Era of Pre-Insolvency Law' (2020) 21 *European Business Organizations Law Review* 829.

Haß, LH, Johan, S and Müller, MA, 'The Effectiveness of Public Enforcement: Evidence from the Resolution of Tunneling in China' (2016) 134 *Journal of Business Ethics* 649.

Hackbarth, D, Haselmann, R and Schoenherr, D, 'Financial Distress, Stock Returns, and the 1978 Bankruptcy Reform Act' (2015) 28 *The Review of Financial Studies* 1810.

Hale, T and White, E, 'Pressure Builds to Resolve Fate of Chinese Bad Debt Manager Huarong' *Financial Times* (29 June 2021).

Halliday, TC and Carruthers BG, *Bankrupt: Global Lawmaking and Systemic Financial Crisis* (Stanford University Press, 2009).

Han, C, 'The Problem of Commercial Banks' Debt for Equity under the Insolvency Law' ['破产法视角下的商业银行债转股问题' (2017) 11 *Law Science* (法学) (in Chinese).

Handa, A, 'An Analysis of the Corporate Insolvency Resolution Process as a Route for Acquisitions' (2020) 29 *International Insolvency Review* 234.

Harner, MM and Marincic, J, 'Committee Capture? An Empirical Analysis of the Role of Creditors' Committees in Business Reorganizations' (2011) 64 *Vanderbilt Law Review* 749.

Hart, O, 'Incomplete Contracts and Control' (2017) 107 *American Economic Review* 1731.

Hart, O, La Porta, R, Lopez-de-Silanes, F and Moore, J, 'A New Bankruptcy Procedure That Uses Multiple Auctions' (1997) 41 *European Economic Review* 461.

—— 'Proposal for a New Bankruptcy Procedure in Emerging Markets' in RM Levich (ed), *Emerging Markets Capital Flows* (Springer US, New York 1997) 401.

Hausch, DB and Ramachandran, S, 'Systemic Financial Distress and Auction-based Bankruptcy Reorganization' (2009) 18 *International Review of Economic and Finance* 366.

He, J, 'Criticism of Guangxi Nonferrous' [广西有色破产点评 – 研发部/何金中] *Shanghai Brilliance Credit Rating & Investors* [上海新世纪资信评估投资服务有限公司] (21 September 2016).

He, LJ and Yuan, M, 'Research on Internet platforms and NPL disposal' [互联网+背景下不良资产业务模式创新研究] (2015) 7 *Internet Finance* [特别聚焦·互联网金融].

He, X. 'A Tale of Two Chinese Courts: Economic Development and Contract Enforcement' (2012) 39 *Journal of Law and Society* 384.

He, Y, Xu, L and McIver, RP, 'How Does Political Connection Affect Firm Financial Distress and Resolution in China?' (2019) 51 *Applied Economics* 2770.

Ho, JKS and Chan, RSY, 'Is Debtor-in-Possession Viable in Hong Kong?' (2010) 39 *Common Law World Review* 204.

Ho, S and Banerjee, SK, 'Indian Bankruptcy Code – How Does It Compare' (2018) 8 *Emerging Markets Restructuring Journal*, available at www.clearygottlieb.com/-/media/files/emrj-materials/issue-8-winter-2018_2019/indian-bankruptcy-codehow-does-it-compare-pdf.pdf.

Ho, S and Marois, T, 'China's Asset Management Companies as State Spatial–Temporal Strategy' (2019) 239 *The China Quarterly* 728.

Hoher, G, 'ESUG: German for "Modernising Bankruptcy Law"' (2012) *Eurofenix* (Spring) 16.

Holderness, CG, 'The Myth of a Diffused Ownership in the United States' (2009) 22 *Review of Financial Studies* 1377.

Hong Kong Monetary Authority, 'Report of the Hong Kong Monetary Authority on Issues Concerning the Distribution of Structured Products Connected to Lehman Group Companies' (2008), available at www.hkma.gov.hk/media/eng/doc/other-information/lehman_report.pdf.

Hong Kong Stock Exchange, 'Consultation Conclusions: Backdoor Listing, Continuous Listing Criteria and other Rule Amendments' (2019), available at www.hkex.com.hk/-/media/HKEX-Market/News/Market-Consultations/2016-Present/June-2018-Backdoor-and-Continuing-Listing/Conclusions-(July-2019)/cp201806cc.pdf?la=en&hash=C0DD7A60622FE2C13EB380DAC231C07EC8953A2A&hash=C0DD7A60622FE2C13EB380DAC231C07EC8953A2A.

—— 'The Rising On-exchange Bond Market in Mainland China and Hong Kong' (September 2020), available at www.hkex.com.hk/-/media/HKEX-Market/News/Research-Reports/HKEx-Research-Papers/2020/CCEO_ExBond_202009_e.pdf?la=en.

HKSAR, 'HKSAR and Mainland Sign Record of Meeting Concerning Mutual Recognition of and Assistance to Insolvency Proceedings (with photos)' Press Release (14 May 2021), available at www.info.gov.hk/gia/general/202105/14/P2021051400219.htm.

Hu, HW and Sun, P, 'What Determines the Severity of Tunneling in China?' (2019) 36 *Asia Pacific Journal of Management* 161.

Hu, T, Lu, Z and Chen, Q, 'A Study of Cinda Asset Management's Restructuring of Guangdong Jiaye Group' [房地产企业破产重整动因与重组经济后果—以信达资产重组嘉粤集团为例] (2021) *China Real Estate* [中国房地] 21.

Hui, R, 'Miclyn Express Offshore Working with SIAS to Engage Bondholders' *The Business Times* (14 November 2017),

Huang, R and Howson, N, *Enforcement of Corporate and Securities Law: China and the World* (Cambridge, Cambridge University Press, 2017).

IBBI and UK Government, 'Handbook on Ethics for Insolvency Professionals: Ethical and Regulatory Framework' (March 2021), available at www.ibbi.gov.in/uploads/whatsnew/0ab3ccba77975afcd9eb7ac679154de8.pdf.

IBBI Disciplinary Committee, Order No IBBI/DC/68/2021 (5 March 2021), available at www.ibbi.gov.in/uploads/order/99021d25ea6922dc843d3c792ef85443.pdf.

INSOL International, 'The New Insolvency and Bankruptcy Code in India: Impact of the Distressed Debt Market' (April 2018), INSOL International Technical Series Issue No 39).

Insolvency and Bankruptcy Board of India, 'Circular – Disclosures by Insolvency Professionals and other Professionals appointed by Insolvency Professionals conducting Resolution Processes' (12 January 2018), available at ibbi.gov.in/webadmin/pdf/legalframwork/2018/Jan/Disclosures-Circular-12.01.2018%20(1)-1_2018-01-16%2018:26:45.pdf.

—— 'Circular on Fee and other Expenses incurred for CIRP' (12 June 2018), available at www.ibbi.gov.in/webadmin/pdf/whatsnew/2018/Jun/Circular%20on%20Fee%20and%20other%20Expenses%20incurred%20for%20CIRP%20[June%202018]_2018-06-18%2014:06:58.pdf.

—— 'Discussion Paper' (21 August 2021), available at ibbi.gov.in/Discussionpaper-CIRP-27Aug2021.pdf.

—— 'Insolvency Professional: A Key to Resolution Information Brochure' (31 March 2021), available at www.ibbi.gov.in/uploads/whatsnew/2021-04-13-163323-pt2ei-a56e6e185a5c5b7e8c7355f7a68f612f.pdf.

—— 'The Report of the Bankruptcy Law Reforms Committee, Volume I: Rationale and Design' (November 2015), available at ibbi.gov.in/BLRCReportVol1_04112015.pdf.

Insolvency and Bankruptcy Board of India and International Finance Corporation, 'Understanding the IBC: Key Jurisprudence and Practical Consideration, A Handbook' (2020), available at ibbi.gov.in/uploads/whatsnew/e42fddce80e99d28b683a7e21c81110e.pdf.

Insolvency Law Reform Committee, 'Report of the Insolvency Law Review Committee: Final Report' (Ministry of Law, 2013), available at www.mlaw.gov.sg/files/news/announcements/2013/10/ReportoftheInsolvencyLawReviewCommittee.pdf.

Insolvency Practitioner Association, Statement of Insolvency Practice 16 (2015), available at insolvency-practitioners.org.uk/uploads/documents/f30389ce35ed923c06b2879fecdb616a.pdf.

International Monetary Fund, 'Selected Issues: People's Republic of China' IMF Country Report No 19/274 (August 2019).

Ivashina, V, Iverson, B and Smith, DC, 'The Ownership and Trading of Debt Claims in Chapter 11 Restructurings' (2016) 119 *Journal of Financial Economics* 316.

Jackson, TH, 'Bankruptcy, Non-Bankruptcy Entitlements, and the Creditors' Bargain' (1982) 91 *Yale Law Journal* 857.

—— *The Logic and Limits of Bankruptcy Law* (Cambridge, MA, Harvard University Press, 1986).

Janger, EJ and Levitin, AJ, 'Badges of Opportunim: Principles for Policing Restructuring Support Agreements' (2018) 13 *Brooklyn Journal of Corporate, Financial and Commercial Law* 169.

Jensen, MC, and Meckling, W, 'Theory of the firm: Managerial behavior, agency costs and ownership structure' (1976) 3 *Journal of Financial Economics* 305.

Jiang, F and Kim, KA, 'Corporate Governance in China: A Modern Perspective' (2014) 32 *Journal of Corporate Finance* 190.

—— 'Corporate Governance in China: A Survey' (2020) 24 *Review of Finance* 733.

Jiang, W, Li, K and Wang, W, 'Hedge Funds and Chapter 11' (2012) 67 *The Journal of Finance* 513.

Keay, A, 'The Shifting of Directors' Duties in the Vicinity of Insolvency' (2015) 24 *International Insolvency Review* 140.

Khaitan and Co, 'All Roads Lead to IBC – RBI Stressed Assets Framework Merges with Debt Resolution under the Insolvency and Bankruptcy Code 2016' (2018) *Lexology*.

Khasawneh, R and Daga, A, 'Banks Accuse Singapore Commodity Trade Agritrade of 'Massive' Fraud' *Reuters* (6 March 2020).

Khosa, A, Ahmed, K and Henry, D, *Ownership Structure, Related-Party Transactions, and Firm Valuation: Evidence from Indian Business Groups* (CUP, Cambridge, 2019).

Kidd, D and Warboys, J, 'Extracting Value for Offshore Creditors Either Side of the Chinese Wall: Restructuring PRC Financing Structures' (2016) 5 *Journal of International Banking & Financial Law* 299a.

Kim, KS, 'Related Party Transactions in East Asia' in L Enriques and T Troger (eds), *The Law and Finance of Related Party Transactions* (Cambridge, CUP, 2019) ch 11.

Klingebiel, D, 'The Use of Asset Management Companies in the Resolution of Banking Crises Cross-Country Experiences' (February 2000), available at /ssrn.com/abstract=282518 or dx.doi.org/10.2139/ssrn.282518.

R Kraakman, J Armour, P Davies, L Enriques, H Hansmann, G Hertig, K Hopt, H Kanda, M Pargendler, W Ringe and E Rock, *The Anatomy of Corporate Law: A Comparative and Functional Approach*, 3rd edn (Oxford, OUP, 2017).

Kraakman, RH, 'Gatekeepers: The Anatomy of a Third-Party Enforcement Strategy' (1986) 2 *Journal of Law, Economics and Organization* 53.

Kumar, D and Sundaresh, G, 'Insolvency Professionals Under India's New Insolvency Regime' (2018) 8 *Emerging Markets Restructuring Journal* 1.

La Porta, R, Lopez-de-Silanes, F and Shleifer, A, 'The Economic Consequences of Legal Origins' (2008) 46 *Journal of Economic Literature* 285.

La Porta, R, Lopez-De-Silanes, F, Shleifer, A and Vishny, RW, 'Law and Finance' (1998) 106 *Journal of Political Economy* 1113.

Lam, F, 'Hyflux says nTan Fees "Fully Justified", Terms from Utico "Best Possible"' *Busniess Times* (5 March 2020).

Lam, NMK, 'Government Intervention in the Economy: A Comparative Analysis of Singapore and Hong Kong' (2000) 20 *Public Administration and Development* 397.

Lam, WR, Schipke, A, Tan, Y and Tan, Z, 'Resolving China's Zombies: Tackling Debt and Raising Productivity' IMF Working Papers (2017) 177.

Law Reform Commission, 'Report on Corporate Rescue and Insolvent Trading' (Hong Kong, Government Printer, October 1996), available at www.hkreform.gov.hk/en/docs/rrescue-e.pdf.

Lee, E, 'The Reorganization Process Under China's Corporate Bankruptcy System' (2011) 45 *The International Lawyer* 939.

Lee, EB, 'Insolvency Law' (2003) 4 Singapore Academic of Law Annual Review of Singapore Cases 263–10.

Lee, J, 'Is Singapore's Insolvency Regime Excessively Pro-creditor' (2003) 12 *International Insolvency Review* 37.

Legislative Council Panel on Financial Affairs, 'Development of the Retail Debt Market in Hong Kong' (7 January 2002), available at www.legco.gov.hk/yr01-02/english/panels/fa/papers/fa0107cb1-716-5e.pdf.

Legislative Council Secretariat, 'Updated background brief on the introduction of a statutory corporate rescue procedure and insolvent trading provisions in Hong Kong' (29 October 2020), available at www.legco.gov.hk/yr20-21/english/panels/fa/agenda/fa20201102.htm.

Lei, P, Luo, Y and Bian J, 'The Evolution of Local AMCs'[当前中国地方AMC高质量发展路径研究] [2020] *Southwest Finance* 69.

Lemmon, ML and Lins, KV, 'Ownership Structure, Corporate Governance, and Firm Value: Evidence from the East Asian Financial Crisis' (2003) 58 *The Journal of Finance* 1445.

Leong, G, 'Embattled Firm Hyflux comes under judicial Management' *Straits Times* (17 November 2020).

—— 'Hin Leong Trading, Once One of Asia's top Oil Traders, to be Wound Up' *Straits Times* (8 March 2021), available at www.straitstimes.com/business/companies-markets/hin-leong-trading-once-one-of-asias-top-oil-traders-to-be-wound-up.

—— 'Hyflux Put Under Judicial Management; Founder Olivia Lum Loses Control Over Firm' *Straits Times* (16 November 2020).

—— 'More than 100 Hyflux Investors Protest at Hong Lim Park' *Straits Times* (31 March 2019).

Leong, H, 'Banks in Crossfire as PwC Plays Hardball' *Lloyd's List* (26 June 2020).

Leroy, A and Grandolini, G, *Principles for Effective Insolvency and Creditor/Debtor Regimes* (Washington, DC,World Bank Group, 2016).

Li, B and Ponticelli, J, *Going Bankrupt in China* (2020) PBCSF-NIFR Research Paper, available at ssrn.com/abstract=3251570.

Li, J, 'Non-Performing Loans and Asset Management Companies in China: Legal and Regulatory Challenges for Achieving Effective Debt Resolution and Recovery' (2013) 1 *PKU Transnational Law Review* 85.

Li, S, 'The Insolvency of the "Zombie Enterprise" through the Insolvency System' [通过破产制度实现"僵尸企业"的破产出清] (2018) 23 *People's Forum* [人民论坛] 98 (in Chinese).

Li, S and Zheng, Z, *Law Review of Corporate Reorganization and Restructuring* [公司重整法律评论：上市公司重整专辑] vol 5 (Beijing, China Law Press [法律出版社], 2019) (in Chinese).

Lin, S, 'The Empirical Studies of China's Enterprise Bankruptcy Law: Problems and Improvements' (2018) 27 *International Insolvency Review* 77.

Lipton, D, 'Rebalancing China: International Lessons in Corporate Debt' (IMF China Economic Society Conference On Sustainable Development in China and the World, Shenzhen, June 2016).

Liu, M and Wei, C, 'Towards a Better Future for Chinese Bankruptcy Law: Problems and Potential' Working Paper No 62 Lau Chor Tak Institute of Global Economics and Finance (2017).

Liu Y, 'Monetary authority pushes back on warning that soaring private-sector debt in Hong Kong could lead to recession' SCMP (22 October 2020).

Lo, SHC, 'Proposal For Insolvent Trading Laws in Hong Kong: A Comparative Analysis' (2020) 7 *Journal of International and Comparative Law* 229.

Lo,SHC and Qu, CZ, *Law of Companies in Hong Kong* (Hong Kong, Sweet Maxwell/Thomson Reuters, 2018).

LoPucki, L and Doherty, JW, 'The Determinants of Professional Fees in Large Bankruptcy Reorganization Cases' (2004) 1 *Journal of Empirical Legal Studies* 111.

LoPucki, LM, 'Strange Visions in a Strange World: A Reply to Professors Bradley and Rosenzweig' (1992) 91 *Michigan Law Review* 79.

LoPucki, LM and Whitford, WC, 'Bargaining over Equity's Share in the Bankruptcy Reorganization of Large, Publicly Held Companies' (1990) 139 *University of Pennsylvania Law Review* 125.

Lubben, S, 'The Overstated Absolute Priority Rule' (2016) 21 *Fordham Journal of Financial and Corporate Law* 5816.

Luo, M and Quan, Y, '"Corrupt Bad Bank Chief Was 'Enemy Within," Watchdogs Say' *Caixin* (21 January 2021).

Ma, G and Fung, BSC, 'China's Asset Management Corporations' [2002] BIS Working Papers No 115 Bank for International Settlements.

Machen, RC, Jones, MT, Varghese, GP and Stark, EL, 'Investigation of Data Irregularities in *Doing Business 2018 and Doing Business 2020* – Investigation Findings and Report to the Board of Executive Directors' (Wilmerhale, 15 September 2021), available at thedocs.worldbank.org/en/doc/84a922cc9273b7b120d49ad3b9e9d3f9-0090012021/original/DB-Investigation-Findings-and-Report-to-the-Board-of-Executive-Directors-September-15-2021.pdf.

Markell, BA, 'Lawyers, Judges and Unwritten Rules' (2020) 36 *Emory Bankruptcy Developments Journal* 719.

McCahill, D and Tracy, A, 'Restructuring Offshore PRC Debt' Skadden Arps Slate Meagher & Flom (2015).

McCormack, G, 'Absolute versus Relative Priority in the Context of the European Restructuring Directive' (2021) 64 *Canadian Business Law Journal* 197.

—— 'Business Restructuring Law in Europe: Making a Fresh Start' (2017) 17 *Journal of Corporate Law Studies* 167.

—— *Corporate Rescue Law – An Anglo-American Perspective (Corporations, Globalisation and the Law)* (Cheltenham, Edward Elgar Publishing, 2008).

—— 'Permanent Changes to the UK's Restructuring and Insolvency Laws in the Wake of COVID 19' INSOL International Special Report (2020).

—— 'Super-Priority New Financing and Corporate Rescue' [2007] *Journal of Business Law* 701.

—— 'Why "Doing Business" with the World Bank May Be Bad for You' (2018) 19 *European Business Organization Law Review* 649.

—— 'The UNCITRAL Model Law on Cross-Border Insolvency Comes of Age: New Times or New Paradigms' (2019) 54 *Texas International Law Journal* 273.

McCormack, G and Wan, WY, 'Transplanting Chapter 11 of the US Bankruptcy Code into Singapore's Restructuring and Insolvency Laws: Opportunities and Challenges' (2019) 19 *Journal of Corporate Law Studies* 69.

McGuinness, PB and Keasey, K, 'The Listing of Chinese State-Owned Banks and Their Path to Banking and Ownership Reform' (2010) 201 *The China Quarterly* 125.

McMahon, D, 'Financial Asset Exchanges: Auctioning Bad Loans to the Masses' Marco Polo (2018).

—— 'Taobao Bad Loan Auctions: What Online Prices Reveal about the NPL Market' Marco Polo (2019).

Mehta, S, 'Conflict of Interest in Resolution Plans may Erode IBC Credibility' *The Economic Times* (5 July 2018).

Miao, C and Liu, H, 'China: Legal Avenues for Foreign Investors to Participate in China's NPL Market' *Mondaq; JunHe Law Office* (3 January 2017).

Miler, HR, 'The Changing Face of Chapter 11: A Reemergence of the Bankruptcy Judge as Producer, Director, and Sometimes Star of the Reorganization Passion Play' (1995) 69 *American Bankruptcy Law Journal* 431.

Milhaupt, C and Pistor, K, 'The China Aviation Oil Episode: Law and Development in China and Singapore' in D Kennedy and JE Stiglitz (eds), *Law and Economics with Chinese Characteristics: Institutions for Promoting Development in the Twenty-First Century* (Oxford Scholarship Online, 2013).

Miller, HR, 'Chapter 11 Reorganization Cases and the Delaware Myth' (2002) 55 *Vanderbilt Law Review* 1987.

Ministry of Corporate Affairs, Press Release, 'IBBI Notifies Regulations for Insolvency Resolution and Bankruptcy Proceedings of Personal Guarantors to Corporate Debtors' (15 November 2019), available at pib.gov.in/Pressreleaseshare.aspx?PRID=1592517.

Ministry of Law, 'Committee to Strengthen Singapore as an International Centre for Debt Restructuring' Report of the Committee (20 April 2016), available at www.mlaw.gov.sg/news/public-consultations/public-consultation-on-the-report-of-the-committee-to-strengthen.

Mo, YK, 'A Review of Recent Banking Reforms' in *Strengthening the Banking System in China: Issues and Experiences*, (Basel, BIS Monetary and Economic Department, 1999).

Modigliani, F and Miller. MH, 'The Cost of Capital, Corporation Finance and the Theory of Investment' (1958) 48 *The American Economic Review* 261.

Mondal, D, 'How IBC Helped Improve India's Ease of Doing Business Rankings' *BusinessToday.In* (24 October 2019), available at www.businesstoday.in/latest/economy-politics/story/how-ibc-helped-improve-india-ease-of-doing-business-rankings-235937-2019-10-24.

Monetary Authority of Singapore, 'Annual Report 2015/2016', available at www.mas.gov.sg/annual_reports/annual20152016/Annual%20Report.pdf.

—— 'CAD, MAS and ACRA Commence Joint Investigation into Hyflux' (2 June 2020), available at https://www.mas.gov.sg/news/media-releases/2020/cad-mas-and-acra-commence-joint-investigation-into-hyflux.

—— 'MAS Takes Civil Penalty Enforcement Action Against China Aviation Oil Holding Company for Insider Trading' (19 August 2005).

Moody's, 'China's New Distressed Bond Market to Boost Liquidity and allow for risk based trading' (31 May 2019).

Morrison, ER, 'Bankruptcy's Rarity: An Essay on Small Business Bankruptcy in the United States' (2008) 5 *European Company and Financial Review* 172.

Morrison, ER and Saavedra, A, 'Bankruptcy's Role in the COVID-19 Crisis' Columbia Law and Economics Working Paper No 624 (7 April 2020), available at ssrn.com/abstract=3567127.

Mrockova, N, *Corporate Bankruptcy Law in China: Principles, Limitations and Options for Reform* (Oxford, Hart Publishing 2021).

Murugaboopathy, P and Galbraith, A, 'China's Corporate Bond Defaults Touch a Record High' Reuters (9 July 2021), available at www.reuters.com/world/china/chinas-corporate-bond-defaults-touch-record-high-2021-07-09.

Nair, V, 'Pending Cases Pile Up at Debt Recovery Tribunals' *Live Mint* (28 August 2015).

—— 'Why RBI Picked These 12 Accounts For Insolvency Action: BQ Explains' *Bloomberg Quint* (17 June 2017), available at www.bloombergquint.com/business/why-rbi-picked-12-stressed-npa-accounts-for-insolvency-bloombergquint-explains.

Narayanan, N, 'A Guide to Special Situations and Distressed Investments in India for International Investors' (2018) 8 *Emerging Markets Restructuring Journal* 1.

—— 'Distressed Debt Investing in India – The Use of Debt Aggregation Vehicles' (2016) 2 *Emerging Markets Restructuring Journal* 6.

Nassiri, A, *The Lending and Secured Finance Review*, 7th edn (The Law Reviews, 2021).

Neemey, P and Sahay, N, 'Indian Corporate Bond Market: An Analysis of Growth and Impact of Macroeconomic Determinants' (2019) 23 *Vision* 244.

Neyens, RL, Samat, DZ, Choi, B, Yang, K and Takagi, S, 'The Successful Asset Management Companies' in M Pomerleano and W Shaw (eds), *Corporate Restructuring: Lessons From Experience* (Washington DC: World Bank, 2005).

'No Guarantees; China's Bond Market' *The Economist* (21 November 2020), available at www.economist.com/finance-and-economics/2020/11/19/chinas-bond-market-is-jolted-by-some-surprising-defaults.

Okazaki, K, 'Banking Reform System in China' RAND Security Research Division (2007), available at www.rand.org/content/dam/rand/pubs/occasional_papers/2007/RAND_OP194.pdf.

Ooi, V, and Tan, CH, 'Singapore Company Law and the Economy: Reciprocal Influence Over 50 Years' (2019) 27 *Asia Pacific Law Review* 14.

Palepu, AR, 'Operational Creditors Recover 42% Of Claims Under IBC, Says ICRA' Bloomberg (19 June 2019), available at www.bloombergquint.com/business/operational-creditors-recover-42-of-claims-under-ibc-says-icra.

Parkin, B and Findlay, S, 'India Bankruptcy Law Faces Vital Test with DHFL Creditor Vote' *Financial Times* (14 January 2021), available at www.ft.com/content/c20e503d-db70-4505-a464-a35b3cdbbc35.

Parry, R and Long, Y 'China's enterprise bankruptcy law, building an infrastructure towards a market-based approach' (2020) 20 *Journal of Corporate Law Studies* 157.

Patel, UR (Governor), 'Resolution of Stressed Assets: Towards the Endgame: Inaugural Session of the National Conference on Insolvency and Bankruptcy: Changing Paradigm' (19 August 2017), available at m.rbi.org.in/Scripts/BS_SpeechesView.aspx?Id=1044.

Paterson, S, 'Bargaining in Financial Restructuring: Market Norms, Legal Rights and Regulatory Standards' (2014) 14 *Journal of Corporate Law Studies* 333.

—— *Corporate Reorganization Law and Forces of Change* (Oxford, OUP, 2020).

—— 'Rethinking the Corporate Bankruptcy Theory in the Twenty-first Century' (2016) 36 *Oxford Journal of Legal Studies* 697.

—— 'The Adaptive Capacity of Markets and Convergence in Law: UK High Yield Issuers, US Investors and Insolvency Law' (2015) 78 *The Modern Law Review* 431.

—— 'The Paradox of Alignment: Agency Problems and Debt Restructuring' (2016) 17 *European Business Organization Law Review* 497.

Payne, J, 'Debt Restructuring in English Law: Lessons from the United States and the Need for Reform' (2014) 130 *LQR* 282.

—— *Schemes of Arrangement: Theory, Structure and Operation* (Cambridge, CUP, 2014).

—— 'The Role of the Court in Debt Restructuring' (2018) 77 *Cambridge Law Journal* 124.

Peck Gek, T, 'ZenRock, Agritrade Face Winding-up; Hontop Put Under JM' *Business Times* (14 September 2020), available at www.businesstimes.com.sg/energy-commodities/zenrock-agritrade-face-winding-up-hontop-put-under-jm-0.

People's Bank of China, 'Financial Stability Report 2019', available at www.centerforfinancialstability.org/fsr/chn_fsr_201911.pdf.

Pistor, K, Guo, L and Zhou, C, 'The Hybridization of Chinese's Financial System' in BL Liebman and CJ Milhaupt (eds), *Regulating the Visible Hand: The Institutional Implications of Chinese State Capitalism* (Oxford, OUP, 2015/16) 353–76.

Povel, P, 'Optimal Soft or Tough Bankruptcy Procedures' (1999) 15 *Journal of Law Economics and Organization* 659.

Press Information Bureau, Government of India, 'India Ranks 63 in World Bank's Doing Business Report – India Improves Rank by 14 Positions' (24 October 2019), available at pib.gov.in/newsite/PrintRelease.aspx?relid=193994.

Puchniak, DW and Varottil, U, 'Related Party Transactions in Commonwealth Asia: Complicating the Comparative Paradigm' (2020) 17 *Berkeley Business Law Journal* 1.

PwC, 'The Chinese NPL Market in 2020: Regulatory Catalyst May Lead to Higher Volumes' (2020), available at www.pwccn.com/en/services/deals-m-and-a/business-recovery/publications/the-chinese-npl-market-in-2020.html.

Qu, CZ, 'The Court's Power to Appoint Provisional Liquidators to Carry Out Rescue Roles: Rethinking Legend' (2019) 28 *International Insolvency Review* 86–102.

—— 'Towards An Effective Scheme-Based Corporate Rescue System for Hong Kong' (2012) 12 *Journal of Corporate Law Studies* 85.

Qi, L, 'The Corporate Reorganization Regime under China's New Enterprise Bankruptcy Law' (2008) 19 *International Insolvency Review* 13.

Rahman, R, 'Indonesian Firms Prefer to Seek Funding from Debt Market' *Jakarta Post* (18 May 2020).

Rajah, I, 'Enhancing Singapore as an International Centre for Debt Restructuring for Asia and Beyond' Singapore Ministry of Law (2017), available at www.mlaw.gov.sg/files/NoteonDebtRestructuring.pdf.

Rajan, RG, 'A Hundred Small Steps: Report of the Committee on Financial Sector Reforms' (New Delhi, Planning Commission, Government of India, SAGE Publications India 2008), available at faculty.iima.ac.in/~jrvarma/reports/Raghuram-Rajan/cfsr_all.pdf.

—— *I Do What I Do: On Reform, Rhetoric and Resolve* (Utta Pradesh, Harper Business, 2018).

Rana, Y, 'Deconstructing Barriers' in *Speeding up Solvency: Bankruptcy Reform in India*, (Columbia Business School Proceedings, 2019) 8.

Rangotra, R, 'A Trend Analysis of Reforms in the Indian Bond Market' in H Chahal, J Jyoti and J Wirtz (eds), *Understanding the Role of Business Analytics* (Singapore, Springer, 2019) 65–86.

Rasmussen, R, 'The Efficiency of Chapter 11' (1991) 8 *Bankruptcy Developments Journal* 319.

Rautray, S, 'Supreme Court Upholds Bankruptcy Code, Rejects Promoters' Challenges' *The Economic Times* (22 January 2019).

'RBI Lists 12 NPA Accounts For Insolvency Proceedings' *The Hindu Business Line* (12 January 2018).

Rebello, J, 'Personal Guarantees May Aid Bad Loan Resolution' *The Economic Times* (20 November 2019).

Regy, P and Shubho, R, 'Understanding Judicial Delays in India: Evidence from Debt Recovery Tribunals' [2017] NIFP Working Paper No 195.

Ren, D, 'Private Borrowers Bear the Burnt of China's Soaring Bond Defaults as Slowing Economy and Trade War put the Squeence on Finances' *South China Morning Post* (24 July 2019).

Ren, Y, *A comparative study of the corporate bankruptcy reorganization law of the US and China* (The Hague, Netherlands/Portland, Eleven International Publishing, 2012).

Research Office of Legislative Council Secretariat, 'Fact Sheet: Bond Markets in Hong Kong and Singapore' (January 2021), available at www.legco.gov.hk/research-publications/english/2021fs01-bond-markets-in-hong-kong-and-singapore-20210128-e.pdf.

Reserve Bank of India, 'Guidelines on Sales of Stressed Assets by Banks' (1 September 2016), available at rbidocs.rbi.org.in/rdocs/notification/PDFs/CIR563104EA2E56CC4305844C469BB753331C.PDF.

—— 'List of Asset Reconstruction Companies Registered with RBI' (as at 31 January 2021), available at rbidocs.rbi.org.in/rdocs/content/DOCs/LSCRCRBI07092016.xlsx.

—— 'Report of the Committee to Review the Working of Asset Reconstruction Companies' (September 2021) available at rbi.org.in/Scripts/PublicationReportDetails.aspx?UrlPage=&ID=1188.

—— 'Report of the Task Force on the Development of Secondary Market for Corporate Loans' (3 September 2019), available at rbidocs.rbi.org.in/rdocs/PublicationReport/Pdfs/DSMCLOANSBB7C3EDF738D4038B734E909AC054D68.PDF.

—— 'Reports on Trend and Progress of Banking in India 2019–20' (29 December 2020), available at rbidocs.rbi.org.in/rdocs/PressRelease/PDFs/PR844B3CEAC37B19548F7B4FA882DB41F08C1.PDF.

Rodano, G and Serrano-Velarde, NAB and Tarantino, E, 'The Causal Effect of Bankruptcy Law on the Cost of Finance' (2016) 120 *Journal of Financial Economics* 363.

Roe, MJ, and Skeel, DA, 'Assessing the Chrysler Bankruptcy' (2010) 108 *Michigan Law Review* 727.

Sahoo, S, 'Financial Intermediation and Growth: Bank-Based Versus Market-Based Systems' (2014) 8 *Margin: The Journal of Applied Economic Research* 93.

Salian, M, 'NPA resolution: Banks go for all cash sale of stressed assets', *Financial Express* (5 December 2018).

Sarra, JP, Payne, J and Madaus, S, 'The Promise and Perils of Regulating Ipso Facto Clauses' (13 December 2021) *International Insolvency Review*, available at onlinelibrary.wiley.com/doi/full/10.1002/iir.1446.

Schwartz, A, 'The Absolute Priority Rule and the Firm's Investment Policy' (1994) 72 *Washington University Law Quarterly* 1213.

SCMP Reporter, 'Xi Jinping's Debt-Relief Recipe: How China's Biggest Bond Defaulter Unloaded its Liabilities' *South China Morning Post* (14 October 2017).

Scott, PC and Risham, G, 'Differential Treatment Among Creditors under India's Insolvency and Bankruptcy Code, 2016: Issues and Solutions' (2020) 94 *American Bankruptcy Law Journal* 123.

Securities and Futures Commission, 'Statement on the SFC's Approach to Backdoor Listings and Shell Activities' (26 July 2019), available at www.sfc.hk/en/News-and-announcements/Policy-statements-and-announcements/Statement-on-the-SFCs-approach-to-backdoor-listings-and-shell-activities.

Securities Investors Association (Singapore) (SIAS), 'Press Statement: SIAS to Hold Independent Briefings to Hyflux P&Ps' (12 March 2020), available at sias.org.sg/latest-updates/press-statement-sias-to-hold-independent-briefings-to-hyflux-pps.

Sengupta, D and Shukla, S, 'Aircel Resolution Plan: RBI Warns UVARCL' *Economic Times Telecom.com* (21 November 2020).

Shen, W, *Conceptualising the Regulatory Thicket, China's Financial Markets: After the Global Financial Crisis* (Abingdon, Routledge, 2021).

Shika, N and Shahi U, 'Assessment of Corporate Insolvency and Resolution Timeline' RP 01/2021, available at ibbi.gov.in/uploads/publication/2021-02-12-154823-p3xwo-8b78d9548a60a756e4c71d49368def03.pdf.

—— 'Policy Inputs on Report on Subcommittee on Pre-packs: Centre for Insolvency and Bankruptcy, Indian Institute of Corporate Affairs' (2021), copy on file with author.

Shorevest, 'China Debt Dynamics: Dealing With a Coming Surge in Nonperforming Loans' (2020) 4 *Shorevest International Finance Center*, available at shorevest.com/wp-content/uploads/2020/11/20.-ShoreVest-China-Debt-Dynamics-Dealing-With-a-Coming-Surge-in-Nonperforming-Loans.pdf.

Shritama, B, 'New Asset Reconstruction Committee: Banks Likely to Ask RBI to Relax Norm' *Financial Express* (4 February 2021).

Shukla, S, 'Budget 2016: Foreign Investors Can Now Establish ARCs in India' *Economic Times* (26 February 2016).

Sina Finance, 'Jiangxi LDK's Reorganisation Plan Crammed Down by the Court' [江西赛维重整计划被法院 强裁 12 家债权银行成冤大头]' *Sina Finance* (October 2016).

Sito, P, 'Shanghai Court's Nod to Hong Kong Ruling on Keepwell Clause Bodes Well for Offshore Creditors of Defaulting Chinese Bonds' *South China Morning Post* (9 December 2020).

Skeel, DA, 'An Evolutionary Theory of Corporate Law and Corporate Bankruptcy' (1998) 51 *Vanderbilt Law Review* 1325.

—— 'Creditors' Ball: The "New" New Corporate Governance in Chapter 11' (2003) 152 *University of Pennsylvania Law Review* 917.

—— 'Distorted Choice in Corporate Bankruptcy' (2020) 130 *Yale Law Journal* 366.

—— 'Taking Stock of Chapter 11' (2021) 71 *Syracuse Law Review* 931.

Skeel DA, Jr and Triantis G, 'Bankruptcy's Uneasy Shift to a Contract Paradigm' (2018) 166 *University of Pennsylvania Law Review* 1777.

Smart, P and Booth CD, 'Reforming Corporate Rescue Procedures in Hong Kong' (2001) 1 *Journal of Corporate Law Studies* 485.

Squire, R *Corporate Bankruptcy and Financial Reorganizations* (New York, Wolters Kluwer 2016).

Steele, S, Godwin, A, Jin, C, Han, C, Ren, Y and Chi, W, 'Trends and Developments in Chinese Insolvency Law: The First Decade of the PRC Enterprise Bankruptcy Law' (2018) 66 *The American Journal of Comparative Law* 669.

Steele, S, Ramsay, I, and Webster, M, 'Insolvency law reform in Australia and Singapore: Directors' liability for insolvent trading and wrongful trading' (2019) 28 *International Insolvency Review* 363.

Somasundaram, N, 'High Costs Hold Back Foreign Funds from Investing in Chinese Debt' *Nikkei Asian Review* (17 February 2020).

Spamann, H, 'Antidirector Rights Index Revisited' (2010) 23 *Review of Financial Studies* 467.

The Supreme People's Court of the PRC, 'Judicial Transparency by People's Court' (14 March 2017), available at english.court.gov.cn/2017-03/14/content_28552039_3.htm.

Tang, A, *Insolvency in China and Hong Kong: A Practitioner's Perspective* (Hong Kong, Sweet & Maxwell Asia, 2005).

Tang, F, 'China's Top Banking Regulator Sees Surge of Bad Loans in 2021 as Effects of Coronavirus Bite' *South China Morning Post* (3 March 2021).

Teloni, F, 'Chapter 11 Duration, Preplanned Cases and Refiling Rates: An Empirical Analysis in the Post-BAPCPA Era' (2015) 23 *American Bankruptcy Institute Law Review* 571.

Thomas, RS and Solomon, SD, 'The Rise and Fall of Delaware's Takeover Standards' in RS Thomas and SD Solomon (eds), *The Corporate Contract in Changing Times* (Chicago, University of Chicago Press. 2019).

Thukral, S, Sridhar, S and Joshi, MS, 'Review of Factors Constraining the Development of Indian Corporate Bond Markets' (2015) 7 *Qualitative Research in Financial Markets* 429.

Tjio, H, 'Restructuring the Bond Market in Singapore' (2019) 14 *Capital Markets Law Journal* 16.

Trebilcock, M and Leng, J, 'The Role of Formal Contract Law and Enforcement in Economic Development' (2006) 92 *Virginia Law Review* 1517.

Triantis, G, 'A Theory of the Regulation of Debtor-in-Possession Financing' (1993) 46 *Vanderbilt Law Review* 901.

—— 'The Interplay Between Liquidation and Reorganization in Bankruptcy: The Role of Screens, Gatekeepers, and Guillotines' (1996) 16 *International Review of Law and Economics* 101.

Trivedi, A, 'China Spins a Trade-deal Trap in Bad Debt Market' Bloomberg (17 January 2020).

Tung, F, 'Confirmation and Claims Trading' (1996) 90 *Northwestern University Law Review* 1684.

Tyler ELG, 'Insolvency Law in Hong Kong' in R Tomasic (ed), *Insolvency Law in East Asia* (Aldergate, Taylor & Francis, 2006).

UK Insolvency Service, 'Graham Review into Pre-pack Administration' (16 June 2014), available at www.gov.uk/government/publications/graham-review-into-pre-pack-administration.

—— 'Insolvency and Corporate Governance: Government Response' (August 2018), available at www.gov.uk/government/consultations/insolvency-and-corporate-governance.

—— 'Insolvency Practitioners: Recognised Professional Bodies', available at www.gov.uk/government/publications/insolvency-practitioners-recognised-professional-bodies.

UNCITRAL, *Legislative Guide on Insolvency Law* (New York, United Nations, 2005).

van Zwieten, K, 'Corporate Rescue in India: The Influence of the Courts' (2015) 15 *Journal of Corporate Law Studies* 1.

—— 'Director Liability in Insolvency and Its Vicinity' (2018) 38 *Oxford Journal of Legal Studies* 382.

Varottil, U, 'The Nature of the Market for Corporate Control in India' in U Varottil and WY Wan (eds), *Comparative Takeover Regulation: Global and Asian Perspectives* (Cambridge, CUP, 2017) 313.

—— 'The Scheme of Arrangement as a Debt Restructuring Tool in India: Problems and Prospects' (2018) 15 *European Company and Financial Law Review* 585.

Varottil, U and Wan, WY, 'Hostile Takeover Regimes in Asia: A Comparative Approach' (2019) 15 *Berkeley Business Law Journal* 267.

—— 'The Divergent Designs of Mandatory Takeovers in Asia' (2021) *Vanderbilt Journal of Transnational Law*, forthcoming, available at papers.ssrn.com/sol3/papers.cfm?abstract_id=3858227.

Vig, V, 'Access to Collateral and Corporate Debt Structure: Evidence from a Natural Experiment' (2013) 68 *Journal of Finance* 881.

Visaria, S, 'Legal Reform and Loan Repayment: The Microeconomic Impact of Debt Recovery Tribunals in India' (2009) 1 *American Economic Journal: Applied Economics* 59.

Waghmare, A, 'Systemic Change: Hits and Misses of India's Bankruptcy Reforms Code' *Business Standard* (5 February 2020).

Walters, AJ, 'Statutory Erosion of Secured Creditors' Rights: Some Insights from the United Kingdom' (2015) 2015 *University of Illinois Law Review* 543.

Wan, WY, 'Recent Developments in Schemes of Arrangement in Singapore: Classification of Creditors and Scheme Manager's Conflicts of Interest' (2013) 2013 *Journal of Business Law* 552.

Wan, WY and Watters, C, 'Mandatory Disclosure in Corporate Debt Restructuring via Schemes of Arrangement: A Comparative Approach' (2021) 30 *International Insolvency Review* S111.

Wan, WY, Chen, C and Goo, SH, 'Public and Private Enforcement of Corporate and Securities Laws: An Empirical Comparison of Hong Kong and Singapore' (2019) 20 *European Business Organization Law Review* 319.

Wan, WY, Watters, C and McCormack, G, 'Schemes of Arrangement in Singapore: Empirical and Comparative Analysis' (2020) 94 *American Bankruptcy Law Journal* 463.

Wang, J, 'The Political Logic of Corporate Governance in China's State Owned Enterprises' (2014) 47 *Cornell International Law Journal* 631.

Wang, L, 'The Law of Secured Transactions in China: Comparison and Future Reform' in L Gullifer and D Neo (eds), *Secured Transactions Law in Asia: Principles, Perspectives and Reform* (Oxford, Hart Publishing, 2021).

Warren, E, 'A Theory of Absolute Priority' (1992) 1 *Annual Survey of American Law* 9.

—— 'Bankruptcy Policy-Making in an Imperfect World' (1993) 92 *Michigan Law Review* 336.

Wei, C and Chen, Y, 'The Predicament of Bank Creditors in Chinese Bankruptcy and the Way Out' (2019) 27 *International Insolvency Review* 110.

Wei, C, Zhao, J and McCormack, G, 'Evolutionary Traditions and Corporate Law: The Effectiveness and Development of Liquidation Duty in China' (2019) 27 *Asia Pacific Law Review* 149.

Wheeler, S, 'Capital Fractionalized: the role of insolvency practitioners in asset distribution' in M Cain and CB Harrington (eds), *Lawyers in a Postmodern World* (Buckingham, Open University Press, 1994).

White, E, 'China's Courts Take Centre Stage as Defaults Shake $17tn Bond Market' *Financial Times* (24 August 2021), available at www.ftchinese.com/interactive/46668/en?exclusive.

White, MJ, 'Bankruptcy Costs and the New Bankruptcy Code' (1983) 38 *The Journal of Finance* 477.

—— 'Measuring Deviations from the Absolute Priority Rule in Chapter 11 Bankruptcy' (1992) 2 *Journal of Legal Economics* 71.

—— 'The Costs of Corporate Bankruptcy: A US-European Comparison' in JS Bhandar and LA Weiss (eds), *Corporate Bankruptcy: Economic and Legal Perspectives* (Cambridge, CUP, 1996).

White & Case, 'Developments on the Chinese NPL Market' (9 November 2018), available at www.jdsupra.com/legalnews/developments-in-the-chinese-npl-market-46283.

Wolf, M, 'Benefits of Intercreditor Agreements in Cross-Border Restructurings' (2017) 5 *Norton Journal of Bankruptcy Law and Practice* 630.

World Bank, 'Principles for Effective Insolvency and Creditor/Debtor Regimes' (2016), available at pubdocs.worldbank.org/en/919511468425523509/ICR-Principles-Insolvency-Creditor-Debtor-Regimes-2016.pdf.

—— 'World Bank to Discontinue Doing Business Report' (16 September 2021), available at www.worldbank.org/en/news/statement/2021/09/16/world-bank-group-to-discontinue-doing-business-report.

Wu, X and Wu, X, 'The Development of Asset Management Companies in the Pandemic' [疫情下不良资产管理行业发展趋势] (2020) 4 *Shandong Finance* [山东国资] 13.

Xie, Y, '"Shell Company" Shares Plunge as China Tightens Back-door Listing Approvals' *South China Morning Post* (20 June 2016).

Xu, H, 'Setting the Tone for 2017 – The Central Economic Work Conference' *China and US Focus* (26 December 2016).

Xu J, 'Promote the Better Implementation of Bankruptcy Law' [依法推动企业破产制度更好实施] *People's Daily* [人民日报] (13 August 2021), available at politics.people.com.cn/n1/2021/0813/c1001-32191458.html.

Xu, Z, 'Discussing Real Estate Bankruptcies' [浅谈房地产企业破产重整实务与要点] *China Law Society* (11 November 2020), available at www.fxcxw.org.cn/dyna/content.php?id=15422.

Yeo, V and Gan, P, 'Insolvency Law in Singapore' in R Tomasic (ed), *Insolvency Law in East Asia* (Aldershot/Burlington, VT, Ashgate, 1986) ch 12.

Yeung, K, 'Coronavirus: China to Open US$1.5 Trillion Distressed Debt Market as it Braces for Bad Loan Blowout' *South China Morning Post* (30 March 2020).

Yiu, E, 'Hong Kong resurrects Chapter 11-style corporate rescue bill after a 24-year hiatus as Singapore powers ahead with reforms' *South China Morning Post* (12 March 2020).

Yu, G, 'Contract enforcement in China: Theory and Evidence' in G Yu (ed), *Rethinking Law and Development* (London, Routledge, 2013) 63–91.

Yu, G, and Zhang, H, 'Adaptive Efficiency and Financial Development in China: The Role of Contracts and Contractual Enforcement' (2008) 11 *Journal of International Economic Law* 459.

Zhan, X, 'Trust company listed after Twenty years [20年来江苏信托成首家借壳上市 但不意味着开闸]' *Investor Journal Weekly* [投资者报] (12 December 2016).

Zhang, C, 'More Chinese Banks Set Up Own Bad-Loan Asset Management Companies' *South China Morning Post* (20 October 2016).

Zhang, S, 'China Adds a Fifth Bad-debt Manager to Prepare for Decade-high Dud Loans as Covid-19 Weighs on Banks and Borrowers' *South China Morning Post* (18 December 2020).

Zhang, W, Lin, W, Zeng, B and Zhang, W, 'Mandatory Bids in China: You can Lead a Horse to Water, But You Can't Make Him Drink' (2021) 22 *European Business Organization Law Review* 351.

Zhang, Z, *Corporate Reorganisations in China: An Empirical Analysis* (Cambridge, CUP, 2018).

—— 'Corporate Reorganisations of Chinese Listed Companies: Winners and Losers' (2016) 16 *Journal of Corporate Law Studies* 101.

—— 'The Corporate Bankruptcy Substitute in China' (2019) 33 *Columbia Journal of Asian Law* 172.

Zhao, H, *Government Intervention in the Reorganisation of Listed Companies in China* (Cambridge, CUP, 2019).

Zhu, C and Dong, D, 'What China's Three Red Lines Mean for Property Firms' Bloomberg (9 October 2020), available at www.bloomberg.com/news/articles/2020-10-08/what-china-s-three-red-lines-mean-for-property-firms-quicktake.

Index

Introductory Note

References such as '178–79' indicate (not necessarily continuous) discussion of a topic across a range of pages. Wherever possible in the case of topics with many references, these have either been divided into sub-topics or only the most significant discussions of the topic are listed. Because the entire work is about 'restructuring', the use of this term (and certain others which occur constantly throughout the book) as an entry point has been minimised. Information will be found under the corresponding detailed topics.

ABC (Agricultural Bank of China) 171, 173, 177
absolute priority rule, *see* **APR**
abstention of voting 96, 146, 286
abusive transactions 62, 76
account creditors 276, 280–81
accountability 32, 189, 191, 201–2, 204, 214–15, 283, 287
  intermediaries 202–4
  lack of 202, 283
accountants 42, 194, 204, 287
accounting firms 193, 207
accredited investors 118–19
active companies 257, 259, 261
active distressed loan markets 153, 181–85, 244
adaptive devices 47, 51, 220, 246, 284
adjudication 141–42, 205, 218
administration 2–4, 9–11, 23, 58, 116, 191–92, 210–11, 270–71
  light-touch 10, 193
  process 1–2, 26, 34
administrative expenses 238, 241, 282
administrators 9–10, 37–39, 191–95, 199, 203–4, 208–11, 214–15, 250–51
advanced jurisdictions 33, 45, 47, 49, 51, 53, 254–55, 262
  development of corporate restructuring law 44–55
advisers 3, 190, 197, 200, 202, 204–6, 217, 224
  financial 95, 190, 199–200, 204, 206, 215–16, 227
  professional 66–67, 189–90, 196, 202–3, 207, 225, 241, 243
affiliates 19, 63, 72, 81, 87–88, 90–91, 139
agency conflicts 17, 251
agency costs 12–13, 32, 57–150, 153–54, 156–86, 190, 239, 276–77
  and AMCs 161–79
  Asia 61–66
  China 64–66
  creditor-creditor relationships 101–50
  heightened friction between creditors and shareholders 70–72
  and hold-outs 66–70
  Hong Kong and Singapore 62–63
  India 63–64
  institutional and organisational background 60–66, 103–14
  manager-creditor and shareholder-creditor 57–100
  and NPLs 152–87
  strategies to deal with conflicts in Anglo-American restructurings 66–72, 114–24
  United States and United Kingdom 60–61
aggregation, debt 154, 162, 166
aggressive screening 138, 251, 261
Agricultural Bank of China, *see* **ABC**
AMCs (asset management companies) 16, 20–21, 28, 30, 153, 172–73, 175–76, 282–83
  and agency costs 161–79
  China, *see* CAMCs
  as debt aggregation vehicles 154–55
  India 162–70
  national 30, 172, 186
  provincial 20, 175, 183
American Bankruptcy Institute 70, 119, 302
amount of NPLs 160
amounts of NPAs 160, 162
analytical framework 17–22
antecedent transactions 86, 198, 209, 213
applicants, resolution 129, 169, 206, 208, 210–11, 232, 235, 287–88
appointment of insolvency professionals, *see also* **advisers**
  intermediaries 202–4
  provisional liquidators 126, 231

receivers 156, 259
soft-touch liquidators 28, 242
appropriate comparators 67, 75–76, 122, 225, 279
APR (absolute priority rule) 8–9, 58–59, 69–70, 76–80, 119–21, 143, 235, 278–79
China 79–82
and distribution in Asia 75–85
and hold-outs 68–70
Hong Kong 84–85
India 82–84
inter-class conflicts 118–20, 138–40
no one-size-fits-all rule 94
Singapore 77–78
ARCs (asset reconstruction companies) 20, 153–54, 157, 162–70, 182, 186–87, 282, 288
arrangement, schemes of, *see* **schemes of arrangement**
Asian economies 18, 46
Asian financial crisis 20, 35, 44–46, 51, 53, 105, 111, 152
Asian firms 7, 12
assessors, independent 142, 147
asset investment companies 174, 176
asset management companies, *see* **AMCs**
asset reconstruction companies, *see* **ARCs**
assets 22–23, 72–75, 113–15, 127–29, 142–47, 196–99, 282–84, 288–92
debtors 8, 57, 117, 120, 125, 188, 224
deployment 32, 146, 283, 286
and reduction of information asymmetry 66–68
distressed 16, 153–55, 157, 163, 165, 171–73, 180–81, 185–86
market for distressed 153, 155, 185
personal 63, 208, 277
profitable 81, 91, 139
sale of 115, 198–99
secured 37, 138, 157, 255
stressed 11, 44, 64, 262
asymmetry, information, *see* **information, asymmetry**
auction 96, 172, 177, 212, 222, 225, 241–42, 263
models 68
process 68, 165
auditors 202, 213
automatic moratorium 115, 125, 221; *see also* **automatic stays**
automatic stays 124, 148; *see also* **automatic moratorium**
average recovery rates 133, 260, 265

backstop fees 117–18, 224
bail-ins 20, 153
bail-outs 91, 98, 247, 286
bank 20, 153
balance sheets 15, 18, 20, 46, 102, 153, 173, 246
bank creditors 20, 123–24, 130, 141–42, 145, 152, 164–66, 260
bank debt 15, 105, 148
bank lenders 61, 104, 162, 167, 282
Bank of China, *see* **BOC**
Bank of Communications, *see* **BOCOM**
banking 159, 163–64, 173, 181
crises 20, 152, 154
regulation 28, 253
regulators 7, 19–20, 152, 185
sectors 6, 16, 40, 154, 178, 220, 282
bankruptcy 1, 4, 36, 217, 224, 226, 238–39, 270; *see also* **insolvency and restructuring laws**
courts 30, 71, 118, 218, 250
law 2, 4, 7, 22, 29, 36, 49, 285
petitions 97, 115, 193, 258, 265–66
practice 6–7, 15, 285
reforms 7, 24, 34, 58, 293, 302
banks 18–20, 44, 105–6, 152–55, 157–59, 161–63, 165–67, 181–85
bail-outs 20, 153
central 171–72
creditor 19, 45, 84, 113, 177, 202–3, 207, 209
foreign 158, 165–67
investment 200, 216
original lending 154, 166, 169
policy 171–72
private sector 162, 166–68, 186
public sector, *see* public sector banks
selling 162, 165, 187
state-owned 21, 25, 28, 153–54, 168, 171–72, 177–78, 186
bargaining 2, 24, 76, 128, 143, 145–46, 211
consensual 8, 57, 101
power 133, 175
process 16, 68, 73–75, 99, 144, 146, 212, 280
behaviour 12, 147, 204, 212, 218, 242, 278, 287
opportunistic 93, 97–98, 189, 219, 242
Bermuda 27, 47–48, 53, 148, 231, 242
best interests tests 8, 68, 123, 190
bias 6, 103, 207, 224, 245
bidders 68, 75, 83–84, 96, 104, 129–30, 206–7, 212
highest 100, 164
bids 64, 68, 82–83, 96, 129, 169, 208, 283
competitive 193, 203
boards of directors 10, 41, 89, 127, 188, 191, 195, 207–8; *see also* **directors**
BOC (Bank of China) 171, 173, 177
BOCOM (Bank of Communications) 172–73, 177

bond defaults 65, 80, 92, 98, 263–64, 285
onshore 19, 65, 108, 113, 263, 265
bond markets 103, 105–6, 110–12, 122, 130, 148, 156, 178
onshore 65, 106–9, 285
bond restructurings 7, 29–31, 50, 90, 146–47, 249, 301
bondholders 96, 103–4, 110, 129–30, 149–50, 225–26, 265, 290
conflicted 96, 146
non-retail 150
retail 16, 118–19
bonds 50, 81, 107–8, 110–13, 149–50, 172–73, 176–78, 263–66
corporate 26, 107, 109, 112
distressed 113–14
foreign currency 106, 109–10
issuances 15, 19, 31, 109, 113
offshore 49–50, 107
onshore 19, 65, 286
book value 163, 181, 183, 187
breach of directors' duties 257, 271–72
bright-line rules 147, 215, 219–20, 233, 280, 283–84
Building an Analytical Framework 17–21
buyers 72, 165, 170, 184, 211, 251
institutional 163

CAMCs (Chinese AMCs) 153–54, 171–80, 183–87
dominance of manufacturing and wholesale/retail NPLs 179–80
fragmentation of industry 179
history 171–76
local 175–76, 179, 186
management of distressed loans 176
as market entities in times of market volatility 177–79
provincial 174–75, 183
variations to agency costs 177–80
capital markets 33, 60, 95, 99, 109, 116
cash 127, 133–36, 162–63, 165, 167, 200–201, 203, 237
flows 23, 49, 104, 202
CBIRC (China Banking and Insurance Regulatory Commission) 128, 160–61, 179, 248
CBRC (China Banking Regulatory Commission) 172, 174–75
CCB (China Construction Bank) 171, 173, 177
central banks 171–72
challenge, Swiss 129, 163–64, 167, 196, 212
Chapter 11 2–3, 6, 8, 21, 24, 128, 218–19, 278
China 2–5, 24–25, 33–37, 91–100, 106–9, 159–61, 254–59, 282–84
agency costs 64–66
APR 79–82
CAMCs, *see* CAMCs
courts 30, 38, 49, 93, 135, 138, 150, 203
court-supervised restructurings 245–51
development of active distressed loan market 183–85
development of corporate restructuring law 36–39
distribution 133–34
effectiveness of practitioners 209
empirical studies 29–30
Hong Kong, *see* Hong Kong
hybrid model 79–82
information asymmetry 127–28
inter-class conflicts 138–39
NPLs 160–61
operational creditors 133–34
practitioners 193–95
reform proposals 285–86
Shenzhen Intermediate Court 81, 193, 204
Shenzhen Stock Exchange (SZSE) 5, 62, 64, 111
small creditors 135–37
state as shareholder 64–66, 89–92
usage of formal insolvency/restructuring law 262–66
China Banking and Insurance Regulatory Commission, *see* CBIRC
China Banking Regulatory Commission, *see* CBRC
China Cinda Asset Management 30, 171, 173, 177–78, 180, 187
China Construction Bank, *see* CCB
China Huarong Asset Management Co Ltd, *see* Huarong
China Orient 30, 172
Chinese AMCs, *see* CAMCs
CIRPs (Corporate Insolvency Resolution Processes) 42–43, 64, 125, 130–33, 164–66, 207–8, 232–34, 258–61
claims 21–22, 68–69, 71–72, 85–86, 88–89, 121–23, 140–43, 147
disputed 140–42, 147
employee 36, 103
release 70–71, 85, 277
secured 124, 255
settlement 70–71, 145
classes 8–10, 71–72, 79–80, 88–89, 119–23, 144–46, 224–25, 278–80
composition 118, 224, 235, 284, 286
dissenting 18, 69, 75, 79, 101, 120, 223, 235
impaired 69, 71, 245
junior 8, 58, 69, 102
senior 8, 58, 68
CoCs, *see* committees of creditors
collateral 22, 140, 144, 173, 176, 255, 259, 280

collateral value 266–67
committees of creditors (CoCs) 42–43, 128–32, 140, 146–47, 196–97, 235–38, 244, 287–89
decisions 219–20, 244
committees of financial creditors 64, 146, 241
commodity prices 111, 209
common law 45, 47, 219–20, 227–28, 231, 238–39, 243, 263
courts 218, 239–40, 281, 284
jurisdictions 32, 40, 156, 219, 228, 241, 247, 259
companies, *see* ***Introductory Note and detailed entries***
company voluntary arrangements, *see* **CVAs**
comparability 3, 107, 109–10, 256
comparators 219, 225
appropriate 67, 75–76, 122, 225, 279
correct 225, 227
relevant 190, 240
compensation 71, 74, 79, 127, 195, 200, 215, 277
packages 61, 67
competitive bids 193, 203
compromise 16, 34, 87, 122–23, 225
compulsory liquidation 258–59
concentrated debt structures 13, 102, 148
concentrated shareholdings 14–15, 17–18, 24, 26, 62–63, 75–76, 98, 291–92
conflicted creditors 147, 219
conflicted pre-packs 72
conflicted transactions 95, 98
conflicts 18–19, 32, 59–60, 146, 189–90, 206–7, 213–15, 283
agency 17, 251
creditor–creditor 18, 27, 102–3, 114, 143, 285
inter-class 118–20, 131, 138, 138–40
of interest 18–19, 21, 146–47, 189–90, 206–7, 211, 213–15, 283
management–creditor and shareholder–creditor 18
within-class 144, 146–47
connected parties 59, 92, 212; *see also* **related parties**
consensual bargaining 8, 57, 101
consent 8–11, 58, 212, 219, 222–23, 236–38, 241, 289
fees 117, 224, 234, 280, 290; *see also* RSAs
consideration 81–82, 121, 269, 271–74, 276, 279, 284–85
contracts 10, 115–16, 142, 212, 217, 255–57, 260, 262–63
construction 141–42
enforcement 4–5, 7, 25, 32, 255–57, 262–63, 266–68, 274–75
executory 8, 195, 199
contractual rights 256, 284, 293
control 4, 6, 59–60, 64, 75–76, 97, 176–77, 202
controlling shareholders 18, 59–64, 70–71, 76–78, 81–82, 85–88, 93–97, 276–79
sales to 72
coordination costs 6–7, 16–17, 21–22, 161–79, 185–86, 218–19, 253–54, 275
AMCs and variations 161–79
creditor-creditor relationships 101–51
and NPLs 152–87
corporate bonds 26, 107, 109, 112
corporate governance 17–18, 59, 62, 64, 94–99, 274, 276, 278
and restructuring law 12–17
Corporate Insolvency Resolution Processes, *see* **CIRPs**
corporate NPLs 153, 178, 184, 187
corporate rescue 23–24, 26–27, 45–47, 50–51, 90–91, 271–72, 289, 302
corporate restructuring law 1–2, 7, 29, 33–34, 36–57, 220, 292
costs 3, 12–13, 143–44, 201, 214–15, 253, 260–62, 268–69
agency, *see* agency, costs
coordination, *see* coordination costs
transaction 1, 3, 15–17, 20, 22, 153–55, 211, 214
counter-parties 115, 126
court restructurings of large companies 23–24
courts 35–41, 84–91, 93–98, 125–30, 138–43, 190–99, 203–14, 263–66
bankruptcy 30, 71, 118, 218, 250
Chinese 30, 38, 49, 93, 135, 138, 150, 203
common law 218, 239–40, 281, 284
Hong Kong 27, 31, 49–50, 188, 201, 243, 290
legislative framework and judicial discretion in United States and UK 220–27
lower 34, 37–38, 42, 219, 247, 288
role in court-supervised restructurings 217–52
Singapore 31, 53, 74, 93, 110, 126, 228–30, 237
United Kingdom 223–26
court-supervised restructurings 188, 217–52
COVID-19 pandemic 10, 43–44, 90, 92, 193, 259, 261, 264
cram-down powers 38, 82, 278–79
cram-downs 45, 71, 79, 82, 94, 128, 139, 278–79
creditor protection 121–23
cross-class 8–9, 58, 68, 70, 77, 120–21, 278, 291–92
and valuation 240–41
within-class 9, 69, 71, 77, 79, 84, 234, 240
creditor approval 122, 196, 198–99, 250, 278
creditor banks 19, 45, 84, 113, 177, 202–3, 207, 209

creditor support 50, 73, 228, 231, 243, 291
creditor-creditor relationships 101–50
creditor–creditor conflicts 18–19, 27, 102–3, 114, 143, 285
creditor-in-control models 4, 27
creditors 70–83, 85–99, 135–52, 188–208, 210–17, 239–51, 253–74, 276–92
account 276, 280–81
bank 20, 123–24, 130, 141–42, 145, 152, 164–66, 260
committees of, *see* committees of creditors
conflicted 147, 219
dissenting 71–72, 77, 128, 130, 236, 239, 278, 280
financial 102–5, 128–35, 137–38, 140, 143–44, 222–23, 279–81, 287–89
heightened friction with shareholders 70–72
institutional 19, 117, 128, 137
junior 15, 18, 58, 60, 68, 70, 119–20, 278–79
new 16, 124, 155, 167, 178, 182
non-adjusting 133, 142–43, 145, 280, 282
non-financial 123, 131, 133–35, 144, 147, 157, 265–66, 280
non-sophisticated 138, 152, 206, 242–43
offshore 49, 149, 290
onshore 49, 148, 243
operational 131–35, 140, 142–44, 147, 241, 260–61, 279, 289
preferential 10, 191, 245
pre-moratorium 10, 116
related party 72, 152, 235, 239–40, 284
secured 22, 119–20, 125–27, 143–46, 253–56, 259–60, 265–69, 287–89
senior 18, 69, 119–20, 148
small 121, 131, 135–36, 138, 144, 147, 265–66, 280
subordinated 49, 137, 145
trade 16, 19, 123, 130, 132–33, 136, 138, 280
unsecured 78–79, 131–32, 138–39, 143–45, 192, 245–46, 265–66, 268
cross-border insolvency 148, 231, 291
cross-class cram-downs 8–9, 58, 68, 70, 77, 120–21, 278, 291–92
CVAs (**company voluntary arrangements**) 2, 23, 258

data, availability 3, 24, 263
datasets 5, 29, 31, 78–80, 135, 165, 194, 265
de facto moratorium 231, 254, 262
debt, *see also* ***Introductory Note and detailed entries***
financial 15–16, 18, 102, 115, 121–22, 135, 276, 282
junior 14, 61, 155
operational 4, 15–16, 18, 27, 102–3, 121–23
pre-petition 124, 145
related party 71–72, 88–89, 277
debt aggregation 154, 162, 166
debt enforcement 36, 156, 181, 185, 254–57, 261
debt markets 19, 26, 103, 130, 175, 181–82
debt recovery tribunals, *see* **DRTs**
debt structures 7, 27, 47, 60, 148, 155
concentrated 13, 102, 148
debt-equity swaps 77, 82, 84–85, 87, 134–36, 174, 176–77, 246
debt-holders 70, 135, 137, 169
debt-holdings 5, 19, 26, 32, 103, 290, 292
debtor companies 46–47, 73–74, 94, 114–15, 138–39, 145–46, 197–98, 204–5
debtor in possession models, *see* **DIP**
debtor management 8, 37, 127, 220, 222, 225, 230, 239–40
leeway granted 239–40
debtors, *see* ***Introductory Note and detailed entries***
deeds, keepwell 107, 149–50
defaults 7, 42, 64–65, 92, 108, 264, 286
bond 65, 80, 92, 98, 263–64, 285
strategic 115, 148
deployment of assets 22–23, 42, 74–75, 115–18, 127, 129, 144–46, 210–13
in Asian restructurings 124–31
and distribution distinguished 22–23, 115, 129, 210
development of corporate restructuring law 33–56
advanced jurisdictions 44–55
China 36–39
emerging jurisdictions 35–44
Hong Kong 44–51
India 39–44
Singapore 51–55
differential treatment 131, 134–36, 144, 280
DIP (**debtor in possession**) 2, 4, 27, 38, 55, 97–98, 269, 276–77
financing 9, 54–55, 63, 124, 145, 150, 236–37, 282
hybrid 27, 34–35, 37, 77, 79, 98, 100, 193–95
lenders 241, 281
loans 9, 145, 241
models/regimes 2–3, 6, 8–9, 18, 58–59, 62–63, 98–99, 277–78
proceedings 47, 74, 189, 202
Singapore 77–78
United States 8–9
directors 71–72, 85–87, 97–98, 190–91, 207–8, 254–55, 269–73, 284–86
boards of 10, 41, 89, 127, 188, 191, 195, 207–8

breach of duties 257, 271–72
duties 95, 97–98, 271, 273
enforcement 18, 98, 243, 271–72, 284–86
and incentives to invoke or use restructuring law 269–74
independent 95, 97–98, 227
disclosure 72–75, 127, 131, 205, 208, 246, 248, 250
early 240, 292
mandatory 8, 58, 73–74, 102, 280
requirements 3, 48, 67, 85, 127, 196, 241
statements 190
discounts 20, 68, 82, 88, 104, 173, 277
discovery, price 58, 99, 167, 250
discretion 121, 123, 126, 129, 214, 218–20, 225, 227
judicial 145, 147, 218–21, 223–37, 251
disincentives 32, 96, 145, 267, 270–71, 281
dispersed ownership 13, 60, 102
dispersed shareholding structures 18, 67, 276
disputed claims 140–42, 147
dissenting classes 18, 69, 75, 79, 101, 120, 223, 235
dissenting creditors 71–72, 77, 128, 130, 236, 239, 278, 280
dissenting votes 80, 278
distress, financial 13–15, 86, 98–99, 104, 123–24, 273–74, 282–83, 292
distressed assets 16, 153–55, 157, 163, 165, 171–73, 180–81, 185–86
distressed bonds 113–14
distressed companies 2, 7, 17–18, 60, 63, 67, 70, 247
distressed debt 25, 104, 113, 176, 181–83, 186
markets 20, 105, 116, 153, 155, 184–85, 282, 302
distressed debtors 176, 187
distressed funds 47, 113–14, 129, 155, 181, 207, 238, 290
distressed loans 16, 44, 114, 154, 176, 181
markets 20, 44, 114, 184, 186–87
active 153, 181–85, 244
distressed SOEs (state-owned enterprises) 36, 90–91, 98, 247
distressed trading 20, 105, 155, 223
distribution 22–23, 58–59, 115–16, 118–21, 143, 196–97, 210–11, 244
and APR in Asia 75–85
Asian restructurings 131–43
and deployment distinguished 22–23, 115, 129, 210
and hold-outs 68–70
India 131–33
DRTs (debt recovery tribunals) 41, 43, 83, 156–57, 159, 260
duties 98, 188–89, 202, 205–6, 254–55, 270–73, 279–81, 284–86
of directors, *see* directors, duties
fiduciary 71, 85, 95, 97, 129, 190, 206, 280

economic interests 18, 119–22, 244, 288
economic policies 276, 285, 293
economies, Asian 18, 46
effective enforcement 241, 285
effectiveness 28, 32, 126, 173, 189, 201, 207, 283
emerging jurisdictions 6–7, 16, 20, 22, 25–26, 33, 43–44, 152
development of corporate restructuring law 35–44
emerging markets 185, 189, 302
empirical studies 29–31, 248
employee claims 36, 103
employee interests 39, 245
employees 38, 40, 46, 133–34, 251–52, 254, 264, 266
enforcement
actions 46, 53, 115, 223, 253, 263
contracts 4–5, 7, 25, 32, 255–57, 262–63, 266–68, 274–75
of creditor rights and restructuring law 255–68
debt 36, 156, 181, 185, 254–57, 261
of directors' duties 18, 98, 243, 271–72, 284–86
effective 241, 285
formal 262, 274
private 214, 254, 271, 273, 302
public 243, 273
of secured debt 27, 41, 259
equal treatment 19, 71–72, 143, 145
equity 14, 61, 69–70, 79–81, 135–36, 164–65, 169, 226
private, *see* private equity
upside 119, 164
executory contracts 8, 195, 199
expenses 72, 129, 206, 246, 266; *see also* **costs**
administrative 238, 241, 282
expertise, judicial 21, 217–18
explanatory statements 31, 67, 85–86, 118, 122, 199
extension 10, 116, 219–20, 228–30, 232–33, 239, 242, 281

families 12, 15, 61–62, 72, 99, 143, 277, 292
feasibility 132, 161, 204, 228, 302
fee arrangements 189, 201–2, 204–6, 215
fees 118, 189–90, 192, 195–97, 201–2, 204–6, 224, 280
backstop 117–18, 224
consent 117, 224, 234, 280, 290
fixed 192, 197, 215

professional 195, 201
restructuring 201, 243
scaled 195, 215
success 197, 200, 204–6, 215, 283
work 117–18, 224, 290
fiduciary duties 71, 85, 95, 97, 129, 190, 206, 280
FIIs (**foreign institutional investors**) 163–64, 168, 184
filing 43, 66, 103–4, 221–22, 258–61, 264–66, 268–70, 301
time of 15, 89, 96, 233, 240
financial advisers 95, 190, 199–200, 204, 206, 215–16, 227
financial companies 109, 129, 162, 168
financial creditors 102–5, 128–35, 137–38, 140, 143–44, 222–23, 279–81, 287–89
financial crisis
Asian 20, 35, 44–46, 51, 53, 105, 111, 152
global 14, 16, 20, 34–35, 41, 44, 51, 152
financial debt 15–16, 18, 102, 115, 121–22, 135, 276, 282
financial distress 13–15, 86, 98–99, 104, 123–24, 273–74, 282–83, 292
financial information 18, 73, 75, 97, 242, 277, 280, 290
financial institutions 22, 25, 40–41, 44, 47, 111–13, 157, 259; *see also* **banks**
financial markets 35, 51, 102, 225, 290, 292–93
financial services firms 25, 183, 225
financial statements 73–74, 139, 229
financing 59, 63, 105, 124, 145, 236–37, 241, 282
interim 237–38
new 118, 124, 202, 204, 237, 292
post-petition 236–38, 241
pre-petition 282
rescue 9, 228, 236, 238, 241, 276, 281–82, 291–92
roll-up 120, 124, 145, 238, 282
super-priority 124, 237–38
fixed fees 192, 197, 215
flexibility 182, 218, 220, 244, 284, 287
flows, cash 23, 49, 104, 202
foreign banks 158, 165–67
foreign currency bonds 106, 109–10
foreign institutional investors, *see* **FIIs**
foreign investors 21, 25, 28, 106–7, 114, 153, 178, 181–86
formal enforcement 262, 274
formal moratorium 45, 230, 251, 289–90
funds, distressed 47, 113–14, 129, 155, 181, 207, 238, 290

gatekeeper intermediaries 188–216
gatekeepers 21, 188, 190, 213–14, 292
enhancing liabilities 214–16
independent 7, 17, 56, 253, 275
GDP (**gross domestic product**) 2, 24, 105–6, 109, 171, 173, 178
global financial crisis 14, 16, 20, 34–35, 41, 44, 51, 152
goals 17, 219–20, 239, 242, 245, 250, 287, 292
national 218–19, 252, 276, 284
good faith 146–47, 205–6, 288
governance
corporate, *see* corporate governance
intermediaries 201–9
Great Wall 30, 172–73
groups, liquidation 39, 209, 286
guarantees 49, 83, 107, 141, 149
implicit 91, 175, 177–78, 186, 283
personal 63, 208, 288

haircuts 19, 80, 86, 134, 136–37, 201–2, 206, 287
hard absolute priority rule 211–12
high-yield debt 15, 178
hold-outs 8, 58, 68–69, 94, 101, 103, 118, 185
and agency costs 66–70
and APR 68–70
Asian restructurings 73–93
and reduction of information asymmetry 66–68
unreasonable 66, 93, 101
home-buyers 16, 144, 206
Hong Kong 26–29, 33–35, 45–51, 109–13, 137–38, 231–32, 243, 290–91
agency costs 62–63
APR 84–85
companies 47, 49–50, 113, 258, 289
courts 27, 31, 49–50, 188, 201, 243, 290
creditor protection 242–43
development of corporate restructuring law 44–51
empirical studies 31
Government 26, 50–51
information asymmetry 130–31
Legislative Council 34, 51, 232, 289
moratorium 230–32
recognition of soft-touch liquidation 28, 41, 47, 50, 69, 231, 239, 243
reform proposals 289–91
related parties 87–89
schemes of arrangement 85, 200–201
secured creditor-in-control model 84–85
small creditors 137–38
Stock Exchange 5, 30, 47–50, 148, 173, 178, 301
usage of formal insolvency/restructuring law 266–69
hostile takeovers 226, 302
Huarong 30, 172–73, 175, 177–80, 183, 187, 283

hybrid DIP/PIP forms 27, 34–35, 37, 74, 77, 98, 100, 193–95
  China 79–82

IBBI (Insolvency and Bankruptcy Board of India) 3, 30, 34, 164, 189, 195–97, 233–34, 258–59
impaired classes 69, 71, 245
implicit guarantees 91, 175, 177–78, 186, 283
incentives 19–21, 75–78, 96–97, 167, 186–87, 202, 204, 282–83
  in Asia 271–74
  economic 216
  to invoke or use restructuring law 269–74
incorporation, place of 47, 49, 127, 242–43
independence 34, 51–52, 72, 190, 203–4, 207, 213, 216
independent assessors 142, 147
independent directors 95, 97–98, 227
independent gatekeepers 7, 17, 56, 253, 275
independent shareholders 93, 95
India 19–22, 24–26, 32–35, 95–98, 156–59, 185–87, 210–15, 277–83
  agency costs 63–64
  AMCs 162–70
  APR 82–84
  certainty and predictability vs flexibility 244–45
  development of active distressed loan market 181–82
  development of corporate restructuring law 39–44
  distribution 131–33
  effectiveness of practitioners 207–8
  empirical studies 30–31
  information asymmetry 129–30
  inter-class-conflicts 140–43
  moratorium 232–34
  NPLs 156–59
  operational creditors 131–33
  PIP model 82–84, 195–97
  promoters 63–64
  RBI (Reserve Bank of India) 40–41, 44, 63, 157–59, 165–67, 169, 182, 187
  reform proposals 287–89
  related parties 89
  resolution professionals 195–97
  Supreme Court 34, 44, 82, 129, 235
  usage of formal insolvency/restructuring law 259–62
industrial companies 25, 40, 63, 156
information 19, 73–75, 138, 167–68, 230, 246–48, 276–79, 291–92
  asymmetry 66–68, 75, 97, 116–17, 146, 185, 277
    Asian restructurings 73–93, 127–31
    China 127–28
    and creditors' decision-making 127–31
    India 129–30
    Singapore and Hong Kong 130–31
  financial 18, 73, 75, 97, 242, 277, 280, 290
  memorandum 42, 196
  relevant 143, 146
  utilities 42, 196
insiders 59, 68, 71
Insolvency and Bankruptcy Board of India, *see* **IBBI**
insolvency and restructuring law 6–7, 29, 35, 59–60, 254–55, 258, 266, 268–69
insolvency law reforms 20, 26, 35, 40, 152, 228, 276
insolvency practitioners, *see* **practitioners**
insolvency proceedings 23, 150, 154, 223, 255, 264, 267–68, 270
insolvent liquidation 13, 16, 116, 122, 189, 226, 271
insolvent trading 46, 271–73
Institute, American Bankruptcy 70, 119, 302
institutional buyers 163
institutional creditors 19, 117, 128, 137
institutional frameworks/structures 3, 27–28, 32, 35, 55, 255, 274
institutional investors 103, 110–11, 134, 137, 163–64, 168, 184
  foreign, *see* foreign institutional investors
insurance, companies 193, 221
interaction between shareholders and creditors 13–14
inter-class conflicts 118–20, 131, 138, 138–40
interim financing 237–38
intermediaries 49, 188–90, 200–201, 203, 205, 207, 209–11, 216
  appointment and accountability 202–4
  fee arrangements 204–6
  gatekeeeper, *see* gatekeeper intermediaries
  governance 201–9
investment banks 200, 216
investors 87, 93–94, 103–4, 106, 112, 130, 184–86, 237
  accredited 118–19
  bond 45, 113
  foreign 21, 25, 28, 106–7, 114, 153, 178, 181–86
    institutional, *see* foreign institutional investors
  new 39, 45, 47, 81–82, 127, 247, 279, 290
  non-sophisticated 137, 151
  retail 19, 109–13, 122, 130, 134, 137–38, 144, 185
  white knight 88–89, 201
IPs (insolvency practitioners), *see* **practitioners**
***ipso facto* clauses** 8, 10, 115–16, 124–26, 146, 148, 151, 281

issuances 77, 84, 93, 96, 107, 109–10, 150, 172
bond 15, 19, 31, 109, 113
issuers 106, 108, 111–12, 134–36, 263, 265, 268, 294–95

JLF (Joint Lenders' Forum) 40, 63, 157
judicial discretion 145, 147, 218–21, 223–37, 251
judicial expertise 21, 217–18
judicial management 5, 26–27, 34, 52, 55, 103, 197–99, 209
judicial managers 52, 54, 86, 103, 197–98, 200, 208–10, 273
judicial oversight 97, 189, 199, 211, 213, 215, 292
judicial process 40, 153, 157, 181
judicial resources 145–46
judicial time 147, 213–15, 254
junior classes 8, 58, 69, 102
junior creditors 15, 18, 58, 60, 68, 70, 119–20, 278–79
junior debt 14, 61, 155
jurisdictions 1–3, 24–26, 31–35, 54–55, 152–54, 211–15, 256–59, 276–79
advanced 33, 44–45, 47, 49, 51, 53, 254–55, 262
choice 24–26
emerging 6–7, 16, 20, 22, 25–26, 33, 35–44, 152
offshore 231, 281, 289

keepwell deeds 107, 149–50

legal proceedings 42, 126, 164, 231–33, 260
Legislative Council 34, 51, 232, 289
lenders 16, 20, 41–42, 140, 144, 236–38, 241, 282
bank 61, 104, 162, 167, 282
new 9, 20, 124, 153, 236–37
original 21, 155, 164, 167–68, 178, 185, 247
secured 72, 241
senior 93, 120, 257
liabilities 23, 66, 70, 87, 214, 222, 225, 272
light-touch administration 10, 193
liquidation 40–43, 115–17, 125–28, 131, 232–33, 258–61, 263–66, 273
analysis 67, 73, 190, 199–200, 279
compulsory 258–59
groups 39, 209, 286
insolvent 13, 16, 116, 122, 189, 226, 271
premature 189, 202
provisional, *see* provisional liquidation
soft-touch, *see* soft-touch liquidation
value 42, 57, 139–40, 235–36, 240, 245–46, 280, 289
waterfall 192, 199
liquidators 49, 198, 200–201, 241, 270–71, 273
soft-touch 127, 242
listed companies 29–31, 59–61, 78, 80–82, 98–99, 245–46, 248–49, 294
listing status 46–47, 49, 84–85, 139, 179, 201, 246, 290
litigation 83–84, 96, 129, 140–41, 144, 176, 208, 211
satellite 96, 126, 143, 147, 280
loans 104, 122–24, 154, 160–66, 172, 176, 178–79, 282–83
crisis 20, 152, 169, 171
non-performing, *see* NPLs
secured 39, 124, 156, 259, 263
local governments 34, 36, 38–39, 90–91, 98, 175–76, 178–79, 194
losses 3, 86–87, 123, 137, 142, 156, 173, 220
lower courts 34, 37–38, 42, 219, 247, 288

Mainland China, *see* **China**
management 12–14, 54–56, 59–63, 66–68, 86, 97–100, 225–28, 239–40
existing 18, 192, 212
judicial 5, 26–27, 34, 52, 55, 103, 197–99, 209
NPLs 19–21, 152–87
teams 72, 119, 187, 209, 212
management-creditor and shareholder-creditor conflicts 18
manager-creditor and shareholder-creditor agency costs, *see* **agency costs, manager-creditor and shareholder-creditor**
manager-in-control models 4, 13, 210, 253, 277
managers 3–4, 12–13, 32, 57, 60–62, 66–67, 101–2, 276–77
judicial 52, 54, 86, 103, 197–98, 200, 208–10, 273
professional 18, 61, 277
scheme 88, 141, 188, 199–200, 205–6
mandatory disclosure 8, 58, 74, 102, 280
Asian restructurings 73–75
manufacturing 169, 179, 187, 283, 295
NPLs 169, 179, 187
market participants 33, 218, 230–31, 253, 255, 275, 284, 286
market prices 146, 177, 186
market reforms 7, 39, 91, 99, 178
market value 23, 49, 120, 173
market-based methods 25, 99, 185, 245, 250, 279, 285–86
market-based reforms 92, 264, 285–86
market-oriented reforms 92, 209, 266
markets 19–20, 32, 87, 91, 98–99, 181, 185, 248–49
active 16, 44, 181
bond 103, 105–6, 110–12, 122, 130, 148, 156, 178
capital 33, 60, 95, 99, 109, 116
debt 19, 26, 103, 130, 175, 181–82

distressed assets 153, 155, 185
distressed debt 20, 105, 116, 153, 155, 184–85, 282, 302
distressed loan 20, 44, 114, 184, 186–87
emerging 185, 189, 302
financial 35, 51, 102, 225, 290, 292–93
NPL 25, 174, 183, 186–87
primary 20, 153, 183–84
retail 26, 111
secondary 20, 111, 114, 154, 183, 185–86

methodology 22–31, 80, 213, 279
non-market 241
valuation 94, 279

minorities 8, 13, 59, 94–95, 103, 108, 224
minority shareholders 12, 64, 78, 84–85, 87, 95, 97–98
misconduct 71, 85–86, 209, 211–12, 241, 277
moratorium 115–16, 125–27, 218–23, 229–30, 232, 248–49, 251, 289–91 (*see also* **stays**)
de facto 231, 254, 262
formal 45, 230, 251, 289–90
Hong Kong 230–32
India 232–34
period 125, 195, 228
Singapore 228–30
statutory 10, 116, 220, 223, 290

National Company Law Appellate Tribunal, *see* **NCLAT**
National Company Law Tribunal, *see* **NCLT**
National Enterprise Bankruptcy Information Disclosure Platform 30, 80, 295
national goals 218–19, 252, 276, 284
NBFCs (non-bank financial companies) 144, 167
NCLAT (National Company Law Appellate Tribunal) 42–43, 83, 129, 131, 140, 142, 236, 244
NCLT (National Company Law Tribunal) 42–43, 83–84, 125, 130, 196–97, 219, 235–36, 244
negotiation costs, reduction 146–50
negotiation processes 16, 37, 165
negotiations 104, 110, 114–17, 137, 153, 155, 176, 184
non-adjusting creditors 133, 142–43, 145, 280, 282
non-bank financial companies, *see* **NBFCs**
non-bankruptcy rules on enforcing contracts and directors' duties 21–22
non-disclosure 96, 205, 225; *see also* **disclosure**
non-financial creditors 123, 131, 133–35, 144, 147, 157, 265–66, 280
non-market methodology 241
non-performing assets, *see* **NPAs**
non-performing loans, *see* **NPLs**
non-related party 89, 284
non-retail bondholders 150
non-sophisticated creditors 138, 152, 206, 242–43
non-sophisticated investors 137, 151
NPAs (non-performing assets) 11, 158–59, 162–63, 181, 187, 285, 288, 292
amounts 160, 162

NPLs (non-performing loans) 19–21, 25, 27–28, 30, 35–36, 152–54, 156–86, 282–83
amount of 160
bank provisioning for 20, 153
China 160–61
corporate 153, 178, 184, 187
India 156–59
institutional and organisational background 154–55, 157, 159
management 19–21, 152–87
manufacturing 169, 179, 187
market 25, 174, 183, 186–87
portfolios 165, 176, 183–84
real estate 169, 179–80, 187

offshore bonds 49–50, 107
offshore creditors 49, 149, 290
offshore jurisdictions 231, 281, 289
onshore bond defaults 19, 65, 108, 113, 263, 265
onshore bond markets 65, 106–9, 285
onshore bonds 19, 65, 286
onshore creditors 49, 148, 243
open-textured rules 242, 245
operating subsidiaries 113, 120, 148–49, 198, 290
operational creditors 131–35, 140, 142–44, 147, 241, 260–61, 279, 289
China 133–34
India 131–33

operational debt 4, 15–16, 18, 27, 102–3, 121–23
opportunistic behaviour 93, 97–98, 189, 219, 242
original lenders 21, 155, 164, 167–68, 178, 185, 247
original lending banks 154, 166, 169
outcomes 22–24, 29–30, 76–77, 144–47, 224–26, 253–55, 276–78, 283–84
better 266, 268, 287
market-based 93, 249
restructuring 153–54, 266, 277

out-of-court processes/procedures 5, 9, 11, 23, 262–63, 265–66, 268, 289
oversight 10, 56, 97, 188–89, 193, 204, 213–16, 251
judicial 97, 189, 199, 211, 213, 215, 292

ownership 7, 13, 32, 35, 62, 64, 105, 165
dispersed 13, 60, 102
structures 59–60, 99–100, 153, 167, 283

parent companies 49, 87, 150
participants 119, 233, 277
market 33, 218, 230–31, 253, 255, 275, 284, 286
parties 87–89, 118–19, 121, 148, 224, 226–27, 240, 242–43
connected 59, 92, 212
non-related 89, 284
payments 8, 39, 111, 115, 118, 122–23, 125, 138
illegal 255, 257
pay-offs 153, 176
People's Bank of China 107, 171, 194
personal assets 63, 208, 277
personal guarantees 63, 208, 288
personal insolvency 46
personal liability 271
petitions 37–38, 46, 221–22, 245–46, 248–50, 253, 258, 265
bankruptcy 97, 115, 193, 258, 265–66
winding-up 46, 48, 50, 141, 231–32, 243, 259, 281
Philippines 47, 113
PIP (**practitioner-in-possession**)
hybrid 27, 34–35, 37, 77, 79, 98, 100, 193–95
India 82–84, 195–97
models 2, 4, 23–24, 26–27, 33–34, 37–38, 188, 276–77
regimes 10, 35, 189, 191, 198, 210, 215–16, 244
role of practitioners 191–99
Singapore 197–99
place of incorporation 47, 49, 127, 242–43
plan confirmations 220–21, 223, 228, 247
plan proposers 138, 246
policy banks 171–72
portfolio companies 14, 18, 61, 67, 98–99
portfolios, NPLs (non-performing loans) 165, 176, 183–84
possession 4, 6, 8, 33, 57, 59, 188, 276
post-petition financing 236–38, 241
powers 10, 22, 190–93, 195–96, 198–200, 208–9, 211–14, 284
cram-down 38, 82, 278–79
of sale 129, 208, 211–12, 283
statutory 40, 190
practitioner-in-control models 253
practitioner-in-possession models, *see* **PIP**
practitioners 2–4, 6–7, 21, 97–98, 189–209, 211–16, 241–42, 283–84
China 193–95
effectiveness 207–9
as gatekeeper intermediaries 188–216
in PIP models 191–99
qualified 10, 46, 52
reconceptualisation of role 210–13
role 35, 188, 191, 191–201
United Kingdom 191–93
pre-bankruptcy entitlements 131, 210
predictability 217–18, 220, 244, 247–48, 250, 252, 284, 286
preference shares 86, 112
preferences, unfair 188, 191, 198
preferential creditors 10, 191, 245
pre-moratorium creditors 10, 116
pre-pack reorganisations 93, 250
pre-packaged schemes, *see* **pre-packs**
pre-packs 88, 92–93, 97, 192, 211–12, 248, 250–51, 291
conflicted 72
pre-petition financing 282
price discovery 58, 99, 167, 250
prices 76, 83, 89, 94, 120, 167–68, 185, 198
commodity 111, 209
market 146, 177, 186
primary markets 20, 153, 183–84
priority 35–36, 68–69, 99, 123, 210–12, 236–38, 241, 281–82
private enforcement 214, 254, 271, 273, 302
private equity 14, 104, 174
portfolios 15, 18, 102, 277
private sector banks 162, 166–68, 186
proceedings 54, 197–98, 219, 221–22, 228, 230, 242, 280–81
insolvency 23, 150, 154, 223, 255, 264, 267–68, 270
legal 42, 126, 164, 231–33, 260
resolution 154, 261
winding-up 28, 50, 127, 138, 231–32, 242
pro-creditor regimes 51–54, 60
professional advisers 66–67, 189–90, 196, 202–3, 207, 225, 241, 243
professional fees 195, 201
professional managers 18, 61, 277
profitable assets 81, 91, 139
profits 16, 104, 142, 164, 267
promoter shareholders 59, 63, 83
promoters 41–43, 73–75, 77, 82–84, 96, 207–8, 212, 287–88
India 63–64
property 27, 59, 193, 195, 255, 257, 263, 267
rights 36, 262, 268
proposers 84, 128, 248
plan 138, 246
pro-rescue culture 34, 41
providers 9, 31, 132, 149–50, 236, 238

provisional liquidation 27–28, 47, 127, 200, 230, 242–43, 289
soft-touch 5, 27, 127, 138
provisional liquidators 28, 46–47, 126–27, 188, 200–201, 230–32, 271
appointment 126, 231
soft-touch 28, 243
provisional supervision 26, 34, 46, 272, 289
PSBs, *see* **public sector banks**
public enforcement 243, 273
public sector banks (PSBs) 157–58, 162, 166–68, 283
purchasers 20, 104, 133, 139, 164, 168, 176, 185
secondary 20, 153, 244

RBI (Reserve Bank of India) 40–41, 44, 63, 157–59, 165–67, 169, 182, 187
real estate 169, 173, 179, 187, 283
NPLs 169, 179–80, 187
reasonable prospect of success 239, 271–72
receipts, security 162–65, 168–69, 182, 186–87
recoveries 19–20, 22, 40, 133–35, 215, 255–57, 260, 262–67
maximising 20, 153, 167, 179, 187, 221
recovery rates 136, 154, 159, 256–57, 260–61, 265, 267, 287
average 133, 260, 265
reform proposals
China 285–86
Hong Kong 289–91
India 287–89
Singapore 291–92
reforms 32, 34–35, 53–56, 58, 92–93, 228–30, 268–69, 275–93
bankruptcy 7, 24, 34, 58, 293, 302
insolvency law 20, 26, 35, 40, 152, 228, 276
market 7, 39, 91, 99, 178
market-based 92, 264, 285–86
market-oriented 92, 209, 266
Singapore 27, 34–35
regulators 3, 39, 49, 168, 175, 178, 186, 195
banking 7, 19–20, 152, 185
related parties
Hong Kong and Singapore 87–89
India 89
related party creditors 72, 152, 235, 239–40, 284
related party debt 71–72, 88–89, 277
related party transactions (RPTs) 13, 95, 240, 255, 267
Relative Priority Rule (RPR) 69–70
release 70–71, 86–87, 95, 143
claims 70–71, 85, 277
remuneration 142, 199, 204, 215
reorganisation 6–8, 17–18, 36–38, 78–82, 104–5, 115–17, 236, 266
plans 79–81, 90, 127–28, 134, 136, 139, 246, 248–49
processes 23, 32, 91, 98, 155, 167, 177, 186
repayment 12, 104, 108, 136, 141, 173, 176–77, 238
rescue 90–91, 94, 99–100, 218–19, 245–46, 250, 286, 289
financing 9, 153, 228, 236–38, 241, 276, 281–82, 291–92
frameworks 34, 46, 51, 271–72, 289
strategies 189, 202–3, 283
Reserve Bank of India, *see* **RBI**
residual claimants 198, 270
resolution applicants 129, 169, 206, 208, 210–11, 232, 235, 287–88
resolution plans 42, 75, 77, 82–83, 129, 140, 196, 233–36
resolution proceedings 154, 261
resolution processes 3, 19, 30, 83, 102, 158, 260
resolution professionals, *see* **RPs**
resources 66, 76, 137, 209, 254, 277
judicial 145–46
restructuring hub 26, 34–35, 63, 78, 197, 220, 242, 292
restructuring innovations 117–18
restructuring models 8–12, 33
transplantation into Asia 10–12, 24
United Kingdom 9–10
United States 8–9
restructuring outcomes 153–54, 266, 277
restructuring plans 2, 70–72, 76, 81–82, 91, 101–3, 115–17, 226–27
restructuring processes 15, 17, 19, 22, 123, 125, 253–54, 268–69
restructuring support agreements, *see* **RSAs**
restructuring tools 96, 220, 242, 275, 278–79, 281, 290
retail bondholders 16, 118–19
retail investors 19, 109–13, 122, 130, 134, 137–38, 144, 185
retail markets 26, 111
reverse takeovers 46–48, 201
review 42–43, 130, 132, 140–41, 186–87, 219–20, 244, 246
rights 23–24, 37, 68, 79, 89, 118–19, 125–26, 280
contractual 256, 284, 293
property 36, 262, 268
voting 74, 230
risks 19, 67–68, 97, 104, 127, 144, 150, 186
role of insolvency practitioners 35, 188, 191, 193, 195, 197, 199
roll-up financing 120, 124, 145, 238, 282
RPR (Relative Priority Rule) 69–70

RPs (resolution professionals) 42–43, 63–64, 142, 195–99, 206–8, 212–13, 234, 287–88
RPTs, *see* **related party transactions**
RSAs (restructuring support agreements) 113, 117–18, 147, 224, 234, 280, 284, 290

sale, power of 129, 208, 211–12, 283
sales 72, 75–77, 119–20, 165–70, 176, 207–8, 211–13, 220–23
of assets 115, 198–99
to controlling shareholders 72
satellite litigation 96, 126, 143, 147, 280
scaled fees 195, 215
scheme managers 88, 141, 188, 199–200, 205–6
schemes of arrangement 4–5, 31, 50–53, 84, 200–201, 223–30, 240–43, 291–92
framework 19, 40, 54, 262
Hong Kong 85
with insolvency professionals having statutory or intermediary role 199–201
sanction 234–36
Singapore 11, 58, 73, 78, 127, 199–200, 277, 280
screening processes 243, 251, 261
secondary markets 20, 111, 114, 154, 183, 185–86
secondary purchasers 20, 153, 244
secured assets 37, 138, 157, 255
secured claims 124, 255
secured creditor-in-control models 9–11, 27, 58, 93, 253, 276–77
Hong Kong 84–85
secured creditors 22, 119–20, 125–27, 143–46, 253–56, 259–60, 265–69, 287–89
secured debt, enforcement 27, 41, 259
secured loans/lending 39, 124, 156, 259, 263
security interests 52, 123, 228, 241, 244, 254, 266, 269
security receipts 162–65, 168–69, 182, 186–87
self-interest 2, 98
selling banks 162, 165, 187
senior classes 8, 58, 68
senior creditors 18, 69, 119–20, 148
senior lenders 93, 120, 257
settlement 36, 70–71, 83–85, 95, 145, 162, 244
Shanghai Stock Exchange 64, 137, 173
shareholder circulars 31, 85
shareholder-creditor agency costs 57–100
shareholders 12–16, 18–19, 54–60, 66–70, 76–80, 93–96, 98–103, 276–78
controlling 18, 59–64, 70–73, 76–78, 81–82, 85–88, 93–97, 276–79
existing 63, 78, 81–82
heightened friction with creditors 70–72
independent 93, 95
interests 18, 98, 270
minority 12, 64, 78, 84–85, 87, 95, 97–98
promoter 59, 63, 83
shareholding concentration 103, 293
shareholding structures 60–61, 104, 152
dispersed 18, 67
shareholdings 3, 5, 12, 14–15, 62, 77–78, 80–82, 99
concentrated 14–15, 17–18, 24, 26, 62–63, 75–76, 98, 291–92
largest 62, 178
shares 47, 77–78, 81–82, 84–85, 87–88, 90, 201, 278–79
preference 86, 112
Shenzhen Intermediate Court 81, 193, 204
Shenzhen Stock Exchange (SZSE) 5, 62, 64, 111
Singapore 2–5, 33–34, 52–53, 61–63, 77, 109–13, 210–12, 239–41
agency costs 62–63
APR (absolute priority rule) 77–78
courts 31, 53, 74, 93, 110, 126, 228–30, 237
development of corporate restructuring law 51–55
DIP (debtor in possession) 77–78
effectiveness ofpractitioners 208–9
empirical studies 31
Exchange 53, 93, 141, 301
information asymmetry 130–31
moratorium 228–30
PIP (practitioner-in-possession) 197–99
reform proposals 291–92
reforms 27, 34–35
related parties 87–89
restructuring hub 242
schemes of arrangement 11, 58, 73, 78, 127, 199–200, 277, 280
settlement and release of claims 86–87
small creditors 137–38
usage of formal insolvency/restructuring law 266–69
single-loan trades 165–66, 181
skin in the game 167, 186
small creditors 121, 131, 144, 147, 265–66, 280
China 135–37
Hong Kong and Singapore 137–38
social unrest 19, 36, 39, 90, 137, 150
socialist market economy 171, 245
SOEs (state-owned enterprises) 36, 64–66, 89–92, 98–99, 171, 177–79, 203, 294–95
central 64, 137
distressed 36, 90–91, 98, 247
listed 89–90
local 64–65

soft-touch liquidation 26, 28, 47, 50, 127, 232, 243, 251
  Hong Kong recognition 28, 47, 50, 69, 127, 231, 239, 243
  process 47–48, 243, 281, 289
  provisional 5, 27, 127, 138
soft-touch liquidators 28, 242
solvent companies 6, 191, 202, 270, 272
special purpose vehicles (SPVs) 122, 222
stakeholders 7, 12–13, 36–37, 68–69, 101, 189, 191, 242
  junior 211
  key 57, 220
  local 184
state as shareholder 64–66, 89–92
statements 66, 192, 198, 222
  disclosure 190
  explanatory 31, 67, 85–86, 118, 122, 199
  financial 73–74, 229
state-owned banks 21, 25, 28, 153–54, 168, 171–72, 177–78, 186
state-owned enterprise, *see* **SOEs**
statutory moratorium 10, 116, 220, 223, 290
statutory powers 40, 190
stays 41, 46, 219, 228, 242, 251, 253, 280–81
  automatic 124, 148
stock exchanges 3, 52, 61, 106, 172, 267
strategic defaults 115, 148
stressed assets 11, 44, 64, 262
structures, ownership 59–60, 99–100, 153, 167, 283
subordinated creditors 49, 137, 145
subscription databases 30–31, 259
subsidiaries 31, 53, 88, 141, 149, 177
  operating 113, 120, 148–49, 198, 290
  PRC 49–50
success 21, 50, 52, 69, 71, 150, 153, 239
  fees 197, 200, 204–6, 215, 283
super-priority financing 124, 237–38
supervision 23, 27, 32, 37, 40, 63, 194, 204
  provisional 26, 34, 46, 272, 289
swaps 135, 164, 174
  debt-equity 77, 82, 84–85, 87, 134–36, 174, 176–77, 246
Swiss challenge 129, 163–64, 167, 196, 212

takeovers 59–60, 93, 220, 227, 302
  hostile 226, 302
  reverse 46–48, 201
theoretical framework 2–32
time of filing 15, 89, 96, 233, 240
time value 3, 66, 137, 287
time-bound periods 43, 125, 251, 268
time-bound processes 42, 181, 260
tools 146–47, 200, 236, 262, 269, 275–77, 286, 291–93
tort victims 133, 142–43, 145
trade creditors 16, 19, 123, 130, 132–33, 136, 138, 280
trades, single-loan 165–66, 181
trading 22, 47, 57, 114, 182–83, 201–2, 204, 270–73
  distressed 20, 105, 155, 223
  insolvent 46, 271–73
  permitted 114, 182
transaction costs 1, 3, 15–17, 20, 22, 153–55, 211, 214
transactions 46–48, 95, 165, 167, 186, 188, 202, 269
  abusive 62, 76
  antecedent 86, 198, 209, 213
  conflicted 95, 98
  related party
  undervalue 191, 198
transparency 25, 92, 97, 147, 247–48, 251, 287
transplantation 17, 59, 73, 218, 292

UK, *see* **United Kingdom**
uncertainty, in valuation 69, 119
UNCITRAL (United Nations Commission on International Trade Law) 33, 36, 148, 231, 243, 291
unfair preferences 188, 191, 198
United Kingdom 1–4, 14–19, 72–73, 102–3, 219–21, 256–59, 261–62, 275
  agency costs 60–61
  courts 223–26
  restructuring models 9–10
  role of practitioners 191–93
United Nations Commission on International Trade Law, *see* **UNCITRAL**
United States 1–5, 14–20, 68–72, 150–52, 255–59, 261–63, 270–71, 275–76
  agency costs 60–61
  Chapter 11 2–3, 6, 8, 21, 24, 128, 218–19, 278
  courts 221–24
  DIP (debtor in possession) 8–9
  Trustee Programme 116, 189, 226
unreasonable hold-outs 66, 93, 101
unrest, social 19, 36, 39, 90, 137, 150
unsecured creditors 78–79, 131–32, 138–39, 143–45, 192, 245–46, 265–66, 268
US, *see* **United States**

valuation 119–20, 138, 211–13, 224, 235, 239–40, 276, 278–79
  and cram-downs 240–41
  disputes 69, 94, 119, 222–23
  methodologies 94, 279
  uncertainty in 69, 119
value 54–55, 69–70, 73, 82–86, 118–20, 138–40, 246, 279–81
  book 163, 181, 183, 187
  collateral 266–67
  destruction 167, 189, 202, 211, 240, 254–55, 266
  liquidation 42, 57, 139–40, 235–36, 240, 245–46, 280, 289
  market 23, 49, 120, 173
  time 3, 66, 137, 287
valuers 42, 119, 127, 139, 196, 212–13, 279
viability 132, 189, 202, 209, 218, 239–40, 242, 247
viable companies 2, 12, 36, 40, 143, 189, 217, 247
votes 78–79, 87–89, 95–96, 129–31, 140–42, 144, 210–11, 277–78
  dissenting 80, 278
voting 15, 71, 73, 88–90, 95, 128, 130, 240
  abstention 96, 146, 286
  purposes 8, 21, 122, 141, 205, 280
  rights 74, 230

white knight investors 88–89, 201
wholly owned foreign enterprises, *see* **WOFEs**
winding-up
  orders 41, 46
  petitions 46, 48, 50, 141, 231–32, 243, 259, 281
  proceedings 28, 50, 127, 138, 231–32, 242
within-class conflicts 144, 146–47
within-class cram-downs 9, 69, 71, 77, 79, 84, 234, 240
WOFEs (wholly owned foreign enterprises) 49, 149
work fees 117–18, 224, 290; *see also* **RSAs**
World Bank 5, 33, 43, 95, 256–57, 259, 262–63, 276

zombie companies 25, 39, 66, 91–92, 98, 108, 245, 250

Lightning Source UK Ltd.
Milton Keynes UK
UKHW020016201022
410785UK00003B/146

9 781509 952335